RECONSTRUCTING IRAQ

RECONSTRUCTING
IRAQ
REGIME CHANGE, JAY GARNER,
AND THE ORHA STORY

GORDON W. RUDD

UNIVERSITY PRESS OF KANSAS

© 2011 by the University Press of Kansas

Published by the University Press of Kansas (Lawrence, Kansas 66045), which was organized by the Kansas Board of Regents and is operated and funded by Emporia State University, Fort Hays State University, Kansas State University, Pittsburg State University, the University of Kansas, and Wichita State University

Library of Congress Cataloging-in-Publication Data

Rudd, Gordon W., 1949–
   Reconstructing Iraq : regime change, Jay Garner, and the ORHA story / Gordon Rudd.
      p.   cm. — (Modern war studies)
   Includes bibliographical references and index.
   ISBN 978-0-7006-1779-1 (cloth : alk. paper)
1. Postwar reconstruction—Iraq. 2. Iraq War, 2003– 3. Office for Reconstruction and Humanitarian Assistance. 4. Garner, Jay Montgomery, 1938– I. Title.
   DS79.769.R84 2011
   956.7044'31—dc22
                         2010048252

British Library Cataloguing-in-Publication Data is available.

Printed in the United States of America

10 9 8 7 6 5 4 3 2 1

The paper used in this publication is recycled and contains 30 percent postconsumer waste. It is acid free and meets the minimum requirements of the American National Standard for Permanence of Paper for Printed Library Materials Z39.48-1992.

CONTENTS

A photo insert follows page 211

PREFACE

The United States invaded Iraq in 2003 to change the regime of Saddam Hussein, prepared for half the job. In less than a month, coalition forces defeated the Iraqi army and drove Saddam into hiding. Yet history shows that regime change must include regime replacement as well as regime removal. American political leaders misread the nature of the Iraqi people and state, and they failed to make adequate preparations to put a new government in place. The loss of lives, treasure, time, and American prestige was a magnitude greater than those leaders anticipated.

The ad hoc organization formed to manage regime replacement was the Office of Reconstruction and Humanitarian Assistance, which came to be called ORHA. The leader was Jay Garner, a retired Army lieutenant general recalled to government service. This is the story of ORHA and Jay Garner, a figure both heroic and tragic, a charismatic leader of great enthusiasm and drive who, in good faith, took on a task of grand proportions and was poorly served by those who chose him and sent him to Iraq.

The rationale for regime change included Iraq's alleged weapons of mass destruction, the view that the Iraqi regime supported terrorism, and other acts that were said to cause regional instability. Yet Iraq had not committed any specific act—nothing comparable to the invasion of Kuwait in 1990—that required the United States to invade in 2003.

The invasion of Iraq was elective and deliberate, following military planning that had been conducted for over a decade. In contrast, the planning for regime replacement was haphazard and grossly inadequate, with far less time for study and debate. Just two months before the invasion, Jay Garner was asked to put together the organization that would execute that planning for the post-conflict phase in Iraq.

In January 2003, I received a call from Jay Garner, asking me—as a historian—to assist him on a project he could not discuss on the phone. I knew Garner as a key figure from Operation Provide Comfort, a 1991 humanitarian intervention to assist Kurdish refugees in northern Iraq following Desert Storm. I had written a book on Provide Comfort based on interviews with many participants of the operation, including General Garner.[1]

I greatly admired Garner, and so—with no sense of the scope of his project—I told him that I would be happy to assist him. Within a week, I found that it would be a full-time endeavor, and I asked those for whom I worked at the U.S. Marine Corps School of Advanced Warfighting in Quantico, Virginia, for a leave of absence to join ORHA. My rationale, beyond assisting Garner, was that ORHA would be a case study in interagency operations and that the experience would yield material we could add to the curriculum at Quantico. My supervisors thus released me from my duties for eight months in 2003 and then for several months more the following year.

When I arrived at the Pentagon that January, Garner had six people with him. I watched as ORHA grew to almost two hundred by mid-March when we flew to Kuwait, then doubled in size by the time we went into Iraq in April. Garner knew no more than a dozen of them prior to their arrival in ORHA. Most of us came from government agencies, mainly from the Departments of Defense and State, and from the U.S. Agency for International Development (USAID). There were also representatives from the Departments of Treasury, Commerce, Agriculture, Justice, and Energy and from the CIA. In the beginning, half of those in ORHA were military personnel from the four American services. As more civilians were added the balance shifted. A few people from the United Kingdom joined as we left Washington.

While there was a growing non-American contingent, ORHA was mainly a U.S. interagency organization, with an exceptionally diverse group of people, just the sort I wanted to study. I had the opportunity to observe their activities in the Pentagon, Kuwait, Baghdad, and other places in Iraq. I got to know some of them well and many became friends. Some were ill suited for the tasks before them and it was sad to see them stumble. Others adapted remarkably well, went into harm's way without apparent reservation, and gave their country and Iraq their best efforts. Sometimes their best efforts were adequate; often they were not.

Garner was replaced by Ambassador L. Paul Bremer III on 12 May 2003. After a three-week transition, Garner left Iraq on the first of June. I rode with him from Baghdad but chose to remain behind at al-Hilla in southern Iraq as Garner continued home. Many of those in ORHA were absorbed into Bremer's Coalition Provisional Authority (CPA), and I wanted to see how that would work. I found that transition neither smooth nor thoughtful, and that is part of the ORHA story. At the end of the summer I left Iraq to resume teaching at Quantico, but returned twice: for a month at the end of 2003 and again in mid-2004 to observe CPA transfer its functions to a new American embassy and to the interim Iraqi government.

My work has been twofold. My first task was to document the experience in the field. For that, I conducted some 280 interviews, many with members of ORHA and CPA while they were serving in Iraq. However, their experiences led to questions that could not be answered there and I have spent much of the past several years conducting interviews—in the United States, in the United Kingdom, and elsewhere—to enlarge upon the context for ORHA. All the interviews were recorded and transcribed, to be placed in appropriate archives for those who would study ORHA and regime change in Iraq.

My second task has been to capture the story of ORHA. Most of this book is devoted to the ORHA story; the Prologue and Chapters 1 and 2 provide a pre-invasion context for the American experience in the liberation and occupation of Iraq and the planning for a new regime. The introduction connects Jay Garner's role in Operation Provide Comfort in 1991 with those in the Department of Defense who asked him in 2003 to form ORHA and to return to Iraq. With reflection, Garner noted to Secretary Rumsfeld, "Marshall had two years . . . you are giving me two months."[2]

Thus follows a prologue that reviews the American post-conflict experience with some attention to World War II. Planning for Iraq included frequent references to American experiences with Germany and Japan. But those were long-term occupations, whereas the focus for Iraq was on liberation. Other experiences, which might have been studied from that period—the liberations of Italy, France, Austria, Korea, and the Philippines (all with aspects of occupation)—arguably had more relevance for Iraq.

Chapters 1 and 2 address the evolution of military and interagency planning for Iraq. Military planning began in the 1990s following Operation Desert Storm, conducted mainly by U.S. Central Command (CENTCOM) in Tampa, Florida. That planning was subject to rigorous review by those in the Pentagon trying to implement a technology-based military transformation. Many at Central Command resisted that transformation. As a result, those in Central Command and in the Pentagon were at cross-purposes on critical issues when planning intensified the year prior to the invasion.

Interagency planning began in 2002, loosely guided by the National Security Council, which proved poorly equipped for the executive management necessary to recruit and guide an interagency body for regime replacement. Few government agencies were fully committed. With no central authority beyond the president to force such commitment, there was no cohesive national plan. Nor was there an adequate effort to bring the international community to join the endeavor.

The story of ORHA begins in chapter 3, as Jay Garner arrives in the Pentagon to form an organization from scratch to manage regime replacement in Iraq. Powerful agendas within the Office of the Secretary of Defense (OSD) provided more obstacles than resources for Garner, while military leaders on the Joint Staff and at Central Command offered little assistance. Other departments and agencies that provided personnel relied on volunteers, useful for their enthusiasm but often junior in rank, many without regional experience and frequently lacking the skills required. Some agencies used contractors or retirees to fill their designated positions. All this compounded Garner's difficulties.

Chapter 4 follows the deployment of ORHA from the Pentagon to Kuwait in March. Accommodations there provided painfully little in the way of communications, intelligence, or access to the military forces in-theater. Last-minute efforts by military planners to coordinate with ORHA lacked central direction. Once in Kuwait, ORHA increased its numbers twofold. The additional personnel were welcome, but their eleventh-hour infusion complicated cohesion and many critical positions still remained vacant. ORHA continued to be crippled by internal OSD agendas, an awkward chain of command, and funding restraints. That did not keep Garner and his team from charging forward, but it ensured their capacity would be limited.

Chapter 5 next tracks the entry of ORHA into Iraq in April after fighting subsided. For three crucial weeks, Garner was the senior civilian responsible for replacing the regime of Saddam Hussein. He formed an Iraqi Interim Authority to assume power as ORHA members attempted to reactivate Iraqi ministries and put essential services back into operation. They found the country in chaos. The physical infrastructure, little damaged by war, had endured years of poor maintenance and international sanctions. The final straw causing its collapse was the extraordinary looting that followed the invasion.

Ambassador Bremer is introduced in Chapter 6. Nominated in late April as Garner's replacement, he arrived in May and imposed a draconian de-Ba'athification policy, which disenfranchised many Iraqi leaders ORHA had just restored to power. Then, he issued an order to disband the Iraqi army, reversing previous plans to retain and reform it. Thousands of bureaucrats and soldiers were suddenly unemployed and angry. Finally, Bremer disbanded the Iraqi Interim Authority that Garner had put in motion, setting the stage for a long-term occupation instead of the liberation that Garner had been instructed to guide. Garner strongly protested each decision, but Bremer was dismissive and Washington backed him. During his final weeks in May, Garner was marginalized by Bremer and left Iraq frustrated and disappointed.

Critical transitions took place as Garner departed, and these are described in Chapter 7. ORHA was quickly subsumed by the Coalition Provisional Authority under Bremer, and the large headquarters in charge of the ground invasion was replaced by the less-capable Combined-Joint Task Force 7 (CJTF-7), under Lieutenant General Ricardo Sanchez. Both transitions included a turnover of personnel, further eroding the capacity for regime replacement. Iraq became more violent, freedom of movement was reduced, and the cost of occupying and reconstructing Iraq put into question the decision to invade.

The final chapter provides an assessment of Jay Garner and ORHA and of the problems with the transitions that followed their work. Necessarily included are analyses of the planning for regime change in Iraq, the prior lessons that might have been incorporated, and the management by the National Security Council and the Department of Defense.

As an observer and participant in ORHA, I have tried to maintain objectivity and detachment in this story. The situation in Iraq and the efforts of those in ORHA were extraordinary, frequently colorful, and often dangerous. It was an honor to have been with those involved and it has been my intention to give them their due. Their efforts were not perfect and I have noted many deficiencies. Others must be included outside of ORHA who bear culpability for the shortcomings of regime replacement. Had those individuals been more forthcoming, the conditions for General Garner and ORHA would undoubtedly have been different and might have achieved more positive results.

Gordon Rudd
May 2010

ACKNOWLEDGMENTS

There are many people who made this project possible, and they fall into several categories. First I must thank General Jay Garner for inviting me to join him and ORHA as the field historian and also those for whom I work at Marine Corps University in Quantico, Virginia, for allowing me to participate in this endeavor. Without that invitation and the support provided by those at Quantico, I would not have been involved in this project.

General Garner allowed me to travel with him throughout his time in Iraq. He was remarkably candid during numerous conversations with me in Iraq and in half a dozen recorded interviews afterward. Those for whom I worked at Quantico not only allowed me to deploy with ORHA and later make two follow-up trips to Iraq during the CPA era, they also allowed me a six-month sabbatical in which to write the initial draft of this book.

This study is based mainly on 282 individual interviews I conducted with participants in ORHA, CPA, and military commands, as well as with those from other governmental departments and agencies and with Iraqis. Those interviews were transcribed by the Special Inspector General for Iraqi Reconstruction (SIGIR), to whom I am also grateful. SIGIR and the British Broadcasting Company (BBC) made about 100 interviews they conducted available to me to complement those I conducted.

In addition to the interviews, I contacted over 100 participants by email or other means for additional details, which were not recorded as interviews but were of significant assistance.

A number of the participants interviewed allowed me access to papers they kept or collected in relation to their work in Iraq. In a few cases these were day-to-day diaries or journals that allowed a sequential understanding of what took place that is often difficult to distill from an oral interview conducted in a single sitting. Those individuals are listed by name in the bibliography.

Several people were generous in providing access to photos used to illustrate this study, notably Colonel Kim Olson, USAF (Ret); Sergeant Major

Glenn Kramer, USMC (Ret); Don Eberly; Colonel Gordon Wells, USA (Ret); Colonel Anthony Puckett, USA (Ret); Colonel Jimmy Rabon, USA (Ret); and Susan Hamrock.

At the University Press of Kansas there are many people to thank, starting with the editor-in-chief Michael Briggs, who encouraged me to submit my manuscript and who guided me throughout the publication process. The marketing manager, Susan Schott, was helpful in the design of the book and allowed for my input. The production editor, Jennifer Dropkin, was patient and helpful throughout the editing process, in which numerous errors were identified and corrected. Kelly Chrisman Jacques managed the photos and illustrations. The anonymous readers who reviewed the manuscript for the Press made insightful comments that led to substantive corrections and adjustments to the final product.

I am also grateful to O'Dell Garrett, a reference librarian with the Gray Research Center, Quantico, Virginia, who assisted me on many research issues for this project.

Throughout the whole process one friend in particular was with me, Colonel John R. Martin, USA (Ret). He was my roommate in Kuwait and Iraq, often traveled with me in Iraq, and accompanied me on a number of important interviews. He read the initial drafts of each chapter and provided critical comments that made this a better work. I am grateful for the time and effort he invested in this project.

Last but not least, I am grateful to my wife, Sevgi Rudd, and my sons Gordon and Russell, who supported me while I was in Iraq and later when I required the quiet time to read, reflect, and write. Without their support I could not have completed this project.

Although I have received critical assistance from those listed here or in the bibliography, any shortcomings or inaccuracies in this work are mine and mine alone.

ABBREVIATIONS

ALOC   Administration and Logistics Operations Center
BIAP   Baghdad International Airport
CA   Civil Affairs
CACOM   Civil Affairs Command
CENTCOM   U.S. Central Command
CFLCC   Combined Forces Land Component Command
CIA   Central Intelligence Agency
CJTF-7   Combined-Joint Task Force 7
CMATT   Coalition Military Advisor Training Team
CMOC   Civil Military Operations Center
CORDS   Civil Operations and Revolutionary Development Support
CPA   Coalition Provisional Authority
CPIC   Coalition Press Information Center
CSI   Combat Studies Institute
DART   Disaster Assistance Response Team
DCHA   Democracy, Conflict, and Humanitarian Assistance
DDR   disarmament, demobilization, and reintegration
DG   director general
EECP   Early Entry Command Post
EIPG   Energy Infrastructure Planning Group
ENCOM   Engineer Command
ESG   Executive Steering Group
FAO   Foreign Area Officer
FBI   Federal Bureau of Investigation
FCO   Foreign and Commonwealth Office
FEST   Forward Engineer Support Team
FOI   Future of Iraq
FSO   Foreign Service Officer
GARIOA   Government and Relief in Occupied Areas
GS   government service

GST	Government Support Team
HOC	Humanitarian Operations Center
ICDC	Iraqi Civil Defense Corps
ICRC	International Committee of the Red Cross
IG	inspector general
IGC	Iraqi Governing Council
IIA	Iraqi Interim Authority
I MEF	First Marine Expeditionary Force
INA	Iraqi National Accord
INC	Iraqi National Congress
INSS	Institute of National Security Studies
IO	international organization
IRDC	Iraqi Reconstruction Development Council
IRRF	Iraq Relief and Reconstruction Fund
JCS	Joint Chiefs of Staff
JIACG	Joint Interagency Coordination Group
JMD	Joint Manning Document
JTF	Joint Task Force
KBR	Kellogg, Brown, and Root
LGT	Local Governance Team
LOGCAP	Logistics Civilian Augmentation Program
MEF	Marine Expeditionary Force
MP	Military Police
MREs	meals ready to eat
NBC	nuclear, biological, chemical
NCO	noncommissioned officer
NDU	National Defense University
NEA	Near Eastern Affairs
NGA	Northern Gulf Affairs
NGO	nongovernmental organization
NIC	New Iraqi Corps
NIST	National Intelligence Security Team
NSC	National Security Council
NSPD	National Security Presidential Directive
OFDA	Office for Foreign Disaster Assistance
ORHA	Office of Reconstruction and Humanitarian Assistance
OIF	Operation Iraqi Freedom
OMB	Office of Management and Budget
OPLAN	Operations Plan
OSD	Office of the Secretary of Defense

OSP	Office of Special Plans
OVP	Office of the Vice President
PAO	Public Affairs Officer
POLAD	Political Advisor
POM	Preparation for Overseas Movement
PPG	Postwar Planning Group
PSD	personal security detail
SAMS	School of Advanced Military Studies
SCIRI	Supreme Council for Islamic Revolution in Iraq
SIGIR	Special Inspector General for Iraqi Reconstruction
SIPRNET	Secret Internet Protocol Router Network
SOE	State-Owned Enterprise
SOLIC	Office of Special Operations and Low Intensity Conflict
TF RIO	Task Force Restore Iraqi Oil
TOC	tactical operations center
UIA	United Iraqi Alliance
UNHCR	United Nations High Commissioner for Refugees
UNICEF	United Nations Children's Fund
USA	United States Army
USACE	United States Army Corps of Engineers
USAID	United States Agency for International Development
USAR	United States Army Reserves
USIA	United States Information Agency
USMC	United States Marine Corps
USNR	United States Navy Reserves
WFP	World Food Program
WMD	weapons of mass destruction

RECONSTRUCTING IRAQ

INTRODUCTION:
A COLD START

After a long day, the general was pleased as his small group boarded the helicopter. Iraqi military forces were cooperating, the refugees had adequate care and were moving home, and Coalition forces would soon depart. The mission was going well and would end successfully within the month. As the noisy aircraft lifted off, he took a three-by-five card from his pocket and wrote on it, "Who Places the Last Tile on the Mosaic?" Then he handed it to me. It was July 1991 and the location was northern Iraq. The Army officer was Major General Jay Garner. I was traveling with him as the field historian for the operation in northern Iraq.

Almost a year earlier, Saddam Hussein had surprised the United States and much of world with the Iraqi invasion of Kuwait. The United States and much of the world surprised Saddam Hussein and Iraq with their response. The American-led Operation Desert Shield contained the invasion and transitioned into Operation Desert Storm, which expelled Iraqi forces from Kuwait. Within a month Shia groups in southern Iraq and Kurds in northern Iraq revolted against the regime of Saddam Hussein. Yet Iraqi forces—beaten, but not destroyed—in Desert Storm were able to overpower both revolts, brutally suppressing the southern Shia and violently driving the Kurds into the mountains on Iraq's northern border, still covered with winter snow.

For the second time in a year, the United States quickly formed a coalition in response to Iraqi aggression, this time against their fellow countrymen. The operation was designated Provide Comfort. Its tasks were to provide humanitarian assistance to the 400,000 Kurds and other Iraqi minority groups in the mountains on the Turkish border. Subsequently, the Coalition sent an intervention force into northern Iraq to coerce the Iraqi forces to allow the refugees to return home. General Garner led that intervention force. His task was far more complex than the size of his forces suggested.

If a mosaic consists of a variety of modular components arranged to form a complex pattern, Garner had dealt with two sets of complex components. His command in northern Iraq approached the size of an infantry division with 10,000 soldiers, Marines, sailors, and airmen from all four American services and from a dozen other countries, all supported by as many Coalition forces working from Turkey. Two of Garner's subordinates in northern Iraq were Colonel James Jones, commanding the 24th Marine Expeditionary Unit, and Lieutenant Colonel John Abizaid, commanding a U.S. Army airborne battalion. In 2003, both would be senior general officers with interests in Iraq.[1]

The other part of Garner's mosaic in 1991 included the components of Iraq. The main focus had been the refugees driven into the mountains, mainly Iraqi Kurds with complex tribal and political differences, accompanied by other Iraqi minority groups and Iraqi army deserters that fled with them. To bring them back into Iraq, Garner had to deal with a hostile Iraqi government and army recently beaten by American and Coalition forces.

Without a written operational plan to guide him, Garner demonstrated great operational acumen and remarkable diplomacy to bring the operation to a successful end. His gift for innovation and personal charisma were key factors working in his favor. The objectives of Provide Comfort had been limited to humanitarian assistance for the refugees and their safe return to Iraq, but Garner knew that the tensions that had caused the crisis had not been resolved; the mosaic in his mind was incomplete. However, there was little reason in July 1991 to assume that he would later return to Iraq in an effort to help resolve those tensions.

Like Desert Storm, Provide Comfort was a success story validating the capacity of American forces to deploy great distances, integrate other Coalition forces, and conduct aggressive operations. Both operations had been guided by astute political, diplomatic, and military leaders who set limited objectives and allocated substantial forces and resources to ensure the achievement of those objectives. It was a high-point for the United States and the Department of Defense. Twelve years later, the United States would again deploy large combat formations to fight the Iraqi Army, achieving decisive operational success within a month. But in 2003, American objectives were grand—to remove and replace the regime in Iraq—while the forces and resources were more limited than those allocated in 1991. Follow-on operations in Iraq—operations in which General Garner would play an important role—would be far more complex than those in Provide Comfort. Garner would find there were still missing tiles on the mosaic in Iraq.

Garner had a larger-than-life personality and a colorful resume. After an enlistment in the Marine Corps, he attended Florida State University, where he earned a degree in history and an Army commission through ROTC. He served two tours in Vietnam and was an advisor to a South Vietnamese formation during the 1968 Tet Offensive. He was twice wounded in combat. Throughout his career, Garner worked successfully with the human and technical dimensions of Army operations. After Provide Comfort he had several assignments on the Army Staff in the Pentagon and was promoted to lieutenant general. He represented the Army before congressional committees on force structure and other matters. Upon retirement from the Army in 1997, Garner went into private business with a senior position in a large corporation. As a civilian he served on several governmental boards, one with Donald Rumsfeld in the late 1990s.[2]

In early January 2003, Secretary of Defense Rumsfeld had his subordinates contact Garner to ask him to form an interagency organization that eventually became known as the Office of Reconstruction and Humanitarian Assistance. With it Garner was to execute—in only a few months—the military and interagency plans for a new regime in Iraq. The planning gestation prior to ORHA, which is part of this story, was short, eclectic, incomplete, and lacking in cohesion, although the aggregate planning was more extensive than many believed. The gestation for ORHA was shorter still, ad hoc, and also incomplete. The ORHA story began with a brief phone call.

Jay Garner took that call on his cell phone at Docks, a restaurant in New York City. It was Thursday, 9 January 2003. Garner was in Manhattan for a business meeting. The caller was Brigadier General Ron Yaggi, an Air Force officer working for Undersecretary of Defense for Policy Douglas Feith.

Yaggi introduced himself and asked Garner to come over to talk, assuming he was in his office in Crystal City, Virginia.

"Well, I'm in New York," Garner responded.

Yaggi paused.

"What's it about?" Garner asked.

"I'm a little hesitant to talk on the telephone."

"Well, that's the only way we're going to be able to conduct this conversation," Garner responded.

"The Secretary," Yaggi struggled, "would like you to consider coming in and begin conducting the postwar reconstruction and things that are necessary in such an environment." Then he added, "I have to tell you up front that you will be the director of this, but . . . the President will probably pick an envoy to replace you, and it most likely will be somebody with name recognition . . . probably a former governor."

Garner pondered. "I'll have to go home. When I get back next week, I'll call you." Home was Windermere, Florida, near Orlando, where he spent weekends with his family. "Back next week" meant Crystal City, near the Pentagon, where Garner was president of SY Coleman, a defense contractor.[3] Yaggi did not mention why Garner had been selected for such a task, nor did Garner ask. At the time he assumed it was due to his role in Provide Comfort in 1991.

A few days after he received the call from General Yaggi, Garner called Doug Feith to discuss the position he had been asked to accept. He said he would have to clear it with his company's directors, but he was interested.

Garner returned to New York and talked to Frank Lanza, CEO of SY Coleman, who responded, "Well, if they ask you to do this, you've probably got to do it. How long do you think it'll take?"

"Probably four months at the most," Garner said.

With a release from his company and the reluctant agreement from his wife, on 17 January Garner went to see Rumsfeld and Feith at the Pentagon. They discussed removing Saddam Hussein and setting up an interagency group under the Defense Department to manage the transition to a stable and democratic Iraq. They did not go into much detail and left many issues unaddressed. Garner said he would take the job, but it was clear he had little time. Thinking back to World War II, Garner mused near the end of the meeting, "Marshall had two years . . . you are giving me two months."[4]

Thus began what would be a five-month odyssey for Garner—to forge an interagency organization from scratch in the Pentagon, deploy it to Kuwait as Coalition forces invaded Iraq, and to follow those forces into the chaos of Iraq to help reestablish order and install a new government. Garner was the agent of Secretary of Defense Donald Rumsfeld, but he would soon be replaced by Ambassador L. Paul "Jerry" Bremer, who, as the presidential envoy, was the agent of President George W. Bush. The transition from Garner to Bremer was disruptive, with dramatic changes that had not been projected in the prewar plans or during ORHA's short preparation.

Those changes would have profound consequences and lead to a much longer ordeal in Iraq than the Bush administration or the American people anticipated. The intended liberation of Iraq became an unintended occupation, with broad aspects of nation building. The United States had not taken on an occupation of that nature and on such a large scale since World War II. For what followed World War II, the United States had made extensive preparations; for Iraq sixty years later, the preparations by the United States were grossly inadequate.

PROLOGUE:
MARSHALL HAD TWO YEARS

In January 1942, General George Marshall had a lot on his mind. The attack on Pearl Harbor had destroyed much of the U.S. Navy's fleet. American forces in the Philippines were under siege, supposedly to be relieved by that fleet, but destined for the largest surrender of American forces in history—to an enemy noted for abusing the vanquished. Germany and Italy had declared war on the United States. American waters were under submarine attack. Yet in that month the Army Chief of Staff had the vision to begin preparation for the liberation and occupation that would come with Allied victory.

In early 1942, the U.S. Army started a new school for military government and established a Civil Affairs branch.[1] It would be well over two years before American forces began to occupy Germany and over three years before the occupation of Japan, but the chores of liberation preceded them. Before 1942 was over, American forces liberated French territory in North Africa. In 1943 Italy was invaded, initially as an adversary, then as an ally under German control, with aspects of both occupation and liberation. France was liberated in 1944 along with other European countries, and the Philippines were liberated from Japan. While Germany and Japan were occupied, so were Austria, Okinawa, and Korea. Each liberation and occupation provided a potential model for the future, yet the lessons offered were often ignored and had to be relearned with each conflict. Such would be the case for Iraq in 2003.

Even during World War II, the political guidance, so essential for tailoring military activity, developed with inconsistency, and military leaders had to work through it. Officers of Marshall's generation had some experience with civil administration from their prewar service in the Philippines, the Canal Zone, and some domestic programs during the Great Depression. But prior to World War II, there had been only one American experience of occupying a modern state defeated in war. Fortunately, the Army had made an effort to learn from it.

As World War I ended, the U.S. Army participated in the occupation of the

German Rhineland alongside British, French, and Belgian armies. The U.S. First and Second Army Headquarters had been formed by General John J. Pershing in France to command the American corps and divisions participating in the war. To prepare for the American share of the occupation of Germany, Pershing formed an additional headquarters as the U.S. Third Army.[2] As war ended in November 1918, American forces fought east to the Meuse River. The Third Army then took control of eight infantry divisions and advanced fifty miles to the Moselle River, in the process liberating Luxembourg, briefly providing military government until a national government could be reconstituted. By December, the Third Army had advanced fifty miles further to the Rhine River opposite Coblenz.[3]

With 250,000 American soldiers, the Third Army had little difficulty establishing security within its zone by early 1919. That allowed a gradual reduction to 120,000 troops by June, a one-to-eight ratio for one million Germans in the American sector. As security remained adequate, additional reductions were conducted throughout the occupation period into 1923. The demands upon military leadership changed, and General Pershing did not hesitate to replace the Third Army's first two commanders when their skills for managing an occupation were shown to be less than their skills in combat.[4]

The Third Army established five departments for occupation: Public Works and Utilities; Fiscal Affairs; Sanitation and Public Health; Schools and Charitable Institutions; and Legal, all of which operated as military staff sections. Some of the officers in those departments were regulars of the Engineer, Medical, and Judge Advocate General branches; some were reservists from comparable civilian professions.[5] Prior to World War I, the Army lacked a modern staff system. When Pershing arrived in France, he chose the French staff system for the American Army with four General Staff sections: G-1 Personnel, G-2 Intelligence, G-3 Operations, and G-4 Logistics. When the Third Army was established, it added a G-5 staff section for Civil Affairs, to control the five civil departments it created. The Assistant G-5, Colonel Irwin L. Hunt, subsequently assumed control of those staff sections through several years of occupation and wrote a multivolume report on that experience, later known as the Hunt Report.[6]

The Hunt Report noted with candor that the "American Army of occupation lacked both training and organization to guide the destinies of the nearly one million civilians whom the fortunes of war had placed under its temporary sovereignty; it [was] deficient in knowledge of German culture, politics, agriculture, and civil infrastructure."[7] But by establishing adequate security with large infantry formations during the initial occupation, the Third Army had time to learn and adapt. Occupation activities were coordinated with

American diplomats in Europe as Herbert Hoover led a civilian relief effort in Germany.

During the 1920s and 1930s, the Army War College curriculum used the original Hunt Report to study the occupation of the Rhineland. In 1939 the Army published FM 27–10, *The Rule of Land Warfare,* a field manual that "provided guidance concerning the rights and obligations of occupied forces," followed in 1940 by FM 27–5, *Military Government,* for the management of liberated and occupied areas. By 1943 the Army had condensed and published the Hunt Report as *American Military Government of Occupied Germany, 1918–1920.* While oriented on Germany, that manual provided concepts that could be used for other occupied or liberated areas.[8]

CIVIL AFFAIRS

Establishing a school system during World War II for a new Civil Affairs branch—to guide humanitarian assistance, liberation, and occupation—was a challenge. Such a branch would require officers with sophisticated training and education. Military schools for the Infantry, Artillery, and Engineers could be expanded from existing installations and cadres, but the new Civil Affairs branch had no base or cadre to expand. As the training and education for Civil Affairs and Military Government was more academic than other military training, the Army turned to American universities, looking for one "at a place easily accessible to the War College," then at Fort McNair in Washington, D.C.[9]

The University of Virginia, two hours southwest of Washington, D.C., in Charlottesville, was quick to offer its services and helped to develop a Civil Affairs curriculum. By the end of 1942, it had graduated 164 officers in two classes, against an assessed requirement of 6,000 officers for 1944. Soon other universities joined the endeavor: Columbia, Yale, Harvard, Pittsburgh, Chicago, Michigan, Johns Hopkins, and Stanford, later Northwestern, Princeton, Tufts, Dartmouth, Boston University, Wisconsin, and Western Reserve. Columbia, and later Princeton, also took on a Civil Affairs program for the Navy to manage islands secured in the Pacific.[10] Those universities were motivated both by patriotism and a concern that the war would deprive them of prospective students. Exploiting university faculties and facilities for the war effort was in the mutual interest of the military services and the universities.

These programs soon encountered political resistance. The New Dealers in the Roosevelt administration questioned the Army lead on Civil Affairs and Military Government. Political figures such as Secretary of the Treasury Henry

Morgenthau, Secretary of the Interior Harold L. Ickes, and presidential advisor Harry Hopkins, among others, felt that the Army "had packed the school with Republicans and anti–New Dealers who are not socially minded." Ickes denounced "military government plans as 'imperialistic,'" and argued that the Interior Department, which included the Bureau of Indian Affairs, should administer occupied territories for "primitive" people.[11]

The Army response was mixed. There was little enthusiasm for liberation and occupation chores, yet older military officers familiar with the management of Indian Reservations were skeptical that the Department of the Interior could undertake large endeavors overseas. Civilian government agencies had made no substantive contribution in the occupation of the Rhineland. During the Depression the Army had managed the Civilian Conservation Corps and other programs to relieve unemployment and to promote public works. Army officers felt they had demonstrated the capacity to set up large programs for civilians, while the federal and state government had struggled with such tasks.[12]

Eventually Secretary of War Henry Stimson brought about a compromise within the government. High-profile speakers were invited to address the students attending the Civil Affairs schools and New Dealers visited to observe classes and meet the faculties. Those from the Department of the Interior realized major operations overseas were beyond their means.[13] But the Army was not prepared with cohesive plans, nor was there an end to political interference.

CIVIL AFFAIRS IN THE EUROPEAN THEATERS

The first experience with occupation did not come with Germany or Japan. Instead it came in French North Africa and Italy. In November 1942, the U.S. Army invaded French Morocco and Algeria, later Tunisia, and began a Mediterranean campaign that it had not anticipated. Humanitarian assistance was the first task for those countries. As American forces provided infrastructure and relief assistance, the debate over civilian versus military control was incomplete. The Army initially allowed the State Department to establish policies and to guide the relief efforts. However, it soon became apparent to the Allied Command, General Dwight D. Eisenhower and his subordinates, that the

> State Department was not an operating agency and dealt only with the relations between sovereign states. On the other hand, the Army had

had experience in doing the thousand and one things that a government must do: it fed men, it housed them, it guarded their health, it operated camps larger than many cities, and it maintained courts and dispensed justice. By any functional standard the Army was infinitely better qualified to administer a local government . . . than [the State Department].[14]

State Department personnel sent to North Africa could not unload ships arriving with relief supplies, set up distribution sites, or transport supplies within the theater of operations. The State Department could conduct diplomacy, but it could not manage the civil infrastructure in Morocco, Algeria, or Tunisia. President Roosevelt prodded the State Department to assume the lead role throughout the summer of 1943, but when it became clear State could not handle it, in November the president imposed that role upon the Army. By that time, the Army had invaded Sicily and the Italian mainland; Italy had surrendered and joined the Allies side. That allowed the pretense of liberation rather than occupation of Italy, but many liberation tasks were comparable with occupation tasks, with Italian political cohesion slow to form and crippled by the war's devastation. Relief operations expanded as the Allies advanced, absorbing Army personnel graduating from the Civil Affairs and Military Government programs.

A key issue for Italy came before it was invaded, when President Roosevelt proposed that all senior Italian political and administrative officials be replaced by Allied military officers, disregarding Army doctrine: "As far as possible deal with the inhabitants through indigenous personnel." Military planners argued for indirect rule using Italian officials, held accountable to the Allies because

- the indirect system economizes on Allied Civil Affairs personnel;
- local subordinate personnel are more likely to obey the orders of their own superiors;
- fewer language difficulties;
- local personnel will remain at work and work loyally if they have a fair chance;
- less danger of a general strike with local administration;
- any administrative breakdown will tend to be attributed by the public . . . to their own officials, rather than to the Allied Military Government;
- Allies will not appear to be implementing a government that appears either colonial or approaches annexation.[15]

Winston Churchill urged Roosevelt to allow the use of Italian leadership when possible and to allow Eisenhower to manage the situation to avoid a drain on Allied manpower. The Combined Chiefs of Staff supported that position, directing the establishment of an Allied Government in Sicily, with the ground commander determining which Italian leaders needed to be replaced. The Fascist Party was to be disbanded with the removal from leadership positions of only those who were party leaders, not nominal fascists in the civil infrastructure.[16]

As Allied forces occupied Sicily, Eisenhower issued a proclamation "to deliver the people of Italy from the Fascist Regime . . . to restore Italy as a Free Nation." But Allied leaders found that Fascism "cannot be broken up or Fascist influence eliminated in a day. Since nearly all Italian administrative officials, at any rate nominally, are members of the Party, it will not be possible to remove or intern all. This would merely cause a breakdown, not only of the whole of the Italian administrative machine, but of all technical services." At the tactical level, Civil Affairs officers followed the Charlottesville dictum of "Put first things first," on the ground restated as "Bury the dead and feed the living" while chaos reigned with "no food, fuel, power, or water; rubble, ruin, and filth were on every hand and looting was rampant." Shortages of food and coal (for electricity) were the biggest challenges. A key lesson was not to promise what could not be delivered.[17]

Political guidance was complicated. Italy began the war as an ally of Germany. Churchill and Roosevelt defined the German Nazi Party as a menace that had to be disbanded and directed the same for the Italian Fascist Party. Their view of the German people was harsh while their view of the Italian people was sympathetic. Roosevelt promoted "the principle of benevolence." He believed Italy could be turned from an adversary into a useful ally against Germany. That would require discretion in dealing with Fascist leaders.[18]

Part of the challenge was determining what kind of government Italy should have and how to deal with the Fascists. Eisenhower's political advisor, Robert Murphy, noted that "the British, especially Churchill, wanted Italy to revert to a British-type monarchy [while] . . . the Americans favored an American-style federal republic . . . and the Russians . . . thinking of imposing their own image, [wanted] Communism."[19] When it was one of many parties in Italy, the Fascist ideology was powerful and consistent in the party. After Italy became a one-party state in 1925, party membership was the only route to advancement in many fields. Many Italians joined the party regardless of their true beliefs and the political ideology was thus diluted. When the Fascists were forced from power in 1943, Italy had been a single-party state for almost two decades. Murphy felt that after so many "years of Fascist dictatorship, every

Italian of consequence who had remained in Italy was tarred in some way or other with the Fascist brush."[20] It was one thing for those in Washington to demand that all Fascists be thrown out and quite another for those on the ground to sustain order and security without Italian management in many spheres. Vetting individual Fascists, in support of Allied political policy, required workable techniques, timely adaptation, and innovation. In the beginning the burden was on military officers to turn the process over to a new Italian government. Two techniques were employed: the Scheda Personale, a political questionnaire, and committees of known anti-Fascist Italians to review the records of Fascists under Allied supervision.[21]

The Scheda Personale consisted of fifty background questions, each answerable with a simple yes or no. Once completed and signed, an individual had defined his political background and staked his public integrity on its veracity. The Allies turned responsibility for vetting Fascists over to Marshall Pietro Badoglio, leader of the new Italian government. Marshall Badoglio wanted to get rid of the Fascists, but he meant the notorious Fascists. His new government was reluctant to dismiss nominal party members that might disrupt civil administration, create unemployment, or impose unnecessary grievances.[22]

Of the Italian armed forces, little was left of the air force and the modest Italian fleet joined the Allied fleets. The Italian army was larger. When Italy surrendered and joined the Allies, part of the Italian army was dissolved, notably factions with strong Fascist identification. Many reservists and conscripts were released from active duty and sent home, some by way of POW camps. The rest were retained in uniform.[23]

When Italy declared war on Germany, Eisenhower thought it would help Italian morale to use part of the Italian army in the war, which would also reduce unemployment, a serious problem in Italy. The most useful were the military service forces: transportation, medical, and engineering units that could assist both Allied forces and the Italian people. Several regimental combat units were embedded in American and British formations to fight the Germans or provide rear security. Keeping an Italian army active also provided a cadre to form the regular army that Italy would raise as the war ended, eventually joining NATO forces in the 1950s.[24]

For the invasion of France, the U.S. Army had 2,500 officers and 5,000 enlisted men in Civil Affairs units, attached to corps and divisions (another 2,700 officers and 5,000 enlisted men were designated for Military Government units designated for the occupation of Germany). The primary mission of Civil Affairs units during the invasion of France was humanitarian assistance and to help French leaders reestablish control of the civil and political infrastructure with the following goals:

- to maintain supervision over local officials and agencies;
- to maintain provost courts;
- to plan and control civilian travel;
- to aid restoration and administration of public health, sanitation, and medical care;
- to reestablish normal financial services;
- to assist in the receipt and forwarding of claims;
- to provide for safeguarding of local records, public monuments, and works of art
- to make recommendations for investigations and surveys.[25]

Establishing political leadership for France was complicated. President Roosevelt was reluctant to accept General Charles de Gaulle as the political leader for France and did not acknowledge him as such until mid-1944. De Gaulle could be difficult, but he was a durable leader and he had the political skills to unify French efforts against the Germans and serve as the figurehead for French resistance. As a French general, he was instrumental in recruiting manpower for a new French army. By the summer of 1944, the Allies had trained and equipped seven French divisions. As the invasion progressed, the French replaced their casualty losses and mobilized three more divisions from the French population as the country was liberated.[26]

As Civil Affairs officers and formations assisted military formations with humanitarian assistance and infrastructure, they also established a section for the protection of "monuments, fine arts, and archives." With the assistance of specialists in the United States and Great Britain, qualified Civil Affairs officers drew up lists of sites to be protected in areas liberated or occupied. They kept Allied invasion forces informed of what should be protected during the fighting.[27]

Allied occupation policy was not yet finalized by the autumn of 1944, when Aachen, near the Belgian border, became the first German town to fall to American forces. In contrast to the benevolent policy that characterized American activities during the occupation of the Rhineland after World War I and for Italy in 1943, occupation of Germany following World War II was intentionally punitive. The Italian people were treated as victims of the Fascist regime, while the German people were held responsible for Nazi activities. The visceral instincts of the Roosevelt administration were harsh, and Secretary of War Stimson wrote General Marshall, "It is very interesting to find Army officers have a better respect . . . in these matters than civilians . . . [who are] anxious to go ahead and chop everybody's head off without a trial or hearing."[28]

At Yalta in 1944 and at Potsdam in 1945, Allied leaders determined that Germany and Austria would be occupied by Allied forces in zones, with Germany as a defeated state and Austria as a liberated state. Denazification would be imposed in both countries with the view that German Nazis had been the greater menace and warranted more draconian measures. Originally, military leaders intended mandatory removal of only those Nazis who were in the party prior to 1933 or were guilty of criminal acts. "Those who had joined the party after the Nazi takeover in January 1933 [when other German parties were outlawed] would not be dismissed or denied employment outright if they could show that they had not been active members and had joined solely to save their jobs."

That critical date was soon shifted to 1937, after which "public employees had been required to join the party or lose their jobs." But even that was deemed too lenient by American political leaders. In 1944, Allied political policy for Germany became more extreme with the intent to remove all Nazi Party members from positions in government and industry—a contrast to Allied policy for Italy where the Badoglio government had been allowed to retain the less offensive Fascists.[29]

Five American field armies fought in the European and Mediterranean theaters during World War II: the First, Third, Fifth, Seventh, and Ninth. When the war ended the Third and Seventh Armies occupied the American sector in Germany and Austria, later reduced to just the Third Army in Germany. The U.S. Fifth Army was to occupy the American sector in Austria, but other units got there first. The Fifth Army provided Civil Affairs teams and headquarters elements in Austria under General Mark Clark, who became the Military Governor of the American zone. As Supreme Allied Commander in Europe, Eisenhower commanded almost three million American and Allied soldiers. When the fighting stopped, the initial requirement was security, effectively achieved with the number of military formations available for occupation.[30]

In July 1945, Eisenhower's Allied headquarters was disbanded and he reverted to commander of American forces in Europe, initially with sixty-one divisions, most to be demobilized. Military planners projected an eventual occupation force of eight divisions for the American zone in Germany, under General George S. Patton's Third Army. Patton was an outstanding field commander, but he did not adapt well to the political nuances and management required for occupation. As General Pershing had replaced several inadequate commanders during occupation in 1919, General Eisenhower replaced Patton with Lieutenant General Lucian Truscott in 1945 as a more suitable commander for occupation. Although demobilization was accelerated, the large infantry formations that invaded Germany remained long enough to reduce chaos and allow Military Government units to adapt.[31]

Overall management of the American occupation zone went to Lieutenant General Lucius D. Clay, Eisenhower's deputy for military government. Eisenhower preferred an early transition to civilian control under the State Department, but the Secretary of State knew his department could not handle that role and deferred to the Army.[32] General Clay believed American civilians should be involved in the military government, and if they could not take over completely he wanted as many as possible in his command. Their contribution would be limited. The military officers noted that many civilians that joined "were not career U.S. Government civil servants; they were only in Germany and other occupied areas on a temporary basis. . . . The situation did not attract the best personnel." Of the 12,000 personnel under Clay by 1946, charged with managing local and national government in Germany, the majority were military with only a few American civilians and an increasing number of German civilians.[33]

With the countryside secured, restoring electricity was a critical objective. German electricity was produced by coal from the Ruhr region. Coal was also used to heat homes. As the war ended, coal production was 15 percent of prewar levels, insufficient to sustain the German infrastructure. Anticipating a cold winter with a coal shortage, in August 1945 Eisenhower told the German population to begin cutting wood. Military units provided the people with saws and axes. Scarcity of food supplies made the winter harsher. Inadequate heat and food led to dysentery, typhoid, and diphtheria, which required additional assistance from occupation forces.[34]

Coal and electricity shortages adversely affected German industry and increased unemployment, which further crippled the economy. So did denazification. Comparable to the Scheda Personale questionnaire used in Italy, military government in Germany used the Fragebogen questionnaire as a requirement for employment in government, industry, and with the occupation forces; it was also required to obtain a ration card. The questionnaire could be usefully checked against 12 million Nazi party registration cards (with photos) found in Munich. Falsifying the Fragebogen was a criminal offense, as it had been with the Scheda Personale.[35]

Denazification went through several phases in Germany. Early in the war, American military leaders knew that the Nazi Party would be destroyed, but assumed the worst Nazis would either be dead or would flee while the lesser Nazis would be retained to help manage Germany. In early 1944, a Civil Affairs unit working on Germany produced a handbook to guide commanders during the initial occupation stage. They were to suspend German courts and educational systems, but it would not be possible to do the same with general administration or services like railroads and public utilities. One section of the handbook instructed Allied commanders to "require all [German] officials to remain at their post until further notice," which suggested the use of German civil servants, many presumably minor Nazi officials.[36]

American political leaders had a more draconian view—of varying degrees. Secretary of Treasury Henry Morgenthau took the harshest position, proposing a plan that would punish the German people, divide the country, reduce industrialization, and make the country much more agrarian. The president and others were more measured, although they demanded sterner measures than the Civil Affairs handbook suggested. That would include the removal of all Nazis from any position in government or business, a policy intentionally punitive. After the initial efforts to comply with American political policy, military government leaders found it necessary to compromise and employ some Nazis for short periods (as in Italy with some Fascists) for essential management.[37]

The final phase of denazification began in March 1946, with quasi-judicial boards composed of Germans without Nazi backgrounds. They divided Nazi Party members into five categories: major offenders subject to prosecution; activists, militarists, and profiteers; probationary offenders; followers; and those exonerated. American policy directed that German boards treat Nazism as a crime and required a schedule of punishments: up to ten years imprisonment for major offenders, five years or less for offenders, fines of 10,000 marks for lesser offenders, and fines of 1,000 marks for followers. But Germans on the boards felt denazification should be a form of rehabilitation with the eventual "removal of the Nazi stigma from the individual and his reinstatement in society." The German boards were lenient and by 1948 had granted amnesty to all but the most criminal Nazis. One American observer noted: "Thus a process was begun with wholesale incriminations turned in the direction of wholesale exemptions and then ended in wholesale exonerations," a significant modification from the intent of American political leaders.[38]

Despite their eventual exoneration, ex-Nazis had been penalized before they were returned to productive society. The conclusion of the U.S. Army official historian was that "denazification was probably the chief, and certainly the most energetically pursued, tactical objective of the early occupation . . . [and] probably the least satisfactory of all military government undertakings. Before the end of 1945, denazification on the terms originally envisioned had been proven impractical; and in the long run, if less had been attempted, more might have been accomplished."[39]

In May 1949, the Federal Republic of Germany (West Germany) was established from the American, British, and French occupied sectors; it joined NATO with rejuvenated armed forces in 1954. Eisenhower had stated as the war ended, "The success of this occupation can only be judged fifty years from now. If the Germans at that time have a stable, prosperous democracy, then we shall have succeeded." The Germans achieved that with Allied assistance in less than ten years.[40] They had done so with hardship, but without violence or widespread chaos.

As the war ended, Austria was separated from Germany. Nazis had competed for power in Austria as early as 1934, and by 1938 that movement led to Austria's seven provinces to be absorbed into Germany as German provinces. At Potsdam in July 1945, the Allies declared Austria's union with Germany null and void and decided that Austria would be occupied as a liberated rather than a defeated country. Austria was not required to sign a surrender document, as some Austrian towns had set up non-Nazi governments before the arrival of occupation forces.[41]

Austria did not, however, experience the same sort of liberation as France, Belgium, Denmark, and Norway. It would go through occupation with an Allied quadripartite system of military administration with Russian, British, American, and French zones. As in Germany, those zones often cut across provincial boundaries and divided the capital city, Vienna. For the American zone, the U.S. Fifth Army had established a school in Italy for the purpose of military government for Austria; 150 Civil Affairs officers and men were ready to go to Austria when the war ended, and more followed. When they arrived they found conditions in Austria austere; people lacked gas, coal, bread, vegetables, meat, clothing, and shoes, and they had only infrequent electricity. During the chaos of the first few months, there was an increase of crime and looting. The harsh winter of 1945–46 was as difficult for Austria as it was for Germany. The Soviets and French imposed reparations on Austria with soldiers of both countries living off the land in their respective areas, which compounded food shortages. The British and Americans did not impose reparations and brought in food for the population and for their own soldiers.[42]

In Austria, the initial phase of denazification in the American sector was as draconian as that imposed in Germany. But in contrast to the extended program in Germany, within a year denazification was turned over to responsible Austrians, with the intent to reform rather than punish the Nazis. When general elections were held in Austria in November 1945, former Nazis were not allowed to vote, but they were allowed to vote in the elections of 1949. As in Germany, there were policy disagreements among the Allies, and when there was agreement, application of policy often differed. The view of Austrian political parties reflected the political inclination of each occupying nation with the American, British, and French inclined to restrain the communist parties and support those more moderate or conservative, some of the latter with aspects of the previous era.[43]

In the American sector there was a succession of military governors beginning with General Mark Clark, aided by civilian advisors from the Department of State and other agencies. As in the American sector in Germany, American forces in Austria were reduced and replaced in part by Army constabulary formations, as Austrian forces were reformed and armed. In 1950, President Truman directed that an American civilian take over as governor of the American sector in Austria, although the Department of the Army retained executive responsibility for the occupation.[44]

With war in Korea that year, American military and political leaders began to manage their policies for Austria more in the light of a growing Cold War. American constabulary formations were reformed as conventional formations and shifted focus from internal to external security. The Soviet Union wanted American, British, and French forces out of Austria just as those countries wanted Soviet forces to depart. Austrians wanted all foreign forces to leave. After extensive negotiations, by May 1955 Austria was restored to full sovereignty and all occupation forces had left by October.[45]

CIVIL AFFAIRS IN THE PACIFIC THEATERS

The Army Civil Affairs program began with a European focus and did not produce officers for the Pacific Theaters until its eighth class; meanwhile, Navy programs at Columbia and Princeton that focused on the Pacific graduated only a small class in August 1942. Despite the Navy having fewer graduates compared to the Army program, the numbers were adequate for the sparse populations in the Marshall, Caroline, Mariana, and Bonin Islands. The Navy turned administration of these islands over to the British, Australians, and Dutch who had prewar interests in them, while MacArthur turned administration of New Guinea over to the Australians and the Dutch. Australia and New Zealand assumed much of the occupation duties for the Solomons, Fiji, and other islands in the South Pacific. The significant U.S. Army liberation in the region came with the invasion of Leyte, a province of the Philippines, in October 1944.

MacArthur lacked a cadre of Charlottesville graduates and until the last minute had to contend with conflicting guidance from the Roosevelt administration over whether American soldiers or civilians were better prepared for such a governance role. Secretary Ickes demanded that a senior civilian representative from the Department of the Interior accompany combat forces ashore and assume responsibility for relief operations in the Philippines. MacArthur objected to such a political incursion, which would bring no administrative capacity.[46] Roosevelt decided in the Army's favor just as the invasion of Leyte was underway, and MacArthur delegated responsibility to his subordinate ground force commander, General Walter Krueger. On its own initiative, MacArthur's command established eight Philippine Civil Affairs Units (PCAUs) to be distributed throughout the Sixth Army, with each unit consisting of ten officers and thirty-nine men, most of them Filipinos. When MacArthur invaded Luzon in 1945, again with Krueger's Sixth Army, he went ashore with thirteen PCAUs. The Filipino population was friendly and military forces were able to turn civil administration over to Filipino authorities. MacArthur also harnessed the resistance movement against the Japanese in the Philippines, both to finish the war and to rebuild the Philippine army.[47]

Engineering projects in the Philippines included constructing airfields and rebuilding infrastructure destroyed during the fighting, particularly in Manila. In the process, MacArthur's command created three Corps of Engineer districts (Leyte, Luzon, and Manila) and in March 1945 formed them into a new Engineer Command, ENCOM, under Major General Leif J. Sverdrup. While Corps of Engineer districts in the United States let contracts for their projects to commercial firms, in the Philippines during and immediately after the war ENCOM used military engineer formations for its projects until commercial firms were available.[48]

To reinforce reconstruction capacity and provide jobs for unemployed Filipinos, Sverdrup organized the Construction Corps of the Philippines (CONCOR) to make use of Philippine labor for ENCOM construction projects. Four CONCOR battalions were formed, each 1,100 strong including 92 American soldiers, organized as civilian variants of military construction battalions. The CONCOR units built barracks, warehouses, and hospitals, maintained roads and utilities, accelerated reconstruction, sustained employment, and put money into the economy as they developed useful construction skills.[49]

As the Philippines were being liberated by MacArthur's Southwest Pacific Command, Admiral Chester Nimitz's Central Pacific Command executed Operation ICEBERG, the invasion of Okinawa (April 1945). This was the last major American campaign of the war and one of the most deadly and destructive. The Navy had responsibility for civil affairs and military government for Okinawa. Nimitz had Civil Affairs officers on his staff; so did the U.S. Tenth Army in charge of ground forces for the invasion of Okinawa.[50]

Although many Okinawans were conscripted for military and labor duties under Japanese control, Nimitz and his staff knew they were a subjected population and not responsible for Japanese atrocities. Nimitz's directed that military occupation be "stern, but just." To offset the initial shortage of Navy Civil Affairs officers in the summer of 1945, the Army provided Civil Affairs officers and teams as they became available.[51] Service formations were attached to the Civil Affairs units: Army quartermaster (supply) and military police battalions, a Navy engineer battalion, six Navy field hospitals, and twenty Navy medical dispensaries. This set a new precedent with Civil Affairs having direct control of supporting formations rather than trying to coordinate with such units through division and corps.[52]

Combat operations on Okinawa lasted three months and produced one of the highest casualty rates of the war for both military and civilian personnel. Most of the fighting took place at one end of the island with much of the Civil Affairs tasks on the other, where the destitute civilian population had fled. The lowest estimate of civilian losses was 42,000 killed; another estimate suggested that "one-fourth of the civilian population perished." The remainder was dispersed in remote areas without shelter, adequate food, or medical facilities. When fighting ended in July, there were 259,000 American servicemen on Okinawa, with 2,600 employed in Civil Affairs and Military Government units. Half the civilian population, almost 300,000, were in temporary refugee camps.[53]

The immediate requirements were food, health services, and shelter. When fighting terminated in August, there were 100,000 Okinawan civilians in Japan and other islands to be repatriated. The influx of additional refugees complicated the challenges of putting the agricultural population back to work, when much of the arable land was consumed by American bases and airfields. Military government officers set up a civil government run by the Okinawan people, an ambitious task given that much of the previous administration had been under Japanese rather than Okinawan leadership. In the interim, military government officials provided intermediate management and government, as they trained the population in administrative skills.[54]

In July 1946, postwar administration for Okinawa shifted from the Pacific Naval command to MacArthur's Far East Asia Command, which also administered postwar Japan. Back in the United States, "Congress established a Government and Relief in Occupied Areas (GARIOA) fund to assist civilians in the Ryukyus [Okinawa], as well as in occupied Japan, Germany, and elsewhere," with $164,500,000 for the Ryukyus "to stimulate the economy with pump-priming projects . . . building roads, hospitals, underwriting the establishment of industries . . . higher education, and funding central banks." As American forces progressed across the Central Pacific during 1944–1945, the U.S. Army established Corps of Engineer districts in the Marianas and Okinawa under the Western Ocean Division, comparable to the Corps of Engineer regional divisions in the United States, and the engineer districts established in the Philippines under ENCOM.[55]

The major occupation of the Pacific Theater came with the surrender of Japan. America's war with Japan lasted three years and eight months. The occupation would last twice as long—six years and eight months—with a profound impact on Japanese society and politics. To complement projected invasion plans, MacArthur's staff had developed a plan to cover a pre-invasion surrender or collapse of Japan: Operation Blacklist. When Japan sued for peace in August, following the use of nuclear bombs on Hiroshima and Nagasaki, Blacklist became the basis for occupation. Emperor Hirohito ordered the Japanese military services and civilians to cooperate with the Allied occupation forces; the Allies in turn allowed Hirohito to continue in his role as emperor.[56]

Japan had over fifty army divisions in the country with much of the Japanese government infrastructure intact. The initial Allied occupation force included sixteen infantry divisions, divided among General Eichelberger's Eighth Army, General Krueger's Sixth Army, and a small Allied force from Australia and Great Britain. In the Philippines, Guam, and Hawaii, other American forces were available if needed.[57]

The first two tasks for the occupation forces were security and humanitarian relief. With Japan compliant, security was manageable and occupation policies were more benevolent than the Japanese anticipated. Allied soldiers were directed not to confiscate personal property or to use Japanese food stocks. But food and other supplies were scarce, water systems were broken and often polluted, sanitation was inadequate, and disease was an immediate health concern. Food had to be imported, water and sewer systems fixed or improved, and health monitored for disease. Shelter was a challenge with some civilian displacement, military demobilization, and repatriation of Japanese soldiers and civilians from overseas.[58]

MacArthur achieved unity of command as Supreme Commander for the Allied Powers (SCAP), through which he commanded all forces and Military Government units in Japan. Although British and Commonwealth troops participated, Japan was not subdivided politically by the Allies as in Germany and Austria. For the Civil Affairs and Military Government units, it was an American show. Japan's civil government was functioning when MacArthur arrived, and he directed that it continue, subject to his supervision and guidance. The policy that Allied military government imposed would be indirect rather than direct. In Japan, there was no political party or ideology comparable to the German Nazi Party. A purge of the senior Japanese leadership, militarists, and ultra-nationalists was conducted on a case-by-case basis by boards of Allied officers, subsequently augmented and later replaced by boards of respected Japanese.[59]

Japanese military formations were regionally distributed throughout Japan with two General Army groups aligned with the provincial regions. As the Allied occupation forces arrived, Eichelberger's Eighth Army was aligned with the Japanese First General Army Group and Krueger's Sixth Army with the Second General Army group, in order to manage demobilization and disarmament. That aligned the respective occupation formations with Japanese provincial governments. That was not the case in Germany and Austria, where conditions of terrain and Allied politics, rather than alignment with provincial boundaries, determined the distribution of occupation forces.

The Japanese military command structure was retained as the control agent for demobilization under Allied supervision. Japanese soldiers were used to dispose of military equipment and munitions, and they assisted with other labor intensive tasks as well. As occupied forces arrived, there had been looting of military stores by Japanese civilians; the main target was foodstuffs and medical supplies rather than weapons and munitions. It also appeared that those in control of the Bank of Japan and other resources passed cash and building materials on to cronies during the period when occupation forces arrived; it would be difficult to identify and recover such assets later.[60]

By the end of 1945 there were over 5,000 U.S. military government personnel dispersed throughout Japan, organized in seven groups and eighteen companies. They were aligned with the occupation divisions and Japanese provincial governments at the local and regional levels. Japanese police forces took direction from the military government teams. As in Germany, the numerous American infantry divisions deployed early in Japan ensured stability. With security achieved, MacArthur's occupation forces were gradually reduced, with the Sixth Army deactivated in January 1946. By 1950 the Eighth Army retained military control of Japan with only four divisions.[61]

MacArthur added eight staff sections to his headquarters: Civil Affairs for humanitarian relief; Government; Economic and Scientific; National Resources; Public Health and Welfare; Civil Intelligence, with a Public Safety Division, which supervised the Japanese Police, Fire Department, Maritime, and Customs; Legal; and Civil Information and Education. While those staff sections focused mainly on policy, the Eighth Army established comparable staff sections to supervise the implementation of those policies. Special expertise was required in those sections, necessitating the use of regular officers from Engineer, Military Police, Medical Corps, and the Judge Advocate General Corps and military reservists with appropriate civilian skills.

MacArthur wanted a large number of qualified civilians from other U.S. departments and agencies for such functions, but few volunteered and they could not be ordered to go. Of those that went, many were not from U.S. government agencies but civilians contracted for such positions. They often lacked the experience and skills required and many were not willing to remain in Japan more than a few months. That caused a high turnover and many vacancies, which put more of the burden on military officers.[62] Obtaining qualified civilians from the American government departments and agencies was a consistent problem in other theaters in World War II.

As in the European theater, once occupation forces provided initial stability, internal security and justice for Japan required three interrelated dimensions: an efficient and impartial police structure, a functional and fair judicial system, and an efficient and humane prison infrastructure. All three components were functional upon arrival of the occupation forces, if lacking democratic and humane traits. With vetting and training by MacArthur's forces and military government teams, an appropriate transition was effectively implemented. Allied military courts augmented Japanese civil courts until the latter were reformed. Prisons were inspected, renovated, and staffed with guards retrained by MacArthur's forces.[63]

MacArthur instituted land reform and promoted labor unions, which helped enlarge and empower the middle class. By 1946 labor unions had 2,700,000 members, over six times the preoccupation number. Intense unionization caused some tension in a country accustomed to a docile labor force, with some communist agitation, closely watched and restrained by the occupation forces.[64]

For long-term legitimacy, it was essential that the Japanese people accept both the policies and the methods necessary for democratic institutions in Japan. The emperor's support ensured general acceptance, but to sustain the process MacArthur wanted a new democratic constitution. Japan had operated under the Meiji Constitution that established a constitutional monarchy in 1890, based on an Imperial German model: the emperor as an active head of state, a strong executive branch, and suffrage limited to land-owning males (most farmers were tenants). Allied leaders wanted Japan to have a constitution with more checks on the executive and greater suffrage. The Japanese leadership that MacArthur had allowed to manage the government was directed to produce such a constitution, but what they offered was conservative and did not transcend their feudalistic concepts of government.[65]

MacArthur rejected their first effort. He had his Government Section draft a constitution and then imposed it upon the Japanese Cabinet and Diet, which reluctantly approved it with a few modifications. One account in a Japanese news magazine published the story of a citizen, who when asked what he thought of the new constitution, replied, "Oh, has it been translated into Japanese?" Despite the heavy-handed approach, the constitution took effect in May 1947 and remained in effect with few changes. While the Japanese elites were conservative and reluctant to make significant changes, the people, weary of war, were ready for change.[66]

Not content to wait for the completion of the constitutional process, MacArthur directed nationwide elections in 1946. Holding elections before a constitution was completed allowed occupation forces to prevent participation by those who had been purged from government or were otherwise considered unsavory. As in Germany and Austria, such people would subsequently join the political process, but not in the formative stages.[67]

A prime concern was economic development, given that the war had badly damaged Japanese industry and trade, and demobilization and repatriation of military personnel had increased unemployment. In order to get the economic engine started, the United States supplied capital through the Government and Relief in Occupied Areas (GARIOA) fund, which assisted in bringing imports such as coal to Japan. This was critical for repairing and expanding electricity systems throughout the country.

The U.S. Tenth Army had been scheduled to invade Korea in 1945, but after Japan surrendered Korea was occupied administratively with reduced forces. The Tenth Army sent its subordinate, the XXIV Corps, to Korea with one infantry division at first and later with two more. The leaner and more junior staff of a corps headquarters was a shoestring operation compared to the numbered Army headquarters in Japan and Germany, given that American objectives were less grand for Korea than for Japan. Initial Allied plans split Korea at the 38th parallel, with Soviet Union forces to occupy the north and American forces the south. As it turned out, the American occupation lasted only three years.[68]

Lieutenant General John Hodge, the XXIV Corps Commander, was appointed at the last minute to command the occupation forces; one historian concluded that the choice of Hodge was made out of sheer political expediency, overlooking the fact that he had no experience with military government or in Asia. Another historian remarked that Hodge "lacked MacArthur's charisma."[69] Ill informed about conditions on the ground and with far too few translators and Korean specialists, Hodge and his command found little favor among the Korean people. The Military Government units had been trained for occupation in Japan, and because the administrative hierarchy in Korea was mainly Japanese, Hodge chose to retain the Japanese Governor General and most of the Japanese administration. Although State Department planners had suggested Japanese administration would be desirable during the initial occupation, protests by the American media led the department to disavow such an approach, and President Truman stated that Japanese officials would be quickly removed. MacArthur directed Hodge to do so immediately.[70]

Replacing the Japanese administration with limited American military forces and poorly prepared military government teams left a serious management void in Korea just as Soviet forces were fomenting fledgling communist movements. Hodge suppressed communist organizations in southern Korea, but his efforts were inadequate for encouraging or empowering political alternatives. When Korea was granted independence on 15 August 1948, the development of South Korea by occupation forces, civil affairs, and military government teams had been limited and less enlightened compared to the occupations of Okinawa and Japan or of Germany and Austria. A constabulary army had been established, but the North Korean invasion in May 1950 proved South Korean forces were insufficiently armed and trained for external defense. Democratic and economic reforms had been less ambitious and developed compared to the other American occupations.

CIVIL AFFAIRS AFTER WORLD WAR II

Shortly after World War II, the War Department disbanded the Civil Affairs Division of the Army Staff and returned responsibility for Civil Affairs and Military Government units to the Provost Marshal Office, with Civil Affairs units established in the Army Reserves. An officer who had served in Civil Affairs in World War II and in Korea wrote that "we are in no better shape to handle military government [in Korea] than we were in 1941." During the Korean War, American forces provided Civil Affairs units for humanitarian assistance but took no role in helping with civil government.[71] After the Korean War, the Civil Affairs and Military Government units faded within the Army structure. In 1959 Civil Affairs was reestablished as a specialty for Army Reserve officers oriented in humanitarian assistance.[72]

Civil Affairs units were activated briefly for American operations in Lebanon in 1958 and the Dominican Republic in 1965. A longer and more developed role during the Cold War came with the Vietnam conflict. Civil Affairs teams were initially deployed there in the early 1960s, followed by Civil Affairs companies and separate platoons for humanitarian assistance.

As the conflict continued, Civil Affairs units and officers were drawn into a program in Vietnam known as the Civil Operations and Revolutionary Development Support (CORDS). Pacification was the general concept associated with CORDS in Vietnam, and it included local and regional aspects of what would later be called nation building. Prior to CORDS, President Johnson watched in frustration as American departments and agencies—Defense, State, USAID, USIA, and the CIA—developed separate and competing programs in Vietnam, all with their own separate budgets. After several studies and recommendations from personnel in Vietnam, Johnson forced an interagency integration. It was clear that the military formations had most of the resources; as a result, CORDS was integrated within the military command with civilian leadership serving in key positions, in some cases comparable to those occupied by general officers. The CORDS program went through several evolutions and was considered a success despite the overall American failure in Vietnam.[73]

In Vietnam, Civil Affairs found a new alignment with Special Forces. In 1972, the Civil Affairs School moved to Fort Bragg, where the Special Forces Schools were located. Civil Affairs became an extension of the Special Forces community to enhance foreign internal defense for developing countries. Most of the units were in the Army Reserves with only one formation, the 96th Civil Affairs Battalion, on active duty. Military government faded from the school curriculum and from the doctrinal tasks.[74]

During the 1980s and 1990s, Civil Affairs units provided humanitarian assistance for operations in Grenada, Panama, Somalia, Bosnia, Haiti, and Kosovo. Although the other American agencies, notably USAID, participated in these endeavors, they did not do so under military command, nor with an integrated interagency structure comparable to the CORDS program in Vietnam. Civil Affairs units and the other agencies assisted often with local government programs, including humanitarian assistance and (rarely after 1945) military government, but all this was meager compared to the grander American efforts involving those countries liberated and occupied following World War II.

By the end of the twentieth century the United States had participated in a wide range of liberation and occupation endeavors, much of that experience coming with the end of World War II. A constant lesson was that there would be surprises and inevitable requirements for more talent, manpower, and funding than initially anticipated. The most consistent requirement was security. Liberation and occupation often took place with civil infrastructure missing or out of service. When government administration was generally intact, it was often dissolved for political reasons. During and following major combat operations, it was essential to provide stability for civilian populations. Experience showed over and over that when large infantry formations were initially available for occupation, stability could be achieved to allow time to assess and determine the appropriate political and military objectives, and to assign appropriate resources to achieve them.

In order to displace military formations for internal security, experience confirmed the importance of effective police forces, functioning courts, and adequate prison systems. Police forces frequently had to be reestablished and reformed, requiring time and resources. Legitimate court systems were necessary to ensure justice and to direct incarceration. To dispose of those incarcerated, a prison system was necessary.

Physical infrastructure had to be put back into operation as security was achieved. In modern states, electricity is essential to sustain water distribution, sewage treatment, hospitals, schools, industry, and some transportation systems, all of which effect employment and economic development. Electricity is normally produced with coal or oil; both in turn require electricity for extraction or refining. Reactivating and sustaining electrical systems was a critical challenge for every liberation and occupation endeavor.

Infrastructure maintenance was often inadequate during and after any lengthy conflict. That in turn required more resources than anticipated to fix infrastructure damaged by war. Ideally, reconstruction would be undertaken by indigenous construction firms, but in most cases they were no longer up to the task. When such firms came from other countries, they often had start-up problems that delayed their contribution and increased costs. Combat engineer units subordinate to military formations could take on limited reconstruction, but far more could be achieved with military construction engineer units consolidated under an engineer command, such as the Engineer Command (ENCOM) that MacArthur established in the Southwest Pacific Theater; or the Corps of Engineer Western Pacific Division established in the Central Pacific Theater. The labor battalions raised by American military engineers in the Philippines provided a means to use the indigenous population for reconstruction as well as to reduce unemployment.

Governance tasks accompanied liberation and occupation. During the liberations of France, Belgium, Netherlands, and the Philippines, governmental transition was swift, with few changes from the prewar systems. Occupations such as those of Germany and Japan were undertaken with the purpose of changing the nature of governments and requiring the use of Military Government units for extended periods: to replace a regime in Germany and to manage the reformation of one retained in Japan. Military officers, apolitical by habit, were more comfortable dealing with the technical rather than political aspects of government. The American and Allied political leadership was more naturally inclined to focus on political parties such as the Fascists in Italy and Nazis in Germany, often with the intent to remove the entire political entity rather than reform it. If the removal of political parties was abrupt, it could complicate transitional stability.

An Army official historian determined that in Germany, "worthy as denazification was in principle, it was not, as military government was painfully aware, realistically conceived. Conducted as a full-scale social revolution, it imposed dangerous strains on the structure of the occupation without necessarily promising any future returns other than more trouble." Clearly, more could have been achieved in Germany with a less aggressive effort to eradicate all administrative personnel with Nazi membership.[75]

The Scheda Personale questionnaire used in Italy and the Fragebogen used in Germany and Austria were useful devices to determine who should be placed or retained in responsible positions. The integration of non-Fascists in Italy and non-Nazis in Austria early in the process led to a more tempered political transition through rehabilitation in contrast with the punitive process imposed in Germany. With a more systematic correction, the Italian and Austrian societies were better able to retain the most useful talent while punishing individually those guilty of atrocities or war crimes. Governance in Japan, which had no political party with the profile of the Fascists or Nazis, was even more successful as MacArthur kept the existing government in place, removing only selected individuals. Military government in Japan was used to guide an existing government rather than replace it, a more effective and less arduous endeavor than military government attempted in Germany.

There was an overriding perception in each experience that governance should be handled by civilian rather than military agencies. But there was no American agency that could take on such a task overseas in an austere environment. Each experience in World War II confirmed that the State Department was not an "operating agency" capable of managing the administration and logistics of national government, much less regional or local government. In the initial phases of an austere environment only a large military formation could undertake such tasks, best managed under the direction of a field army headquarters. This was demonstrated with the U.S. Seventh Army in Sicily, the Fifth Army in mainland Italy, the Seventh and Third Armies in Germany, and the Sixth and Eighth Armies, first in the Philippines, then in Japan.

By doctrine, a field army headquarters connects the tactical and operational with the strategic level of war. With a shift in focus the same headquarters can be used as a base to functionally assist or directly manage local, regional, and national government. The disappointing experience with the XXIV Corps in

Korea in 1945–1947 indicates that the corps headquarters is inappropriate, as by doctrine it is oriented at the tactical level of war, has a smaller and more junior staff, and is far less capable of implementing or guiding governance, engaging major reconstruction projects, and completing other complex and expensive endeavors for a nation-state in a post-conflict transition.

When military leaders wanted to pass humanitarian assistance, reconstruction, and governance on to civilian agencies and found no such agency capable of replacing them, they requested civilian augmentation for the military staffs. The response was consistently limited in numbers and capacity as civilians in government departments cannot simply be ordered overseas as with military personnel. Those that did choose to go were often young volunteers, retirees, or contract personnel who were enthusiastic but often poorly qualified; furthermore, many chose to leave after a brief stay rather than remain to make a major contribution.

The American experience from World War II offers several models for liberation and occupation. The liberations of France, Belgium, Netherlands, and the Philippines were successful examples of restoration. With regard to Japan and Germany, the results were models of long-term reformation, with at least the latter case having been intentionally punitive. Intermediate models are both more complex and perhaps more useful for the contemporary era: Italy, Austria, Okinawa, and Korea were all liberated in theory but occupied in the process, in each case with some institutions restored and others reformed. For those interested in the study of these experiences, it is not necessary to go to the archives or classified material. There is substantial coverage of these experiences in the published memoirs of the participants and the official, social, and political histories.

Unfortunately in 2002 and the first few months of 2003 — the period when the United States conducted its planning to invade Iraq and impose regime change — little attention was given to historical experiences with liberation and occupation. Stated American policy was that Iraq was to be liberated, not occupied,[76] yet when American officials considered historical case studies, they looked only to Germany and Japan, which were not examples of liberation but of intended long-term occupation. It is difficult to find evidence that American officials made a determined effort to study just what liberation would mean for Iraq based upon historical context. Many challenges of the World War II post-conflict experiences would all be encountered anew in Iraq without the benefit of learning from those earlier experiences.

1
MILITARY PLANNING

The invasion of Iraq in March 2003 was the product of extensive planning, including significant work devoted to what would follow. The purpose of the invasion was to remove one regime and replace it with another. The military planning covered removal and replacement, although it was heavily weighted on removal. Military planners assumed that other agencies would work closely with them and focus on regime replacement, an assumption that would not be well validated. Nevertheless, those who believe—and they are legion—that there was little or no attention devoted to replacing the regime of Saddam Hussein prior to the invasion in 2003—are uninformed.

The crucial questions should seek to determine why so little of the planning for regime change in Iraq benefited Jay Garner and ORHA. Clearly, the first group of Americans specifically charged with putting a new Iraqi regime into operation were poorly supported in their efforts. This profound deficiency must take into account both civilian agencies and the military establishment that planned for regime replacement. While planning by civilian agencies was conducted only within a year prior to the 2003 invasion, military planning had been evolving for over a decade. During that decade, the military establishment was driven by complex and competing agendas.

At the beginning of the 1990s, two events had a significant impact upon the Department of Defense and the military services: the end of the Cold War and Operation Desert Storm. With the former came the call for a so-called peace dividend that would include a massive reduction within the American force structure. With the latter came a validation of American military doctrine and equipment that had been designed to defeat the Soviet Union, with the Iraqi army as a surrogate for Soviet doctrine and equipment. To some degree, these experiences were at cross-purposes. The end of the Cold War suggested there would be changes in the nature of national security tasks. Success in Desert Storm confirmed the proficiency of American military forces—based on a Cold War standard. Rather than adapt for the future, much of the energy of those guiding American national security was devoted to enhancing the capacity to fight a Cold War–type conventional adversary.

This was all the more remarkable given the military experience that followed Desert Storm: military operations in Somalia, Haiti, Macedonia, Bosnia, and Kosovo. For a full decade prior to the invasion of Iraq in 2003, American forces were occupied with ethnic conflict and peace operations, with many aspects of nation building. What became known as military operations other than war, or MOOTW (which did include combat and many elements of war), was treated as a backwater compared to continued preparation for a future variant of Desert Storm. As a result, by 2003 American military forces were well prepared to invade and remove the Iraqi regime, but poorly prepared to help replace it.

Much has been said about an "American Way of War." Assessing the application of any such method against recent American military performance in Iraq may be useful. Yet consensus has been elusive for such an American method, as the changes in warfare and the unique context of each conflict make the reduction of common traits debatable. Russell Weigley, a respected military historian, has suggested that the American Way of War has "an attritional impulse even in those instances when a more strictly modulated application of violence may have been more appropriate."[1]

That attritional impulse is commonly aligned to methods employed in the American Civil War and World War II, the two most studied American military experiences. In both cases, exceptionally large armies were raised, equipped, and sustained with a massive industrial base. Others disagree, pointing out that the Civil War and World War II were aberrations in the American military experience, given that the United States has more frequently been involved in smaller conflicts, often driven by guerrilla warfare or insurgencies. However, even in those more numerous experiences, the American method was often to use larger forces to wear down and eventually overwhelm the adversary. In truth, the frequency of the American involvement in small wars and insurgencies has produced no refined method, and with each small war or insurgency, American military leaders and doctrine seem to be starting anew.

Technology became a critical ingredient during the Cold War when the American Army prepared for conflict with the even larger forces of the Soviet Union, both sides supported by large alliances that in terms of numbers favored the Warsaw Pact over NATO. The Cold War produced no major military engagements between American and Soviet forces. The best lessons seemed to come from the Israeli campaigns against Egypt and Syria in 1967 and 1973, when Israel relied as heavily on American weapons as Arab forces relied on Soviet weapons and tactics. From those lessons came the American concept that, through superior training and enhanced technology, America could "fight outnumbered and win."

With technology came efforts to integrate advanced management concepts, an American business attribute notable during Robert McNamara's tenure as Secretary of Defense during the Vietnam conflict. Yet the failure of technology and management techniques to defeat North Vietnamese forces did not deter the effort to continue to promote them as key components in an evolution in the American Way of War. The real war was anticipated against the Warsaw Pact, where American technology and management would have to offset opposing numbers. Fortunately that war never took place.

The demonstrated capacity of the U.S. Army, Navy, Marines, Air Force, and Coast Guard to effectively work together during warfare has a lower profile in American military history. This became most remarkable during World War II with the development of Unified Commands integrating the efforts of the service formations within each theater. Unified Commands were institutionalized with the 1947 National Security Act, which created the Department of Defense and subordinated the service departments to a single cabinet official, the Secretary of Defense, one of the most powerful positions in American government. The Goldwater-Nichols Act of 1986 further enhanced the management and operational aspects of joint warfare.

With Operation Desert Storm came the concept of "overwhelming force," occasionally referred to as the Powell Doctrine after General Colin Powell, the Chairman of the Joint Chiefs of Staff. While Iraq fielded the larger army, certainly if measured in divisions, the greater depth of American air and sea forces, and the vast American advantage in military technology, allowed the American-led Coalition ground forces to overwhelm Iraqi forces. Kuwait was liberated as Iraq was dealt a devastating blow with remarkably few Coalition losses. Evaluations of important lessons were naturally weighted by each service community. Those with the greatest investment in technology, the Air Force and Navy and their supporting industries, argued that technology was the dominant factor in Desert Storm. In contrast, those in the Army and Marines believed it was a combination of training, leadership, and articulated mass on the battlefield that was dominant; as one American division commander stated, "We could have beat them with their equipment."[2]

With the end of the Cold War came a drive to reduce not only American military forces but also those of other NATO countries upon which the United States had long relied. The American military services were reduced from 2.1 to 1.6 million military personnel with the Army taking the biggest cut: divisions were reduced from eighteen to ten and it was with some difficulty that the Army was able to resist the elimination of two more.

Within the Pentagon and the defense industry, the zeal to leverage technology supported the concept of a projected "revolution in military affairs," or RMA, which assumed enhanced intelligence systems, more capable precision weapons, and information technology that could be used to defeat any potential adversary. In 1996, the Pentagon produced *Joint Vision 2010,* a thirty-four-page glossy pamphlet that proposed a "conceptual template for how America's Armed Forces will channel the vitality and innovation of our people and leverage technological opportunities to achieve new levels of effectiveness in joint warfighting." To promote the joint aspect of future warfare, the cover was purple, the color associated with joint commands, and the text repeatedly emphasized the concepts of "precision strike, dominant maneuver, enhanced communications, and focused logistics." Such notions had the greatest utility in conventional operations oriented against an adversary with inferior ships, planes, and tanks. The photos in *JV2010* included modern American equipment projected against an adversary with tanks and other armor vehicles operating in the open desert, comparable to the Iraqi army of Desert Storm.[3]

The pamphlet had no pictures or reference to U.S. operations in Somalia, Haiti, or Bosnia, where American forces had more recently been deployed. Nor was there any mention of ethnic conflict, peace operations, or nation building. *JV2010* was signed by Chairman of the Joint Chiefs of Staff, General John Shalikashvili, but it clearly had the imprint of the Vice Chairman, Admiral William Owens, a prolific writer on futurist topics exploiting technology.[4]

Admiral Owens had a background in submarine operations, one of the most technologically advanced forms of warfare and the most removed from the human dimension of ethnic conflict and insurgency. In 1995, the year before *JV2010* was published, he had promoted cohesive joint warfare to respond "quickly to disrupt, delay, or defeat a regional predator's ground-force operational scheme . . . without sustaining heavy casualties." The emphasis was on speed of deployment and technology. No mention was made of ethnic conflict, insurgencies, or post-conflict operations.[5] The zeal in the Pentagon for enhanced technology and RMA was not fully replicated in the military establishment beyond the Pentagon. And that did not bode well for the world of military planning.

Military planners are generally a faceless lot. During World War II, the most senior American military leaders were well known by their last names—Marshall, King, Arnold, Eisenhower, MacArthur, and Nimitz—as were their most colorful subordinates—Stilwell, Bradley, Patton, Doolittle, and Halsey. But even the full names or nicknames of the key military planners before and during the war—Stanley Embick, Charles "Soc" McMorris, Joseph McNarney, or Charles "Savvy" Cooke—remain unknown to the general public and for many historians. Planners that did gain some name recognition, such as Krueger, Wedemeyer, Gerow, Turner, and certainly Eisenhower, did so for their subsequent roles as commanders, not for their substantive contributions as planners.[6]

Such would be the case sixty years later in the war against Iraq. There would be frequent reference in the media to America's senior commanders through 2003: Franks, Abizaid, McKiernan, Sanchez, Casey, and Petraeus. But the names of key planners before and during the conflict remain elusive — Richard Stouder, Roland Tiso, Steve Kidder, Mike Fitzgerald, Kevin Benson, Paul Shelton, Tom Fisher, and Wesley Odum. Only the outspoken and profane John Agoglia, Fitzgerald's assistant at Central Command, achieved much recognition as books on Iraq were published, and even he was relegated to sound bites and footnotes.[7] Though the role of military planners did not receive much attention in popular accounts on Iraq, their efforts were profound and might have been even more influential had their military and civilian commanders given them more attention.

Military planning at the highest levels is conducted by the Unified Commands, which develop plans and pass them to the Joint Chiefs of Staff in the Pentagon for review and then on to the Secretary of Defense for formal approval. Military planning for Iraq was the responsibility of U.S. Central Command. From Desert Storm (1990–1991) to the invasion of Iraq in 2003, Central Command had five commanders: Generals Norman Schwarzkopf, Joseph Hoar, Binford Peay, Anthony Zinni, and Tommy Franks. During that period the Central Command senior officer in the J-5 Plans and Policy staff section was always a Navy rear admiral, often with little planning experience; the subordinate Chief of War Plans was always a senior Army colonel with significant planning experience. From 1992 to 2003, Army officers serving as Chief of War Plans included Richard Stouder, Roland Tiso, Steve Kidder, and Mike Fitzgerald. All of them came to Central Command upon graduation from the Army War College.

Richard Stouder arrived in 1992 to take over responsibility for planning prospective operations in Iraq. He had served as a battalion commander and then as a planner during Desert Storm. At Central Command headquarters in Tampa, he was assigned to work on Operation Plan 1002-90, which had been developed in 1990 and was implemented later that year against Iraq for Desert Shield and Desert Storm. In 1992, with Saddam Hussein still in power and Iraqi forces still formidable, the plan warranted an update.[8]

Once it had been reworked as 1002-92, Colonel Stouder accompanied General Hoar, who had replaced General Schwarzkopf, to present the plan to Secretary of Defense Dick Cheney. Those present included the Chairman of the Joint Chiefs of Staff, General Colin Powell, and Undersecretary of Defense for Policy Paul Wolfowitz. The plan entailed a projected response to a subsequent Iraqi invasion of Kuwait or Saudi Arabia. The presentation went well until Stouder and Hoar laid out the amount of ground forces that would be employed: two Army corps and one Marine Expeditionary Force (MEF) with nine American divisions.

Wolfowitz questioned the size of the projected American ground forces in light of the destruction of much of the Iraqi army in Desert Storm. He argued that the number and size of Coalition ground forces could be reduced with enhanced air power using precision guided weapons. That resulted in a spirited discussion with General Hoar, who argued that the intelligence assessment of Iraqi capability merited the large American ground forces. General Powell sided with Hoar. When Wolfowitz saw the discussion going against him he became prickly, until Cheney stepped in and said, "That's enough Paul." Despite Wolfowitz's objections, Cheney approved the plan.[9]

Later, Colonel Roland Tiso arrived at Tampa from the War College and was assigned by Stouder to work on the next variation of the plan, designated 1002-94. It was a new era, with William Perry now Secretary of Defense in the Clinton administration and General Peay having replaced General Hoar at Central Command. Peay had commanded an Army division during Desert Storm. At that time, the Department of Defense was grappling with a shift in two major regional contingency scenarios. During the Cold War, that meant engaging the Warsaw Pact in Europe while simultaneously engaging other Communist forces in Asia.[10]

After the Cold War, the concept of fighting two major wars simultaneously was retained but altered for a war in the Middle East (with Iran or Iraq) and a war with North Korea. As American forces were reduced in the 1990s, Pentagon planners expressed concern that plans for the Middle East and Korea relied on the same forces with no provision that the conflicts could take place concurrently. To address those concerns, Stouder directed Tiso to rework 1002-94 as 1003-94 with the assumption that the latter plan for Iraq had to be coordinated with a possible conflict in Korea. Stouder found that some Pentagon leaders wanted to reduce the threat from Iraq to a minor regional contingency, which presumably would require fewer forces to confront.[11]

The basis for defining a regional threat as major or minor was the National Intelligence Estimate (NIE), produced by the Central Intelligence Agency with input from other intelligence agencies. For the threat posed by Iraq, Stouder found that in discussions with senior members of the CIA there was a political aspect to the NIE process. In Stouder's view, those preparing the NIE seemed to adapt it to favor what senior executive or political leaders wanted to hear so that it could be used to support the policies and acquisition programs they favored.[12]

The NIE predicted that for a future Desert Storm scenario, American ground forces could be reduced by relying on other Coalition forces from Middle Eastern countries. Stouder was skeptical that such a coalition could be easily formed or effectively employed against Iraq. General Peay shared that skepticism along with the Chairman of the Joint Staff, General John Shalikashvilli. Again, the chairman supported the position of the commander at Central Command.[13]

But that did not settle the issue as Stouder, Tiso, and others at Central Command continued with "spirited debates with the Policy component of the Office of the Secretary of Defense. The argument was over the number of ground and air forces. Those in Policy thought we could reduce the number of ground battalions by employing more fighter squadrons since we could count on the use of precision munitions." Those at Central Command used war gaming data to defend their force requirements. When Peay and Stouder went to Washington to brief 1003-94, the Pentagon senior leadership included Secretary Perry, Undersecretary of Defense for Policy Walt Slocombe, and General Shalikashvilli. General Peay provided an introduction and Stouder presented the new variant of the plan, which would respond to an Iraqi invasion of Kuwait and Saudi Arabia with a Coalition counter-invasion of Iraq.[14]

Stouder projected ground forces that had been comparable to earlier plans, supported by large air forces. Although the requirement was mainly for heavy armor and mechanized formations, General Peay was concerned with stability operations that would follow invasion, assuming "we had to put that country back together. . . . I don't need all heavy divisions." He wanted forces for dismounted patrolling to "provide some confidence and stabilize the country."[15]

No one disagreed that a future conflict with Iraq would include an invasion of that country, but Secretary Perry "argued that we could do with less ground forces while increasing the number of Air Force Wings." Perry was suggesting that "Air Force fighter wings were cheaper than Army or Marine divisions." Generals Peay and Shalikashvilli argued for the ground forces in the plan. Stouder observed that "Perry was clearly disgusted and left the room." Shalikashvilli told Peay and Stouder that the senior civilians would not approve the plan until they were convinced that the proposed ground forces were essential.[16]

Stouder left Central Command in 1996 for an assignment in Alaska; in 1998 he went to the Third Army to become the G-3 Operations officer. There he continued his work on Iraq until he retired in 2001. Colonel Tiso had replaced him as Chief of War Plans at Central Command as Colonel Steve Kidder arrived from the War College. Tiso directed Kidder to work on planning for Iraq. Kidder knew that the United States had imposed a UN-sanctioned no-fly zone for Iraqi aircraft above the 36th parallel to protect the Kurds in northern Iraq. In 1992 a no-fly zone had been imposed on southern Iraq as well, below the 32nd parallel in reaction to the atrocities Saddam Hussein imposed on the Shiites in the region.[17]

In 1996 the southern no-fly zone was moved up with UN approval to the 34th parallel in response to Iraqi provocations, further reducing the use of Iraqi airpower. American and Coalition aircraft patrolled the no-fly zones, on occasion challenged by Iraqi aircraft and air defense systems. Meanwhile, the U.S. Army began storing equipment ashore in several Persian Gulf countries and with additional Army and Marine equipment pre-positioned aboard ships. In the Gulf, there was enough heavy equipment to equip two divisions, one Army and one Marine, on short notice. Those at Central Command wanted more, but Kidder noted that some in the Pentagon preferred technology over numbers.[18]

Kidder was present on one occasion when Admiral Owens visited General Peay at Central Command to promote *Joint Vision 2010,* which relied heavily on advanced technology to reduce the number of combat formations. Peay responded with caution and told Owens that they might be putting too much stock in technology: "To tell you the truth, I'd be a fan of just buying a bunch of old cheap tanks and airplanes and have more volume."[19]

In March 1996, General Peay had Central Command conduct a war game, Internal Look-96, with commanders from the U.S. Third Army, the U.S. Ninth Air Force, and the U.S. Navy Fifth Fleet; each would serve as component commanders under Central Command for potential operations against Iraq. Lieutenant General Anthony Zinni, then commanding I Marine Expeditionary Force, represented the Marines. While the war game focused on combat operations, Peay told his commanders that if an American-led Coalition invaded Iraq, they would need more forces to secure the country than they required for invasion; those present agreed. Air and naval power could help defeat Iraqi forces, but a stability phase would have to rely on substantial ground forces.[20]

When General Peay retired in 1997, he sent Defense Secretary William Cohen an end-of-tour report that included challenges with Iraq stating that Saddam Hussein "recognizes that he has survived through three U.S. administrations" and was still a serious threat in the region, with an army of 420,000 in seventeen regular and six Republican Guard divisions, "capable of launching a 12-division attack into Kuwait, with a subsequent assault . . . into Saudi Arabia." However, the report stated that Hussein "is intimidated by military strength . . . the most effective deterrent to Iraqi adventurism. Our current forward presence costs our nation around $500 million per year" in contrast to fighting a war with Iraq, which the report estimated could "cost nearly $100 billion."[21]

The report stated that a major conflict with Iraq would require about ten American Army and Marine divisions. Peay expressed reservations about defense experts, those in the "military and civilian[s] who seek an elusive 'silver bullet' . . . [a] precision strike as one method for decreasing the size of our service." Experience showed that precision firepower "is most effective in the early hours of conflict, but it has never, in and of itself, been fully decisive." Peay addressed a Pentagon scenario that relied on precision weapons and airpower with "relatively small numbers of active and reserve forces [that] can then 'mop up' a defeated enemy, occupy ground, and secure national ends." Peay stated that such a "scenario is terribly flawed. Military history, simulations, and recent experience in war underscore . . . [that] precision strikes are best exploited in the context of a comprehensive military campaign. We must recognize that high-technology systems are not a panacea for protecting our national interests or reducing high defense costs—there are limits to leveraging technology to reduce force structure. . . . I don't see any way out of this dilemma and, frankly, feel we have [already] cut defense too far."[22]

In the conclusions of the report, General Peay noted, "Our nation does not accept . . . the morally and militarily bankrupt notion of destroying a nation to save it. Our countrymen know that our victory over a foe will inevitably require us to assist in his post-war recovery—an expensive affair." The prescience of the report predicted challenges that would be encountered in 2003, but General Peay received no feedback on the report and would later wonder if it had even been read in the Pentagon.[23]

In 1996 General Zinni became the Deputy Commander for Central Command and replaced General Peay a year later as Commander. Colonel Tiso departed for a new assignment and was replaced by Colonel Kidder as Chief of War Plans (Tiso later returned as General Zinni's executive officer). Kidder worked closely with General Zinni on war plans for the next three years.[24] He continued to monitor planning for Iraq, as Zinni directed his staff to establish a target list for radar stations and other military facilities; when Iraq violated the no-fly zone, those targets would be hit. Such strikes degraded Iraqi military capabilities and forced Saddam Hussein to pull much of his ground forces into central Iraq, making a surprise attack on Kuwait or Saudi Arabia more difficult for Iraq and easier for those at Central Command to monitor.

Assessments indicated that Iraq would be unable to deploy more than two divisions on short notice against Kuwait, rather than the twelve divisions predicted earlier. Any movement of Iraqi formations into southern Iraq could be attacked with American air forces well before they could close on Iraq's borders with Kuwait or Saudi Arabia. During the next planning cycle, OPLAN 1003-96 was redesignated 1003-98, with preemptive options against Iraq. The plan included increased use of precision weapons but still required substantial ground forces—two Army corps and a Marine Expeditionary Force—to be used for the invasion and a subsequent occupation, with the number of divisions reduced from ten to seven.[25]

When Iraqi forces fired upon Coalition aircraft patrolling the no-fly zones, and when Saddam Hussein threw the United Nations weapons inspectors out of Iraq, Central Command responded with Operations Desert Thunder in 1997 and Desert Fox in 1998, respectively, using air and naval forces with precision weapons. Zinni had been told that Iraq had weapons of mass destruction, and yet he noted that the intelligence agencies' target lists did not include the sites for such weapons; as such he wondered if Iraq's WMD program was active. And, as with General Peay before him, Zinni expressed concern about a potential occupation of Iraq. What if the air attacks led to regime turmoil or regime change? How would the United States respond, Zinni asked Kidder following a briefing in November 1997, "if Iraq collapses like a cheap suitcase?"[26]

One assumption General Zinni made about a post-conflict phase in Iraq included the retention of Iraq's regular army to provide external and internal security under Coalition control until a new regime could be put into place. To shape such a situation, Central Command had begun a long-term Information Operation to convince the Iraqi army that if the Coalition invaded, it would not attack Iraqi formations that did not fight, with the implication that the Iraqi army would be retained afterward.[27]

A year later, in November 1998, as Kidder was briefing Zinni, a call came in on the "Bat Phone"—the direct line to Zinni from General Hugh Shelton, Chairman of the Joint Chiefs of Staff. Kidder started to leave, but Zinni motioned for him to stay. Shelton asked Zinni what would happen if Saddam Hussein's regime were to collapse as a result of Desert Fox air operations the next month. When the conversation ended, Zinni passed the question to Kidder, who in turn took the issue to the 352nd Civil Affairs Command, an Army Reserve formation aligned with Central Command. Many of the reservists in the 352nd held jobs in other government agencies, mainly in the State Department, the CIA, and the FBI. As Kidder explained the anticipated occupation requirements for OPLAN 1003-98, those present told him that obtaining significant participation from their respective civilian agencies would be difficult.[28]

Kidder prepared a briefing for Zinni titled Desert Crossing, a rough concept proposing actions for securing Iraq if the regime collapsed. But the briefing did not constitute a plan or designate specific formations or agencies to be employed. Indeed, he told General Zinni that the officers of the 352nd Civil Affairs Command had predicted that interagency support would be limited under that scenario. In any case, when air operations in Desert Fox terminated that month, although Iraq had been hit hard, the regime did not collapse. Still, Zinni wanted more attention given to reconstruction in postwar Iraq. He directed a series of conferences for the Desert Crossing project; six would be conducted over the next year.[29]

As Kidder requested interagency support through the Pentagon, Zinni reinforced his efforts with calls to senior officials in the Departments of State, Justice, and Treasury, as well as to the CIA and USAID. He wanted senior players from those agencies to participate in the conference, not merely their subordinates. To make such participation convenient, Central Command had Booz-Allen, a defense contractor, set up the conference in northern Virginia in June 1998. Seventy participants from the civilian agencies in Washington discussed a plausible scenario that projected a Coalition takeover of Iraq with a stability period with military, political, and humanitarian tasks.[30]

It became clear that deliberate planning for Iraq required interagency cooperation, with a political-military plan necessary to achieve unity of command. Key issues included the retention of a strong Iraqi army for security; restraining Iran as a new regime for Iraq was installed; and acknowledgment that Iraqi exiled opposition groups were weak and would be unable to provide substantive assistance for a new regime. During the conference, General Zinni told those from the Department of State that Central Command should work with their planning component. He was surprised when they told him that State did not do such planning. Zinni gently suggested that they should.[31]

The first conference drew senior personnel from the other agencies, but subsequent seminars drew more junior participants. Kidder tried to obtain participation from other countries but received no response. For military operations, there was little interest from America's allies other than Great Britain, which developed its own plan for Iraq, designated JCP 502. Saudi Arabia, which had provided bases for Coalition forces during Desert Storm, began to send signals that those bases might not be available for a future conflict against Iraq. Central Command thus began to look for other options among the Persian Gulf states. Kuwait remained supportive, and air and naval bases in Qatar and Bahrain were arranged to replace those in Saudi Arabia. Kidder continued work on Desert Crossing until June 1999, when he was reassigned as an instructor at the Army War College.[32]

Lieutenant Colonel Mike Fitzgerald graduated from the Army War College in 1999 and went to Central Command, arriving a few weeks after Kidder departed; he would play a key role in planning for Iraq through 2003. Initially Fitzgerald was responsible for plans on Iraq; a year later he was promoted to colonel and took over as Chief of War Plans. He found that most of the Desert Crossing conferences had been restricted to fifty participants, many of them coming from other agencies or military commands such as the Third Army; only a few participants had come from Central Command, which restricted its institutional experience with Desert Crossing. He also noted that with the diversity of participants, conference seminars tended to bog down on minor details about responsibility for specific tasks rather than how to achieve them.[33]

Fitzgerald found that war plans were often tied to the force structure that each military service wanted to retain or expand during a period of reductions. Any service that did not have substantial forces committed to a war plan against Iraq or Korea could find them at risk during the Pentagon's efforts to downsize. It was not a problem to get the services to allocate forces for planning against Iraq; the problem was getting other agencies involved. Annex V, Interagency Participation for 1003-98, had been drafted by military planners, but they needed involvement from the other agencies to add substance to it. Military planners assumed that at some stage an ambassador from the State Department would take over responsibility for Iraq, but Fitzgerald was not sure anyone at State was aware of that assumption. Earlier, in fact, Colonel Kidder had asked a contact at the Pentagon when he would get more feedback from the civilian agencies; he was told not to count on a serious effort from them.[34]

In the spring of 2000, General Zinni spent little time at Tampa. His tour at Central Command would soon terminate and he was to retire that summer. He was frequently out of town attempting to seal relationships he had established with the military and civilian leaders in the countries for which Central Command was responsible. As such, after February 2000 there were no more Desert Crossing seminars. Even the changes to 1003-98 were not complete when he left, and his successor, General Tommy Franks, signed off on OPLAN 1003-98 and sent it on to the Pentagon for approval. All that was available from the Desert Crossing seminars and war games was the After Action Report of 28–29 June 1999. The title of the thirty-six-page document was *Desert Crossing Seminar;* it had never been developed as a plan or even as an annex to a plan.[35]

As those at Central Command worked on 1003-98, their military counterparts in the Pentagon tracked the drafts. There were no surprises about the final copy when it reached the Chairman of the Joint Chiefs of Staff, General Shelton. He recommended approval and sent it to Secretary of Defense Donald Rumsfeld, as the Bush administration took over in 2001. Rumsfeld did not disapprove the plan, but he would not sign it. The planners at Central Command did not understand why. Fitzgerald thought perhaps 1003-98 represented "old think," a term new officials in the Pentagon were using as they promoted transformation.[36]

A year earlier, the Pentagon produced *Joint Vision 2020,* a reworking of its 1996 predecessor, *JV2010.* It added two pages on interagency operations with one photo of a relief operation, but most of the document remained devoted to the themes of technology for enhanced weapons systems aligned against a platform-centric adversary. Clearly, the Pentagon remained focused on conventional opponents, despite recent experiences in Somalia, Haiti, and the Balkans.[37] Secretary Rumsfeld was on board with the technology agenda and within a year of taking office he stood up the Office of Force Transformation under retired Admiral Arthur Cebrowski, a naval aviator. Like Admiral Owens, Cebrowski was an advocate of technology over numbers to achieve greater military capacity for conventional operations.

The Pentagon office that oversaw unconventional operations was the Office of Special Operations and Low Intensity Conflict, known as SOLIC. The new administration had an interest in empowering Special Operations forces, although not for anything related to nation building, which they were determined to avoid. What the civilian officials wanted were large formations of highly trained Special Operations forces that could displace the role of more numerous conventional ground forces.

In August 2000, the destroyer *USS Cole* was struck by a small boat in a suicide attack off the coast of Yemen. It was clearly a deliberate attack on America, and intelligence indicated the culprit was Osama bin Laden and his al-Qaeda group, based in Afghanistan, where the Taliban controlling the country supported them. Many of those in the Pentagon and at Central Command shifted their attention to such groups and away from 1003-98.

Al-Qaeda struck again a little more than a year later at the World Trade Center and the Pentagon. American military planners were immediately consumed with operations in Afghanistan against al-Qaeda and the Taliban, which was in the Central Command's area of responsibility. Secretary Rumsfeld and others favoring transformation did not want to employ large numbers of American ground forces in Afghanistan. They preferred to rely on Special Forces to integrate the efforts of the Air Force using precision weapons with armed

Afghan opposition groups. The initial success in Afghanistan seemed to validate a new era that relied less on conventional ground forces.

Fitzgerald found there was also renewed Pentagon interest in Iraq. A message through channels from the Office of the Secretary of Defense at the end of September 2001 asked what plans were available to seize the southern oil fields in Iraq. Fitzgerald thought there had to be a mistake as that had no obvious relationship with operations in Afghanistan, which were then about to begin. When he requested clarification, his counterparts in the Pentagon simply told him that Central Command was to develop a plan for the seizure of Iraq's southern oil fields, and that direction came from beyond the Joint Chiefs of Staff. As seizure of the oil fields would be dominated by ground forces, Central Command passed the requirement for tactical planning on to the Third Army, its designated ground component.[38]

On 27 November, General Franks was working with his staff on Afghanistan when he received a call from Rumsfeld, who told him the president wanted to know about options for Iraq. Franks told him Central Command had OPLAN 1003. When the Secretary of Defense asked for an assessment of the plan, Franks replied that it was essentially Desert Storm II, out of date and under revision. (Later he said the same thing to President Bush.) Rumsfeld told Franks to study the plan and get back to him the following week. With operations beginning to surge in Afghanistan, Franks gathered together a select group of officers at Central Command and told them Secretary Rumsfeld wanted to begin new planning for Iraq. The group included the Deputy Commander, Lieutenant General Michael DeLong; Major General Eugene Renuart and Colonel David Halverson from J-3 Operations; Major General Jeff Kimmons from J-2 Intelligence; Brigadier General Mark Scheid from J-4 Logistics; and Colonel Fitzgerald from J-5 War Plans.[39]

Rumsfeld participated with the group through a series of televised exchanges with those at Tampa on four Thursday afternoons. The discussions centered on an invasion of Iraq and regime change. Initial guidance from the Pentagon was not directive; it was more a dialogue to explore options. For Fitzgerald and others at Central Command, 1003-98 was the base from which to start, but Rumsfeld was not interested in that base. Neither was General Franks, who told him that "it's too big, too slow and out-of-date."

The plan would require a large buildup in the Gulf to support combat operations. The secretary asked how visible such a buildup would be, how much it would cost, and how long it would take. The questions suggested that a leaner force was in order, one that could be assembled and deployed at less cost and, most important, more quickly. During conversations with Rumsfeld, Franks suggested that the objectives for Iraq should be the removal of

Saddam Hussein and ensuring that Iraq would not have access to weapons of mass destruction or otherwise be a menace in the region; Rumsfeld agreed. At that time there was little focus on what a future Iraq would look like.[40]

Rumsfeld wanted to begin with a clean slate. In lieu of 1003-98, the officers at Tampa began using the term "1003 Generated Start" to acknowledge a new track. To Colonel Fitzgerald, the secretary focused on the removal of Saddam Hussein, not overall regime replacement. In response to questions addressing the latter from the military officers, one morning prior to the meeting, General DeLong told the group that Rumsfeld had just threatened to "fire the next person" who talked about a postwar plan. The response of Fitzgerald and others was mixed; in general they decided to "let soldiers be soldiers, and carry out what we are told." The planners assumed their tasks during post-hostilities would be humanitarian assistance with some other organization responsible for regime replacement.[41] Generals Peay and Zinni had placed emphasis on planning for what would come after combat operations and the number of ground forces required for stability in Iraq. That focus was not apparent with those that replaced them.

Officers at Central Command asked what they could expect in terms of staging bases in Kuwait, Saudi Arabia, Jordan, and Turkey, which would require diplomatic assistance. Planning required basing options. As the discussion continued through the fall of 2001, the planning group was expanded at Tampa with planners in the subordinate ground, air, and maritime commands. For ground operations, much of the planning would be the responsibility of Halverson in the J-3 and Fitzgerald in the J-5, both Army colonels. General Franks referred to them as his lead planners, "the most selfless, hardest working colonels I had ever known."[42]

In the summer of 2001, Army Lieutenant Colonel John Agoglia was assigned to work for Fitzgerald and would soon play an important role in planning for Iraq. Agoglia had attended the Army's School of Advanced Military Studies, SAMS, where many Army planners were educated; he subsequently had served as a planner in Korea and Japan. Well educated and experienced as a planner, Agoglia could be candid and profane, often quick-tempered. Soon after he arrived at Tampa, he became consumed with planning for Afghanistan. Early in 2002, Fitzgerald designated Agoglia his lead planner for Iraq. Lieutenant Colonel Eric Yonkee, a Marine logistics officer, joined Agoglia. Yonkee's expertise was in the deployment of forces to the Middle East. General Franks initiated a request for additional planners who had attended the Army SAMS course or the Marine or Air Force counterparts; soon there was a large planning cell for Iraq. Franks referred to his planners as the "fifty-pound brains."[43]

As the lead planner for Iraq, Agoglia began a dialogue with his military counterparts in the Pentagon and learned that the political appointees working with them did not want to see the -98 on the Iraq 1003-98 OPLAN, which represented General Zinni's work on the plan. Agoglia kept 1003 designation for the plan as it was worked at Central Command, but he dropped the -98 from the briefing slides and working papers. Over the next year the plan would have several names, including 1003 Generated Start, 1003 Running Start, and 1003 Hybrid, variants of the earlier 1003-98 with reduced force structure. The essence of these plans was that the Coalition would fight with forces on hand in theater as other forces flowed in to join the fight. This was a major shift from the Desert Storm concept of a full buildup of forces in theater before major operations would be conducted, allowing a smaller footprint in the region and a lower profile before an invasion; it might bring an element of surprise that had been lacking in Desert Storm. A key issue for the follow-on forces was that they would enter the theater as planned, something military planners assumed would take place as indicated, while others in the Pentagon considered the follow-on plans an option that might be discarded in order to reduce the overall cost of the operation. These different views would lead to a serious reduction in occupation and security forces for Iraq once Baghdad was secured, a reduction many planners and even some commanders did not anticipate.

Later in the year the developing plan appeared on a briefing slide as 1003V, a designation that in October was listed as the title of the plan. Neither Agoglia nor Fitzgerald could later recall who first put the V on the plan, but it stuck. The nature of the plan no longer assumed an initial defense of Kuwait and Saudi Arabia; it would be a preemptive invasion of Iraq. Coalition ground forces would not be staged from Saudi Arabia; they would be staged through Kuwait and perhaps through southeastern Turkey. Special Operations forces might work from Jordan and Turkey; air and naval forces would be based in Qatar, Bahrain, and Kuwait.[44]

Conventional ground forces—Army, Marine, and Coalition—would serve under the Third Army headquarters, which would be redesignated as the Combined Forces Land Component Command (CFLCC). In the transition to CFLCC, the Third Army staff would have staff augmentation from the U.S. Marines as well as the United Kingdom and Australia, the key nations prepared to commit ground forces for the Coalition. These ground forces would serve under CFLCC with Army formations for operations in Iraq. The main contact for Fitzgerald and Agoglia at the Third Army as it became CFLCC would be Army Colonel Kevin Benson.

In the summer of 2002, Colonel Kevin Benson joined the Third Army staff at Fort McPherson, Georgia. Prior to his arrival, the Third Army Plans section was part of the G-3 Operations staff section and the Third Army G-5 was the Civil Affairs staff section, in accordance with Army doctrine (on an Army staff, G represents General Staff section). In the 1990s, Benson had served as the Plans officer in the Third Army G-3. Now Benson was back as a full colonel with the Third Army restructured as CFLCC and Plans as a separate (Coalition) C-5 staff section; the Civil Affairs staff section became the C-9.

Benson had been requested by name by the Third Army commander, Lieutenant General Paul T. Mikolashek, based on his reputation and previous assignment with the Third Army. For a field army headquarters, the primary staff positions are held by full colonels. But when the Third Army was redesignated a CFLCC staff, several staff positions were upgraded with general officers: Brigadier General James A. "Spider" Marks became the C-2 for intelligence; Major General James "J.D." Thurman became the C-3 for operations, Major General Claude Christianson became the C-4 for logistics, Major General Lowell C. Detamore became the C-6 for communications, Major General William "Fuzzy" Webster became the CFLCC Deputy Commander, and Marine Major General Robert R. "Rusty" Blackman assumed the chief of staff position. While Benson had clout with Mikolashek and had served in the Third Army previously, he would be junior in rank to other primary staff officers on the CFLCC staff.

As with Agoglia at Central Command, Benson arrived at CFLCC with experience in planning. An armor officer who had attended SAMS, he had served as planner with the XVIII Airborne Corps, which included planning operations in Bosnia and Haiti, before his first assignment to the Third Army. While Agoglia was outspoken, Benson was mild-mannered, deliberate, and spoke with a gravity that befitted a senior Plans officer. Upon arrival, he began working on plans for Iraq generated by Central Command, with guidance from General Mikolashek. To Benson, it appeared that Mikolashek did not get on well with Tommy Franks, so he was not surprised when later Mikolashek was replaced by Lieutenant General David McKiernan.[45]

As McKiernan replaced Mikolashek, Benson and others argued for a larger force for the buildup and initial invasion. By the end of July a new variant of the plan, designated 1003 Hybrid, was developed with more time for forces to move into theater. However, the American ground forces scheduled to invade Iraq in 2003 would be less than half the size of the American ground forces employed for Desert Storm. Furthermore, for Desert Storm the Coalition had included eight non-American divisions; in 2003 the Coalition had only one, the United Kingdom 1st Armor Division.

In 2003, American military doctrine designated four operational phases for the invasion of Iraq:

- Phase I: Deter/Engage
- Phase II: Seize Initiative
- Phase III: Decisive Operations
- Phase IV: Transition[46]

Phases I and II would include mobilization, deployment, and defensive operations as required. Offensive combat operations—the invasion of Iraq—were the core of Phase III. Phase IV—Transition—included different tasks for each subordinate formation. For most formations during Desert Storm in 1991, transition meant redeployment as Kuwaitis resumed control of their country. Some military engineering, Civil Affairs, and other support units remained to assist with reconstruction and a United Nations observer force to assume border control. Those units that remained in Kuwait for such operations in 1991 were a small fraction of those used for combat operations.[47]

During the first half of 2002, much of the military planning for Iraq was devoted to forward basing, forces to participate, and deployment priorities—tasks associated with Phases I and II. The planning for the invasion of Iraq, Phase III operations, also consumed significant energy given that it was clear that ground forces would be greatly reduced from the projections for Iraq developed in the 1990s, and thus to be successful the invasion would have to be well designed and executed. Phase IV operations were not so clearly defined. Military planners assumed some residual forces would remain as in Desert Storm, with a handoff to a United Nations military formation or other Coalition forces. During operations in Afghanistan beginning in 2001, Phase IV was listed as Reconstruction. For Iraq, planners at Central Command begin listing Phase IV as Post-Hostilities. During a briefing for President Bush at his Texas ranch in December 2001, General Franks defined Phase IV for Iraq as both Post-Hostilities and as Reconstruction. He vaguely suggested that Phase IV operations for Iraq include humanitarian assistance and the establishment of a representative form of government without weapons of mass destruction. Thus General Franks could talk in detail about how combat operations in Phase III would be conducted, but his concept of Phase IV for Iraq was poorly defined, with no projection of how it would be managed or what the military contribution would be.[48]

By mid-summer, Agoglia's main interest in Phase IV planning was on the regular Iraqi army. Consistent with General Zinni's initiative several years earlier, he assumed the Republican Guard formations, intensely loyal to Saddam

Hussein, would have to be destroyed or disbanded, but he felt that much of the regular army might not fight. If Central Command's information campaign convinced the regular forces not to fight, the Coalition invasion could be conducted with fewer forces and with reduced risk. If the Iraqi army did not fight, it would not have to be destroyed and therefore could be used to help provide internal security after the invasion. Agoglia requested that Psychological Operations units further enhance the information campaign.[49]

Meanwhile, as Benson developed a CFLCC plan for ground operations based on 1003V, he learned of an aggressive dialogue between Franks and Rumsfeld over the forces to be employed. Franks had inherited a number of close to 400,000 combat troops from a decade of planning with the 1002–1003 series; that period covered his tour as Third Army commander. Rumsfeld, however, relentlessly challenged these numbers. Benson never saw any of the work on Desert Crossing, but that did not surprise him: "When I got to CFLCC, the guys in the Central Command J-5 were so busy responding to requirements from OSD, no one was really thinking very deeply about the scope of the campaign." Planners assumed that General Franks would resist any effort to seriously limit ground forces. There is little evidence that Franks did so for the initial invasion, however, perhaps in part because there would be follow-on divisions to support those operations. Furthermore, in contrast to his predecessors at Central Command, Peay and Zinni, Franks seemed to agree with Rumsfeld that leaner forces with precision weapons could displace the numbers for ground formations previously programmed for an invasion of Iraq. To some planners it appeared that General Franks did not share the concern repeatedly expressed by Peay and Zinni that large ground formations would be necessary to provide security in Iraq after an invasion. On the other hand, General Franks would later note that he "chafed at the intellectual arrogance of some in [the Bush] Administration" and that Rumsfeld's management style was too centralized.[50]

In May 2002, Agoglia asked for an interagency link for Phase IV planning. His contacts in the Pentagon told him that those in the OSD and NSC were working on a provisional Iraqi government in exile, but no details were forthcoming. By late summer, Agoglia determined such a government in exile was problematic and that "Phase IV was going to fall squarely in the lap of the military." He later noted that "there wasn't a lot of intellectual energy focused on Phase IV." Planners anticipated there would be aspects of occupation, but OSD was saying only that Iraq was to be liberated. Indeed, those who had worked for General Zinni at Central Command disclosed to him that they were not even allowed to use the term "occupation." Based on its role in other conflicts, Agoglia assumed that the United Nations would play a substantive role in Phase IV, but until linkage with Central Command and the UN was developed, such detailed planning would have to wait.[51]

During the summer of 2002, military planning for an invasion of Iraq that included the post-invasion period was conducted in several military headquarters and would continue into the early months of 2003. The process was complicated and often driven or obstructed by strong personalities, both military and civilian. To address the impact on Iraqi civilians, on 9 July General Richard Myers, Chairman of the Joint Staff in the Pentagon, issued a planning order to Central Command to include planning for the use of military Civil Affairs to assist with basic services in Iraq following an invasion.[52]

Brigadier General John H. "Jack" Kern commanded the 352nd Civil Affairs Command in 2002, an Army Reserve formation aligned with Central Command for operations in the Middle East. General Kern and the 352nd deployed for operations in Afghanistan. Kern had argued with the senior U.S. Army commander over the employment of Civil Affairs units and was sent home early, although he was not relieved of command, which would have caused an uproar that his superiors wanted to avoid. There was no press sensation, but word spread throughout Central Command and CFLCC that Kern had been marginalized as a general officer, a situation that would not be favorable for operations in Iraq.[53]

In October 2002, Colonel Aldo Calvi and Colonel James Owens, Army reservists with the 352nd, went to Central Command to begin planning just as Major Ray Eiriz, another Civil Affairs reservist, joined Agoglia's planning team. With the 352nd then returning from Afghanistan, it was clear that it would soon mobilize again for an invasion of Iraq. Calvi and Owens anticipated that the requirements would be much greater for Iraq. As they began planning, they determined that four Civil Affairs brigade headquarters and ten Civil Affairs battalions would be required. That would be close to half the Civil Affairs inventory that included eight brigade headquarters and twenty-three battalions in the Army Reserves, two reserve Marine Civil Affairs Groups (comparable to an Army CA battalion), and the only active-duty formation, the Army's 96th Civil Affairs Battalion.

Calvi and Owens knew that one Civil Affairs battalion was still in Afghanistan, another battalion was working in the Horn of Africa, and part of a third was in the Balkans. In the Army and Marines there were fewer than 6,000 Civil Affairs personnel altogether, virtually all reservists. Over 30 percent were still in basic training or otherwise non-deployable. Of those trained, some were overseas already or had just returned and were unavailable for deployment to Iraq.[54]

The designation of a Civil Affairs brigade and Civil Affairs battalion are frequently misleading for active-duty officers. Civil Affairs personnel are mainly advisors and Civil Affairs battalions and brigades are formations made up of teams of advisors to work with conventional forces. An infantry or armor brigade would normally consist of a brigade headquarters with three to five subordinate infantry or armor battalions for a total of 3,000 to 5,000 soldiers, whereas a Civil Affairs brigade in 2003 with several subordinate Civil Affairs battalions would have an aggregate strength of about 500, with only 100 or so light vehicles and a few medium trucks. In 2003 those vehicles were not armored and had no mounted weapons; many were without radios.

The Civil Affairs units would work for the ground component, and General Mikolashek recruited Colonel Marty Stanton to serve as his C-9 Civil Affairs staff officer. An infantryman and Middle East Foreign Area Officer, the outspoken Stanton arrived with a colorful background. He had been captured by the Iraqi army in 1990 and spent several months as a POW, and had also served in Saudi Arabia, Pakistan, and Somalia. He had no Civil Affairs experience, but Mikolashek told him he would have little difficulty picking up the required expertise.[55]

As the CFLCC C-9 officer, Stanton became the point of contact for Calvi, Owens, and Eiriz. But as the 352nd commander, General Kern should have been designated the C-9 officer for CFLCC, with Stanton becoming his deputy. Stanton, however, had higher standing than Kern with many general officers and thus retained the primary C-9 staff position. It was not a match made in heaven: Stanton, despite having no background in Civil Affairs, would become the senior CA staff officer for CFLCC, while Kern, the only Civil Affairs general officer headed to Iraq, would have less prestige.[56]

By November, Calvi and Owens had put together a task force, designated TF 167, to deploy as the Civil Affairs advance party. It arrived in Kuwait on 13 January 2003 and set up at Camp Arifjan, a logistics base south of Kuwait City and forty miles from Camp Doha, where the CFLCC headquarters was located.[57] Over several months 1,800 Army and Marine Civil Affairs reservists flowed into Kuwait. The active-duty 96th Civil Affairs Battalion deployed to Jordan to work with Special Forces. The total Civil Affairs personnel would soon number almost 2,000 for operations in Iraq. That was less that 1.5 percent of the total American forces deployed, yet they accounted for half the deployable Army and Marine Civil Affairs personnel. No one anticipated that they would be in theater more than a few months; most would remain for a year.[58]

General Kern arrived in February to assume command of the 352nd and Colonel Calvi became his deputy. Yet all Kern would really command was the 352nd headquarters and two subordinate units, fewer than 400 personnel.

The other Civil Affairs brigades and battalions were attached to maneuver formations that would control them. The CA units were to plan for humanitarian assistance for Iraqi civilians adversely affected by the invasion. While the alignment and tasks were consistent with Civil Affairs doctrine, there was not much left to prepare for other post-conflict tasks.

The directive to develop a plan to secure Iraq's southern oil fields had been the first notice Colonel Fitzgerald had that there would be an invasion of any kind for Iraq. Oil was not the reason for invading Iraq, but it was clear that Iraqi oil fields had to be protected for a follow-on regime, a task Agoglia and Fitzgerald did not address until the fall of 2002. That task soon went to Major Paul Shelton, a Marine intelligence officer who arrived at Central Command on temporary duty to assist with planning. Shelton told Agoglia he wanted to do something different and interesting.[59]

Agoglia found it for him. In late October, Agoglia and Fitzgerald asked him, "Paul, what do you know about oil?"

"Well, sir, I change it every 3,000 miles."

Fitzpatrick said, "You're hired."

He showed Shelton a "Rumsfeld snowflake—one of those little hand scrawled questions." Shelton later learned that "they are called snowflakes because they drift slowly down through the atmosphere of the chain of command until they land on some poor lieutenant colonel or major's desk like a snowflake." The one Shelton was given directed Central Command to brief those on the National Security Council on plans to secure and repair Iraqi oilfields.

Shelton smiled at Fitzgerald and Agoglia. "Let me guess. There is no plan."

They laughed. "That's why we hired you—because you're so damn smart."[60]

Shelton soon had others join him to form an operational planning team. A key participant was Cliff Fowler, a GS-14 civilian from the J-2 Intelligence staff section. Fowler had been an oil analyst for Central Command since 1988 and knew his subject. Shelton learned that Iraq had twenty-two major oil fields with some 1,500 oil wells, about 1,000 in southern Iraq and 500 in the north. He also learned that Iraq had thirty-four gas-oil separation plants, known as GOSPs, particularly vulnerable if targeted. The planners knew that during Desert Storm, Saddam Hussein had ordered the destruction of 700 oil wells in Kuwait, which led to a financial and environmental disaster that took over a year and a fortune to clean up.[61]

Shelton knew that those contemplating an invasion wanted to protect the Iraqi oil infrastructure so that a postwar Iraq could generate revenues from oil to cover costs of the war. The problem was preventing the destruction of the Iraqi oil infrastructure during an invasion. Oil fields could not be targeted by Coalition forces and they had to be protected from Iraqi forces that might try to set them on fire as a smoke screen or obstacle for Coalition forces. That led to Shelton's first challenge, and perhaps a significant contribution to the overall planning.

By October, the Coalition offensive plan was for the Army's V Corps in Kuwait to invade Iraq just west of all major population centers. The First Marine Expeditionary Force (I MEF) would make a supporting attack east of V Corps, an area including the southern oil fields. Shelton contacted planners in I MEF to discuss those oil fields. During Desert Storm, Coalition aircraft had bombed Iraq and Kuwait almost a month before the ground forces invaded. Many Air Force officers assumed that would be the case in 2003, a role they wanted. At Central Command, the J-3 Operations officer, Air Force Major General Renuart, and the J-5 Plans and Policy officer, Rear Admiral James Robb, were both fighter pilots. As the J-5, Robb was Fitzgerald and Agoglia's boss; through them he was Shelton's boss.[62]

Shelton went to Agoglia and Fitzgerald and to Colonel Halverson in the J-3, all Army officers, to propose that an invasion of Iraq should commence with air attacks supporting, but not preceding, a ground attack. Otherwise there would be little opportunity to prevent Iraqi forces from firing the oil wells. The three Army officers concurred and for other reasons had already argued for opening the invasion with ground forces. Aviators at Central Command, however, as well as those in the Ninth Air Force, which would provide air support for the invasion, were hard to convince. Fitzgerald sent Shelton to brief General Renuart, who wanted a substantial air attack to precede ground operations, perhaps for thirty days. Shelton made a strong case for protecting the oil wells and avoiding early use of air forces. Renuart objected and the question went to General Franks, who eventually decided to have the air and ground attacks begin at the same time. Protecting the oil wells was one of several issues in that determination.[63]

As Calvi and Owens planned for Civil Affairs operations and Shelton worked on oil fields, military officers at several levels began to concentrate on the interagency operations that would come with or follow invasion. At Central Command, a key player would be Major Tom Fisher, who arrived there just after Shelton. Fisher would take on a role that that might have gone to an officer of higher rank: writing the Phase IV Plan for 1003V. Fisher had enlisted in the Army to serve in a Ranger battalion and was later commissioned as an armor officer. Rather than training for operations against the Warsaw Pact armies, Fisher served in armor units sent to Bosnia for peace operations in the mid-1990s, then returned a few years later to the Balkans on a similar operation in Kosovo. Subsequently, he attended the Naval Command

and Staff Course and was selected for the Naval Operational Planners Course, the Navy counterpart to the Army's SAMS program. He graduated in August 2002 and reported to Central Command. In November, he was working on 1003V with the forward headquarters in Qatar. In December he returned to Tampa to work on Phase IV planning.[64]

Earlier in October, planners had produced Annex V (Interagency Coordination) for 1003V, which listed eight Phase IV objectives:

1. Establish a permissive environment for recovery and reconstruction
2. Establish an Iraqi military capable of defending the territorial borders of Iraq and maintaining internal security
3. Support establishment of a provisional/permanent Iraqi government
4. Ensure that the territorial integrity of Iraq remains intact
5. Transition civil-military operations to international and nongovernmental organizations
6. Ensure that weapons of mass destruction capabilities are destroyed, removed, or transitioned to competent authority
7. Detain terrorists and war criminals and free individuals unjustly detained
8. Redeploy forces

Some of those tasks could be undertaken by military forces, while some were appropriate for other governmental agencies. A Joint Interagency Coordination Group was proposed in Annex V as a means through which to coordinate those tasks, but no such group had yet been formed. A Central Command planning session conducted in Germany, with planners in V Corps, noted that without such an interagency group there was little basis for the Phase IV concept in the plan. Major Fisher's task was to get such a group off the ground and to provide linkage with the tactical formations, V Corps and I MEF, to identify the full range of Phase IV tasks and procedures to implement them.

Joined by Ray Eiriz, Agoglia's Civil Affairs planner, Fisher put together a planning team with forty participants: thirty military officers and ten civilians. The military officers included three from the UK and one from Australia. The civilians came from the Departments of State, Treasury, and Energy and USAID, all Americans. Much of the work focused on humanitarian assistance, less on regime replacement. Fisher ran a working conference over 9–12 December 2002 and briefed Admiral Robb and General Renuart two days later. General Franks was not present, nor was his deputy, General DeLong. Copies of the Phase IV work were forwarded to OSD and the Joint Staff in the Pentagon. Colonel Benson had some of his planners coordinate with the Central

Command effort and received a copy of Fisher's final concept in December. Then with the emergence in the Pentagon of another component (Jay Garner and ORHA) designated to prepare for Phase IV, Fisher was taken off Phase IV planning and assigned to other tasks.[65]

As military officers at Central Command and the subordinate headquarters were planning for Iraq, Lieutenant General George Casey began to weigh in. General Casey was in charge of J-5 Strategic Plans and Policy on the Joint Staff in the Pentagon. Remarkably, that staff section had not played a key role in planning for Iraq through the first half of 2002. During the summer of 2002, Casey went to Lieutenant General John Abizaid, the Director of the Joint Staff, to whom Casey normally reported. Casey had been heavily involved in writing a strategy for counterterrorism and was not convinced that an invasion of Iraq was probable. "I am not paying attention to all this chatter I hear about Iraq going on in the background," he told Abizaid. "If I need to start paying attention, you need to tell me." In early August Abizaid told Casey to start paying attention and specifically to concentrate on what would have to be done following an invasion.[66]

In the Pentagon, Casey set up a group of military officers from the J-5 to work on interagency aspects for Iraq called the Post-War Planning Group. By September the group was in full operation and bringing in senior members of other government departments and agencies. In October Casey went to the White House to brief the president on the status of postwar planning for Iraq, recommending that a government department, probably State or Defense, should be given the lead, though he noted that senior civilians at State and Defense disagreed as to which department that should be. Rather than resolving the question, the president and others on the NSC were reluctant to get too far ahead in planning for what would follow an invasion of Iraq when it was not confirmed that there would be an invasion at all. In Casey's view, these dilemmas led to the administration squandering two months that could have been used to better prepare for what would follow an invasion.[67]

In late September, the Joint Staff held a planning seminar called Prominent Hammer II to analyze resources and risks of an invasion of Iraq. The seminar identified a requirement for a headquarters to help Central Command plan for complex Phase IV requirements. Later on 19 December, General Myers, Chairman of the Joint Chiefs of Staff, directed General Franks to further refine planning for Phase IV operations. Myers would not receive a copy of those plans until March, just days before the war started.[68]

Concerned that the work on Phase IV operations was insufficient, General Casey decided to establish a task force to assist Central Command. First he tried to activate the Standing Joint Task Force (JTF) Headquarters, a

subordinate unit of the Joint Forces Command in Norfolk that was specifically designed for crisis operations. But when Casey asked for that JTF, Admiral Edmund Giambastiani, the commander in Norfolk, declined to provide
the JTF. It was unclear if this reflected less substance to the JTF than had been
advertised or if Giambastiani wanted to reserve it for another role. Rebuffed,
Casey decided to stand up an ad hoc JTF, designated JTF-4, for Phase IV
planning and operations. Forming such a command element from scratch is
a challenging endeavor. While Casey could provide the top-down authority,
others would have to pick up the momentum. Casey chose Brigadier General
Steven Hawkins, a military engineer officer, to command JTF-4.[69]

During the 1980s, Hawkins spent three years in Saudi Arabia working on
construction projects. He later commanded an engineer battalion during Desert Storm, and then served as the Chief of Staff for the 3rd Infantry Division
during a deployment to Kuwait in 1998. Hawkins had more experience in
the Middle East than many other military engineers. He also had had a tour
as an observer-controller at the Army's National Training Center in Fort Irwin, California, where he determined that the cardinal error of most military
formations was "a lack of mental preparation for follow-on tactical operations
after the objective was taken."[70]

In the 1990s, Hawkins commanded an engineer brigade in the 1st Infantry
Division under General Casey. When the United States deployed forces into
Bosnia in 1995, Hawkins was in charge of bridging the Sava River and subsequently worked with engineer units from a dozen countries in Bosnia. Later,
he participated in reconstruction projects in Kosovo. When General Casey
called him on 15 December 2002, Hawkins was commanding a regional engineer division with the U.S. Army Corps of Engineers (USACE) in Cincinnati,
an experience that had exposed him to contracting with large civilian engineer
projects.[71] In 2002, it would have been difficult to find a general officer with
more exposure to combat and construction, post-conflict situations, and the
Middle East than Steve Hawkins. By that criteria, General Casey had made a
good call.

Casey obtained Colonel Jimmy Rabon, then teaching at the National War
College, as a deputy for Hawkins. Rabon had worked for Casey in Germany
and knew Hawkins. Casey had the Joint Staff create a Joint Manning Document (JMD) with fifty-eight officers and soldiers from the Army, Air Force,
Navy, and Marines who would join Hawkins and Rabon in Tampa to form
JTF-4. Hawkins flew to Washington to check in at the Pentagon and visit appropriate agencies.[72]

Colonel Tom Baltazar, working in the Office of Special Operations and
Low Intensity Conflict in the Pentagon, picked Hawkins up at the airport. He

took him to see a group of civilians with an umbrella organization for non-governmental organizations (NGOs) called INTERACTION. Baltazar was also an engineer officer and had served in Civil Affairs, commanding the 96th CA Battalion. He had been monitoring planning for Iraq and would soon join General Jay Garner and ORHA. Baltazar wanted Hawkins to establish contact with the NGOs that could assist with humanitarian and other tasks in Iraq. Hawkins had worked with NGOs in the Balkans, but the exchange did not go well that day in Washington. Baltazar noted Hawkins had a condescending tone that put off many of the civilians present with the implication that he intended to control their efforts. It was not a good sign for other relationships that would follow.[73]

Hawkins flew on to Tampa, but found he was not welcome. With Tom Fisher and others working on Phase IV, staff planners at Central Command had not asked for JTF-4, nor did they ask for Hawkins. Casey, as a three-star staff officer, had imposed Hawkins and fifty-some personnel on a four-star commander and his staff with the implication that they were not thinking ahead. The planners there did not believe they had dropped the ball on Phase IV planning. Furthermore, Central Command Headquarters did not have the assets at Tampa to stand-up a JTF headquarters.[74]

When Hawkins and Rabon arrived there, they found a shortage of office space due to the staff augmentation supporting operations in Afghanistan and the Horn of Africa and pending operations in Iraq. No arrangements had been made to receive Hawkins or those that would soon join him to form JTF-4. To Agoglia, Fitzgerald, and others at Central Command, it appeared that General Franks considered General Casey's efforts more interference than assistance. What Casey considered self-confidence in Hawkins, others would soon consider arrogance.[75]

With difficulty, Hawkins was able to obtain a warehouse on the installation for JTF-4. Staying at a nearby hotel, he picked up office supplies from civilian conferences there. When he learned JTF-4 was coming to Tampa, Lieutenant Colonel John Agoglia assumed JTF-4 would arrive with some cohesion rather than "come in here and build this group from the ground up. Central Command as a staff was not prepared for it."[76] Hawkins was indignant with the lack of assistance, and it showed. It appeared to Agoglia that Hawkins soon annoyed "every general officer in Central Command . . . [and] soured relationships."[77]

Still, Hawkins and Rabon put the JTF-4 headquarters together in record time. Within several weeks, they had assembled all their personnel and put them to work. Hawkins asked an officer to prepare a large binder on Iraq called the "Brain Book. . . . It started with 2500 B.C. and went all the way to modern day. So we tried to learn everything there was about [Iraq] . . . how they governed and why they governed, what the military role could be, and what the headquarters would have to move to get the country up and running again beyond Saddam Hussein." It was an impressive endeavor, but the necessity for it confirmed that those in charge of post-conflict operations began knowing little about Iraq.[78]

Those in JTF-4 reviewed the work conducted by Central Command. Hawkins was unimpressed: "They had done some Phase IV cursory planning [and] convinced themselves it was more detailed than it really was. . . . You [need] experts across the core of the skill sets and expertise, from how to reestablish schools, how to reestablish transportation systems, how to reestablish governments, how to reestablish infrastructure, how to reestablish water, power and sewer, road systems and all that stuff."[79]

Hawkins was correct: Phase IV planning for regime change should cover many dimensions. Arguably, Tom Fisher had made an effort to do that by bringing in interagency and other participants for his December Operational Planning Team. But few of the military participants and none of the civilians were in Tampa when Hawkins arrived and he was unable to replicate an interagency component. Prior to deployment to Kuwait in January, Hawkins encountered another surprise. He assumed that JTF-4 would eventually replace General McKiernan and CFLCC in Iraq and be augmented with substantial engineer, medical, transportation, Civil Affairs, and MP units.[80]

But Central Command made no such assets available to Hawkins, nor would it promise any. Instead, Central Command assigned Hawkins and JTF-4 to McKiernan's command as a subordinate unit. Hawkins was incensed; he resisted and lost. According to Agoglia, Hawkins "went down to work for the CFLCC kicking and screaming. They were not happy with that decision," and soon Hawkins managed to annoy most of the general officers there including General McKiernan.[81]

On 28 January, Hawkins, Rabon, and Colonel Mike Williams, the JTF Chief of Staff, flew ahead to Kuwait. Their arrival was a surprise for the CFLCC staff, which had been there since October preparing for the invasion. Colonel Benson had a Phase IV component in his plan, but it did not include Hawkins and JTF-4. When word arrived that Hawkins and his two officers were coming, arrangements were made to pick them up at the Kuwaiti airport. At that time military personnel traveling in Kuwait had to have two armed soldiers in every vehicle and CFLCC had a duty roster of NCOs and drivers that would go to the airport to pick up arriving military personnel. By chance, the NCOs next on the duty roster came from Benson's C-5 staff section.[82]

Before departing Tampa, Hawkins, Williams, and Rabon had studied the planning that CFLCC had done for Phase IV. On the ride from the airport to Camp Doha they discussed it in the vehicle driven by Benson's NCOs. The discussion was caustic and critical, addressing how they would have to readjust the thinking of the CFLCC staff. The NCOs driving them to Camp Doha did not say a word. After they delivered their passengers, however, one of the NCOs went to see Benson. He was livid and told Benson what had been said. Ever the professional, Benson told the NCO to keep it to himself as they had enough problems already. But it was too late. The other NCO that had been in the van had already begun to pass the word around Camp Doha that some new staff had arrived and thought CFLCC "was all fucked-up."[83]

The reception Hawkins and JTF-4 had encountered with Central Command at Tampa would be replicated in Kuwait. The experience, expertise, and energy Hawkins brought to the post-conflict challenges and his relationship with General Casey were not enough to get JTF-4 properly established. It was not a good situation for JTF-4, CFLCC, or Central Command, and it would not be good for other planning efforts in Washington, including Jay Garner's ORHA, then forming in the Pentagon.

In January 2002, General Casey replaced General Abizaid as Director of the Joint Staff. Abizaid was reassigned to Central Command as a second deputy commander for General Franks to work in Qatar and Kuwait on operations for Iraq (Lieutenant General DeLong, the original deputy, would manage operations in Tampa). Agoglia, Garner, and others assumed Abizaid would be the follow-on Coalition commander in Iraq.[84]

As military commanders and planners were striving to implement an operational campaign with incomplete strategic guidance, retired military officers were expressing reservations. Their views were sometimes supportive of the administration. At times they were critical, in some cases with remarkable prescience.

In a *Wall Street Journal* op-ed on 15 August 2002, Lieutenant General Brent Scowcroft, a former National Security Advisor in the George H. W. Bush administration, made a strong argument against war with Iraq: it would "divert us for some indefinite period from our war on terrorism. Worse, there is a virtual consensus in the world against an attack on Iraq at this time. So long as that sentiment persists, it would require the U.S. to pursue a virtual go-it-alone strategy against Iraq, making any military operations correspondingly more difficult and expensive." Condoleezza Rice, who held Scowcroft's former post in the current administration and who had worked for him years earlier, was incensed at the article and called her old mentor to complain.[85]

On 11 September 2002, exactly one year after the attacks on New York and the Pentagon, General Zinni came to Quantico, Virginia, to speak to an assembled group of five hundred military officers attending military courses there. After retiring two years earlier, Zinni had served briefly as the Secretary of State's Special Envoy for assisting with the Palestinian-Israeli peace process, and he was in Quantico to speak on that topic. But he surprised his audience by stating that he had decided to speak on another topic—Iraq.[86]

Two weeks earlier, on 26 August, General Zinni had attended a Veteran of Foreign Wars ceremony in Tennessee to receive an award. The function was also attended by Vice President Richard Cheney, who gave a speech with Zinni sitting near him. About halfway through the speech, Cheney began to talk about Iraq and Zinni soon had the feeling that Cheney was making a case for invasion. The vice president said that Saddam Hussein was stockpiling weapons of mass destruction along his borders to use against his neighbors. Zinni was shocked. Since his retirement from the Marines, he had been working with the CIA trying to provide a "sanity check" for the agency's analysts studying Iraq. He was not aware of any intelligence on Iraq stockpiling weapons of mass destruction along its borders. He knew that American planes patrolling the no-fly zones over the border areas could have identified such actions if that had been the case. When he returned to the CIA after the ceremony, he asked if there was any intelligence he had missed on Iraq.

He was told there was not. George Tenet, the Director of the CIA, was also surprised at the vice president's statements and later wrote, "The speech went well beyond what our analysis could support."[87]

At Quantico, Zinni spoke for thirty minutes. He told the audience that America's political leaders intended to invade Iraq. He said it would be the first time the United States had conducted such an invasion without first being attacked. Only a clear and present danger to the United States could justify such an attack. While Saddam Hussein and his regime were a menace to the region, Zinni argued that there was no compelling evidence that Iraq posed a clear threat to America or that an invasion was warranted. Zinni could not mention the information he had received from the CIA, but he made it clear there was reason to doubt that Iraq was about to endanger the United States.

The attacks on the United States the previous year had been conducted by al-Qaeda, supported by the Taliban in Afghanistan. Zinni said that the American attack on Afghanistan was clearly in order, but the task was incomplete. Operations there should not be compromised by an unnecessary campaign in Iraq. Zinni noted that many of the Americans of his generation in political power who wanted to invade Iraq had not served in Vietnam and did not fully appreciate the consequences of war. He suggested that those political leaders believed an invasion of Iraq would stabilize the region and help the Palestinian-Israeli peace process. Zinni stated firmly that the opposite was true: an invasion would only increase tensions and destabilize the region. Using a metaphor for an attack by a pack of wolves, he said the goal should be to "first shoot the wolf on the sled." For Zinni, the wolf on the sled was in Afghanistan, not in Iraq.[88]

Less than two weeks later on 23 September, four retired military officers testified before the Senate Armed Services Committee on the subject of war with Iraq. General John M. Shalikashvili had served as the overall commander for Provide Comfort, the operation on which Jay Garner led a division-size formation to assist Kurdish refugees driven into the Iraqi mountains after Desert Storm. Shalikashvili subsequently served as the Chairman of the Joint Chiefs of Staff. General Wesley J. Clark, like Shalikashvili from the Army, had been the NATO commander and had extensive experience in the Balkans. Marine General Joseph P. Hoar had served as commander of Central Command when it managed operations in Somalia. General Thomas G. McInerney had served as the Assistant Vice Chief of Staff of the Air Force.[89]

In their opening statements, all four generals acknowledged the menace Iraq posed in the Middle East and its potential to produce weapons of mass destruction, but each added caveats about invading. Shalikashvili stated that a war with Iraq should have the full support of Congress, the American people, and the United Nations. It would entail risks and bring the unexpected; it should not be undertaken on the cheap. Clark concurred, adding that there must be a plan for a post-conflict phase in Iraq as there had been for the intervention in Kosovo. Such an invasion should include a large force, but Clark cautioned that it could "distract us from Al-Qaeda with a diversion of effort."

Hoar stated that the Muslim world was suspicious of unilateral action by the United States and that the main effort should be against al-Qaeda. Second priority should be the peace process for resolving the Palestinian-Israeli conflict. Any operations against Iraq should be third priority. Hoar also noted there was no evidence of a connection between al-Qaeda and Iraq, and several times he expressed concern that there was little support in the Middle East for an American invasion of Iraq.

McInerney took another track, stating that an invasion would be preceded by a massive air campaign with precision weapons that would cripple Iraq. It would then require no more than 30,000–50,000 American ground troops; Coalition forces could bring that up to more than 100,000. He said there were two million Iraqi-Americans who could return to Iraq to help with the liberation and that a year after the invasion the impact of Iraq's liberation on neighboring Iran would lead that country to overthrow its religious leadership. Making McInerney's remarks more striking in comparison with those of the Army and Marine generals who had also testified was that he was an

Air Force general citing precision weapons as a decisive factor in a potential invasion of Iraq.

When one senator asked if reliance on Coalition forces was overrated, Shalikashvilli, Clark, and Hoar suggested that such a coalition was essential. Only McInerney expressed little interest in Coalition forces. General Hoar was the most cautious of the group and politely expressed skepticism with McInerney's views.[90]

General Zinni testified separately before the Senate Foreign Relations Committee. When Senator Richard Lugar asked if Saddam Hussein posed an imminent threat for the United States, Zinni responded there was no such threat. "It's not there."[91]

For a decade prior to 2002, military commanders at Central Command—Generals Hoar, Peay, and Zinni, along with their planners—had developed a concept for invading Iraq with two Army corps and a Marine Expeditionary Force, originally with nine American Army and Marine divisions—to defeat twenty-three Iraqi divisions. By the end of the 1990s, OPLAN 1003-98 had reduced the ground formations to seven American divisions and assumed the UK would provide a division. With Coalition air and naval dominance, those eight divisions should have been enough to successfully invade and occupy Iraq. The plans of that period had been approved by each Secretary of Defense, but with the arrival of Rumsfeld in 2001 those plans were declared dated. That coincided with the arrival of General Franks at Central Command, who also considered the troop-heavy plan out of date.

The commanders and planners at Central Command had competed with Pentagon policy makers, both military and civilian, who had a zeal for technology and considered the projected ground forces for Iraq excessive. In 2002, Rumsfeld and other key political leaders in the Pentagon and the White House assumed that the operative concept was liberation of Iraq and hence large occupation forces would not be required. That view was consistent with their intention to avoid nation-building tasks, particularly with military forces. The collective experience from Bosnia, Somalia, Haiti, and Kosovo should have been useful for planning for a postwar Iraq, but that was ignored.

Initially, when planners at Central Command asked about guidance for a post-hostilities phase in Iraq, they were directed to focus their energy on planning for the invasion rather than what would follow. As it became clear that no other U.S. government agency or international organization could take on such a task, there was a rush by Central Command, the Joint Staff, and others late in 2002 to develop appropriate plans and establish a military headquarters to assume that role. Most of that effort focused on humanitarian assistance, rather than governance, civil administration, or reconstruction.

While military commanders and planners had little recourse but to obey orders from their civilian leaders, retired Army and Marine officers advocated caution for an invasion of Iraq and urged preparation for the unexpected that was inevitable with war. Brent Scowcroft made a much more public protest. Civilian leaders running the Pentagon, however, did not want to hear it. The military planning and preparation for Iraq, though extensive, was insufficient, with the post-conflict planning poorly coordinated. Interagency planning and preparation would turn out to be worse.

2
INTERAGENCY PLANNING

Interagency planning for regime change in Iraq was initiated by the National Security Council. Established in 1947, the NSC had gone through a steady evolution by the time George W. Bush was sworn in as president in 2001. Then, within weeks of taking office, he signed National Security Presidential Directive 1 (NSPD-1), which established the specific guidelines for the NSC during his administration.[1] As in earlier administrations, it would be a multilayered organization managed and staffed by some of the most senior and talented personnel in the American government. Yet the NSC would prove incapable or unwilling, through inadequate structure and leadership, to provide the executive management necessary to properly guide the planning and execution of the post-conflict operations for Iraq.

NSPD-1 confirmed two tasks for the NSC: to advise the president on the integration of domestic, foreign, and military policies relating to national security; and to provide a process to implement that integration, known as the Interagency Process. The regular attendees of the NSC were the president, vice president, Secretary of State, Secretary of Defense, Secretary of Treasury, National Security Advisor, Chairman of the Joint Chiefs of Staff, and the Director of the CIA. The White House chief of staff and the Assistant to the President for Economic Policy were normally included, as were other senior officials in the administration as deemed necessary. When this group met without the president it was referred to as the Principals Committee, chaired by the National Security Advisor. The respective deputies for each of the principals would meet as the NSC Deputies Committee, chaired by the Deputy National Security Advisor, to "ensure that issues brought before the NSC/PC or the NSC have been properly analyzed and prepared for decision." In 2001, the NSC was supported by a staff with six regional and eleven functional Policy Coordination Committees (see Figure 1).[2]

Despite the broad representation of senior officials across the government and the depth of its staff, the NSC did not have a structured planning system

National Security Council – NSPD 1 (13 Feb 2001)

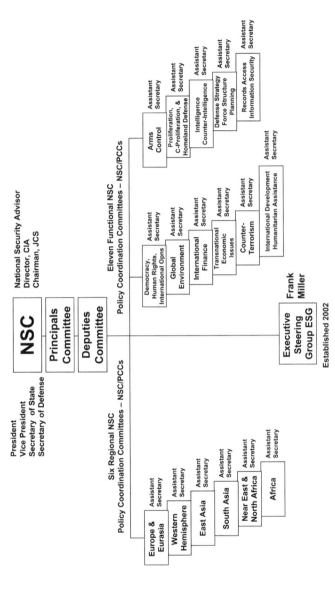

Figure 1. National Security Council, National Security Presidential Directive 1 (13 February 2001).

or methodology comparable to the military components of the Department of Defense. There was no counterpart within the NSC staff, or elsewhere in the American government, to a military J-5 Plans and Policy staff section to manage the conversion of policy into a planning effort, or a J-3 Operations staff section to resource and implement such plans. Furthermore, only the military services had a professional education system with year-long staff colleges, war colleges, and other service schools specifically designed to prepare officers to serve as planners and strategists. The absence of a cohesive interagency planning methodology with those trained to implement it led to considerable inefficiency in 2002 vis-à-vis preparation for regime replacement in Iraq and efforts to manage it over the next year.

When the World Trade Center and the Pentagon were attacked on 11 September 2001, the U.S. response was to attack al-Qaeda and the Taliban in Afghanistan, which it did with remarkably modest forces. This was followed by even more modest contributions from the other American agencies for regime replacement in Afghanistan. In contrast, the American objectives for regime change in Iraq were grander than in Afghanistan and thus required larger military formations, despite efforts to keep the numbers limited. These objectives for Iraq would also require significant contributions from civilian components of the American government. This would become more critical when other nations, as well as international and nongovernmental organizations (IOs and NGOs), failed to respond to the situation in Iraq as many American leaders had anticipated. The invasion of Iraq came with over a decade of military planning behind it, but those involved in interagency planning had only a year to prepare for regime change, without a comparable planning system.

When other agencies plan, they frequently begin with a dialogue between the key personnel at several levels rather than with decisive, top-down direction that defines the initial stages of military planning. Such interaction took place to address regime change in Iraq in 2002. Those efforts were often driven by competing political and departmental agendas, influenced by strong personalities. During 2002, the civilian agencies undertook significant work on Iraq, but the NSC did not establish a single cohesive interagency plan for regime replacement.

Early in 2002, the Principals Committee directed the Deputies Committee to begin a study of regime change for Iraq. Stephen Hadley, the Deputy National Security Advisor, scheduled twice-weekly meetings, initially luncheons in the White House Situation Room, known as the Deputies Lunches. Attendees included Richard Armitage and Marc Grossman from the Department of State; Paul Wolfowitz, Doug Feith, and either General Peter Pace or Lieutenant General George Casey from the Department of Defense; John

McLaughlin from the CIA; and Lewis "Scooter" Libby from the Office of the Vice President (OVP). Of the NSC staff, General Wayne Downing, USA (Ret), and Zalmay Khalilzad joined the meetings. Downing had a background in Special Operations and counterterrorism. Khalilzad had regional experience in Afghanistan and had played a key role in the recent developments there.[3]

Much of the policy discussed by the Principals Committee was to be worked out by the Deputies Committee, an eclectic group with diverse agendas who were to convert the general policy decisions of the Principals into detailed guidance for the appropriate departments and agencies. The high-energy Feith was a critical player at these meetings. But Feith and those in his office had limited linkage with General Franks, who preferred to work directly with Rumsfeld. Franks wrote that his "dealings with [Feith] had left me ambivalent. . . . I wasn't convinced that the Secretary [Rumsfeld] was always well-served by his advice. Feith was a master of the off-the-wall question that rarely had relevance to operational problems. . . . I generally ignored his contributions, and focused on what the Secretary had to say. And Rumsfeld never allowed Feith to interfere in my business."[4]

Franks could be caustic and profane about Feith and those who worked for him in Policy, and he also did his best to keep them from interfering with his military planners. Franks held Feith responsible, among others, for the poor working relationship and occasional bad blood between the Departments of State and Defense. Of the senior policy advisors like Feith, Franks stated, "In many cases these advisors' deep and inflexible commitment to their own ideas was disruptive and divisive, as they sought to influence their bosses—and ultimately George W. Bush—with respect to Iraq policy. On far too many occasions the Washington bureaucracy fought like cats in a sack."[5] The linkage in the Deputies Committee meetings between the respective departments was tense and contentious on the topic of Iraq, as was the linkage between OSD-Policy and Central Command, a situation that would not improve over the following year—with profound complications for Jay Garner and ORHA.

Once the Deputies Committee had been meeting for several months, Hadley informed Frank Miller of the NSC staff about the developing work on Iraq and instructed him to be prepared to put together working groups to support it. "We will call you when the time is right," Hadley told him.[6]

Miller had little Middle East experience and his selection for such a role was more a tribute to his management capacity and connections. After initial service in the Navy in the 1970s, Miller joined the Civil Service, worked briefly in the Department of State, then moved to the Department of Defense, where he worked for Walt Slocombe, then Deputy Undersecretary for Policy, and for

Richard Perle, Assistant Secretary of Defense for International Security Policy, responsible for arms control (Hadley later took Perle's position and became Miller's boss). Miller's specialty was arms control, which kept him in contact with others working in that field: Perle, Hadley, Slocombe, and Condoleezza Rice when she served on the NSC staff in the 1980s and early 1990s.

When Rice became the National Security Advisor with Hadley as her deputy, Miller moved to the NSC as the Special Assistant to the President and Senior Director for Defense and Arms Control Policy. In that role Miller worked directly for Hadley and Rice. By that time, Miller had spent over twenty years working in the Pentagon and knew most of the senior civilians there and many of the senior military officers. Miller's deputy was Colonel Tom Greenwood, a Marine infantryman with a background in military planning and post-conflict experience from the 1990s. He had also served on the NSC staff during the Clinton administration. Like Miller, Greenwood was well connected in Washington.[7]

In the fall of 2001, Rice and Hadley tapped Miller to manage an inter-agency working group for operations in Afghanistan, with Greenwood as his right-hand man. Arguably, that role might have been assigned to another NSC office with more regional experience for Afghanistan with someone such as Khalilzad in charge. But in the view of some of those on the NSC, the affable Khalilzad often acted as a free agent and did not display developed management skills. Miller and Greenwood had better connections with the Department of Defense and were considered good managers. They worked on Afghanistan for five months through March 2002.

When Hadley directed Miller to reestablish such a group for Iraq in the summer of 2002, it became the Executive Steering Group (ESG). Miller was aware that General Casey had set up a group of military officers to work on interagency issues in the Pentagon. Miller felt that group should be better connected to the White House and the NSC and he convened the ESG in the Pentagon, incorporating the group General Casey had set up. Doug Feith had discussed the merger with Generals Pace and Casey and they agreed it was a good idea. Feith considered Miller "immodest, even aggressive" and often "flouted the chain of command" in the Pentagon, which annoyed Rumsfeld, but overall Feith thought Miller made a useful contribution to the interagency efforts on Iraq.[8]

Meeting several times a week, senior ESG members from the Pentagon included Assistant Secretary Bill Luti from OSD-Policy and General Casey. Ambassador Ryan Crocker and Lincoln Bloomfield (and later Debra Kagen) represented the Department of State. Bob Grenier came from the CIA. To keep a low profile on planning involving Iraq, Miller kept the ESG meetings in the Pentagon. Several agencies set up working groups that provided reports to the ESG, but Miller exercised little control over them.[9]

There was only one component directly subordinate to the ESG—the Humanitarian Relief and Reconstruction Working Group co-chaired by Elliot Abrams and Robin Cleveland. Abrams was the Senior Advisor to the President for Democracy and Humanitarian Affairs on the NSC staff and Cleveland was an Associate Director for National Security in the Office of Management and Budget (OMB) responsible for funding national security and overseas programs. Abrams had worked in previous Republican administrations and was known as a neoconservative ideologue. Cleveland had worked on economic issues as a congressional staffer before moving to OMB and was described by one NSC staff member as "outspoken, hard-nosed, and sharp-elbowed."[10]

Cleveland began hosting weekly meetings of the working group in early September 2002 in her corner office in the Old Executive Office Building (OEOB), adjacent to the White House. Representatives came from State, Defense, USAID, and CIA. Some meetings included officials from the Departments of Justice, Treasury, and Commerce, among others. The Abrams-Cleveland working group never exceeded twenty people, and its linkage with the agencies was essentially through individual association rather than any specific guidance or tasking. Cleveland and Abrams set up two subordinate working groups: one for Humanitarian Relief under Jonathan Dworken, and another for Reconstruction under Wendy Chamberlin. Dworken worked on the NSC staff for Abrams, a civil servant on loan from USAID. Cleveland recruited Chamberlin, who had recently returned from Pakistan where as ambassador she had played a substantive role in operations in Afghanistan. When Chamberlin joined Cleveland and Abrams she was serving as an assistant administrator for USAID and head of the USAID Asia and Near East Bureau, which included responsibility for Iraq and Afghanistan.[11]

The initial guidance to Dworken and Chamberlin was to consider Afghanistan the model for postwar Iraq and to keep commitments limited. Dworken and Chamberlin were accustomed to working with the United Nations and international and nongovernmental organizations for relief and reconstruction work. They were encouraged to consider contractors based on the assumption, perhaps questionable, that contractors would be more reliable than the UN, IOs, and NGOs and would not require as much security. Dworken and Chamberlin were told that security was not their task. Those serving with working groups from the Departments of State and Justice proposed setting up a plan to reform the civilian police in Iraq; however, those from OSD-Policy in the Pentagon, reinforced by Cleveland and Abrams, dismissed the idea, feeling that it would be too expensive. Frank Miller from the NSC concurred, believing that any police training effort by NSC would be inappropriate, based on ill-suited Western models and with non-Arabic-speaking training personnel.[12]

Dworken wanted to know how relief operations would fit in with military operations, and in early November he flew to Tampa to get a grasp of the military planning. With military planners absorbed with reworking the forces allocated for the invasion, he found little substantive planning for post-conflict operations. Yet the president was committed to humanitarian assistance and Robin Cleveland arranged for $200 million dollars to support it. Dworken lined up the World Food Program to convert that money into pre-positioned food supplies in countries surrounding Iraq so that they could be moved in quickly following an invasion. Chamberlin asked for $10 billion for reconstruction, but Cleveland would only provide $2 billion. Others in the administration felt that Iraqi oil revenues could cover such costs, but Dworken and Chamberlin did not believe such revenues would be available in time for their tasks.[13]

THE FUTURE OF IRAQ PROJECT

With those on the NSC tending toward a military option for dealing with Iraq, in addition to supplying humanitarian assistance for the Iraqi people, the Department of State initiated an ambitious study of what should follow regime removal in Iraq. That task went to Tom Warrick, who set out to develop a multi-dimensional concept to shape a replacement regime for Iraq by working with the Iraqi people. Warrick's venture was soon known as the Future of Iraq (FOI) project. There were other studies before the war, including military planning that went back a decade and additional interagency working groups set up by the NSC and ESG, but none would match the FOI's interaction with people who knew Iraqi institutions firsthand. While Warrick's project was broad in scope, it would be disappointing, controversial from the beginning, and dominated by strong personalities. That included Tom Warrick.

A graduate of Harvard Law School, Warrick practiced international law for seventeen years with a specialty in litigation involving Middle Eastern oil and gas. In the 1990s, he worked for the United Nations investigating war crimes in the former Yugoslavia, then joined the State Department in 1997. His work on war crimes in the Balkans led to a study of ethnic conflict in the post–Cold War era, including the regime of Saddam Hussein. In May 2001, Warrick moved to the Near Eastern Affairs Bureau (NEA) at State as a civil servant, GS-15. Within NEA, Warrick was assigned to the Office of Northern Gulf Affairs (NGA), which covered the Persian Gulf states.

At NGA, Warrick found that his superiors "were not sure what to do with me as a war crimes expert." Forty-nine years of age, he was unusual because he was not a Foreign Service Officer, had only been at State for six years, and had no appreciable service overseas beyond working trips. His expertise was functional rather than regional. But he was a quick study and found his niche on Iraq, eventually being assigned to the sub-bureau with the Iraq portfolio. His immediate boss was David Pearce, the head of NGA, but Warrick's title was Special Advisor to the Assistant Secretary, meaning Ambassador Ryan C. Crocker, who was in charge of the NEA Bureau. Crocker reported to Undersecretary for Political Affairs Marc Grossman, the senior State Department official after Secretary Colin Powell and Deputy Secretary Richard Armitage. With responsibility for Iraq within the NEA Bureau, Crocker had a high profile in 2002 and remarkable credentials. He spoke Arabic and had previously served as ambassador to Syria, Lebanon, Kuwait, and Afghanistan. Warrick was in talented company.[14]

After the attacks of 11 September 2001, Warrick and several others on the Iraq desk began discussions about what would happen to Iraq if an American-led coalition invaded. In Warrick's view, the Future of Iraq project had begun as a bottom-up effort. By January 2002 he was putting together papers on Iraq for a select group that included Pearce, Crocker, Armitage, and Powell.[15]

In February, the State Department authorized Warrick to put together conferences for Iraqi opposition groups. The initial meeting of 9–10 April 2002 was hosted by the Middle East Institute, a think tank that received funding from the State Department and other organizations. Ned Walker, the president of the Institute, was a former assistant secretary of state. But Walker had made some negative comments about the Bush administration and Warrick soon had to find another host for future meetings. Several of the Iraqi opposition group leaders, notably Ahmad Chalabi of the Iraqi National Congress (INC) and Ayed Allawi of the Iraqi National Accord (INA), wanted to run the conference, but Warrick found the groups contentious, and if one were given the lead, one or more of the others would refuse to participate. Warrick's superiors decided that the State Department would have to host the meeting with Warrick in charge of the project. Within six weeks he had a $5 million budget from Congress and had held the first working group over 7–8 July, just as military planning was surging within Central Command.[16]

Warrick initially structured seventeen working groups comprising two hundred Iraqis living in the United States, Europe, and the Middle East, including the autonomous Kurdish region of northern Iraq. Many were doctors, engineers, lawyers, and business people, and Warrick organized them into working groups based on their backgrounds and interests. Joining these groups were forty non-Iraqi specialists in functional areas. Warrick's team would put together papers related to a specific group and then would convene a two-day conference. Often the agenda and related issues were discussed with the participants in advance so as to preclude surprises and to establish consensus beforehand. The meetings were held in Washington and London, the latter to accommodate Iraqis using Iranian passports, which complicated entry into the United States. Each conference was conducted in Arabic and English. Additional participants often joined from the Pentagon, the Office of the Vice President, the Treasury, and USAID.[17] Representation from Defense was limited and Civil Affairs personnel did not join until the project was well underway.[18]

Of the seventeen projected working groups, three never met. Of those that did, six groups had a high profile and met three or four times: Transitional Justice, Public Finance, Economy & Infrastructure, Democratic Principles, Public Outreach, and Oil & Energy. Others met only once or twice: Agriculture, Water & Environment, Defense Policy & Institutions, Local Government, Transparency & Anti-Corruption Measures, Public Health & Humanitarian Needs, Education, Free Media, and Civil Society Capacity Building.[19]

The Transitional Justice group was the first to meet, on 7–8 July 2002. Participants were lawyers, judges, and a few former ambassadors; they were familiar with the Iraqi judicial, police, and prison systems. Their main interest was legal reform and they drafted papers for a proposed Iraqi judiciary. The special and intelligence court systems that had been used for repression would be disbanded. The criminal, civil, juvenile, and family court systems would be retained and reformed with new legal codes. The judiciary branch would have its own budget to ensure its independence.[20] The group knew that there had been significant looting, vandalism, and revenge killing in Iraq during the Shiite and Kurdish revolts following Desert Storm in 1991, and thus recommended an interim government in Iraq following regime change in order to reform the police, courts, and prisons.[21]

The Iraqi police presented a special problem. The members of the force were underpaid and corrupt and lacked credibility with the Iraqi population. Neither the police nor the army would be able to help with chaos in the beginning and the group suggested there be "an international protection force under the auspices of the United Nations, after regime change. . . . Iraq must be at peace with itself, its neighbors and the world. . . . While focusing on democracy . . . the [working group] sees no need for compulsory military service. Instead there should be a professional army of volunteers to defend the country against external aggression."[22]

Such a protection force would allow time to convert the Iraqi army into a volunteer force. The UN had provided such protection forces in the Balkans and for other conflicts; it would be appropriate that it do so for a transition period in Iraq. The group addressed de-Ba'athification but with limited scope. The intent was to disband the party, and through a "truth and reconciliation" process bring party members back to a more balanced society. Those guilty of criminal acts would be tried and punished.

The group proposed that a new constitution be drafted, since any previous Iraqi constitutions would not receive sufficient consensus among the diverse populace.[23] A new constitution should include a constitutional process with full participation of the Iraqi population. It should also include executive, leg- islative, and judicial branches with checks and balances, a bill of human rights, and acknowledgment of the multi-ethnic and multi-religious nature of the na- tion. Such a process would be time-consuming. Thus a transitional period was proposed, with an interim presidential council of three statesmen representing northern, southern, and central Iraq, as well as a transitional constitution.[24]

The Public Finance group met on 6–7 August, the first of its four meetings. Warrick chaired the first meeting with Deputy Assistant Secretary of State Elizabeth Cheney, the vice president's daughter. Warrick asked what the top financial priorities should be for Iraq. Several people suggested sustaining a strong Iraqi dinar and restructuring the nation's debt. A young woman in the group, Ahlam al-Shibib, disagreed. She suggested that the top priority should be job creation in order to preserve social peace. Cheney was the first to back her position and the others quickly agreed.[25] The group also wanted to re- capture assets controlled by Saddam Hussein, his family, and his cronies, and proposed banking reforms as well as transparency and accountability of public expenditures to restore confidence in Iraq's domestic finances.[26]

The next three meetings of the Public Finance group were integrated with the Economy and Infrastructure group. U.S. Department of Treasury rep- resentatives monitored the sessions to correlate their understanding of eco- nomic factors with statistics provided by the UN on Iraq. As the two working groups merged their efforts, they drew a wider assortment of Iraqi academics, economists, businessmen, and engineers and split into seven subgroups to study specific topics.

A subgroup on electricity estimated that Iraq could produce only 3,500 constant megawatts but needed 6,200 for industrial and domestic consump- tion; the cost for an increase to 6,200 MW was estimated at $6.2 billion.

The electricity grid had to be protected during any invasion and from the chaos that might follow.[27] Another subgroup noted that the UN Oil for Food program had provided $60 billion to Iraq, with $40 billion for humanitarian goods and services, mainly food. The subgroup recommended continuing the program several months after a regime change to sustain the distribution of food and to fund the health care system.[28]

A third subgroup worked on proposals to convert the Iraq Ministry of Industry and Military Industrialization to civilian purposes, although not necessarily through privatization. That ministry had some of the best and brightest Iraqis working on weapons programs, talent that could be reoriented toward more useful programs. One subgroup drafted proposals to improve the communications infrastructure, while another studied how to improve the training and employment opportunities for women in Iraq. One subgroup proposed an Iraqi Development and Reconstruction Council (IDRC, later changed to IRDC) to manage economic and social tasks during a transitional period for twenty-four to thirty-six months with "an implicit political role."[29]

A colorful Iraqi businessman, Rubar Sandi, suggested setting aside $3 billion to employ those in the Mohabarat security service and the Republican Guards, whose jobs would have been liquidated. Warrick was incredulous: was Sandi suggesting that the Mohabarat be given jobs before the chronically unemployed? Sandi replied that those security forces should not be left on the streets to go into organized crime. Few took his suggestion seriously.[30]

The Democratic Principles group met only twice—in September and December, both times near London. David Philips, a specialist on conflict resolution at Columbia University, was asked by Grossman and Crocker to serve as a facilitator in the group. Philips later wrote a book, *Losing Iraq,* in which he stated Warrick was unhappy with Philips's role and "knew that I had friends in the upper echelons of the State Department. As a consultant, I could operate outside the envelope that constrained career personnel. . . . I did not allow [Warrick] to bulldoze decisions that I thought were detrimental to the Iraqis." Philips described Warrick as "too protective of his ties with the Iraqis and overly possessive of the Future of Iraq project. His reluctance to communicate and share work products exacerbated interagency tensions." Philips felt that if the U.S. government was serious about the post-conflict phase, it should have assigned someone more senior than Warrick to the project, "a heavyweight who could command greater respect from the Iraqis and who might have kept the interagency work on track."[31]

The Democratic Principles group had a high profile; more than a dozen U.S. officials planned to attend the first conference. Philips objected that so many observers would "result in grandstanding by Iraqis." The number was cut and limited to representatives from the Office of the Vice President and the Department of Defense. Of the thirty-two Iraqis, twelve came from the United States, ten from the UK, four from Kurdish Iraq, and the rest from countries bordering Iraq. Absent was Ahmad Chalabi, who had objected to any conference he could not control. But when it was clear how important the Future of Iraq project had become, he sent several of his senior associates from the INC to represent his views and to keep him informed.[32]

Philips had visited Iraq's Kurdish areas and believed Iraq's internal problems had resulted from the abuses of a strong central government. With others he argued for power-sharing through decentralization and federalism, which suited the Kurds who wanted autonomy if not outright independence. Other Iraqis wanted only limited decentralization, with provincial and local governments empowered but without a federalism that would empower ethnic groups. Many Americans who had been to Iraq had only visited the Kurdish areas and tended to see Iraq from a Kurdish perspective, and thus they were positive about federalism. Decentralizing the government of Iraq would be a challenging endeavor, leading to more turmoil than anticipated.

For Warrick, the Democratic Principles group was divided into two schools of thought. One, represented by Kanan Makiya and Rend al-Rahim Francke, would turn Iraq over to the external opposition groups selecting Iraqis for the executive and the legislature. Warrick believed Makiya's views reflected those of Chalabi and his INC supporters. The second school included Laith Kubba from the National Endowment for Democracy and others in the working group who felt that that would be a recipe for civil war, as the external opposition did not have credibility with the Iraqi people and they would reject leaders imposed from outside.[33]

Philips also observed that those from the INC wanted to empower the expatriates to rule Iraq and that this was not just a difference among Iraqis. He felt it was a defining current throughout the U.S. interagency process in 2002. Philips described the Democratic Principles group as the "mother of all working groups," while Warrick thought it drew too much attention from the other groups.[34]

The Oil and Energy group met four times during the year and included petroleum economists, engineers, and other oil specialists. They wanted to establish Iraq as a leader in international oil: to get the oil revenues flowing, increase production and marketing efficiency, and obtain a strong position within OPEC. Warrick and others were concerned about perceptions of some secret plot to take over Iraqi oil. Everyone had a keen interest in Iraqi oil, not to steal or manage it, but to have oil sustain reconstruction costs and aid regime transition. They wanted to protect it from the damage inflicted on oil fields in Kuwait in 1991.[35]

The Defense Policy group included Iraqi military officers who had left the country and some Kurdish Peshmerga military leaders. The group met twice. The key issues included how to structure Iraqi forces so as not to threaten its neighbors and to ensure that the role of the military forces was to defend the constitution rather than political leaders. The group agreed that Iraqi military policies and adventures had caused instability for Iraq and the region. Yet they knew that Iraqi forces, which had been used to repress the Iraqi population, would be required for internal security during a transition phase. They wanted an army as a national unifying force. Arab Sunnis and Shiites wanted a unified army, while the Kurdish representatives wanted a regionally based army. They wanted to have the Iraqi army switch sides and join the Coalition during an invasion. No one suggested disbanding the regular army.[36]

The Public Outreach and the Free Media groups, meeting separately, wanted to train Iraqi media personnel in free-world methods and temporarily retain the Ministry of Information to help establish a new media system in Iraq. They proposed a code of media ethics to assist a public debate for a new regime, all transparent to the Iraqi people, the region, and the world.

The Education group met only once; its aim was to advance Iraqis' self-image through better teaching methodologies, particularly with regard to primary and secondary education, reeducating teachers, and replacing textbooks for history and social studies. The group was concerned with the high number of Ba'athists in the teaching community; many had joined the party merely to obtain employment, while others were true believers and would have to be removed.

Warrick wanted to have city managers for the Local Government group, but it was composed of academics and religious leaders. The group considered how de-Ba'athification would work at the local level. Some in the group had extreme views, notably those representing Chalabi's INC; others were more moderate. They were interested in following the model of denazification following World War II. Warrick thought the Ba'ath under Saddam Hussein were more comparable to communists and suggested they consider German unification in the 1990s as more relevant.[37]

The object of the Transparency and Anti-Corruption group was to reduce corruption to gain public confidence, attract foreign investment, and sustain the rule of law. They felt the key problem was not the Iraqi laws, but their lack of systematic enforcement. They proposed a European-style code of conduct and an anti-corruption task force with broad powers during the transition.[38]

During his past work at the Department of State, Warrick had studied regime change in Bosnia, Kosovo, East Timor, and west Africa; he believed those experiences had led him to his role with the Future of Iraq project. In his view the Balkans experience had the most to offer on the mechanics of regime change with Coalition assistance. But he felt that those in political power in the Bush administration lacked that experience or were otherwise dismissive of it.[39]

In Bush's 2000 presidential campaign, such experience had indeed been dismissed as nation-building projects inappropriate for America and its high-tech military forces. Many in the new administration thought that if such projects were undertaken at all, they should be managed by the United Nations or regional coalitions. The United States could assist on the margins, but otherwise it should preserve its independence for larger tasks befitting a superpower. Warrick worried that the Bush administration would take on regime change and the nation building that came with it with little regard for the lessons learned during the Clinton administration.

The Iraqis he worked with wanted the United States to devote the same kind of effort toward Iraq that it had devoted to postwar Japan and Germany, but they did not want an occupation or a military governor. They wanted American resources with Iraqi control. If a non-Iraqi had to serve as an interim leader, they wanted a civilian. Warrick wanted "a level playing field. We wanted to make sure that no one, none of the Iraqi participants . . . were allowed to high-jack the agenda." Although Chalabi kept his distance, members from his INC were aggressive in trying to wrest control from other Iraqis who wanted a balanced approach.[40]

Several Future of Iraq conferences were conducted late in 2002 in London that included members of Iraqi opposition groups. David Pearce representing NEA at State and Bill Luti representing Doug Feith's Policy office from the Pentagon went to the conference with a letter addressed to the opposition groups signed by Armitage, Wolfowitz, and Libby, the deputies at State, Defense, and the Office of the Vice President. The letter stated that Washington was not ready to form a provisional government for Iraq or to create an interim national assembly. Both should come after Saddam was removed from power. What the Bush administration wanted to form was an Iraqi advisory group with broad representation. From the National Security Council, Zalmay Khalilzad was appointed as a Special Envoy and Ambassador-at-Large to work with the Iraqi opposition.[41]

Khalilzad, an American citizen and Afghan Sunni from Kabul, had a Ph.D. from the University of Chicago. He was in a unique position to join the chemistry in London. According to David Philips, "Khalilzhad's Farsi language skills and Afghan sensibilities endeared him to Iraqis." He had a long history with American conservatives, having served with Richard Perle and Paul Wolfowitz in the Pentagon in the early 1990s. He also had ties with Vice President Cheney. Ryan Crocker and David Pearce were happy to see Khalilzad align himself with the NEA Bureau and the Future of Iraq project.[42]

When Pearce and Luti read the letter during a presentation, the Iraqi response was mixed. Some agreed it was premature to create a provisional government while Saddam was still in power. Others resented American efforts to dictate ground rules and written instructions. But they agreed that there should be no military occupation. A representative of the Supreme Council for Islamic Revolution in Iraq (SCIRI) opined, "We want the Americans to help us overthrow Saddam. They seem to want to do it themselves."[43]

David Philips noted that "Chalabi was furious with the United States for its decision to scale back the role of the Iraqi exiles." But Philips also observed that Chalabi was smooth and through his representatives tried "persuading the conference to endorse a transitional authority to be formed just before the U.S.-led invasion . . . [and] concluded that his best chance to establish himself in power would come before Iraqis in Iraq could organize themselves. Chalabi envisioned himself at the head of a nucleus transitional authority that would follow on the heels of U.S. Forces entering Baghdad . . . [and he] demanded his own militia so that he could garner credibility with Iraqis." As if in response to Chalabi, during the conference, "a U.S. Army general arrived to finalize arrangements for training a 5,000-man force to be called the Free Iraqi Forces."[44]

Although Chalabi had not participated in the Future of Iraq project, he called a press conference one morning at the London Conference with Kanan Makiya and Rend al-Rahim, two INC members who had participated, and had Kanan present a draft report by the Democratic Principles Working Group, "summarizing the INC's plan for a nucleus transitional authority to be installed in Baghdad." Philips was "shocked that Chalabi would hold a press conference to present the Working Group's report as the agenda for the whole conference." Iraqis from other groups "were infuriated that the INC would attempt to hijack the conference."[45]

The Future of Iraq project would have additional sessions through mid-2003, but the high water point of its activity and impact came at the London Conference. Some felt little of substance had been achieved. There was no government-in-exile as Chalabi and the INC wanted, nor was a transitional group established. The working groups produced studies and proposals, but they lacked cohesion and consensus. The Iraqi members were far from united on how to impose democracy, de-Ba'athification, and defense and economic policy for Iraq. Those involved with the Future of Iraq project were an eclectic group of ambitious and contentious expatriates. Yet 200 Iraqis had come together to explore a broad range of issues that should be addressed with regime change.

Remarkably, few State Department personnel participated with Warrick. He had only two career officers with him full-time: Andrea Gastaldo, a junior Foreign Service Officer (FSO), and David Staples, a junior government service (GS) press officer. Warrick's deputy was Sahar Khoury Kincannon, a Palestinian American, Arabic speaker, and the wife of an FSO, John Kincannon, then serving in Pakistan. But Sahar was neither an FSO herself nor on a GS career track at State. Ryan Crocker and David Pearce monitored the FOI Project, but not on a daily basis. Warrick had only four other assistants for the project that were, in State Department jargon, WAEs ("while actually employed") and a few specialists who joined for short periods. Warrick had managed an important project for State, but few from the department had been involved and the experience was not institutionalized there or elsewhere within the government. Some observers, like David Philips, felt that Warrick was too possessive and kept others out. [46]

The project did not constitute structured planning. The combined products from the working groups came to over 1,200 pages — 15 percent of which were Arabic translations. There was much unresolved disagreement and no uniform format. There was no consolidated summary beyond a set of PowerPoint slides. Warrick had played the dominant role and only he could effectively brief the summary slides or make full sense of the Future of Iraq project. But others at State were interested in Warrick's work and attempted to join.

ANOTHER DEPARTMENT OF STATE INITIATIVE

In 2002 Mike Ayoub was a civil servant (GS-14) in the Department of State Bureau of Political-Military Affairs. Over the next year he would have several roles on Iraq. The first was his effort to update State's Political-Military (Pol-Mil) plan for Iraq. Potentially that plan could integrate classified military planning with the unclassified Future of Iraq project, and Ayoub tried to bring that about. Of Palestinian heritage, Ayoub spoke Arabic, although he had learned it while attending the Defense Language Institute during his earlier military service. He joined the State Department in 1991 and as an FSO he had served in diplomatic positions in Europe, Saudi Arabia, and Oman, and had also worked in Algeria and the Balkans. He continued his military service with the Army as a military intelligence reservist; in 2002 he held the rank of major. He was one of the few working on Iraq who had a connection with both the Departments of State and Defense.[47]

In February 2002 Ayoub began writing papers on Iraq for his superiors when he picked up the Pol-Mil plan to work on. It was classified as secret with eleven appendices: International Diplomacy, Regional Engagement, Internal Political situation, Public Order, Regional Security, Weapons of Mass Destruction (WMD), Counter-terrorism, Human Rights, Economics and Finance, International Public Information, and Humanitarian Assistance. While the State Pol-Mil Bureau had overall responsibility for the plan, responsibility for the appendixes fell to other components within State; Ayoub began coordination to get them updated.

Ayoub obtained updates from several offices at State. He then took it to Tom Krajeski, deputy of the Near East Asia/Northern Gulf Affairs (NEA/NGA) Bureau, where Tom Warrick worked. Krajeski told Ayoub that NGA had its own effort for Iraq and did not have time for the Pol-Mil Bureau. Ayoub left him a copy of his plan anyway. Krajeski called Ayoub the next day and asked him to come back. He apologized for being abrupt the day before and said he was impressed with Ayoub's work. He cleared Ayoub to attend Future of Iraq conferences. Although Ayoub would not work for Warrick, they were authorized to share information.

Ayoub wanted to link the Future of Iraq project with the Department of Defense, which had little representation with it through the summer of 2002. In October, Ayoub went to the Pentagon and met Brigadier General Kern, commander of the 352nd Civil Affairs Command. Kern complained that his Civil Affairs units would be the first line of governance into Iraq and that he had been excluded from planning on Iraq. Ayoub was unaware that the U.S. Army commander in Afghanistan had sent Kern home from Afghanistan. He was surprised when a colonel working on the J-5 staff told him not to put much stock in Kern because "he isn't a player." Ayoub wondered "how could someone in that position—not be a player?"[48]

The following day, Ayoub contacted Colonel Margo Sheridan, a reservist with the 352nd, and gave her a copy of the Pol-Mil Plan for Iraq that he had been trying to update. His intent was to bring Civil Affairs officers into the Future of Iraq project, and soon he had Warrick's permission to do so. Ayoub attended a weekend meeting with the 352nd at its headquarters in College Park, Maryland, to coordinate the integration of additional personnel with appropriate working groups. They in turn gave him his first look at the Central Command 1003 plan for Iraq. Ayoub studied Annex V for interagency operations, which he found "rather flimsy," but he was pleased that State and Civil Affairs were working together. When several colonels became aware that

Ayoub held a reserve army commission, they asked him to join the 352nd and go with them to Kuwait, where they were soon to deploy. Ayoub deferred, assuming he could make a better contribution at State to sustain the connection with the Department of Defense. The following week he attended a conference with Warrick's Economic and Infrastructure Working Group "to help ease Colonel Sheridan into the group." It was the first Civil Affairs connection, driven by Ayoub and Civil Affairs officers, rather than by the Pentagon.[49]

By November, Joe Collins in OSD-Policy at the Pentagon learned of the Civil Affairs connection with Warrick's group. That did not surprise him since he believed Civil Affairs officers were "military entrepreneurs" looking for such connections. Collins wanted linkage at a higher level, however. He met Warrick, whom he found positive about such a connection, but nothing came of it and no senior official from the Pentagon or Central Command joined Warrick as a full-time participant.[50]

In October, Ayoub flew to Heidelberg, Germany, to participate in planning with the army's V Corps, one of the tactical formations that would invade Iraq. Ayoub asked about rear area operations, constabulary forces, currency, and the UN Oil for Food network, but those issues had received little attention in the military planning. Returning to Washington, Ayoub went to the Defense Intelligence Agency to obtain material on the military forces of Iraq and its adjacent neighbors. He passed that on to Warrick's working group that was attempting to determine the appropriate size of the Iraqi army. In early November, Ayoub escorted General Kern to the State Department to meet Tom Warrick; Kern was the most senior military officer Warrick had worked with at that stage. But with two complex and intense personalities, Ayoub was concerned about their capacity to work effectively together.[51]

USAID PLANNING

As State was working on Iraq through the efforts of Warrick and Ayoub during the fall of 2002, Wendy Chamberlin had USAID stand up a working group to address the reconstruction tasks that could fall to it. This would be an extension of the ESG working groups she had joined. In 2003 USAID was a semi-autonomous agency aligned with the Department of State, with its own culture and procedures—oriented on grass roots foreign assistance rather than political diplomacy. Mid-level personnel from USAID had participated in several of the Future of Iraq working groups: Public Health & Humanitarian Needs and Local Government. These corresponded with two USAID organizations: the Bureau of Democracy, Conflict and Humanitarian

Assistance (DCHA), and its subordinate, the Office for Foreign Disaster Assistance (OFDA). OFDA was preparing to deploy Disaster Assistance Relief Teams (DARTs), small groups of assessment specialists for immediate humanitarian requirements following an invasion of Iraq. DCHA would assist with mid-term reconstruction and local government development.

The senior position at USAID was the USAID administrator, at that time Andrew Natsios. Remarkably, Natsios was not included on the Principals or Deputies Committees—in his view because Secretary Rumsfeld wanted to exclude him.[52] Natsios could be preachy and academic and that alienated those on the NSC. Natsios had two deputies or assistants; one was Wendy Chamberlin, also the head of the USAID Bureau for Asia and Near East. As such, Chamberlin took the lead on planning for Iraq for USAID.

In November 2002, Chris Milligan and Ross Wherry joined Chamberlin to plan for Iraq. Milligan had been an FSO with USAID since 1990. He had worked briefly in Vietnam, followed by three-year tours in Ecuador and Zimbabwe. He was completing another such tour in Indonesia with USAID when the terrorist bombing in Bali in mid-2002 led to the evacuation of many Americans stationed there. Milligan assumed when he joined Chamberlin's team it was merely to help with the planning while he was waiting to return to Indonesia; little did he know that he would spend the next year in Iraq. His first task was "to write an analysis of a future governance framework for Iraq, based upon experience working [de-]centralization in Indonesia." After he wrote the paper, he joined Chamberlin in November and set up teams for functional sectors: education, health, infrastructure, agriculture, and economics.[53]

Milligan participated on the Future of Iraq project as a USAID representative with the Local Government Iraqi Working Group. With little background in the Middle East, Milligan was soon exposed to Iraqi expatriate views, their talents, experiences, and agendas for regime change. Milligan worked well as a team player. He had a serious, engaging, and self-effacing personality. Articulate, honest, and direct in style, he was passionate about his work and rarely lost his temper. People naturally liked him and those much his senior frequently sought his advice.

Through Chamberlin, Milligan made contact with Frank Miller's Executive Steering Group and the subordinate group on humanitarian assistance with Robin Cleveland and Elliot Abrams. This was the group where the two sides of the USAID strategy came into play, one for humanitarian relief and one for reconstruction. Milligan felt the OMB connection through Robin Cleveland was extremely important. Setting up procedures for USAID projects, early enough to allow for timely movement of money, ensured that USAID received those projects rather than another agency. Milligan had experience moving money through the grant process for reconstruction projects. Others working on Iraq did not, a cause of frustration and friction over the next year.[54]

OSD PLANNING

While State and USAID were attempting to prepare for postwar Iraq, Doug Feith's Policy office in the Pentagon was generating several projects for the Defense Department. Most of the military planning was conducted through U.S. Central Command with some guidance from Feith's office. Those in Feith's office worked with other agencies in Washington, as Feith represented the Department of Defense in the Deputies Committee meetings with Deputy Secretary Paul Wolfowitz. Feith's office had subordinate regional offices, with Iraq covered by the Near East and South Asian Affairs Office under Deputy Assistant Secretary Bill Luti, a retired Navy captain. With fewer personnel, it was comparable to Ryan Crocker's NEA Bureau at State.

With the developing interest in Iraq, Feith had Luti form a Near East Office, a South Asia Office, and an office focused just on Iraq, designated as the Office of Special Plans, known as OSP (in 2003, it was renamed the Office of Northern Gulf Affairs, or NGA, using the same acronym as its counterpart bureau at State). When OSP was formed, Feith added twelve people to the four Luti already had working on Iraq. Abram "Abe" Shulsky was the senior member. An academic with connections at think tanks and Defense, he had been Wolfowitz's classmate at the University of Chicago.[55]

Feith had Luti and others represent his office on the Executive Steering Group while he set up the working group on oil under Michael Mobbs in the fall of 2002. Mobbs would play several key roles over the next year on Iraq. His undergraduate work at Yale was in Russian studies and he graduated from law school in 1974 from the University of Chicago and worked for several years on international law issues related to Eastern Europe. In 1981 Mobbs was contacted by Assistant Secretary of Defense for International Security Richard Perle, who asked him to work on Strategic Arms Reduction Talks (START) with the Russians. Mobbs remained at Defense through 1987 and then joined a law firm with Doug Feith. When Feith joined the Bush administration, he asked Mobbs to join him, which he did—just after the attacks of 9/11.

Mobbs worked on legal issues with maritime interception in the Indian Ocean, targeting terrorist organizations working from Pakistan and

Afghanistan, as well as legal issues involving captured terrorists. On 30 September, Rumsfeld sent a memo to the Joint Staff, Central Command, and Feith with directions to prepare plans for safeguarding the Iraqi oil infrastructure in the event of hostilities, a snowflake that eventually landed on Major Paul Shelton's desk at Central Command.[56]

By the end of September 2002, Mobbs was assembling a team that took on the title Energy Infrastructure Planning Group (EIPG) within OSD-Policy. The EIPG members came from Departments of Defense, State, and Energy, the CIA, and the Army Corps of Engineers. Executives and specialists from the oil industry participated, some with experience in Kuwaiti oil fields, some with experience in Iraq. Except for Gary Vogler, whom Mobbs hired in early November, those from the oil industry participated infrequently.

Vogler was a graduate of West Point and an Army reservist who had recently retired as an Exxon-Mobil executive. He had worked in Saudi Arabia during the first Gulf War. Mobbs requested someone from the Department of Energy and soon had Clarke Turner on his team. Turner had served in the Army for nine years as a quartermaster officer with a petroleum specialty before he left to join the Department of Energy; by 2002 he was responsible for the strategic oil reserves in several states in the northwest. Vogler and Turner would deploy to Kuwait in March 2003 and to Baghdad a month later as the senior advisory team for the Iraqi Ministry of Oil.[57]

Seneca Johnson, a career FSO with a background on oil issues, joined them from the Department of State. Richard Frost joined as a Middle East oil specialist from the CIA and provided access to maps and satellite pictures of oil facilities in Iraq. Barbara Glotfelty, a contracting officer, joined from the Department of Defense.[58] She helped pre-position firefighting equipment with specialists sent to Kuwait to train soldiers to safely shut down oil production facilities.

Mike Makovsky joined the group with less obvious credentials. In the summer of 2002, he began working for Abe Shulsky and was assigned to the EIPG planning cell later in November. He had just completed a Ph.D. with a dissertation on Winston Churchill. Not much was known about Makovsky's oil experience other than that he had spent some time with an oil trading firm in New York. Vogler noted that Makovsky had difficulty obtaining a top secret clearance. Upon returning from his third security interview, he mentioned to Vogler that he had been asked a lot of questions about his acquaintances in Israel. Later in 2005, Vogler read a story about a 1989 *St. Louis Post-Dispatch* article stating that Makovsky had left a congressional staff position to join the Israeli army and then worked for several senior Israeli politicians. Later that year, Vogler ran into Makovsky at a meeting in the Department of State and asked him about the story. "I refuse to confirm or deny such stories," Mak-ovsky replied.[59]

Mobbs and his team planned for repair operations of Iraqi oil fields after an invasion and determined they would need an American corporation that could work with classified matters. Three were considered: Bechtel, Fluor, and KBR, a subsidiary of the Halliburton Corporation. The latter had a standing contract for Defense work through the Logistics Civilian Augmentation Program, known as LOGCAP, which managed many of the large Defense contracts overseas. Mobbs was concerned that Vice President Cheney's prior association as an executive with Halliburton might appear as a conflict of interest if KBR received the contract. Mobbs was told, however, to select the best company regardless of appearances, and so KBR was awarded the contract. The next task was to integrate Central Command's efforts to secure the oil fields with those of KBR to repair damage.[60]

In November 2002, Major Shelton and Cliff Flower, developing plans at Central Command for the Iraqi oil fields, went to the Pentagon to brief Mobbs and his team. At the Pentagon, Shelton and Flower learned about the LOGCAP contract and the role KBR would play. After they returned to Tampa, Shelton was instructed by his boss to fly to Houston to brief those at KBR who would work on the Iraqi oil fields. Shelton objected. Briefing a civilian organization on military plans for an upcoming operation made no sense to an intelligence officer naturally concerned with operational security. But Colonel Fitzgerald told him he had to go and bring KBR into CENT-COM planning. When Shelton went to Houston, he took his class B formal uniform and wore it to meet the KBR engineers. To his surprise, he found that the Houston KBR office had a secure area where the government had authorized them to conduct classified briefings with those KBR personnel with top secret security clearance, the same level at which Shelton had been working at Tampa. If that altered his disdain for bringing the dozen civilian engineers into classified military planning, Shelton was slow to show it.[61]

"Gentleman, this is serious business and we're in the planning process," Shelton began. But as the briefing continued the KBR personnel became excited and began articulating their need for various equipment—a valve here, a pump there. As the engineers defined more tasks than anticipated, Shelton stopped them for a moment and said, "Okay, how many 18-year-old lives is it worth for you to have this valve? That's what we're talking about, killing 18-year-old Iraqis and losing 18-year-old Americans to secure this infrastructure. You need to be very sober about this. If it's not critical, don't tell me it's critical because people may die to get it." The KBR people then became more restrained about what was critical.[62]

Some government component with engineering experience would have to manage the KBR project on the oil wells, and by late December Mobbs requested assistance from the Army Corps of Engineers. Brigadier General Robert Crear was appointed to form what became known as Task Force RIO (Restore Iraqi Oil). In 2002, Crear was in charge of the Corps of Engineer Southwest Division with headquarters in Dallas, one of seven such engineer divisions. The Southwest Division was aligned with Central Command and its region if the Corps' engineers were needed overseas. Crear had already made a trip to Kuwait in September on a related task. He formed TF RIO in January 2003 and deployed it to Kuwait the following month to assess the oil situation in Iraq.[63]

TWO MILITARY THINK TANKS

As military and interagency planning surged for an invasion of Iraq, several government studies were conducted to explore preparations necessary for regime replacement. Those studies were conference-based with participants (mainly Americans) of diverse backgrounds from academia, law, diplomacy, military service, international and humanitarian assistance organizations, and the private sector. They provided useful concerns and ideas. Many would go unheeded.

Joe Collins had an interest in potential operations in Iraq, which he had already attempted to explore with Warrick's Future of Iraq project. Collins was Deputy Assistant Secretary Defense for Peacekeeping and Humanitarian Operations within OSD-Policy and a retired Army colonel who had taught political science at West Point. He went to Dr. James Schear, Director of Research at the Institute of National Security Studies (INSS) at the National Defense University and Collins's predecessor at OSD. Collins asked him to organize a workshop to study the requirements of regime replacement in Iraq. Schear took on the task and assigned it to Colonel Paul Hughes.[64]

Hughes had served as an Army planner in Europe and later with the Third Army during Desert Storm in the 1990s. Like Collins and Schear, Hughes had served in the Office of Peacekeeping and Humanitarian Affairs. That was followed by an assignment on the Army Staff working on policy issues. Hughes moved to INSS during the summer of 2002 as the Army Senior Fellow. Schear directed him to pull together a conference with the title "Iraq After Saddam."

Hughes would face numerous challenges. The workshop group would be diverse, and few among them would have security clearances. As the project commenced, senior personnel in OSD began to have reservations about the conference. The Bush administration wanted to present the facade that there was no planning underway for an invasion of Iraq, a position openly questioned by the media and reinforced by Warrick's Future of Iraq project (also conducted in an unclassified setting). While Collins believed a conference could develop ideas and concepts to support military and interagency planning, others at the Pentagon did not want such ideas and concepts to appear part of a larger national security agenda. Not only did that constrain Hughes's ability to manage the conference, but it would hinder the dissemination of conference reports to those responsible for planning.

On 20 November 2002, the two-day conference opened with seventy-nine participants. Laith Kubba, an academic with the National Endowment for Democracy, was the only Iraqi-American; he had also participated on the Future of Iraq project. About half of those attending were academics from military and civilian think tanks, war colleges, and civilian universities. About twenty came from the Pentagon, including Joe Collins and Colonel Tom Baltazar. Nine came from the Department of State and USAID, including Mike Ayoub, but not Tom Warrick. Robin Cleveland came from OMB. Catherine Dale, the Political Advisor (POLAD) for the U.S. Army V Corps in Germany, flew in to attend.[65] There were a few participants from international organizations and NGOs. Their background experience included international relations, stabilization, oil, the Middle East, and, in a few cases, Iraq. Many would be in Iraq six months later. Only a few had participated on Warrick's Future of Iraq project—Laith Kubba, David Pearce, Mike Ayoub, and several Civil Affairs officers, but none of them brought any reports from FOI, nor was it discussed in any detail.[66]

The conference began with several guest speakers and panels, then it was divided into three working groups: Military and Security Stabilization; Political Stabilization; and Humanitarian, Infrastructure, and Economic Stabilization. Four assumptions about the situation the United States would be facing were established for each group:

- U.S. forces are in Iraq
- the Iraqi regime has been defeated and its military forces have surrendered
- Saddam Hussein is no longer in power
- Iraq has suffered light to medium collateral damage as a result of the military campaign[67]

Each working group had to propose policy and guidance for Iraq. The Military and Security Stabilization Group determined that the "primary post-intervention focus of US military operations must be on establishing and maintaining a secure environment [in Iraq]." It assumed the invading force would be an American-led coalition with possible military participation by Egypt and Jordan along with Western nations, ideally authorized by the United Nations, with a follow-on multinational force to legitimize and assume much of the security task. It also assumed the U.S. forces would have to remain for several years with substantial military police, engineer, medical, and transportation units.

Significant attention was given to defeated Iraqi military forces, with the assumption that the Iraqi army would be retained, vetted, reformed. The Iraqi internal security forces and the Republican Guards would have to be disbanded. Detailed planning for the Iraqi army should precede an invasion. Most of the domestic Iraqi police force would be put back to work, initially under U.S. Military Police supervision—an ambitious task imposed on MP formations. Overall the object was to reconstruct an Iraqi military establishment that "should be a smaller, higher quality, non-offensively oriented force led by a de-politicized officer corps capable of securing Iraqi territory [and] maintaining Iraq's territorial integrity and domestic security."[68]

The Political Stabilization Group proposed that the political goals include transformation with a new Iraqi government that had "sovereign legitimacy with its citizens, its neighbors, and the international community." It proposed that a senior American civilian be appointed as governor to administer Iraq and "report directly to the commander of U.S. forces until a stable security environment is established; at a later stage, a non-U.S. civilian (perhaps an Iraqi) should be appointed." Civil and military authorities would rely on "unity of effort over unity of command." An effective governor would have his office "resourced with appropriate quick-impact funds."[69]

No estimate was provided for such funds. The group stated that the "transformation process must provide for Iraqi participation," initially with advice, later with a constitutional council, followed by ministerial control. There should be "no hidden agendas" such as establishing a Kurdish state or taking control of Iraqi oil.

The report emphasized that "an integrated planning effort must start before the conflict begins, and Central Command's war planning must include the requisite civil-military planning." Remarkably, the group felt that the situation in Iraq would be so unique that lessons of postwar Germany and Japan, and more recently in Afghanistan, would not apply. It was clear that elections alone would not establish a democracy, and that "Iraq will require some interim governance structures" to determine its eventual political makeup. Outsiders, presumably Iraqi expatriates or other Arab states, should not be allowed to overly influence the natural evolution that would take place. Governmental reform must include judicial reform to eliminate corruption in the court system. There was little mention of the Ba'ath Party or how to deal with senior Ba'athists.[70]

The working group on Humanitarian, Infrastructure, and Economic Stabilization addressed humanitarian assistance and the institutional changes that should follow. Coordination with International Organizations and NGOs would be required. Humanitarian assistance would be coordinated with the military forces throughout Iraq to avoid damage to physical infrastructure. In the interim the UN Oil for Food program would continue to sustain the Iraqi people.[71]

On the economic front, protecting oil production received the most attention, including keeping key Iraqi personnel in charge. Iraqis in other sectors would be retained to help jump-start the economy; no mention was made of their political connections with the Ba'ath Party. Inflation would have to be controlled in a postwar environment and micro-credit systems would have to be established. Agriculture was addressed as a means to sustain employment, but there were no proposals to develop the agricultural sector of the Iraqi economy.[72]

Colonel Hughes had assembled a broad-based group interested in Iraq and produced a forty-one-page report by December. The report was a set of ideas, concerns, and proposals, not a plan with defined resources to support it. No end-state for Iraq was identified and no conditions were established for a handoff to the UN or to the Iraqis, although that was intended. Though unclassified, the report was not distributed widely beyond the Pentagon due to its sensitivity. Hughes made sure a copy went to Doug Feith and Joe Collins, but he was not invited to give a briefing of it and he was unsure of its impact.[73] Colonel Hughes had little experience with Iraq beyond his tour in Desert Storm, but the conference gave him the opportunity to discuss post-conflict issues with Middle East and Iraqi specialists, which would soon position him for a key role in Iraq.

In October 2002, Colonel Robert McClure, Chief of War Plans for the Department of the Army, contacted the Army War College to request a study for post-invasion planning for Iraq. This action came from discussions between Lieutenant General Richard Cody, the Department of Army G-3 for Operations, and Major General Robert Ivany, the Commandant of the Army War College on the topic of managing Iraq after an invasion. In making that call, McClure was representing the Army Staff, not those on the Joint Staff or from Secretary Rumsfeld's office. The study was assigned to Dr. Conrad Crane, an analyst with the Strategic Studies Institute (SSI) at the Army War

College. Crane was a retired Army officer and a military historian with a doctorate from Stanford. His resume included an extended teaching tour at West Point and a long list of publications. He had also conducted recent studies on peacekeeping and nation building at SSI and been a participant at Colonel Hughes's INSS Conference in November.[74]

Crane asked Andrew Terrill, a Middle East specialist with SSI, to join him. After an initial study, they held a conference in December with specialists on post-conflict issues and the Middle East. Among those attending were Colonel Hughes from INSS and Colonel Steve Kidder of the Army War College faculty and previously a planner at Central Command; Kidder sent drafts of the study as they were produced to those he knew at Central Command. In February 2003, Crane and Terrill published a seventy-eight-page monograph, *Reconstructing Iraq: Insights, Challenges, and Missions for Military Forces in a Post-Conflict Scenario.* The monograph included three sections: a historical overview of American occupations; challenges of an occupation of Iraq; and a list of 135 tasks for an occupation of Iraq with phases identified for transition.[75]

The historical section was a succinct fifteen pages covering the American experiences in the Philippines, Germany, Japan, Panama, Haiti, Bosnia, and Kosovo. Crane and Terrill dismissed contemporary rhetoric about liberation and assumed Iraq would have to be occupied to consummate regime change. They suggested "transitional operations" as an appropriate term rather than "post-conflict operations," with some violence probable after major combat operations. "Transitional" was consistent with the term used in Phase IV of the 2003 Army and Joint Staff doctrine, but Crane and Terrill proposed that such transitional operations be implemented incrementally as combat operations were executed rather than as a distinct follow-on phase.[76]

They cited the early example of the occupation of the Philippines (the first American experience with an Islamic subculture), arguing that a military commander is the best agent for local pacification, armed with clear directives and some autonomy for their implementation. Such a commander should be sensitive to cultural differences and "accept some decline in the combat efficiency of [his] units in order to keep them in lengthy occupation duties."[77]

To emphasize planning, the monograph noted, "By the time Germany surrendered in May 1945, detailed Allied planning for the occupation of that nation had been ongoing for 2 years." When Allied forces moved into Germany in 1944, small military government "detachments were sent out immediately to every town in the U.S. occupation zone" and imposed authority over the civilian leaders. After Germany's surrender, the main effort was to change Germany from the bottom up through local elections, followed by regional elections, then national elections, while "political life was strictly controlled to prevent any resurgence of radicalism." Opinion polls were used "to monitor what the German people thought about occupation policies."[78]

Addressing denazification, the monograph stated, "One of the most vexing problems for occupation authorities was how to dismantle the Nazi Party and its security apparatus while retaining the skills of some members who performed important functions." To identify the prior political activities and associations of important Germans, they were required to fill out the Fragebogen questionnaire to determine who should be allowed to participate in important roles in society and government and whose past activities should preclude them from such roles. The later stages of the Allied denazification program did not prevent former Nazis from rejoining productive society once the Germans took over the process, but it did ensure that they were isolated from the political process during the formative stages immediately after the war. It suggested that a similar questionnaire, polling data, and other policies used in Germany "might work to demobilize and reintegrate members of the Ba'ath Party and security forces in Iraq."[79]

The attempts to reform the German legal system in the American occupation zone were compared to those employed by the British and Soviets in their respective zones. The British tried to retain selected Nazi lawyers and judges, while the Americans tried to reform the entire system. But "the best solution was probably the one the Soviets applied, where they found educated and politically loyal people and gave them six weeks of legal training. Their system built around these 'lay judges' got criminal and civil court systems working very quickly."[80]

For Japan (a country smaller than Iraq in area), the study noted that initial occupation forces included twenty-three American divisions with over 500,000 soldiers. A purge list restricted certain people from political activity, basic services were soon restored, the police were reformed, the economy was restarted, and land reform was initiated as Japan adopted a democratic constitution. Crane and Terrill noted that in October 2002 the Bush administration reviewed the Japanese occupation as a potential model for democratization and demilitarization in Iraq, but by December it appeared that the Japanese model had been largely dismissed.[81]

Crane believed the White House had been influenced by Professor John Dower, a specialist on Japan at the Massachusetts Institute of Technology. In October 2002, Dower had written a *New York Times* op-ed piece that asked: "Does America's successful occupation of Japan after World War II provide a model for a constructive American role in a post–Saddam Hussein Iraq? The short answer is no." Dower stated that while the occupation of Japan was a success, the country was weary of war and had surrendered unconditionally. The occupation was legitimate in the eyes of the Japanese as well as the international community. Dower questioned if the Iraqi people or the international community would find such legitimacy in an American occupation of Iraq. Emperor Hirohito's compliance and support of the occupation could not be anticipated by Saddam Hussein or anyone comparable in Iraq. Nor would the United States have anyone comparable with MacArthur's stature and charisma "authorized to rule by fiat" in Iraq, with little outside interference.[82]

Dower noted that the lack of natural resources in Japan had been a positive factor that reduced outside interest in the occupation; it would be just the opposite for Iraq given its oil wealth, which might be improperly exploited or lead to the perception of exploitation. MacArthur had over 5,000 personnel working on civil affairs and military government, whereas Dower doubted that that many people could be mobilized for such tasks in Iraq (he would be proven correct). Furthermore, he stated that the "suicidal fanaticism that characterized Japanese behavior on the battlefield did not survive the war," whereas such suicidal fanaticism might remain prevalent in an occupied Iraq.[83] As such, in his quest to define the Japanese situation as significantly different from that of Iraq, he may have led policy makers to assume that the American experience there had no relevance for their own plans. Yet it should have been just the reverse—many of the criteria that made Japan a different model for occupation were exactly those that were necessary for a successful occupation leading to the establishment of a new regime. The Crane-Terrill monograph did not address other World War II occupation experiences at all—Italy, Austria, Okinawa, or Korea—which, like Iraq, were to be liberated, but had to be temporarily occupied first. Nor would others in the military or civilian government look at those experiences.

From World War II, the monograph jumped to a discussion of Operation Just Cause in Panama in December 1989 that removed General Manuel Noriega from power and installed a democratic regime. Military commanders conceded poor planning for what followed regime change there and noted that the army should "remedy that situation in the future."[84] Five years later, Operation Uphold Democracy was conducted in Haiti to replace the corrupt regime of General Raoul Cedras. The removal of Cedras was well executed, but there were problems similar to the experience in Panama despite efforts to avoid them in Haiti. Pre-invasion planning allowed USAID responsibility to reestablish public administration, conduct elections, restore information services, run airports, care for refugees, and assist the Department of Justice in setting up a reformed police force. Military leaders intended to avoid nation building, entrusting such tasks to USAID and other agencies. But security was inadequate with the limited troops deployed and USAID could not perform all the tasks assigned; many chores had to be undertaken by military engineers, military police, and military field hospitals. Those and other military units would remain in Haiti longer than planners had intended.[85]

There were serious problems with the planning and execution of American and Coalition operations in the Balkans in the 1990s, but results were generally successful by the end of the decade and the experience there would have application elsewhere. Again it was clear that civilian agencies require freedom of movement secured with adequate ground forces and domestic law enforcement. In addition, when security was inadequate military police, engineer, medical, and Civil Affairs units had to augment or temporarily replace civilian organizations. Even with a secure environment, the civilian organizations were often insufficiently robust to relieve military forces. In contrast to operations in Panama and Haiti, which were designed according to a specific timeframe for withdrawal without regard to whether the goals of occupation had been achieved, in the Balkans the criteria was the opposite. Coalition forces that included a substantial American component set their goals and then remained long enough to see them achieved.[86]

In the second section of the monograph, Crane and Terrill proposed that preparation for a postwar occupation in Iraq was as important as preparation for war—in order to avoid winning the war and losing the peace. The Iraqis would be grateful for the removal of Saddam Hussein and his regime, but such gratitude would be fleeting. With occupation of some sort inevitable, it would become more difficult the longer it lasted—particularly without a significant international component. An Iraqi culture unaccustomed to democracy would pose special challenges. An early shift from a single repressive party to pluralistic politics, while attractive, could lead to political parties forming along ethnic and religious lines and thus be potentially divisive. The resulting tensions that could accompany free elections would pose a challenge to a people conditioned to authoritarian leadership. Voting alone would not ensure democracy. The monograph also noted that the Iraqi army was one of the few unifying forces in the country and thus must be preserved and reformed.

All the historical studies showed that an occupying force could not abruptly hand off nation building to civilian agencies, which would have difficulty providing personnel in sufficient numbers to replace the military forces. The NGOs that often assist in such a role might be reluctant to participate in an Iraqi transition if the environment was dangerous and unstable, as had occurred in Afghanistan.[87]

In January 2003, Crane gave a draft copy of the monograph to Colonel McClure in the Pentagon, with the expectation that he would pass it along to

Lieutenant General McKiernan, who would command the ground force that would invade Iraq and whom Crane knew was in Washington at the time. It was published in March, and its succinct conclusions were remarkably prescient regarding the challenges that would soon be encountered in Iraq. Crane was told later that the creation of ORHA had killed army interest in his project because it appeared the army would not be in charge of the post-conflict phase in Baghdad. Crane had Steve Kidder continue to pass on the results of their study to his contacts at Central Command.[88] There is little evidence, however, that their monograph reached far beyond the Department of Army Staff, nor is it apparent that the monograph's insights made an impact on the preparation for operations in Iraq.

Of the three governmental conference studies conducted to address a replacement regime for Iraq—Warrick's Future of Iraq project at the Department of State; Hughes's INSS report at the National Defense University; and the Crane-Terrill monograph from the SSI[89]—the FOI project was the most extensive, with 200 participants, over a dozen working groups, and a final report topping 1,000 pages; it was also the most eclectic and controversial. Even in its final version, the report was disjointed and lacked a common format or useful summary. Warrick briefed Frank Miller's Executive Steering Group, but Miller was unimpressed with the work and did not monitor its progression. Ultimately, the Future of Iraq project had little impact within the NSC, the Department of Defense, or those who would go into Iraq.[90]

Without Warrick providing briefings, the FOI papers were difficult to digest; in contrast, the INSS report and the SSI monograph did not require explanations from Hughes or Crane. There was some linkage between these projects through a few common participants (Ayoub and Crane attended Hughes's INSS conference and Hughes participated in Crane's SSI study), but those projects did not include Warrick. And while the FOI project exploited Iraqi knowledge and experience, the other conferences did not. Finally, none of these efforts from Warrick, Hughes, Crane, and Terrill represented actual planning or detailed preparation for the tasks at hand in Iraq. The reports could have been useful for planners, but they were not widely distributed and rarely reached those that might have best used them.

The extensive interagency work on Iraq in 2002—planning by some and study by others—lacked integration and resources. Frank Miller and his Executive Steering Group might have brought such efforts together, but the ESG did not have control of all the working groups on Iraq, nor did it monitor them sufficiently. The most cohesive planning was conducted by working groups run by Robin Cleveland, Elliot Abrams, and USAID, which arranged for prepositioned food supplies for humanitarian assistance and made arrangements for some basic reconstruction, but much of their work would turn out to be inapplicable: there would be no humanitarian crisis in Iraq and reconstruction tasks would be several magnitudes greater than envisioned.

Even within the Pentagon there was a lack of cohesion. The effort by General Casey, Director of the Joint Staff, to set up a command element known as JTF-4 to help manage post-conflict operations under General Hawkins received little interest by those at the OSD-Policy. Perhaps the senior civilians in the Pentagon envisioned a requirement beyond what a purely military staff could manage. In December 2002, Feith had his office draft a proposal that Rumsfeld would take to the president to form an interagency group that would work under the control of the Department of Defense. Feith asked Steve Hadley to assist him with the draft, which then went to Frank Miller, who in turn staffed it among the other agencies.[91]

The draft indicated that the Department of State would set up an embassy in Iraq, initially subordinate to the Department of Defense, that would assist in establishing a new Iraqi regime. But State objected to having an embassy subordinate to Defense. In Miller's view, when the Pentagon refused to share control with State, Powell, Armitage, and Grossman essentially responded, "Okay. You guys want Iraq, over to you." The final paper was sent to the White House as NSPD-24. It was signed by President Bush on 20 January and provided the Pentagon the basis for standing up an interagency component with a broader focus on regime change than what General Casey had planned with JTF-4 (Feith did not consult or involve Casey in the new project). But Miller's work to ensure that it was properly staffed with the other agencies could not overcome the heavy-handed approach of Defense to control the effort. As a result, the enthusiasm of the other agencies to participate in the effort was greatly reduced, which the National Security Council could not overcome.[92]

3
IN THE PENTAGON

When Jay Garner accepted the task to form an organization to prepare for regime replacement in Iraq, he began with no staff, no workspace, no funding, no knowledge of what planning been done, and little insight of the situation in Iraq. His first undertaking in mid-January 2003 was to build a team that would represent half a dozen government agencies. Garner's base was and would continue to be the Department of Defense. He would soon find that those in the Pentagon were more anxious to provide guidance and restrictions than provide him assistance or resources. Those joining Garner were naturally loyal to their respective agencies. Garner would have to win them over to mold an inherently diverse group into something cohesive. Winning people over was one of Garner's long suits, but he had little time to find the right people. It was a daunting task—but Garner took it on with enthusiasm.

The scope of Garner's task was grand: to create and prepare an organization to manage the dimensions of a nation-state about to go through the chaos of invasion and regime removal; to put that state back into operation, in part as it had been, in part with new institutions, not yet clarified or agreed upon. The work would be done within the complexity of an international coalition, not fully formed, with contributions anticipated but not yet available. The object—to recruit personnel with broad capacity from a large and sophisticated government—would be poorly supported, despite presidential guidance.

Looking for a deputy to assist and complement him, Garner called Lieutenant General Ron Adams, recently retired from the Army. It was not a welcome call. Adams wanted a second career; he had just applied for a senior administrative position at a public university a few blocks from his house. He knew the position would be filled soon and that accepting a position with Garner for several months would take him out of the running.[1]

Garner had good reason to go to Adams, who had served in Operation Desert Storm with the 101st Air Assault Division in 1990–1991 and had seen much of Kuwait and the southern portion of Iraq. Garner was familiar with northern Iraq through his experience with Operation Provide Comfort, but nothing further south. Later in the 1990s, Adams served as the NATO Chief of Staff for Allied Forces Central Europe and oversaw the planning for the NATO force that would intervene in Kosovo, known as KFOR. Adams subsequently served a year as the commander of the Stabilization Force in Bosnia, known as SFOR, in 1999–2000. When he retired in 2002, Adams had experience with two complicated post-conflict operations.

That experience included an understanding of ethnic and religious divisions in the Balkans; disrupted civil infrastructure that had to be repaired; the challenges with establishing democratic government at local, regional, and national levels; and military forces providing essential security and some services. Adams had managed the difficult integration of military and civilian resources, the former complicated by a multi-national coalition, the latter by the diverse nature of United Nations and European civilian agencies, along with other international and nongovernmental organizations, known as IOs and NGOs. Successful experience at the executive level with such complex organizations made Adams an attractive, arguably essential, leader within Garner's emerging organization.[2]

Adams had worked for or with Garner twice in the 1990s on the Army Staff in the Pentagon. Their traits and styles were different yet complementary. Garner was gregarious, charismatic, intuitive, and highly energetic. Adams was serious by nature with a business-like demeanor and an attention to detail, a self-described "process guy." He was not a micro-manager, but he had the penetrating capacity to see through a complex situation to important aspects, particularly when at a formative stage.[3]

Garner sent Adams a line diagram that Abe Shulsky in the OSD Office of Special Plans had proposed as Garner's organization with three components: humanitarian assistance; reconstruction; and civil administration of Iraq. Garner had added an expeditionary staff to manage the overall effort. Adams made notes on the diagram about issues not clearly addressed (see Figure 2). The initial concept struck him as loosely thought out and in need of revision and greater detail. The lack of preparation and detail for a project of such immense importance alarmed and annoyed Adams, but that made his role all the more important. With reluctance, Adams agreed to join Garner.[4]

When Adams joined him in Crystal City, Garner said they had a few months to get ready and that once in Iraq their work would probably take two to three months. The next day they went to the Pentagon to see Secretary Rumsfeld, but the meeting was postponed and they went to see Undersecretary of Defense for Policy Doug Feith. Adams politely asked Feith to "clearly define their

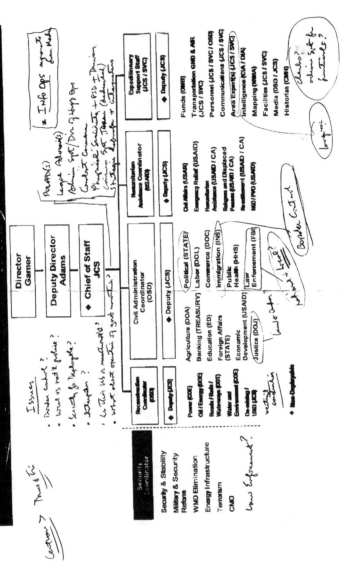

Figure 2. Proposed organization with Adams's notes.

mission." He told them their mission was to put together an interagency team and prepare it for deployment to the Middle East to "operationalize the planning that has been done." That suggested to Adams that substantial planning had been done, but Adams found Feith to be vague and unclear regarding who had conducted such planning. Feith said that Garner would eventually be replaced, either before the interagency team deployed or soon afterward in Iraq, but no timeline was established for deployment or a transition for Garner.[5]

Adams was a good listener and took notes in his meetings with Feith. He found Feith intelligent but erratic, shifting from one topic to another. It was clear to Adams that Feith had a critical role in the decisions on Iraq even if he lacked the appropriate rigor for sound planning. Adams tried to attend relevant meetings that Feith convened, which was possible in the beginning before his access was reduced for reasons that were not clear to him.[6] Garner and Adams understood Pentagon bureaucracy, yet they were apolitical by habit. They did not use the "neocon" term when referring to political appointees in the Pentagon or the Bush administration, a term frequently used to describe Feith and others with whom he identified.[7] Their world was executive leadership and management, not policy or ideology. In terms of getting things done, that was a plus; but in terms of anticipating policy development or changes, Garner and Adams may have been naive.

Larry Hanauer and Colonel Tom Baltazar were the first to join Garner and Adams from the OSD staff. Hanauer was a civilian administrator working for Feith and would assist Garner in the Pentagon, but he would not deploy with him. Baltazar would play a much larger role and joined Garner at the recommendation of Feith's Deputy Assistant Secretary for Stability Operations, Joe Collins. With a degree in civil engineering and early assignments as a military engineer, Baltazar in mid-career had shifted to Civil Affairs and commanded the 96th Civil Affairs Battalion, the only such active duty formation in the Army (there were twenty-three Civil Affairs battalions in the Army Reserves). Two months earlier Baltazar attended a conference at Fort McNair run by Colonel Paul Hughes on "Iraq: Looking Beyond Saddam's Rule." Baltazar held strong views and did not think highly of Feith or many of his civilian associates. Like Adams, Baltazar found Feith erratic with a poor understanding of the Pentagon and the military establishment.[8]

Colonel Paul Hughes soon joined Garner. With his background as a planner in Desert Storm, work on the Army and OSD staffs in the Pentagon, and more recent work on Iraq at the National Defense University (NDU), Hughes set up a Strategic Initiatives Group for Garner, soon known as the "Law Firm," to study Iraq. As Baltazar and Hanauer obtained furniture, phones, and computers, Garner and Adams worked from Feith's office. Hughes and others who joined them worked from their original offices until sufficient space opened up.[9]

On 20 January 2003, President Bush signed NSPD-24, which directed the Department of Defense to establish a Post-War Planning Office to begin preparation for the transition that would follow a potential invasion of Iraq. It was a classified document addressed to a dozen government agencies directing them to assist the Department of Defense, but without specific guidance. The directive was written as if originating from the White House, but it had been drafted by Feith and staffed with a few agencies by Frank Miller in December. Secretary Rumsfeld took it to the president to be signed, which caused some animosity with the other agencies that might have been involved in the drafting. Garner's group was originally designated the Postwar Planning Group (PPG). It was not a designation that many would use or recognize within the Pentagon. That was useful to keep the profile low; it would be replaced with another designation a few weeks later.[10]

The next day Garner and Adams went to Washington to meet Zalmay Khalilzad and Elliot Abrams, who were responsible for the Middle East on the NSC staff. Khalilzad told them that the NSC wanted to get the UK and Australia to provide Garner personnel. Some would work on civil administration in Iraq; others might assist in potential war crimes trials for Iraqis. Abrams talked about the UN Oil for Food program that might be extended under the UN or taken over by the Coalition.[11]

On 24 January, Adams and Garner went to see Frank Miller and two key members of his Executive Steering Group: Elliot Abrams, whom they had met three days earlier, and Robin Cleveland, who managed national security funding for OMB. They had been working on humanitarian assistance requirements that would come with an invasion. Adams attended the ESG meetings until they were discontinued. The chemistry between Garner and Miller, however, was not positive. NSPD-24 essentially degraded Miller's role on Iraq. He said Garner had an impossible task but offered little help. When Garner expressed concern about Miller's attitude to National Security Advisor Condoleeza Rice, she told him to work directly with her and her deputy, Stephen Hadley. Miller then stopped the ESG meetings. Cleveland and Abrams continued to meet over the next few months with Adams and others on Garner's team to discuss humanitarian assistance, but the linkage between the ESG and ORHA was weak and the good will limited.[12]

On 26 January Hadley set up a Deputies Committee meeting for Garner involving senior representatives from the departments and agencies of the government that would support ORHA. In addition to Rice and Hadley, those present included Wolfowitz from Defense and Armitage from State, Wendy Chamberlin from USAID, and their counterparts from Treasury, Justice, Energy, Agriculture, Commerce, Education, CIA, and OMB.

Garner handed out paper slides with the tasks assigned to him in NSPD-24, involving reforms of the political, economic, and security components of Iraq.[13] Political liberation would be conducted in five phases: proclamations to establish Coalition intentions and the Iraqi role within it; the establishment of Iraqi consultative and judicial councils to begin the government transition; bureaucracy reform; municipal elections and a constitutional convention with several hundred Iraqi delegates; and national elections. Local elections would precede national elections to provide a delegate base for a constitutional convention. A constitution would in turn provide the form of a new government and for national elections.[14]

On economic reconstruction, the Iraqi banking system would be reformed with the currency standardized to allow financial progression to a free-market system from a centralized economy. Iraq had significant international debt which the Coalition sought to have forgiven so as to shift resources to internal development and to stimulate the private sector. Construction projects would improve the infrastructure, notably electricity and water systems, and would also provide employment.[15]

Much of the presentation addressed security and how the Iraqis would participate. Security agencies that had suppressed the Iraqi people would be disbanded: the secret police, the special and intelligence court systems, and the Republican Guard formations. The civil police and much of the regular army would be put back to work. To reduce the size of the army, activated reserve formations would be demobilized and many conscripts would simply be sent home; some desertions were anticipated. Most of the regular soldiers, NCOs, and officers would be retrained. Many formations would work on infrastructure reconstruction. It was not clear how large a reformed army should be, however. Should it be adequate only for the defense of Iraq or should it be larger to participate in regional security? The intention was not to use it for internal security; presumably the police would handle that.[16]

As Garner took questions, the overall response was positive and those present indicated they would provide personnel and resources. The greatest numbers would come from State and USAID, with the other agencies represented at the meeting contributing only a few personnel.[17] Wendy Chamberlin told Garner she had a team at USAID working on reconstruction for Iraq and that she would give the team to him. Garner was grateful and impressed with her direct, no-nonsense style. After the meeting Garner asked her to lunch and she invited him to visit USAID to learn more about its work for Iraq.[18]

Chamberlin had been surprised with NSPD-24 and the plan to put Garner in charge of reconstruction and humanitarian assistance for Iraq. She had assumed the job might go to a general officer with the Department of Defense in the lead, not a retired general, nor did she anticipate that he would subsequently be so poorly supported by the military establishment. She was not the only one at the meeting surprised by Garner's appointment. Robin Cleveland was visibly annoyed that much of the responsibility of her ESG working group was suddenly being shifted to a new organization in the Pentagon. At a subsequent meeting of that working group with Garner in attendance, Chamberlin noted that Cleveland went out of her way to be rude to Garner. She went to see Cleveland after the meeting and told her that while they might not like the shift to Garner, they had to support him. But she found Cleveland reluctant to change. It was not a good sign for the future relationship between Cleveland and Garner.[19]

On 29 January, Garner and Adams went to see Andrew Natsios, the head of USAID, and then had a longer meeting with Chamberlin. With her were Bernd "Bear" McConnell and Chris Milligan. McConnell was in charge of USAID's Office of Foreign Disaster Assistance, concerned with humanitarian assistance in Iraq. Milligan had joined Chamberlin's team in November and was working with her on reconstruction tasks for Iraq. In Garner's view, McConnell tended to dominate Chamberlin in the discussion but otherwise remained aloof. Garner and Adams, however, were impressed with Milligan, who had significant experience in local development, and when Chamberlin suggested he join their team, he was immediately accepted.[20] One of the youngest on Garner's team, Milligan became the first person to join from a non-Defense agency.

Garner accepted the three-pillar organizational structure that OSD had proposed: Humanitarian Assistance, for anticipated challenge with Iraqi refugees; Reconstruction, to rebuild any infrastructure damaged during the war or otherwise necessary to enable Iraq to get back on its feet; and Civil Administration, to assist with the management of the governmental infrastructure of Iraq. Garner assigned Milligan the job of deputy for the Reconstruction pillar. The lead for the group would be Lew Lucke, who had been recalled by USAID from retirement in November. Lucke had already gone to Kuwait to determine what the military forces were planning; he would not meet Garner for another month. Milligan would serve in his stead in the Pentagon. With his passion for work and overseas development, Milligan was soon a favorite with Garner.[21]

Garner and Adams had added the Expeditionary Support Staff for management of the pillars and the regional components that would extend from them. Assuming he would lead a multinational effort comparable to what he had known during Operation Provide Comfort in 1991, Garner wanted a coalition team and so designated a C-staff as the core of his Support Staff, structured along military lines for a coalition: a C-1 staff section for personnel, a C-2 for intelligence, a C-3 for operations, a C-4 for logistics and transportation, a C-5 for plans, a C-6 for communications, a C-7 for engineer, and a C-8 for comptroller, plus public affairs, foreign area specialists, even a historian.

By the end of January, Garner and Adams proposed a Joint Manning Document (JMD) for a C-staff with about 100 military officers and NCOs. They submitted it to Lieutenant General George Casey, Director of the Joint Staff. Casey had already set in motion a military headquarters, JTF-4, for post-conflict operations in Iraq, under Brigadier General Steve Hawkins. Garner's group had been packaged by OSD, however, and Casey had not been consulted about it. To Garner's surprise, Casey had no enthusiasm for Garner's task and was initially unsupportive.[22]

Garner asked Lieutenant General Jared "Jerry" Bates, another retired officer, to join him to run the C-staff. Bates was the financial operations officer for MPRI, a defense contractor. He was not looking for a job or thinking about going to Iraq. Bates had served as the Army Inspector General before his retirement; Garner and Adams had worked with him on the Army Staff. Garner's call caught Bates in the parking lot of a Target department store. When Bates hesitated to join him, Garner said, "Jerry, I am offering you a chance to go soldiering again." It was the right line for Bates.[23]

Garner told Bates he needed two more senior leaders; Bates recommended Brigadier General Buck Walters and Major General Bruce Moore, also retired Army officers. When they both agreed to join, Walters was designated to manage the southern region in Iraq and Moore the northern region. Adams had no involvement in their selection, but he had known Moore in the Army and the military bond was useful. Later the media would dub the retired generals the "Space Cowboys," a reference to a recent movie about retired astronauts returning to space. That designation amused them but seemed to fit Bates, Walters, and Moore more than Adams.[24]

Garner took Bates with him to see General Casey one morning to discuss communications support and military personnel they needed. Casey had reviewed their proposal for personnel and asked them if they really needed so many military personnel: would they be running a 24/7 operation? Garner and Bates were incredulous; Casey was concerned that so many ad hoc staffs were taking military officers from other positions. To Garner and Bates, Casey was reluctant to help them when Defense had the lead for their project. When they asked for a military signal unit, Casey denied the request and suggested they get a contractor for communications. The meeting was not a success.[25]

Later that day, Garner called Casey and said he would see Rumsfeld that evening. "It's hardball time," Garner said. If Casey would not support the JMD, he would take it up with the Secretary of Defense. Within an hour a major general from the Joint Staff J-1 Personnel staff called Garner: "I understand you need some people?" Casey had caved, and Garner would get the military personnel he wanted, divided among the four services. The colonels for intermediate leadership came from within the Pentagon. Those more junior came from nearby military bases. They would be new to each other.[26]

From the Air Force Staff came Lieutenant Colonel Dennis DeGraff as the C-1 Personnel officer. The Army Staff provided Colonel Deborah Taylor, an intelligence officer, as C-2. From the Joint Staff came Colonel Robert Costello, a logistics officer, as the C-4. OSD provided Colonel Randy Conway, a signal officer, as the C-6, and Colonel Craig McLane, who would serve as Bates's deputy to manage the staff. DeGraff and McLane were Air Force officers and the rest were from the Army; none had ever met before.

Taylor and McLane would be replaced, causing some turmoil later. Costello and Conway were the dominant personalities. A large man with an imposing manner, Costello could be loud, demanding, and stubborn. He was also gregarious with a good sense of humor. He was tough on his subordinates but they loved him. Costello wanted an assignment that would let him work what he called operational logistics in Iraq, but he would be disappointed. The nature of what Garner needed was support for his emerging team and Costello would have his hands full with that.

As a signal officer, Conway had a background in special operations that shaped his views on communications support, views that would have a critical impact over the next few months. During Conway's formative years in Special Forces, it was assumed that communications would often be inadequate and units would have to learn to get by without consistent linkage to higher units. Even as communications technology for Special Forces improved, some officers with Conway's background continued to believe that linkage between units would often be inadequate and that they would have to adapt accordingly. Like Costello, Conway was tough on his subordinates; unlike Costello, Conway's subordinates did not learn to love him. Another trait that later became evident was Conway's dislike for civilians, the very people he was to support in Kuwait and Iraq.

Lieutenant Colonel Bob Polk arrived with a background as an Army planner with a year in Bosnia under his belt. He had graduated from the Leavenworth School of Advanced Military Studies (SAMS), and had a tour as a planner at Fort Lewis. Afterward he was selected for a fellowship with the Department of State Foreign Service Institute outside Washington, where he participated in long-range policy and interagency issues. Headed for the Army Staff, he was redirected to join Garner as his C-5 planner.[27]

Lieutenant Colonel Jim Torgler, a reservist who had recently been activated for duty on the Army Staff, was assigned as Garner's initial C-3 Operations officer. His manner and style were low key and his reserve status and rank put him at a disadvantage with strong-willed personalities on the C-staff such as Costello and Conway.

The rest of the JMD positions were spread among the four services. Those that joined ORHA did not know each other nor Bates who would manage them. It would take time to develop staff cohesion among so many personnel not previously known to each other. In the meantime, despite the 'C' in C-staff indicating a Coalition or multi-national staff, it would be several weeks before many non-Americans joined.

As Garner added more military personnel through the JMD, civilians slowly joined from other government agencies. Some were recalled from retirement and others joined on individual contracts. Obtaining qualified civilians would be challenging and lead to friction, which Garner and Adams did not anticipate. The cause was subtle. Many of those affected by NSPD-24, particularly at State and USAID, were annoyed that such an important document would be drafted by OSD and signed by the president without their input. Garner had assumed the president's signature would ensure cooperation rather than the resistance he encountered.

Garner and Bates went to see Secretary of State Colin Powell and his deputy, Richard Armitage. They all knew each other. Powell and Armitage told Garner they would do their best to support him and understood that Defense had the lead on postwar Iraq. While Powell and Armitage accepted that view, that was not the case throughout their department. Unlike Defense, it was not common for State to order its personnel to deploy to a particular country, much less to a war zone. As in other civilian agencies, State asked for volunteers, but only a few came forward. Middle East specialists in the department who spoke Arabic were already in short supply. While State wanted to fill Garner's senior positions, it would not provide many of the middle-level personnel required. Part of the reason was there were fewer than 10,000 Foreign Service Officers (FSOs) at State and only 1,000 in USAID. Most of the FSOs were already serving overseas. A surge of FSOs for Iraq would require assistance from retirees and contractors.

Given the personnel challenges, Powell had Undersecretary of State for Political Affairs Marc Grossman manage the effort to assist Garner. Grossman had met Garner in Turkey in 1991, where he had served as the embassy's deputy chief of mission while Garner led the intervention force for Provide Comfort in northern Iraq. Grossman attempted to define and fill the positions that seemed appropriate for State and to monitor the positions that USAID filled. With Lew Lucke recalled from retirement for Garner's Reconstruction pillar, Grossman wanted to fill the other two positions at the top of Humanitarian Assistance and Civil Administration.

For the former, Grossman contacted George Ward, a retired ambassador working for the United States Institute for Peace. Ward was not a Middle East or Iraqi specialist; his only tour as an ambassador was to Namibia in southern Africa. But Ward had served as a Marine in Vietnam, and at State he had experience in peacekeeping and governance. Ward agreed to go to the Pentagon for an interview on 29 January. Garner liked Ward and appointed him to run the Humanitarian Assistance position. Ward, however, felt his background was better suited for Civil Administration and asked for that position instead. Reluctantly, Garner told him that OSD wanted to fill it. A week later Ward went to see Grossman to say he would take the position offered.[28] The position Grossman wanted most for State was Civil Administration, but Doug Feith did not want someone from State in that post. Over several weeks, OSD hedged on the position, eventually offering it to David Kay, who had participated in arms inspections in Iraq. Kay agreed to serve, but he would not last long enough to deploy to Iraq.

By early February, Garner, Adams, and Bates were starting each day with a round of meetings. After an early breakfast meeting with a select few at a nearby hotel, Garner would arrive at the Pentagon for a meeting with key personnel, a group that soon grew to over twenty people. Bates would meet afterward with the C-staff. Those in the Humanitarian Assistance, Reconstruction, and Civil Administration pillars soon were having their own meetings during the day. There were meetings for functional tasks, such as funding, engineering, and NGOs, that drew participants from each subgroup.

Throughout each day Garner received individuals and small groups, either those already working for him, those interviewing to join him, or those in the Pentagon and Washington with an interest in his project. In late January Garner began a series of meetings in the White House with Condoleezza Rice to define his challenges to her and to seek assistance. Garner put together a "big five" list of his most important requirements each week. Each requirement was to come off the list as it was resolved. If it was not resolved, it would stay on the list for the next meeting along with five more challenges. Baltazar soon noted the list grew longer and longer each week.[29]

Later Garner added a daily director's meeting at 5:00 P.M. to update his main subordinates on his activities of the day and to get feedback on theirs. The meetings were unrestricted and lasted about an hour, often leading to off-line discussions. As a result, the days grew longer. Garner and others were arriving by 6:30 A.M. and rarely left before 7:00 P.M.; many worked further into the night on the phone and reading papers. In Crystal City Garner met others in the evenings. During the day Garner left the Pentagon to attend meetings in Washington or Crystal City. By February, Frank Miller had terminated the ESG meetings, but Cleveland and Abrams continued with working groups into February with several from Garner's team attending in the Old Executive Office Building next to the White House.

With an invasion of Iraq more imminent and the knowledge that preparations for regime replacement were behind schedule, activity began to surge and soon the workweek for Garner and his team included Saturdays and Sundays. But the excessive meetings kept many participants in a passive listening role during much of the day. Often the meetings tended to recirculate the same issues and precluded reading and research that might have been conducted instead.

On the last day of January, Garner and Adams had a list of twenty-six tasks to be undertaken in Iraq. Half were on transitional security: constabulary forces as the Iraqi police were vetted and retrained, and security for oil fields, government buildings, and warehoused supplies. Looting and revenge killing were projected problems. Weapons of mass destruction (WMD) had to be located and secured. Most of the other tasks were for civil administration in Iraq: reforming and developing local and provincial government as an interim national government laid out transitional laws and policies. Ba'ath Party members had to be vetted and many retained in order to keep the ministries functioning. Governance required legitimacy with the Iraqi people and international conventions. The remainder of the tasks related to reconstruction: quick-start projects for essential services and keeping the ports, airfields, and road systems functional. Food and fuel distribution systems had to be sustained as well.[30]

None of the tasks on the list included humanitarian assistance, surprising given that Garner would later be accused of an early preoccupation with humanitarian tasks commensurate with those he took on during Provide Comfort in 1991. But Garner and Adams from the beginning focused on regime replacement as their fundamental assignment. The tasks on their list clearly defined that as security, governance, basic services, and legitimacy. At a meeting with Secretary Rumsfeld, Garner told him he would not have the resources to handle the WMD tasks or to protect and restart the Iraqi oil industry. Rumsfeld agreed and designated others for those responsibilities.

On Saturday, 1 February, those that had joined Garner attended a classified briefing on the current military situation in Iraq, followed by an unclassified political background presentation. By that time Garner had just over twenty-five members on his team, most of whom were in attendance that Saturday. They represented half a dozen American agencies and were just getting to know each other. There were no Iraqis or other Coalition members present. Garner tried to keep the tone friendly and told everyone to call him Jay. Bates did, but Adams pointedly referred to Garner as "the Boss," perhaps to sustain a more serious setting. To some present at the time (and later), there appeared to be some tension between Bates and Adams. Their styles differed: one smooth and casual, the other direct and formal.[31]

The classified briefing was not impressive, with the intelligence team only regurgitating information from other sources and displaying no first-hand knowledge of Iraq. More interesting was the presentation that followed by Judith Yaphe, a senior fellow at INSS. She was a specialist on Iraq who had previously been a CIA analyst; she had also participated in the workshop on Iraq at NDU run by Colonel Paul Hughes. In her presentation she played to her strengths as an academic, essentially providing an Iraq 101 lecture to a group with broad experience but little knowledge of Iraq. She went over the geography of the country, its population, religion, and culture with the obligatory emphasis on the ethnic breakdown of Kurds, Shiites, and Sunnis. Yaphe did not recommend any books on Iraq, nor did anyone ask for one. Everyone seemed conditioned to learn through briefings and meetings rather than individual study. While some appreciated Yaphe's general overview, others were less patient and wanted specific information with currency.

Dick Mayer, representing the Department of Justice, asked about the police system in Iraq, how big it was, how centralized, the nature of its components, and the depth of police training and education. Yaphe could not provide answers, which did not embarrass her. She had little to offer on Iraqi infrastructure, the information most needed by the group. And when General Adams asked what lessons from the Balkans would be useful for Iraq, she did not seem to anticipate the international infrastructure that might follow a Coalition invasion of Iraq.

Like the others in the room, Adams was in civilian clothes and only a few people knew of his extensive background in the Balkans. Yaphe was not one of them. She said that the Balkans were "absolutely different" and had nothing to offer a study of Iraq. As she turned to look for another question, it was clear her response had left Adams stunned and embarrassed. Some present wondered if Yaphe knew enough about the Balkans to dismiss its history of ethnic tensions, the Islamic component, UN peacekeeping efforts, NATO intervention, or the civilian relief agencies that had tried to relieve the suffering there.

There was indeed much the Balkans could have offered a group that would have to pick through the debris of regime change in Iraq. It was partly his Balkans experience that led to Tom Warrick's selection to manage the Future of Iraq Project; it was a similar experience there that led to Major Tom Fisher's selection as the Phase IV planner at Central Command. As an academic specialist, Yaphe demonstrated little understanding of Iraq's infrastructure, and it was clear she knew less about the Balkans. Adams may have been put off by Yaphe's dismissal, but that did not deter his efforts to learn.

Earlier on 28 January, Adams had gone to the Army War College to met Con Crane and Andy Terrill, whose study of post-conflict for Iraq was not yet published. The briefing, based on twelve slides, began with historical post-conflict experiences. Crane noted that Adams seemed troubled by the costs of the Marshall Plan to rebuild Europe, because comparable funds would not likely be available to ORHA for Iraq. Another slide had a long list of post-conflict tasks for Iraq they had adapted from a previous study of such tasks for Haiti. The briefing was useful, but Crane and Terrill were not asked to provide it to others in ORHA. Later in February, Crane participated in a conference on Iraq at the Wilson Center in Washington with George Ward present. But when Crane presented the results of his study, Ward "downplayed our work, and emphasized very strongly that our study 'was not the plan' that would be used to reconstruct Iraq." Crane later regretted he had not pushed "to find out exactly what the plan was going to be."[32]

David Kay joined Garner the first week in February to lead the Civil Administration pillar, with Marc Powe arriving the next week as his deputy. A retired Army colonel with an intelligence background, Powe had served as a provincial advisor in Vietnam, then in attaché positions in Baghdad (1985–1987) and Tunisia (1988–1991) with exposure to Arab culture. After leaving the Army, Powe spent eight years with the United Nations working on Africa before joining OSD-Policy just in time "to watch the lights going out for the Clinton team, and to watch with little enthusiasm as Rumsfeld came on board." Pleasant, unassuming, low-key, yet outspoken, Powe was unimpressed with the civilian leadership in the Pentagon. "As the acting Deputy Assistant Secretary of Defense for Africa (DASD), I had enough contact with Feith to know that he was an ass."[33]

Powe also had contact with Rumsfeld and Wolfowitz. He felt both were smart, but "demonstrated repeatedly that they wanted information/advice that fit with their pre-conceived ideas." Powe liked Garner and quickly became a positive member of the team. Adams took Powe with him to meetings in Washington. Powe was impressed with Kay and disappointed to see him leave within the week. "Unfortunately, he was so turned off by Feith that he told me he just wasn't willing to work with or for a person of such little intelligence." Powe briefly took over Civil Administration until Feith found a replacement for Kay. When Kay quit, Feith replaced him with Michael Mobbs, and Marc Powe became his deputy. Garner had met Mobbs earlier in January when he and Adams received a briefing from his Energy Infrastructure Planning Group (EIPG), studying the oil infrastructure in Iraq.[34]

After he heard the briefing, Garner asked, "Okay, who's going to Iraq with me?"

At first no one responded. Then Gary Vogler, a retired oil executive said, "Sir, I'm here for some adventure. If we're going to have some adventure over there, I'll go."[35]

Vogler had served eight years in the Army during the 1970s, then was hit with cancer before eventually beating it. That experience was life-changing for him, and he saw Garner's offer as a means to again provide service for his country. He reflected that after twenty years in the private sector, he had not had a real adrenaline rush since 1975, when his main parachute failed to open over Fort Bragg and he had to pull his reserve ripcord. Going to Iraq with Garner was something he suddenly wanted to do. Garner told him there would be adventure.

Clarke Turner was more cautious. Aware that Turner had also served in the army, Garner asked him directly, "You're going with us, aren't you, Clarke?"

"Well, I need to check with two people, my two bosses," he paused, "my wife and my boss in Department of Energy." Turner had been sent to Washington to help with planning, not to go to Iraq.

Turner recalled later that he "was trying to size up Garner and his crew to . . . see how he operated and after watching him for about a week, I decided that, yeah, it was probably a pretty good thing to do. He seemed like . . . the right personality for something like this. So, I told Mike Mobbs after about a week I would join."[36]

Later, Richard Frost, the oil specialist from the CIA, joined ORHA and Garner had a team to work on oil in Iraq. Everyone at the meeting that day with Garner eventually went to Iraq except for Mike Makovsky and Seneca Johnson. Johnson was pregnant. Makovsky did not offer a reason for not going. When Mike Mobbs took the senior role for the Civil Administration pillar, he requested that responsibility for oil be moved to his pillar from Reconstruction. It seemed to make sense and no one objected.[37]

There were objections, however, from Grossman and others at State who wanted the Civil Administration pillar to be headed by one of their own. But Feith and civilian leaders in the Pentagon did not want that position filled by State. Mobbs had been a law partner with Feith in civilian practice and at Feith's request had followed him to the Pentagon at the beginning of the Bush administration. Mobbs was self-effacing, quiet, and unflappable, useful traits, perhaps, in legal negotiations, but his style would not track well with the aggressive, high-energy group Garner was forming.[38]

If Mobbs had remained as the leader of the working group on oil, his contribution might have been less problematic. Feith took Mobbs off oil and put him in charge of Civil Administration when Kay quit; he wanted someone in the position he could trust. Garner did not anticipate the animosity between State and Defense that developed over the position; as far as he was concerned, if the Pentagon leadership thought Mobbs was the right man for the job he was grateful to have him—in the beginning. Soon the Mobbs-Garner relationship would begin to suffer and create a serious void.[39]

As Mobbs and Powe tried to get a handle on Civil Administration, Dayton Maxwell joined George Ward as the deputy for Humanitarian Assistance. Maxwell was a long-serving FSO for USAID with experience going back to Vietnam. In 1991, he joined Garner for Operation Provide Comfort in northern Iraq representing USAID. Garner had a high opinion of Maxwell then and felt lucky to have him a second time. Maxwell had retired from USAID, then volunteered to come back to work for JTF-4 under General Hawkins, but JTF-4 deployed to Kuwait before he could get to Tampa. When USAID shifted assistance to Garner, Maxwell was redirected to the Pentagon. By the beginning of February, Garner had a small skeleton team. With the JMD, approved military personnel were arriving and civilians volunteering from the other agencies continued to join up.[40]

Garner had begun a dialogue with General Franks at Central Command. They had served together in the 1980s in the same division, although their prior association was limited. In the early fall of 2002 Franks had asked Garner to give a brief at Tampa on Provide Comfort; Garner had given a similar briefing to Wolfowitz in 2002. When Rumsfeld consulted Franks on the selection of Garner, Franks was positive and told Rumsfeld a story about Garner. "When [Garner] retired, a reporter asked him whether he would change anything about his life if he had it to live over again. 'Sure, I would change a lot of things,' Jay answered. 'But I'd marry the same woman and I'd join the United States Army.'" Rumsfeld told Franks that Garner "will be your subordinate, but he'll be my man in Iraq."[41]

In January, when Franks met Garner in the Pentagon, he told him, "We both work for the same guy," meaning Rumsfeld. With the assumption that combat operations would be over quickly, Franks was more interested in a handoff of Iraq to Garner than having Garner as his subordinate. He said he "wanted the interagency off his ass" and needed Garner to handle them until the dust settled in Iraq. When Garner asked him about Hawkins and JTF-4, which was forming at Tampa, Franks said he "didn't like JTF-4. . . . It was shoved up his ass by the JCS," specifically by General Casey. Franks told Garner, "I don't have any use for George Casey. . . . This is his goddamned idea . . . from Bosnia, and this ain't Bosnia."[42]

On 26 January Garner went to Tampa to meet Hawkins and his JTF-4 staff. Garner suggested that JTF-4 should be rolled in with the group he was organizing. Hawkins and his staff were torn between working with Garner and keeping their distance, an awkward relationship that would continue into April.[43] Garner was concerned that Franks and Central Command considered the transition as sequential with military forces redeploying as the fighting terminated. Garner felt the roles should overlap and substantial military forces should remain to assist him. He went to Rumsfeld to discuss General Abizaid's role. Abizaid had recently been designated as a second deputy commander for Central Command. Garner and others assumed Abizaid was positioned to become the Coalition military commander in Iraq. He felt that Franks should keep military forces in Iraq for six months into the Phase IV period under Abizaid, as the sub-Unified Commander for Iraq responsible for stability operations.[44]

Throughout January and February, Garner repeatedly discussed that with Rumsfeld, Wolfowitz, and Feith, as well as with Generals Myers, Franks, Pace, and Abizaid. It was clear to Garner that Franks and the Central Command were not focused on Phase IV, nor interested in assisting the interagency effort. He assumed that when Abizaid was sent to Central Command's forward headquarters in Qatar, it was to prepare him to manage Phase IV. In Garner's view of post-conflict operations, "You've got to have a military guy in charge. I couldn't do that. I didn't own any helicopters, and I didn't have any fuel, and I didn't own any trucks, or any of that kind of stuff." He knew and trusted Abizaid with his experience in the Middle East.[45]

Garner had other concerns in early February, closer to the immediate tasks. With his skeleton staff still building, he needed to prepare for deployment to the Gulf, to Qatar or Kuwait, where his organization would stage in-theater.

He also had to determine when and how he would move into Iraq following an invasion. Garner wanted to get into Iraq early, before conventional operations terminated to assess the situation on the ground and to get established. He preferred to deploy to Qatar, where Central Command had established a headquarters, but Franks told him Kuwait, where the ground forces were staging for Iraq, was more appropriate. Garner later conceded that Franks was correct, but he wanted to see for himself. On 5 February Garner and Bates flew to Qatar.[46]

They knew that Abizaid would be there and wanted to discuss their plans with him. The evening they arrived they met Lew Lucke for the first time. When Lucke was recalled from retirement by USAID, he had gone to the Gulf to survey the situation. By the time he met Garner, he knew he was to take over the Reconstruction pillar. He also knew that all post-conflict operations would be dependent on military support. The next day Garner and Bates sat through a series of briefings and talked to Abizaid. Both knew Abizaid from prior assignments; Garner had Abizaid under his command on Provide Comfort in 1991. Abizaid stated that as soon as the invasion was over they would need to "put an Iraqi face on it." They should provide an Iraqi political entity to ensure the population acknowledged that Iraq had been liberated, rather than defeated and occupied. It would also ensure that other Middle Eastern countries would acknowledge the liberation.

Abizaid was concerned about the Iraqi army. After the invasion he wanted it used as part of a liberated Iraq as soon as possible, a view shared by the think tanks and working groups in Washington, including Warrick's Future of Iraq project. Garner fully agreed. Garner and Bates suggested Abizaid should have some role as the senior military officer in Iraq when the invasion was over. Abizaid would not confirm such a role for himself. Abizaid gave Garner and Bates a tour of the headquarters and showed them a communications package that Raytheon had put together for Central Command the previous year. All the bugs had been worked out and it was working fine. Garner and Bates flew back the next day. They did not go to Kuwait or meet General McKiernan or General Hawkins.[47]

Upon Garner's return to Washington, he was informed the Pentagon had once again renamed his organization, this time as the Office of Reconstruction and Humanitarian Assistance (ORHA). By 13 February Baltazar and Hanauer produced the first ORHA personnel roster as an expanded JMD with 37 people on hand, 22 more identified by name, and vacancies for 85. Of the 144 positions on the roster, 80 were military. About 20 of the civilians were from the Department of Defense or were retired military officers.

Some of those beyond the Department of Defense that joined Garner in early February came from the Department of State, mainly from functional bureaus rather than from the Near East Bureau. From State's Bureau of Population, Refugees, and Migration (PRM) came Jan Beltz and Ananta Hans, both middle-rank civil servants. Their background led to assignment to the Humanitarian Assistance pillar under George Ward.

Drew Erdmann and Meghan O'Sullivan had been with State only a few years when they volunteered to join ORHA. Both had Ph.D.s and worked for Richard Haass, an academic who had a senior policy position at State. Both had interests in terrorism, WMD, and strategy. Erdmann had worked briefly on a study related to Iraq, but that was enough to get him into ORHA, where he was assigned to the Civil Administration pillar. O'Sullivan had written a book on sanctions and was assigned initially to the Humanitarian Assistance pillar; she would gradually move on to other positions. Both Erdmann and O'Sullivan told Haass that the endeavor in Iraq "was likely to be the defining experience for their generation and they wanted to be part of it."[48]

Mike Gfoeller came from State's Political Military Bureau, where he had an office near Mike Ayoub. Gfoeller was one of the few Arabists to join ORHA, with a degree in Arabic Literature and another in Middle Eastern Studies from Georgetown's School of Foreign Service. He had the highest Arabic score in the State Department, had served in Saudi Arabia and Bahrain, and had studied in Egypt and in Yemen. He had also served in Eastern Europe and dealt with transitional issues, with some generic relevance to Iraq: the collapse of the dictatorial government, emergence of the democratic government, and economic transition from centrally planned to capitalist economies. Heavy-set with a monotone voice, Gfoeller was initially unimpressive to military officers who tended to judge people by their bearing. He was assigned to the Civil Administration pillar. His star would soon rise in ORHA and later with the Coalition Provisional Authority (CPA), but few in the Pentagon would have anticipated that.[49]

One of the junior members from State and the youngest to join was twenty-nine-year-old Sherri Kraham. A GS-13 civil servant, Kraham would play a key role in Iraq beyond what her age and rank suggested. She was industrious and had completed law school while an intern at State. In early 2003, she was working for Undersecretary of State for Arms Control and International Security Affairs John Bolton. There she oversaw International Military Education and Training programs. Her interest in Iraq extended specifically to Qubai Talabani, son of Jabal Talabani, head of the Kurdish PUK Party, whom she would marry in 2004.

A description of Kraham absorbed adjectives: she was attractive, articulate, politically savvy, assertive, and blatantly ambitious. She knew Larry

Hanauer and contacted him in January to see if she could join Garner's group. Hanauer sent a memo to General Adams recommending her. A week later she joined ORHA and Adams assigned her to the "Law Firm" under Colonel Paul Hughes.[50] When Garner assigned Bob Polk, the ORHA C-5 officer, the task to study the Iraqi ministries, Kraham volunteered to assist him. Soon they had a wall plastered with paper slides of each of the twenty-some Iraqi ministries. Kraham cultivated a close working relationship with Garner, and with her industrious work ethic she soon became a favorite. But her ambitious cultivation of those in the top ranks of ORHA led others to consider Kraham a poor team player.[51]

Lee Schatz came from the Department of Agriculture, where he was a GS-15 civil servant with the Foreign Agriculture Service, which he joined in 1975. He went to Iraq on business in 1977, worked for several years in south and southeast Asia, then transferred to Iran in the fall of 1979 in time to be among the American hostages seized in the embassy in Tehran. He managed to get out with the help of the Canadian embassy. Schatz was likable and competent, but few in ORHA were interested in Iraqi agriculture.[52]

Dick Mayer and Bill Lantz came from the Department of Justice. Experienced and intense GS-15s, their task was to reform the Iraqi police. They would develop a plan for police training but would have difficulty selling it even with Garner's support. Their failure to obtain the resources would lead to great frustration on their part and a serious deficiency for the overall endeavor.

In March the Department of Treasury would provide personnel for ORHA to work on finance and banking for Iraq. Earlier in February, Dorothy Mazaka had volunteered. Mazaka was a GS-14 civil servant in the Treasury's Office of Technical Assistance with regional expertise in Saudi Arabia, where she had worked from 1995 to 2000 on development programs. She spoke Arabic, had connections with USAID, and wanted to return to the Middle East. Her specialty was health and education programs overseas, and she was assigned to the Civil Affairs pillar to work on education issues.[53]

Of the civilians that joined ORHA by mid-February, only a few were Foreign Service Officers with Middle Eastern experience, such as Gfoeller from State and Milligan from USAID. Gfoeller and Mazaka were among the few Arabic speakers. As the military personnel assigned to ORHA, most of the civilians were unknown to each other, not to mention new to the Pentagon and the military environment. The learning curve was steep.

General Adams wanted legal and auditing personnel on board early and initially relied on military officers. Lieutenant Colonel Brett Barkey, a Marine reservist activated from his GS-15 position at Treasury, was the first lawyer to join. Colonel Michael Murphy, an Air Force officer on the White House legal staff, came for an interview in January, but he was not released to ORHA until mid-February. While happy to have Murphy and Barkey, Adams wanted civilian attorneys; the State Department promised one, but she did not arrive until mid-March. In late February the first comptroller arrived, Air Force Colonel Kim Olson. But a week later Garner assigned Olson as his executive officer; she was replaced as a comptroller in early March by Air Force Colonel Gary Minor, designated as ORHA's C-8. At the same time Navy Captain Richard Kiser, a quiet Seabee engineer, joined as the ORHA C-7 Engineer staff officer.[54]

Adams requested Public Affairs Officers and Middle East Foreign Area Officers, known as PAOs and FAOs. Garner personally interviewed several PAOs and eventually selected Captain "Nate" Jones, a Navy reservist; Jones ran a family newspaper and had been activated for military duty after 9/11. The Pentagon provided two FAOs: Majors Fadi Petro and Chris Herndon, both Arabic speakers. Herndon had participated with Colonel Paul Hughes with his NDU workshop the previous November.[55]

February arrivals also included Colonel Tom Gross, an infantryman teaching at the Armed Forces Staff College who joined Paul Hughes and Sherri Kraham in the Law Firm. In January Adams had requested Colonel John "JR" Martin from the Army's Strategic Studies Institute (SSI), and Colonel George Oliver from the Peacekeeping Institute at the Army War College. Martin had worked for Adams before, in Bosnia and in the Pentagon, and had recently returned from a tour in Afghanistan and prior to that had a tour in Kosovo; while at SSI he had worked with Crane and Terrill on the study of Iraq. Oliver had previously worked for General Bates and was assigned as a deputy for George Ward in the Humanitarian Assistance pillar. But the War College squabbled over who would pay the expenses for Martin and Oliver, and they were not released to join until mid-February.

Two officers with Civil Affairs backgrounds were Majors William Butcher and James Wolff; both were soon promoted to lieutenant colonel. They were regular officers who had served under Tom Baltazar when he commanded the 96th Civil Affairs battalion. They were aligned with two regional components of ORHA, Butcher as the operations officer for Bruce Moore with ORHA-North, and Wolff in the same role for Buck Walters with ORHA-South (later South Central). Once General Casey agreed to fill slots on the JMD, the real challenge was with the other agencies.[56]

By mid-February there were thirty civilians on the ORHA roster, mainly from State and USAID. But only a few designated by name from USAID had arrived; some were still working overseas. David Nummy and Van Jorstad from Treasury joined ORHA in early March; they had already done some work on Iraq, but had little time in the Pentagon to master the nature of the tasks they would take on in Iraq. No one had yet arrived from the Departments of Transportation, Labor, Commerce, or Health, or from OMB, CIA, or FBI.

As ORHA was forming and word spread about the tasks it would undertake, Major General Carl Strock of the Army Corps of Engineers (USACE) took an interest. Strock was the Deputy for Civil Works at the Corps's headquarters in Washington. In 2002 he had been involved in a dispute with USAID about construction of a major road in Afghanistan. USAID managed to keep the task and forced an early completion of the road, which pleased senior USAID personnel. But Strock and other engineers knew the road contract had not been properly supervised and the project was not a success.[57]

Strock and others from his organization believed few planners were aware that USACE had several overseas districts and significant overseas construction experience. He anticipated USAID would get the lead for construction in Iraq, and he thought it might bite off more than it could chew. During the Cold War USAID had been a large organization with some depth for reconstruction tasks. But by 2003 USAID had only 1,000 Foreign Service Officers and another 1,000 civil servants compared to the 37,000 members (mostly civilians) of the Corps of Engineers. Even those numbers were deceiving as few of the USAID personnel were engineers, while most of those in the Corps were engineers. Strock felt most of those in USAID had expertise weighted in what he called soft reconstruction: governance, human rights, democracy, and so on. But for hard reconstruction—water and sewer systems, transportation nets, and electricity grids—USAID had little expertise for large-scale projects that should be anticipated in Iraq. With the approval of Lieutenant General Robert E. Flowers, the Chief of Engineers, one day Strock went to the Pentagon and walked the halls until he found the ORHA offices.

Garner had not met Strock before, but when he did he took to him right away. Strock had such an effect on people. With a boyish grin, he had a demeanor both informal and engaging that belied an articulate command of what USACE had to offer for reconstruction tasks. Strock told Garner that ORHA should include some civilian engineers from the Corps; most of those engineers had contracting experience on large engineer projects. Strock selected one for Garner with overseas experience.[58]

Steve Browning was a regional engineer director in San Francisco; his specialty was environmental engineer and he had worked for the Corps for fifteen years. His work overseas included assignments in Afghanistan, Israel, Australia, New Zealand, India, Korea, and Germany. He represented the Corps during Hurricane Mitch in Central America and Hurricane Jorge in Haiti. Like Strock, Browning had a winning personality, great confidence, and no shortage of ambition; he had impressed Garner earlier when they had both participated on the Defense Science board. Browning had been designated for Afghanistan to work on reconstruction, but had not yet deployed when Strock asked him to check in with ORHA. On the February day he arrived for an interview, Garner told him simply, "I want you working here." Browning flew home to California, packed his bags, and by 11 February was at work in the Pentagon.[59]

Originally Browning was to work with Lew Lucke, but Browning felt Lucke had a parochial view of reconstruction as exclusively the domain of USAID and "was not really receptive to the notion of me working with him." Instead Browning joined Buck Walters and ORHA-South. In the Pentagon, Browning and Strock monitored Task Force RIO (Restore Iraqi Oil) under Brigadier General Robert Crear, another formation from the Corps of Engineers preparing to go into Iraq. TF RIO was not under Garner's control, but through Strock Garner would monitor its work and progress.[60]

As ORHA began to study possible reconstruction projects, General Flowers directed Strock to stay in contact and the charismatic Strock soon had a high profile in the meetings. One Saturday morning, Garner asked him, "Well, Carl, you're going with us, aren't you?" Strock was surprised. "I don't think so. I have a full-time job here." But Garner went to Flowers and had him release Strock to join ORHA.[61]

Most of the civilians and many of the junior military members had never worked in the Pentagon before; they had to get special access badges to the Pentagon in a system increasingly regimented after 9/11. They learned the idiosyncrasies that came with the cavernous Pentagon: byzantine parking, fast-food cafeterias, and the ultra-thin toilet paper in the restrooms (perhaps once a day they might wonder about the utility of contracts going to the lowest bidder). As more joined ORHA, each cubicle soon had several people squeezed together sharing desks, phones, and the unclassified and classified computer systems, the latter known as SIPRNET, on which much of the DOD digital traffic moved. Meetings were conducted around a table that seated a dozen people with thirty chairs along the wall for others. Most meetings lasted an hour in a military format with all key players providing an update and others asking questions that those from other agencies found plodding.

During February, Colonel Tom Greenwood began grooming a new Marine assistant, Major Jeff Kojac. Those on the NSC staff had difficulty tracking the military plans for Iraq, because the NSC did not maintain copies of the relevant plans within its staff sections, and because Rumsfeld and others did not want to share their planning products. To keep Rice and others on the NSC informed and up to date, Frank Miller sent Greenwood to the Pentagon to work his military contacts and get the copies and updates they needed; Major Kojac would assist Greenwood in that task.

Greenwood and Kojac had worked together before. A newly promoted major, Kojac was a speechwriter for General James Jones, the Commandant of the Marines. He had also completed research on stabilization operations while working with the Center for Strategic and International Studies (CSIS). When General Jones gave up his position as Commandant in January 2003 to take the senior NATO position, Greenwood requested Kojac by name to join him on the NSC staff. Kojac arrived the last week in January and soon found that what "I really did there was Iraq, 99.9% Iraq."[62]

As he began to study Iraq combined with his prior study of post-conflict operations, Kojac told Colonel Greenwood that he was beginning to have "visions of Mosul being very ugly, of Kirkuk being very ugly, Baghdad being very ugly—because of the inner sectarian [strife] . . . in all three of those cities." Greenwood told him to prepare a briefing for the NSC staff on stabilization issues to be considered for Iraq. With the title "Force Security in Seven Recent Stability Operations" Kojac included data on the military forces used for stabilization in Northern Ireland, Sierra Leone, Bosnia, Kosovo, East Timor, Afghanistan, and Haiti. With significant disparity in the nature of each situation and the forces employed, Kojac tried to establish discriminators based on the size of the country, the population, how urban or rural it was, and the nature and intensity of the conflict—to allow useful comparisons for Iraq. He made his presentation on 7 February to Rice, her deputy Hadley, Eric Edelman from the Office of the Vice President, Miller, and Greenwood.[63]

For Kojac, the dominant factors for Iraq were the potential for communal strife and the degree to which the population was urbanized; by comparison, Bosnia and Kosovo could be useful models for stabilization. Based on the population ratios in those experiences, the number of troops needed to stabilize Iraq should have been between 364,000 and 480,000. But Hadley was more interested in the figures for Afghanistan, a more recent experience for the Bush administration. At that time the American forces in Afghanistan were about 17,000 for a country with a population slightly larger than Iraq. The Pentagon had programmed 30,000 American troops for Iraq by the fall of 2003. Compared with the Afghanistan model, the troop projections for Iraq appeared generous.

Kojac had reservations about using Afghanistan as a model for Iraq. Afghanistan was far more rural with a decentralized population that should make stabilization less challenging, a point he tried to set up in the presentation. In

Afghanistan, the United States had relied heavily on tribal forces for stabilization. Perhaps most important, Kojac felt stabilization in Afghanistan was still an "experiment as it had only been in effect for a year," with success and its full costs yet to be determined. But for Hadley and others comparing the force ratios, the case studies that took place during the Clinton administration—notably Bosnia and Kosovo—had been poorly managed and wasteful. In their view the American experience in Afghanistan was a success story attributable to more effective management by the Bush administration. Looking back, Kojac noted that he had "just arrived at the NSC [at] the end of January. This was the first brief I gave to Rice and Hadley. My approach was understated."[64]

On 12 February, Garner had a series of eventful meetings. At 1:00 P.M., he met Major General Tim Cross of the British army, the first and most senior Coalition member to join ORHA. Originally Cross was to lead two brigades through northern Turkey to invade Iraq from the north, but by February, with over 80 percent of the Turkish population opposed to an invasion through their country, UK forces were sent to Kuwait under another commander and Cross joined ORHA. He had a serious air that some incorrectly took for British formality. Those who worked closely with him soon noted his cerebral nature, reflecting an astute and penetrating mind, which fit his first role in ORHA as a member of the Law Firm, subsequently called the ORHA Strategic Initiatives Group.

At 1:30 Garner and Bates met in General Casey's office to address vacancies on JMD and for a second time to ask for an Army signal company to provide classified and unclassified computers and satellite radios for ORHA until conventional systems were available. Casey had agreed to fill the military positions requested, but on a military formation for communications, Casey again told Garner and Bates, "I don't see you running a 24/7 operation." Garner was frustrated that Casey did not appreciate the importance of communications for ORHA starting work in an austere environment. Casey said the Army was overextended and could not provide a signal unit to a civilian organization like ORHA. It was an interesting setting. Casey had been a colonel when Garner and Bates had been active-duty lieutenant generals. Now Casey held military power; Garner and Bates were civilians. Casey's refusal not only ordained a future communications failure for ORHA; it also suggested that the retired generals might not be able to leverage prior rank and associations with senior military leaders.[65]

Garner and Bates decided they could get the communications support through outsourcing. They had been impressed with the Raytheon communications package that General Abizaid showed them in Qatar, but they may not have appreciated the year it had taken to get it up and running effectively there. They contacted a Raytheon executive, Paul Blackwell, also a retired lieutenant general. Garner told him they needed three mobile communications platforms for the three regional components that ORHA had planned. With only a few weeks before ORHA would deploy to Kuwait, then deploy again into Iraq, there would be little time to work out the bugs from the systems Raytheon provided.[66] After the meeting Bates informed Colonel Randy Conway, the ORHA C-6 Communications officer, that they would have to go with a Raytheon contract rather than a military signal unit.

Garner's next meeting was with Dick Mayer and Bill Lantz on a plan to reform the Iraqi police force. Mayer and Lantz wanted money appropriated to mobilize 5,000 police trainers who would deploy to Kuwait and follow military forces into Iraq. Both were concerned that Iraq could quickly slip into chaos if the Iraqi police stopped operating. Keeping them on the street and working in accordance with Coalition procedures would be challenging. In addition to moving police trainers into Iraq early, they had to make arrangements to see that the Iraqi police were paid to keep them on the job. Garner shared their concern and intended to take it up with those senior to him.[67]

His next meeting was with Catherine Dale, the political advisor (POLAD) for the U.S. Army V Corps in Germany, the formation that would conduct the main attack into Iraq. Normally a POLAD was a serving FSO or ambassador from the Department of State, but in the 1990s personnel reductions at State reduced the number of such positions it could fill—and V Corps had to contract their own POLAD. With a Harvard Ph.D., Dale had worked with international organization in the Balkans, but she was not a Middle East specialist and had never served in the State Department; nor did she have strong contacts there. She had attended key conferences in Washington on Iraq and would continue to work with ORHA and others in Iraq—but her limited credentials in government and on the Middle East would restrict her overall contribution.[68]

Garner's last meeting of the day was with Secretary Rumsfeld. Garner went into the meeting planning to ask for only what he needed most. He did not comment on the meeting with General Casey and his refusal to provide an Army signal company; he was resigned to going to Raytheon for communications support. But he needed help with police. Rumsfeld asked what it would cost; Garner estimated it would come to about ten million dollars. Rumsfeld scoffed. The United States, he said, would not pay that kind of money for police forces in Iraq; Iraq's oil revenues would pay for it. Garner was surprised. Even if there were no oil well fires, it would take time to get oil revenues flowing into Iraq. Mayer and Lantz needed funding in advance to pre-position police trainers. The secretary was unmoved and Garner's request for police assistance went unaddressed. The other topics Garner addressed each day crossed a wide spectrum. Constantly he searched for people and resources. Frequently he had to accept less than what he needed. The consequences would be severe.[69]

During the third week of February, Marc Powe represented ORHA at a meeting in Washington, met Tom Warrick, and offered Warrick a ride to the State Department afterward. When Warrick told him about the Future of Iraq project, Powe was impressed that he had studied Iraq more than anyone in ORHA. When he told Adams about Warrick the next day, Adams told Powe "to get him over here." Baltazar scheduled a meeting with Warrick for Garner and Adams, but Warrick missed the meeting. Garner would not learn about his project or meet him until later.[70]

On 19 February, Garner again briefed Rumsfeld on his recent and projected activities. He noted that ORHA had received most of the military personnel projected on the JMD but had few civilians from other agencies, and fewer still of those with senior credentials for Iraq. His dominant concerns were transitional security and civil administration for Iraq and the funding necessary for both. Garner addressed preparations for retraining and reforms for the Iraqi army and the Iraqi police forces, as well as putting Iraq's civil servants back to work. Plans had to be accompanied by preparation and preparation required funding. Again Rumsfeld demurred on the costs Garner projected.[71]

The next day, Garner and Baltazar went to the White House, to see Rice and to address many of the same issues. Garner made it clear he did not have the personnel required and needed more interagency support. Funding and preparations were required for law enforcement in Iraq. He asked what the United Nations could provide. While Rice was generally positive, Baltazar thought there was more talk than action and was concerned that Rice was not aggressively working the funding and interagency support. In his meetings with Rumsfeld and Rice, Garner told both that ORHA would soon conduct a large two-day conference to further explore the tasks ahead of them.[72]

THE ROCK DRILL

On Friday and Saturday, 21–22 February 2003, ORHA conducted a large conference billed as a rock drill, which in military parlance refers to a rehearsal. It was held in a large lecture room in the Eisenhower Building at NDU in Washington beginning at 8:30 in the morning with all one hundred seats filled and twenty people standing. Sixty members of ORHA were present. The rest came from military commands and government agencies; some of them would soon join ORHA. The rock drill laid out much of ORHA's work and was to integrate assistance from others working on Iraq. It turned out to be one of ORHA's most critical meetings.[73]

Defense had the largest contingent. From OSD came Assistant Deputy Undersecretary of Defense Bill Luti and Abe Shulsky from the Office of Plans, but neither Feith nor Wolfowitz attended. Central Command was represented by Rear Admiral James Robb and Major Ray Eiriz of J-5, but absent were Ambassador David C. Litt, the Central Command Political Advisor (PO-LAD), and Robb's key planners—Mike Fitzgerald, John Agoglia, and Tom Fisher; they were all in Qatar. The Third Army augmented and designated as CFLCC had four U.S. Army officers present: Brigadier General Steve Hawkins; his Plans officer, Colonel Anthony "Tony" Puckett of JTF-4; Colonel Marty Stanton, C-9 Civil Affairs; and Lieutenant Colonel Robert Newman, a Middle East Foreign Area Officer serving as Political Advisor for General McKiernan; also present was Major General Albert Whitely of the UK Army, McKiernan's deputy for Phase IV operations. Absent were Kevin Benson, C-5 Plans officer, and his planners who had been working on Phase IV—they were all in Kuwait.[74]

The rock drill was the first time ORHA members had significant face-to-face contact with military officers from CFLCC. Earlier in January, when General Adams received a briefing from Con Crane and Andy Terrill at the Army War College on their study of Iraq, Adams had shown Crane a line diagram that placed ORHA subordinate to CFLCC, but he told Crane that the ORHA leadership would resist that arrangement, preferring to work directly for Central Command. The issue did not come up at the rock drill and none of the officers from CFLCC indicated they were aware that ORHA might be placed under CFLCC control—a command relationship that Central Command would later impose on both CFLCC and ORHA, causing significant friction and turmoil.[75]

Wendy Chamberlin, the deputy at USAID, was present, but those representing the Department of State were middle management and did not include senior diplomats such as Marc Grossman or Ryan Crocker. Those representing the Office of the Vice President, CIA, Treasury, Justice, Agriculture, Commerce, the UN mission, and the U.S. Embassy in Kuwait were also middle management rather than senior decision makers. For a short period Elliot Abrams from the NSC staff attended, but Robin Cleveland did not attend, nor did Rice or Hadley.[76]

Buck Walters was the first up and opened with a funny story. Walters had a good sense of timing, and his jokes went over well—with most of those present. When he walked on stage, everyone knew the next round was about to begin and quickly sat down expecting to resume work with a good laugh. But it was serious business; everyone knew ORHA had started late and had a lot to do. Garner followed Walters with a general introduction, defining his role as an interim administrator during the regime replacement period in Iraq; several times he suggested he would be involved for a few months and return in July. The format began with a discussion on security issues, followed by briefings under three headings: Humanitarian Assistance, Reconstruction, and Civil Administration, ORHA's three functional pillars. Briefers were to follow a standard format: planning assumptions; requirements, including money and staff; high-impact actions; and measures of effectiveness, specifically what they expected to achieve in 30 days, 90 days, 180 days, 270 days, and 360 days. Policy decisions were included with any showstoppers that would cause notable problems.[77]

Garner and Adams had expressed concern about security for ORHA personnel, but Admiral Robb told Garner that Central Command would not have enough military forces to provide security for ORHA in Iraq. He suggested Garner should outsource the task as soon as possible. Funding for such security went unaddressed.[78]

George Ward was next. He stated that this could be "the largest humanitarian crisis we have ever faced." He went on to predict major shortages of water and food, refugee displacement within and beyond Iraq, and the possible Iraqi use of WMD and oil well fires to endanger the Iraqi people. The immediate effects of a humanitarian disaster would not only impede military operations, they would require military forces to provide the emergency assistance in the initial period. Civil Affairs units and military formations of medical, engineer, and transportation units would be required. They needed an integrated plan for ORHA and the ground forces to take on such tasks.

A speaker representing USAID stated that a large Disaster Assistance Response Team (DART) of some sixty-two personnel would follow military forces into Iraq to make assessments for humanitarian assistance. But there was no indication that the DART would come under Garner's control, nor was that an issue at the rock drill. It would become a serious issue later. The implication was that military forces would have to take on immediate humanitarian tasks and ORHA would pick it up when able. But ORHA was little more than a headquarters. Undertaking significant humanitarian tasks in Iraq, even with a secure environment, would require military support, presumably followed by NGOs and the United Nations, which would not be forthcoming if Iraq was not secure. Those representing the Pentagon, Central Command, and CFLCC made no comment.

The data on food distribution came mainly from the UN Oil for Food program. The Iraqi Ministry of Trade was responsible for food distribution, but Garner did not yet have a designated senior advisor for that ministry. Of greater concern were intelligence reports that indicated the Iraqi people would have four weeks of food on hand when an invasion might commence. Studies indicated it would take seven weeks to start moving food convoys into Iraq, assuming the money was soon made available to stockpile food in the region for such a contingency. That left a potential three-week gap in food distribution, perhaps six weeks for some areas in Iraq. No one questioned the intelligence reports, however, and no one offered a satisfactory solution.[79]

Sustaining potable water would be a challenge if combat operations disrupted electricity necessary to operate water and sewage systems. If the water systems were already fragile, combat operations could only make them worse, which might lead to an outbreak of disease. Refugee displacement would also compound the situation. Iraqi suppression of Shiite and Kurdish revolts after Desert Storm resulted in over a million refugees fleeing Iraq. Ward estimated an invasion of Iraq could lead to two million displaced refugees, encumbering military operations. Central Command estimates were 10 percent of what ORHA projected based on classified plans for a wide sweep into Iraq bypassing major population centers. But those plans could not be included in an unclassified setting; thus ORHA anticipated a scenario worse than did Central Command.[80]

During the discussions on the first morning, one man in the audience was remarkably vocal and impatient, asking hard questions and speaking with authority. During a break Garner approached him to find out that he was Tom Warrick. Garner asked how he knew so much about Iraq. Warrick told Garner about his Future of Iraq project. It was the first time Garner had heard of either Warrick or his project, a month after Garner had taken on his task with several visits to the Department of State and the NSC. Incredibly, no one had mentioned the FOI project to him. Garner was interested and asked Warrick to join him. Warrick said he would report to the Pentagon the next week.[81]

The next set of speakers represented USAID with a quest to define the scope of reconstruction tasks: was it to simply fix damage caused by an invasion, fix them to a level comparable to what it had been prior to Desert Storm in 1991, or include fundamental improvements in the Iraqi infrastructure? Determining appropriate reconstruction tasks was problematic without an assessment of the infrastructure or knowledge of how much funding would be available. The issues were broad in scope, covering oil, electricity, health care systems, agriculture, education, industry, and housing. Few of those from USAID were engineers, and although General Strock was present as an observer there was little mention of the Army Corps of Engineers during the conference. Strock did not provide a presentation or interact in the discussions, but he monitored the developing chemistry in ORHA and the many challenges before it.

Oil had received significant attention in OSD under Mike Mobbs, and there were military plans to protect Iraqi oil wells. There was an assumption that Iraqi oil would provide revenue to fund reconstruction. Electricity received less attention; the Coalition did not plan to target the electricity grid as it had during Desert Storm, so it was assumed that electricity would remain in operation. Iraqi agriculture also received little attention during the rock drill, though there was some discussion of reflooding the southern marshes that Saddam Hussein had drained a decade earlier to drive out the marsh Arabs. Rather than address relevant details with such a venture, the discussion centered on whether such a move should be left for Iraqis to make on their own.

On the subject of health care, beyond humanitarian assistance, some of those present were in favor of universal coverage within a year of invasion, an interesting proposal in that the United States had no such universal health care plan of its own. Again, many present assumed the availability of massive oil revenues. There was no suggestion of a possible breakdown in Iraqi health care after invasion.

Education also struck an idealist chord. One briefing made it clear that there were two education systems or ministries in Iraq, one for primary and secondary education and another for higher education. Garner emphasized the objective to get schools up and running as soon as possible after the invasion, partially to keep people off the streets and teachers employed. He also wanted to ensure a school year was not lost. Speakers suggested the Iraqi education system relied heavily on rote memorization and suggested more contemporary methods be incorporated. Textbooks with Ba'athist ideology should be replaced. A briefer noted that many teachers were Ba'athists, without indication of how that should be addressed by ORHA. Little notice was taken of Dorothy Mazaka in the audience, who would take over responsibility for the Iraqi Ministry of Education.

Higher education received less attention, although one voice suggested that any science program related to nuclear energy should be stricken from the university curriculum. Much of the audience was aghast at such a draconian suggestion and it was quickly dismissed. No mention was made of the depth of the university system in Iraq, nor was there a vision of how higher education could be harnessed during the post-conflict period.

A presentation on Iraqi industry noted that much of it was under government ownership (the term used later was State-Owned Enterprises, or SOEs). Suggestions that government-owned industries should be privatized as soon as possible were countered by those who had observed how accelerated privatization in the Soviet Union caused unanticipated chaos in the 1990s. They also expressed concern that returning expatriates might exploit such a situation for personal gain with further turmoil. A briefing on the Iraqi Housing Ministry suggested that war damage and refugee displacement could create a housing shortage. Some of those present expressed concern with resettling one ethnic group at the expense of another, a sensitive issue given that Saddam Hussein had forced certain ethnic groups into some areas in order to disperse dissension, most notably in Kirkuk, where an Arab population had been used to displace part of the Kurdish population.

During the reconstruction briefings, Ron Adams asked how they were to deal with the multiple currencies in Iraq: two separate currencies used within the Arab areas and a third currency used in the Kurdish areas. Hard currency would be crucial in Iraq until the banking system could implement an effective credit system. The object was a single Iraqi currency, but it was not clear what procedures should be used to reduce it to one.

Civil Administration presentations followed the Humanitarian Assistance and Reconstruction briefings. Mike Mobbs had only recently taken on the lead for Civil Administration, and he was the least known of the senior leaders in ORHA. But rather than establish himself through the presentations at the rock drill, he had been designated by OSD to go to Turkey and on into northern Iraq to establish contact with Iraqi opposition groups. Garner introduced him at the beginning of the rock drill, but Mobbs left without a substantive role in the conference. Of all the presentations at the conference, those for Civil Administration were the least developed.

A report after the conference noted that it "did not take up the most basic issue: What sort of future Government of Iraq do we have in mind, and how do we plan to get there? For months and months the Interagency has debated different approaches—naming a provisional government, or instituting a process leading from census to local elections to constitution to national elections," but there had been no resolution. Garner did not take a position on the issue at the conference, nor did any of his subordinates.[82]

There were several off-line meetings, mainly with military representatives from Central Command and CFLCC so that classified issues could be discussed. They were not planning meetings, nor did they integrate the efforts of Hughes, Gross, and Polk of ORHA with those of Admiral Robb and Eritz from Central Command, or Stanton and Newman from CFLCC. Some attention focused on General Hawkins and the mission of JTF-4. There had been a number of phone conversations with JTF-4 personnel before the conference, but few knew much about Hawkins, his views or intentions. Nor were many in ORHA aware of the difficulties those in JTF-4 had encountered with Central Command in Tampa, or with CFLCC in Kuwait.

When Major General Whitley arrived with Hawkins, many in ORHA wondered what Whitley's role would be. So did Hawkins. Whitley had joined CFLCC as General McKiernan's deputy in December, but McKiernan already had two American deputies, Major General William C. "Fuzzy" Webster for Operations and Major General Henry W. Stratman for Logistics. McKiernan knew Whitley from a previous tour in Europe and referred to him as "my Brit minder." Whitley was an engineer and McKiernan decided to assign him to be the deputy for Phase IV operations. When Whitley arrived in Kuwait in December, he was a brigadier general—the same rank as Hawkins. To give him clout in the headquarters, the UK promoted Whitley to major general; it was not a promotion that pleased Hawkins.[83]

With the lead for Phase IV operations, Whitley assumed he would become the commander of JTF-4 (reflagged as CJTF-4 to indicate a Coalition headquarters) with Hawkins as his deputy. Hawkins did not see it the same way. He had no intention of moving down a notch in the organization he had raised with so much difficulty. All the original JTF-4 personnel were Americans; Whitley brought only two UK officers with him. It did not make sense to Hawkins for JTF-4 to have a British general imposed upon it. The situation was awkward for Whitley. During the rock drill, Hawkins and Whitley sat together but said little during the conference and less to each other. It was not long before those present could sense a problem, but it was not a problem Garner could correct: neither JTF-4 nor the two generals were under his control, despite the common focus of ORHA and JTF-4. Some of the Americans present considered Hawkins the rightful commander of JTF-4. Some ORHA members felt Hawkins and JTF-4 should be integrated with ORHA with or without Whitley. A meeting that should have clarified command relationships for those working on regime replacement in Iraq began and ended without such a resolution.[84]

Garner had recently designated General Tim Cross (the other UK representative at the rock drill) the ORHA Deputy for Coalition affairs. At the conference Cross laid out two themes he would continue to promote, but with limited success. First, he argued that ORHA had to add more civilians to its core from the other agencies in order for those agencies to play the roles for which they were considered best prepared. Second, he argued that ORHA needed a larger coalition, meaning a non-American component. Both shifts in personnel would add greater diversity of talent and capacity to the ORHA mission and greatly enhance its legitimacy. Cross intended to increase the UK contingent of ORHA with civilian rather than military personnel consistent with his first objective and had requested his Foreign Office to provide them. Several would join by March, but they would be the only non-Americans to join before the deployment.

At the rock drill one observer representing a military command noted that "there was no side-by-side walk-through of the plans for each line of activity. . . . The purpose of this rehearsal was to gather all the key players involved in post-war planning in the same room at the same time . . . to identify the gaps." Garner had described his role as an interim civil administrator for Iraq, but much of the conference focused on humanitarian tasks with the expectations of a thousand oil well fires, a six-week food shortage, two million displaced refugees, and possible use of WMD. Those challenges had been defined mainly by George Ward and his Humanitarian Assistance team.

Much of the discussion on reconstruction addressed the most immediate requirements in Iraq and overlapped with talks on humanitarian tasks. The Civil Administration team presentation was the least developed, with Mike Mobbs attending only the beginning of the conference. While Garner and Adams had spent much of their time prior to the conference working on civil administration for Iraq, the substance of the rock drill suggested that Garner and ORHA were distracted by humanitarian assistance.[85]

USAID

During the month of February, USAID was completing a parallel project that would have a significant impact upon Garner's efforts for Iraq, a document with the grandiose title "USAID's Vision for Post-Conflict Iraq." Wendy Chamberlin had managed the project earlier in the fall and had foreseen expensive reconstruction projects in Iraq after the initial humanitarian tasks were addressed. She had requested $10 billion, but Elliot Abrams and Robin Cleveland had no intention of allowing such funding, assuming that Iraqi oil revenues would be able to cover any such costs. Chamberlin was less optimistic, but her arguments and those of others led to a request to Congress for just over $2 billion, soon to be known as the Iraq Relief and Reconstruction Fund, subsequently passed by Congress in April as the IRRF.[86]

In January, before Garner had an office in the Pentagon, the National Security Council instructed USAID to initiate contracting related to Iraq, and on the sixteenth of that month the USAID administrator authorized "less than a full and open competitive process" in the interests of time. At a Washington meeting, Chamberlin observed while Andrew Natsios briefed potential contractors about potential business in Iraq in the auditorium of the

Ronald Reagan Building. "Lines were out the door . . . an auditorium filled with 6,000 greedy people." Uncoordinated with Garner or ORHA, USAID awarded eight major contracts from February through May related to work in Iraq, one to the Bechtel Corporation with an initial allocation of $680 million, one-third the money Congress was to provide.[87]

The USAID Vision Statement listed ten sectors for those contracts: water and sanitation, health, transportation, electricity, local development, economic governance, payroll management, food, education, and shelter. With little detail to support it, the Vision Statement indicated 3,000 schools would be repaired and within six months basic health services would cover half the population with maternal and child care available to all. Within a year electricity generation would be increased from a prewar standard of 4,500 constant megawatts to 6,750 constant megawatts.[88]

Chris Milligan had been a planner for reconstruction, and the previous November he had written much of what was contained in the Vision Statement on reconstruction. But Milligan had little information on Iraqi infrastructure or a basis to project war damage or to anticipate the looting that followed. Much of his work was based on conjecture for the planning, contracting, and requests for funding. When Milligan joined Garner in late January, Chamberlin intended that he would be the connecting link between USAID and ORHA, but Milligan felt that others at USAID working on humanitarian assistance would resist funding for reconstruction in Iraq. With Chamberlin, he wanted to preserve the planning that had been done, and while Milligan was criticized by others at USAID, he told them that Garner and his project was "our Trojan Horse—it's how we get to Iraq."[89]

Chamberlin knew that Frank Miller, Robin Cleveland, and some members of USAID were angry that Defense, and subsequently Garner, had been given the lead role for Iraq. Chamberlin had her own reservations: she felt that Garner disregarded USAID, in spite of the work they had done the past few months. When one of Buck Walters's jokes made fun of USAID and another disparaged women, Chamberlin took offense. She was one of the most senior government officials to attend the rock drill and, like Tom Warrick, had been working on Iraq longer than many others present, yet neither were asked to make a presentation of their work. This was yet another misunderstanding that did not help Garner or ORHA and that reinforced the perception that the Department of Defense was usurping others' authorities.[90]

The following week Garner and others in ORHA returned to the Pentagon with a better sense of their overall focus (or lack of it). It had not been a planning conference, as few decisions were made and relationships were still undetermined with other organizations. But there was a sense of what information was available and what was not. During the last half of February, Garner and his planners learned that Central Command and the Bush administration were concerned that Turkey would not allow Coalition forces to pass through its territory to invade Iraq, which would mean that more forces would invade through Kuwait. Those in ORHA who had been to Kuwait knew that the military bases there were already packed with military personnel preparing for the invasion, with more coming daily. It was clear that there would be little room for ORHA personnel on those bases. George Ward knew that NGOs were also arriving in Kuwait and planned to take Garner with him to the UN in New York to determine what support ORHA could anticipate and how it should be coordinated.

Later in March, Undersecretary Paul Wolfowitz had a meeting with Garner to discuss Iraqi expatriates, suggesting that "a group of these people could be useful." Garner agreed and Abe Shulsky of the OSD Office of Special Plans took the lead to set them up as the Iraqi Reconstruction Development Council (IRDC) in an office in Crystal City. Some had served with Tom Warrick and the FOI project, but Warrick was excluded. Apparently he had expressed reservations about political agendas in OSD, which led to OSD reservations about Warrick. Security made it difficult to organize the IRDC in the Pentagon, yet Crystal City kept it physically remote from ORHA. Garner met briefly with some of the IRDC members, but they were not subordinate to ORHA. Whereas Warrick's FOI project had substantial input from Iraqi expatriates familiar with the culture and governmental infrastructure in Iraq, ORHA had little or no comparable counterpart.[91]

Garner soon encountered another political agenda with Meghan O'Sullivan, who had joined ORHA the week before the rock drill, and Tom Warrick, who attempted to join the week after. O'Sullivan and Warrick were both GS-15s from State, although at thirty-four O'Sullivan was fifteen years younger than Warrick. While Warrick was intense and crusty, O'Sullivan was attractive and pleasant. With an Oxford Ph.D. and several years at the Brookings Institute, she was more an academic than a diplomat and defined her specialty as ethnic conflict and constitutional design, with consideration of its mitigation or exacerbation of conflict. Her regional specialty before joining the Department of State was Asia, where she had worked in Sri Lanka, India, and Indonesia.[92]

At Brookings she had written articles that challenged the UN sanctions imposed on Iraq, arguing the effects were counterproductive. She promoted what she called "smart sanctions," a position she thought some interpreted as being soft on Iraq.[93] She observed Tom Warrick for the first time at the rock drill. Remarkably, given her growing interest in Iraq and her short tenure at State, she had neither heard of him nor the FOI project. But she was impressed and thought "he had more knowledge than anyone else in the room" and wondered "why he wasn't up there on the stage rather than in the audience."[94]

General Adams was skeptical of the utility of the FOI project and wanted Warrick to assist in making it useful for ORHA. Before Warrick arrived at the Pentagon, Adams went to visit him at the State Department. Warrick was willing to share his work with ORHA, but he wanted a senior position under Garner. Adams suggested he come to the Pentagon to work that out; Warrick spent a few days in the Pentagon without a specific position when he was suddenly ordered back to State.[95]

On the first Thursday after the rock drill, 27 February, Garner met Secretary Rumsfeld to provide him an update on ORHA. At the end of the meeting, just as Garner was leaving, Rumsfeld beckoned him back as he picked up a note he had just written: "Oh, by the way, you will have to get rid of these two people." Garner looked at the note and read the names: Tom Warrick and Meghan O'Sullivan. "You can't be serious," Garner exclaimed. "These are two of the most well informed people we have."

Rumsfeld shook his head. "It's well above me. You have to get rid of them."

Garner left the room determined to resist. He went to see Deputy National Security Advisor Steve Hadley and told him he needed to keep O'Sullivan and Warrick. But Hadley begged off and without explanation said there was nothing he could do. It appeared to Garner that it was not the White House that objected to O'Sullivan and Warrick but the vice president's office. Garner knew Baltazar had a contact working for Scooter Libby, the vice president's chief of staff. Baltazar called him and was told the objections indeed came from the OVP.[96]

Warrick and O'Sullivan were sent back to State. Warrick was furious, O'Sullivan embarrassed. Secretary Powell supposedly was trying to provide good people for ORHA, but the Defense Department was rejecting them. Garner later learned that Powell put in a call to Rumsfeld to object, telling him that "we can take prisoners too." Apparently the greater objection lay with Warrick. At his next meeting with Rumsfeld, Garner argued that Warrick and O'Sullivan should be reinstated. Rumsfeld said, "You can have the woman if you keep it quiet, but you cannot have Warrick." Within a week O'Sullivan rejoined ORHA, unsure where to focus her anger, but otherwise she was pleased to be back.[97]

Warrick would not rejoin, however, nor would his FOI work make much of a contribution, an avoidable tragedy. Baltazar looked over hard copies of Warrick's papers, thirteen binders worth. But without Warrick to help interpret the ponderous material and align it with the relevant components in ORHA, the reports had little utility. The papers had no common format and were not structured as any sort of planning document. It was so voluminous and eclectic that it was unclear where to start or how to use it. Later, part of the report was sent to some members of ORHA but with limited use.[98]

The day after Rumsfeld told him Warrick could not stay with ORHA, Garner had an interesting interview with another State Department official, Ambassador Barbara Bodine. In her initial interview with Garner and Adams, Bodine laid out her Middle East credentials, which began with a tour as the U.S. Embassy Deputy Chief of Mission in Iraq in 1980–1983, followed by a tour in the embassy in Kuwait, where she was under siege during Desert Storm. In 1997 she was ambassador to Yemen when the USS *Cole* was attacked offshore by a suicide bombing (she did not mention an altercation she had with the FBI during the investigation of the bombing).[99]

Bodine had seen a wire diagram of ORHA and asked if she could have the lead position for Civil Administration. Garner explained that it had been filled with Mike Mobbs and offered her instead the Baghdad central region, comparable to ORHA-South under Buck Walters and ORHA-North under Bruce Moore; this she accepted. She asked for a personal staff, but Adams explained that no one had a personal staff in ORHA. It was an issue that did not go away; she continued to badger Adams for a personal staff.

Baltazar told Garner that Bodine would be high maintenance. Security at the Pentagon was strict and Baltazar had escorted her into the building when she arrived for her interview. Halfway to Garner's office she realized she had left her purse in her car and asked Baltazar to get it for her. Baltazar stopped and looked at her. "I can't do that for you, ma'am," he said, thinking it would take him forever to find her car in the parking lot; furthermore, he was not her assistant. Bodine was visibly annoyed, not a good sign. Shortly afterward, Mike Ayoub wrote in his journal, "Former Ambassador Barbara Bodine is seconded to ORHA. The announcement is met with mixed reviews among the group."[100]

Bodine became one of Garner's key leaders and sat at the main table with him and others during key meetings. But soon she got into her first of several altercations. Early upon arrival, she convened a meeting with those from State working for ORHA. She wanted to make it clear that she was the senior representative from the department. Many of them came from George Ward's Humanitarian Assistance pillar. When Ward found out about the meeting, he asked her about it with some irritation prior to one of Garner's morning meetings. Bodine was incensed at the question and began to berate Ward. As others entered the room, Ward tried to terminate the discussion, but Bodine persisted even after Garner and Adams arrived. Garner listened to Bodine as Ward hung his head in embarrassment. "Some kind of family spat going on here?" Garner asked half-playfully. The minor event set the tone for Bodine's tour in ORHA.[101]

Yet Bodine could be insightful. On the question of Ba'athists, Bodine forcefully noted that all senior Ba'athists were not guilty of atrocities or corruption, nor were all junior Ba'athists innocent. Garner also tried to defuse the Ba'athist issue. Several times he stated in meetings that after an invasion the worst of the regime members would either be dead or would have fled. Any bad ones that remained would soon be turned in by other Iraqis. Garner was not concerned about those politically tainted by Saddam Hussein, and he discouraged those in ORHA from wasting energy on de-Ba'athification.[102]

With a lower profile, three British civil servants joined ORHA in March. Graham Rowcroft came from British Trade International and quietly joined those working on economic issues. Somewhat more colorful were Philip Hall and Simon Elvy from the UK Foreign and Commonwealth Office, known as FCO—the UK counterpart to the Department of State. Hall was tall and sophisticated, with a Cambridge accent and law degree; he had overseas service in Europe and Africa. More recently, he had studied while working in London. He was pleasant and unflappable, taking challenges in stride, finding humor where others found frustration. In contrast, Elvy was short and portly with a British working-class accent; he had dropped out of a university and took a Foreign Service exam on a whim, surprised when he was accepted. In the 1980s he served in the British embassy in Iraq; following some unpleasant experiences, he left with no intention of ever returning. But when General Cross asked the FCO for volunteers, Elvy signed up with Hall and Rowcroft.[103]

On 24 February, Mike Ayoub at State sent Colonel Baltazar a copy of the Pol-Mil Plan on Iraq he was trying to update, requesting input. Ayoub thought Baltazar was still working at OSD and had not tracked the evolution of ORHA or been invited to the rock drill. Baltazar was more interested in Ayoub than his Pol-Mil plan. He had Larry Hanauer contact State to have Ayoub released to ORHA. Ayoub was "distressed at departing without a completed Pol-Mil plan," but reported to the Pentagon a week later, assigned to work with the Civil Administration pillar.[104]

MEETINGS WITH THE WHITE HOUSE AND
UNITED NATIONS

Garner went to the White House to meet President Bush for the first time at an NSC meeting on 28 February. He entered the conference room and sat at the opposite end of the table from the president. When the president entered and noticed Garner, he asked, "Who are you?" Rumsfeld introduced him with reference to his leadership in northern Iraq in 1991. The president was attentive and took a liking to him when he learned that Garner had lived in Texas. But there was no developed discussion of ORHA or the problems Garner was having with personnel and funding.[105]

A week later Garner and Bates went to the State Department to see Secretary Powell and Undersecretary Armitage. All knew each other from previous military tours.It was more relaxed than Garner's visit to meet the president. Powell and Armitage wanted to help ORHA, but they made it clear that Rumsfeld, Wolfowitz, and Feith were stiff-arming their efforts at State in order to keep control within the Defense Department. It was another indication that Garner would have difficulty with support.[106]

When Garner and George Ward went to the United Nations after the rock drill to discuss NGO and international support for ORHA, they met UN Deputy Secretary General Louise Fourchette. With her were representatives of the UN agencies. Garner asked for a UN liaison officer but was turned down, an ominous sign. While the UN officials said they were preparing for what might take place in Iraq, they were not actively seeking a role aligned with the United States and told Garner they had no authority to seek such a role. Garner had anticipated more enthusiasm and found the exchange with UN officials lukewarm.[107]

The choke point was a UN resolution that would sanction an invasion of Iraq. Until that was consummated, the UN would keep its distance. The British ambassador to the UN, Jeremy Greenstock, met Garner and made it clear that Great Britain was "in this with the US" and said, "You will get whatever you need." Like Tim Cross in ORHA, Greenstock wanted to internationalize the effort and energize UN involvement with rehearsals to address food, water, oil, and electricity—part of a relief and reconstruction plan. Ideally, such rehearsals would assign tasks and address duplication, seams, and shortfalls, but none were conducted.

Garner was disappointed that Greenstock's zeal was not matched by his American counterpart at the UN, U.S. Ambassador John Negroponte. When

Garner met Negroponte and told him what he needed from the UN, the latter merely said, "Good luck" and left without even shaking his hand. Garner was disappointed Negroponte did not go with him to meet Fourchette and the UN officials. When he briefed Condoleezza Rice about his visit to the UN on 5 March, he had little to show for the trip. He told members of ORHA that he was troubled "that the UN resolution might be rejected," denying both the support he had needed from the international community and legitimacy for an invasion of Iraq.[108]

Garner continued to meet with OSD officials and attend meetings at the White House and Old Executive Office Building next door, but there was no direct linkage with Frank Miller, who was a key player on the NSC staff. That was unfortunate, as Miller was more effective than Rice or Hadley at coordinating with the other agencies. Neither Garner nor Miller liked Doug Feith and bypassed him whenever possible. Garner preferred to deal with Wolfowitz and Rumsfeld, and Miller worked with other senior contacts in the Pentagon. The cool relations among key players added a dimension that complicated Garner's ability to get the right people, the necessary funding, or support for specific projects, such as rebuilding the Iraqi police forces. Earlier in January, Colonel Baltazar had started an ongoing "ORHA Wants List" for unresolved requests for each scheduled meeting with Condoleezza Rice. Initially the dominant items included the following:

- Non-Iraqi police are needed to enforce laws while Iraqi police are trained.
- What determined how suspected war criminals are to be apprehended?
- How is the Iraqi army to be reformed with some part demobilized?
- How is a single currency for Iraq to be established?
- Could electrical power for Iraq be obtained from Kuwait and Turkey?

By March, those issues were still unresolved while Garner and Baltazar added more:

- How would prisoners found in Iraqi prisons be handled?
- What governed restrictions on local Iraqi media? Could Iraqis take over as the agent for the UN Oil for Food program? How could oil revenues support Humanitarian Assistance and Reconstruction? What international assistance and reconstruction would be authorized for Iraq? How were border control and regional boundaries to be established? How was the right of return of

refugees and displaced persons to be managed? What Coalition political element would manage Iraq in an interim period?

Each issue or question required an answer, a policy, a plan, or, most important, resources and a designated component to work it. Rice was sympathetic with the personnel problem and acknowledged the list of issues and questions, but she was either unable or unwilling to provide answers and resources from the NSC or the appropriate government agency—and there was little evidence that she took them to the president for resolution. By March Garner was frustrated with the poor response from Rice.[109]

As Garner struggled with support in Washington, he had to arrange for the deployment for ORHA. He knew there was no room for ORHA in Kuwait at Camp Doha, the military installation where CFLCC and JTF-4 were established. It appeared military leaders there were uncomfortable with a large interagency group of civilians, many without security clearances, and did not want them at Doha. Garner had to find another place for ORHA in Kuwait and sent an advance party under Buck Walters to find adequate accommodations. Walters took with him Steve Browning, Marc Powe, and Colonel John "JR" Martin. They departed on 7 March, nine days before Garner and his main body would deploy.[110]

Funding was a constant concern. In January, Garner had met with Robin Cleveland, the OMB point of contact for funding national security operations and related programs, but little funding was being allocated for ORHA. When Garner complained to Rice about inadequate funding, she had Cleveland attend their next meeting and told her several times that funding had to be forthcoming for ORHA. Baltazar noted that Cleveland looked down at her notes rather than provide a positive response. As they departed, Cleveland told Baltazar in the hall that Garner would not get the money they wanted. Baltazar was shocked that she would deny ORHA funding support just after Rice had directed her to provide it and questioned the capacity of Rice to manage the NSC effort. As Wendy Chamberlin had noted earlier, Cleveland was angry that the project she had worked on for a year had passed to the Department of Defense and ORHA.[111]

Security remained a concern, and to Garner internal security for Iraq meant police. The Iraqi police would have to be reformed and thus a training package would need to be in place before the invasion with a designated interim force to provide law enforcement. In March 2003, there was no intention to use the Iraqi army for internal security; almost everyone in Washington concurred that should be a police task. Planners at Central Command had come to the same conclusion, but assumed that police would be the responsibility of ORHA. They knew that police salaries would have to be paid right away to keep the police on duty, but they considered that was for ORHA to manage.

Unknown to Garner, Frank Miller had earlier taken a hard position on the Iraqi police in discussions with Rice and Hadley. He was convinced the United States should not get involved with reforming or training police forces for Iraq. He felt it would be too difficult to put together an adequate package of police training and that should not be a Coalition responsibility. Rice and Hadley seemed to defer to Miller on the police issue, and were passive when Garner repeatedly brought it up. Yet Garner had an unlikely ally on the issue in Miller's military assistant, Colonel Tom Greenwood. During earlier service in Haiti in the 1990s, Greenwood knew firsthand how critical an effective police force would be for internal security. He knew that following an invasion of Iraq there would be a critical period of chaos; it would continue unless preparations were made to put Iraqi police forces back into operation.[112]

Major Jeff Kojac, who had worked for Greenwood and Miller, saw their disagreement build to a major argument that erupted into a yelling match in mid-February. Kojac recalled it taking place in Miller's third floor office in the Old Executive Office Building with windows that overlooked the West Wing of the White House. Kojac felt that to Greenwood, "it was clear that the Iraqi police were discredited by their association with the Saddam regime. Moreover, the Iraqi police were a 'fear and punishment' organization, not trained or proficient in Western notions of community policing . . . He wanted to mitigate the approaching chaos."

Kojac noted that Miller's "position was that the United States was not going to send 7,000 civilian police to Iraq—and it was futile to argue for it" within the Bush administration. Miller understood the reality of Washington. First, there were not 7,000 American police (who exist for domestic municipal use, not federal overseas deployment) available to deploy to Iraq. Second, the administration's mindset was that once regime change took place, the United States would withdraw and the Iraqis would govern themselves. In this light, there would be no need for American police in Baghdad. Third, the administration leadership had complete distain for the Clinton program in the Balkans of peacekeeper and police post-conflict work. There was no way the administration wanted to repeat the Clinton post-conflict reconstruction that the Republicans had criticized so heavily the proceeding five years.

Kojac felt that Greenwood "was right about the requirement and Iraq, but Miller was right about the lack of resources and the art of the possible in DC." What fascinated Kojac was the intensity of the argument and Greenwood and Miller's apparent loss of control. Kojac assumed that Greenwood would be fired and reflected later that "whereas [Eric]Shinseki [Army Chief of Staff] was ridiculed and hated and thrown into darkness by Rumsfeld and Wolfowitz for representing an alternative view," Frank Miller "continued to work with and respect Greenwood, and ask his counsel on all matter of concerns."[113]

Resistance came from other sources. While Miller was convinced the United States lacked the capacity to reform or train Iraqi police, Robin Cleveland felt the cost was too high. She was not the only one. When Dick Mayer and Bill Lantz presented a plan for thousands of police trainers for Iraq, Garner discussed the plan with Rumsfeld. When Rumsfeld was told what it would cost, he was dismissive and said the United States would not pay for it. No one senior to Garner was concerned about the Iraqi police forces sustaining internal security after an invasion.[114]

Garner also wanted funding ready for the estimated two million government employees in Iraq who should be kept on their jobs to keep the country operating. That meant money had to be available for salaries. Garner kept asking, but with no response from the NSC or OSD. Following that would be a broad array of reconstruction projects, many of which could not be identified in advance; some would have to be implemented immediately. Where would the money come from? Garner was frequently told by those in OSD that Iraqi oil revenues should finance such projects, as if such revenues could be activated immediately after an invasion.

General Tim Cross suggested operational considerations were driving strategy, not the reverse. It was clear to him that regime removal must be integrated with regime replacement; instead, it was sequenced in time with a transition from Central Command to ORHA, suggesting ORHA was more than a small headquarters. Cross knew that Great Britain wanted a UN resolution supporting a war in Iraq with the commitment of UN support. But that was not the view of senior officials in the Bush administration Garner went to for support. Both Garner and Cross continued to plead for more internationalization and civilianization of ORHA, but without greater UN involvement there were few non-Americans coming forward to join the Coalition. And with the bad blood between the Pentagon and the rest of Washington, there were few civilian specialists joining ORHA in the numbers required.[115]

George Ward and Chris Milligan were concerned about getting into southern Iraq as an invasion force advanced toward Baghdad. The crucial period for humanitarian assistance could develop before the war was over; critical reconstruction tasks might be required early. They wanted to know if ORHA personnel could follow the invasion forces into the southern populated areas around Basra. Ward was monitoring a humanitarian operations center (HOC) that Lew Lucke had helped establish in Kuwait. With a few humanitarian groups in Kuwait augmented by Civil Affairs military personnel trying to bring them together, the HOC had potential. Ward wanted to get ORHA personnel to Kuwait to provide organizational assistance.[116]

Compared to Ward and Milligan's aggressive efforts on humanitarian assistance and reconstruction, the Civil Administration pillar was lagging in early March, but not because Garner reduced it to a lower priority. From the beginning Garner and Adams were focused on regime replacement, but they were not supported by policy guidance and resources from OSD and the NSC. Wolfowitz and Feith suggested the Iraqis aided by expatriates and projected oil revenues would put the country back on its feet with little assistance from the Coalition. Garner and Adams were not so sure.

Iraq had some twenty-three Iraqi ministries. With Garner's approval, Bob Polk, his C-5 planner, and Sherri Kraham divided responsibility for the ministries between the Reconstruction and Civil Administration pillars. Ministries with hard infrastructure, such as Housing and Transportation, were aligned with the former and those related to governance were aligned with the latter. When Polk moved on to other tasks, Kraham became Garner's principal coordinator for the ministries. The critical shortcoming was specialists who understood the nature of the respective ministries from comparable U.S. government agencies. Those who had joined often had little or no regional understanding of Iraq or the nature of its ministries. USAID, aided by those from the Corps of Engineers like Browning and Strock, could tackle the ministries that involved hard infrastructure, but Garner had less expertise with the governance of Iraq.

He went to Wolfowitz and Rumsfeld and suggested that someone should put together a world-class group of experts—some academics, some practitioners—to guide governance policy for Iraq. They suggested that Liz Cheney, an assistant secretary of state, might take on that role. Garner was enthusiastic and met with Cheney, who brought with her Scott Carpenter, an assistant secretary of state from the department's Bureau of Democracy and Human Rights. As the vice president's daughter, Cheney would not herself deploy to Iraq, but she worked with Carpenter to set up an appropriate group. Garner wanted the group to deploy with ORHA, but Carpenter needed time to assemble it; the group would arrive after Garner was replaced.[117]

During the first few weeks in March there was a flurry of meetings in the NSC about Iraq. No one from ORHA, including Garner, was invited. One of the key issues at the meetings was who to put into power in Iraq after Saddam Hussein was removed. Doug Feith and those in his office had developed a proposal for a group they referred to as the Iraqi Interim Authority, soon known as the IIA. Feith knew Rumsfeld was "convinced that the United

States should hand authority over to the Iraqis as quickly as possible." The question was who to put on the IIA.[118]

Other than the senior Kurds, it would take time to identify capable leaders in Iraq—those Feith and others referred to as "internals." The discussion among the Principals and Deputies concerned the Iraqi opposition leaders who were not in Iraq, referred to as "externals." Those from State and the CIA had strong reservations about the externals, and, in one exchange, Deputy Secretary of State Armitage declared that the externals would lack legitimacy with the Iraqi people and should be excluded from the IIA. Feith observed that Rumsfeld bristled and responded that the IIA would be a temporary body and that its success would determine its legitimacy. Rice asked Feith to work with Zalmay Khalilzad to discuss the issue with the opposition leaders.[119]

Miller and Greenwood set up NSC meetings for President Bush on 10 and 12 March that would cover a number of topics on Iraq. On the tenth, they would address how the Iraqi Foreign Ministry would be represented in international bodies; the administration of justice and police; and de-Ba'athification. Feith would also address the IIA. On the twelfth, they would cover the defense establishment: intelligence services and the Iraqi army. Feith later wrote that the IIA concept was approved by President Bush at the meeting with these key points:

- The IIA should be formed as soon as possible after liberation and include internals, Kurds, and externals.
- The internals were to be fully represented, which could be ensured by convening a political conference on liberated Iraqi territory.
- The United States should allocate responsibilities with the IIA by agreement.
- The IIA would serve only in the interim, until a more fully representative government could be established through elections.
- The United States and IIA should work together on appointing ministry officials and the United States should transfer each ministry to Iraqi control as soon as possible.
- The United States should sponsor a UN Security Council resolution that would authorize the IIA and otherwise support Iraqi Reconstruction after Saddam's overthrow.[120]

Although Garner did not attend the meeting, he and Feith had previously discussed an interim Iraqi government and agreed on the use of Kurds, externals, and internals. It would soon be up to Garner to put the IIA into operation.

During the 10 March meeting, Rumsfeld told Miller, "I'm not going to let you brief the [Iraqi] army. That's a Defense issue." Greenwood had made the slides for that briefing and Miller felt they were his to brief. When they sent the slides to the Pentagon, those working for Feith put an OSD logo on them and it was Feith who gave the briefing on 12 March. Miller detested Feith and was livid that Rumsfeld passed the slides to him to brief. Beyond the logo, however, Feith made no changes and the key points were unchanged: the Iraqi intelligence services, Republican Guards, and any intelligence organization guilty of atrocities would be disbanded. But the Iraqi regular army would remain; one slide bullet stated that they could not "afford to put 300,000 men [the Iraqi army] on the street with rifles."[121]

Miller knew that Garner had told the Principals and Deputies Committees that he wanted to retain the regular army and use them as construction battalions and for other tasks, while vetting the officers and NCOs to determine whom to keep. Despite the tension among some participants in the NSC briefings, they agreed that the regular Iraqi army could not be disbanded with the other military and intelligence organizations.[122]

As the NSC worked on last-minute policies and with the invasion of Iraq imminent, General Eric Shinseki, the U.S. Army Chief of Staff, took an interest in post-conflict plans for Iraq. When General Steve Hawkins returned from Kuwait with Colonel Tony Puckett, his Plans officer, to attend the ORHA rock drill, they stopped by the Pentagon to see General Casey on the Joint Staff and told him about their difficulties with Central Command. Then they went to see General Shinseki. All four of them had served in the Balkans during the 1990s. Shinseki asked Hawkins and Puckett about their plans. Puckett had been working on projections for stability operations (he did not use the term occupation forces) in Iraq following the invasion. The figures they gave Shinseki were 207,000 American forces and 80,000 other Coalition forces, almost 300,000 altogether. As they were unsure what countries would provide the 80,000 troops, the American portion was all the more critical.[123] The number was close to that which Major Kojac had provided to the NSC earlier in 2002.

On 25 February, less than a week after the rock drill, Shinseki testified before the Senate Armed Services Committee. When asked about the size of occupation forces for Iraq, he replied that it would probably take several hundred thousand soldiers. The numbers he had from Hawkins and Puckett had been reinforced by the U.S. Army Center of Military History, which had provided comparable figures from historical models. Within days, Paul Wolfowitz testified before Congress that such figures were far higher than required. At the time those in OSD were projecting that only about 30,000 troops would be required in Iraq by the fall of 2003.

When Rumsfeld heard about Shinseki's testimony, he called Garner late the following evening. "Did you see the Shinseki statement?" he demanded, referring to the numbers of forces the general had said would be required after the invasion. Garner answered that he did.

Rumsfeld: "Do you believe that?"

Garner referred to his time in Iraq with Operation Provide Comfort in 1991. "I owned 5% of the real estate in Iraq and we had 22,000 soldiers in our Coalition. Never did I have enough troops for what I was doing. If you work all the real estate [in Iraq], Shinseki is right on."

Rumsfeld was unmoved. "Thank you very much. That's all." And he hung up.[124]

As Shinseki monitored the planning conducted by JTF-4 and ORHA, he directed his staff to form a "post stability operations subgroup" to assist Garner and ORHA. Eleven Army officers were pulled from West Point, the war colleges, and other military schools and sent to the Pentagon the second week of March. It was a well-intended effort, but it was too late to make a substantive contribution. Garner did not know about the group; Shinseki was not aware Garner was due to fly to Kuwait in mid-March. Once Garner and ORHA departed, the group Shinseki had directed to assist him was disbanded and the members returned to the respective schools.[125]

THE MEDIA

With war imminent and his profile rising in Washington, it was inevitable that Garner would have to deal with the media. Through early February, senior PAO personnel in the Pentagon told him to keep a low profile and avoid the press. But articles were appearing about ORHA and Garner. He knew that if he did not talk to the press, they would write about ORHA anyway but would get the facts wrong and perhaps become hostile. Nate Jones, Garner's PAO, had been meeting with Torie Clarke, the Defense Department spokeswoman. He requested assistance, but there was only one PAO slot on the JMD and those in the Pentagon told him to get PAOs from other agencies.

Jones tried going directly to the State Department, but when Barbara Bodine joined ORHA, she made it clear that any requests for personnel from State would go through her. In compliance, Jones asked her for four PAOs, one to work with each of the three functional pillars and one to work for him. Bodine knew the importance of PAOs and forwarded his request to State. The first volunteer released to ORHA was Caitlin Hayden, but when she arrived Bodine assigned Hayden as her aide rather than to Jones. She promised him more PAOs from State, but none would arrive until ORHA was in Kuwait weeks later; Bodine's personal staff had trumped the requirement for a PAO section.[126]

Jones obtained approval from Torie Clarke for Garner to provide a background briefing to the press. Clarke wanted to be open and support Garner, but others in OSD were reluctant. A press meeting was not approved and scheduled until 11 March, just days before ORHA was to deploy. Garner and Bates went to the Pentagon PAO office to discuss what they could say with an Air Force colonel. He took them to a briefing room and introduced Garner and Bates to a group of nineteen journalists. Garner made an opening statement on the purpose of ORHA and its functional pillars and regional components.[127]

When asked if ORHA was big enough, Garner said, "You are never as big as you would like," and explained they would rely on contractors, ideally Iraqi contractors, to assist with the work. When asked about Ba'athists, Garner said he might use some of them, but he thought that "the bad ones would be gone," consistent with what he had said during ORHA meetings. When asked what sort of government would follow an invasion, Garner said any elective government the Iraqis wanted should evolve naturally. When asked about funding, he indicated that that had not yet been worked out in detail, but he anticipated a supplemental budget from Congress. When asked about Iraqi oil, Garner made it clear that the oil belonged to the Iraqi people, although it should be used to help fund reconstruction projects in Iraqi and civil infrastructure, particularly the police and the other ministries, specifically to pay salaries to keep them on the job.[128]

When asked how much time would be required, Garner said that while he intended to remain for several months only, he anticipated the full task of regime replacement could take years. When asked to compare Iraq to Afghanistan, Garner replied that Iraq was much more sophisticated than Afghanistan and would require a more sophisticated response on the part of the United States. Bates added that there would have to be interim evaluations and international involvement.[129]

A seemingly innocent question related to the role of Iraqi expatriates. Garner said a group of Iraqis based in Michigan could probably provide some assistance, but when pressed on details about Ahmed Chalabi's Iraqi National Congress, Garner responded, "There is no specified role for the INC, there is no specified role for Chalabi. I don't have a candidate. The degree to which those people play or are allowed to play, we'll determine later."[130]

That night Feith called Garner in a rage. "You've done some real damage to the INC and to Ahmed. . . . You were very non-supportive in your press conference. And by the way, who told you—you could have a press conference?"

"I didn't know I had to ask, number one." Garner responded. "Number two, if we're getting ready to go somewhere we ought to tell everybody what we're doing because the word is going to get out anyway. But the fact of the matter is I'm neither a supporter nor a non-supporter of the INC or Ahmed Chalabi. I don't have a candidate. And by the way, your boss doesn't either. Because I have heard Rumsfeld say several times, 'I don't have a candidate.' And Doug, if this really is bothering you so much . . . then you have a choice. You can say you don't want me and I'll go back to my company. I don't have a problem with that at all and you can put another guy in my job."[131]

Feith backed down, but the next day Garner found he "was embargoed from speaking to the press." Wolfowitz also called to express concern but was smoother than Feith: "Maybe we just need to be more careful next time when we refer to the INC, because they've been very supportive." Garner refused to be scolded by Feith, but Nate Jones took the rebuke as a bad omen. Jones anticipated a more draconian response to the interview and he would be proven right.[132]

A challenge Garner had not anticipated just prior to deployment was a request from Senators Joseph Biden and Richard Lugar to appear before the Senate Foreign Relations Committee. That committee had interviewed those opposed to an invasion of Iraq, notably General Tony Zinni, who had testified in February that the planning for post-conflict Iraq was inadequate and that an invasion would be a mistake.[133] Some ORHA members suggested Senators Lugar and Biden could be potential allies. But Garner had been in front of congressional committees before; he knew that it would not be a simple office call and could easily absorb a full day. He knew he would have to clear with the Pentagon the positions he might take or be asked about before he testified. After his encounter with the media and the response from Feith and Wolfowitz, preparing for congressional testimony could become complicated and time consuming. In Garner's mind, it was too late for such an appearance and no one in the Pentagon or the NSC encouraged one. But putting off Senators Lugar, Biden, and others on the committee would not gain him congressional allies for the future.

PREPARING FOR DEPARTURE

During his last few days in the United States, Garner wanted to focus on pre-deployment training and processing. By the first week in March, Colonel

Costello, the colorful and forceful C-4 for ORHA, had made arrangements for a chartered aircraft and a departure date of Sunday, 16 March. Everyone had to have a medical exam, shots for the region, passports, visas, and military orders. They also had to go through Preparation for Overseas Movement (POM), which included an issue of individual equipment and training for chemical protection. Military personnel would go through weapons qualification; civilians would do so as an option. Costello made arrangement for equipment issue at Fort Myer, Virginia, and the training at Fort Meade, Maryland, just north of Washington for 12–13 February. At Fort Myer everyone was issued two sets of military uniforms, chemical protective equipment, sleeping gear, and mosquito nets—enough to fill three military duffel bags. Some chose not to draw all the equipment, such as the mosquito nets—and would suffer for it later. Military personnel helped civilians pack their duffel bags as lines moved briskly. Then everyone was off to Fort Meade for NBC (nuclear, biological, chemical) training.

The group was accommodated in a nearby motel; that evening was the first time ORHA had a group meal together. Military lawyers assisted with wills and powers of attorney. Garner, Adams, and Bates organized last-minute meetings. The next day there was more NBC training. Afterward Garner gathered everyone together for a pep talk. Barbara Bodine appeared in her camouflage uniform with her name over one pocket and "Ambassador" over the other. Before Garner could finish his talk she asked, "How long do we have to wear theses costumes?"

Garner replied, "Barbara, those are not costumes; they are uniforms. And you don't have to wear one if you don't want to do so." It was an unfortunate exchange.[134]

Simon Elvy and Philip Hall, the two British diplomats with no prior military experience, were fascinated with the experience of being under military control with sergeants giving everyone orders. They were surprised to be issued American uniforms and wondered if they could wear them legally. They enjoyed going to the pistol range to fire their fifteen rounds for familiarization. Elvy had never fired a pistol before. But they could not imagine carrying a weapon in Iraq given their diplomatic status.[135]

The Raytheon contractors came to see Garner to discuss the communications package for Iraq. They brought a prototype of the mobile communications platform built onto the back of a large pickup, soon dubbed the "Batmobile." Garner and Bates were more comfortable with the Raytheon contract than others in ORHA, in part because General Abizaid had shown them what Raytheon had packaged for Central Command.

Colonel Randy Conway, the C-6 Communications officer, had little problem with the communications arrangements if Garner and Bates were satisfied. But that was not the case for his subordinate communications personnel. Differences would intensify in Kuwait, the more so once ORHA deployed into Iraq. Major Keith June, Conway's deputy, had a conventional background and more experience with high volume communications. He had strong reservations about outsourcing communications support, but his views were unknown to most of those in ORHA at the time.[136]

More people joined ORHA just prior to deployment. At Fort Meade, Garner was approached by Ambassador Robin Raphel, then serving as the vice president of NDU. She said she would like to join ORHA. Raphel had served in Pakistan and as ambassador to Tunisia. She was an economist and suggested she could work with the Iraqi Ministry of Trade. Garner liked her and signed her up. She would fly to Kuwait after the ORHA main body.[137]

Sue Hamrock, a GS-14 civil servant from the Department of Commerce, joined ORHA just in time to go to Fort Meade. Her specialty was Asian trade issues, but when asked to volunteer for ORHA, she signed up and joined the Civil Administration pillar. When Hamrock and Raphel met in Kuwait they would make a good team, and when they deployed into Iraq, they would stay on for most of a year, longer than many others.[138]

On the firing range at Fort Meade, Mike Ayoub met Terry Sullivan, a former Vietnam-era SEAL and a civilian contractor who said he had no idea why he was with ORHA. Another latecomer with Sullivan was Harold Rhode from a think tank within OSD. A talkative academic type, Rhode contrasted with the stoic Sullivan. Both were joining as part of Mike Mobbs's Civil Administration pillar—with no obvious role. Later Ayoub learned that Sullivan and Rhode were sent by OSD to support Ahmed Chalabi and the INC in Iraq.[139]

When buses took everyone back to the Pentagon on Friday, 14 March, they loaded duffel bags into their cars, cleaned out their desks, and signed off their computers. Their temporary spaces in the Pentagon would soon be undergoing renovation again for someone else. There were a few final meetings, but they were short as everyone wanted to get out of the building by late afternoon to spend some time with their families before the Sunday departure. The last event on Friday was a large meeting in an auditorium in the Pentagon. It was really a pep talk with Garner as the key speaker. He talked about their mission, the opportunity to help change Iraq and the Middle East for the better, and how proud he was of those who had joined ORHA to go with him. Everyone was euphoric and Garner's charisma flowed.

Earlier that Friday morning, Garner left Fort Meade for the Pentagon with a small group to brief Rumsfeld on the Iraqi ministries. Petite Sherri Kraham had fired a pistol for the first time that morning and hit her target each time. For the meeting with Rumsfeld she wore her new military uniform and made the main presentation. Kraham made a cute figure and was articulate, but it was clear there was much yet to be done.

Of the twenty-three Iraqi ministries, Garner would deploy with senior advisors for only seven: Agriculture, Education, Health, Finance, Central Bank, Irrigation, and Housing, with Steve Browning responsible for the last two. Bob Gifford from Justice had been identified for the critical Ministry of the Interior, which controlled the Iraqi police, but Gifford would deploy later. Of the remaining sixteen ministries, Garner had requested assistance from the State Department, which had proposed eight names, most of them retired ambassadors. Garner had aligned their names with several ministries. That left eight more to fill (see Table 1).

Rumsfeld said little during the briefing, but on Saturday morning he called Garner and said he had some problems with some of the people listed as ministry advisors. Garner expressed surprise and frustration. He had less than half of those he needed on hand. It had taken significant time and energy just to get names for those who would follow. For Garner it was too late to restart the process; he was not leaving behind an adequate rear party that could line up more people.

When Garner met Rumsfeld on Saturday, the secretary expressed concern with the ministry advisors scheduled to join ORHA, particularly the eight designated to come from the State Department. He wanted the senior positions filled by personnel from Defense, his people. It made no sense to Garner to have such diverse positions for Iraq filled from a single agency of the U.S. government. ORHA was supposed to be an interagency organization and he knew that Defense did not have the aggregate talent to fill all the key positions, and he said so.

"Who will you find in Defense to work with the Agriculture Ministry? Who will you get for Education? Who will you get for Electricity?"

Rumsfeld admitted that he had not spent enough time with Garner discussing the issue and asked him to think it over on his way to Kuwait and consider filling some of the positions with Defense personnel.

Then he asked Garner, "How are you going to handle de-Ba'athification?"

"Well, I need a policy on that from you," Garner responded.

"I don't have one, but we will get you one," Rumsfeld responded. "How will you handle it until we do?"

Garner paused and thought, "Well, the Kurds will take care of the bad ones in the north and the Shiites will take care of the bad ones in the south. Those in Baghdad we will have to deal with." Remembering what he had learned

Table 1. 16 March 2003: ORHA Senior Advisors for Iraqi Ministries

Ministry	Senior Advisor
Ministry Coordinator	Sherri Kraham
Reconstruction Pillar	Lew Lucke; Deputy Chris Milligan
1. Agriculture	Lee Schatz: USDA
2. Education	Dorothy Mazaka: USAID (via Treasury)
3. Electricity Commission	TBD: USAID*
4. Health	Skip Burkle: USAID
5. Housing & Construction	Steve Browning: USACE
6. Industry & Minerals	Tim Carney: DOS Contractor**
7. Labor & Social Affairs	TBD: USAID*
8. Irrigation	Steve Browning: USACE
9. Military Industry	TBD: DOS*
10. Higher Education/Sci Research	TBD: USAID*
11. Information	TBD: DOD*
12. Defense	TBD: DOD*
Civil Affairs Pillar	Mike Mobbs; Deputy Marc Powe
13. Planning	David Dunford: DOS (Ret)**
14. Trade	Robin Raphel: DOS**
15. Justice	Williamson: DOJ**
16. Transportation & Communications	TBD: USAID
17. Culture	John Limbert: DOS**
18. Foreign Affairs	Keith Kenton: DOS (Ret)**
19. Interior	Bob Gifford: DOS**
20. Central Bank	George Mullinax: Treasury Contractor
21. Finance	David Nummy: Treasury Contractor
22. Oil	TBD: DOD*
23. AWQAF/Religions Affairs	David Jamison: DOS**
Governance	Scott Carpenter, DOS**

NOTES. AWQAF = Ministry of Religious Affairs; TBD = to be determined; USDA = U.S. Department of Agriculture; USAID = U.S. Agency for International Development; USACE = U.S. Army Corps of Engineers; DOS = U.S. Department of State; DOJ = U.S. Department of Justice; DOD = U.S. Department of Defense.
*Not designated.
**Not ready to deploy.

from an intelligence briefing on the Ba'athists, he added, "We know that in each ministry the Minister and the senior personnel manager are hard core Ba'athists. We will remove those and retain the rest to keep the ministries operating."

Garner knew there were others who were bad, but they would be removed as they were identified. Rumsfeld did not suggest otherwise.[140]

On Sunday morning at 8:00, 167 people arrived in the Pentagon South

Parking lot, each with their duffel bags and suitcases; four had already gone forward on the advance party and twelve others would depart on a military aircraft carrying equipment for ORHA. Of those then with ORHA, half were active-duty military. Of the civilians, only fifteen came from the Department of State, less than 10 percent of the total, and only three of those were Foreign Service Officers (Bodine, Ayoub, and Gfoeller); a few more FSOs would follow later. The rest from State were civil servants, many with limited overseas experience. Most of those from USAID were contractors; Maxwell, Lucke, and Milligan were the only FSOs, and Maxwell and Lucke had retired and were technically recalled in a contractor status. From the other American agencies, there were only one or two representatives each. Only a dozen spoke Arabic and none did so as their first language. There were no Iraqis in the ORHA main body; those in the IRDC would depart later.

In the parking lot there were a dozen men in ill-fitting suits with plastic transmitters in their ears, each with a bulge on his hip; they were not ORHA personnel. They were a personal security detail. Word spread that the Secretary of Defense would soon be there to send them off. A car arrived and Secretary Rumsfeld emerged and moved comfortably to the center of the ORHA group. Garner quickly announced his arrival and Rumsfeld shook some hands, made a few remarks, and was quickly whisked away. Bags were loaded onto trucks, there were last-minute goodbyes to family and friends, then everyone boarded buses for Andrews Air Force Base. During the waiting period Kim Olson, Garner's executive officer, began a journal that later became the basis for a book on her experiences in Iraq. The chartered aircraft had twenty first-class seats that went to the general officers, ambassadors, and full colonels, the latter gaining influence in ORHA at the expense of their counterparts from the other agencies.

Garner had told everyone several times they would make history. In general there was an apolitical atmosphere within the group. The notable exception was Harold Rhode, who had just joined ORHA with no designated role. Waiting in the terminal, he told one member of the group from the UK that the operation in Iraq was just a battle, not the whole war: "The goal is Tehran." The diplomat was more amused than concerned by the comment. Rhode was seated next to Ayoub on the plane and Ayoub learned more about him and noted in his journal:

> I spend the 14-hour flight in the company of Harold Rhode. An ardent Zionist and ideologue, Rhode was tasked by OSD/Feith's Office to serve as liaison to the Iraqi opposition parties. (This function doesn't appear on any of the ORHA org charts.) Our seats being adjacent to

one another, I have no place to hide, and we spend the hours debating Mid-East politics. . . . He said the real objective was not Baghdad, it is Tehran, and after that Assadville [Syria]. . . . In the course of his diatribe I learned Tom Warrick was branded persona non-grata due to his bias against Chalabi. Hence he and his plan were left on the curb in DC. No loss there either as OSD, according to Rhode, considers the State Near East Asia (NEA) Bureau as the enemy.[141]

For others the flight was enjoyable, social, and uneventful. The service was good and several people had brought scotch or bourbon along, only to be told they could not enter Kuwait with alcohol. They promptly broke out the bottles and shared the contents. Soon it was clear who drank scotch and bourbon and who did not drink. It was a long flight, but there was camaraderie with much to discuss and many experiences anticipated.

While on the plane, Garner reflected on his meeting with Rumsfeld and the latter's desire to have the senior advisors for the Iraqi ministries come from within the Department of Defense. Garner and Ron Adams reviewed the list of positions and appropriate skills they would require. Garner called General Strock over and asked him to help him fill in names of engineers for senior advisors for the Ministries of Irrigation, Housing and Construction, Transportation and Communications, and Electricity. Then he looked at Strock and said he needed someone for the Iraqi Ministry of Defense until Walt Slocombe deployed. He knew Strock had served in infantry and Special Forces assignments before becoming an engineer and had served in combat in Panama and Desert Storm. Furthermore, Strock had established strong rapport throughout ORHA; Garner felt he could handle several roles concurrently.

As an organization, the original OSD design for ORHA had three functional components (humanitarian assistance, reconstruction, and civil administration) and three regional components (ORHA-South, ORHA-North, and Baghdad Central), not dissimilar to the bureau system in the NSC and other government departments and agencies. Ron Adams brought in specialists— legal, PAO, contracting, and auditing sections to aid and complement the functional components, and several Middle East military Foreign Area Officers to complement the regional components. Garner and Adams added an operational staff with a C-1 for personnel, a C-2 for intelligence, a C-3 for operations, a C-4 for logistics, a C-5 for plans, and so on, common to military commands but foreign to civilian government. Those with a military background considered the C-staff an appropriate addition for staff management. To those from other parts of government, the C-staff was not only foreign; it appeared to dominate the functional and regional components without appreciating their requirements, setting up friction that would follow during deployment.

The grand scope of tasks for ORHA—engaging the political, economic, and social structure of a foreign country and culture—required a broad range of talent. From Garner's first meetings with the Deputies Committee, he sought personnel from across the spectrum of government, although his inner circle was heavily weighted with his military peers, which some civilians and the media considered cronies. Garner resisted the efforts of Rumsfeld and Feith to have a disproportionate number come from the Department of Defense, but when the other agencies were reluctant to provide the personnel requested the contribution from Defense was disproportionate for interagency balance. Although a coalition, ORHA was almost exclusively American except for a few from the United Kingdom; there was no UN representation and initially no one of Iraqi extraction.

In March, Garner had few specialists on Iraq. In uniform, he had only two Foreign Area Officers. Most of those from State, USAID, and other agencies were civil servants; only half a dozen were Foreign Service Officers. Altogether he had only a dozen that spoke Arabic with varying proficiency.

With a monumental task and so few people, ORHA's relationship with other organizations in Washington was critical and awkward. The NSC had functional and regional officers, but no counterpart to the C-staff, thus the substantive connection was limited to Garner's visits to see Rice or Hadley, and Adams's visits to those a level lower. But Rice did not wield the organizational clout Garner needed. The real management drive was a level lower with Frank Miller and the ESG. When Garner went directly to Rice, Miller felt bypassed and stood down the ESG as ORHA stood up; Miller also objected to funding for an Iraqi police program. Cleveland and Abrams remained involved longer, but they were disappointed when ORHA displaced their work and Cleveland blocked the money ORHA needed.

The work on Iraq by State and USAID was of marginal value to Garner. Powell and Armitage wanted to help, but they were at odds with Rumsfeld and the Pentagon. The FOI project was voluminous and eclectic but had no planning format; without Warrick, who was not allowed to join ORHA, it had little utility. The efforts by Mike Ayoub to update State's Political-Military Plan for Iraq received little support and made no contribution. Wendy Chamberlin, at USAID, helped Garner in the beginning, but she shifted to other projects after she felt marginalized at the rock drill. Overall the interagency support for Garner and ORHA was inadequate.

Garner's relationships within the Pentagon were also problematic. He did not like Doug Feith or those under him in the Policy component of OSD, and he preferred to work directly with Rumsfeld and Wolfowitz. Supposedly Feith's office had developed plans for a new regime in Iraq, but no such plans were passed to ORHA. Nor did Garner have a developed relationship with the Joint Staff or General Casey. Only reluctantly did Casey support Garner with the Joint Manning Document and he had refused military communications support. The decision to outsource communications to Raytheon would lead to serious problems.

Those in ORHA left for Kuwait with enthusiasm, and with a popular and respected leader in Jay Garner. But they were poorly prepared and lacked support in Washington for the tasks ahead of them. They anticipated the military commands would provide the assistance they needed once they arrived, but they would be poorly supported there, too.

4
IN KUWAIT

I don't have the intellectual energy to talk about Phase IV right now.
—Lieutenant General David McKiernan, 16 March 2003

Kuwait was the primary staging base for the invasion forces. The main ground attack would be conducted from there by General McKiernan's Combined Forces Land Component Command (CFLCC). Special Forces formations would invade from Jordan and would guide and support Kurdish formations from northern Iraq. There were substantial supporting units to assist the combat forces with regime removal, and those units could play a key role with regime replacement. The complexity and management of the latter would require imagination and energy—which would be slow to appear.

Jay Garner and ORHA arrived in Kuwait just a few days before the invasion, an operation that would overwhelm Iraqi forces and take Baghdad in less than a month. During that period, ORHA would continue to plan, prepare, and build cohesion, as it more than doubled in size. Its members sought common purpose with their military counterparts for Phase IV operations, originally defined as Transition, then as Post-Hostilities, and by spring as Post-Conflict. No one used the term "regime replacement." Several military organizations had a critical contribution to make alongside ORHA: JTF-4 under Generals Whitley and Hawkins and the 352nd Civil Affairs Command under General Kern; to be effective, they would have to be supported by engineer, military police, transportation, signal, and logistics units. But that linkage did not develop.

The emphasis on invading and defeating the Iraqi army absorbed much of the attention and energy of senior military commanders and their staffs, leaving too little for what would follow. Many military officers knew ORHA was deploying to Kuwait and would move into Iraq when combat operations were complete, but they had little grasp of the small size of ORHA or its limitations. They assumed that responsibility for Iraq could simply be handed off, allowing Coalition military formations to go home. In Washington, senior political and military leaders either did not understand the deficiencies and time constraints with which Garner had to contend, or they chose to do little to assist him.

Nor would the traditional civilian organizations associated with post-conflict—agencies of the United Nations, other international organizations, and NGOs—contribute as much as anticipated. Garner and those in ORHA sought to be the catalyst for a unifying effort, but there were many obstacles, a few of their making but most beyond their control. Inattention and inadequate support for ORHA while it was in Kuwait laid the seeds for additional challenges.

At the Kuwaiti International Airport on 9 March, Colonel Mike Williams met the advance party Garner sent to Kuwait: retired General Floyd "Buck" Walters, Colonel John R. Martin, Steve Browning, and Marc Powe. Williams was the Chief of Staff for JTF-4 and he was accompanied by two contractors from Kellogg, Brown, and Root, better known as KBR. It was soon clear that traveling in Kuwait was complicated as the Coalition had imposed a two-vehicle rule for local transportation, with each vehicle required to have one shooter. A shooter was anyone armed with a pistol or rifle. Several months earlier, two American contractors had been shot and killed while driving in Kuwait. Contractors were free agents and on their own as far as American military commanders were concerned, but any time Americans were killed, it received attention in Washington. As a result, force protection standards were increased for all American military and government personnel.[1]

The two KBR contractors would quickly recruit a crew to support ORHA. The Department of Defense LOGCAP system normally arranged such support overseas, and KBR held the major contract under LOGCAP. In the Pentagon, Colonel Robert Costello, Garner's C-4 Logistics officer, had projected $68 million for ORHA life support with 350 people for one year. If the number exceeded 350 or the time and nature of support had to be altered, the LOGCAP task order would be amended.[2]

With the ORHA main body a week behind him and aware there was no space available for it on the Coalition military installations, Walters had KBR arrange accommodations for ORHA at the Hilton Hotel south of Kuwait City. He then took his advance party to network with the military commanders and staffs located at various locations in Kuwait. When the ORHA main body arrived on 17 March, Walters and the advance party met them with a convoy of vehicles on the taxiway, having made arrangements to bypass customs at the airport. Accompanying the charter flight was a military cargo aircraft with an officer and NCO from Costello's C-4 shop with supplies and equipment; also on that plane was a National Intelligence Security Team (NIST) that included representatives from several intelligence agencies. The NIST kept a low profile and many in ORHA would take little notice of it—and consequently made little use of it.

With the advance party, the main body, and those on the cargo aircraft, the total strength of ORHA upon arrival in Kuwait was just under two hundred, half active-duty military and the rest civilians. Two-thirds of the military personnel were officers, with fourteen full colonels and Major General Strock. The civilians were also rank heavy, with ten of senior executive service or ambassadorial rank; another twenty were GS-14/15s. There were twenty-eight women, most of them civilians from State and USAID. Only three were non-Americans, all diplomats from the UK. Major General Tim Cross, who had been with ORHA in the Pentagon, and his executive officer, Lieutenant Commander Lewis Notley, arrived a few days later, increasing the number to five. There were no Iraqis then with ORHA.[3]

Over the next five weeks, ORHA would double in size; most of the additions would be civilians, mainly Americans with a few Australians and later with a few Iraqi expatriates. There was no substantive rear party for ORHA in Washington beyond Colonel Craig McLane, Larry Hanauer from OSD, and Mike Shane, a contractor for administrative support. Liz Cheney's group under Scott Carpenter had little interaction with ORHA as it formed in Washington, nor did the IRDC expatriates in Crystal City under Abe Shulsky: some would join ORHA in Kuwait later in April.

While it was disappointing that Camp Doha could not accommodate ORHA personnel, the Hilton was not unpleasant. At one end of the complex was a tall hotel building with several restaurants, boutiques, and a large swimming pool; the front entrance had a security detail, and the complex was already surrounded by a steel fence. There were fifty separate villas, each with three to six bedrooms along the beach south of the main hotel. ORHA occupied twenty of the villas at the far end of the complex, providing some isolation from the journalists living in the main hotel building.

Each villa was designed for luxury, but ORHA needed to exploit the space; soon the bedrooms were crammed with extra beds and the living rooms converted into office spaces, operations centers, and meeting rooms. The kitchens were packed with cases of meals ready to eat (MREs), bottled water, plastic plates, and flatware. Private baths became communal. Internally, the villas gave up luxury for function. Those from USAID with Lew Lucke and Chris Milligan in the Reconstruction pillar chose to go to the Radisson Hotel a few miles north closer to Kuwait City. Many of them would work at the

Humanitarian Operations Center (HOC) in downtown Kuwait rather than at the Hilton.

The evening the main body arrived, they attended a buffet and met military officers who came from Camp Doha. In contrast to the formal attire in the Pentagon, the group dressed more casually, some more than others. Barbara Bodine attended the buffet barefoot with her toenails freshly painted. The meal was followed by a general meeting to address specifics about Kuwait. The meeting opened with two directives: "Manage your expectations" and "It does not have to make sense—it's policy." Living arrangements at the Hilton were addressed: where and when to eat, laundry, the lack of phones and computers, and no access to the internet or SIPRNET.[4]

Military pistols would be issued to military personnel and civilians with military or police experience. All travel would be in convoys of at least two vehicles. Because war could commence any time and Iraqi missiles with chemical warheads could reach the Hilton, everyone was to have their protective masks available at all times. Costello described the large logistics compound at Camp Arifjan south of the Hilton, but few beyond his C-4 section would ever go there. Of interest to those from State was information about the U.S. Embassy, which some would visit for coordination and to use its facilities.[5]

Military personnel in the other commands in Kuwait were subject to General Order Number One, which specified there would be no alcohol in theater. But Colonel Mike Murphy, the ORHA judge advocate, determined that it did not apply to personnel assigned to ORHA. It was a fine distinction that would not be challenged, but it would later cause some friction with military commands.

The day the main body arrived in Kuwait, President Bush announced that Saddam Hussein and his two sons should leave Iraq within forty-eight hours or the United States would attack at a time of its choosing; American citizens in Kuwait, Jordan, and Israel were advised to depart those countries for their safety. At the UN, the secretary general directed the withdrawal of UN peacekeeping forces on the Kuwaiti border and WMD inspectors from Iraq. Meanwhile in the UK, there was turmoil in Parliament over the invasion with one cabinet minister, Robin Cook, resigning in protest.[6]

The next day at breakfast, there were few Kuwaitis or other Arabs present in the Hilton's restaurant. The friendly waiters and waitresses were from the Philippines; the hotel guests were Westerners, mostly American, and half of those from ORHA. The rest were contractors working for the Coalition, other businessmen, and journalists. Navy Captain Nate Jones, the PAO for ORHA, determined that 2,000 registered journalists were in Kuwait covering the approaching conflict, many living in the Hilton. When they learned more about ORHA their interest would grow, but in mid-March media attention was on the impending war, not on its aftermath. Later, when journalists expressed indignation that the Coalition had not taken a greater prewar interest in postwar Iraq, few would remember their own lack of interest.[7]

COORDINATION WITH MILITARY COMMANDS

On 19 and 20 March, four senior officers came to the Hilton: Major General Albert Whitley, McKiernan's British deputy for post-conflict operations, Brigadier General Steve Hawkins of JTF-4, Brigadier General Jack Kern of the 352nd Civil Affairs Command, and Colonel Kevin Benson, the C-5 Plans officer for CFLCC. Only two other staff officers from CFLCC had previously made direct contact with ORHA, Colonel Marty Stanton and Lieutenant Colonel Bob Newman, who attended the rock drill in February. They all knew that CFLCC and ORHA were subordinate to Central Command.

Garner and others in ORHA knew that the Central Command plan for Iraq was designated 1003V, and that the CFLCC supporting plan was designated COBRA II, signed 13 January, a week before ORHA was established. In the Pentagon, Garner had received a copy of Annex V to 1003V which addressed Interagency Cooperation, but it was dated 1 October 2002, with little guidance for Phase IV Post-Hostilities.[8]

COBRA II briefly addressed Phase IV with three sub-phases to stabilize Iraq and to support "an emerging provisional government" assisted by "a Coalition Joint Task Force-4" and then to "conduct redeployment operations." CJTF-4 was the element General Hawkins or General Whitley would control; most officers still called it JTF-4. No mention had been made of ORHA in the COBRA II plans or annexes. It was unclear to Benson what relationship there would be between CFLCC, JTF-4, and ORHA. It was anticipated that international organizations and NGOs would play a role in Phase IV, but arrangements for that role were undeveloped.[9]

Benson knew that the October 2002 Annex V to 1003V was a shell, and he had begun work on a supporting plan for Phase IV in January designated Eclipse II, which he wanted to show to ORHA. By that time, JTF-4 under General Hawkins was in Kuwait under CFLCC control. The day the ORHA main body arrived in Kuwait, Benson approached General McKiernan for guidance.

McKiernan, ready to launch his attack, tried to put him off. "Kevin, I don't have the intellectual energy to talk about Phase IV right now."

When Benson persisted, McKiernan said, "Kevin, soldiers are going to die in Phase III. I have to work on that."

"But sir," Benson responded with extraordinary clairvoyance, "soldiers are going to die in Phase IV!" McKiernan just walked away.[10]

During the meeting with ORHA, Benson opened with a PowerPoint slide presentation with six conditions for Eclipse II:

- Key [Iraqi] regime leadership removed;
- Coalition forces physically controlling Iraq;
- Iraqi army and Republican Guards defeated or capitulated;
- Vital life support infrastructure sustained;
- Stability operations ongoing;
- Conditions established for CFLCC Battle Handover to CJTF-7.[11]

No one in ORHA had heard of CJTF-7. Presumably it was a large headquarters that would replace CFLCC, comparable to a field army. It should be a considerably more capable headquarters than General Hawkins's and General Whitley's CJTF-4, which COBRA II had originally designated to take over from CFLCC. But after studying the fifty-eight-man JTF that Hawkins brought to Kuwait in January, it was clear something larger would be required, commanded by someone senior to a one-star; thus the designation CJTF-7 in Eclipse II, with additional assumptions:

- Policy guidance and Endstate will evolve;
- Asymmetric threats to CFLCC forces will exist in Phase IV;
- Non-DoD agencies will contribute to Iraq recovery operations;
- Some essential infrastructure (rail, airports, power generation, bridges) will be damaged due to combat operations;
- IO/NGO will request CFLCC support with at least force protection, CSS [Combat Service Support], and HA [Humanitarian Assistance] supply distribution;
- Coalition will participate in Phase IV;
- The TPFDL flow (modified) will continue until completion;
- IO/NGO already operating in Iraq, but some will cease activities by A-day.[12]

The presentation stated that CFLCC would establish unity of effort with Coalition government agencies, IOs/NGOs through the HOC, and existing Iraqi organizations and administration, such as the Iraqi provincial administration. Upon regime collapse, they would help establish an interim authority for Iraq to interface with Iraqi ministries and assist with reintegration of Iraqi military forces.[13]

One of Benson's slides indicated that twenty maneuver brigades would be required for Phase IV, remarkable as only fourteen maneuver brigades were under CFLCC control for the invasion of Iraq.[14] No mention was made of where the additional six brigades would come from. Two slides listed six lines of operation for end-state conditions:

- Security
- Rule of Law
- Governance and Administration
- Infrastructure Recovery
- Perception
- Humanitarian Relief and Assistance[15]

It was clear Benson was grappling with the scope of regime replacement. He assumed other government agencies would participate, but the presentation did not specify any organization to manage an interagency effort. To assist a transition from CFLCC to another organization, Eclipse II indicated that Phase III (Decisive Operations) and Phase IV (Post-Hostilities) would overlap in time as maneuver forces advanced into Iraq, and rear areas would be handled as part of Phase IV while areas in which combat was conducted would still be part of Phase III. Within Phase IV, Eclipse II identified three sub-phases: IV-A (Stability Operations), IV-B (Recovery), and IV-C (Transition). The slide indicated CJTF-7 would begin assuming control during IV-A. During the transition, CFLCC formations would shift from offense to stability, then to support operations.[16]

In his part of the briefing, General Whitley indicated the military ground forces would establish a forward headquarters at the Baghdad airport that he referred to as the Early Entry Command Post, or EECP. Once it was established, it would include work and living spaces for 100 members of ORHA during the period necessary to establish a more substantial headquarters in the city. Those present from ORHA asked what military formations would remain in Iraq once ORHA was on the ground and what the command relationships would be between those formations and ORHA. Benson could not provide answers as he had little information or guidance from General McKiernan or from Central Command. Benson did not know what headquarters would be designated CJTF-7. For those in ORHA, the Eclipse II presentation suggested more questions than it answered. Benson would return to the Hilton for subsequent meetings in an effort to resolve them.

Officers from Hawkins's JTF-4 and Kern's 352nd Civil Affairs Command also attended the meetings. Garner and others in ORHA knew there were problems with Hawkins and Kern that would influence what their organizations could contribute. From the rock drill, they learned that JTF-4 had difficulties with Central Command in Tampa and with CFLCC in Kuwait, driven by the late formation of JTF-4, its lack of material assets, and the awkward personal relations Hawkins had established there. On a weekend trip home to Orlando in January, Garner drove to Tampa to meet Hawkins and his deputy, Colonel Jimmy Rabon, before they deployed to Kuwait. Garner liked Rabon, but felt it might be hard to work with Hawkins. Putting General Whitley in charge of Phase IV operations for CFLCC had not improved the situation. The tension observed at the rock drill in February between Hawkins and Whitley was not resolved by March.

At first glance, the situation with General Kern and his 352nd Civil Affairs Command appeared better than for JTF-4. There would soon be four Civil Affairs brigade headquarters and close to a dozen Civil Affairs battalions in theater with almost two thousand Civil Affairs soldiers and Marines, while Hawkins had only fifty-eight military personnel for JTF-4. But most of those CA units had been attached to other commands, leaving Kern only a few hundred soldiers under his control, not a great deal more than what Hawkins had. There were pros and cons with the distribution of CA units. The traditional CA task for several decades had been humanitarian assistance, with CA units attached to the maneuver formations. The military government function was resident in the staff sections of the 352nd and the CA brigade headquarters, but it was an undeveloped capability. With the CA battalions detached, the 352nd and several of the CA brigade headquarters could have oriented their efforts on the more complex aspects of regime replacement; but that was slow to materialize.

In part that was due to Kern's inability to get on well with senior officers in Kuwait and his earlier command problems in Afghanistan. Kern objected to his loss of control of the CA battalions, which absorbed energy he might have better devoted to governance tasks the Coalition would soon take on. The overall focus on invasion was instrumental in retaining the use of the Civil Affairs efforts for humanitarian assistance.

For humanitarian assistance and civil administration tasks, both JTF-4 and the 352nd would require other military formations they could manipulate if not fully control: military engineers, medical, MP, and logistical units. There were substantial numbers of those units in Kuwait, but like the CA battalions, they were attached to the maneuver formations to support the invasion. The Eclipse II plan Benson presented did not address a handoff of such support formations to JTF-4 or the 352nd Civil Affairs Command (CACOM). Nor was there a provision for such formations to join ORHA.

On 24 March, just after Whitley and Benson provided the briefings on what the military commands had planned, Garner received a fax from Doug Fcith's Policy office in the Pentagon proposing a modification to Garner's organization. The wire diagram showed three organizations under ORHA: the Operations staff, the pillars (Humanitarian Assistance, Civil Administration, and Reconstruction), and an added component for Policy with four subordinate elements of its own: Executive Infrastructure, National Governance, Local Governance, and External Relations. But there were only two names on the list for the additional structure: Scott Carpenter for National Governance and Steve Goldsmith for Local Governance. Neither had yet deployed to Kuwait. The policy component on the wire diagram was an outgrowth of what Garner had originally called the Liz Cheney group to establish governmental policies for Iraq. In that sense the information in the fax was positive, but there was no indication as to who would come with that component beyond Carpenter and Goldsmith.[17]

Another addition on the line diagram adjacent to the Policy Component connected by a dotted line was something listed as IIA. On a subsequent slide, IIA was defined as the Iraqi Interim Authority, with several subordinate components: Interim Political Governors, Municipal Authorities, a Constitutional Commission, a Judicial Council, and National Ministries, all presumably Iraqis. There were no names associated with the IIA module, nor significant detail to further define it. Other slides addressed the ministry advisors for Iraq, indicating that the Defense Department and the White House (rather than State or USAID) would fill fifteen senior positions for the ministries, but without people yet identified for those positions. Feith's advice grated on Garner; the good ideas for demanding tasks were not resourced with the people ORHA needed.

Subsequently, Garner received more information from Feith on the IIA concept: it was to be "the legitimate governmental authority of Iraq, pending the Iraqi people's ratification of a new constitution and election of a new government in accordance with that constitution" recognized by the U.S. Government. No mention was made of the Coalition. The proposal suggested the IIA would have a twenty-one-person council, which would elect from among themselves a presiding chairman. Eleven of the twenty-one seats will be allocated to Free Iraqis, those who had lived outside areas controlled by Saddam Hussein's government.[18]

The documents from OSD-Policy focused at the national level, suggesting that the Iraqi government would be reformed top-down with the provincial and municipal governments to follow. Garner's concept had been just the opposite: to implement local elections to develop a basis for a constitutional convention of delegates from local elections, then move on to national elections, a bottom-up approach. It was a profound difference that should have been settled months earlier. Separately, military planners within Central Command were thinking about a bottom-up approach similar to Garner's.

EXPANDING AND REORGANIZING ORHA

As Benson, Hawkins, Kern, and their officers converged on ORHA, it was clear Garner needed a better connection with the Central Command headquarters in Qatar to achieve the unity of effort everyone required. Within two days, he sent Ron Adams and a small group to fine-tune guidance and support. Concurrently, he needed to reorganize his C-staff for greater efficiency and establish relations with the media. He also needed to establish security for his people. When Admiral Robb told him at the rock drill in February that Central Command could not provide security for ORHA, Garner did not challenge him. But the war had started and there were limitations to the protection provided by the Hilton Hotel and the two hundred pistols that Colonel Costello had brought.

Major Larry Miller, a Marine infantryman in the ORHA C-2 section, was directed to develop a security plan. He put together a small team and worked with Colonel Costello to contract for a security detachment that Central Command would not provide. Miller wanted internal security within the Hilton complex and a personal security detail (PSD) for Garner. In the Pentagon, Miller had tried without success to obtain security teams through American contractors DynCorp or SAIC. Finally he arranged a contract with a UK firm, Global Risk Security, for twenty guards from Nepal, retired soldiers from the Gurkha regiments; eventually ORHA would have a hundred Gurkhas for internal security.[19]

Miller wanted American military rifles for the Gurkhas, but U.S. military commands in Kuwait refused his request for automatic rifles and a few light machine guns, forcing him to go to a contractor in Pakistan. The weapons had to transit Pakistan and Kuwait with customs costs before they arrived at the Hilton. Miller was annoyed at such complications considering there were American weapons in storage at several locations in theater and in the United States. Miller also needed uniforms and related gear for the Gurkhas. He could not dress them in American uniforms because they were not American soldiers. In Kuwait he found a source that could make tan uniforms with accessories. [20]

Eight bodyguards arrived within a few days to serve as the PSD for Garner. Led by Lyon Olivier, seven were South African ex–special force police officers; another was from the UK with a similar background. They were large, powerful men who kept to themselves. Two or more were always on duty near Garner and tried to be within sight of him at all times; they also served as his drivers. At first their attention annoyed him, but eventually Garner developed a bond with them as a stoic part of his inner circle.

At the Hilton, each C-staff section was established in one of the villas along the beach, with their personnel packed into the bedrooms upstairs. A military style tactical operations center (TOC) was set up in one villa and would soon operate seven days a week with someone on duty twenty-four hours a day, which might have surprised General Casey, who had questioned if ORHA would run 24/7. In another villa, the C-4 and C-1 staffs combined to form an Administration and Logistics Operations Center (ALOC). It was the most crowded building at the Hilton, as Colonel Costello wanted all his people in the same building and chose to live there himself rather than with the other colonels. Lieutenant Colonel Robert Mott, ORHA's military doctor, set up a medical aid station in such a villa. The C-2 established the NIST in another, which few would visit. A villa that many ORHA personnel would visit in a quest for computer support, often in frustration, was occupied by the C-6 Communications section.

Next there was a staff reorganization driven in part by Tom Baltazar's role (see Figure 3). In the Pentagon, Garner referred to Baltazar as his chief of staff, but Jerry Bates was in control of the Operations Group, now called the C-staff and in that sense Bates was the chief of staff. Recognizing Baltazar's experience and talent, Bates offered him two positions on the C-staff, deputy chief of staff working directly for Bates to help manage the staff, or C-3 Operations officer to manage the operations in ORHA. While other primary staff officers were full colonels, Jim Torgler, the C-3, was a lieutenant colonel, somewhat marginalized by the more dominant personalities of the colonels on the staff. Baltazar chose the C-3 position and Torgler became his deputy.

Colonel Glen Collins joined ORHA just prior to deployment and took the deputy chief of staff position. Paul Hughes, who had led the Strategic Initiatives Group, aka the Law Firm, was redesignated the ORHA C-5 Plans and Policy staff officer, and Bob Polk was reduced to a planner working as much for Baltazar as for Hughes. Tom Gross was designated the Strategic Communications staff officer. [21]

Under George Ward and Mike Mobbs, the Humanitarian Assistance and

Office of Reconstruction and Humanitarian Assistance

as of 1000/14 April 2003

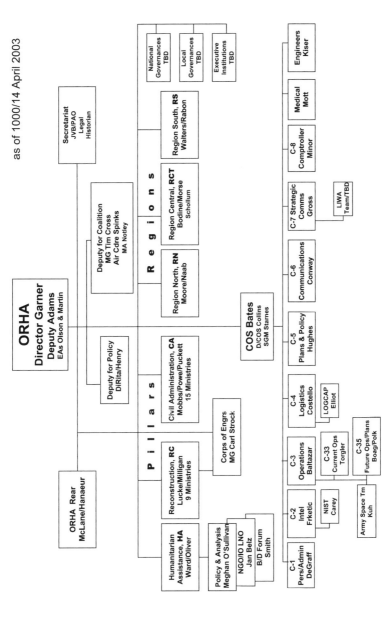

Figure 3. Office of Reconstruction and Humanitarian Assistance, as of 1000, 14 April 2003.

Civil Administration pillars were each allocated a villa for their offices. The Reconstruction pillar under Lew Lucke and Chris Milligan set up at the Radisson Hotel; having a separate location from the rest of ORHA initially left them out of some meetings. But much of their work was in the HOC downtown closer to the Radisson. Those in Ward's Humanitarian Assistance pillar also had interests at the HOC, and many commuted there daily by an escorted hotel bus. Those associated with the three pillars were slower to get established than the C-staff sections, partially as they were last to obtain computer support.

When the C-6 section arrived in Kuwait, it issued eighty-eight laptop computers, mainly to the staff sections to get them up and running. Only a few laptops were left for the three pillars. That seemed appropriate to Colonel Randy Conway, as little could be achieved without operational staff sections. But everyone needed a computer in Kuwait, and it would take several weeks to obtain more. The priority given to military personnel for computers sent the unfortunate message to the civilians in ORHA that they were second-class citizens.[22]

As a coalition, ORHA expanded incrementally with the arrival of Andrew Goledzinowski, a diplomat from Australia. Cordial in style and with an easy smile, he was willing to do whatever Garner asked but expressed a preference to serve as the senior advisor for the Iraqi Ministry of Culture. Garner chose to use him to form a secretariat for Garner's inner circle that would include Cross, Adams, and Bates, the ORHA legal section under Colonel Mike Murphy, the PAO under Navy Captain Nate Jones, and a Joint Visitors Bureau. A week later another Australian, Colonel Keith Schollum, joined Goledzinowski's Secretariat. When it became clear that Colonel George Oliver could not work effectively for Barbara Bodine in the Baghdad Central group, Schollum replaced him as Bodine's deputy.[23]

THE INVASION OF IRAQ

On 19 March, the war began with Coalition air attacks throughout Iraq. Marines quickly secured the oilfields just across the border. Some oil wells were rigged with explosives, but only a few were on fire when taken. From the Hilton, jet aircraft bombing Iraq could be heard passing overhead from bases south of Kuwait. The next day several Scud missiles from Iraq hit Kuwait and Saudi Arabia but with little effect. Missile attacks continued for the next week with the threat of chemical warheads, and ORHA personnel went through frequent masking drills in response. Only a few Scuds passed near the Hilton and none hit nearby. Concerned with chemical attacks that never materialized, Garner had Buck Walters sustain NBC training that had begun a week earlier at Fort Meade.

The day the war began, General Adams with six others flew to Qatar where Central Command had its forward headquarters. It was the first direct contact with that headquarters since Garner and Bates visited in early February. Admiral Robb met Adams with Colonels Fitzgerald and Halverson, Lieutenant Colonel Agoglia, and Majors Tom Fisher and Ray Eiriz. Fisher's Phase IV briefing impressed Adams, but it was clear the concepts presented were not reinforced with preparation and resources. Much of the assets in theater useful for Phase IV tasks—engineers, civil affairs, military police—were attached to maneuver forces for the invasion. There was no clear plan to pass them to ORHA, JTF-4, or the 352nd CACOM for Phase IV tasks. Admiral Robb was aware of disconnects and told Adams he would send a planner to Kuwait to sort them out.[24]

When Adams returned to the Hilton, the reorganization of the C-staff was complete, but it did not please Adams. He had had greater access to Baltazar, Hughes, and Gross when they were independent of the C-staff, but now they were all under Bates's control. As Adams told Garner about his trip to Qatar, he did not say much about the changes in ORHA and avoided the appearance of any internal friction. But it was not clear to Adams what his role was. With Bates in charge of the C-staff and most of ORHA's military personnel, Adams shifted his focus to the three pillars, to working with the government in Kuwait, and to the NGOs setting up at the HOC in Kuwait City.

Soon he was making daily trips to the HOC to assess its potential and manage the ORHA relationship. The HOC had been set up in a new elementary school in Kuwait still under construction. Furniture and phones were scarce. But otherwise the school classrooms and offices were adequate for the NGO and other international groups trying to prepare for the aftermath of war. It was not clear that anyone was in charge of the HOC, but with ample space every group found a place to set up. Civil Affairs officers tried to provide coordination without seeming to take over, a sensitive issue with NGOs. George Ward wanted a strong UN presence, but the UN sent only a few people to Kuwait with a few more working from other countries in the region, all of them trying to keep their distance from the Coalition.

On one visit, Adams met the Spanish ambassador to Kuwait. He told Adams that the Spanish government wanted to assist the Coalition, but he explained that the Spanish population was opposed to the invasion and Spain could not provide forces for that role. If the invasion went well and received positive media coverage, he thought Spain could send forces for the stability phase. Adams was courteous; he acknowledged the complexities faced by the Spanish government and told the ambassador that he believed Spain could make a substantial contribution to the Coalition.

Thinking about what might be needed most after the war, Adams asked the ambassador about providing Spanish Guardia Civil police forces to help establish law and order in Iraq and to assist with retraining the Iraqi police forces. From his experience in Bosnia, Adams knew that Spain, Italy, and Argentina had paramilitary national police for which there was no counterpart in the United States. Police forces in those countries had a cohesive command structure in contrast to the eclectic American law enforcement system. Adams knew Spain had a track record for deploying such paramilitary police in cohesive modules to assist with law enforcement on peacekeeping operations as he had observed in the Balkans. Such paramilitary police forces could potentially assist with interim law enforcement and train an Iraqi police force to replace them. Adams had been disappointed in American efforts to take on such police tasks in previous operations.

The Spanish ambassador had assumed the American-led Coalition would want a military contribution from Spain such as an infantry brigade; initial queries from the Pentagon and State Department had suggested as much. The NSC and OSD had shown little imagination about internal security requirements for Iraq and had refused funding for interim police and police trainers. Adams suggested the best contribution for Spain was not maneuver forces, but deployable police forces. The exchange with the ambassador was positive and informative, but it consummated no commitment or design. Spain's eventual contribution for the Coalition was an infantry brigade, not a police formation.[25]

Captain Nate Jones, the PAO for ORHA, wanted to have Garner talk to the media. He considered Garner and ORHA a good news story. But after the Pentagon briefing in which Garner denied a Chalabi connection and annoyed Feith and others, he had been forbidden to speak to the media. Jones knew that avoiding the media would eventually hurt Garner and ORHA and pleaded with Torie Clarke, the senior PAO for Defense, for a reprieve. Each time Clarke responded that OSD, probably meaning Feith, did not want Garner talking to the press. Jones felt Clarke was sympathetic but had her hands tied.[26]

At the Hilton, Jones found Colonel Guy Shields with the Coalition Press Information Center (CPIC). Shields had with him thirty-five members of the 328th Public Affairs Operation Center, an Army Reserve unit. The CPIC was in Kuwait to provide media support for the CFLCC, but it remained under the control of Central Command. With overcrowding at Camp Doha, the

CPIC went to the Hilton as had ORHA. Shields gave Jones a workstation within the CPIC with a classified internet capability. Both Jones and Shields coordinated with Torie Clarke at the Pentagon, who in turn worked with Ari Fleischer, the spokesperson for the White House, who was later replaced by Scott McClellan. Jones knew Dan Bartlett, Fleischer's assistant and other PAOs at the Pentagon, Brian Williams and Colonel George Rhynedance. He knew the PAO at Central Command, Colonel Jim Wilkinson, and Colonel Rick Thomas at CFLCC. Each of them had a PAO team except for Jones upon his arrival in Kuwait.[27]

Jones had requested interagency support from the Department of State through Barbara Bodine, but when State sent Caitlin Hayden, Bodine took Hayden as a personal aide. Upon departure from Washington, three more PAOs joined ORHA and two more joined a few days later in Kuwait. Portia Palmer and Joanne Giordano came from USAID, but they were assigned to the Humanitarian Assistance and Reconstruction pillars. Juliet Wurr and Meghan Gregonis arrived from State. Gregonis, who spoke some Arabic, had been working in the embassy in Israel. But Bodine also took Wurr and Gregonis to expand her staff, just as she had taken Hayden.[28]

Of the six PAOs joining ORHA, only John Kincannon ended up with Jones. Coming directly from the U.S. embassy in Pakistan, most of Kincannon's eighteen years of service had been in the Middle East: Jordan, Yemen, and Saudi Arabia. He spoke Arabic and his wife was a Palestinian American; she had been with him in Pakistan until they were evacuated after the 9/11 attacks (later, in Washington, she joined Warrick's Future of Iraq project). Kincannon was quiet and worked well with Jones with a moderate workload in March due to the media embargo; that would change in April with an important arrival.[29]

While Jones encountered challenges putting a PAO shop together, ORHA's staff sections had their own communications problems. The C-6 staff section was responsible for computer and phone systems. Colonel Conway had a dozen military personnel in the C-6, four officers and a group of junior NCOs. Major Keith June was Conway's deputy. Although Conway and June were both from the army, their backgrounds were different. Conway spent his career in Special Forces with a low-volume communications requirement; June spent his in conventional Army formations that had greater demands.

In February, Major June was on the Army G-6 staff in the Pentagon before going to Kuwait to work on communications at Camp Doha, noting the large number of American communications formations in Kuwait. He then received a call from the Pentagon stating that on his return he would be assigned to ORHA and would ship back to Kuwait with it. June asked instead to remain in Kuwait and link up with ORHA when it arrived, but his request was refused. He returned to Washington and reported to Conway on 3 March, then deployed back to Kuwait two weeks later.[30]

In contrast to the stoic Conway, June was appalled by the communications arrangements for ORHA. He urged Conway to request a military signal unit, but Conway knew such a request from Garner and Bates had been rejected by General Casey, and he was resigned to go with Raytheon as Garner and Bates directed. June believed such a course would be a serious error given the robust support ORHA would need. He continued to urge Conway to put in a request for such support to Central Command or CFLCC, arguing there were lots of military communications units in theater. He was convinced contractor support would be inadequate. Conway did not think ORHA would be in Kuwait long and require extensive communications support; what was required could be handled by his small staff section until Raytheon personnel arrived in April.[31]

Like Major June, Lieutenant Commander Angela Albergottie joined the C-6 just prior to deployment; her role was obtaining and issuing communications equipment. Once in Kuwait, she quickly issued the laptops the C-6 had brought to Kuwait and then ordered more. As the computers arrived in batches of twenty over several weeks, Albergottie continued to meet the demand, also supplying related equipment required as ORHA expanded. The initial allocation of laptops went to military personnel, however, before civilians in ORHA came to the C-6 villa to request their own. In this it was apparent that Conway did not care for civilians. Albergottie's crusty personality made her appear adversarial to some civilians, but that was the way she treated everyone. She worked hard to get them what they needed; often it just required time.

With computers came the requirement for email and internet capability, which was not available in the Hilton beyond a few workstations in the lobby. Conway never established a networked system at the Hilton for internal ORHA email, but by the end of March his NCOs had set up an internet café with a dozen workstations in one of the villas. It required ORHA personnel to rely on personal email accounts for message traffic, however. With a limited telephone system in the Hilton, the C-6 staff obtained cell phones, but these could not reach the military command posts in Kuwait nor would they work in Iraq; the C-6 shop had to obtain another set for the next deployment.

Email communication with military units in Kuwait was also challenging. Military units used two systems, unclassified (NIPRNET) and classified (SIPRNET); in Kuwait most of the work was done on the classified system.

Conway could not get approval to set up a SIPRNET system in the Hilton for ORHA, partially because many of the civilians lacked the security clearance required for SIPRNET use. But without such a system it was almost impossible to communicate with military units in Kuwait or on classified matters with those back in the United States, even if one had the right clearance. Major June finally got Conway to allow him to ask Major General Lowell Detamore, the C-6 for CFLCC, for SIPRNET support, but Detamore denied the request because ORHA was not a subordinate unit when the request was made. Conway was not surprised by the response and made no effort to force the issue. The CFLCC staff did offer ORHA some workstations with SIPRNET at Camp Doha, but with the hour drive and the two-car and shooter requirement, no one took advantage of the offer. The several classified computers that were in the Hilton were not managed by the C-6 staff.

The C-2 Intelligence staff section set up a SIPRNET workstation in the villa it occupied in the Hilton. Conway thought they were violating security procedures, but he did not push the issue. Colonel John Frketic had joined ORHA, replacing Colonel Deb Taylor as the C-2 officer just prior to deployment to Kuwait. Frketic had a counter-intelligence background and was naturally suspicious of everyone. He was smart, but his intensity and self-important manner put people off. He was an authoritarian leader and tended to bully his staff, which was soon unhappy.[32]

Frketic was obsessed with operational security and he had a condescending disdain for anyone without a top secret clearance. Those without the highest clearances were not allowed to enter the C-2 villa. By the end of March, some of them became aware that the C-2 had a SIPRNET station and asked to use it. Under pressure, Frketic reluctantly set aside an hour each morning and each evening for those with the proper clearance. But two hours a day was inadequate for those who needed access. Guy Shields allowed only Nate Jones to use the SIPRNET workstation in the CPIC.[33]

ORHA members from USAID, State, Treasury, and Commerce had worked with classified computer systems compatible with the SIPRNET system, available at the U.S. embassy. Bodine, Raphel, Ayoub, Hamrock, and a few others went to the embassy to use the classified system there, but going to and from the embassy was almost as time-consuming as going to Camp Doha; and even there access was limited.[34]

Those from the UK and Australia, as well as other non-Americans who would join later, were not authorized to use SIPRNET. The UK sent out a communications team with their counterpart system known as FIRECREST and set it up where Cross shared an office area with Garner, Adams, and Bates.

But FIRECREST worked only with other UK elements and was not compatible with SIPRNET. Coalition members from other countries would not have access to any classified system.[35]

All forms of communication for ORHA were inadequate. There were challenges with the media due to the misuse of PAO personnel and restrictions imposed by the White House and Pentagon. There were challenges for internal communications with limited computers, phones, and the lack of a LAN. And there were challenges communicating with classified systems; those problems would continue with greater consequences as the mission progressed.

COMMAND RELATIONSHIPS

On 29 March, just a few days after Adams returned from Qatar, Admiral Robb at Central Command sent his lead planner for 1003V, Lieutenant Colonel John Agoglia, to resolve complications identified in the meetings with Benson, Hawkins, Whitley, and Kern. As a lieutenant colonel, Agoglia was the junior officer in his first meeting at the Hilton. Having reviewed the situation with others at his headquarters, he proposed that ORHA be placed under the operational control of CFLCC. Bates, Hughes, and others were opposed to such a move. When Agoglia persisted, Hughes told him ORHA would not acknowledge such a command shift without a formal order. Hughes argued that ORHA had been formed by the NSC and the Pentagon and had comparable status to Central Command. McKiernan had been a colonel when Garner, Bates, and Adams were active duty generals. To place ORHA under McKiernan and CFLCC did not make sense to Hughes.[36]

Agoglia argued that the military assets that could best support ORHA were under CFLCC control. Putting ORHA under CFLCC would be the best way for CFLCC to manage support for ORHA. Agoglia's proposal took Colonel Benson and others on the CFLCC staff by surprise. The war was on and there was no zeal to take charge of ORHA or the fuzzy tasks that came with it. Benson's Eclipse II plan made no provision for ORHA, and with McKiernan fully focused on the war, Benson could not obtain guidance or authority to support or otherwise integrate ORHA with JTF-4 or the 352nd CACOM (see Figure 4).[37]

Merging the three would appear logical, if one did not have to take into account the personalities involved and the lack of command attention by Generals Franks and McKiernan. Even if they were merged as a single headquarters, they still had no subordinate MP, engineer, or logistic units necessary for humanitarian assistance, reconstruction, and civil administration in Iraq.

CFLCC Phase IV Assets

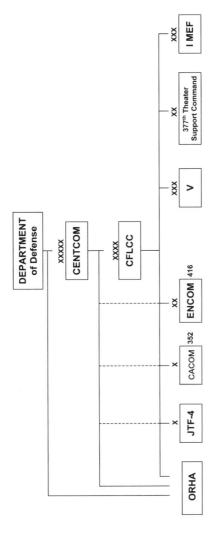

- ORHA was not under CFLCC control until April 2003; other units were under CFLCC control as they came into theater

Figure 4. Combined Forces Land Component Command (CFLCC) Phase IV Assets.

By the end of March, it was apparent that JTF-4 might be dissolved. Garner wanted personnel from JTF-4, but he did not want Hawkins. He contacted General Abizaid to request some of the JTF-4 colonels for ORHA. Abizaid was lukewarm and said he would look into it. A few weeks later, CFLCC sent four JTF-4 colonels to ORHA. The 352nd CACOM provided several Civil Affairs officers as liaison officers to ORHA, whom Baltazar placed in his C-3 Operations section. He had already gone to Camp Arifjan to visit the 352nd (see Figure 5).[38]

Meeting with several colonels there, he confirmed that CFLCC had distributed most of the Civil Affairs brigades and battalions to the maneuver formations. At Arifjan, General Kern had fewer than 350 soldiers under the 352nd. Baltazar knew Kern had been sent home from Afghanistan by the JTF commander there. Baltazar also knew that Colonel Marty Stanton, an infantryman serving as the C-9 Civil Affairs officer for CFLCC, had the confidence of General McKiernan, while General Kern did not. When Kern complained about the situation, Baltazar had little sympathy for him and felt the serious flaw was not replacing Kern in command if he was not respected by his boss.[39]

At Camp Arifjan, Baltazar learned about other formations located in Kuwait: military police and engineers. Of the former, there were three MP brigade headquarters in Kuwait: the 18th, 220th, and 800th, with seventeen tactical MP battalions, and other MP units for internment of prisoners of war. Altogether there were fifty MP companies, counting those with the maneuver divisions. For static security, the MP brigades were reinforced with six National Guard infantry battalions with a total of eighteen infantry companies (see Figure 6). Later, in Baghdad, one of those infantry companies would be assigned to provide perimeter security for ORHA, a task that might have been assigned earlier in the Hilton, rather than being forced to contract that task out to the Gurkhas.

There were also a large number of military engineer formations in Kuwait, including forty-two battalions and many separate companies, the majority attached to maneuver formations like most of the CA and MP units (see Figure 7). A notable exception was the 416th Engineer Command (ENCOM). In 2003, there were two ENCOMs in the Army structure, both in the Army Reserves: the 416th ENCOM aligned with Central Command and the 412th ENCOM aligned with the Pacific Command and Korea. Both were commanded by major generals. Each ENCOM was capable of managing up to sixteen engineer construction battalions.

The 416th ENCOM had deployed in 1990 during Desert Storm, and Central Command had attached it to the Third Army to provide construction support. The 416th remained in Kuwait after the war as part of Task Force

OIF CFLCC Civil Affairs Units

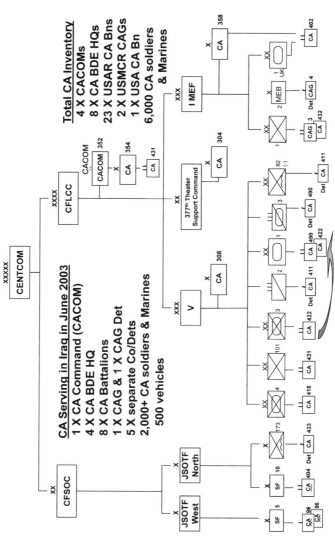

Figure 5. Operation Iraqi Freedom (OIF) Combined Forces Land Component Command (CFLCC) Civil Affairs Units.

OIF CFLCC Military Police Units

3 X MP BDE HQs
17 X MP Battalions
7 X MP separate Companies
(Total 50 MP companies)
7,000+ Military Police
As of 1 May 2003

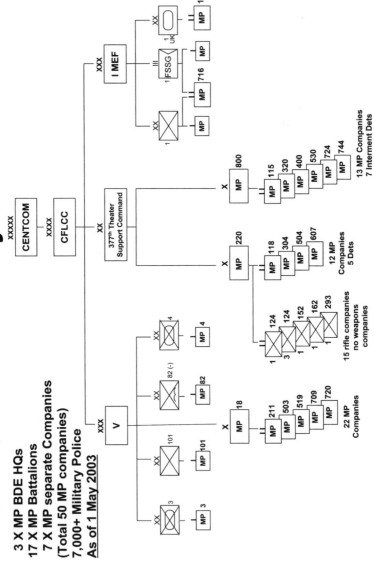

Figure 6. Operation Iraqi Freedom (OIF) Combined Forces Land Component Command (CFLCC) Military Police Units.

OIF CFLCC Engineer Units

1 X ENCOM HQ
4 X BDE HQ
7 X GRP HQ
42 X Battalions
16 X separate Companies
As of 1 May 2003

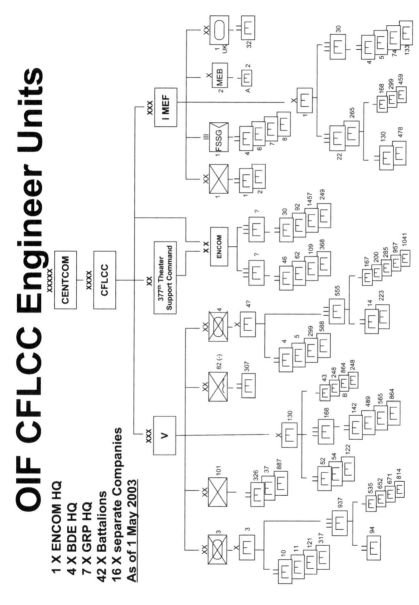

Figure 7. Operation Iraqi Freedom (OIF) Combined Forces Land Component Command (CFLCC) Engineer Units.

Freedom, which also had the 352nd CACOM, MP, signal, transportation, and other support formations under its control. The mission of TF Freedom was reconstruction in Kuwait following Desert Storm, which involved substantial contracting with civilian organizations. With its subordinate engineer battalions, the 416th ENCOM helped restore electrical systems for hospitals, fire and police stations, bakeries, schools, and other buildings; they repaired roads, plumbing, and other construction or reconstruction tasks. It worked with the 352nd CACOM in assessing postwar reconstruction, establishing work priorities, and arranging much of the contracting support required to fulfill its mission of rebuilding Kuwait.[40]

In January 2003, the 416th ENCOM was again activated and deployed to Kuwait to support Central Command, and again it was attached to the Third Army, reconfigured as CFLCC. By the time Baltazar visited Camp Arifjan, the 416th ENCOM had under its control two engineer groups and eight engineer construction battalions. Its tasks were to assist with the arrival of Coalition formations deploying into theater and to set up base camps for them in Kuwait as they prepared for combat operations; much of the work involved contracting.[41]

The senior engineers in ORHA were Major General Carl Strock and Steve Browning, both from the U.S. Army Corps of Engineers. They were trying to prepare for anticipated reconstruction work in Iraq. In accordance with the Bush administration and Pentagon policy, reconstruction tasks for Iraq would be outsourced to firms in the private sector. But the NSC had designated USAID with leading reconstruction efforts and managing the contracting process. Strock and Browning wanted to assist USAID, but it would take some time for them to adapt to the personalities involved. In the process, they worked on other engineer-related tasks.

Prior to Garner leaving for Kuwait, Rumsfeld had asked him to consider people in the Department of Defense to serve as senior advisors. On the plane to Kuwait, Garner turned to General Strock, who was to find senior advisors from the Corps of Engineers for four ministries. Shortly after arriving in Kuwait, Strock lined up Eugene Stakhiv for Irrigation, Pete Gibson for Electricity, and Dan Hitchings for Housing and Reconstruction, and moved Steve Browning from the latter to Transportation and Communications. That gave four of the twenty-three positions to civilians from the Corps of Engineers (Strock himself initially was to be a senior advisor to the Defense Ministry, but this position would go to Walt Slocombe when he arrived later for this purpose).[42]

Strock had a colorful background that soon became known around ORHA. In the early 1970s he served in Special Forces. According to one story, as a lieutenant he took his A-Team on a training exercise one winter at Fort Bragg, North Carolina, and during a night patrol approached a wide stream that had to be crossed. As the tallest member of his team, Strock waded across the chest-high, ice-cold stream. Reaching the other side he dropped his rucksack, crossed back over, and carried each of his team members on his back across the stream. It was only a training exercise, but the word spread throughout the Special Forces community, making Strock into a minor hero at Fort Bragg. Later Strock transferred to the engineer branch and commanded an engineer battalion in the 82nd Airborne Division in Panama during Operation Just Cause in 1989 and in Iraq during Desert Storm in 1990–91. When he was promoted to general officer, he moved to the Corps of Engineers Headquarters in Washington; from there he was tapped to join ORHA to assist with reconstruction and related tasks.[43]

As Strock and Browning lined up personnel from the Corps of Engineer for ORHA, they continued to find Lucke and Milligan from USAID reluctant to allow the Corps of Engineers a larger role in reconstruction for Iraq. Strock and Browning knew there would soon be plenty of reconstruction work to go around and so did not force the issue. They also knew that Lucke and Milligan were convinced that USAID personnel understood the nuances of construction projects in non-Western countries better than the engineers. That may have been true for some in the Corps of Engineers who had never served overseas, but not for Strock and Browning, who had extensive time working in other countries. Until he could gain acceptance with the USAID crowd, Strock monitored the engineer activities of Brigadier Generals Steve Hawkins and Robert Crear with their roles in JTF-4 and TF RIO.[44]

During one meeting in March, several military officers from CFLCC came to the Hilton with a presentation that laid out their reconstruction concept. Strock identified gaps between what CFLCC and ORHA were preparing and expressed concern that too much work was set aside for contractors early in the operation, when turmoil should be predictable and security questionable. Others in ORHA noted that funding for such contracting was not yet in place. Strock tried to coordinate the components that would begin reconstruction in Iraq, an enormous task without something like the TF Freedom formation used for reconstruction in Kuwait in 1991.

In late March, as the invasion was closing on Baghdad, Strock made a trip into southern Iraq with several personnel to observe the efforts to put out the oil well fires started upon the Iraqi withdrawal. The Coalition had anticipated as many as 1,000 oil well fires in Iraq based on Saddam Hussein's destruction of Kuwaiti oil fields during Desert Storm, but the plan was to have the Marines secure the oil fields early in the conflict and minimize the fires.[45]

Strock and his group drove north to the main border crossing into Iraq, an inconsequential location with little more than a customs office and a truck stop. There were only a few civilian cars and trucks parked at the border with little military presence. Kuwaiti border officials appeared uninterested and imposed no delay. There were only a few buildings on the Iraqi side of the border, with children along the road waving and hoping someone would throw them food or candy. Some did.

Once out of the small urban area, the surroundings reverted to the dusty, bleak terrain that had led to the border on the Kuwaiti side. The concrete highways in Iraq were better than expected. As the oil fields came into view, several fires could be spotted. Strock's group went to one oil well fire with trucks and heavy equipment nearby. A group of men tried to approach the fire to cap it. Cameramen and journalists were present as Strock made contact with General Crear of Task Force RIO, responsible for dealing with the Iraqi oilfields. The crew at that fire site was from the Kuwaiti Oil Company. Crear's address to the media explaining the oil situation in southern Iraq was formal, deliberate, and articulate. He stated that up till then there had been little damage to Iraqi oil production. Many in Iraq and Washington thus assumed that Iraqi oil exports would resume soon, providing a major source of revenue to cover the costs of regime change. There was no indication at the time that the flow of oil would be a problem later or that oil would not produce the anticipated revenues.

By the end of March, noticeable tension had developed in ORHA between the civilians and the military C-staff. Despite the effort to provide proper support, the C-staff encountered many delays that frustrated the nonmilitary members throughout ORHA. Some officers felt the civilians were whining, and it did not take long before their NCOs felt the same way. Garner had meetings with his key leaders each morning and there were also daily meetings for each of those within the pillars and regions, but the daily C-staff meeting, in which the civilians had little representation, was the basis for conducting much of the business in ORHA. To reduce the tension, Bates restructured the C-staff meetings with the primary C-staff officers seated on one side of a long table and civilian representatives from each of the three pillars and regions seated on the other. But even with each component at the table, military officers at the meetings outnumbered the civilians.

When squabbles surfaced, the response was to assign responsibility ("pin the rose" in colloquial terms) for researching or working out an issue. C-staff meetings often lasted an hour, covering issues that did not necessarily relate to everyone present. Military officers were accustomed to such meetings, but many civilians found the format onerous. Garner rarely attended C-staff meetings, and when he did Bates still sat at the head of the table and ran the meeting; Garner observed and spoke by exception.

A frequent problem at the C-staff meetings was someone getting carried away with their particular issue, as with Colonel Costello on a detailed logistical issue or Lieutenant Colonel Polk with an arcane planning concept. Costello had a forceful personality and a thick skin, oblivious to the annoyance he caused. His particular pet peeve was the irregular flow of people joining ORHA in Kuwait, which caused a constant search for accommodations and increases to personnel support. He was at odds with what ORHA really needed—more people and sooner rather than later.

Polk could be long-winded. On one occasion, he droned on about promoting a fusion cell to integrate the efforts of ORHA's components—a good concept but the wrong forum to discuss it. Bates suggested the issue had been covered adequately, but Polk persisted. Finally Baltazar, impatient, exclaimed, "Cut away, Bob, cut away," a metaphor relating to a freefall parachute malfunction that required the main parachute to be cut away in order to open the reserve. Colonel Jimmy Rabon, representing JTF-4 at the meeting, then muttered from the back of the room, "Put that shovel down, Bob. Put it down." Embarrassed, Polk sat down.

Polk's inability to make a more compelling case for a fusion cell was unfortunate. Since joining ORHA, Polk was constantly aware that it had inherited few planning products from OSD or any other military or civilian agency, nor had ORHA created many. He knew that the fast pace of building, organizing, and deploying ORHA to Kuwait had made mid-term and long-term planning nearly impossible. Although ORHA had people with experience and talent, they had not been harnessed for detailed planning.

In an ideal situation, the resident planner would have greater access to the senior leaders to provide guidance and mentorship for planning, but Polk did not establish such a relationship with ORHA's busy leaders. Garner talked frequently to Paul Hughes, but Polk did not work for Hughes in the Pentagon, and after the staff reorganization, when Hughes was designated the C-5 Plans officer, Polk was assigned to work for Colonel Baltazar, the C-3 Operations officer.[46]

The Humanitarian Assistance pillar group also met daily. Their object was to empower the UN and NGOs to aggressively participate in the post-conflict tasks, but those organizations did not want to be controlled by the Coalition. The best that could be done was to coordinate with them at the HOC. By design, no one was in charge of the HOC and interaction was by consensus, although CFLCC had provided a few Civil Affairs officers to help with coordination at the HOC. It was only as a meeting center for sharing information and coordinating efforts that it resembled the operations center suggested by its acronym.

Garner understood the reluctance of the UN and NGOs to come under his direct control, but what he wanted was control over the Disaster Assistance Response Team (DART), which USAID had deployed to Kuwait. Normally a DART had no more than a dozen people, but USAID had sent sixty-five people for this one, which would follow combat forces into Iraq and make assessments for humanitarian assistance. Garner was annoyed when the DART wanted the same autonomy as the UN and NGOs, preferring to work directly for USAID headquarters in Washington. In protest, Garner called Andrew Natsios, the administrator of USAID, but to his surprise Natsios balked at putting the DART under Garner's control. Finally, Garner called Secretary of State Powell, to whom Natsios was responsible. Under pressure, Natsios told the DART to work with Garner, but the lack of enthusiasm there led to poor linkage, and the DART nevertheless remained independent.[47]

General Kern and other Civil Affairs officers were concerned that there would be security problems for civilian groups attempting to provide humanitarian assistance. The military plan was to bypass populated areas and rush to Baghdad, but much of the humanitarian work would be in the urban areas where there would be no military forces to provide security. Military reserves for the invasion were limited and Kern had to make it clear, as it had been made clear to him, that those reserves were to be used to support military operations, not to provide security for bypassed areas.

After Desert Storm in 1991, Shiite and Kurdish revolts in southern and northern Iraq were brutally repressed by the Iraqi army; over a million civilian refugees fled toward the borders of Turkey and Iran. Those in ORHA and Civil Affairs anticipated that, in response to the invasion, large numbers of Iraqis would either flee internally or cross Iraq's borders to escape violence. The situation might require temporary camps to care for refugees, like those Garner established in northern Iraq in 1991 during Operation Provide Comfort. Kern argued such camps should be established by exception due to the limited forces and equipment available to set them up and run them; he did not believe the relief organizations could tackle those tasks.

Modest relief supplies were pre-positioned in Jordan and Kuwait. Additional supplies would require more funding. Such funding could not be programmed by the international community until an assessment determined what was needed. That reinforced Garner's intention to control the DART as it deployed into Iraq. USAID had emergency funds for immediate relief and reconstruction tasks, but those tasks required contractors who would require security. But what if security was inadequate?

General Strock consulted General Whitley about damaged infrastructure that would have to be repaired during the first thirty days following the invasion—before contractors could begin work. They both knew that most of the military engineers were committed to support the combat forces and that it would be difficult to use them for reconstruction during the fighting. Those in the Bush administration had optimistically assumed that outsourcing reconstruction to large contractors would take the load off military forces, but they did not anticipate security challenges that would prevent contractors from operating.

ORHA, JTF-4, and the 352nd CACOM were all concerned with humanitarian and reconstruction tasks, but they had no engineer, MP, medical, or logistic units. Colonel Benson's Eclipse II plan made no provisions to pass such units to them. Benson assumed that CFLCC would hand off the Phase IV mission to CJTF-7, for which no specific formation or headquarters had been identified.

For the mid-term tasks of regime replacement, Garner needed more senior advisors for the Iraqi ministries, those Rumsfeld had promised. He also needed the Governance Team that Liz Cheney and Scott Carpenter were putting together. Garner had one phone call with Carpenter when he got to Kuwait, who indicated he had eight people on his team with more to come, but no one knew when Carpenter would bring them to Kuwait or Iraq. Garner needed Arabic interpreters and translators, but the only Arabic speakers that arrived the last two weeks in March were several members of Chalabi's INC, unwilling to serve as interpreters. Colonel Dennis DeGraff, the C-1, could assist with the arrival and reception of additional personnel, and Colonel Costello, the C-4, could house and sustain them, but neither could recruit them. Sustaining those in the Hilton was expensive. The twenty villas that ORHA occupied cost $1.5 million a month (about $3,750 per person) with ORHA now having expanded to 400 people.[48]

The ORHA communications were dependent on the Raytheon contract, signed only the previous month. There would be no Raytheon personnel and equipment in Kuwait to service that contract until April, however. With ORHA's communications problems well known beyond the Hilton, Timothy Phillips, a GS-15 communications manager, arrived to join ORHA in early April. Phillips was a retired Marine lieutenant colonel with a communications background. He had continued working in the communications field in the Pentagon as a civil servant. But he had not gone straight to Kuwait. First he stopped in Qatar to see Brigadier General Dennis Moran, the J-6 Communications officer for Central Command.[49]

Moran told Phillips there were communications problems in ORHA and it was his understanding that these included a conflict between the military and civilian components. Moran told Phillips his priority task with ORHA was communications planning, but as a civilian with a military background Moran expected Phillips to bridge the apparent gaps between the military C-staff and the civilians in ORHA. Moran also told Phillips that Colonel Conway had a strained relationship with McKiernan's C-6 Communications officer, Major General Lowell Detamore. An Army reservist, Detamore had been activated to upgrade the CFLCC communications staff when general officers were added to the other staff sections of the Third Army. When Phillips arrived in Kuwait, he learned that Detamore felt Conway demonstrated a lack of protocol by not stopping by to check in with him for an office call as the senior communications officer in Kuwait.[50]

Later, when Conway, at Major June's urging, went to Camp Doha to ask Detamore for communications support in the Hilton, Detamore informed him that he was fully committed to the invasion and if ORHA needed communication support, they would have to move to Camp Doha. That was not feasible because there was insufficient room for ORHA there. Detamore thus made it clear he was not interested in helping ORHA. Phillips also found problems with the Raytheon contract. The original proposal was for $20 million, but when Jerry Bates reviewed the details of the contract with Conway, he felt they were getting gouged and he told Raytheon they would pay only $14.5 million. To Raytheon, that meant something had to be dropped from the contract. Conway selected several items he thought he could handle through other means. One was a computer help desk that Raytheon would have provided; Conway thought he had enough talent among the NCOs on his staff for that task.[51]

Another component dropped from the Raytheon contract was generator support to service the communications system. Presumably Baghdad would have electrical power that ORHA could use for its communications. ORHA communications would require substantial electrical support, and if it was not immediately available in Baghdad, field generators would be required. If those did not come from Raytheon, they would have to come from another source, and the only available source would be the military command in Iraq. With the poor relationship Conway had established with General Detamore, Phillips was concerned that military generators might not be forthcoming.[52]

Through March, news coverage of the invasion showed Coalition forces advancing on Baghdad. Colonel Frketic provided intelligence updates in the C-staff meetings and gave classified briefings privately to Garner, Bates, and Adams. Frketic described the tactical events he could monitor through intelligence channels, but he did not seek information relevant to regime replacement in Iraq; nor did anyone ask him for any. Few knew the details of the Coalition maneuver plan except that the main attack would swing to the west to avoid population centers, with a supporting attack by the U.S. Marines and UK forces through Basra and the southern oil fields. No one was surprised when the Iraqi Army and Republican Guards melted away with little resistance. Many were surprised when the irregular Fedayeen forces put up a suicidal defense, but it was unclear what that suggested for the future.

Few in ORHA pondered a U.S. military transformation in the campaign. But Operation Iraqi Freedom (OIF), as the campaign was called, did include a transformation. For some that meant greater reliance on precision weapons and other new technology. There was also a significant shift from the overwhelming force used during Desert Storm a decade earlier to Rumsfeld's "more strictly modulated application of violence," which military commanders and planners unsuccessfully resisted. At the time, this seemed to vindicate Rumsfeld, perhaps because only professional soldiers anticipated the utility of large formations when the fighting was over.

Of course, after Desert Storm, American military leaders had a better sense of the hollow nature of the Iraqi army and knew that fewer forces would be required to defeat it the second time around. But an invasion of Iraq would include greater distances with the task of liberation (or occupation), even though Rumsfeld had discouraged attention to such challenges.[53] During Desert Storm, the Third Army played a crucial role in managing the deployment and assembly of the Army ground forces, but not of the Marines. For OIF, the Third Army formed the core of CFLCC and again took on such a role and fought those forces all the way to Baghdad. Yet in 2003, it was poorly prepared to take on the occupation tasks the Third Army had undertaken at the close of World War I and World War II. And there was no formation configured in advance for reconstruction tasks such as TF Freedom, which helped rebuild Kuwait in 1991–92. The military deficiencies of 2003 would be more expensive at several levels than anyone anticipated.

The three regional groups in ORHA had begun to form with more depth in Kuwait: ORHA-North under Bruce Moore, ORHA-South under Buck Walters, and Baghdad-Central under Barbara Bodine. Moore and Walters had formed small operational staffs with positions comparable to the C-staff. Moore's deputy was Dick Naab, a retired Army colonel who had served with Garner in northern Iraq in 1991 and had remained an additional year to work with the Kurdish groups. His Operations officer was Lieutenant Colonel Bill Butcher, an active duty Civil Affairs officer who had served under Baltazar in the 96th CA Battalion.

Buck Walters had a comparable group for the southern region with Marc

Powe as his deputy, also a retired Army colonel with previous experience in Iraq. Lieutenant Colonel Jim Wolff, another CA officer who had served under Baltazar in the 96th CA battalion, served as the Operations officer for ORHA-South. A dozen military officers and civilians rounded out each staff with components that lined up with the C-staff. Garner wanted to send Walters and Moore into Iraq before the fighting was over to get them positioned early. He planned to fly Moore's team into an airfield in the Kurdish areas in the north with Walter's team driving into southern Iraq behind the Marines.

ORHA's third region, Baghdad Central, could not deploy until the fighting there was over. Bodine needed an operational staff for her region comparable to Moore and Walters. But she did not ask for a colonel as her deputy, nor did she want a staff built along military lines. She wanted Meghan O'Sullivan as her deputy, but Garner assigned her Colonel George Oliver instead. Bodine and Oliver clashed and Garner replaced him with Colonel Keith Schollum, the collegial Australian who joined ORHA in Kuwait (Oliver was reassigned as George Ward's deputy with the HA pillar). Bodine would have fewer military officers and more women with her than Walters or Moore. She was popular with the career-oriented women in ORHA and worked well with them, but her staff lacked operational structure and had less linkage with the ORHA C-staff. Garner had divided Iraq's eighteen provinces between Moore, Walters, and Bodine, but Bodine continued to think of herself as the mayor of Baghdad; Garner felt she focused on the capital at the expense of the provinces assigned to her.[54]

Moore, Walters, and Bodine were accommodated together in one of the beachside villas, but they did not get along well. For one thing, Bates, Moore, and Walters liked to play practical jokes and Bodine became one of their targets. Bodine could laugh at others but not at herself; furthermore, she could be intolerant and was easily angered. She did not like military people and made her contempt known, and also considered her status as an ambassador the equivalent to that of a major general. All in all, she continued to be as difficult to work with in Kuwait and later in Iraq as she had been in the Pentagon.

Colonel Kim Olson, Garner's military assistant, sympathized with Bodine. Olson found her a bottle of scotch, rare in alcohol-free Kuwait, and one evening Bodine shared it with Bates, Walters, and Moore as the latter were telling stories. The gift took them by surprise and they allowed her to tell some of her own from her thirty-year career at State, from which she had some good ones. Whatever the positive effects from that evening, however, they were fleeting, and she continued to find herself frequently at odds with military officers in ORHA.[55]

Mike Mobbs also had problems with acceptance in ORHA. He had neither a military nor an executive leadership background and little experience over-seas. He was a skilled legal negotiator and his quiet, unflappable style may have been effective in small conference settings, but he was ill at ease with larger groups, poorly prepared to take charge of the Civil Administration pillar that Feith had demanded for him. For his part, the energetic Garner was frus-trated with Mobbs's apparent lethargy. When Powe went to work for Walters, Garner did not provide Mobbs with a new deputy. Finally, after a few weeks, Mike Ayoub emerged as the acting deputy for the Civil Administration pillar. But Garner did not know Ayoub, and he had far less clout within ORHA than the other deputies there—Powe, Naab, Schollum, Oliver, and Milligan.

The Civil Administration pillar had the task to manage senior advisors for the Iraqi ministries involved with governance. Working informally as the dep-uty, Ayoub found himself in frequent disagreement with Sherri Kraham, who had positioned herself as the gatekeeper between Garner and the ministries' staff. Ayoub had known Kraham at State when she worked in Undersecretary John Bolton's office, where he had considered her Bolton's gatekeeper; he felt she was now trying to be Garner's gatekeeper in Iraq for those in the Civil Administration pillar who wanted access to him.[56]

With the Iraqi ministries split between the Reconstruction and Civil Ad-ministration pillars, Garner needed an overall coordinator to integrate the ministry effort; Kraham worked her way into that position. But if Garner ap-preciated her industrious work ethic and forward style, that did not endear her to others. Kraham had a tendency to speak in Garner's name that oth-ers found grating. She would demand that information to Garner be filtered through her, but she did not provide information requested from Garner in return. There was often a palpable tension in the air as she entered the Civil Administration working area and talked about what "Jay needs." Ayoub tried to counsel her on this several times but with little effect.[57]

An important issue Ayoub had to work through Kraham was a list Gar-ner wanted of the key sites in Baghdad that should be protected by Coalition ground forces immediately upon taking the city. Those in the Civil Adminis-tration pillar were working that issue aggressively. On 22 March, Mike Ay-oub, Drew Erdmann, Simon Elvy, and Philip Hall had a list of fifteen ministry buildings that should be secured, with the Central Bank listed as number one and the Ministry of Oil as number fifteen. When Mike Gfoeller saw the list, he insisted that the National Museum should be added near the top of the list, which was then expanded to sixteen sites with the museum listed second.[58]

Ayoub passed the list to Kraham, who gave a copy to Garner, but she did not forward it any further. A few days later, when Garner found the list had not left ORHA, he admonished those in Civil Administration for the delay;

they were in turn incensed with Kraham. Ayoub decided to send the list through multiple channels, including Paul Hughes in the C-5 and Colonel Richard Burton, a British officer serving with the political component to General McKiernan's command. Hughes challenged Drew Erdmann on why the museum should be number two on the list, but he was receptive to the ranking when Erdmann said it was a symbolic site and that protecting it would confirm to the Iraqis and others of the Coalition's altruistic intent.[59]

By 9 April, as Coalition forces were taking Baghdad, the media began reporting widespread looting and accused the Coalition of standing by as government buildings on the ORHA list were looted. Ayoub, Erdmann, and Elvy went to Camp Doha to determine what happened. They were joined by Colonel Tony Puckett, who was moving from Hawkins's JTF-4 to ORHA and the Civil Administration pillar to replace Ayoub as deputy to Mike Mobbs. When they complained to Lieutenant Colonel Ernst Isensee at Camp Doha, the officer told them angrily, "We can't guard everything!"[60]

Over several days, media reports indicated that the Ministries of Trade and Planning and the Museum of Music and Art were ransacked, the latter as television cameras showed Marines standing by. Ayoub, Erdmann, and Elvy returned to Camp Doha to protest to Colonel Burton, who admitted he had lost the original ORHA message and had just found it. Incredulous that their efforts to protect key sites in Baghdad had gone unheeded, they sent another message to the military command on 16 April with an updated list. It was a tragic affair that implied to Iraq and to the world that the Coalition did not care about Iraq's government buildings and museum treasures.[61]

Concerned that the Civil Administration pillar lacked information available in Washington, Ayoub contacted Tom Warrick at State and asked about his Future of Iraq project. Warrick had brought a copy to the Pentagon when he joined briefly in February, but took it with him when he was forced to leave. Ayoub had Warrick fax most of the study a page at a time to the embassy in Kuwait, a clumsy process. But without Warrick in person to help make sense of the papers, they could make only a marginal contribution.

Of those working with Ayoub, the most frustrated were Dick Mayer and Bill Lantz, representing the Department of Justice; they had been designated as interim senior advisors for the Iraqi Ministries of Interior and Justice. In the Pentagon they had proposed a plan to bring in an interim police force and police trainers to respond to the predicable chaos that would follow invasion. They knew that the State Department Bureau of International Narcotics and Law Enforcement had experience with police forces in other countries, and they went to Barbara Bodine several times to brief her on their efforts to obtain funds and police trainers. But many of the scheduled meetings were canceled because she was busy. When Mayer finally met with her to enlist her support, she cut the session short before he could complete his presentation. He felt she was not interested in a training package for the police in Iraq.[62]

It was easier to deploy Coalition military formations than an interim police force. Mayer and Lantz were unaware of the discussion Ron Adams had with the Spanish ambassador about the possibility of deploying paramilitary Spanish police forces to Iraq. Their proposal for civilian police trainers required advance funding that Garner requested repeatedly, but it was turned down by Secretary Rumsfeld and aggressively resisted by Frank Miller at the NSC. Mayer and Lantz were appalled that they would be a two-man operation to take on the tasks of two important Iraqi ministries with no projected funding. They saw a train wreck coming while few others were paying attention.

As the maneuver formations entered Iraq, the supporting Civil Affairs battalions and brigades moved with them to provide humanitarian assistance. But their tasks were not as demanding as anticipated. There was no major population displacement as Coalition forces successfully avoided most population centers. Nor was there resistance by the Iraqi people other than the Fedayeen irregulars. There was no use of WMD (weapons of mass destruction) with the disasters that might have come with them. There were no imminent food shortages as the intelligence agencies had indicated. In fact, there was plenty of food for the first month after the war because Saddam Hussein had ordered bulk food supplies to be issued to the population prior to the invasion. As this became apparent in ORHA, there was a shift in attention from humanitarian assistance to reconstruction and civil administration.

On 1 April, Garner, Walters, and a few others made a day trip into Iraq to visit the port of Umm Qasr, which had been taken by the UK forces a week earlier. The port was not damaged and, with some work, it appeared that it could be in operation soon. Two days later, Garner received a briefing by the ORHA-North and ORHA-South teams on their plans to enter Iraq. Bill Butcher, the Operations officer for ORHA-North, laid out a plan to fly eighty-four personnel into northern Iraq in several increments. Initially they would stay in a Kurdish hotel under construction a few miles north of Erbil. They would focus on six cities, each with a population of over 100,000, three in Kurdish areas and three in Arab areas. For their first thirty days, they planned to work in the Kurdish areas, then move to the Arab areas. The briefing went well and Garner was pleased.

Garner was less pleased with the briefing that followed, however, which Walters chose to give on behalf of ORHA-South himself. His area included nine of the eighteen provinces in Iraq, including nine cities with over 100,000 people, a larger region in area and population than what ORHA-North would tackle. Walters noted their reconnaissance two days earlier, and contacts with the UK soldiers in the area indicated that the Iraqis in the South were afraid of what was to come. The few NGOs that had been in the South said the Iraqis they encountered were not very friendly. Lew Lucke interjected that security had become a big issue, with the NGOs preparing to enter Iraq, a bad sign for those who wanted to see more NGOs participate. Bates added that military forces would soon shift from area to point security, a move that should provide more protection to the NGOs.

Walters said there would be sixteen in his initial group with more to follow. He enthusiastically added that his Arabist from State, Mike Gfoeller, "would find the first Iraqi to help re-shape a new nation." General Tim Cross suggested they would need positive media coverage right away. General Carl Strock added such coverage should address the positive status of the southern oil fields he had recently visited. Walters's briefing was more complicated, drawing more discussion than Butcher's had for ORHA-North. Deployment into the South would take place first, without a friendly population base. While it was assumed the Kurds would provide security for ORHA in the North, it was not clear who would provide security in the South, and there was no obvious coordination with the Marines or UK forces who occupied those areas.

There were differing views about carrying weapons. Cross, Bodine, and Adams felt ORHA's status should be comparable to the DART and NGOs: they should be unarmed. That did not sound like "going soldiering again" to Walters, who strongly disagreed. Military members asked if they should wear uniforms or civilian clothes. Cross, Bodine, and Adams argued that uniforms were inappropriate for ORHA personnel, but that led to questions about the status of soldiers traveling in civilian clothes in a combat zone. Garner felt there were too many unresolved issues and was dissatisfied with the preparations to enter southern Iraq. Much of the ORHA support would be dependent on KBR, and it was not clear when their contractors would be in place. Walters was embarrassed as Garner demanded another briefing that evening.

Walters and his staff had not asked the C-staff for much assistance for their briefing, but Baltazar and Costello piled on to help now. They spent the day coordinating with the military forces for security and with KBR for support. Thus when Walters gave Garner the second presentation, he allowed others to participate rather than do it all himself, with Baltazar addressing security arrangements and Costello contract support through KBR. Walters won his point on taking weapons, but he left unresolved the question of uniforms for military personnel, which allowed them to make their own call on how they dressed in Iraq. Garner was more comfortable, but he still had questions.[63]

On 5 April, a third meeting addressed in greater detail the move into southern Iraq. Walters had made direct contact with the First Marine Expeditionary Force (I MEF), which had control over the UK forces in southern Iraq and confirmed that they would provide protection for his group. He had also tightened up the KBR support. Garner told Lew Lucke and General Strock that he wanted the DART team to work with those from the FESTs (Forward Engineer Support Teams, from the Corps of Engineers) to support Walters. Everyone knew the DART was there to make assessments and provide immediate assistance; FESTs could make more detailed reconstruction assessments than the DART could. With Garner's approval, Strock had quietly brought in several FESTs to send into Iraq, and Garner wanted to ensure that the DART and FEST teams worked together.

Later that day, Catherine Dale visited ORHA. Dale was the political advisor (POLAD) for the V Corps commander, although she had no formal connection with the Department of State. Because V Corps was a tactical headquarters subordinate to General McKiernan's CFLCC, it was not clear what interest Dale had in ORHA and few took notice of her. Her role would become notable in May, when V Corps was designated to become the senior headquarters in Iraq, replacing General McKiernan's command.[64]

When the ORHA main body arrived in Baghdad, they would need a base to live and work from, but by late March no facility had been identified. General Whitley told Garner on 19 March that the main military headquarters would be established at the Baghdad airport and that they would set up an interim headquarters there to accommodate a hundred of Garner's people, allowing him time to set up a more permanent base. But Garner wanted to get set up in downtown Baghdad right away. Some wanted a large hotel that would have rooms for offices, accommodations, conference rooms for meetings, restaurants, lots of bathrooms, and a large parking lot. Getting two such hotels in the same vicinity would be better. But Major Peter Veale, the engineer studying the issue, was leery of hotels and suggested the Republican Palace in Baghdad. It might not have had the ideal interior configuration for offices and bedrooms, but it had a better security layout than a hotel. The debate on the appropriate location for ORHA continued into April.

Adams had listened closely in the meetings and expressed concern that the staff action process for ORHA was inadequate for the anticipated support requirements. Most important, communications were unsatisfactory. Once the regional groups were in southern and northern Iraq, staff support would have to increase considerably. But before he could take action, Adams became ill and had to leave Kuwait. He had had a bad cough for over a week and a doctor told him it might be serious and wanted him to see a specialist at Walter

Reed Hospital in Washington. He made plans to return home with Colonel Martin, an absence that would leave a critical void in ORHA. Adams and Martin departed Kuwait on 6 April, the day Ted Morse arrived.

Morse was a senior USAID official. Garner assigned him to be deputy for Baghdad Central under Barbara Bodine; Colonel Schollum was designated her Operations officer. Morse had an easygoing personality, but working with Bodine would be a trial. He knew Bodine only by her reputation as ambassador to Yemen. When Morse met her in the Hilton, he asked her penetrating questions: "What's your management style? How do you learn? How do you make decisions?"

Bodine was surprised with the questions. "In terms of management style, well, I never thought about that," she replied.

So Morse went to two other American ambassadors who knew Bodine and was told that "her management style is egocentric. . . . Everything about her . . . is interpreted in terms of her power, her position, her decisions. . . . Within the [State] Department . . . she's known as a very difficult person to work with." Morse soon found they were right.[65]

Mike Page came to the Hilton the day after Morse arrived. Page was joining not ORHA but KBR as the new project manager supporting ORHA, now expanded to eighty people. The initial tasks for KBR had been billeting and local transportation for ORHA. But as ORHA expanded and prepared to move into Iraq, the KBR support also expanded, with staff sections for Human Resources, Finance and Accounting, Project Controls; Logistics, Materials and Procurement; Information Technology and Communications; a security coordinator; an engineering section; and, later in Iraq, a base camp maintenance section; these were all staff sections similar to those on the C-staff.[66]

Page was a 1977 graduate of West Point. He left the Army as a major in 1994 to join KBR, for which he would work in Somalia, Haiti, Bosnia, and Hungary; then he left KBR to work for an Alaska Native Corporation employed in government services work. There he was contacted by KBR and asked if he would become its project manager supporting ORHA. He agreed and deployed to Kuwait, where he coordinated directly with Colonel Costello. During March and April, the KBR team was expanding but with some friction and personnel turbulence. Some KBR personnel came to Kuwait from other projects supporting American military forces; some were non-Americans and came from the Balkans where KBR had recruited many locals (presumably paid at lower rates than Americans). But over half the team Page put together was recruited in the United States, particularly in Texas, where the KBR headquarters was located. Page estimated that half his people had some military service and all had agreed to go into Iraq with ORHA.

KBR worked on a cost-plus-contract, which meant that the costs of its services, its personnel, what it procured for ORHA, and other overhead were billed directly to the government through Costello's C-4 shop, with a base fee and a fixed profit margin. There was also an award fee if the service provided was exceptional. If ORHA needed transportation, KBR rented buses, trucks, and cars. In Iraq, ORHA would need a fleet of vehicles that the military commands would not provide. Costello requested 200 SUVs. Page found a General Motors dealer in Kuwait that had just received a big shipment of SUVs and quickly bought them for ORHA.[67]

With such requirements, Garner needed to set up a formal process for support, and on 9 April he signed a memorandum establishing a Procurement Management Review Process under Jerry Bates and Colonel Costello. The memo provided guidance for assessing requirements, requests, and accounting to streamline the contracting process.[68]

In the Civil Administration pillar, Mike Ayoub had to contend with two individuals assigned to his group who were not aligned with an Iraqi ministry: Harold Rhode and Terry Sullivan. Ayoub was convinced they were sent by OSD to assist Ahmed Chalabi and his INC as a political solution for postwar Iraq, even though Garner had taken no position to support Chalabi or the INC. On 19 March, Rhode interrupted a meeting Ayoub was having with the Civil Administration members to "exuberantly announce that Feith has just told him that six OSD sponsored Iraqi expatriates (IRDC) have just gotten their visas and will soon be here to help us!" Ayoub liked Sullivan but did not approve of his apparent role as the "operations officer for the Chalabi group." When those from the IRDC arrived in Kuwait, they received little attention from those in ORHA, perhaps in part because of the way Rhode had promoted them.[69]

On 8 April, Ayoub observed Sullivan slip out of the Hilton with Salem "Sam" Chalabi and a few other Iraqis to join his uncle Ahmed Chalabi in Tallil, near Nasiriyah. Sullivan used two Chevrolet Suburbans that Ayoub had just signed for in his role in the Civil Administration pillar. With a hundred Iraqi exiles recently trained as soldiers, the elder Chalabi had flown into the Tallil airbase near Nasiriyah a few days earlier on U.S. Air Force aircraft, supposedly at the direction of Feith. Ayoub later found that only Rhode was aware that this would take place. Ayoub noted that Sullivan's "trip was unauthorized within ORHA and involved more than a little subterfuge. It was becoming increasingly apparent that OSD has a separate agenda going within the cover of ORHA." A few days later Chalabi announced through the media, "I'm here [in Iraq], where is Garner? Why is he in Kuwait?"[70]

In early April, Lieutenant Colonel John Agoglia returned to the Hilton from Qatar. He confirmed the subordination of ORHA to CFLCC. He said a formal order would soon follow; it arrived a few days later, dated 6 April. In the Central Command order, ORHA was placed under the operational control of McKiernan's CFLCC and McKiernan was directed to provide logistical support and force protection for Garner and his team in Iraq. With ORHA now subordinate, CFLCC was suddenly responsible for it and its mission. Neither General McKiernan nor Colonel Benson had anticipated the order. If ORHA had been placed under CFLCC control upon arrival in Kuwait three weeks earlier, Benson's planners might have been able to integrate ORHA with other units under its control: JTF-4, the 352nd CACOM, the 416th ENCOM, an MP formation, some logistical and signal units. But it was late to form such an organization. Within a few days McKiernan put out a fragmentary order, FRAGO 254, acknowledging operational control of ORHA.[71]

McKiernan and his staff knew that ORHA had three sub-regional elements and they tried to align each one with a military formation: ORHA-South under Buck Walters aligned with I MEF; ORHA-North under Bruce Moore initially aligned with the Special Operations command in northern Iraq, later with V Corps; and Baghdad-Central aligned with the 3rd Mechanized Infantry Division in Baghdad. Such regional alignment would help integrate the efforts of ORHA with the CFLCC Eclipse II plan. The order directed the respective military commands to provide ORHA convoy escort, protection, and other support, but such support would be slow to materialize.

By 9 April, Baghdad was secured and Coalition military forces were spread out all over Iraq. Soldiers and commanders were tired and in many cases content that they had achieved all their objectives. It was challenging for Colonel Benson to get McKiernan and his subordinate commanders to make additional preparations necessary to integrate Garner's group into the military command, but there were a few exceptions. The day ORHA received the order placing it under CFLCC control, Garner sent Jerry Bates to see Major General Rusty Blackman, McKiernan's chief of staff, to discuss the new command relationship. Blackman told Bates that CFLCC was going to dismantle JTF-4 and offered Bates three of its colonels. He also directed the 352nd CACOM to send ORHA several CA officers who joined ORHA in the Hilton prior to its departure for Iraq.[72]

As the war terminated, a Spanish ship arrived at Umm Qasr on 9 April to unload relief supplies, and Australia had a ship en route with a shipment of wheat. Soon other ships would be arriving, but it was determined that the port had silted up and would require dredging to become fully operational. It was an early signal that infrastructure challenges lay ahead in Iraq, a symptom of inadequate maintenance rather than war.

The next day, Garner sent a memorandum to Ryan Henry, Feith's deputy in the Pentagon, based on initial reports from the military commands, the DART, and NGOs: "The general security situation is unstable and tense, as a result of continued fighting, a breakdown in law and order, and extensive looting. . . . There is a lack of confirmed information about the humanitarian situation." In northern Iraq, the reports indicated that "the governorates of Dahuk, Erbil, and Sulaymaniyyah [Kurdish areas] remain stable, but tense." In the southern areas around Basra, security "has begun to stabilize, with the military assessing the situation to be permissive in Umm Qasr, Az Zubayr, and Safwan. Humanitarian supplies (food, water, fuel, and medical supplies) are now moving into those areas."[73]

Security in other areas was noted as "uncertain," but there were no indications of the massive humanitarian disaster or displacement of civilians that many had anticipated. Donor contributions were arriving: "A shipment of 50,000 tons of wheat is being unloaded in Kuwait," with a second shipment due soon after. A ship from the United Arab Emirates with "aid workers and 700 tons of food" was due the next day. Organizations in Europe were sending 9.5 million euros with as much to follow. Japan had pledged over $20 million and Norway $56 million to relief agencies preparing to come forward from Kuwait and Jordan. There were even reports that Russia intended to send "500,000 tons of grain to Iraq in the next six months." Overall, the humanitarian assistance activities immediately following the war appeared under control, allowing Garner and his team to shift their focus to reconstruction and civil administration in Iraq.[74]

The day Garner sent the memo to Ryan Henry, he attended a meeting with his ministry advisors. Of the twenty-four Iraqi ministries (the Ministry of Youth had been added), Garner had only eleven designated senior advisors in Kuwait: Lee Schatz for Agriculture, Dorothy Mazaka for Education, Skip Burkle for Health, Tim Carney for Industry and Materials, David Dunford for Planning, Robin Raphel for Trade, John Limbert for Culture, Bob Gifford for Interior, George Mullinax for the Central Bank, David Nummy for Finance, and Don Eberly for Youth. Two more had been identified by name but had not yet joined ORHA: Walt Slocombe for Defense and Phil Carroll for Oil. Thus Garner did not have senior advisors on hand for thirteen ministries, or even designated personnel for eleven of them. He would have to appoint junior personnel in ORHA as interim ministry advisors until more senior personnel were identified and arrived in theater (see Table 2).

Steve Browning was already holding the interim positions for three ministries: Irrigation, Housing and Construction, and Transportation and Communications. From those with him in Kuwait, Garner assigned interim positions

Table 2. Mid-April 2003: ORHA Senior and Interim Advisors for Iraqi Ministries

Ministry	Senior Advisor	Interim Senior Advisor
Ministry Coordinator	Sherri Kraham	
Reconstruction Pillar	Lew Lucke; Deputy Chris Milligan	
1. Agriculture	Lee Schatz: USDA	
2. Education	Dorothy Mazaka: USAID	
3. Electricity Commission	TBD: USAID*	Tom Wheelock: USAID Contractor
4. Health	Skip Burkle: USAID	
5. Housing & Construction	TBD: USAID*	Steve Browning: USACE
6. Industry & Minerals	Tim Carney: DOS	
7. Labor & Social Affairs	TBD: USAID*	Karen Walsh: USAID Contractor
8. Irrigation	TBD: USACE*	Steve Browning: USACE
9. Military Industry	TBD: DOS*	COL Paul Hughes, USA
10. Higher Education/ Scientific Research	TBD: USAID*	Mike Ayoub: DOS
11. Information	TBD: DOD*	Bob Reilly: Contractor
12. Defense	Walt Slocombe: DOD**	MG Carl Strock: USACE Asst.: COL Paul Hughes Asst.: Mike Ayoub: DOS Asst.: LTC Torgler

to Tom Wheelock for Electricity, Karen Walsh for Labor and Social Affairs, Mike Ayoub for Higher Education and Scientific Research, Dick Mayer for Justice, and Gary Vogler for Oil. Sherri Kraham had penciled herself in as the interim advisor for Foreign Affairs, but after objections from several people at State who felt more qualified and wanted the position, Ambassador Dunford took the job and was replaced in Planning with Simon Elvy. That left two senior advisor positions that Garner chose to delay filling: the Ministry of Military Industry and the Ministry of Religious Affairs, with the assumption that the former would be disbanded and that it was inappropriate to impose a Coalition member on the latter.

Walt Slocombe had been designated by the Pentagon to take the senior advisor position for the Ministry of Defense, but he would not arrive for several weeks. In the Pentagon, Garner and Colonel Paul Hughes had put in motion two contracts to deal with the regular Iraqi army. One contract with RONCO

Table 2 (*continued*)

Ministry	Senior Advisor	Interim Senior Advisor
Civil Affairs Pillar	Mike Mobbs; Deputy: COL Tony Puckett	
13. Planning	TBD: DOS*	Simon Elvy: UK FCO
14. Trade	Robin Raphel: DOS	
15. Justice	TBD: DOJ*	Bill Lantz: DOJ
16. Transportation & Communications	TBD: DOS*	Steve Browning: USACE
17. Culture	John Limbert: DOS	
18. Foreign Affairs	David Dunford: DOS (Ret)	
19. Interior	Bob Gifford: DOS Asst.: Philip Hall: UK FCO	Dick Mayer: DOJ
20. Central Bank	George Mullinax: Treasury Contractor	
21. Finance	David Nummy: Treasury Contractor	
22. Oil	Phil Carroll: DOD Contractor**	Gary Vogler: DOD Contractor
23. AWQAF/ Religions Affairs	TBD: DOS*	
24. Youth	Don Eberly: SAIC Contractor	
Governance	Scott Carpenter**	

NOTES. AWQAF = Ministry of Religious Affairs; TBD = to be determined; USDA = U.S. Department of Agriculture; USAID = U.S. Agency for International Development; USACE = U.S. Army Corps of Engineers; DOS = U.S. Department of State; DOJ = U.S. Department of Justice; DOD = Department of Defense; UK FCO = UK Foreign and Commonwealth Office.
*Not identified.
**Not in theater.

would be responsible for disarmament, demobilization, and reintegration (DDR); another with the defense contractor MPRI was to retrain those Iraqi soldiers retained for active duty. In Slocombe's absence, the interim position went to General Carl Strock, assisted by Colonel Paul Hughes and Lieutenant Colonel Jim Torgler, all of whom had other important responsibilities.[75]

Garner was concerned and frustrated with his perception of obstruction and lack of support from the Pentagon, and he complained about it to Rumsfeld frequently since his arrival in Kuwait. The State Department, USAID, and the Corps of Engineers had been the most forthcoming, with seven senior advisors (including three interim advisors designated by Garner); Treasury and Justice each provided two senior advisors; and one advisor each came from Agriculture and the NSC. The Department of Defense had provided only one name for a senior advisor—Slocombe, and he had not arrived. With news that humanitarian assistance would require less work than anticipated, the need to move forward with the ministries was of paramount importance—at least to those in ORHA. That said, there was no demonstrated sense of urgency in Washington to fill the vacant positions.

Garner was really irritated by the assignment of Slocombe as senior advisor for the Ministry of Defense, partially because he was not consulted on such an important position. Slocombe had served as the Deputy Undersecretary of Defense for Policy in the Clinton administration, Feith's current job. Although a Democrat, Slocombe had previously been asked by Rumsfeld to serve on the Defense Policy Board and subsequently offered to assist with Iraq. In March Feith asked him if he would take on the position for senior advisor of the Iraqi Ministry of Defense.

Garner was not consulted even though he was working in the Pentagon at the time. When he was informed of Slocombe's selection he did not protest, but he had reservations. In the 1990s, when Garner was the Army Assistant Vice Chief of Staff, Slocombe had tried to reduce the size of the Army by 45,000 soldiers. The Army had already been cut from eighteen to ten divisions earlier in the decade and the additional reduction Slocombe and others were proposing would cost the Army two more divisions. Garner did not believe Slocombe appreciated the importance of infantry formations for national defense and he had actively resisted that reduction. In the end, Garner and the Army were successful, but the experience did not endear Garner to Slocombe.[76]

Secretary Rumsfeld did not inform Garner about Slocombe's selection until early April, after Garner had been deployed to Kuwait. At that time, it was too late for Garner to resist. Once Slocombe accepted the assignment, Army Colonel Greg Gardner was assigned as his assistant in the Pentagon. Slocombe made several brief phone calls to Jerry Bates, who suggested he use Colonel Paul Hughes as his primary point of contact for the Ministry of Defense, as General Strock had several other demanding tasks. Once Hughes was involved, he sent a message to Colonel Gardner with the details of the planning that had been done for the Ministry of Defense and for the Iraqi army, including Garner's intention to use the Iraqi army for assistance with reconstruction; separately, Lieutenant General John Abizaid wanted to use the Iraqi regular army for internal security.[77]

By that time, there had been some progress with RONCO and MPRI to demobilize and retrain the Iraqi army. Hughes wanted to get Slocombe and Gardner up to date with that progress as well as the intent to use the Iraqi army for stability operations. Much of the exchange was by email, but soon included televised conferences with Slocombe, Gardner, Hughes, Torgler, and occasionally General Strock; General Abizaid and Colonel Agoglia represented Central Command. Hughes and Strock had earlier proposed to Abizaid and Agoglia that a reconstituted Iraqi army could be used for external security and border control only. General Abizaid aggressively contradicted such a limited role and stated that the Iraqi army would be essential for stability operations.[78]

Colonel Hughes had worked with Slocombe during an earlier tour in the Pentagon. He contacted him from Baghdad: "Sir, you've got to get over here. There are a lot of people over here waiting for you to make decisions." But Slocombe was reluctant to come right away. He asked about food arrangements and if he could bring his own cook to Iraq while Colonel Gardner asked about drivers, transportation, and a manning document. Hughes tried to focus on the details of a training package and was concerned that Slocombe and Colonel Gardner were more interested in amenities than the Iraqi army.[79]

During the second week of April, Colonels Jimmy Rabon, Tony Puckett, and Colin Boag left JTF-4 to join ORHA. Rabon was assigned to Buck Walters as the deputy for ORHA-South, displacing Marc Powe to another position. Puckett was assigned to Mike Mobbs as the deputy for Civil Administration; Mike Ayoub became an interim senior advisor. Boag, a UK military engineer, moved into the C-3 shop to work with Bob Polk and the future Operations section. Boag was soon sent to Baghdad to find a headquarters for ORHA. Colonel Mike Williams, the Chief of Staff for JTF-4, came by to see Baltazar to determine what job ORHA might have for him, but all the best positions had been filled and Williams was unwilling to serve under another colonel. He returned to Camp Doha and continued with General Hawkins.

Early on 13 April, Bruce Moore, Dick Naab, and several others with ORHA-North flew by military aircraft to Erbil in northern Iraq where they were met by Kurdish leaders anxious to receive them. Naab recognized many faces and friends among the Kurds he had known a decade earlier. Those contacts would be both a blessing and a handicap for Naab over the next eight months.

The day prior, Ambassador Margaret Tutwiler arrived in Kuwait to join ORHA. As spokesperson for the State Department when James Baker was secretary during the George H.W. Bush administration, Tutwiler not only had senior level experience working with the media, but also had strong political connections with the Bush administration. She had a forceful personality and was direct to the point of bluntness, prone to short sentences and answering questions without elaboration. She was serving as ambassador to Morocco when the White House asked her to join ORHA, adding depth to her new assignment while altering ORHA's relationship with the media. She had never met Garner before, but they soon hit it off and she became a loyal supporter.[80]

When Tutwiler arrived, Garner placed her atop Strategic Communications, giving her control of Nate Jones and the Public Affairs Office. Tutwiler also inherited two new Public Affairs civilians whom General Cross had brought from the UK: Charles Heatly and Emily Hand, both from the UK Foreign and Colonial Office (FCO). Hand would remain only a month, but Heatly would stay in theater for the next year working on media issues. An Oxford graduate who had studied Arabic and by most accounts spoke it well, Heatly was in his early thirties, confident and brash. His relations with the media would be heavy-handed.

In the Pentagon and Kuwait, the Department of Defense had imposed a media embargo on Garner through Jones. Tutwiler, however, was reluctant to take guidance from Defense, and yet her views on the media were conservative. When Jones proposed to embed the media with ORHA as the military formations had done during the invasion of Iraq, Tutwiler was not interested. She agreed with Jones that Garner needed to better his relationship with the media; it would be her job to control the media in that relationship, working around the restrictions that had been placed on Garner. She contacted members of the media living in the Hilton and told them that if one or two were to follow Garner from the restaurant as he walked back to his quarters, he would probably talk informally. They were quick to respond. Tutwiler also made it clear she would be with Garner and if she waved them off, they were to walk away. As a result, Garner had discussions with the media almost every evening for the next week.

As he began these informal sessions, Garner was contacted by Dr. Frederick "Skip" Burkle about a situation he did not need reported in the media. Burkle, Garner's senior advisor for the Ministry of Health, told Garner there could be a cholera outbreak in Iraq. Garbage had not been picked up in several weeks and there was potable water for only about 60 percent of the population. Burkle felt they were facing a crisis and wanted to go to Baghdad right away. Garner told Major General William "Fuzzy" Webster, McKiernan's deputy for operations, about the situation. A few days later Burkle was in Baghdad. Garner had a high regard for Burkle, a senior USAID official and a Navy reservist. He had been with Garner in northern Iraq in 1991 and later served in Somalia and Kosovo. He was also one of several senior advisors Washington wanted to replace.[81]

On 13 April, General Strock went to the HOC for a meeting on reconstruction in Iraq. He met Tom Wheelock, who was representing the ORHA

Reconstruction pillar, and Major General Albert Whitley, representing CFLCC. A number of NGOs and other international representatives who wanted to help with reconstruction were present. Strock had attended other such meetings as an observer and was concerned that while the meetings were useful to identify problems, they lacked the leadership needed to assign responsibility for resolutions, "pinning the rose," as many in ORHA called it. Strock was not in charge of the meeting, but he managed to get seated at the head table with General Whitley.

During the meeting, the group would identify a problem but then, without resolving it, start to move on to another topic. Each time, Strock tactfully interrupted to ask who was going to take the problem on. In each case, everyone stopped and looked around before eventually someone volunteered or suggested someone else. Through Strock's interaction, the group made progress, but otherwise the reconstruction effort for Iraq lacked leadership. Strock had a private meeting with Wheelock afterward to discuss this void.[82]

Strock had been tactful with Lew Lucke and Chris Milligan of the Reconstruction pillar when they tried to keep the Corp of Engineers out of their projects. But neither Lucke nor Milligan were engineers and it was clear that reconstruction tasks would be much larger than those USAID normally took on. USAID had contracted Wheelock specifically because he was an engineer; he was to work on the Bechtel contract reconstruction in Iraq. But Wheelock thought more like Strock than Lucke or Milligan. A West Point graduate with a Harvard degree in government, Wheelock knew that Strock and the Corps of Engineers could offer significant help with reconstruction in Iraq. Wheelock's dilemma was that the ORHA Reconstruction pillar had no control of the military engineer units for the reconstruction, and contracting Iraqi workers through Bechtel and other civilian firms would take precious time. The only engineer capability that could be put into operation right away in Iraq, particularly if the stability was in doubt, were military engineers.[83]

Coalition military forces in Kuwait and Iraq included forty-two military engineer battalions. There were half a dozen engineer general officers in theater, including Strock, Whitley, and Major General Robert L. Heine, USAR. Heine commanded the 416th ENCOM, with eight construction battalions. Whitley represented CFLCC at the HOC meetings on reconstruction, but like Strock his status was more observer than participant. General Heine did not attend the HOC meetings, nor was his command represented there. The 416th had not been designated to play a substantive reconstruction role in Iraq as it had for Kuwait following Desert Storm in 1991.

Strock felt reconstruction planning for Iraq lacked cohesion. USAID had the task for reconstruction and the authority to contract, but it needed time and assumed a stable environment. The Army Corps of Engineers had General Robert Crear working on the Iraqi oil fields with Task Force RIO, and Strock had a few FEST teams supporting ORHA. The only robust engineer capability in theater was the military engineer formations, particularly those in the 416th ENCOM, but those formations were not projected for reconstruction. There was no unity of effort or leadership tying the engineer capacity of the Coalition to the post-conflict reconstruction tasks.

David Dunford arrived in Kuwait on 14 April; ten days later he would fly into Baghdad. His adventures had begun in Washington as a pawn between the Departments of State and Defense. Dunford was a retired ambassador with twenty-nine years of service and tours in Egypt, Saudi Arabia (during Desert Storm), and Oman. Gifted in languages, he had picked up Arabic during his assignments without attending a formal course. Jim Larocco of the Near East Asia Bureau called Dunford just as ground forces invaded Iraq to see if he was interested in going over to help. Dunford had reservations as he had opposed the war, and at sixty he had made a recent adjustment to retired life in Tucson, Arizona. But he knew that the endeavor in Iraq was important. He discussed it with his wife, who told him it would be a wonderful opportunity.[84]

Dunford was one of eight senior diplomats State nominated for ministry advisor positions for Iraq; most of them were retired. Only four would make it to Iraq, however. Inspired by his wife's enthusiasm, Dunford agreed to participate and flew to Washington in late March for meetings with Larocco, Ryan Crocker, David Peace, Tom Warrick, and others at State. He was told that the neocons in the administration were determined to get Ahmed Chalabi into power and that Crocker, who had expressed reservations throughout 2002 about invading Iraq, would probably not get a senior position despite his high qualifications.[85]

Dunford contacted Barbara Bodine and Robin Raphel in Kuwait, but administrative preparations took longer than anticipated; Dunford used the time in Washington to indulge his passions for basketball, in the midst of the championship period, and for bird watching. Then he was told he would not be permitted to go, as Secretary Rumsfeld felt some of the nominees were "too low profile and too bureaucratic for the job." Raphel had apparently passed the OSD test through her recent assignment as the vice president of the National Defense University, and Dunford assumed Tim Carney passed muster for having served with Wolfowitz when he was ambassador to Indonesia.[86]

The rejection of those State had nominated did not go uncontested. Secretary Powell was livid, and Hadley called Feith to set up a meeting with Marc Grossman and try to sort it out. But Grossman apparently arrived angry, and as Feith began to speak he walked out, stating they had nothing to talk about.

Hadley went to some effort to get them reconnected, but there was bad blood between State and Defense over the issue.[87] Kenton Keith, who had been acceptable, could not go for medical reasons, and so Dunford's nomination was resurrected.[88] By the time he arrived in Kuwait he was assigned as the senior advisor for the Ministry of Foreign Affairs, which Sherri Kraham had initially reserved for herself.

At the Hilton, Dunford was greeted by Ted Morse, an old friend with whom Dunford would share a room for the next week. The next day he joined those from State and USAID for a birthday photo for Secretary Powell. Dunford thought he would work for Barbara Bodine but found his ministry aligned with the Civil Administration pillar under Mike Mobbs. He then met Garner, Bates, and Cross. When Cross, who struck Dunford as unusually intelligent, asked what he thought of their chances for success, Dunford was not optimistic. He conceded that he had been opposed to the war, but the endeavor was too important to stand by and watch. Dunford continued to make the rounds in Kuwait, checked in at the embassy, met the U.S. ambassador, and tried to decipher the ORHA organization. He had a few books on Iraq and information from Tom Warrick and others in Washington, but his preparation for Iraq was as limited as others waiting to go forward.[89]

When the Treasury team arrived in Kuwait—David Nummy, Van Jorstad, and George Mullinax—they had an incomplete understanding of the Iraqi financial structure. They wanted information about the budget, the revenue stream, how the government was organized, how the banks functioned, and the Central Bank. They were disappointed with the lack of information, however. Nummy had served as an assistant secretary in the Treasury Department in 1988–1992 and had worked in Treasury's office of Technical Assistance for Budget Policy to assist government development and transition. He had worked overseas in Russia, Montenegro, Bosnia, Kosovo, and Serbia in the Balkans and after 9/11 with Afghanistan. He had experience in three areas: how the U.S. Treasury Department worked, the financial challenges for countries going through critical structural transitions, and the strengths and weaknesses of the NSC to manage the financial endeavors.[90]

Nummy was assigned as the senior advisor for the Ministry of Finance; Mullinax would work with the Iraqi Central Bank; Jorstad would serve as an economic counselor. Mullinax and Jorstad also had experience with developing countries in Eastern Europe and the Balkans. They knew each other and had an amicable working relationship that did not require one to be in charge of the other two, although Garner normally consulted with Nummy. In Kuwait they had found themselves under the Reconstruction pillar, which they argued was not appropriate and so were moved to Mobbs's Civil Affairs pillar. When they needed guidance on financial issues, they went to Garner or Adams or called back to the Treasury Department. They assisted Buck Walters with financing to put the port of Umm Qasr into operation for arrival of relief supplies.

The ideal manner for putting the port into operation was to activate the Iraqis who had managed it prior to invasion. Making it clear that port workers would receive their salaries was essential to getting them back to work. That assumed a salary system, records, and funds. When Garner had asked in Washington about funding to sustain Iraqi salaries, the NSC and the Pentagon's response was lukewarm. Nummy knew that moving money into Iraq would be important, and so when he arrived in Kuwait he went to Camp Arifjan to meet Brigadier General Edgar E. Stanton, the senior Army finance officer in theater. Stanton was positive about helping. He had under his control vaults for securing large amounts of cash, critical in a situation where there would be no credit. Stanton volunteered to store any cash that Nummy could acquire from the United States or elsewhere.

Nummy knew that during Desert Storm the United States had frozen $1.7 billion dollars in Iraqi assets held in the United States. After the attacks on New York and the Pentagon on 9/11, Congress passed legislation that any funds frozen by the U.S. government by a terrorist state could be used to combat terrorism, and President Bush had already declared Iraq a terrorist state. That made the frozen funds available for "reconstruction, humanitarian assistance, and other activities to benefit the Iraqi people." Nummy wanted those funds in Kuwait as cash reserves for immediate use, with Stanton providing the vault to hold such cash. Nummy's next objective was to get Washington to move it to Kuwait, a task with more bureaucratic potholes than he expected.[91]

Nummy knew that control of money within the Bush administration was power. He found that the NSC and the Office of Management and Budget were chary about the release of funds for Iraq, despite congressional legislation and the president's intentions. For the NSC, the issue was oversight; the OMB, for its part, wanted accountability. In the latter case, Robin Cleveland was a central figure; she was the OMB representative for oversight for Iraq, and was apparently resentful that her working group under Frank Miller had been displaced by ORHA. Several people in ORHA felt that Cleveland was going to make funding difficult. Nummy appreciated Cleveland's position on accountability, but he still found her difficult.[92]

Before releasing money for salaries in Umm Qasr, OMB wanted to know who was going to be paid, according to what pay rate, and how it would be managed. Nummy did not know the answers to any of these questions.

General Stanton was sympathetic and offered to assist with military finance officers. It took Nummy several weeks to get Washington to release $20 million of the frozen Iraqi funds and fly pallets of cash to Kuwait, which Stanton secured. That allowed salary payments for Umm Qasr. As the Coalition gained control of Iraq, however, ORHA would have to pay salaries on a much larger scale.[93] Meanwhile, as Nummy began to pay salaries in Iraq, others in ORHA were trying to determine how to jumpstart the economy and the banking industry in a country without a functioning credit system.

On 14 April, the topic of the C-staff meeting was the ORHA move into Iraq. Colonel DeGraff, the C-1, reported there were 360 in ORHA, a 100 percent personnel increase in a month, mostly of civilians. Colonel Costello had a fleet of 100 SUVs for the move and was sending Lieutenant Colonel Glen Cook to Baghdad to set up their quarters. Garner himself needed to set up the IIA, and with a small team he went to a meeting near the Tallil airbase near Nasiriyah, recently liberated, to discuss regime replacement.

Zalmay Khalilzad and Sherri Kraham would join him there by military aircraft with a group of Iraqi expatriates. President Bush had appointed Khalilzad as Special Envoy and Ambassador at Large for Free Iraqis in December 2002.[94] Charles Heatly and Emily Hand went along to manage the media. The group with Garner included his executive officer, Kim Olson; General Tim Cross; the ORHA historian; and four Arabic-speaking ORHA members: Mike Gfoeller and Andy Morrison from State and two Army Foreign Area Officers, Majors Chris Herndon and Fadi Petro. They flew to Tallil on board an army CH-47 helicopter from Kuwait with the back ramp down and a tail gunner seated on an improvised cushion tied to the middle of the ramp. Rather than the small windows that lined the side of the aircraft, the best view was over the tail gunner. The flight covered 120 miles. The terrain was almost featureless: tan, dusty, habitually flat, with a few oilfields. Roads and villages were scarce.[95]

The South African bodyguards with three SUVs had driven ahead and were waiting for the group at the airfield with Jennifer Glass, an American reporter working for the BBC who had been with ORHA-South at Umm Qasr. They drove through the airfield complex to the meeting site at Ur, the birthplace of Abraham. Two large tents had been set up for the conference with carpets covering the ground; a long line of outdoor toilets were nearby. There was no air conditioning and the next day would be hot. With what daylight remained, Garner and the group toured the large pyramid at the site and wandered through the ruins nearby. Mike Gfoeller had developed an interest in such ruins and served as a guide. Later they returned to the vicinity of the airfield where camping tents had been set up for them. After a modest dinner, Gfoeller, Morrison, Herndon, and Petro worked on some documents that Garner wanted translated into Arabic. The two FAO officers were in awe of Gfoeller's mastery of Arabic.[96]

An hour later, Buck Walters arrived from Umm Qasr to update Garner on the activities of ORHA-South. His appearance was remarkable; he wore blue jeans, a tropical shirt, a bush hat, and a long grey scarf with his pistol in a fast-draw holster. He told Garner that ORHA-South should move further north into Iraq; Garner and Walters discussed where that should be. An hour later several other vehicles arrived. A man in an American uniform without rank approached the gate and asked if General Garner was present. He indicated that Ahmed Chalabi was in one of the cars and wanted to speak to Garner. It would be the first time they had met.

Garner was not anxious to meet Chalabi, and the latter was reluctant to approach the gate. Everyone watched as the two awkwardly walked around in separate circles within fifty meters of each other. Finally, Garner approached the gate and Chalabi slowly responded by entering. The normally gregarious Garner was cautious and reserved. Chalabi was dressed in an elegant black suit, shirt, and tie, out of place with the austere surroundings and the casual clothes of the others. The dark shirt gave him the aura of a mafia don, and his demeanor was serious and calculating. After Garner and Chalabi solemnly shook hands, Garner offered him a seat at a small table in the compound.[97]

Chalabi had been in and out of Iraq the previous months and had intended to fly with his Free Iraqi Forces into Baghdad as it was captured. They were a motley group of poorly trained soldiers whom the Coaltion forces would soon identify as thugs. General Franks had refused Chalabi access to fly into Baghdad, but at the urging of Paul Wolfowitz he had been allowed to fly into Tallil on 6 April. Chalabi then made his way by car to Baghdad and back and told Garner there was little requirement for humanitarian assistance. Nor was it time to work on democracy: chaos reigned all over and the greatest need was for law and order.

Buck Walters agreed, indicating that his observations near Basra were comparable. But they disagreed on the appropriate response. Walters argued for a bottom-up approach relying on the military forces. Chalabi argued for a complete restructuring of the Iraqi government, a top-down approach to be led by Iraqi expatriates. Garner listened and said little. It was obvious that he was ill at ease with Chalabi, but he was polite and did not interrupt or argue. After Chalabi left without commitments from anyone, Garner and Walters talked through the events of the day and the challenges ahead.

The next morning, Garner and the group arrived early at the meeting site. Soon, about a hundred Iraqis arrived on three buses from the liberated areas of the country. The expatriates flying in from Qatar with Khalilzad and Kraham were delayed and arrived several hours later. The press pool arrived with Khalilzad's group. Fans in the tents kept the air circulating, but by noon the temperature was over 100 degrees. Euphoria in the air neutralized the heat.

At 1:00 P.M., Garner spoke to great applause. He was followed by Khalilzad, who made a long speech, followed by political representatives from the UK, Poland, Australia, Spain, and Czechoslovakia, all Coalition participants. Each addressed three issues: Iraq's future, a democratic government, and an Iraqi interim authority. The audience represented Iraq's ethnic and religious groups. Most spoke in Arabic. To ensure that American and other Coalition members present could understand, Mike Gfoeller served as translator. Soon word spread around the group that Gfoeller's command of Arabic and the quality of the interpretations he rendered were both superb. Prior to the meeting, Gfoeller had a low profile in ORHA; after the conference in Nasiriyah he was a Garner favorite. Gfoeller's star would continue to rise over the next year.

The first Iraqi to speak, a Shiite cleric from Nasiriyah, opened with a plea for democracy without a confessional system, with political positions allocated by ethnic group. He quoted Abraham Lincoln and advocated a constitution that did not discriminate between Shiite, Sunni, and Kurds and that erected a separation between church and state. In the future there would be no Iraqi refugees in the world thanks to the Coalition, he said. The second speaker introduced himself as a teacher and stated that what divided Iraq and Iraqis was not religion but policy. He argued that if anyone thought they could separate religion from government in Iraq, they were dreaming. He was followed to the podium by a doctor from Tikrit, Saddam Hussein's hometown. He said that his father had been imprisoned there and executed by being torn apart by mad dogs. It was time now for Iraqis to enjoy the riches of nature given to them by God. He quoted John F. Kennedy that Iraqis should "ask not what your country can do for you; ask what you can do for your country."

Kanan Makiya rose to speak next. He was a professor who taught at Brandeis and Harvard Universities, had served on the Democratic Principles Working Group with the Future of Iraq project, and was a member of Chalabi's INC. He asked what democracy should mean to Iraqis, and then suggested the answer was justice and the rule of law, which would provide a basis for equality. Democracy should not simply mean the rule of the majority. He was followed by a Shiite from the Shamar tribe who stated that Islam must be the state religion because it was fundamental to Iraq's beginnings. The next speaker was an Assyrian Christian who said there was religion in Iraq 7,000 years before Islam; an Iraqi constitution should thus respect diversity.

Hoshyar Zebari, a Kurd representing the Barzani faction with the KDP political party, wanted a federation in Iraq. Like Makiya, Zebari had served on the Democratic Principles Working Group of the Future of Iraq project. He stated that the Kurds wanted a united Iraq with rights for all, but they could not simply start from "ground zero" with the autonomy the Kurds had established over the past decade. He suggested the regional government that the Kurds had established could serve as a model for the rest of Iraq, a somewhat leftist philosophy. But he promoted a united Iraq, perhaps to appease those who might question Kurdish autonomy. Later in 2003, Zebari would become Iraq's foreign minister.

The meeting broke up at 5:00 P.M., with everyone tired from the heat and the excitement of the day. All the participants seemed pleased, perhaps because the meeting was a series of platitudes rather than a structured plan that would have required wide agreement. Garner would return to Tallil tired but relaxed, and in general he was satisfied with the meeting. Kim Olson directed everyone in Garner's group to the CH-47 aircraft, whose engines were throwing about sand and dust in a wide circle. Jennifer Glass managed to break away from the press pool and join Garner. For her part, Sherri Kraham, who had arrived with the Khalilzad group, suddenly hesitated as she began to board. She looked deathly ill, her makeup running and her face distraught. She was not ill, however; she had just never been on a helicopter before.

Garner overheard Loutjie Horn, one of his bodyguards, whisper to another bodyguard, Lyon Olivier, "Lyon, she's scared. I think she's going to cry."

Olivier responded matter-of-factly, "That's OK, Loutjie, you can't hear with the engines running."

But Kraham was not forced to fly that day after all: the flight was canceled due to a sandstorm. The group returned to their tents from the previous night and stayed over till the next morning. Olson, Glass, and Kraham shared a tent, laughing and giggling as if at a girl's slumber party, much to the amusement of the others. The next day they all drove back to Kuwait. The roads were better than anticipated and went through few populated areas. The terrain was as bleak, tan, flat, and dusty as it appeared from the air. There were a number of American military vehicles and trailers abandoned along the road, stripped of tires, wheels, and anything else of value.

Garner arrived at the Hilton in the mid-afternoon, pleased with the trip to Iraq. As he settled in for the evening, he received a call from Bruce Moore in northern Iraq, who told Garner that the Kurdish leaders, Barzani and Talabani, were preparing to go to Baghdad to set up an interim government. Garner wanted such a government, but he wanted to shape it, not inherit it. He told Moore to ask them to hold their trip to Baghdad until he could get to the Kurdish region and meet with them. Then they would set up the IIA as proposed by the Pentagon. To harness the momentum for an interim government, Garner altered his itinerary and took an immediate side trip to the Kurdish region. That seemed logical at the time, but it would leave Garner open to charges of cronyism with the Kurds at the expense of the larger tasks in Baghdad.

At the C-staff meeting on 17 April, Colonel DeGraff noted that personnel for ORHA had grown to over 430, with 386 in Kuwait at the Hilton or the Radisson Hotels. The rest were distributed in Umm Qasr with ORHA-South and in Erbil with ORHA-North, with a half dozen others in Baghdad looking for quarters. The increased number included the expanding Gurkha security detail, Raytheon contractors, and the IRDC expatriates from the United States. But only a few more senior advisor positions were filled; Defense still had not provided those promised.

Colonel Conway said his staff was shutting down the internet café and packing up the equipment for the move; he had received a small team from Raytheon a week earlier, but they would not be operational until later. His staff assumed they would set up an interim base at the airport as General Whitley proposed a month earlier. Gary Minor, the C-8 Comptroller, said he needed volunteers to pay Iraqi government civilians to keep them working. It was announced there would be two Easter services at the Hilton on Sunday, 20 April.

Larry Di Rita had arrived and joined ORHA; he was a special assistant to Secretary Rumsfeld. Garner and others assumed Di Rita had been sent as Rumsfeld's spy. It was a perception that Di Rita would overcome with Garner and Bates but not with everyone. On the seventeenth, Di Rita attended a meeting with Garner and some of those who would fly with him to Baghdad: Tim Cross, Barbara Bodine, Margaret Tutwiler, Sherri Kraham, and Kim Olson. They discussed the Kurdish leaders' desire to form an interim government. Kraham had strong views on the Kurds and was outspoken on their behalf. Di Rita disagreed and said the Pentagon wanted a more neutral position with the Kurds and did not want to alienate the Arab groups.

Tutwiler wanted to take a press pool. Di Rita weighed in again about how the media should be handled. Garner was visibly uncomfortable, in part due to fatigue from the previous days in Iraq and in part from Di Rita's aggressiveness. General Cross tried to speak several times, too much a gentleman to interrupt, though none hesitated to interrupt him.

General Franks wanted Garner to wait another month to bring ORHA into Iraq. Military commanders did not want a bunch of civilians in Baghdad or anywhere else in the country until it was secure. Others in ORHA had reservations about going in too soon. Costello argued that he needed time to distribute his SUVs and other equipment. Coalition aircraft would move some of them to Baghdad, but he had to drive in with their equipment. Jerry Bates agreed and wanted Garner to wait a few more days.

Garner was visibly annoyed with those who urged delay. He flew to Qatar to see General Franks to force the issue. Garner said he was less concerned about security than getting to Baghdad late. He felt he should have been there a week earlier, after Coalition forces had taken the capital city. So did some in Washington, who thought he was stalling. But Garner was not stalling; others were. Franks hesitated and then told him, "You are cleared to go. McKiernan will help, but there is much he can't do for you." Franks did not share Garner's concern about what would follow an invasion, nor was ORHA provided much in support through the ground commander.[98]

The movement preparation was dominated by Colonels Costello and Baltazar. The reconnaissance element under Colonel Boag in Baghdad had identified two locations for a headquarters: the Republican Palace and the high-rise Al-Rashid Hotel. Garner preferred the horizontal Republican Palace, concerned that a vertical structure like the Al-Rashid could be more easily targeted (as it would be in August).

A quartering party under Colonel Glen Collins was to drive up on 20 April to lay out a floor plan for the headquarters. Accompanying Collins were Captain Jones, the Public Affairs Officer, and three civilians: Steve Browning, Bob Gifford (both to serve as ministry advisors), and Andy Morrison, who would work with Baghdad Central; Skip Burkle had flown up earlier because of his concern about a cholera outbreak. They would be followed by an advance party with representatives of each ORHA component. The main body would then drive up in groups of SUVs, several days apart. KBR would go separately, bringing furniture, supplies, and equipment. Those still arriving in Kuwait to join ORHA would go with one of the serials of SUVs or by military aircraft.

This movement would split the pillars and staff sections, but those destined for Baghdad would soon be back together. Most of those in the Humanitarian Assistance, Reconstruction, and Civil Administration pillars would go to Baghdad with the C-staff; a few from each pillar would join the regional components. Those in Baghdad Central under Bodine, Morse, and Schollum would be with the C-staff in the Republican Palace. Those going to ORHA-South and ORHA-North would not see their peers again for some time. There would only be a few administrative personnel remaining in Kuwait to help those arriving to move on into Iraq. Once the main body was in Baghdad, those designated to work with the Iraqi ministries would have to travel into the city to find them.

On 20 April, there were two Easter services by the Hilton swimming pool; half of those in ORHA attended one or the other. The chaplain's sermon about the effects of war was sobering. An Army soldier sang several hymns a capella, the striking splendor of her performance standing in marked contrast to the assembled congregation's off-key attempts at singing other hymns. Later that day, Garner had all the ORHA members in Kuwait gather at a tennis court at the Hilton. About 300 were present. Without notes, Garner spoke at length, articulately and with inspiration. He talked of their mission, the opportunity to help change Iraq and make a contribution to history. It was a clear day and his voice carried well. There was excitement in the air and Garner's charisma was dominant. He seemed to know everyone's name and almost everyone felt they knew him personally. There was much to be done, he stressed, but the opportunities seemed more important than the challenges. Afterward, Garner's inner circle packed their things and prepared to fly into Baghdad. The quartering party would drive up in four SUVs; others would soon follow.[99]

The five weeks Garner and ORHA spent in Kuwait were crucial, offering many opportunities; a few were exploited, some only partially, but many were missed. Personnel expanded from 167 to 430, mostly civilians. Uniformed personnel accounted for half of ORHA in March; a month later they were only a quarter. In February the C-staff had only half a dozen officers occupying cubicles in the Pentagon. By mid-April it had full staff sections and some cohesion (communications were still poor). C-staff cohesion, however, had come at the expense of servicing the civilians with an unfortunate "we-they" divide.

ORHA civilians included those contracted for security and communications support, plus another hundred KBR civilians, who were not counted as ORHA but provided crucial support. Although the contractors worked hard and suffered the same hardships as the rest of ORHA, their roles would have been more effectively handled by military units.

The civilians that joined from other American governmental agencies enhanced the interagency component of ORHA, as a few counterparts from the UK and Australia marginally enhanced the Coalition component. Of the three pillars, Humanitarian Assistance and Reconstruction initially had the most personnel, but by mid-April Civil Administration had expanded and filled half its senior advisor positions for the Iraqi ministries. The Department of Defense had not yet provided the people it had promised. In their absence, Garner appointed junior personnel as interim advisors. Iraqi expatriates from the IRDC also increased ORHA personnel numbers, but the expatriates were not well integrated with the pillars.

In Kuwait, those in ORHA had some exposure to the military commands, but Central Command did little to assist Garner. The order placing ORHA under the control of CFLCC followed major operations rather than preceded them, taking General McKiernan and their staffs by surprise. Eclipse II, the CFLCC plan for post-conflict, did not address ORHA or the role it was to play in Iraq. Nor did CFLCC adjust to integrate ORHA into its plans or provide ORHA a useful relationship with JTF-4, the 352nd Civil Affairs Command, or the 416th Engineer Command. Giving ORHA several key colonels from JTF-4 was useful, but it degraded the formation General Hawkins had put together. When Colonel Benson, the CFLCC Plans officer, sought a better arrangement, he could not obtain the intellectual energy of his commander for key decisions.

In Kuwait, those from the Humanitarian Assistance and Reconstruction pillars sought to mobilize international agencies and NGOs through the HOC, but that had little utility when there was no humanitarian disaster. Little progress was made to integrate the civilian and military capacity for reconstruction. Those from USAID were possessive of their warrant from the NSC for reconstruction, leaving the Army Corps of Engineers only a minor role, despite its greater experience with large construction projects. There was no vision to integrate military engineer formations such as the 416th ENCOM in Iraq, when it should have been clear that outsourcing reconstruction would be challenging.

Inadequate preparation for security in Iraq after the invasion would become a damning Coalition deficiency. Despite repeated pleas by Garner, the NSC and Pentagon refused funds for interim police forces and trainers to reform Iraq's police. Ron Adams was perceptive enough to ask the Spanish ambassador if Spain could send their paramilitary police rather than an infantry brigade, but little came of that suggestion. General Abizaid intended to retain the Iraqi army for internal security; Colonel Hughes was working to obtain contractors for that role. Certainly no one in ORHA intended to disband the Iraqi army.

When OSD sent Garner a concept for an Iraqi Interim Authority to assume control in Iraq, it came with little substance or resources. When Garner and Khalilzad had their initial meeting with Iraqis in Nasiriyah, no one attended from OSD or from the Liz Cheney–Scott Carpenter Governance Team. When OSD managed to get Ahmed Chalabi and his freedom fighters into Iraq, there was no effort to coordinate them with Garner. Larry Di Rita joined Garner in Kuwait too late to learn much about ORHA before going into Iraq. The Pentagon and White House had muzzled Garner from talking to the media. Margaret Tutwiler tried to improve media relations, but her efforts came late. The invasion itself went much as projected, with Baghdad secured within a month. The surprise was that there was no refugee crisis, only half a dozen oil well fires, and no evidence of WMD, much less of their use.

Garner sent a team to Umm Qasr to help open the port, an experience that suggested problems and solutions for the rest of Iraq. To get Iraqi personnel to run the port, salaries had to be paid; to pay them, cash was required. David Nummy and General Stanton were ready to store and move the money, but Washington was reluctant to provide the money. For those with interagency skills to make a contribution, security was required, but the military formations that could provide security were reluctant. Recent damage to the infrastructure was caused from looting more than combat, but there were insufficient forces to prevent looting.

Garner had difficulty obtaining military support for ORHA before he went into Iraq, and it would be just as hard once he got there. ORHA preparations had been incomplete, which would lead to many surprises and inadequate responses. But all the problems Garner had experienced in Kuwait did not discourage him from going forward in Iraq. In fact, he could hardly wait.

ORHA senior leaders. *Left to right,* Lieutenant General Jay Garner, USA (Ret), in charge of ORHA; Brigadier General Floyd J. "Buck" Walters, USA (Ret), in charge of ORHA South-Central; Lieutenant General Jared "Jerry" L. Bates, USA (Ret), ORHA Chief of Staff; and Major General W. Bruce Moore, USA (Ret), in charge of ORHA-North. (Photo courtesy of Kim Olson)

Lieutenant General Ronald E. Adams, USA (Ret), ORHA deputy for operations. (Photo courtesy of Ron Adams)

State department personnel with ORHA in Kuwait, later in Iraq. *Seated left to right,* Caitlin Hayden, Ambassador Barbara Bodine. *Standing left to right,* Mike Ayoub, Ambassador Robin Raphel, Meghan O'Sullivan, Andy Morrison, Sandy Hodgkinson, Frank Oslander, woman unknown, Ambassador David Dunford, woman unknown, man unknown, woman unknown, Ambassador John W. Limbert, Sherri Kraham, Ambassador Tim Carney, woman unknown, man unknown, Drew Erdmann, last woman on the right Juliet Wurr, rest unknown. (Photo courtesy of Mike Ayoub)

ORHA leaders visit U.S. Embassy in Kuwait. *Left to right,* Ambassador Barbara K. Bodine, Colonel Kim Olson, USAF, Ambassador Richard H. Jones, ambassador to Kuwait, and Jay Garner. (Photo courtesy of Kim Olson)

ORHA leaders visit U.S. Embassy in Kuwait. *Left to right,* Ambassador John W. Limbert, Ambassador George F. Ward, Jay Garner, Buck Walters, and Major General Tim Cross, British Army, ORHA deputy for coalition operations. (Photo courtesy of Kim Olson)

ORHA Oil Team members. *Left to right,* Richard Frost, Clarke Turner, Gary Vogler, and Mike Taylor. (Photo courtesy of Gary Vogler)

Loutjie Horn and Lyon Olivier, South African bodyguards for Jay Garner, with him on a flight to Nasiriyah, Iraq, mid-April 2003. (Author photo)

Jay Garner at Ur, near Nasiriyah, Iraq, for the April conference with Iraqi leaders on Iraq's future, mid-April 2003. (Author photo)

Jay Garner and Mike Gfoeller, Foreign Service Officer, with others at Ur, near Nasiriyah, Iraq, April 2003. (Author photo)

Jay Garner speaking to ORHA members at the Hilton in Kuwait, 20 April 2003, just before departure to Baghdad. (Photo courtesy of Glenn Kramer)

Garner arrives in Baghdad, 21 April 2003, met by reporters, Major General William "Fuzzy" Webster, USA (next to Garner), deputy for operations, Combined Forces Land Component Command. Major General Albert Whitley, UK Army, deputy for reconstruction, is on the right in the picture. (Photo courtesy of Kim Olson)

ORHA members at luncheon with Kurdish leaders near Sulaymāniyyah, Iraq, 22 April 2003. *Seated on the right side of table in photo from the front*, Colonel Kim Olson, Major General Carl Strock, Ambassador Margaret Tutwiler, Larry Di Rita, Jabal Talabani, Jay Garner, Massod Barzani, and Major General Tim Cross. *Seated at front left in white*, Sherri Kraham. (Author photo)

Major General Tim Cross, Jay Garner, Major General Carl Strock talking to reporters in Erbil, Iraq, 23 April 2003. (Photo courtesy of Kim Olson)

Colonel Tom Baltazar, USA, organizing a ground convoy in Kuwait to drive to Baghdad, April 2003. Gene Stakhiv is leaning on the vehicle to the right. (Photo courtesy of Glenn Kramer)

ORHA convoy headed to Baghdad, April 2003. *In the foreground,* Meghan O'Sullivan in white jacket with Colonel George Oliver, USA. (Photo courtesy of David Nummy)

ORHA Treasury team flying to Iraq on a C-130, April 2003. *Left to right,* Van Jorstad, George Mullinax, and David Nummy. Gary Vogler of the ORHA Oil Team is on the right. (Photo courtesy of David Nummy)

The ORHA Treasury team: David Nummy, holding a radio, George Mullinax to his right, Van Jorstad to the right of him; Colonel Tony Puckett, holding a map. (Photo courtesy of David Nummy)

Colonel John R. "JR" Martin, USA, executive assistant to Lieutenant General Ron Adams. (Author photo)

Dayton Maxwell, strategic planner for U.S. Agency for International Development and ORHA, on a helicopter over Iraq. (Photo courtesy of Robert Polk)

Lieutenant Colonel Robert B. Polk, ORHA strategic planner, with children in Baghdad. (Photo courtesy of Robert Polk)

Steven E. Browning, senior advisor to the Health Ministry, and Dr. Said Haki, an Iraqi American working with ORHA. (Photo courtesy of Steve Browning)

Jay Garner with Iraqis in Baghdad, April 2003. (Author photo)

Don Eberly, senior advisor for the Ministry of Sports, with children in Baghdad. (Photo courtesy of Don Eberly)

Dorothy Mazaka, ORHA senior advisor for Education, seated with a Kurdish schoolboy in northern Iraq. (Author photo)

Ambassador David Dunford, senior advisor for the Ministry of Foreign Affairs, with members of that ministry in Baghdad. (Photo courtesy of David Dunford)

Lee Schatz, senior advisor for Agriculture, in an Iraqi wheatfield. (Photo courtesy of Lee Schatz)

Susan E. Hamrock, senior advisor for the Ministry of Trade. (Photo courtesy of Susan Hamrock)

David Nummy with an NBC reporter. (Photo courtesy of David Nummy)

Brigadier General "Buck" Walters, USA (Ret), in charge of ORHA South-Central, with a reporter from FOX News. (Photo courtesy of Glenn Kramer)

Jay Garner and Secretary of Defense Donald Rumsfeld in Baghdad, May 2003. (Photo courtesy of Kim Olson)

Jay Garner with Major General Carl Strock, USA, and Ambassador Ted Morse in Baghdad, late May 2003. Steve Browning, senior advisor to the Ministry of Health, is on the left holding a can; Major Larry F. Miller, USMC, in charge of security for ORHA, is in the right rear. The occasion is Garner's departure from Iraq. (Author photo)

Jay Garner, upon his departure from Iraq, accepting a gift from the Gurkhas, who were responsible for providing security for ORHA. (Photo courtesy of Tony Puckett)

The author in northern Iraq near Iranian border, August 2003. (Author photo)

Republican Palace, Baghdad, Iraq: headquarters for ORHA in 2003 and, later, for the Coalition Provisional Authority, 2003–2004. (Photo courtesy of Glenn Kramer)

Jay Garner on the road, departing Iraq, 31 May 2003. (Author photo)

5
IN IRAQ: GARNER'S FIRST THREE WEEKS

You have three weeks. If you cannot secure Baghdad by then, you will lose the support of the people and they will go to those who can.
—Iraqi Ministry of Health official[1]

For twenty-one days, Jay Garner was the senior civilian of the Coalition in Iraq before the arrival of his replacement, Ambassador L. Paul "Jerry" Bremer. It was a crucial three weeks, full of opportunity, obstacles, surprises, and disappointments, all with profound consequences for the Coalition and for Iraq. Garner's overarching plan, based on Washington's guidance, was to put Iraqis in charge of their country within a few months of the invasion. By doing so he hoped to empower the Iraqis living there over the expatriates who were attempting to return, but he tried to work with all groups. His assumption was that although Coalition forces would remain in Iraq for some time, it would be to assist with security rather than to dominate or occupy. As for the size of the Coalition's forces or their tasks over the long term, Garner did not forecast, nor did anyone in Washington provide him a roadmap.

Garner's team came from half a dozen government agencies and beyond: some were in uniform, some were contractors, and some were Iraqi expatriates. Most of Garner's people were driven and quickly adapted to the austere conditions in Iraq; only a few were petty or obstructive. It was a period of chaos that would test each of them, Garner most of all. Simon Elvy noted that Garner was comfortable with chaos—an assessment proven throughout this period.[2]

Lieutenant General McKiernan, the ground force commander, was busy with the invasion. Given the limited forces available to him, he wanted the occupation to be short-lived. He provided only meager support to Garner and ORHA upon the latter's arrival in Iraq. General Franks, the overall commander for the invasion, paid even less attention to Garner. Ironically, the Pentagon had placed Garner and ORHA under the operational control of

Franks and McKiernan, which made them responsible for his support, and yet the military commanders were anxious for Garner to take over in the shortest possible time so the military forces could go home sooner; perhaps they felt that if more substantive assistance were provided to Garner, it would commit them to remain longer. Meanwhile, no one in Washington attempted to correct the inadequate support given to ORHA. In fact, many there made it worse, with the result that unintended chaos would reign supreme in Iraq.

GARNER ENTERS IRAQ

From Kuwait, Garner flew to Baghdad with a small group early on 21 April. The group included General Tim Cross, ORHA Deputy for Coalition issues; Ambassador Margaret Tutwiler, media relations; Larry Di Rita, representing Secretary Rumsfeld; and Ambassador Barbara Bodine, who would manage Baghdad. Others included Colonel Kim Olson, Garner's executive officer; Mike Gfoeller, State political officer and Arabic linguist; Sherri Kraham, also from State and the ORHA coordinator for Iraqi ministries; and several South African bodyguards. A press pool joined them, comprising half a dozen print media personnel and several cameramen, managed by Charles Heatly and Elizabeth Hand, from the UK Foreign and Colonial Office (FCO).[3]

The sun was up for the last hour of the flight to Baghdad and several people took turns at the few small windows on the plane. From there they could glimpse Iraq's dominant color—tan. Most of it is sand. The monotony extends to the buildings in Iraq, nearly all the same color. In some areas the green from the fronds of date trees is prevalent, but even those trees were covered with the ubiquitous tan dust, dulling any addition to the uniform color scheme. Except for the northernmost areas, most of Iraq is flat and desolate. The dominant features observed from the air were the skeletal road system, sparse urban areas, and a few canal-like waterways.

At Baghdad International Airport (BIAP, pronounced "Bi–Ap"), Garner was met by Major General "Fuzzy" Webster, General McKiernan's deputy. Webster would be the most frequent point of contact Garner would have with any military command. Despite the friction between ORHA and CFLCC, everyone liked Webster. Having flown up earlier, Steve Browning and Dr. Skip Burkle also met Garner at the airport. Browning was designated the senior advisor for the Ministry of Transportation and Communications; Burkle was the senior advisor for the Ministry of Health.

Loaded onto half a dozen military trucks, the group drove the six miles from the airport into Baghdad. There was an armed escort but little sensation

of threat. The highway was littered with damaged civilian and military vehicles. Soldiers were observed along the way, sleeping, washing clothes, or
relaxing. It was clear the fighting was over and they were waiting to go home.
Iraqis along the road waved to Garner's convoy as it passed by, a few with
apparent reluctance. Surprisingly, there were many Iraqis driving around the
city, although no one seemed to be in a hurry. Coalition vehicles and Iraqi
traffic merged together without the aid of traffic lights or police.

The first stop was al-Yarmouk Hospital, with the entrance guarded by a
pair of Bradley-armored vehicles. They were there to protect Garner, not to
secure the already-looted hospital. A crowd gathered as Garner entered the
compound. Burkle and several Iraqi doctors provided a tour. Garner was
gregarious and friendly. The Iraqis could tell he was the senior person and
his charisma reached through the language barrier. Their welcoming remarks
were followed by complaints about the looting and condition of the hospital.
Garner promised to help. The visit was short and the convoy next drove to the
east side of Baghdad, crossing the slow and muddy Tigris. A dozen boys were
swimming along the banks.[4]

The next stop was one of the main power plants in Baghdad. Brigadier General Steve Hawkins was there to lead Garner on a tour of the facility. Those left
with JTF-4 were working on electricity. Hawkins had renamed it Task Force
Fajr, which meant "new dawn" in Arabic (though it also had a more profane
meaning). A week earlier, Hawkins had deployed with TF Fajr to BIAP, the
site of one of Saddam Hussein's palaces; there Hawkins established his task
force near McKiernan's headquarters, soon designated Camp Victory.[5]

There were fewer Iraqis at the power plant than at the hospital, and most
of those were employees of the plant. Since it was out of operation, there was
little activity. In contrast to the hospital, there was no sign of looting, but it
was dirty and appeared antiquated. Garner mixed easily with the Iraqis and
he and General Strock visited the plant manager to discuss electrical requirements for Baghdad's five million inhabitants. Within a few days, Hawkins, his
team, and a few Iraqis had turned on enough electricity in Baghdad to service
8 percent of the city's requirements; he intended to bring it up to 25 percent
within a week. But Hawkins said they had tackled the easiest obstacles first
and that getting additional electricity would be difficult. Prior to the invasion
in March, the electricity requirement for Baghdad was 1,400 constant megawatts, but the summer heat would demand well over 2,000 megawatts, about
half the electricity produced in the whole country before the invasion.[6]

From the power plant, Garner's convoy traveled to the edge of town to visit
a water treatment facility that had also been looted. No Iraqis were present

and Garner allowed his group an hour to eat the military rations they were issued. From there, they drove to Camp Victory near the airport; Heatly took the journalists to a location nearby for the night. Garner and his group spent the night in the airport palace, which had a huge rotunda and a high dome, several floors of large rooms, but no furniture beyond a few army cots. There was no working plumbing or electricity, and all the doors had been removed. Damage was limited to what appeared to be a master bedroom where an aerial bomb had penetrated the ceiling and gone through the floor. Broken stones, bricks, and twisted steel were spread all over.

At the entrance of the building were two large stacks of boxes, one containing military rations, the other cases of bottled water, available to anyone passing through. Barbara Bodine had subsisted on such rations during the siege of the U.S. Embassy in Kuwait in 1990; she picked out the meals with fruit. Garner, Di Rita, Cross, Tutwiler, Kraham, and a few others joined her in front of the palace for their second meal of the day. It was a quiet evening and they talked about what they had observed and the plan for the following morning: to fly north to the Kurdish area to determine what sort of interim government Talabani and Barzani were planning.

Late that night, the departure time from Baghdad was moved up and Olson had to wake the group at two in the morning. With no electricity, the group relied on pen lights to get packed. Olson got the word to Heatly in time for him to have the press pool ready just as a C-130 picked everyone up for the trip. The first stop was Erbil in northern Iraq. There was no airport there, just a long asphalt airstrip with some American military personnel set up in tents to manage air operations. Arriving as the sun came up, Garner's party shifted to two U.S. Air Force Special Operations MH-53 helicopters. There were no seats in the cargo area, so the crew chiefs directed everyone to sit on the floor and then draped a long cargo strap across them as a common seatbelt. The two aircraft flew close to the ground across the irregular terrain of the Kurdish region. It was fortunate, perhaps, that there had been no time for breakfast that morning before the roller-coaster ride.

The flight went from Erbil, the stronghold city of Barzani's KDP, to Sulaymāniyyah, the stronghold city of Talabani's PUK. At the latter, the airfield was comparable to the one at Erbil, a long asphalt airstrip with no terminal. This time there were no obvious American military forces on the ground. But there was quite a party to greet Garner. From ORHA-North, Bruce Moore and Dick Naab were waiting with a large number of Kurdish leaders. There was an honor guard of Kurdish Peshmerga awkwardly dressed in ceremonial uniforms at attention along the road, and a long line of brand new Japanese SUVs. As Garner stopped to talk to the Kurds, Charles Heatly strictly marshaled the journalists in another direction and prohibited them from taking pictures or talking to anyone on the airfield.

Without the media, Garner and his party drove to the University of Sulaymāniyyah in the center of town. They entered an auditorium designed for about 500 people, with every seat filled and people crowded into the aisles. Garner had been in the Kurdish region in 1991 when he commanded the ground intervention force in Operation Provide Comfort, assisting the Kurds driven into the mountains by Saddam Hussein after Desert Storm. Now Garner was being treated as a returning hero. He moved to the center of the stage; no one seemed disturbed that he was surrounded by guards carrying assault rifles. There was loud cheering and applause. With no introduction or notes, Garner spoke for thirty minutes. He discussed in broad terms the liberation of Iraq and the important role the Kurds would now play. He told the many students present that they were the future leaders in Iraq. The overwhelming euphoria in the crowd surprised those who had traveled with Garner. Several people commented that it must be akin to Americans entering Paris in 1944. Garner introduced General Cross, in civilian clothes, as the senior UK representative. Though less gregarious by nature than Garner, Cross too was caught up in the moment, speaking with strong words and powerful gestures, clearly enjoying himself. He emphasized the role of his country in the Coalition with both enthusiasm and eloquence. Even Garner's stoic South African bodyguards were caught up in the emotions of the moment. The cheering was nonstop. Few would remember later exactly what Garner and Cross had said. But it was not what they said that mattered: it was what they represented.

The American invasion the previous month was a major event for the Kurdish population, bringing an end to an oppressive regime. Recording the moment with Garner and Cross were Kurdish photographers and journalists, the only members of the media allowed into the auditorium, and their many flashing cameras added to the excitement. Some in the audience called out the word for "federation," suggesting Kurdish autonomy within Iraq. Garner did not use the word himself, but to many Kurds that was what liberation meant.

Leaving the auditorium, Garner and Cross made a brief visit to a local primary school and then returned to the airfield where the group flew by helicopter to Lake Dokan, a resort area west of the city. Again, the journalists that had traveled with him were left behind. At the resort Garner and Cross were greeted by more Kurds. Around the hotel, there were over a hundred guards armed with assault rifles. As Garner waited, Larry Di Rita and Margaret Tutwiler went outside to call Washington on their satellite phones.

Subsequently, everyone moved to another building, with a large conference-style banquet room.

In the lobby, Garner met Barzani and Talabani. Kurdish journalists abounded and jockeyed for position as Garner talked to the two Kurdish leaders. After brief comments, they went into the banquet room where there were more well-armed bodyguards. The meal included lamb, beef, and fish amid colorful vegetables and fruits. There were plenty of soft drinks but no alcohol, perhaps in deference to the devout Barzani, who did not drink. After the meal, Garner, Cross, Talabani, and Barzani returned to the lobby for more photographs for the eager Kurdish media.

When they retired to a conference room, they quickly got down to the reason Garner had left Baghdad right after his arrival—to discuss an interim government of Iraqi leaders. Barzani and Talabani would represent the Kurdish population of Iraq. Garner assumed there would be several Iraqi expatriates in an interim government, probably Ayad Allawi of the INA and Ahmed Chalabi of the INC. Garner and Cross wanted more leaders who had been in Iraq. Talabani told him they would bring in Ibrahim Jaafari of the Dawa Party and Abdul Aziz Hakim of SCIRI, and perhaps a Christian Iraqi.

"That's fine," said Garner. "I don't have a problem with anybody in the group except Hakim. . . . Hakim is too Iranian for me."

Talabani put his hand on Garner's knee. "Jay, think about this. It's better to have Hakim inside the tent than outside the tent."

"You know," replied Garner, "that's damn good advice."

Several times Talabani and Barzani told Garner he could pick whomever he wanted for the group or reject anyone they suggested. Within a few weeks there would be seven members of Garner's Iraqi Interim Authority: Barzani, Talabani, Chalabi, Allawi, Jaafari, Hakim, and Nassir Chadurchi, the latter a Sunni rather than the Christian Talabani had suggested.[7]

Afterward, Garner talked to Tutwiler and Di Rita about what was said. Di Rita called Paul Wolfowitz at the Pentagon to keep those in Washington up to date. Then they returned to Sulaymāniyyah. At their hotel, Garner and Cross met another group of Kurds. The mood approached what had been experienced at the university earlier. As Garner and Cross talked about liberating Iraq and the important role of the Kurds in a new regime, again there were cries from the crowd for federation. The journalists present were all from the Kurdish region, while Garner's press pool was again kept away. That evening, hotel televisions had nonstop coverage of the day's events: Garner's arrival at the airfield, his talk at the university, the visit with Barzani and Talabani at Lake Dokan, and the talk that evening in the hotel. But all the TV channels

were Kurdish stations. There was no CNN or other international coverage of
the day's events; the news went no further than northern Iraq.

That evening, after Garner and others in his entourage took their first
shower in three days, Talabani hosted a meal in the hotel restaurant with local
leaders, academics, and journalists from Sulaymāniyyah. Those present were
mainly from Talabani's PUK, with little or no representation from Barzani's
KDP. In contrast to the luncheon, that evening the alcohol flowed freely and
waiters went from table to table dispensing glasses of scotch, wine, and beer.
Jalal Talabani was the center of attention, well dressed and doting on Garner
and his party, going from guest to guest shaking hands and making small and
not-so-small talk. Garner was relaxed and enjoyed the evening, his view of
Talabani as the consummate politician confirmed.

The next morning, 23 April, Garner and his party, finally joined by his press
pool, flew CH-53 helicopters back to Erbil, the capital of Iraqi Kurdistan. The
first stop there was a school where Garner talked to teachers and students.
Banners hung from the walls praising the United States and United Kingdom for the liberation of Iraq. From the school, Garner went to the Kurdish
regional parliament, which included all Kurdish parties, to meet with more
political leaders.

After the meeting, Garner held a press conference in the garden courtyard,
with both the Kurdish media and his own press pool present. Garner talked
about Iraqi sovereignty rather than Kurdish autonomy. Tutwiler managed the
questions from the media, which were aggressive but not hostile. After another banquet in the parliament building, Garner's group was flown by helicopter to a nearby Arab village on a road north of Mosul. American aircraft
had destroyed a bridge near the village a month earlier. A large crowd gathered as the helicopters landed. In contrast to those in the Kurdish areas, the
Arab villagers were more subdued. There were no banners or cheering. Major
General Carl Strock, who had been with Garner since he left Kuwait, took
charge of the bridge tour.

At the bridge were several members of a FEST-A (Forward Engineer Support Team–Advance) from the U.S. Army Corps of Engineers. Strock had sent
the team to northern Iraq earlier to work with ORHA-North; they provided
information about plans to repair the main span. A U.S. Army engineer unit
had already put a single-lane military bridge into operation to allow one-lane
traffic. Through an interpreter, Garner tried to engage several Arabs nearby,
but they were reluctant to warm to him. The experience underscored the fact
that northern Iraq had large Arab as well as Kurdish communities, and the
Arabs did not share the Kurdish enthusiasm for the Coalition.

When they returned to Erbil, Garner's group was split for accommodations at two locations, both about ten miles north of Erbil. Garner and his senior members stayed in the guest houses of Kurdish leaders and continued discussions into the evening. More junior members of the group and the accompanying media were sent to a new hotel still under construction two miles away. A dozen members of ORHA-North staying in the hotel were reunited with those from Garner's group with whom they had worked at the Pentagon and in Kuwait. The press pool sent to the hotel again missed Garner's interactions with the Kurdish leaders, but they were stoic about their situation and mixed easily with those from ORHA.

Garner had come to Kuwait and Iraq with little guidance on how to form an Iraqi government. The pro-Chalabi pressure in the Pentagon from Doug Feith and Paul Wolfowitz[8] had not been reinforced by Rumsfeld or the NSC; nor had Chalabi made an effort to promote himself to Garner prior to their meeting at Tallil a week earlier. Garner was more comfortable with the Kurdish leaders with whom he had worked before, such as Talabani. At Sulaymāniyyah Garner had asked him if he was going to Baghdad.

"Yes, initially," he answered. "Mr. Barzani will remain here in charge of Kurdistan and I will represent the Kurds in Baghdad."

For Garner, the gregarious and dynamic Talabani had more political utility than the reserved Barzani, whom Garner described as more warrior than politician. Garner was already thinking of Talabani as a key figure for a future interim government.[9]

Early on 24 April, Garner returned to Baghdad by C-130 and went to the Baghdad Convention Center to speak to leading Iraqi professionals. Barbara Bodine, who remained in Baghdad when Garner had gone north to meet the Kurds, rejoined him. The Convention Center was a large modern complex across from the Al-Rashid Hotel, less than two miles from the National Palace, which together defined much of what would soon be known as the Green Zone in the city. The Convention Center had survived the war with no obvious damage and little looting, secured by a tank platoon. An Army signal unit had set up a sound system in the main auditorium. When the Iraqis arrived they were dignified and restrained, almost sullen. They were dressed in business suits or formal Arab attire, while Garner and his party wore casual clothes. The Iraqis spoke little to each other, making it difficult to determine their respective backgrounds or relative status.

Garner's opening remarks were gracious, humble, and subdued—neither as emotional nor as ambitious as his statements in Sulaymāniyyah and Erbil. In contrast to his audience in the Kurdish areas, Garner did not know any of the Iraqis present, nor was he well known to them. Garner informed them that the purpose of the Coalition was to remove Saddam Hussein from power, to set conditions for democracy, and to get Iraq on its feet. He said Iraq was a rich country with enormous oil wealth and stressed that the oil was for the Iraqis, not for the Coalition. The Coalition's interest in the oil was only to get it flowing so Iraq would have revenues for reconstruction. General Cross spoke next; he made clear that the UK was a key member of the Coalition and wanted to assist Iraq to move toward democracy and prosperity. Garner then introduced Bodine as his senior representative in Baghdad. He told the Iraqis present that she needed the names of the key leaders in Baghdad to help them get the city administration running. Bodine spoke briefly, her serious and direct mien drawing no response from the all-male audience.

The audience listened without apparent emotion. One person introduced himself as Riyadh Aziz, a professor at Baghdad University. He expressed concern about human rights and security and asked that students be allowed to complete the academic year so they would not have to repeat it the following year. He added that the Iraqi people wanted an elected government as soon as possible. Garner said getting the schools reopened was a high priority and that the Coalition was working to establish security to make that happen; they also wanted to get the Iraqi ministries restarted.

The next Iraqi who spoke from the audience thanked Garner "for removing the dictator," and then requested that the Iraqi media be activated to inform the population of their future, a concern echoed by others in attendance. The Iraqi also expressed apprehension about the number of privately owned weapons; the postwar chaos and insecurity could lead to their misuse.

Another Iraqi opened with a gracious statement acknowledging what the Coalition had done for Iraq. He also asked to help get students back into school, which would get them off the streets and out of mischief. He said Iraq needed a temporary government for stability and for hope, and also because the people were accustomed to getting news and guidance "from the top." Garner acknowledged the internal media issue and said he would get someone working on it.

The Baghdad manager for electricity then introduced himself and said that although electricity was not a political issue, it still warranted immediate attention given the many sectors of the economy that depended on it. It was thus necessary to pay the salaries of the electrical workers—and by implication other government employees—to keep them on the job. Meanwhile, most Iraqis had not been paid for several weeks.

The next Iraqi to speak introduced himself as a judge. He complained that there was too much attention on democracy, when what Iraq needed most was law and order in the face of all the chaos and destructive looting that the invasion had unleashed. He warned Garner that the looting was more serious than the Coalition appreciated. Many Iraqis did not really understand all the talk about new liberties. Liberty, he said, must have its limitations; otherwise some would assume liberty included the right to steal. The judge also complained that Chalabi's people were moving into Baghdad as if they were going to take over the country. Garner stated firmly that Chalabi was not the Coalition's candidate for national leader in Iraq—that was something the Coalition expected the Iraqis to work out for themselves. He said that if Chalabi caused problems the Coalition would have him leave. Garner could see clearly that while those in Washington were obsessed with installing democracy in Iraq, the responsible members of the audience and others throughout Iraq were more interested in security, essential services, and salaries.

One of the last speakers from the audience pointed out that the Iraqi army was formed in 1921 as an Iraqi institution and that the country was proud of it. Similarly, the Iraqi police forces had been set up by the British over eighty years ago. Neither was an institution created by Saddam Hussein. Therefore, the speaker said, both the army and the police forces should be put back into operation as soon as possible rather than disbanded. If the Coalition were to follow this advice, it would see that "this is a rich country with frozen assets." In all, the meeting was cordial and serious, with suppressed emotion; the Iraqi Arabs were more cautious about the Coalition and uneasy about the future than the Kurds had been.

After the meeting, Garner went to the National Museum in Baghdad. Earlier in the month, the international media had complained about the military's failure to secure the museum when the city was taken, with much of the blame directed at ORHA. While some criticism was justified, ORHA's Drew Erdmann, Simon Elvy, Philip Hall, Mike Gfoeller, and Mike Ayoub had made multiple efforts to have military forces provide security for the museum when Coalition forces took Baghdad. That security had not been provided, however, in part because the military command paid little attention to ORHA's multiple requests, and in part because the military forces available to provide security for such sites were inadequate, a deficiency of prewar preparation.

Three days earlier, Colonel Matthew Bogdanos had arrived in Baghdad with a small team known as the Joint Interagency Coordination Group (JIACG). Bogdanos was a New York City prosecutor and a Marine Corps Reserve officer who had been activated for the invasion of Iraq. His team included members of the military services, Treasury, FBI, CIA, and the Bureau of Immigration and Customs Enforcement. The JIACG had many tasks in Iraq, but Bogdanos had a particular interest in antiquities. After reports of looting at the National Museum, he requested permission to add it to his responsibilities. When his team came in on 21 April, a platoon from the 3rd

Mechanized Infantry Division was also arriving to secure the compound. By then, however, the museum had already been looted. Press reports indicated that 170,000 museum pieces were lost. It took Bogdanos's team several weeks to determine that the actual number was less than 10 percent of that because many artifacts had been placed in storage for protection or taken by Iraqis for safekeeping. To encourage the artifacts' return, Bogdanos implemented an amnesty program.[10]

When Garner arrived at the museum, there were still Bradley fighting vehicles on the grounds, but otherwise the site was almost deserted. The grounds were in poor condition and the building inside was dirty and sparsely furnished, with few pieces still on display. Garner's media pool had accompanied him, but they were not allowed to go in the building. An hour later Garner left for his new headquarters at the National Palace.

ORHA ARRIVAL IN BAGHDAD

The first ORHA group arrived in Baghdad on 16 April, with the Coalition's Early Entry Command Post (EECP). Under Colonel Colin Boag, it included Lieutenant Colonel Glen Cook of the C-4 Logistics staff; Major Keith June of the C-6 Communications staff; and Major Pete Veale of the C-7 Engineer staff. Their purpose was to find a headquarters for ORHA. After considering the Al-Rashid Hotel, they settled on the National Palace, often called the Republican Palace, later just called the palace. While undamaged by bombing and structurally sound, the interior was in disarray.[11]

The nearby power plant had been bombed, which cut power for water and sewage. Most of the furniture had been removed by the Iraqis or by American soldiers to be used at other locations. There were no functioning communications, all the interior doors had been removed, some of the windows were broken, and a recent sand storm had left a thick layer of talcum powder–like dust throughout the building, which quickly turned to mud when the floors were washed. Mosquitoes swarmed throughout much of the compound. Major June was amazed at the size of the palace and wondered how they would wire it for the extensive computer connections that would be required. Major Veale suggested they should wire only the central portion of the building for the first phase and use the rest for sleeping quarters, which made sense at the time but would soon lead to friction within ORHA.[12]

A few days later, Cook and June caught a flight back to Kuwait to prepare their staff sections for the work to be done in the palace. June managed to attend a meeting at CFLCC Headquarters at Camp Doha on Saturday night, 19 April, to discuss the status of the palace and the complications for their communications. Raytheon had sent eight of their contractors to Kuwait on 7 April, but they had not fully anticipated ORHA's needs and the rest of their team had still not arrived. General McKiernan directed his staff to provide communications assistance, but the support was modest. When Major June returned to Baghdad on 23 April, a detachment of seventeen soldiers from the 86th Signal Battalion were at the palace. The signal unit set up two servers with thirty classified and thirty unclassified computers, as well as thirty military phone lines that could network with military units in Iraq and Kuwait (there were no communications systems to link with Iraqis). That was more capacity than had been available to ORHA in Kuwait, but by the end of April ORHA's growth to some five hundred people at the palace, with more to follow, would make it insufficient.[13]

After Colonel Boag selected the National Palace for ORHA headquarters, Colonel Glenn Collins, the ORHA deputy chief of staff, decided to lay out a floor plan for the staff sections. As Cook and June returned to Kuwait, Collins left for Baghdad on an early flight on Easter Sunday. He took Steve Browning and several others with him and linked up with Colonel Boag, Major Veale, and Skip Burkle, who came up earlier. Browning and Burkle found Hawkins's Task Force Fajr at the airport. Since the officers in TF Fajr had been in Iraq a week, Browning wanted to discuss the electricity situation and the Ministry of Transportation and Communications, for which he was to be the Senior Advisor. Burkle met Navy Captain Dennis Ammundson, a doctor and Hawkins's medical staff officer, who took an interest in Burkle's role as senior advisor for the Iraqi Ministry of Health.[14]

Barbara Bodine, who remained in Baghdad when Garner flew to Erbil, met Browning and Major General Buford "Buff" Blount, commander of the 3rd Mechanized Infantry Division, on 21 April at Camp Victory. Blount took them to see the palace in Baghdad, where they met Colonel Collins as he was laying out the floor plan for the ORHA C-staff. Browning and Bodine objected to putting the C-staff in the main office spaces in the central part of the building, the only part of the building that would initially be wired for computers, while those in the three pillars would be set up in the wings of the building without computer support. Browning felt that Collins "just got it absolutely wrong; this was going to lead to dysfunction and chaos. . . . The biggest problem at ORHA from the very beginning was there was never a recognition that the C-staff was there to support the mission." Browning felt problems with the C-staff in Kuwait would be replicated in Baghdad and

"Barbara Bodine was in . . . absolute agreement with me and tried to reiterate the point that I was making when Glenn [Collins] . . . blew her off. . . . This dysfunction [with communications] caused incredible tension."[15]

Meanwhile, on 22 April, the advance party departed from Kuwait under Jerry Bates and headed for Baghdad. Costello and Baltazar had planned for sixty-four personnel in the advance party, with the main body to follow in three serial convoys, several days apart. That plan was based on the condition that Garner would initially stay with General McKiernan's headquarters at the Baghdad airport while the group with Bates set up operations in the Republican Palace. But when it was clear that Garner intended to move directly into the palace, each component in ORHA wanted to get more people into Baghdad as soon as possible. With Bates's concurrence, the advance party was expanded to 120 personnel with thirty Chevrolet Suburbans, each carrying four people and their baggage. To prevent congestion on the road, the convoy was split into three smaller groups, known as serials, of ten vehicles each with a gap between them, out of touch with the others until they linked up at the airport outside Baghdad.

There were no assigned drivers as there were in military formations; most of the drivers were majors, colonels, and senior civilians from the Departments of State, Commerce, Agriculture, and Treasury and from USAID. No one asked to see a license. There were no radios attached to the Suburbans, though the advance party did have a few walkie-talkies of limited range and reliability. Printed maps were scarce, while some groups made do with hand-drawn maps. Lieutenant Colonel Bob Mott, the Army doctor with ORHA, put together some first-aid kits, which were scattered throughout the convoys, about one per four vehicles. Colonel Baltazar had asked the military command for an armed escort for the ORHA vehicles, but that was refused.[16] Major Larry Miller took a few of his Gurkhas, the only convoy members with rifles. Others that were armed had only a pistol. Most of the civilians were unarmed. None of the vehicles were armored.

Colonel Tony Puckett rode in the convoy serial with Bates; later he recalled making a stop as they crossed into Iraq. "I walked off the road thirty meters to take a photo of our convoy. Jerry [Bates] went nuts, thinking there could be mines around. . . . [He] started screaming at me like I was a private. I realized then that they were under a lot of stress. Every time we stopped, Iraqis swarmed around us. No one seemed happy about our presence. . . . We had no security escort."[17]

During the last week of April, over 130 SUVs packed with ORHA personnel drove from Kuwait to Baghdad in serials of ten vehicles with no military escort. Those relying on hand-drawn strip maps often missed turns that would have taken them around Basra and Nasiriyah; as a result, many serials endured unintended tours of those cities. What was projected to be a ten-hour drive often took fourteen. Fortunately, there was only one accident and no fatal injuries. Many making the trip were appalled that the military command provided no armed escort and that the serials were so poorly equipped with maps and communications.[18]

By late April, when it was time for ORHA to move into Iraq, the military commanders made it clear they were not anxious to have the civilians come forward, yet they were anxious for ORHA to take over so they could return to the United States—a contradiction imposed upon Garner and ORHA. As such, Garner, Bates, Baltazar, Costello, and others had become conditioned not to ask for much assistance from the military command—perhaps too conditioned.

While most of those in ORHA drove to Baghdad, some flew. On 24 April, eighteen people left on a military aircraft; most of them were designated as senior or interim advisors for the Iraqi ministries. They included Ambassador David Dunford for the Ministry of Foreign Affairs; Ambassador Robin Raphel for the Ministry of Trade; Ambassador Tim Carney for the Ministry of Industry and Minerals; Lee Schatz for the Ministry of Agriculture; Don Eberly for the Ministry of Youth and Sport; Dorothy Mazaka for the Ministry of Education; and Gary Vogler for the Ministry of Oil. Their first aircraft was taken by a general who had missed his flight, forcing them to wait several hours for another. When they finally arrived at the airport in Baghdad, it took several more hours to arrange ground transportation to the palace in the Green Zone.[19]

When Garner returned from Erbil on 24 April, there were 150 ORHA personnel in Baghdad; 300 more were still in Kuwait. A KBR convoy had arrived separately on 21 April with food, equipment, furniture, and eighty personnel soon crammed into several rooms in the palace. KBR support was sustained by a steady flow of trucks, initially driven by Americans, later by other nationals as well.[20]

As ORHA moved into the palace, the American soldiers who had initially occupied it moved out. They remained nearby to secure the Green Zone, but Colonel Collins had to establish perimeter and internal security for the palace. By the time Bates and Costello arrived with the advance party, Collins located a warehouse with the furniture and heavy eight-foot doors that had been removed. It took a week to have the doors replaced. Collins learned that the center section of the palace had been built in the 1950s and had been bombed in 1991 during Desert Storm. When it was repaired in 1995, two wings had been added and four large statues of Saddam Hussein were erected on the roof. While some believed Saddam Hussein had used the palace as his head-quarters, Collins learned that it served as meeting center for the Republican Guard, with conferences held in the large ball rooms.

Major Veale had to get the electricity and plumbing in the building work-ing. It took a week to locate all the critical plumbing and electrical lines and longer to get them repaired with a working electrical source. The large kitchen in the palace was full of food that had rotted, creating an incredible odor. The first arrivals had boarded up the kitchen; when they began to clean it they found not only decayed food but also the corpse of an Iraqi man.[21]

When Major Miller arrived with the advance party, he set up security with his Gurkhas at the entrances to the palace building. He established quarters for the Gurkhas in the dank basement of the main section of the palace, but the stoic Gurkhas did not complain; the location of their quarters ensured they were always nearby. After several requests for more security, Miller added two military units to his security force. For external security around the com-pound, he obtained 127 soldiers from Company C, 3rd Battalion, 124th Infantry, a Florida National Guard regiment. That unit had followed inva-sion forces into Iraq, initially to secure an air defense unit at Tallil Air Base. Eventually it joined ORHA to secure the palace. When many regular army formations redeployed to the United States during the summer of 2003, the National Guard Company remained for most of a year to provide perimeter security for the palace.[22]

Miller also picked up a military police company with two platoons to pro-vide security for ORHA SUVs that would soon be driving all over Baghdad. The MP Company had its own communications and vehicle maintenance. Miller had the company set up in adjacent buildings to the palace where it maintained a motor pool and its own operations center. Miller used the MPs to help him set up his own small operations center on the second floor of the palace near the C-2 and C-3 staff sections. Soon after arrival, Miller had in-ternal security of the palace established with the Gurkhas, external perimeter security with Company C, and movement security with the MP Company. But it was a modest force to protect and assist the eclectic ORHA organiza-tion. The rush to Baghdad and the zeal to get to work led many in ORHA to disregard their own safety. When they arrived in Baghdad, Miller felt that many in ORHA were overly concerned with their living and working condi-tions rather than their security.[23]

Living and working conditions over the first week in Baghdad were challenging. Before the plumbing was fixed, there were half a dozen porta-potties available for several hundred people. As the dining facility was put into operation, there were two mountains of boxes in the palace basement: one with bottled water; the other with military rations. No one would starve or go without water, although the latter was restricted for drinking, not to be used for bathing. By the time Garner arrived from Erbil, KBR had a grill set up outside offering hamburgers and hot dogs for lunch. Even after the kitchen was in operation, the fare remained hot dogs, hamburgers, and chicken nuggets through the end of April. But no matter how modest the food was for ORHA, it was better than what the American soldiers in Baghdad were eating through May.

Next to the bedroom he would share later with Ron Adams, Garner had a meeting room with a few couches and chairs Colonel Collins had found. The first evening in the palace, Garner, Bates, Cross, Tutwiler, and Di Rita opened a bottle of scotch someone had found. Lacking glasses or cups, Tim Cross cut up plastic water bottles to make crude bowl-like containers for the warm whiskey. Any drink was a treat. But that could not be shared with the American soldiers who were subject to General Order #1, which prohibited the consumption of alcohol by Coalition military personnel in Iraq.

That evening Garner took a phone call from the Secretary of Defense. Rumsfeld complimented Garner on his work in Iraq and the efforts of ORHA; Garner brought him up to date on issues he was working, including the Iraqi Interim Authority (IIA) he was trying to form with Barzani, Talabani, Chalabi, Hakim, Jaafari, and Chadurchi. Rumsfeld offered no objection to the IIA, which Garner assumed constituted approval. At the end of the conversation Rumsfeld told Garner, almost as an afterthought, that President Bush would soon announce the new presidential envoy to Iraq, Ambassador L. Paul "Jerry" Bremer.[24]

Garner was taken aback. He had just gotten on the ground in Iraq and it was his first night in the palace. He had been working with the assumption that he would have sixty to ninety days to get ORHA focused and moving in the right direction before he departed. He did not know Bremer. Announcing the replacement would make Garner a lame duck just when he needed all the clout he could muster with the Iraqi population. He expressed his concerns and asked Rumsfeld to delay the announcement and Bremer's arrival in Iraq until 1 July.

"I can't," Rumsfeld responded. "The President has already selected Bremer and it's up to him." He asked Garner to stay for an interim period with Bremer.

Garner objected. "You can't have two bosses in one command." Again he asked for more time. Rumsfeld said it was out of his hands and reminded

Garner that a replacement for him had always been the plan. When Garner asked how he was to work with Bremer if he remained, Rumsfeld simply told him they should just "work it out."[25]

The next day Garner called Bremer at the Pentagon to discuss their transition. Bremer said Garner was doing important work and asked him to stay. With the positive exchange, Garner assumed they might be able to work together. But the situation was less positive than it appeared; Bremer would not only be difficult for Garner, he was planning to reverse many of the initiatives Garner had put in motion.[26]

BURKLE, BROWNING, AND THE MINISTRY OF HEALTH

Skip Burkle had had a similar surprise two days earlier when he learned that he was to be replaced as senior advisor to the Ministry of Health by James K. Haveman, a politically connected social worker from Michigan. Garner was not informed about the change until days later, only hearing it through CNN at one of the military locations with better communications. Burkle believed Haveman was less qualified and was so furious about the replacement that he went to the Baghdad airport and left the next day. Perhaps thinking Garner had something to do with Haveman, Burkle did not notify Garner of his departure. He did, however, tell Steve Browning and asked him to attend a meeting at the Health Ministry for 24 April that he had scheduled.[27]

A few days earlier, General Steve Hawkins, with his chief of staff, Colonel Mike Williams, was visiting a power plant in southern Baghdad when an Iraqi handed Williams a message. It said senior Iraqi officials at the Ministry of Health wanted to talk to someone about getting their ministry operating. That message set in motion a series of unanticipated problems within the Coalition. Williams consulted Hawkins and took two of the doctors he had retained from his medical personnel with JTF-4, Captain Dennis Ammundson, USN, and Charles Fisher, USAR, to the ministry, where three Iraqis were waiting. They told Williams they wanted the ministry to be able to provide spring vaccinations for children. Williams returned to report to Hawkins and later to British Major General Albert Whitley, McKiernan's deputy for post-conflict operations. Subsequently, McKiernan directed Hawkins to add the Iraqi medical community to his tasks in Baghdad; it was not clear why McKiernan did not direct his own large military medical command to take on such a mission. Williams called his group the Medical Support Team. With Ammundson and Fisher, he looked for Skip Burkle, just as the latter had left

Iraq. Williams then went to Steve Browning, who had arrived to work with another ministry and asked him to join them in representing Garner and ORHA. Browning agreed; they made their first visit to the ministry the next day.[28]

Williams, Browning, and the two military doctors went to the ministry building to find that it had been severely looted and damaged; debris was scattered throughout and there was no one to protect what was left. But there were senior ministry representatives there to meet Browning and his group. The senior administrative ranks in the Iraqi government had the title of Director General (DG), roughly comparable to a U.S. government assistant secretary. Several DGs from the Ministry of Health were present with Dr. Ali Shanan al-Janabi, the deputy minister prior to the invasion. They met in a small room with broken windows, using some chairs and a table that had not been looted. They were joined by Chris Giannou, a doctor and representative of the International Committee of the Red Cross (ICRC), then working in Baghdad.

Browning introduced his team and delivered a prepared statement that indicated that he would serve as an interim ministry advisor, with the objective to get people back to work and the health system functioning. He said the Coalition would help with rebuilding and that groups of NGOs would soon be arriving in Baghdad. But Browning did not want to disrupt efforts by those in the ministry to regain control, nor did he want to alter the health policies in Iraq. Browning told them that it was the Coalition policy to "work with Ba'athists or former Ba'athists as long as they had not been engaged in the development of weapons of mass destruction, atrocities, criminal behavior, or violations of human rights"—a policy that would be changed several weeks later, with no advance warning for Browning or the Iraqis in the Ministry of Health.[29]

The Iraqis were receptive, courteous, and nervous. When Browning asked what they needed most, they all stated the same thing repeatedly—security. Looting had crippled the health care system throughout Iraq, particularly in Baghdad. Security was required to protect the buildings and equipment as well as the personnel that worked in the hospitals and the Health Ministry. Browning learned that there were thirty-three hospitals in Baghdad and that eleven of them were then under the control and protection of Hawza, an organization run by Shia clerics. He thought control of the hospitals by a conservative religious group was undesirable and initially started to take action to replace them, but he soon realized that he could not replace the security they provided the hospitals that they controlled.[30]

ORHA ACTIVITIES IN BAGHDAD

An early morning ceremony on 25 April commemorating ANZAC Day, the date Australian and New Zealand forces landed at Gallipoli in 1915, was planned at Camp Victory, and the Australians Andrew Goledzinowski and Colonel Keith Schollum managed to get a vehicle so they could attend. They had a couple of pistols but no military escort. About fifty people gathered at the rear of the airport palace, where Garner had spent his first night in Baghdad. Half of those were British officers, including General Albert Whitley, and the few Australians in Baghdad; the rest were Americans from the headquarters staff. Michael Gordon, the *New York Times* journalist embedded with McKiernan's headquarters, also attended. As the sun came up, the weather was clear and the compound was quiet. Lieutenant General McKiernan appeared and spoke briefly about the events of ANZAC Day and tried to relate them to recent operations in Iraq. It was a modest but moving ceremony.[31]

Back at the National Palace, everyone was up early. The night had been hot but not excessively; soon the temperature would reach over 100 degrees, day and night. Standing water around the palace bred mosquitoes, leading many to regret that they had not taken the mosquito nets offered at Fort Myer in March. Everyone missed the air conditioning and showers at the Hilton, among other amenities. Breakfast and dinner were MREs, with another lunch of hot dogs and hamburgers in the KBR tent for those who arrived before the food ran out.

Colonel Tony Puckett, the deputy for the Civil Administration pillar, was on the receiving end of complaints from many of the senior civilians serving as ministry advisors. Initially with no staff of his own, Puckett was soon running errands for the ambassadors and others in his pillar, such as assembling their beds and arranging their bedding. A few helped him—Simon Elvy, Drew Erdmann, and Mike Ayoub—but many did not. Puckett was well liked by his peers and in time became a favorite of many civilians. He was a steady performer who rarely complained. But the complaints imposed upon him were a trial when air conditioning, washing facilities, or laundry service were simply unavailable. One ambassador went directly to Garner to demand a better room. Taken aback, Garner offered to exchange rooms with him, but when it was clear that even Garner had no air conditioning, the ambassador recovered to make the best of it until conditions improved.[32]

The daily routine was a round of meetings comparable to those held in Kuwait and the Pentagon, but in markedly less comfortable conditions. Each morning Garner had a brief session in his office at 7:00 with half a dozen of his most senior personnel; a larger meeting with fifty immediately followed in the main conference room, attended by representatives of the three pillars, senior advisors for the ministries, and a few colonels from the ORHA C-staff. This meeting normally lasted only forty-five minutes, with many participants anxious to get downtown to meet with their Iraqis counterparts. At 8:00, the full ORHA C-staff met in the same room with Bates in charge. Those attending would spend most of their day in the palace working on support issues to sustain the civilians. It was beginning to sink in that supporting the civilians, particularly those working with the ministries, was the primary task for the C-staff. Other meetings were scheduled throughout the day. Garner wanted the meeting schedule to be loose—to fully address issues rather than simply terminate at a specific time to allow for a follow-on meeting, a subtle technique that Garner's successor would not sustain a month later.

Within a week, other rooms in the palace were cleaned up and meetings were held throughout the building. Jerry Bates was one of the few people who attended all the morning meetings; it was his role to integrate efforts within ORHA and play the honest broker who would sort out conflicts. The move into Iraq only partially tempered the military-civilian divide within ORHA. The complaints about the living and working conditions in the palace led Colonel Costello, the logistics manager, to propose that follow-on convoys be delayed until there was more order and more furniture in the building.

On Friday, the first of several afternoon meetings was convened to coordinate the efforts for the Iraqi ministries with C-staff support. Many of the designated senior advisors had just arrived and were anxious to get to work. The ministries were still split between the Reconstruction and Civil Affairs pillars, and it fell to Sherri Kraham to manage the meeting. But because she had been traveling with Garner in the Kurdish areas until the day before, she was not on top of some of the ministries' issues. As the meeting began, the ministry advisors requested information and support, but Kraham could provide little information and had no support to offer. In his notes Ambassador Dunford wrote that "Sherri is point of contact for everything, something that will quickly be unworkable."[33]

Mike Mobbs, the reticent head of the Civil Affairs pillar, wanted priorities established for the limited support available. David Nummy from Treasury complained that with inadequate work spaces and no internet or phone communications, there was little they could do. Steve Browning said they must get out into the city, find their respective ministries, contact the appropriate Iraqis, and get working. That led to a discussion about transportation and the lack of maps to get around the city, the limited number of interpreters for talking with the Iraqis, more questions about when computer and phone communications would be available, and how to coordinate with the Civil Affairs units in Baghdad.

Kraham could only pass requests for transportation and communications to the C-staff, a deflection that raised the frustration in the room. Again Costello said that until additional beds and office furniture could be delivered to the palace they should delay those in Kuwait from coming forward. General Strock had just joined the meeting and took the opposite view: it was more important to get everyone in Kuwait up to Baghdad in order to get Iraq back into operation. He added that they all had a sleeping bag from Fort Myer and he offered to take volunteers and sleep outside the palace to make more room available. The momentum to restrain the flow of personnel from Kuwait was strong, however. Costello complained that he had not yet established control over the several hundred vehicles that had been driven to Baghdad and were now parked all around the palace.

Colonel Randy Conway agreed with Costello. With the military signal detachment, he had just managed to provide enough communications to support the C-staff and could not yet support all the civilians in the palace, nor those waiting to come to Baghdad. The small Raytheon team, hired to provide communications support for ORHA, was still forming and only part of it had arrived. To provide the computer support required, they needed to set up a server system, which required air conditioning to operate properly. There was no air conditioning available in April. As the civilians arrived in Baghdad, they all wanted computer support, which Conway was ill prepared to provide. In the midst of the uproar, Garner entered and had a calming effect, albeit a temporary one. He said the C-staff would address many of the concerns expressed, but it was difficult to simply mandate better support. Nevertheless, the civilians remained dissatisfied and the military officers on the staff were annoyed with what they considered constant whining in the palace about living and work conditions.

Colonel Collins had begun to manage the palace as if it were a hotel and office complex—which it had indeed become. He even referred to himself as the mayor of the palace. But that orientation divorced him from the larger task as Bates's deputy for the C-staff. To those on the staff, support meant improving living conditions: food, showers, toilets, laundry services, and security. Those tasks would intensify with several hundred more people arriving from Kuwait and converging on the palace.[34]

On 26 April, Garner seemed to be everywhere. He attended many of the meetings, talked constantly with key subordinates, and tried to maintain contact with Talabani and Barzani as they assembled other Iraqi leaders to form an interim government. Restless by nature, Garner roamed the halls of the palace and stopped frequently to talk to people to get an update or to issue instructions. He remembered names and almost always had something positive to say. Many fancied themselves a favorite, which in turn led some to accost Garner in a friendly manner to tell him about their problems or what they had accomplished. Sometimes Garner would grab people in the hallways to assign them a task that did not always line up well with their positions, but often a task for which there was no appropriate position.

That morning he stopped Don Eberly, recently designated the senior advisor for the Ministry of Youth.

"Don, I've got a job, and it's got your name on it: organizing trash removal in downtown Baghdad."

Eberly paused, unsure what to say; Garner added impatiently, "Eberly, you're dancing." Eberly reflected that Garner made him "feel like a little boy standing there having to pee." But the enthusiastic Eberly recovered, took on the task, and was designated the Minister of Rubble by an amused David Dunford.[35]

At one meeting, George Ward revealed that a group of fifty-five NGOs had arrived to work on de-mining. They would begin by sweeping the palace compound and nearby areas. For Garner, that was a good signal. He wanted more NGOs, but their numbers would not increase significantly as many anticipated. Larry Di Rita said that Ambassador Ryan Crocker would arrive soon with someone from the governance group Liz Cheney and Scott Carpenter had put together. That was news for Ambassador Dunford, who had been told in Washington that the skeptical Crocker would not be employed in Iraq.[36]

Margaret Tutwiler complained about the media entering the palace grounds. She wanted them under escort and requested military personnel for the task. Few others in ORHA had noticed the international journalists arriving in Baghdad, whose interest had shifted from the invasion of Iraq to what the Coalition would do next. Someone mentioned that the PUK had a newspaper operating in Baghdad and that a radio station was to start operating soon. But if the international media received little attention from those in ORHA, the Iraqi media received less.

General Cross said that a C-130 load of British civilians would arrive soon to join ORHA. Some would go to Basra, where they would help establish the new ORHA-South regional component; the rest would go to Baghdad. The British civilians headed for Basra would fill the gap Buck Walters had left as he moved the original ORHA-South to Hilla, redesignated ORHA-South Central. That had left the UK military command responsible for Basra and southern Iraq without an ORHA contingent. The southern region in general received less attention than the other regional components. Many in ORHA, if they thought about the southern region at all, assumed the UK military command could cover the appropriate tasks there. In reality, military commanders from the UK were no more inclined to support ORHA than the American commanders; ORHA-South would suffer accordingly.

Chris Milligan said members of the International Committee of the Red Cross (ICRC) were coming in to assist with garbage and rubble removal in Baghdad, but it was unclear how a few civilians would be able to undertake such a task without resources. General Strock provided an update on the bridge repair project north of Mosul. Barbara Bodine talked about the zoo in the Green Zone near the palace, where they were trying to provide proper care for the animals, in particular a lion and her cub. With so many infrastructure tasks in Baghdad, Bodine's attention on the animals in the small zoo seemed both a novelty and a distraction.

Garner said on Sunday he intended to have a meeting with Talabani, who had arrived in Baghdad. He wanted to use the Kurdish leaders as a catalyst to get the IIA organized. Discretely, Garner began to ask those he trusted what they thought about Talabani as an interim president of Iraq, a concept that took many by surprise given the autonomy the Kurds had established in the previous decade. Garner's intuition would be validated over the next decade, however, as Talabani took on several senior positions in the Iraqi government, including the presidency.

Few in the palace paid much attention to the IIA. The more dominant task was linking up the senior advisors with their respective ministries. The governance group Garner had requested while in the Pentagon had been slow coming together and there had been little contact with it when Garner was in Kuwait. Without such a policy body in Baghdad, Garner would have to do much of the work himself. He reminded the ministry advisors that while they were responsible for getting the ministries up and working, ultimately their task was to guide and advise. To make that transition, they needed to get capable Iraqis into senior positions as soon as possible. The leaders they put into power would eventually be vetted by the Coalition, but the immediate task in late April was to get Iraq up and running.[37]

During the C-staff meeting, Colonel DeGraff announced that the total strength of ORHA had reached 902, with close to 500 in Baghdad and 350 attached soldiers from the U.S. Army providing perimeter security and communications support. There were still 300 in Kuwait waiting to come forward and about 100 with ORHA-South Central and ORHA-North. Colonel Costello announced that a shower unit and a flush toilet unit, both mounted on trailers, had arrived with a KBR convoy. A dozen shower stalls would have to service 500 civilian and 350 military personnel as more arrived, initially with alternating hours for men and women based on proportional numbers, until the women complained and the hours were modified to allow them more time. Colonel Collins put a sign on the toilet trailer that read, "Coed Toilet, Coed Head, Coed Latrine," indicating that adjacent toilet stalls in the tight trailer would service both genders concurrently.

Costello complained that there were 150 ORHA vehicles parked all over the palace area. He wanted them turned in to the ORHA C-4 section as they arrived from Kuwait. But no one who had keys to a car wanted to give it up. Costello wanted a military-style motor pool to centralize control and allocate vehicles on a priority system, as well as to provide appropriate maintenance for them, but he did not have military personnel to manage a motor pool. Even with such a system, it would require those needing a vehicle to submit a request to the C-3 Operations section, which would prioritize the requests for daily allocation. Costello made arrangements for KBR to set up the motor pool he wanted, even though they were poorly prepared to do so. The system eventually worked for Costello's purposes, but it created a transportation chokepoint for civilians who preferred having their own vehicles.

Later that day, a dozen officers from the 352nd Civil Affairs Command came to the palace for a meeting managed by Colonel Puckett, deputy for the Civil Administration pillar. Lieutenant Colonel Erickson of the 352nd opened with a briefing that laid out the distribution of the four Civil Affairs brigades and ten Civil Affairs battalions in Iraq aligned with maneuver formations. In Baghdad the 354th Civil Affairs Brigade was working with the 3rd Mechanized Infantry Division. General Kern had set up his 352nd Headquarters within the Green Zone a quarter mile from the palace, having arrived in Baghdad a week earlier. With most of the Civil Affairs brigades and battalions under control of the maneuver formations, General Kern had little more than his residual headquarters with about 200 officers under his control to work with ORHA.

The purpose of the meeting was to determine how to integrate those officers with the ORHA components to achieve a unified effort, a task that many believed should have been done months before. Colonel Stanton, the C-9 Civil Affairs officer on McKiernan's staff, had been in Baghdad for several weeks and was there to help manage the effort. He noted that his "fun meter was pegged," as virtually all the ministry buildings in Baghdad had been badly looted. It would take a lot of work to get them operating.[38]

During the meeting, Puckett and Erickson aligned Civil Affairs officers with ministry senior advisors as much as possible based on their individual skills, either as reservists or their civilian occupations. Within a month, sixty

Civil Affairs officers were working in the palace. They remained on the unit Civil Affairs rosters, not ORHA's, although they were clearly working for ORHA. Puckett's role was complicated because the pillar he represented was not responsible for all the ministries; they were still split between Civil Administration and Reconstruction. Mike Mobbs wanted Puckett to manage all the ministry coordination tasks, which Sherri Kraham was supposed to do.[39]

Several people told Garner that the coordination task exceeded Kraham's capacity and that the ministry coordination role should go to someone more senior. Ambassador Dunford described one of the meetings run by Kraham as a slugfest, with many of those present frustrated that she could not provide useful coordination or support. The obvious person for that position was Mike Mobbs, with the Civil Administration pillar.[40]

Garner was dissatisfied with the energy and leadership Mobbs displayed in Kuwait and Iraq. Furthermore, he was reluctant to demote the industrious Kraham, who had been trying to manage the ministries since February. He moved Meghan O'Sullivan over to work with Kraham. Since joining Garner, O'Sullivan had worked briefly in turn for George Ward, Barbara Bodine, and Paul Hughes. It was an unusual working relationship as Kraham was a GS-13, whereas O'Sullivan was two ranks her senior as a GS-15. O'Sullivan, however, was less rank conscious than most and was happy to have a useful role where she could exercise her interest in policy, which would come with managing the ministries. But that arrangement would continue only until Mobbs's unexpected departure a few days later.[41]

Garner spent the rest of the day driving around Baghdad, with Olson and his bodyguards in two SUVs. He wanted to assess the situation in the city. Although there were constant reports of shooting, there was no obvious organized resistance and the greater concern was the looting. To most Westerners looting generally meant the theft of furniture, clothes, computers, and appliances. In Iraq, it also included fixed infrastructure, wiring, generators, toilets, and whole fleets of government cars and trucks. What was not taken was often vandalized or sabotaged, with many government buildings and installations set on fire.

Garner stopped frequently to talk to Iraqis through an interpreter. Not until late May would he take members of the media with him on his trips in the city; the media thus missed some colorful experiences. On one occasion, an excited Iraqi grabbed Garner by the arm and said in Arabic, "I believe in two things: Allah and you. And I need you now!" Garner was moved. The Iraqis were normally polite and friendly. When Garner asked if they had problems, they consistently asked for better security, more electricity, and jobs. Garner enjoyed interacting with Iraqis, but he was concerned there was insufficient momentum for the interim government he wanted to activate. He needed political movement on the part of the Iraqis if the Coalition was going to be able to depart within the intended timeframe, and that was beginning to appear elusive.

Garner went to the Ministry of Health where Browning, Williams, Ammundson, and Fisher were conducting their third meeting. Browning introduced Garner to the Iraqis and Garner repeated Browning's message that the Coalition wanted to put the Health Ministry back into operation with an Iraqi doctor in control. He said he would work on security and implement a salary plan for the ministry, but he asked them to manage their expectations about what the Coalition could provide. In the ensuing dialogue, one Iraqi asked if the health care system for Iraq would be free. After some discussion, Browning suggested a three-tier system, with the first tier of basic health care provided free, a second tier paid equally by the patient and government, and a third tier of care covered by patients. Garner said they should continue to discuss the issue and the Coalition would study it. Putting the ministries back into operation would require more policy direction.

Browning wanted to put an Iraqi in charge as an interim minister. He had been most impressed with Dr. Ali al-Janabi, whom he called Dr. Ali, the deputy minister for health before the invasion. The doctor seemed to have the good will of the ministry officials and was cooperative with Browning and his team. Browning consulted officials in Baghdad from the Cooperative for American Relief Everywhere (CARE), the International Committee of the Red Cross (ICRC), the World Health Organization (WHO), the United Nations Children's Fund (UNICEF), and other IOs and NGOs, who told Browning that Dr. Ali was a good choice. At Browning's recommendation, Garner appointed him as the interim minister, a decision that would subsequently cause some controversy and require a replacement.[42]

On the same day Garner visited the Ministry of Health, Lee Schatz went to the Iraqi Ministry of Agriculture. Schatz was from the U.S. Department of Agriculture and Garner's designated senior advisor for the Iraqi counterpart. In Kuwait, Schatz had made contact with two Civil Affairs reservists, Danny Woodyard and Ken Rudisill, who had connections with agriculture. Woodyard was an attorney for the U.S. Department of Agriculture in Arkansas. Rudisill was an agriculture extension agent in Florida.[43]

In Kuwait, Schatz told them they would "need pay records, employee records, and an understanding of what kind of condition the Ministry might be in." They knew the ministry was "less than two blocks from where Saddam's statue was pulled down in the circle . . . [near] the Sheraton Hotel." When Schatz made it to Baghdad on 24 April, he found that "Danny and Ken had already made an appointment with a group of people they had run into down at the Ministry." While Browning relied on military officers from Hawkins's TF Fajr to assist him with his work at the Ministry of Health, Schatz relied on Civil Affairs officers from the 352nd to work with the Ministry of Agriculture.

When Schatz and his two Civil Affairs officers arrived the next morning, they met a "self-appointed committee of employees. Everything had been trashed from top to bottom—files on the floors, planters thrown all over, some windows broken out—[but] the main building had no damage from fire. The smaller building had been trashed and vandalized with half the desks and almost all the chairs taken. Half a dozen rooms had been burned; but there was no structural damage." Ministry employees had taken their computers home before the building was looted, and through them Schatz was able to obtain the ministry records he needed. He told those at the meeting to start cleaning up the building. All the vehicles had been stolen, but there was a large generator left that could be put into operation. Schatz learned that someone had attempted to take it with a crane truck, but the truck turned over in the effort to lift it.

Until the buildings could be cleaned up, Schatz arranged for Iraqis from the ministry to meet him at the Baghdad Convention Center. Schatz soon found there were two groups from the ministry vying for control. Coolly, he played one group off against the other to determine who was more honest and capable, and then he brought the best of each group together to rebuild the ministry. Once organized, the ministry leaders wanted to provide services to the farmers with two priorities: getting the poultry industry functioning to address the meat shortage in the country, and purchasing the wheat and barley crops under harvest. The latter was a priority Schatz had identified in the Pentagon with some interest from Garner, who had played a role with the wheat harvest in northern Iraq in 1991. Schatz told the group that once the ministry building was back in operation his advisory team would need a room from which to work. The Iraqis suggested the minister's office, a very grand room. Thoughtfully, Schatz declined, making it clear the Iraqis were to take over soon; his group would take a smaller room.[44]

As Browning and Schatz found their respective ministries, so did Robin Raphel, responsible for the Ministry of Trade. Colonel Puckett took her to the ministry in a Suburban using a city map that Ambassador Tim Carney had given her. When they arrived, Raphel noted that "the building was still smoldering. . . . We went around the back of the building, found a bunch of people who had been coming to work . . . waiting for something to happen, keeping a list of who turned up for work." With the ministry building unsuitable for work, Raphel arranged for the Iraqis to meet her at the Convention Center the following day, as Schatz had done. Later Raphel met with them in a farm silo complex managed by the Ministry of Trade in northern Baghdad.[45]

On 26 April, Colonel Greg Gardner arrived in Baghdad as the lead member of the Coalition Military Advisor Training Team, soon known as CMATT. It would be responsible for rebuilding the Iraqi army. Colonel Gardner was working for Walt Slocombe, a former Undersecretary of Defense for Policy in the Clinton administration, who was to be in charge of that effort. Colonel Paul Hughes, the ORHA C-5 Plans officer tasked to assist with the planning for the Iraqi army, had sustained a dialogue with Slocombe and Colonel Gardner for several weeks. But Gardner and Hughes would not meet in Baghdad, which would soon lead to serious consequences.[46]

Previously Hughes had explained to Slocombe and Gardner that ORHA had two contracts in motion to deal with the regular Iraqi army: one with RONCO for disarmament, demobilization, and reintegration (DDR); and another with MPRI to retrain the Iraqi army. Hughes had Lieutenant Colonel Jim Torgler working on the RONCO contract, but arrangements were far from complete because money had not yet been allocated and specific Coalition policies for the Iraqi army were not defined. Consummating plans required active input from Slocombe and Gardner.[47]

Since his assignment as the senior advisor for the Ministry of Defense, Slocombe had spent his time in Washington consulting think tanks and other commands about rebuilding the army. He had a particular interest in the disposition of the East German army during German reunification, a process greatly enabled by a stable West Germany, for which there was no counterpart in Iraq. With Colonel Gardner, Slocombe worked up a joint manning document for ninety people to staff the advisory section for the Iraqi military forces, more than ten times the size of any other ministry advisory group in ORHA. Colonel Gardner introduced himself to Garner, who objected to the ninety people Gardner wanted to bring given the lack of room in the palace, but Garner said he wanted Slocombe to get a ministry advisor team to Iraq right away.[48]

Rather than scale back numbers, Colonel Gardner spent most of his second day in Baghdad driving around the Green Zone looking for a building suitable for the staff Slocombe and he had designed. Colonel Hughes drove up to Baghdad in a convoy the same day, but he missed seeing Gardner before the latter flew to Qatar to discuss his plans with Central Command. From there, Gardner flew back to the United States and would not return to Iraq with

Slocombe for almost three weeks. While ORHA had other senior advisors working to get their ministries up and operating, the senior advisor for the Ministry of Defense and his deputy remained in Washington.[49]

The day Colonel Gardner drove around the Green Zone looking for office space, David Dunford was in downtown Baghdad trying to find people at the Ministry of Foreign Affairs. Dunford arrived in Baghdad with only Drew Erdmann to assist him; Erdmann would soon be designated the interim advisor for another ministry. Upon their arrival, Dunford and Erdmann had no transportation, no computers, and no functional office or phone. Dunford shared a small room with Ambassadors Tim Carney and John Limbert, all three of whom were in their sixties and in some distress with the heat.[50]

Dunford made a list of what he needed for his ministry: a determination of its current status, local contacts, a place to meet, transportation and security, interpreters, communications, and salaries. Unpretentious and almost proud of the "low-profile" description Rumsfeld allegedly had bestowed upon him, Dunford was determined to get on with his task. At a meeting with the Civil Affairs officers on 26 April, he was told that they had an officer designated for the Foreign Ministry but who was not yet available. Undeterred, Dunford walked up to another Civil Affairs officer, Lieutenant Colonel Alex Sonski, and asked for a ride into Baghdad. Sonski was surprised at the request, but he took Dunford and Erdmann to the Foreign Ministry the next day. As with other ministry buildings in Baghdad, they found theirs "badly burned . . . papers strewn everywhere, and . . . all of the windows broken. We climbed over the rubble and entered the main Foreign Ministry building. . . . We looked through the Diplomatic Institute the first day, the equivalent [of which] in the United States would be the Foreign Service Institute." When communications could be established with Iraq's embassies overseas, Dunford could exercise control of their property and assets, but he had no policy guidance from Washington to establish foreign policy for Iraq. In contrast to the other ministries there, Foreign Affairs would have little impact on getting the country running.[51]

Sunday, 27 April, was another long day in Iraq with a never-ending flood of information and requests. The Bechtel Corporation was setting up contracts to dredge the Iraqi port of Umm Qasr, a project the Japanese had agreed to help fund. Shipments of wheat were in-bound, with pressure to increase the port capacity. The Australian Wheat Board, which had a contract with Iraq before the invasion, was pushing grain to Umm Qasr to consummate that contract. By that time, it was clear that there was no food shortage in Iraq, and so Garner preferred that Iraqis harvest and distribute Iraqi wheat rather than rely on imported food. This was complicated, however, by Iraqi price controls that had kept the cost of grain down as a food subsidy for the population, which led Iraqi producers to export their crops to adjacent countries where they received higher prices, which in turn caused Iraq to import food. Senior advisors would have to establish common policies for Iraq's economy.[52]

Tim Cross wanted to add more personnel to ORHA from other Coalition participants. Jerry Bates, representing the C-staff, indicated there was still insufficient room and furniture in the palace for more people. Barbara Bodine and Mike Mobbs sided with Cross; they wanted more people right away. They also wanted to put more Iraqis to work, including working for ORHA. One person noted that news stations in the United States indicated that no one was in charge in Iraq, leading Tutwiler to warn everyone to be careful what they said to the aggressive international media in Baghdad. For his part, Garner was more concerned about getting Iraqi television and radio stations operating to inform the Iraqis about current events in the country.[53]

At the C-staff meeting, Colonel Baltazar emphasized that the staff must support the ORHA civilians more aggressively. Their requests for transportation and security had to be met for them to do their work. He understood the need to bring in more people, but that put him at odds with the other staff sections, concerned that bringing in the 300 personnel from Kuwait too quickly would lead to more chaos in the palace.

During their first week in Baghdad at the end of April, most of Garner's ministry advisors found their buildings and some of their employees. The ministers appointed by Saddam Hussein were gone, but some of the deputy ministers and many of the directors general had remained. Although most DGs were Ba'athists, frequently that was but a nominal designation; many were simply technocrats, the personnel Garner sought to empower as they were vetted. The object was to get the government up and functioning, no small challenge with most of the buildings looted and damaged and with little available power, water, or security.

COMMUNICATIONS PROBLEMS

Computer and phone communications for ORHA had been a challenge in Kuwait and would continue to be so in Iraq. The causes were outsourcing communications to Raytheon, inadequate support from military commands, changes in plans, turmoil in Iraq, and clashing personalities. John Bulla, a retired army officer, was the Raytheon team leader. He had been hired only a month earlier—as were most of those on his team. Bulla arrived in Kuwait the first week of April. Within two weeks of partially assembling his team, they all drove to Baghdad with their equipment. Tim Phillips, Colonel Conway's deputy C-6, had already gone to Baghdad with the quartering party. The Raytheon contract required ORHA to provide a secure working environment, temperature control for their server, and a reliable source of electricity for their equipment.[54]

Earlier in Kuwait, one of Conway's officers, Captain Macias, proposed purchasing an air conditioning unit to regulate the temperature for the equipment, but Conway felt they could get by with fans through April. By the end of April, the temperature was hot, and hot air aggressively circulated was not sufficient for cooling the computer servers. Air conditioning for communications equipment would not be available until 28 April, but even afterward it broke down several times, which in turn shut down the server. Electricity had not been available either, and ORHA had to bring in generators, which they had not anticipated.[55]

The original concept had been for 100 ORHA personnel to join the military command structure at the Baghdad airport, allowing time to set up a structure for 300 additional personnel in a vertical office or hotel-like building for which the Raytheon team had precut their wiring. Changes to that plan began with the move into Baghdad in mid-April. When Colonel Boag selected the National Palace for ORHA's headquarters, Garner decided to move ORHA in right away. The transition at Camp Victory was eliminated to get people working in Baghdad early. Without an intermediate period working from the airport, there was less time to prepare the main facility with a communications system. When the palace was selected with a horizontal rather than vertical layout, the wiring had to be recut to fit the building.[56]

In the original plan, the heavy communications equipment was to be set up on the main floor, but competition for working space in the palace was such that the equipment had to be moved to the second floor, which required a crane, another unprojected task that caused delay. And as Conway's staff was unpacking and issuing equipment in Baghdad, it also had to assist the Raytheon team with wiring the central section of the palace.

Military communications support had been haphazard. General Casey had refused to allocate such support to ORHA and Colonel Conway had been reluctant to ask CFLCC for help in Kuwait despite Major June's pleas that he do so. When General McKiernan directed his command to provide communications support, ORHA received only seventeen soldiers and enough computers and phones for the C-staff but not much more.

When those in the Civil Administration, Reconstruction, and Humanitarian Assistance pillars were told to locate in the south wing of the palace, they encountered two problems. They no access to the computers the military detachment brought because the wiring did not reach to their assigned areas, and thus could not plug into the initial system in the palace. Second, those that had used the internet café system Conway had set up in Kuwait had computers that were "dirty" and so had to be "ghosted" so they would not contaminate the ORHA server; this required each laptop to be turned into the C-6 staff for several days, during which the hard drives were cleaned, another labor-intensive chore. With time required to ghost the laptops and wire the palace, combined with the problems of air conditioning and electricity, the ORHA computer system would not be operational and reliable until the second week in May.

There was soon friction between Conway and Bulla over electricity and the air conditioning necessary to support an integrated computer system, given Bulla's incomplete team that had to adapt to the situation. The members of the Raytheon team had been told that they would work in a modern "multistory hotel that was up to or would exceed commercial standards, but [the palace] was a great deal smaller" and certainly more austere than projected when they arrived in Baghdad. From Bulla's perspective, his team adjusted well considering the working conditions and the changes they encountered; from Conway's perspective, they were another group of civilian complainers expecting amenities in a war zone.[57]

Conway also knew there would be no commercial phone system available in Baghdad and that ORHA could not plug into the Coalition military classified communications system. He bought Thuraya cell phones that could work from satellites and by the end of April had issued over a hundred of them for use in Baghdad. But the Thurayas operated on line of sight, requiring the operator to be outside to make a connection with a satellite. Only a few base stations were set up inside with an external antenna outside the building; most people thus had to go outside to make a call, and the person receiving the call had to be outside as well.

There were also difficulties with the televised conferences that took place with key leaders in Baghdad, Kuwait, Qatar, and Washington. When Garner was in Kuwait the system had worked fairly well, but there had been difficulties in Baghdad. On one occasion, the link on the Baghdad end failed to operate properly when senior officials in Washington were involved. That led to the involvement of senior communications officers in theater to try to fix the systems serving ORHA to prevent future embarrassment. Previously when there had been such problems, Brigadier General Dennis Moran, the senior communications officer at Central Command, simply called Tim Phillips and told him, "Fix your gear." But when communications failed involving the more senior officials in Washington, Moran flew to Baghdad to check on it himself.[58]

Major General Detamore, Moran's counterpart on McKiernan's staff, came with him. For Phillips it was amusing to see two general officers on the roof of the palace with several technicians studying the antenna system and trying to realign it for better reception. Phillips could tell that Detamore and Moran were not impressed and thought that ORHA communications was poorly managed. They would be back—and the next time they would try to make changes in the leadership of the ORHA C-6 staff.[59]

ORHA CONSOLIDATION IN BAGHDAD

Early on 28 April, the third convoy of the ORHA main body left Kuwait with 125 people in some thirty commercial SUVs broken into serials as the previous convoys had done. One serial with Mike Ayoub missed a turn near Basra and was stopped and turned back by a UK army unit at the Iranian border. The serials regrouped at the airport outside Baghdad and drove into the city together, arriving well after dark. Colonel Collins gave them a tour of the palace, but most just wanted to know where they were to sleep.

Ayoub moved into a room with Drew Erdmann, Mike Gfoeller, Simon Elvy, and Philip Hall, whose combined snoring drove him to move into Colonel Puckett's room nearby; Puckett was "also a serious snore meister, but better one than dueling snores on either side of me all night long." The following day Mike Mobbs asked Ayoub to shift his position from the Ministry of Higher Education to work with the Ministry of Defense. When Colonel Gardner left the day before, Mobbs knew there was no one to monitor the Ministry of Defense until Colonel Gardner returned with Walt Slocombe. Ayoub had reservations about the position change as he had a developed interest in the Scientific Research component of the Ministry of Higher Education, which he believed was a cover for the development of nuclear, biological, and chemical weapons. In 1994, Ayoub had studied Iraqi weapons of mass destruction and wanted to exploit that experience, but he recognized the importance of the Ministry of Defense in the critical days in April.

He began a dialogue with Colonel Hughes, Garner's senior planner, and Lieutenant Colonel Torgler; the latter had been assigned to work on the Iraqi army. Within a few days Ayoub managed to meet with five former Iraqi officers, led by Major General Ma'an Al Jibouri, with Brigadier General Al Muhalib Kalaf Salman, Brigadier General Khatan Kalf Salman, a military engineer, and Colonels Riad Abdulah Kawan and Rhahem Obied, the latter "a nervous officer from Iraq's security services."[60]

Ayoub found them credible:

> We spoke of the future of the Iraqi Army, the need for change within the structure and a realignment of the Sunni/Shia Officer to Enlisted ratios. We also discussed . . . a new NCO Corps where the sergeants would be empowered to take initiative and assume responsibilities previously reserved for officers. We made follow-on plans to meet again and I requested copies of all MOD payroll records available. General Ma'an indicated that the records still existed and were retrievable.

Ayoub retained his interest in nuclear weapons in Iraq and kept a dialogue going on that topic with his roommate, Colonel Puckett, who had commanded an artillery unit with a nuclear mission during the Cold War.[61] Ayoub's proposal for an empowered NCO corps was ambitious given that it was foreign to most Arab armies other than Jordan's, but with Jordan as an example Ayoub's proposal was not unreasonable.

As Ayoub, Hughes, and Torgler developed contacts with the Iraqi army, so did others in the Coalition military forces. In mid-April, General Abizaid informed those in Washington that the Iraqi army had gone home. But Abizaid and other officers knew Iraq would need an army for external and internal security. Officers working for General McKiernan made contact with Iraqi general officers to reconstitute a portion of the regular army, a brigade at a time in three cities: Mosul, Baghdad, and Basra. McKiernan assumed Iraqi soldiers were disillusioned and that bringing them back onto active duty in an organized manner would give them a purpose. They could provide a service to Iraq and the Coalition by "guarding infrastructure, guiding traffic, and border security."[62] But there was no integration of such efforts with ORHA, nor was there policy guidance from the national level. Slocombe was responsible for the policy to put the regular Iraqi army back into operation, but he was not present in Iraq to assist Garner when progress for the army was desperately needed.

On 28 April, Ambassador and birdwatcher David Dunford noted in his diary the gulls, crows, and towhees he had seen in Iraq; his first shower in four days; and Saddam Hussein's birthday. Only a few were aware that Saddam Hussein, at sixty-four, was the same age as Jay Garner (and also Ambassador Bremer, who would arrive in a few weeks).[63] The same day, Don Eberly set off to take on the Baghdad garbage collection task Garner had assigned him, a project that would illustrate many of the dilemmas in Iraq. He was accompanied by Colonel Keith Schollum, the Australian working for Baghdad-Central. They drove to Baghdad City Hall to find the building secured by a few tanks and soldiers from the 3rd Mechanized Infantry Division (3ID). They were happily surprised to find it in reasonable condition compared to most of the ministry buildings that had been looted and vandalized. An army engineer showed them around the empty building and introduced them to an Iraqi who had been coming daily looking for someone trying to take charge. Through that Iraqi, Eberly and Schollum were able to set up a meeting the next day with key administrators for the city, including six directors general, some city engineers, and related personnel.[64]

Eberly and Schollum let the Iraqis run the first meeting and observed a more authoritarian manner on the part of some Iraqis than they had anticipated. They would try to change the tone and procedures later, but for the first meeting they wanted to determine how the city was organized and how the leadership worked. Despite terms such as mayor and deputy mayor, it soon became apparent that the senior Iraqis present were more comparable to city managers oriented on civil infrastructure than city politics; several held functional positions for water and power, while others were in charge of the infrastructure of city precincts. All had been appointed rather than elected and did not think of themselves as political leaders. Eberly and Schollum asked the group how the trash removal system worked.

Eberly determined that there were about 60,000 tons of garbage to be removed from the city; another 2,500 tons were accumulating daily. Virtually all of the 600 trucks the city owned for trash removal had been stolen or displaced to other areas in Iraq during the invasion. No loaders or trash compactors were available. But Eberly learned there had been a contract system in place with 30 percent of the trash subcontracted to drivers who owned their own trucks. Many of those had not lost their trucks, but to activate the subcontracts Eberly would need money.

Eberly and Schollum decided to go to the U.S. Army units occupying the city. Individual officers and soldiers tried to be helpful, but there were complications. Military units did not have authority to commit trucks and engineer loaders to trash removal without approval from McKiernan's headquarters. Getting that required a formal request from the ORHA C-3 Operations section to the CFLCC military command, which took time. Even then the military response was less than enthusiastic; military and transportation units were not in the business of moving garbage, and such assistance would have to be for only a few days.

Eberly requested money through ORHA to activate and expand the contracts for trash removal across the city. He also coordinated with Civil Affairs detachments to assist. Soon he had military trucks and Iraqi contractors picking up the garbage. The Baghdad municipal assets would have to come later. Paying the Iraqis to pick up their own trash would be a long-term project for both ORHA and the military forces in the city, with much initiative required at the local level. The lack of proper equipment made trash removal labor intensive, a short-term advantage if it put people to work when most of the country was unemployed. Eberly found there was more to remove than normal garbage: unexploded ordnance, human bodies, burned out military and civilian vehicles. Eberly requested a military mortuary unit to assist with the removal of bodies, which had to be handled in accordance with international law.

Eberly put his project in motion on 30 April, advertised as "trash day," which he sought to portray as a good news story for the media. Organizing and moving a media pool safely across town to monitor the event was difficult, however. Dan Senor, a White House press officer, had arrived in Baghdad to join Margaret Tutwiler and her media team. Eberly knew Baghdad was unsafe and warned Senor to be careful when he went out with the press pool. Senor returned that evening and told Eberly that he had been fired upon while trying to cover the trash story. Senor also told him that he had been told by the White House communications staff that Iraq was in danger of becoming a "rolling political disaster." Eberly found it ironic that once those in Washington took notice of the problems Garner was having in Iraq, they provided more blame than assistance.[65]

The trash project was indicative of the challenges in Iraq, the lack of centralized control, and the problems with achieving unity of effort. Garner had no trucks or equipment capable of moving trash, and the military command was reluctant to provide military equipment to do so. Eberly had no background in such projects despite the enthusiasm he dedicated to the task. In the short term, Eberly's trash removal project was a success story. But removal of the garbage had only a token effect on the broken infrastructure in the city.

By the end of April, Garner had moved all those in ORHA from Kuwait to Iraq. Most were in the palace in Baghdad; about 100 were with ORHA-North and ORHA-South Central. The conditions were austere and the temperature was above 100 degrees. There was no air conditioning (except for the server), no indoor plumbing, and only limited communications. Bates insisted they arrange to air condition the entire palace, but it would be well into the summer before that was possible. Within a week KBR brought up more shower and toilet trailer units and installed them behind the palace. They would service close to a thousand civilians and attached military personnel working in the compound. Laundry service was on the way, but through April it was not uncommon to see colonels and ambassadors sharing buckets to wash their clothes. Meals were still field rations with lunches of hamburgers, hot dogs, and chicken nuggets.

Security, transportation, and communications were greater obstacles than living conditions. The military police company could only provide armed escorts for two dozen independent trips downtown when ORHA needed twice as many each day. While some complained when they did not get the escorts they needed, others just took a SUV and went out anyway, violating the security procedures. It was the civilians, particularly those in the growing Civil Administration pillar, that needed to get into the city the most. Much of the C-staff work could be conducted within the palace. There were tasks the civilians might have accomplished in the palace when they could not get into the city, but those tasks required computer support that would not be well provided until May.

By the end of April, Garner realized he had to reorganize ORHA by dismantling the Humanitarian Assistance pillar, distributing its personnel to other components in ORHA, and consolidating all the ministries under a single leader. By position, that might have been Mike Mobbs and the Civil Administration pillar. But Garner did not think Mobbs was capable of the task and decided to relieve him and send him home. On the last day of April, Garner caught Mobbs in the palace hallway. He told Mobbs he would have to go and asked if there were any family issues that would seem to justify his departure. Mobbs said there were and he appeared content to leave.[66]

The previous day, Colonel Tony Puckett, the deputy for Civil Administration, had chaired a meeting of the senior advisors and lost his temper when one advisor complained about having to meet Iraqis dressed in suits when he had no clean laundry. Fed up with complaints and demands he could not rectify, Puckett chewed the advisors out as if they were privates. Remarkably, the ambassadors and the others present calmly took it all in. They were suddenly aware they had pushed a good man too far. The next day the meeting began soon after the word was out that Mobbs was leaving. As Puckett was about to open the meeting, the ambassadors and other civilians in the room stopped him, then gave him a standing ovation for all his work. Puckett was humbled at the gesture.[67]

That day Garner asked Ambassador Robin Raphel, the senior advisor for Trade, to take charge of Civil Administration pillar, which would be renamed Ministry Coordination and include all Iraqi ministry advisor teams. The Reconstruction pillar would continue work on reconstruction tasks without responsibility for any ministries. With Raphel in charge, the ministry meetings David Dunford had described as slugfests became more productive. Puckett became Raphel's deputy and handled the administration for the ministry advisors, with Sherri Kraham and Meghan O'Sullivan coming under his control.

Puckett was a stoic and serious leader. He believed in discipline and the use of organizational procedure to get things done. Like others, he had been annoyed with Kraham for her inability to properly manage and support the senior advisor teams. When O'Sullivan started work with Kraham, Puckett felt the two were operating as free agents in ORHA without proper coordination. They also complained frequently about the limited support they were getting from the military forces. Puckett, however, had little patience for their complaints, while neither Kraham nor O'Sullivan had ever been subject to the rage of a full colonel. One evening Puckett shut the door and chewed them out until they both broke down and cried—then he stormed out. Even with the door shut, Puckett could be heard by others outside the room. Many, like Ayoub and Baltazar, felt Kraham had it coming. A year later when O'Sullivan was working for the president in the White House, some would recall Puckett reading her the riot act. It was a tribute to Kraham and O'Sullivan that they both bounced back and worked their hearts out for the demanding Puckett.[68]

Garner had frequent meetings with Major General Webster, McKiernan's deputy for operations, who had replaced General Whitley as the senior officer from CFLCC working with ORHA. Webster was more formal in style than Garner, yet more outgoing than McKiernan and better connected within the American-dominated military coalition than General Whitley. Webster told Garner's team that the military forces were trying to secure 150 buildings in Baghdad and had set up two confinement facilities in Iraq to secure the 46,000 Iraqi prisoners captured during the invasion. On a visit to the Convention Center, he gave an assembled group of Iraqis the same message.

Webster did not make excuses, but it was clear that the military coalition was overstretched for the required tasks in Iraq. Two heavy divisions, the 4th Mechanized Infantry Division and 1st Armor Division, were just beginning to arrive and would take several weeks to deploy into Iraq; the 1st Cavalry Division (an armor division) was supposed to follow from Kuwait, but earlier in April Secretary Rumsfeld and General Franks agreed not to send it. McKiernan had been counting on that division to assist with the security of Iraq.[69]

Webster and other military leaders were aware that their civilian counterparts under Garner numbered fewer than 1,000 by the end of April, and that they had limited assets beyond a few hundred vehicles and their individual equipment. Security was the overwhelming challenge in Iraq, and that fell on the military coalition. Garner and Webster told the Iraqis that they would need the Iraqis to help solve problems in the country. An Iraqi woman at one conference proposed that the Coalition empower the neighborhoods in

Baghdad to take on much of the management. Garner agreed and directed Bodine as his lead for Baghdad to move in that direction—a task that seemed to suit her.

On the last day of April, Rumsfeld flew into Baghdad. Garner, Bates, and Larry Di Rita met him at the airport; Rumsfeld did not visit the palace or meet with others from ORHA. Garner told him that in a few days he would stand up the Iraqi Interim Authority with seven Iraqi leaders, but he added with frustration that it was coming together slowly. While the exchange was frank, Garner felt Rumsfeld did not grasp the depth of the problems in Iraq. He was disappointed that Franks and Rumsfeld had decided not to send the 1st Calvary Division to Iraq, and more so when they sent the 3rd Mechanized Infantry Division home as the 1st Armor Division arrived, leaving fewer forces in Iraq than called for in the original plans. That was apparently driven by the desire of political leaders in Washington, reflected in the original operational plans to reduce military forces in Iraq to about 30,000 by the fall of 2003.[70]

At the next meeting in the palace, Larry Di Rita stated that those in ORHA should get better aligned with U.S. policy, but he did not go far to define that policy. Jerry Bates wanted more coordination with the U.S. military command and its subordinate units working in Baghdad; he also wanted more infrastructure support and knew that the C-staff had hit a wall with the limited assets on hand. Others were making incremental progress. Chris Milligan had started work on a town council system in Baghdad supporting the task Garner had given Bodine. General Strock had three more FEST teams arriving to assist with reconstruction assessments; that sounded good, but few in ORHA understood what the FESTs offered. Bates, Baltazar, and George Ward all expressed concern about the lack of cohesion for all of ORHA's projects. No one mentioned the fusion cell Bob Polk had proposed earlier in Kuwait. The senior advisors for the ministries wanted funding and a plan to pay Iraqi civil servants to get people back to work. They also wanted pensions for those that needed them, a system for food distribution, and a solution to the long lines of Iraqis trying to buy gasoline. There were many problems facing Iraq and ORHA and too little assistance.

At the end of the month, Colonel Mike Williams, working with the advisory team at the Iraqi Ministry of Health, was handed a note by an Iraqi that indicated Dr. Oumid Mubararak wanted to turn himself in. For several years, Mubararak had served as the Minister for Health and had been at least a nominal Ba'athist. He was also a Kurd from a family with a distinguished record in Iraqi medicine. Williams knew that Mubararak was number 230 on the "Black List" of important Iraqis the Coalition wanted to capture. That posed a dilemma for him and others on the advisor team. They had an obligation to assist the military coalition with incarceration of designated Iraqis, but they wanted to be fair with Iraqis that contacted them.[71]

Two days later, Williams and other members of his team met Dr. Mubararak at the office of the ICRC, a neutral location. Mubararak was escorted by Dr. Ali, the previous deputy minister and Garner's interim minister of health. Williams read Mubararak a formal statement noting the sanctity of the Red Cross office and the Coalition's interest in him. Dr. Ali asked to make a comment and noted for the record that Dr. Mubararak was loved by Kurds and Arabs alike and that a large number of important Iraqi people belonged to the Ba'athist party, yet only a few of them were irredeemable. Williams told Mubararak that if he turned himself in to the Coalition, he would be treated fairly. The doctor was nervous but said he was proud of his record and wanted to clear his name and cooperate. They agreed that the doctor could leave to go home, then meet Williams later at the ICRC building.

True to his word, Mubararak met them that afternoon in the company of his son-in-law, who asked Williams to keep the doctor's family informed about his whereabouts and situation; Williams agreed. From the ICRC building, they drove Mubararak to the appropriate intelligence agency and from there he was incarcerated in a military police facility. Williams visited the doctor several times and noted that the interned Ba'athists slept on a concrete floor with only a blanket. On one trip Williams brought him a cot, which he, in turn, shared with others. After the doctor was interrogated, the intelligence agency notified Williams they had no further use for him. The MPs told Williams that the doctor was a model prisoner and had provided medical assistance for other prisoners. Williams consulted Browning, the senior ministry advisor, who reviewed the situation and signed a letter of release for Mubararak. The intelligence agency had no objection and Captain Ammundson took the letter to the MPs, who were happy to release Mubararak to make room for others. But not everyone was so happy.[72]

Soon Browning was notified that only Secretary Rumsfeld was authorized to sign a release for a Ba'athist on the wanted list, and that Rumsfeld was furious when he was informed that Browning had usurped his authority. Garner's legal officer, Colonel Mike Murphy, subsequently contacted Browning and went through token motions of scolding him. He said that Rumsfeld and Browning were the only ones that had signed a release for any incarcerated Ba'athist, and that Rumsfeld would be the only one to do so in the future. Browning considered it a hand slap, but the issue would later resurface after Murphy left and other members of the advisory team involved with Mubararak's release were counseled with more seriousness.[73]

Colonel Williams conceded that by some standards Mubararak "had blood on his hands," for as a Health Ministry official, the Iraqi had signed phony death certificates for those killed through torture by other Iraq agencies and had condoned other such atrocities. But Williams believed that, as with many Iraqis in the government, Mubararak had done what he had to do to survive and to manage the Ministry of Health.[74]

By early May, Browning and Williams were making frequent visits to hospitals in Baghdad, many of them in the impoverished Shiite section on the northeast side of the city, previously designated Saddam City. Since the invasion it had been renamed Sadr City in honor of a Shia religious leader who had been tortured and murdered several years earlier. Browning and Williams found that the hospitals in the Shiite areas were often managed by armed religious groups, which also protected schools and other infrastructure from the looting rampant in Baghdad. The most notable of the religious groups they encountered was the Hawza, which had a seminary base in Najaf for traditional Shiite Islamic studies.

Browning and his team soon found they were perceived by the Hawza as interfering. Browning was notified by Iraqis in the Ministry of Health that a fatwa, a declaration threatening Browning with violence, had been declared. A few days later a military vehicle carrying several Civil Affairs medical personnel was attacked, using a route that Browning had often taken to the Health Ministry. Several of the soldiers in the vehicle were wounded, but one of the military doctors drew his pistol, killed several of those attacking them, provided immediate aid to the Americans who had been wounded, then took them to safety.[75]

WORKING WITH THE MINISTRIES

David Nummy, Sue Hamrock, Dorothy Mazaka, Drew Erdmann, Gene Stakhiv, Donald Campbell, Philip Hall, and Raoul Stanley were a diverse group who had never met before joining Garner and ORHA. Their academic degrees were from different fields—economics, business, foreign affairs, history, engineering, and law—and they represented different government agencies: Treasury, Commerce, USAID, State, the Army Corps of Engineers, and the Army Civil Affairs. Hall was British and came from the UK Foreign and Colonial Office (FCO). Stanley was Australian and came from his country's counterpart to USAID, known as AUSAID.

In some cases, they had specific skills for what they would do in Iraq. In other cases, their experience would only loosely align with their assignments and they would have to leverage what skills and education they had. Only

Campbell had been to Iraq before and that was for a brief foray into northern Iraq with Garner on Provide Comfort in the summer of 1991. Only Mazaka had expertise in the Middle East, mainly in Saudi Arabia where she had learned Arabic. Mazaka and Erdmann had joined Garner in February; Nummy, Hall, and Hamrock joined just prior to the ORHA departure from Washington, D.C., in March; Stakhiv, Stanley, and Campbell joined in Kuwait, Campbell the day before he was to drive to Baghdad. They were all employed by agencies of the American, UK, and Australian governments, and had credentials and instincts that were altruistic and apolitical. Each was determined to go into harm's way to make a contribution.

David Nummy, senior advisor for the Iraq Ministry of Finance, had his share of challenges in Baghdad. As with many of his peers working with other Iraqi ministries, when he got downtown he found that looting and vandalism had disrupted the use of many government buildings. It took several trips to schedule meetings with his Iraqi counterparts, and together they decided on three initial projects: salaries, currency, and the use of available funds for the Coalition in Iraq.[76]

From his previous work in Eastern Europe, Nummy knew that to jump-start a government paralyzed by sudden change, civil servants had to go back to work. The incentive would be salaries, an issue that Garner had raised with the Pentagon and NSC. Overcoming bureaucratic resistance in Washington, ORHA had paid Iraqi salaries at the port of Umm Qasr in mid-April and stockpiled cash in the army vaults in Kuwait. The release of that money was subject to the approval of Robin Cleveland and others at OMB and NSC. They wanted to know in advance how the money would be spent, information Nummy and Garner could not provide in a fluid environment with constant surprises.

As in Umm Qasr, paying government salaries in Baghdad or elsewhere in Iraq required access to pay records and scales with a Coalition policy determination on what would be retained or changed of the old salary structure. With many government buildings looted and vandalized, Nummy's first concern was that pay records might have been destroyed. But within a few weeks most of the ministries were able to find enough personnel data to provide a basis for compensation. In the process, Nummy set in motion an interim system of four levels with monthly payments of $50, $100, $150, and $250, in contrast to the pre-invasion system that had ten levels across a greater range (the lowest level had been only $4 per month). Nummy also wanted to sustain and improve the Iraqi pension system (some recipients had received as little as $2 per month). The changes in the salary and pension system that Nummy put in motion in April, however, would generate some controversy in May.[77]

Before salaries or pensions could be paid, Nummy and his team would need cash, far more than the $20 million that had been authorized by OMB earlier in April, which had been used in part to pay emergency salaries at Umm Qasr. As Nummy worked the issue with Washington, an intermediate opportunity came with a surprise call from General Webster to Jerry Bates during the last week of April. Coalition military units had found substantial cash in a number of buildings and other locations, including $700 million in U.S. dollars in one of Saddam Hussein's palaces. Within the month, the total assets confiscated by the military coalition, soon known as "seized assets," amounted to $900 million. Nummy later learned that before the invasion Saddam Hussein had authorized the release of about $1 billion, mostly in U.S. dollars, from the Iraqi Central Bank to selected cronies. That accounted for most of the money recovered and sent to Brigadier General Stanton, who secured the cash in his vaults in Kuwait. The question was who was authorized to use that money.[78]

Garner, Nummy, and many of the senior military commanders in Iraq assumed that the seized assets recovered in Iraq would be more accessible than the vested Iraqi assets frozen in American banks. But there were complications with the seized assets. First, OMB tried to assume control over those funds, and it took several weeks for Garner to get it to back off and allow him to use the money. By then the U.S. Bureau of Engraving and Printing had weighed in, expressing concern that the large amount of U.S. dollars might be counterfeit and asking to inspect it with special machines that would have to be shipped to Kuwait. That would take several months. Nummy would have to rely initially on the vested funds, subject to the OMB requirements for its expenditure.

The majority of the seized assets and all of the vested assets were in American dollars rather than in Iraqi dinars, the national currency. Nummy had several concerns about currency use in Iraq. He knew there would be virtually no credit instruments such as checks, credit cards, and bank drafts available in Iraq for some time after the invasion. Hard currency would be essential for market transactions, complicated by variants of the Iraqi Dinar. When the Kurdish areas in Iraq achieved limited autonomy in 1991, they kept the original Iraqi dinar for their currency; this became known as the Swiss dinar, allegedly because it had been printed in Switzerland. There had been no recent issues of that currency and the supply in Iraq was fixed. After a decade of wear and tear, the notes had decreased in number, which led to an increase in its relative value.

In the 1990s, Iraq issued a new dinar known as the Saddam dinar, with Hussein's face on each note. Within a decade that currency was overprinted, resulting in inflation. The highest denomination was the 500 dinar note, by 2003 worth about twenty-five cents in U.S. currency. Prior to the invasion, Iraq had issued a new 10,000 dinar note, worth about $5 US, to make transactions easier. With such a gap in denominations, normal transactions were still difficult, further complicated by lack of confidence in the recently issued denomination. Nummy wanted to avoid a currency collapse with massive inflation, a situation not uncommon in post-conflict situations. Prior to entering Iraq, he had "primed Garner to state publicly that all currencies in Iraq would be considered valid in Iraq, including existing Dinars, to avoid rumors that the Coalition would repudiate the Saddam Dinars." There was little doubt that Iraq would not long use a currency with Hussein's picture on it, but its replacement would have to be delayed.[79]

While there were lots of American dollars in Iraq, they were mainly $100 bills and were rarely used for local transactions. As the Coalition had no substantial number of dinars of any variant in April 2003, American dollars would have to serve as Iraq's dominant currency for the first several months, but the Coalition also would need smaller denominations. Pallets of dollars in denominations of $20 and below were flown into Kuwait for ORHA from the Federal Reserve Bank in New York. General Stanton had the cash stored in his vaults at Camp Arifjan. General Stanton assumed responsibility to secure and move the cash for ORHA.[80]

In an early meeting in Baghdad, Garner asked Nummy about setting an exchange rate for the two dinar variants and the dollar. The normally poker-faced and unflappable Nummy responded as if spring-loaded. "We must let the currency float," he stated emphatically.[81]

The issue had come up before. Nummy and others from Treasury knew that "the only way to fix an exchange rate and prevent a split between official rates and black market rates was if a Central Bank had large amounts of foreign reserves in hard currency willing to buy a currency at the fixed rate any time anyone wants to sell it."[82] They also knew it would be difficult to get the Central Bank operating after widespread looting and chaos. Establishing public confidence in a banking system with multiple currencies would be an additional complication. Those from Treasury wanted to avoid a black market in currency that could "feed criminal activity . . . with damaging economic distortions." The most effective way to avoid a currency black market was to let the currency rates float rather than fix it.[83]

Nummy's team discussed banking and finance issues with their Treasury counterparts in Washington, occasionally disagreeing but overall maintaining a positive relationship. Nummy felt they "always got the issues worked out in a way that recognized the pragmatic realities on the ground . . . without much acrimony . . . a different situation than what some of my colleagues experienced from other agencies."[84]

Garner accepted the advice and let the exchange rate float with the uncertainty that came with it. Nummy knew that currency exchange rates would be in the hands of a few Iraqi bulk currency traders, often working from street corners with no policy guidance and a limited capacity to communicate and anticipate the future. The prospects for the Iraqi dinar against the dollar did not appear positive in April 2003, but that would change later.

While Nummy had a good dialogue with Treasury, relations with OMB were another matter. He found that OMB exercised excessive restraint in allowing ORHA to allocate the money set aside for reconstruction. Nummy noted that military commanders were given hundreds of thousands of dollars for reconstruction and jobs programs, but Garner had difficulty obtaining funds in late April just to have the streets cleaned. The restrictive supervision by OMB, mainly through Robin Cleveland, would continue into the following year. Those in ORHA viewed that as obstruction.[85]

Sue Hamrock arrived in Baghdad with the last large convoy on 28 April and moved into the palace with Robin Raphel as her roommate. Raphel was senior advisor for the Iraqi Ministry of Trade; Hamrock was her deputy and later her replacement. Earlier in Kuwait, Raphel had taken the measure of Hamrock, whom she described as "having a serious dose of common sense." Hamrock did not know much about Iraq or the Middle East, but her experience in Asia provided her an understanding of technical aspects of international trade that exceeded Raphel's economic experience, making Hamrock valuable despite her lack of regional knowledge. In Kuwait, Hamrock studied Iraq's Central Organization for Standards and Quality Control, a standalone agency that controlled international trade and economics that otherwise aligned with the Ministry of Trade. Hamrock worked with two others on her team: Frank Oslander, an attorney from the Department of State, and Nic Harvey from the United Kingdom. Later, when Oslander and Harvey left Iraq along with Raphel, Hamrock would remain as the senior advisor for the Ministry of Trade.[86]

When Raphel arrived in Baghdad on 24 April, she went downtown to find her ministry building smoldering and unusable. By the time Hamrock, Oslander, and Harvey arrived, Raphel had arranged a meeting with senior officials from the ministry at the Convention Center. On 29 April, with an interpreter in tow, they met four Iraqis there. The minister of trade was on the Coalition's wanted list and, like many other ministers, was not to be found, but the second order ministry leadership, the directors general, were there waiting for them.

Raphel and her team oriented their efforts on international trade for Iraq to activate the economy. In Kuwait they had learned that the Ministry of Trade handled food distribution for the country, an additional task their team assumed. As with other ministry advisors, they had to determine which Iraqi leaders to retain in position, which to move into other positions, and which to remove from the ministry. They determined that most of the Iraqi oil revenues went to the Ministry of Trade, which in turn was the government agency responsible for procuring food, equipment, supplies, and services from international markets, making the Ministry of Trade a central vehicle for many governmental activities within Iraq as well as beyond it. As the ministry acquired so much material it was responsible for initial storage, particularly of food, for which it had large warehouses, though the warehouses were highly vulnerable to looting that was then rampant in the country.

For several years, the ministry warehouse system had been integrated with the UN managed Oil for Food program (OFF), moving essential goods into Iraq for distribution to the population. Raphel and her team soon found that the UN program was profoundly inundated with graft and corruption. With experience in third-world countries, Raphel had anticipated some corruption with a totalitarian regime such as Iraq that had been subject to economic sanctions. But the full magnitude of the extraordinary corruption within the OFF program by UN officials was just beginning to emerge.[87]

When Mike Mobbs left Baghdad and Raphel replaced him to coordinate all the Iraqi ministries, she retained her position as senior advisor for the Ministry of Trade, spreading her efforts in two directions. For ministry coordination, she had Puckett as her deputy as well as O'Sullivan and Kraham, soon joined by Captain Brad Clark. At Trade, she could count on Oslander, Harvey, and Hamrock, with the latter gaining Raphel's confidence and taking on more of the work, eventually replacing her (see Table 3).

Dorothy Mazaka was the only woman other than Raphel initially assigned a role as ministry senior advisor—for the Ministry of Education. Shy and modest by nature, she did not mention to others her original position with the Department of Treasury, her prior experience in Saudi Arabia, or her knowledge of Arabic. In February, USAID assumed responsibility for providing a senior advisor for the Ministry of Education and arranged for Treasury to release Mazaka for that role while Garner was still in the Pentagon. From Kuwait, Mazaka flew into Baghdad with the other senior advisors on 24 April.

Upon arrival, Garner told his senior advisors about the chaos in Baghdad.

Table 3. Mid-May 2003: ORHA Senior and Interim Advisors for Iraqi Ministries

Ministry	Senior Advisor	Interim Senior Advisor
Director of Ministries	Robin Raphel	
Deputy Director	COL Tony Puckett, USA	
Program Coordinator	Sherri Kraham, DOS	
Transition Coordinator	Meghan O'Sullivan, DOS	
Legal Coordinator	CPT Brad Clark, USAR	
1. Agriculture	Lee Schatz: USDA	
2. Education	Dorothy Mazaka: USAID	
3. Electricity Commission	Pete Gibson: USACE	
4. Health	James K. Haveman**	Steve Browning: USACE
5. Housing & Construction	Joe Morgan > Dan Hitchings: USACE	
6. Industry & Minerals	Tim Carney: DOS	
7. Labor & Social Affairs	TBD: USAID*	Karen Walsh: USAID Contractor
8. Irrigation	Eugene Stakhiv: USACE	
9. Military Industry	TBD: DOS*	
10. Higher Education/ Scientific Research	Drew Erdmann: DOS	
11. Information	Bob Reilly, Contractor	
12. Defense	Walt Slocombe: DOD	
13. Planning	Simon Elvy: UK FCO	
14. Trade	Robin Raphel: DOS	
15. Justice	Donald Campbell: USAR	
16. Transportation & Communications	Steve Browning: USACE	

He wanted them to get downtown and establish contacts with their respective ministries. On 26 April, escorted by several Civil Affairs officers, Mazaka found her ministry buildings looted and smoldering, but was able to arrange a meeting at the Convention Center for the next day with representatives of the Education Ministry. The senior Iraqi present was Dr. Sulayman al-Dhari. Mazaka knew through an intelligence briefing that he was the ranking director general of the ministry, after the minister and two deputy ministers who had disappeared. Al-Dhari had been in charge of Technical Affairs, which included vocational training, a subset of the secondary education system in Iraq.[88]

Mazaka did not find al-Dhari sufficiently energetic and looked for others in the ministry whom she could rely upon for the necessary work to get the ministry functioning. They would soon find the shy Mazaka had a sterner side. Those included the directors general in the ministry headquarters in Baghdad and their nineteen counterparts responsible for education in each of the Iraqi

Table 3 (*continued*)

Ministry	Senior Advisor	Interim Senior Advisor
17. Culture	John Limbert: DOS	
18. Foreign Affairs	David Dunford: DOS (Ret)	

19. Interior	Bob Gifford: DOS >
	     Bernard Kerik:
	     DOD contractor	

Interior: Sanitation services	Raoul Stanley: AUSAID	
20. Central Bank	George Mullinax: Treasury Contractor	
21. Finance	David Nummy: Treasury Contractor	

22. Oil	Phil Carroll:
	     DOD Contractor
		Deputy: Gary Vogler:
		     DOD Contractor

23. AWQAF/Religious Affairs	TBD: DOS*	Andy Morrison: DOS
24. Youth	Don Eberly: SAIC Contractor	
Atomic Energy Commission	Mike Ayoub: DOS	
Governance	Ryan Crocker: DOS Deputy: Scott Carpenter: DOS	

NOTES. AWQAF = Ministry of Religious Affairs; TBD = to be determined; USDA = U.S. Department of Agriculture; USAID = U.S. Agency for International Development; USACE = U.S. Army Corps of Engineers; DOS = U.S. Department of State; DOJ = U.S. Department of Justice; DOD = Department of Defense; USAR = U.S. Army Reserve; UK FCO = UK Foreign and Commonwealth Office; AUSAID = Australian Agency for International Development.
*Not identified.
**Not in theater.

provinces. There were four DGs devoted to the large Baghdad school system (the three Kurdish provinces were not represented at her initial meetings). Mazaka knew that the Iraqi primary, intermediate, and secondary education system included six million students and 280,000 teachers and administrators, making the Ministry of Education the largest employer of government civilians in the country. It also accounted for much of the government real estate, with 15,000 school buildings.[89]

The Iraqi education system resembled the UK system with a tier of examinations that determined when students terminated their education, who went to vocational programs, and who continued with university preparation. The key examinations took place at the end of the sixth, ninth, and twelfth grades. In 2003, school was mandatory only through the sixth grade and the system was designed for only half the students to continue after that point. The ninth grade examinations determined which students would go into vocational training or for university preparation. The twelfth grade examinations were used to determine which of the twenty Iraqi universities each student would attend.

The examinations were normally held at the end of the school year, in late May or early June, but prior to the invasion all schools in Iraq had suspended operations. Garner wanted them back into session as soon as possible to ensure the students did not lose credit for a school year, an expensive proposition for six million students plus those in universities. The importance of putting the teachers and school administrators back to work was crucial.

Mazaka found that much of the education infrastructure had been underfunded for years and the recent looting and vandalism would require extensive repair of the schools to put the system into operation. If a higher percentage of children were to continue their education after the sixth grade, the school system would require expansion. Within the 15,000 school buildings, there were over 18,000 schools, with one-fifth of the buildings housing two schools, one for the morning and one for the afternoon, each with its own teachers, administrators, and students—a system that worked but that warranted modification.

USAID had projected construction for 3,000 schools within the large Bechtel contract, an unusual task for a company that normally undertook high-tech projects rather than more basic construction. Coalition forces in Iraq wanted the schools back into operation to get children off the street and teachers employed. With poor communications throughout the Coalition and Iraq, much of the effort to put the Iraqi school system back into operation was decentralized, but by 3 May almost 90 percent of the primary and secondary schools were back in operation.[90]

Progress was slower with the Iraqi Ministry of Higher Education. With no developed interest in the Iraqi university system, or perhaps an understanding that it was managed by a separate ministry, no one had appointed a senior advisor. In Kuwait, Mike Ayoub had been designated as interim advisor for that ministry, a decision that was driven by Ayoub's quest to quietly search for nuclear weapons given the belief that Iraq's WMD program was embedded in the Higher Education Ministry. But when Ayoub was moved to work with the Iraqi Ministry of Defense, Higher Education was left uncovered until the end of April. After Robin Raphel replaced Mike Mobbs to manage the ministry senior advisors, she assigned Drew Erdmann as the interim senior advisor for Higher Education. At the time, Erdmann had been working for Dunford on the Ministry of Foreign Affairs. Although Erdmann had been with ORHA in the Pentagon and Kuwait, he had taken no interest during that period in the Iraqi university system and would be starting at ground zero in Iraq. He was an interesting choice for the position. At thirty-six and as a GS-14, he was both one of the youngest and most junior of Garner's civilians to serve as an interim advisor, a position he would hold until his departure in the fall of 2003.

To assist in the transition, Raphel took Ayoub and Erdmann to Baghdad University on the afternoon of 30 April to meet representatives of eleven of Iraq's twenty universities. Ayoub was surprised that the meeting took place in the same auditorium he had used during his UN Special Commision inspection tour a decade earlier. Raphel introduced Erdmann as Garner's senior representative for the Ministry of Higher Education and Scientific Research and then went into a general discussion on higher education issues. The Iraqis present expressed concern about the looting and vandalism and some indicated that religious clerics in the Shia areas were trying to assume control of the universities and had intimidated the students.[91]

Erdmann had a doctorate in history from Harvard and had done some teaching, but he had no experience with large-scale administration for such a system. He was soon joined by Major Steve Kurda, a Civil Affairs reservist with a background in education from his civilian occupation in Florida. Together they made contact with the twenty universities throughout the country. They found that half of them had been established in the decade following Desert Storm and lacked the prestige and development of the older institutions. Like the primary and secondary schools in Iraq, the universities had been underfunded and poorly maintained. Recent looting and vandalism compounded the situation, which included the ministry headquarters in Baghdad. Needing a location to coordinate with the Iraqis in the ministry, Erdmann arranged to use conference rooms in several Baghdad universities.[92]

Just as Garner wanted to get the elementary and secondary schools operating, he wanted to reopen the universities to avoid having students repeat a full school year. Putting university students back in classrooms and getting them off the street was as important as putting younger children back into school. Inadequate communications throughout the country made that difficult. In contrast to money budgeted for primary and secondary schools, USAID had not projected early funding for higher education. The Coalition planned a conference in Madrid to solicit contributions for Iraq and assumed an international audience would assist the universities. Erdmann's immediate task was to establish contact with all the universities and assess each one for damage and potential. The main effort in early May was simply to get them up and running. At that time there was little vision on how the universities might be further harnessed to help Iraq.

Eugene Stakhiv arrived in Kuwait on 21 April. With a doctorate in engineering, he had served as a civilian with the Corps of Engineers for twenty-five years when he volunteered to go to Iraq. But those with the highest priority from his organization were to serve on FESTs to provide assessments for the reconstruction; he could only follow. His specialty was hydrology and river systems. He had never worked in the Middle East, but he had experience with water programs in Bangladesh, Uzbekistan, Kazakhstan, and Ukraine (where he had been part of a project to save the Aral Sea). He had worked with engineers from the World Bank and respected their work on overseas projects more than those of the United Nations or in his own Department of State, the latter of whom he referred to as "pompous turds." He got his call in early April and with some delay made it to Kuwait just as the other personnel were headed for Baghdad; his convoy arrived on 26 April with Stakhiv designated as the senior advisor for the Ministry of Irrigation.[93]

After talking to a contact with USAID, he determined that his ticket downtown was through General Steve Hawkins, who bore responsibility for electricity. The next morning, as Hawkins passed through the palace, Stakhiv introduced himself and asked for a ride into the city. Hawkins took him along and together they found that his ministry building had been looted and vandalized as so many others had. But the determined Stakhiv found officials from his ministry and an office in Baghdad to begin daily meetings. There had been 18,000 people employed by the ministry, many of them working in ten state-owned companies (known as State-Owned Enterprises or SOEs) that the ministry controlled. While irrigation in the ministry title suggested an orientation in agriculture, the Coalition's interest (and that of Hawkins) was the ten major hydro-electric dams on Iraq's inland waterways, which could produce up to 1,500 megawatts, about a third of Iraq's daily electricity production in April and May 2003. Coalition military forces had secured the dams to prevent sabotage during the invasion. With the high demand for electricity in Iraq, Stakhiv was soon pressured to increase the electricity produced.

From TF Fajr, General Hawkins provided Major Regan MacDonald to assist Stakhiv. MacDonald also had a background in hydrology. With a crusty no-nonsense style, Stakhiv was not discouraged with the austere working condition in the palace or the damage to his ministry. He was in his early sixties, older than the others under Garner, and was no complainer. He put in his requests, fought for what he needed, and got to work. He had little patience with the diplomats working with the other ministries, whom he considered whiners, or those on the C-staff, whom he considered unresponsive. Stakhiv and MacDonald obtained several SUVs and were soon driving into the city to work with their ministry personnel. In little time their small office in the palace was plastered with maps and diagrams of the water systems in Iraq. When

Stakhiv learned that the Soviet Union had conducted a study of Iraq's water system in the 1980s, he obtained a copy in English from Washington.[94]

Stakhiv studied the broad aspects of the Tigris and Euphrates river systems to include where the two rivers originated, with water programs and policies in Turkey, Syria, and Iran. There were problems with raw sewage dumped directly into Iraq's rivers, particularly in Baghdad, with the challenges of purifying water. Although the sewage treatment plants were not working in Baghdad due to the looting and lack of electricity, Stakhiv observed that the Iraqis were smart enough to take their water out above the city and dump the sewage below it. But the water still required purification, which could only be done with massive amounts of chlorine. Chlorine was expensive and required significant electricity to produce. Stakhiv's solution was to ensure enough bottled water for drinking, while the rest of the water supply only had to be clean enough for washing and uses other than consumption, referred to as "grey water."

Stakhiv knew that most of the sewage flowing into Iraq's rivers was organic—human or animal waste—and would decompose as it moved toward the Gulf; in theory, without treatment, it would be pure enough to use 100 miles down river, assuming no other large amounts of sewage were added on the way down. Toxic sewage from chemical plants and other industries would be a greater threat to the water system, but that was not a problem: those plants and industries had not been operating since the invasion. What was a problem, however, was the lack of oil storage facilities in southern Iraq. Oil waste dumped into the river system around Basra could pollute the Gulf ecosystem, an issue that put the interests of Stakhiv's ministry at cross-purposes with others who wanted to get oil flowing and the revenues that came with it.[95]

Just like his peers with their ministries, Stakhiv had to put his back together, find responsible people to take charge, get thousands of ministry people back to work, and pay their salaries. With ministry installations spread throughout Iraq, he would have to develop a security system to protect them. Iraq's southern marshes, which had been drained over the past decades, was another issue that few fully understood but were not hesitant to politicize. Stakhiv the engineer complained little and worked hard; he suffered no fools and few wanted to tangle with him.[96]

Major General Donald Campbell arrived in Kuwait the afternoon of 27 April, joining Garner for the second time. In 1991 as an Army reservist, he commanded the 351st Civil Affairs Command in support of Operation Provide Comfort and supported Garner's intervention force into northern Iraq to assist Kurdish refugees. This time Campbell would serve in a capacity more aligned with his civilian position as a New Jersey superior court judge. Garner requested Campbell by name to serve as the senior advisor for the Iraqi Ministry of Justice. Although activated as a soldier, Campbell chose to work in civilian clothes and few knew he was a serving major general. As he arrived in Kuwait, he found the airlines had lost his personal baggage. That did not stop him from departing early the following morning in a convoy to Baghdad, riding alongside Mike Ayoub.[97]

In the 1990s, Campbell had several experiences overseas with post-conflict situations and nation building. After northern Iraq, he was activated for service in Haiti, Bosnia, and Kosovo. When he arrived in Baghdad, he knew that a system of law and order required a cohesive "three-legged stool" with a police system, a legal system, and a prison system. Any missing leg would be disruptive for the other two. If those systems were under separate ministries — as they were in Iraq — cohesion would be more challenging: the Ministry of Justice had the court system; the Ministry of Labor and Social Affairs had the prisons; and the Ministry of the Interior had the police. Campbell initially assumed responsibility for the Ministry of Justice and subsequently picked up responsibility for the Iraqi prison system despite its alignment with another ministry.

With the other senior advisors, Campbell made his way into Baghdad to find the Ministry of Justice, a complex of buildings within sight of the palace that included the Supreme Court and the Judicial Institute, the latter an advanced law school for judges. As with the other ministry buildings, the Ministry of Justice had been looted and vandalized, but the ministry's large auditorium had little damage and could seat 500 people. Campbell convened a meeting there of the Iraqi Bar Association to develop a dialogue with the lawyers, prosecutors, and judges. They had many questions for Campbell and were skeptical of the Coalition's motives and capacity to reform Iraq.

Campbell knew that, like most Arab countries, Iraq had a French-style Napoleonic Code legal system. Trials were normally conducted by a panel of three judges and, as in France, there were no jury trials in Iraq. While Iraqis in other professions such as engineering and medicine often went to the United Kingdom or the United States for graduate work, those in the Iraqi legal system who studied overseas did so in France. Campbell had observed a comparable system in Haiti, which had a French heritage. Although more comfortable with the American system, Campbell believed that the French-style system would work in Iraq and should be retained.

The framework of the Iraqi judicial system had a Supreme Court, twelve appellate regions, with four subordinate systems: civil, criminal, family, and juvenile courts. The military and security services had run three additional systems: security, special, and intelligence courts, which had been responsible for most of the legal abuses in Iraq under the Saddam Hussein regime. By the time the invasion was over, the three military and security court systems had dissolved on their own. Each of the four remaining court systems were legitimate without major reforms, but they would require substantial assistance to renovate facilities and pay the salaries necessary to get those in the court system back to work. While others in the Coalition wanted to reform the Iraqi government, set up political parties, and write a constitution, Campbell simply wanted to get the residual Iraqi judicial system working again.[98]

Before Garner requested and received notification that Campbell would join him, Dick Mayer of the U.S. Department of Justice had been the interim senior advisor for the Iraqi Ministry of Justice, but Mayer's real interest was the Iraqi domestic police. Bob Gifford from State Department's Bureau of International Narcotics and Law Enforcement Affairs (INL) was designated as the senior advisor for the Iraqi Ministry of the Interior, responsible for the centralized police system throughout Iraq. But until Gifford arrived in late April, Mayer served as the interim advisor for Interior. Philip Hall, who had a legal background with the UK Foreign Ministry, shifted to cover Justice in Kuwait. When Campbell arrived to take Justice, Hall joined Mayer with the Interior Ministry. Hall learned that, in addition to police, the Ministry of the Interior was responsible for border control, immigration, passports, and customs. He tried to cover those areas, leaving Mayer to concentrate on the police. When they arrived in Baghdad, Hall and Mayer found the ministry buildings looted and vandalized. There was widespread chaos in the city with no law and order, much as Mayer had predicted at the Pentagon and in Kuwait.

Hall found that the ministry advisors with Interior did not want to work on border control; Hall argued that without such regulation anyone could enter Iraq. Paul Hughes, monitoring the policy for the Iraqi army in the absence of Walt Slocombe, felt border control could be a useful task for the army as it was reconstituted. A few days later, Mayer became ill and had to return to the United States; he would not return to Iraq.

As Mayer left, Bob Gifford arrived in Baghdad. Assisted by Hall, Gifford was able to make contact with second-tier Iraqi officials in Interior. With the ministry building unusable, they conducted their initial meetings in the Baghdad Convention Center (as did other ministry advisory teams). Their initial and most pressing goal was to get the Iraqi police operating in Baghdad. They tried to coordinate with the 3rd Mechanized Infantry Division occupying the city, but they could not find anyone focused on police issues for the whole city. Soon they met Colonel Terry Spain, commander of the 18th Military Police Brigade, part of V Corps. There were three MP brigades in theater with a total of seventeen MP battalions and fifty MP companies. Spain's brigade consisted of five MP battalions with twenty-two of the MP companies, but just as McKiernan's command had taken most of General Kern's Civil Affairs battalions and attached them to the maneuver formations, so had most of Spain's MP units been farmed out. That left Spain with his brigade staff and a handful of MP units to assist with law and order in Iraq. Much like Mayer and Hall, Colonel Spain's main focus was bringing the chaos in Baghdad under control.[99]

Working with Spain, Gifford and Hall found a police academy in the city used for training and educating police. Despite some looting, those buildings had more utility than the main ministry buildings. By 4 May, they were able to arrange a meeting with the precinct police chiefs in Baghdad and agreed to issue a call through a radio station in Kuwait that could reach Iraq for the police to return to duty. They soon found that most of the police stations throughout the city, and throughout Iraq, had been looted and would therefore have to be renovated and reequipped before police services could be restored.

A few days later, Gifford and Hall were joined by Jim Steele, a retired army colonel, supposedly sent to Iraq by Rumsfeld to work on electricity in Iraq. When Steele arrived, Garner saw him in the palace and asked what he was doing. Steele said he was working on electricity. Garner later learned that Steele had a direct line to Secretary Rumsfeld and may have been sent over to keep Rumsfeld informed. From prior Army assignments Garner knew and respected Steele. He told Steele there were enough people working on electricity and so moved him to Interior. Steele was an armor officer with service in Special Forces; he had worked with police in Latin America during the 1980s and 1990s. As Steele joined them, Gifford and Hall received word that Bernard Kerik, previously the New York City Police Commissioner, would arrive soon to serve as the senior advisor for the ministry. For the rest of May, their main effort was activating the police in Baghdad.[100]

Hall was not the only one curious about the Ministry of the Interior and what it controlled beyond the police. Raoul Percy Stanley took an interest in the ministry's Department of Technical Services, responsible for water, sanitation, and roads throughout the country. Stanley was an Australian civilian from AUSAID. He had field experience in the Solomon Islands and New Guinea and would be one of the few non-Americans to serve as a ministry senior advisor. When he joined ORHA in Kuwait, he was originally assigned to the Humanitarian Assistance pillar based on his background, and he had driven to Iraq in one of the first convoys from Kuwait. When he determined that there was no humanitarian crisis in Iraq, he went looking for another job. With a developed interest in water and sanitation, he searched for the ministry responsible for that sector. He learned that those functions had previously been managed by the Ministry of Local Government and Technical Services, but that ministry had been disbanded (prior to the Coalition invasion) and its responsibilities absorbed by the Interior Ministry.[101]

As he observed Mayer and Hall, then Gifford and Steele, orient their efforts on the police, Stanley informally managed his way in to work with the subordinate Department of Technical Services. He found that the buildings housing Technical Services had not been looted when he arrived in Baghdad, and to protect them he requested military forces to secure the buildings. The request went to the 3rd Mechanized Infantry Division, which supported the request. But Stanley found only one tank parked in front of the building while it was being looted from the opposite side. Once again, the Coalition military effort to secure Baghdad was insufficient.[102]

Locating senior Iraqis associated with Technical Services, Stanley found their credentials were in engineering (whereas others in the ministry had credentials in security). He also found a small group from UNICEF working in Baghdad that shared his interest in water and sanitation, and through them he learned more about the structure of the Technical Services and the Iraqis that worked within it. Stanley's contacts in UNICEF provided him an office to manage his first meetings with Iraqis in the Technical Services Department. His efforts would eventually lead to the creation of the ministry status for Technical Services, for which he would become the senior advisor.[103]

Garner spent the first four days of May in Baghdad. Restless to see what was going on outside the palace walls, he went into the city for several hours each day to mix with Iraqis and made a few day trips out of town to adjacent areas. The daily meetings in the palace continued, with the senior advisors going downtown daily to reestablish the ministries or bring Iraqis to the Convention Center for meetings. By the beginning of May, Garner had a thousand people working for him in Baghdad: some were military officers from McKiernan's command, mainly Civil Affairs officers; most of the civilians came from government agencies in the United States. Contractor support came from Raytheon, providing communications for ORHA and KBR with more general support. Most of the military and civilian personnel were American; about a hundred were non-Americans, half from the UK. The dominant challenges were security, electricity, communications, money, and organization.

The Iraqi police system remained dysfunctional, leaving domestic security to Coalition military formations throughout Iraq. The 3rd Mechanized Infantry Division had responsibility for Baghdad (until it was replaced by the 1st

Armor Division), divided into brigade, battalion, and company sectors. Civil Affairs, MP, engineer, medical, and other supporting formations were integrated into each brigade sector. Linkage between Garner in Baghdad and the division commander, Major General Blount, was almost nonexistent. Blount worked for General McKiernan. So did Garner, nominally, but McKiernan did not choose to exercise control over ORHA. Garner continued to talk to the Secretary of Defense, whereas McKiernan answered to General Franks, commander of U.S. Central Command, a situation that would continue through May.[104]

After security, electricity was the most pervasive challenge, necessary for utility systems: water, sewage, hospitals, schools, and every home, building, business, and industry in Iraq. With the summer heat rising, electricity became a measurement of Coalition success. When Garner met Iraqis downtown, the common complaint other than security was inadequate electricity or none at all. Garner had responsibility for managing the Electricity Commission (with ministry status), but he had nothing to fix the system in Baghdad or elsewhere in Iraq.

That task had fallen to General Steve Hawkins and his TF Fajr, working for General McKiernan, who had directed him to get the electricity working. Hawkins was driven, but his team was small and his assets limited. As soon as he got one part of the electricity system working, another part would fail due to years of poor maintenance, looting, or vandalism. Under Garner, Steve Browning had oversight for electricity, transportation, and communications, but Browning's time was dominated by his work as the acting senior advisor for the Ministry of Health. James Haveman, designated to replace Skip Burkle as senior advisor for the Ministry of Health, would not arrive until mid-July.

Representing ORHA, Major General Strock worked closely with General Hawkins on electricity. On the first of May, Strock announced at a meeting that Hawkins had five power stations running, although not at full capacity, and they broke down frequently. Strock also took an interest in the petroleum products used in Iraq. While the country had enormous oil reserves, Iraqi access to fuel for consumption relied on its refineries. An inadequate number of refineries was one bottleneck; another was the limited storage capacity. The distribution system and pumping stations were poorly maintained, so the movement of crude oil to refineries (and to ports) was slow. Without a steady source of fuel, electrical power plants could not operate at full capacity. They could operate with several types of fuel oil, some forms far more efficient than others. Those less efficient variants were often the most available; use of those variants reduced potential electricity output when the power plants were in operation.

Coalition convoys had to import gasoline, diesel, and natural gas from Kuwait and other Gulf countries to meet Iraqi internal demand—at significant cost to the Coalition. While Hawkins worked on electricity, Brigadier General Crear and his Task Force RIO continued to tackle the fuel challenges. Crear did not work directly for Garner, nor was he tightly under McKiernan's command; technically he worked for the Headquarters of the Army Corps of Engineers in Washington. Strock as the senior Corps representative in theater had a good relationship with Crear that sustained a link between ORHA and RIO.[105]

Garner had given Strock another assignment as one of Barbara Bodine's deputies for Baghdad. While Bodine was interested in community governance, Strock tried to get the electricity and other utilities in the capital in operation. That might have made Strock and Bodine complementary, but it would soon lead to conflict. Ted Morse, Bodine's other deputy, helped her with "soft reconstruction" in Baghdad, but he too would have difficulty working with Bodine. Garner held Strock and Morse in high regard. When both had problems with Bodine, Garner anticipated he would have to change the leadership.[106]

Work and living conditions for ORHA slowly improved. There would be no air conditioning until mid-summer, but a palace dining facility opened with a hot breakfast on 4 May. Food was imported from Kuwait or the United States. Fresh Iraqi bread and produce could not be procured due to the strict sanitary conditions imposed by Coalition food inspectors (the same standard applied to the military formations). Laundry service was established for those in the palace with a five-day turnaround through Kuwait. The KBR subcontract for laundry went to a firm in Kuwait rather than one in Baghdad, which might have been cheaper and faster; it would also have employed Iraqis.

Communications within the palace improved but at an agonizingly slow pace. After the computer servers were set up, it took several weeks to fully wire the palace, an annoyance for civilians with offices beyond the central area that had been wired in late April. Lack of a functional phone system was also a problem. Colonel Conway received more Thuraya phones to issue, but with the line-of-sight satellite requirement they were inadequate for normal office work in Baghdad. There would not be a cell phone system in operation until late May, which restricted communications within the Coalition and with Iraqis.

International organizations and NGOs were arriving to complement the few such organizations that were in Baghdad before the invasion, but the numbers were far below what Garner had anticipated. When the UN announced it would send a civilian contingent to Iraq, it insisted that the UN compound and offices be distant from any Coalition military formations (which led to disaster in August with a suicide bombing). Without assistance from the UN or related organizations, ORHA had to rely on the military formations, already overloaded and reluctant or unable to provide such support.

Getting around Baghdad was another problem. KBR brought more SUVs to Baghdad, but the ORHA personnel expansion and transportation requirements exceeded the increase in vehicles. Limitations on armed escorts added to the complication. The military command reinforced the MP company supporting ORHA with a third platoon, a modest increase when there were fifty MP companies serving in Iraq. Civil Affairs officers working with ORHA tried to assist with vehicles as escorts, though they often lacked mounted radios and weapons.

More Iraqi expatriates arrived in early May, but their contribution had mixed results. One case that made many from ORHA skeptical of expatriates came with an experience Don Eberly had when he took one of them with him as a back-up interpreter into Baghdad. Eberly's primary interpreter caught the expatriate telling Iraqis, "Don't worry about what this guy [Eberly] says. This isn't the real agenda and he's really not in control." The patient Eberly took it in stride. But when Garner was informed of the incident, it confirmed his reservations about the motives for some of those coming to Iraq. He had Colonel Mike Murphy, the ORHA legal officer, talk to the IRDC group. Murphy read them the riot act, making it clear that Garner was in charge and that the IRDC was to support him, not the reverse. It was an appropriate correction, but it left those in ORHA uneasy about the expatriates and reluctant to empower them, unfortunate given that many were talented and had come to Iraq for the right reasons.[107]

A larger issue was the inability to get the IIA off the ground. Garner met with Talabani and others of the group, but they lacked a cohesive agenda. Without the governance pillar promised by OSD, Garner could not provide policy guidance for the Coalition. At multiple levels, he had to find the right Iraqis and get them to take charge of Iraq. He needed more expertise and support from the Coalition. Garner had frequent assurances from the Pentagon that more senior advisors were on the way, but those with the appropriate qualifications were slow to arrive. Indeed, Coalition personnel with inappropriate qualifications would be a problem long after Garner's departure from Iraq.

During April and early May, Garner monitored his regional components and was anxious to get out and see them. His April trip to northern Iraq to meet Talabani and Barzani was brief and provided a first-hand perspective of the operations under Bruce Moore and Dick Naab with ORHA-North. Initially, military support for Moore and Naab came from the 10th Special Forces Group, during the period when ORHA-North worked with the Kurds, and perhaps it remained focused on the Kurds too long. The day Garner arrived in Iraq, Colonel Joe Anderson had taken a reinforced infantry brigade to Mosul. Anderson had the lead component of the 101st Air Assault Division under Major General David Petraeus, deploying to northern Iraq. There were two formations in Mosul when Anderson arrived, a battalion of the 10th Special Forces and an infantry battalion from the 26th Marine Expeditionary Unit, flown in from the Mediterranean as reinforcements.

When the Marines entered Mosul, they ran the American flag over city hall, an action McKiernan's command had prohibited. The Iraqis protested the flag raising, which led to a riot in which the Marines allegedly shot a dozen people, then withdrew to the airfield. Anderson had no command relationship with the Marines in Mosul and he was thankful when they left a week later. When Petraeus moved into northern Iraq, his focus was on Mosul and the Arab areas to the northwest. At that time, ORHA-North was working from Erbil, oriented on the Kurdish areas to the northeast. Petraeus was subordinate to General McKiernan, while ORHA-North was subordinate to Garner. It would take another month to better integrate their efforts in northern Iraq.[108]

In early May, Garner made a day trip to Hilla, about 100 miles south of Baghdad, to see Buck Walters with ORHA-South Central. Walters had moved his group to Hilla at the suggestion of General James Conway, commander of the 1st Marine Expeditionary Force. The Marines had invaded from the south, taken the eastern half of Baghdad, and then occupied several provinces south of the city. Just as Moore and ORHA-North were loosely aligned with Petraeus's command, Walters and ORHA-South Central were loosely aligned with Conway's command, with its headquarters next to the main historic site of Babylon, a few miles outside Hilla. General Conway did not impose control over Walters, but he suggested it would be useful if they were located near each other; Walters concurred.

That coincided with Garner's decision to split the more populous southern Iraq into two subordinate regions: the newly designated ORHA-South Central with six of Iraq's eighteen provinces under Walters aligned with Conway's command; and another region inheriting the ORHA-South title with the six most southern provinces in Iraq aligned with the British division stationed there. Garner went to see Walters at the Babil Tourist Hotel on the Shat al-Hilla River of the Euphrates River system, two miles from General Conway's headquarters. Both were located north of Hilla, a city of 400,000. Walters's sixty-room hotel had been the property of the Ministry of Tourism. It was in poor condition and Walters had his hands full to get it cleaned up as he began to work with the Iraqis in the six provinces he had been assigned.

Next to the hotel was another building Walters used to establish a Civil Military Operations Center (CMOC). He intended to bring Iraqis there for meetings with ORHA and Civil Affairs personnel working for Conway. By the end of April, Walters had his team at the Babil Hotel with thirty Gurkhas for security and the Marines nearby. Garner returned to Baghdad satisfied that Walters was headed in the right direction. Garner had given him Mike Gfoeller, the Arabist from State who soon became one of Walters's favorites; Gfoeller would replace Walters in July.

On 5 May, Garner flew to Basra to see how the new regional component had developed. With him he took Margaret Tutwiler, Larry Di Rita, and Tim Cross. The British forces had their main headquarters at the international airport at Basra, several miles outside of the city. Garner met several senior British officers there and decided to spend the night, a delight for Cross, who told the Americans what he missed most from his home country was "a good cup of tea, which is only available in two places—in England and in any British Army mess."[109]

The ORHA-South counterpart for Moore and Walters was Ambassador Ole Olsen, a Danish diplomat. Only a week earlier, Olsen had been the Danish ambassador to Syria. Prior to the invasion he had visited Baghdad frequently to monitor Denmark's economic interests in the UN-sponsored Oil for Food program. Olsen had previously served as Denmark's ambassador to several other Arab countries. He spoke Arabic, had married an Algerian doctor, and had allegedly converted to Islam. He began with a broader understanding of the Middle East and Iraq than Walters, Moore, or even Bodine. But his ORHA component was well behind the other three and he was slow to catch up.

Olsen was not sure why he had been selected for such a senior position within ORHA and assumed it was to expand its international depth. He flew to Baghdad on 2 May to meet Garner, Bates, and Cross and left the next day for Basra, where he moved in with the UK's 1st Military Police Regiment in a building previously used by the Basra Electrical Company. He had security through the British MPs, rooms and a mess hall he could use as he built up his staff. Two colonels joined him from Baghdad, and a third joined from the Civil Affairs command. When Garner arrived three days later, Olsen had fewer than a dozen people with him. ORHA had not provided any vehicles, security, communications, or money. Buck Walters had gone to Hilla with all his people and equipment. Garner and Cross were sympathetic and promised

Olsen they would make arrangements for more support, but ORHA-South would continue as the leanest of all Garner's regions in terms of people, equipment, and capacity.[110]

Initially Olsen used his personal funds to buy his team basic amenities. He rented half a dozen land cruisers from a dealer in Kuwait with Danish funds. Within the month, he received half a dozen SUVs from ORHA as he accumulated more people. Many of those in Baghdad assumed the British military command would provide more support, which they provided to an extent. Within a few weeks, KBR provided Olsen a support team and Captain Macias from the C-6 staff installed a communications package linking Olsen with Baghdad.[111]

Before he left Basra, Garner and his group toured the city, which was more humid, dirtier, and more impoverished than any other place they had been in Iraq. They visited a school, a hospital, and one of Iraq's largest oil refineries. The latter was a large complex, poorly maintained and in disrepair. Garner met the manager of the refinery, who explained many of the challenges they faced. Again Garner was sympathetic and promised assistance. The group returned to the airport, where they had dinner with several British officers, including Brigadier Andrew Gregory. During the invasion, Gregory had been the artillery commander providing fire power, then provided what he called "soft effects"—information operations, psychological operations, media relations, and humanitarian aid. Gregory took an interest in Ambassador Olsen's task and sent some UK officers to join ORHA-South. Gregory subsequently became Olsen's deputy.[112]

The next morning Garner and his group returned to Baghdad, where he was met at the airport by Jakob Knellenberger of the ICRC. During the twenty-minute meeting, Garner and Knellenberger discussed what they each wanted to accomplish in Iraq. They agreed the anticipated humanitarian crisis in Iraq had not materialized. For Garner, that meant moving on to larger tasks of nation building. He needed help from international organizations like the ICRC. But the ICRC representative and others had reservations about larger aspects of nation building with the United States in control. Garner was disappointed with the meeting.[113]

After a quick stop at his headquarters in the palace, Garner went downtown for a tour of Sadr City, increasingly concerned about that section of Baghdad. Garner knew General Franks was going to send the 3rd Mechanized Infantry Division home to be replaced with another division in Baghdad. Garner visited McKiernan at the airport and appealed to him to move the 101st Air Assault Division into the capital city. Garner knew the differences in the structure of army divisions that would affect their capacity for occupation.

In 2003, the Army had several types of divisions: half were heavy divisions—armor and mechanized infantry divisions—and half were airborne, air assault, or light infantry. The heavy divisions had lots of tanks but less than half the infantry of the other divisions. In Garner's view, the most useful forces for stabilizing Baghdad would be infantry, which could most effectively patrol the city streets. Armor and mechanized divisions have a mix of tank and mechanized battalions but do not have non-mechanized battalions, which are found only in infantry, airborne, air assault, and Marine divisions.

Garner believed that the 101st with nine infantry battalions would be more useful in Baghdad's large urban environment than the heavy formations. Security in Baghdad would be a function of dismounted patrolling, which required more infantry. For the same reason, Colonel Benson, McKiernan's senior planner, also advised McKiernan to assign the 101st to Baghdad.[114]

McKiernan's concern was quickly distributing his limited forces throughout Iraq, and the agile 101st Division (with twice as many helicopters as other divisions) could be moved north quickly by air because it did not include tank or mechanized units. Furthermore, McKiernan was an armor officer, comfortable with the heavy formations, and he did not share Garner's reservation about the use of armor in Baghdad. For the next seven years, all the American divisions assigned to Baghdad were either armor or mechanized infantry divisions, with less capacity for dismounted patrolling than infantry, air assault, or airborne divisions.[115]

Ron Adams rejoined ORHA in Baghdad the day Garner flew to Basra. He had left Kuwait a month earlier to go to Walter Reed Hospital to address several illnesses, and Colonel Martin had returned with him. Adams began to recover while undergoing tests. By 11 April, with Martin, he began making day trips from his home in Carlisle, Pennsylvania, to Washington to work for ORHA. Garner had given Adams no specific instructions other than to get well, but Adams had three objectives he defined for himself: obtain more qualified personnel for ORHA; represent Garner in the Pentagon and with the staff of the National Security Council; and bring in more international support, NGOs, and other organizations.

Adams found there were two offices in the Pentagon sending people to ORHA. One was managed by Colonel Chris Leins and Mike Shane, a contractor, both working for Colonel DeGraff, the ORHA C-1 Personnel officer. Leins and Shane recruited some of those headed for Iraq and arranged for them to get orders, medical checks, and pre-deployment training. The office that recruited the senior positions in Iraq was run by Jim O'Beirne, who worked as the White House personnel liaison in Doug Feith's Policy shop. Adams met O'Beirne on 14 April to discuss the people Garner needed from the other agencies to serve as senior advisors for the Iraqi ministries. Adams soon suspected, as DeGraff learned separately, that those working with O'Beirne to recruit personnel for Iraq were more concerned about political alignment with the Bush administration than with the developed and diverse skills Garner needed.[116]

After meeting with O'Beirne, Adams had an office call with Walt Slocombe, who had been designated the senior advisor for the Ministry of Defense with responsibility for the Iraqi army. Adams had met Slocombe several years earlier when Slocombe was Undersecretary of Defense for Policy and Adams was about to take command of the NATO headquarters in Bosnia. Slocombe might have acknowledged the experience Adams had in post-conflict operations; instead he took little interest in the role Adams had with ORHA. He did not share with Adams his developing intention to disband the Iraqi army and rebuild a new one from scratch.

Adams tried to see Doug Feith several times, but on each occasion he was told Feith was too busy. He did see Ryan Henry, Feith's deputy, but even Henry was almost inaccessible to him. Adams tried to attend the meetings scheduled in Washington that addressed ORHA, meetings he had attended earlier in January through March, but he found he was excluded from those meetings in April and May; he did not know why.[117]

When Colonel Martin returned to Kuwait in mid-April as ORHA began to deploy into Iraq, Adams remained behind, awaiting medical clearance from Walter Reed. When he found he was excluded from meetings in the Pentagon and with the NSC staff, he met with officials from the World Bank and with Japanese, Romanian, and other foreign government representatives interested in providing assistance for Iraq. But it was difficult for Adams to coordinate significant contributions from other countries and organizations when he lacked a formal connection with OSD and the NSC.

While Adams was in the Pentagon, L. Paul "Jerry" Bremer was selected as Garner's replacement. Remarkably, no one in the Pentagon arranged a meeting for Adams with Bremer as the latter was receiving briefings on Iraq. Frustrated in Washington, Adams decided to rejoin Garner in Baghdad. He was skeptical of his government's intention or capacity to support operations in Iraq.[118]

Colonel Martin was serving as Jerry Bates's deputy chief of staff, while Colonel Collins managed administrative activities in the palace. Collins was also renovating the Al-Rashid Hotel nearby as additional accommodations for ORHA. Upon Adams's return, the energetic Martin split his efforts between serving Bates and resuming his role as Adams's executive assistant.

When Garner returned from Basra, his attention was again dominated by the many challenges in Baghdad; one of those was Barbara Bodine. When she joined ORHA in the Pentagon, Colonel Baltazar told Garner that she would be high maintenance, and he was right. She had taken several of the Public Affairs Officers for her personal staff at the expense of the ORHA media program. She picked fights with the senior leaders in ORHA and had a blatant disdain for military officers. Her end in Iraq was driven by three incidents. The first was a morning encounter on 7 May with Steve Browning in the parking lot; the second occurred the next day during a staff meeting with Garner; and the third was an altercation with General Carl Strock that evening.

Context for the parking lot incident developed a week earlier. On a trip to the Ministry of Health, Steve Browning was approached by several Iraqis representing the Ministry of Religious Affairs and Endowments. They told Browning no one from ORHA had been to see them and that they too wanted their salaries paid. Browning said he would look into it and get back to them. When he told Garner later that day, Garner said he would have Andy Morrison of Bodine's Baghdad Central unit take care of it. Morrison had been appointed the interim senior advisor for that ministry in addition to other tasks. Browning told the Iraqis they would hear from someone in a few days.[119]

Three days later, they again approached Browning and said no one had been to see them. Browning went to Morrison, whom he found dismissive, with little interest in the ministry. After a third contact from the Iraqis indicating no one had been to see them, Browning took the issue to Garner, who was annoyed that Morrison had not taken the action directed. Garner told the energetic Browning to visit the ministry and establish contact. Browning set out to do so the morning of 7 May from the parking lot in front of the palace. He was accompanied by Colonel Mike Williams and the TF Fajr Medical Support Team that normally escorted Browning to the Ministry of Health. Browning was seated in a military vehicle with Said Haki, a doctor and Iraqi expatriate with the IRDC. They were then approached by Bodine with Andy Morrison in tow. She was obviously upset and Browning got out of the vehicle to talk to her. Soon so did Dr. Haki.[120]

Bodine asked Browning if he was going to the Ministry of Religious Affairs. When Browning said that he was, she ordered him not to do so and stated that he was certainly not to take Dr. Haki, a Shia from the IRDC. As Browning explained he was going on Garner's explicit direction, Bodine became enraged and began stomping her foot in a manner Browning found unnatural. She became profane, called Browning offensive names, said she was a major general, and stated emphatically that she was ordering him not to go. Obviously she was not a military officer, but her rank in the Department of State was comparable for protocol purposes to a major general. Browning offered to see Garner to ensure that his guidance had not changed, but Bodine continued to scream at him, catching the attention of those with Browning and others in the parking lot. At one stage she called Browning a "mother fucker," which led Dr. Haki to place himself between Bodine and Browning as if to defend Browning.[121]

Browning assumed the stress and heat was causing Bodine some sort of breakdown. He ceased arguing, said he would discuss it with Garner, and went into the palace to find him. Dr. Haki went with him and quickly drafted a one-page letter stating that Bodine "insulted me in front of many witnesses. This slanderous behavior was totally unprovoked." When Browning and Haki explained what had taken place in the parking lot, Garner looked down and said quietly that Bodine "has to go."[122]

The next day Garner had a meeting with senior members of his team, including Bodine. During the discussion, Bodine went into a long and unusually harsh diatribe criticizing the Coalition and ORHA performance in Iraq. While she had been critical before, often with useful insight, those present found her more irate than thoughtful. Garner said nothing and merely looked away as she droned on; eventually someone else took up another issue; no one responded to Bodine's comments.[123]

That evening General Strock had a long discussion with Bodine on Iraqi leadership in Baghdad. Strock was concerned about Bodine's efforts to use one of the city's senior leaders to manage political change. Strock had spent some time with the leader and found that he was in essence a city manager for Baghdad's physical infrastructure, with little political experience and no interest in a political role. Bodine was determined to use him to implement social programs she was trying to develop. When Strock objected to such a role for a city manager, Bodine became adversarial. Strock was perplexed and got up, believing they had reached an impasse. As he was leaving, Bodine said something Strock took to be conciliatory. He turned around ready to restart the discussion. But he soon realized he had misread her comment and that she was now making fun of him for attempting to restart the discussion. Strock stormed out of the office.[124]

Strock had a room near Garner's and, as he passed by, Garner called him. Still angry, Strock tried to defer but Garner insisted, sensing something was bothering him. After he gave Strock a drink, Garner prodded him until he opened up about his discussion with Bodine. It was unlike the congenial Strock to speak about anyone in such a manner, and all the more so when he blurted out, "If she had been a man, I would have hit her."[125]

Garner said little in response. After Strock left, he called for Colonel Martin, who helped manage his schedule. Garner told Martin to get Secretary

Powell on the phone. Garner had already discussed his concerns about Bodine with Margaret Tutwiler, Larry Di Rita, and Robin Raphel. All agreed that Bodine had become a problem. Tutwiler had called Powell to prepare him for what might be coming.

When Garner got through, Powell said, "I understand you've got some problems."

"My problem is Barbara Bodine," replied Garner. "I have two solutions. We can do it hard or we do it easy. Hard is I'll just relieve her and put her on the next aircraft. Easy is you can reassign her."

Powell told Garner he would take care of it and have her reassigned. The next morning Garner walked into his office and found Bodine waiting. She told him she wanted to stay but she had been reassigned and had to return to Washington.

"Barbara, we really appreciate what you've done," Garner said. "You have a lot of knowledge of the area and a lot of Iraqis look up to you and are glad you were here, so I'm sorry you're leaving, but I wish you the best. Thank you for your service."

Later Garner recalled the conversation. "She knew I was lying. I knew she was lying and we parted ways."[126]

Bodine left a few days later after telling others that she had to leave to take a new assignment at State as the Assistant Secretary for the Political-Military Bureau, a position that surprised many in ORHA given her disdain for military officers. Few knew that Garner had fired Bodine or the specific reasons, but when the word was out that she was leaving, hardly anyone was surprised.[127]

Garner had now fired two senior people in Iraq—Mike Mobbs and Barbara Bodine. In both cases he waited too long. Within a few weeks in Kuwait, Garner knew that Mobbs was ineffective with his passive management style when ORHA needed someone dynamic for the Civil Administration pillar. Reliance on the industrious but junior and inexperienced Sherri Kraham to add momentum for the ministry effort had not been effective and the planning and preparation had suffered. Raphel and Puckett made a good team for what became the Ministry Coordination cell, but it came late.

Bodine's management style was not passive but lacked method and was too contentious for effective interagency teamwork. Since she joined Garner in the Pentagon, she had become increasingly disruptive and occasionally erratic. In contrast to many in ORHA, she had previously served in the Arab world and specifically in Baghdad. She spoke some Arabic and was hard-charging. But she did not understand the leadership dynamic of the Iraqis in Baghdad and could not work effectively with those like Strock and Ted Morse assigned to help her. Bodine left Iraq a more tragic figure than Mobbs, as she might have contributed much more.

On 3 May, Mike Ayoub, Paul Hughes, and an interpreter went to the Ministry of Defense, which like many government buildings had been looted and burned. They found it guarded by American soldiers. With flashlights, they went through several rooms and discovered a large trove of documents marked "Top Secret" in Arabic. They assumed those documents might include information about weapons of mass destruction. Ayoub and Hughes took all they could carry and told the lieutenant in charge of the complex to protect the remainder.

Dated 23 January 2003, one of the documents was an emergency plan anticipating "the fall of the Iraqi leadership" from the al-Ististkbarat and al-Mokabarat security services with directions for government officers:

1. Loot and burn all government offices in our area and other.
2. Change places every now and then.
3. Damage all electricity plants.
4. Damage all water plants.
5. Arm related members and sources and hide them in Mosques.
6. Go to the Hawza Alelmea in An Najef.
7. Go to the National and Islamic parties.
8. Cut all communications national and international.
9. Buy weapons from residents.
10. Get close to the people coming back into the country.
11. Assassinate all mosque leaders and (Imams).[128]

When Ayoub read the letter (in Arabic) and translated it for Colonel Hughes, they understood that some of the looting and vandalism they had observed and would continue to see in Iraq was directed sabotage. Some of the Iraqi classified material might be outdated, but they assumed some would be useful for the Coalition. When they returned to the palace, they passed the documents they had collected to the intelligence personnel in the C-2 staff section, and Ayoub "tried to arrange for an Intel team to be sent out to the bunker only to learn they were tied up working on a project for Harold Rhode."

Ayoub learned that Harold Rhode and Terry Sullivan had taken Judith Miller, a reporter from the *New York Times,* to "one of the Iraqi Intelligence Headquarters in search of an ancient Talmud [Jewish law book]." Eventually Rhode and Sullivan found some Jewish artifacts in Baghdad and sent them back to the United States. Later that summer, those artifacts would become a hot potato for the NSC.[129]

Ayoub directed his efforts to the Iraqi army and met several Iraqi officers at the Convention Center, whom he had begun to refer to as the "al-Jibouri Group," as they were from the al-Jibouri tribe. The group included Major General Aamer Sheaa Abdula, whom Ayoub found articulate, witty, bright, and the apparent leader of the group. They discussed the deteriorating security situation, and Ayoub directed their attention to three tasks: to formulate a plan to mobilize some former Iraqi military police to assist with the security threat in Baghdad; to find a suitable site to train those MPs; and to find and bring him Ministry of Defense payroll records. Ayoub told them he needed the latter so the Coalition could provide emergency payments to military personnel, as such payments were being made to Iraqis associated with other ministries. When Ayoub offered to provide those in the group an emergency payment, they declined, stating that "as senior officers they are better off than the troops and low level civilians, and will accept payment when everyone else receives it."[130]

Despite the enthusiastic response of the Iraqi officers he was working with, Ayoub was concerned that progress with the Ministry of Defense was slipping behind the other ministries. Hughes and Ayoub were working in a vacuum with the Iraqi army. Neither had the status of senior advisor for the Ministry of Defense, a position held by Walt Slocombe, still in Washington. Nor were Hughes or Ayoub aware that McKiernan's command had established contacts with several Iraqi generals interested in working with the Coalition and reconstituting the army.[131]

By the first week of May, the military command and ORHA were working more closely. On 7 May, General Kern announced that his Civil Affairs command would open a Humanitarian Operations Center in Baghdad. General Hawkins kept those involved with electricity under Garner up to date with his progress and challenges, just as General Crear kept others updated with his efforts to get oil flowing. General Webster, McKiernan's representative to ORHA, met frequently with Jerry Bates and occasionally with Garner, but his role tended to focus more on security rather than Civil Affairs, electricity, or oil.

Garner directed his energy toward the Iraqi ministries and making progress with an interim Iraqi government. Robin Raphel reported that contact had been made with all the ministries, with seventeen of twenty-three ministry building complexes unusable. Each ministry required a headquarters, and Garner asked for money to renovate their buildings or put them in new ones. For the ministries to become operational, the Coalition had to provide security,

Table 4. Garner's Ten Tasks

Task	ORHA Lead	Military Lead
1. Salaries paid nationwide	David Nummy	BG Edgar E. Stanton
2. Police, courts, prisons	Bob Gifford	BG Howard B. Bromberg
3. Restore basic services in Baghdad	MG Carl Strock	BG Steven Hawkins
4. Fix fuel crisis	Gary Vogler	MG Claude Christianson and BG Robert Crear
5. Purchase crops (in Iraq)	Robin Raphel	COL Marty Stanton
6. Solve food distribution challenges	Robin Raphel	COL Marty Stanton
7. Install town councils, GSTs/LGTs	Chris Milligan	BG John H. Kern
8. Meet pressing public health needs	Steve Browning	LTC Stafford
9. Ministries to functional level	Robin Raphel	BG John H. Kern
10. Security		MG William Webster

NOTE. GST = Government Support Team; LGT = Local Government Team. Both teams with Civil Affairs personnel.

salaries, and budgets; fix infrastructure, water and sewage, power and fuel, telecommunications and public information; and vet the Ba'ath leadership. Life support to the ministries was challenging. Substantive progress would require more money and resources, more than Garner had available.

To better integrate the military coalition with his team, Garner determined that they had ten key tasks to manage the transition. General Webster and Garner identified members of their respective staffs to assume responsibility for each task (see Table 4).

Garner also wanted to harness the agencies of the United Nations starting to flow into Iraq. On 8 May, he met with the UN special representative for Iraq, Sergio de Mello. Like Knellenberger of the ICRC, de Mello did not want a tight relationship with the Coalition. In contrast to the international cooperation Garner had experienced in northern Iraq in 1991, little international assistance was forthcoming in 2003. The United States accounted for over 85 percent of the Coalition contribution in personnel and resources, with the United Kingdom the only other substantive participant and their contribution almost exclusively in southern Iraq. General Cross announced that the UK was opening an embassy in Baghdad, which would likely expand UK interests in Iraq. Other embassies were beginning to open, but few offered assistance to the Coalition.

Tied down in Baghdad with important daily meetings in the palace, Garner continued to drive into the city each day to assess the situation, talk to Iraqis, and visit the ministries in whatever buildings they were in. He liked to talk to soldiers and noted that those occupying Baghdad were anxious to go home.

The Deputy Commander for Central Command and designated replacement for General Franks, Lieutenant General John Abizaid, flew into Baghdad to discuss the situation with Garner and senior military commanders. Garner met Abizaid at the airport on 9 May for the meeting attended by Generals McKiernan, Webster, Hawkins, Crear, and Strock, as well as senior staff officers.

Abizaid was gracious and made it clear that the Coalition constituted the government of Iraq, a message that resonated more with Garner than with McKiernan and his staff. A veteran of operations in the Balkans, Abizaid stated that Bosnia had been a marathon, but Iraq was going to be a sprint. He wanted to know about the security situation and how the military forces could be more supportive. He requested information about the storage of crude oil that was complicating refinery operations in Iraq. He asked if they could bring tankers in to store fuel until it could be refined rather than have it imported from other countries.[132]

McKiernan said little in the meeting and offered little in return, which agitated Garner, who was animated and more emotional than normal. Several times he spoke out to Abizaid and pleaded for more assistance. At one stage he told Abizaid if he looked outside he would see every vehicle in the 3rd Mechanized Infantry Division with a trailer behind it pointed south: they were anxious and prepared to leave Iraq when the Coalition desperately needed them in Baghdad. Abizaid was visibly surprised at Garner's emotion and evident frustration. He wanted to help but had to absorb more information to make decisions. The senior military officers were anxious for Garner to take over so they could go home. Yet they offered little assistance, perhaps because they believed that was the role of other U.S. departments and agencies, or because they believed that if they became more involved with ORHA, it would unduly extend their time in Iraq.

At one stage in the meeting, Garner talked about bringing in the Iraqi wheat harvest, a vestige of his experience from 1991 in putting the Kurds back to work on a profitable basis. There was no obvious way senior military officers could assist with an agricultural endeavor. The harvest issue was an indication that some of the frustration Garner vented at the meeting probably should have been directed elsewhere. The National Security Council and the Pentagon, not McKiernan's command, had promised Garner qualified people, information, money, and international support. While people were joining ORHA daily, too few had the qualifications Garner needed.

What Garner desperately needed from Generals Abizaid and McKiernan and the other military officers at the meeting in May was greater security and assistance to get the Iraqi ministries on their feet and aligned with the regional governments. The military ground command had over 130,000 uniformed personnel in Iraq with substantial arms, equipment, communications, and supplies; Garner had 1,000 working for him with little assets. The military command had not planned support for Garner and there was pressure in Washington to reduce forces to 30,000 by autumn. Such a reduction assumed Garner could stand up an interim authority or government to assume control of Iraq.

As Garner spoke to the collected military leadership in Iraq, his plea was directed at General Abizaid. Garner and others had assumed that Abizaid would become the senior commander in Iraq, but by May it was clear he would soon replace General Franks at Central Command. Until then, as the Deputy Commander for CENTCOM, Abizaid's authority was limited. He could not yet provide directives to properly align the military efforts to support ORHA, and he could not yet stop the flow of forces preparing to leave Iraq.

The overall response of the other military officers present was not resistance—it was indifference. Garner left the meeting feeling more alone than when he arrived. On Sunday, 10 May, three weeks after his arrival in Baghdad, Garner left Iraq to meet Ambassador Bremer in Qatar.

6

BREMER ARRIVES

After Bremer arrived in Iraq, Garner remained for another three weeks through the end of May 2003. It was not a smooth transition and involved major shifts in policy without clear oversight or assistance from Washington. While Garner had two months in the Pentagon and six weeks in Kuwait to prepare for his entry into Iraq, Bremer had only two weeks in the former and a day in the latter before he arrived in Baghdad. There was little question, though, that Bremer was in charge from the moment he arrived.

Bremer left Washington on 10 May and flew to the forward headquarters of U.S. Central Command in Qatar, arriving early the next morning. Garner arrived later that morning from Baghdad via Kuwait just as the briefings were starting for Bremer. In General Franks's absence General Abizaid led the briefing team. At one stage, Abizaid made reference to the "leadership group" of Iraqis that Garner had helped to form. Garner interjected to say that he had scheduled a meeting with them within a few days.[1]

"I'm not sure that meeting will ever take place," Bremer stated abruptly.

"Well, you've got to speak to these people," Garner responded.

"I told you I'm not sure that meeting will ever take place," Bremer repeated pointedly. "And if it does take place, I don't think it's going to occur when you said it would."

Garner did not understand why Bremer was disdainful toward the IIA. The Pentagon had used the term Iraqi Interim Authority earlier and Garner had kept Secretary Rumsfeld informed as the IIA began to form after his visit to northern Iraq. Larry Di Rita also kept Rumsfeld and those in the Pentagon up to date on the IIA, just as Margaret Tutwiler kept others informed at State and in the White House. Garner thought then that Bremer might make decisions prematurely and that the transition would be difficult. After the initial comments about the IIA, however, Bremer lightened up and became friendlier as the briefing progressed.[2]

That afternoon, Bremer and Garner flew together to Kuwait, where they spent the night. Bremer wanted to see Basra en route to Baghdad. The trip was scheduled for the next morning. In addition to a few assistants, Bremer was accompanied by General Richard Myers, Chairman of the Joint Chiefs of Staff. They were joined by Lieutenant Colonel John Agoglia from Central Command, who would become a liaison officer to Bremer.

The next day in Basra they met the British military commanders and Ambassador Ole Olsen, who was in charge of ORHA-South. After a stop at the military headquarters at the airfield and Olsen's headquarters downtown, they toured the city and then flew to Baghdad. Bremer later wrote that as he landed he could see that Baghdad "was burning." Later when Garner read what Bremer had written in his book, he reflected on their arrival in Baghdad and felt that such an observation would have been difficult to make from the small windows in the military aircraft they were using. Furthermore, by the time Bremer arrived in Baghdad, virtually all of the fires had been put out or had burned out. From the airport, the group made a brief tour of the city before going to the palace. Jerry Bates had an "all-hands" group of available ORHA members meet them in the ballroom next to the rotunda.[3]

Garner introduced Bremer, who told everyone what a fine job they had done. He was particularly gracious to Garner. As Ron Adams left the meeting, he told Garner, "I was dreading this, but I feel better about him now."

Garner said, "He's a good diplomat." But Garner would soon challenge Bremer's policies and the diplomacy with which he implemented them.[4]

In mid-April, Deputy Secretary of Defense Paul Wolfowitz and Scooter Libby of the Office of the Vice President contacted Bremer to see if he was interested in taking the senior Coalition position in Iraq. After talking to his wife, Bremer expressed interest and a week later discussed it with Secretary Rumsfeld, who asked him how he got along with the other senior members of the National Security team. Bremer said that when he was ambassador to the Netherlands he had known Secretary of State Powell briefly, then serving in Germany; they also had both served on the NSC staff. He knew National Security Advisor Condoleezza Rice from the first Bush administration, but he was unsure about George Tenet, the Director of the CIA. As chairman of a Commission on Terrorism, Bremer had been critical of the CIA, which he thought had annoyed Tenet. He had never met the president.[5]

Bremer assumed Rumsfeld was considering others for the position, but later that day he received a call from the secretary's office telling him he was to see President Bush. This first meeting with the president, Rumsfeld, and Rice lasted half an hour. Bremer assumed the president wanted to size him up. By then he knew that "there had been a considerable debate in the administration about what kind of an occupation it was going to be . . . very short, very quick," or something longer. Bremer felt the president was suggesting the longer view; Bremer said he agreed and understood that the object was to replace Garner in mid-June with somebody with more political experience.[6]

Bremer assumed that he was being offered the position because he had a great deal of interagency experience. During his twenty-three years with the State Department, he had served in Afghanistan, East Africa, Norway, and, as ambassador, the Netherlands. But it was the tours he had in Washington that raised his profile, serving as a special assistant or chief of staff to Secretaries of State William Rogers, Henry Kissinger, Cyrus Vance, Edmund Muskie, Alexander Haig, and George Shultz. His last assignment was as ambassador for counterterrorism. In the Washington assignments he worked with the National Security Council and other agencies.[7] Remarkably, no one seemed concerned that Bremer had never served in an Arab country and that his service in Afghanistan was over thirty years behind him.

As Bremer left the White House, he was aware that he would work for Rumsfeld, but he knew that he had been personally selected by the president. Bremer's background in the State Department led to the general perception that his appointment signaled a shift to State for political management in Iraq. And among the first people he recruited were Ambassadors Clay McManaway, Hume Horan, and Pat Kennedy. McManaway and Horan had retired from the State Department; neither was current with planning for Iraq. Kennedy's credentials were administrative rather than political. Bremer's base, to the degree that he had one, would be the Department of Defense, which provided him an assistant, Air Force Colonel Scott Norwood, and an aide, Navy Lieutenant Justin Lemmon, to manage his schedule, transportation, and other personnel needs. Rumsfeld, not Powell, had proposed Bremer to the president, although Powell did not object to Bremer. There was no shift from Defense to State as some supposed.[8]

During his two weeks in Washington, Bremer prepared for his assignment in Iraq by consulting selected people in the Pentagon and from Washington think tanks who would influence his initial policies in Iraq. Those policies would change the direction set in motion by the key leaders that preceded him: General Franks, the commander of Central Command; Garner, in charge of ORHA; and Zalmay Khalilzad, a senior member of the NSC staff and presidential envoy to Iraq working with Iraqi opposition leaders.[9]

While Bremer was in Washington, he had several brief phone calls with Garner, but there was little substance to the conversations. Remarkably, Bremer did not meet or consult Ron Adams, the one man in the Pentagon who knew the most about Garner and ORHA. Bremer met Slocombe, Feith, and Ryan Henry in the Pentagon several times, but none of them introduced Adams to

Bremer. Adams had one brief visit with Walt Slocombe but was provided no details about his plans or thoughts on the Iraqi army.[10]

Together Slocombe and Bremer began to form their views on the Iraqi army, independent of some at Central Command such as General Abizaid and the military planners, whose views were comparable to those of Garner and his planners. All the critical Central Command military officers intended to reconstitute the Iraqi army and put it to work on reconstruction and security. On 12 March Doug Feith briefed President Bush on that position and the president approved it as policy. When General Abizaid told those in Washington in April that the Iraqi army had gone home, Abizaid (and Garner) assumed the Iraqi army would be recalled and put to work, but Slocombe and Bremer were developing other plans.[11]

Bremer and Slocombe also joined discussions in the Pentagon about how to handle the Ba'athist party members. Bremer's short preparation for his assignment was driven by civilian leaders in the Pentagon with developed, if flawed, political agendas on how to manage Iraq. The original concept that a handoff to Iraqi leaders might be swift was changing. But that change was not passed on to Garner as he proceeded with his initial guidance to put an Iraqi interim government in place. Bremer developed his own concepts with the view that the Coalition might remain in control of Iraq for as much as two years, whereas Garner was working toward a political transition to take over within months. Bremer's concept would allow more time to reform Iraq.[12]

Rather than allow Iraqis to manage such projects as de-Ba'athification and restructuring the Iraqi army, the Coalition would play the dominant role. No one informed Garner of such a shift in policy. Nor had anyone informed Ron Adams while he was in the Pentagon in April and early May. Zalmay Khalilzad, the president's Special Envoy and Ambassador at Large for Free Iraqis (appointed in December 2002), was also out of the loop. Khalilzad anticipated he would soon convene an assembly of Iraqi leaders to form a new Iraqi government. Furthermore, a shift from liberation in a few months to several years of occupation would require a large military occupation force, which the Pentagon did not intend to provide at that time.[13]

A self-styled historian with a Harvard MBA, Bremer exuded confidence with a business-like manner and take-charge style, qualities that made him attractive to President Bush, Rumsfeld, Wolfowitz, Feith, even Powell. He set out to take decisive control of Iraq. On 6 May, he had his second meeting with President Bush. He told the president what he had learned over the previous ten days in the Pentagon, using the term "occupation" when those before him had used "liberation." Iraq was going to be challenging and would require more time than had been originally anticipated. The president agreed and told him "to get it right," but he was lukewarm to Bremer's second concern: the number of troops in Iraq. Bremer expressed concern that a Pentagon briefing indicated that the forces could be reduced to 30,000 by September. That was in contrast to a RAND study that indicated that an occupation would require at least twice as many troops as the 130,000 in Iraq. The president said he would look into it.[14]

Bremer took up an organizational issue, based on his experience in government and the private sector: unity of command was essential for success. That principle would be compromised if Khalilzad retained the designation of presidential envoy to Iraq. With no further consultation, the president said he would terminate Khalilzad's role in Iraq to give Bremer a free hand. But neither Bremer nor the president took on the issue of unity of command for the organization Bremer would lead and the military command in Iraq. After the meeting, the president formally announced Bremer's appointment to the media, an announcement that had already been leaked.[15]

No one anticipated Khalilzad's termination. Khalilzad stated that he assumed that Bremer would "run things and [Khalilzad would] convene the Loya Jirga," to put Iraqi leaders in charge. "Then the game plan suddenly changed. Powell and Condi were incredulous. Powell called me and asked, What happened? And [I] said, You are Secretary of State and you are asking me what happened?" As far as Powell was concerned, "The plan was for Khalilzad to go back [and work in Iraq]. . . . He was the one guy that knew [the Iraqi people] better than anyone. I thought this was part of the deal with Bremer. But with no discussion, no debate, things changed. I was stunned."[16]

What appeared a subtle change for the sake of good management in Iraq in effect deleted much of the work Khalilzad and Garner had in motion to put Iraqi leaders to work. Powell subsequently reflected on the early decisions for Iraq: "It was a mistake not to move more rapidly to put an Iraqi face on it." General Abizaid had argued for months that they must "put an Iraqi face" on the liberation, which seemed sound to everyone in Iraq. Suddenly the Coalition was on a different track without all the key players properly informed or fully on board.[17]

On the day before Bremer left for the Middle East, Doug Feith gave him a document on de-Ba'athification drafted by his office, essentially a policy to remove Ba'athists from power in Iraq. Feith was about to send the document to Garner to announce the policy, but when Bremer saw it, he asked Feith to hold the document. He wanted a vehicle with which to make a major impact upon his arrival. By making the de-Ba'athification announcement himself, he would put political change in motion in Iraq and establish himself as the dominant leader in the Coalition, clearly in charge.[18]

Walt Slocombe was involved in the discussions on de-Ba'athification; his main role was to set up a new Iraqi army without the abusive dimensions associated with Saddam Hussein. When Bremer joined the discussion on the Iraqi army, Slocombe was proposing a small motorized force of 40,000 soldiers in three infantry divisions without artillery or armor, structured as the New Iraqi Corps, to be known as the NIC. His studies of post-conflict situations in Eastern Europe, the Balkans, and Africa shaped his views more than studies conducted by those in the Coalition that focused on the needs of Iraq and the role its army should have. He did not share the view that the Iraqi army was a useful means to deal with post-invasion unemployment, nor did he think it should be involved with internal security. Slocombe learned little from Iraqis or Arab specialists in his preparations. It would be several weeks before he learned that the pronunciation of NIC in Arabic meant "fuck." The name was changed to the New Iraqi Army.[19]

To reinforce the impression he wanted to make upon arriving in Iraq, Bremer intended his second major announcement to address the security forces. With the concept developed with Slocombe, Bremer sent a draft to Rumsfeld and a copy to Wolfowitz with the awkward title "Dissolution of Entities." While the document for de-Ba'athification was produced by Feith's office, the proposal for the army was more a product of Slocombe and Bremer. The Iraqi army was not mentioned in the title or anywhere on the first three pages; it was listed on an annex to the document halfway down the fourth page. Anyone reading the document quickly could miss the profound implications for the Iraqi army. Garner was not consulted during the discussions on the Ba'athists and the Iraqi army during Bremer's ten days of preparation in the Pentagon.

Colonel Paul Hughes had left Baghdad with Garner on 10 May to go to Kuwait to work on contracts with RONCO and MPRI, both defense contractors for the Iraqi army. Remarkably, RONCO, with expertise in de-mining operations, won the contract to design a plan to both disarm and reform the Iraqi army. MPRI, with a track record for training foreign armies, would have the contract to reform the Iraqi army. Hughes would continue working on those contracts in Washington in conjunction with an untimely leave to attend his daughter's graduation from college. His absence from Baghdad during two critical weeks in May put him out of touch with the plans Bremer and Slocombe were developing for the Iraqi armed forces. The memo Bremer attached to the draft order to disband the Iraqi army indicated he would show it to Central Command that weekend. No senior military officer in the Pentagon appeared to take notice.[20]

A few days before Bremer arrived in Iraq, Scott Carpenter and an advance team moved in with ORHA in the palace. Carpenter had put together the Governance Team to provide policy guidance for the political changes to be imposed in Iraq. Along with him came junior people to serve as an immediate staff for Bremer. Some of those serving as assistants to Bremer, in their twenties and thirties, would refer to themselves as senior advisors, a title Garner had reserved for ambassadors and those of comparable rank in their fifties and sixties to manage Iraqi ministries. Among those arriving with Carpenter was Kristin Silverberg, a thirty-two-year-old lawyer from Texas who had worked for political advisor Karl Rove in the White House. Her task was to set up an office for Bremer, apparently without knowing that the ORHA staff had already set up a large office for him on the first floor of the palace. Silverberg asked Colonel J. R. Martin if Garner could move out of his office to make way for Bremer. Martin tersely replied that an appropriate office had been set up for Bremer, one of several curt encounters between Garner's staff and those arriving with Bremer.[21]

Among the first in Baghdad to appreciate the impact of Bremer's arrival was Robin Raphel. She was one of the few in Iraq who had worked with Garner and knew Bremer. In little more than a month Raphel had impressed Garner so much he had her replace Mike Mobbs and gave her responsibility to manage the senior advisors for the Iraqi ministries. Raphel had known Bremer through their service in the Department of State. She had also been a dinner guest at his home. When Raphel heard that Bremer was coming to Iraq, she called him from Baghdad and told him to wear a suit and tie and to bring plenty of clothes as laundry service was slow. Raphel knew that the austere conditions in Iraq had made formal dress difficult for Coalition members. She also knew that formality could be an advantage at the highest levels in the Arab world. A shift in apparel was in order, something easy for the preppy Bremer in contrast to the more casual Garner.[22]

After Bremer's initial meeting in the palace, Raphel and several others went to his office to learn about the incoming team and new developments that might come with it. For Raphel, Bremer's "briefcase exploded with documents" that would soon alter the policies Garner had been trying to put in place. The one "on top of the pile" was the draft order for de-Ba'athification that Doug Feith had handed Bremer on his departure. Skimming it, she quickly made two observations. First, it was poorly written, in her view almost incoherent. She assumed it did not come from State. Second and more important, it signaled a profound shift toward an arbitrary and draconian policy with the projected removal of all senior Ba'athists from government positions. When she showed it to Colonel Tony Puckett, her deputy, he was incredulous. He knew what an adverse impact such a plan would have on the senior advisors working with the ministries. Puckett wanted to see Bremer to protest, but Raphel was concerned that Puckett might be too forceful; she told him she would handle it.[23]

When she met with Bremer she told him point-blank, "We can't do this." It was too severe and would have a crippling effect. Bremer was impatient with the objection and told Raphel the decision had been made by those in Washington and the Coalition must simply get on with it. Raphel was appalled at Bremer's dismissive attitude toward their work in progress in Baghdad. When she protested that the format and wording in the document must be improved, Bremer allowed her to redraft it. In the process, she wanted others to see it, both to make it read more clearly and to get their input before it went for final signature.[24]

Raphel was assisted by Meghan O'Sullivan from the Ministry Coordination Team. O'Sullivan liked and respected Garner and had no prior connection with Bremer, but she wanted to assist with the transition that was to take place. Together, Raphel and O'Sullivan worked through the night to redraft the document to prepare it for Bremer's signature. At an initial briefing on the new draft, Bremer took note of O'Sullivan's intellect and demeanor. Soon he had her moved to work in Governance with Scott Carpenter; within a month O'Sullivan would be a member of Bremer's inner circle. Earlier O'Sullivan had told Richard Haass, her boss and mentor in the Pentagon, that Iraq would be one of the defining experiences for her generation. She was in the process of making Iraq a defining experience for herself.[25]

Since leaving Secretary Powell's policy office as a GS-15, O'Sullivan had been moving down by positions to get involved with Iraq. She had begun working with Ambassador George Ward in the Humanitarian Assistance pillar, and then with Colonel Paul Hughes in the C-5 Plans staff section. Finally, in Baghdad, Garner had her work for Sherri Kraham, a GS-13 from State, before Raphel took charge of the ministries. With Bremer's arrival, O'Sullivan was back on an upward glide path. In the policy shop in Governance, she would have frequent contact with Bremer and travel with him to many of his most important meetings; a year later she would continue into the inner circles of the White House as one of the senior policy specialists on Iraq.

O'Sullivan's first assignment for Bremer was managing de-Ba'athification for the Coalition, a task that Raphel considered should be undertaken with more tenacity than finesse.[26] De-Ba'athification was not a task for which O'Sullivan had prepared, nor one that she wanted. While her ambition was to work in governmental policy, her views on Iraq were not as ambitious or as strident as those of Feith, Wolfowitz, and others in Washington. In fact, it was the perception that her political views were opposed to the policies of the Bush administration that had led Rumsfeld to direct Garner to send her back to Powell's office in February. Rumsfeld allowed her to go back to ORHA under the condition that she keep her profile low. Until Bremer's arrival in Baghdad, her profile had indeed been low within Garner's team. When Bremer arrived in Iraq with few people of his own, however, he looked for capable people on Garner's team who would shift their loyalty to him. For O'Sullivan, it was not a shift in loyalty as much as an opportunity to work on policy issues.

As Raphel and O'Sullivan redrafted the document known as Coalition Provisional Authority Order Number 1, Bremer told Raphel that he would sign and announce it publicly on 16 May and it was dated accordingly. The key provisions of the order were to "disestablish the Ba'ath Party of Iraq . . . eliminating the party's structures and removing its leadership from positions of authority and responsibility in Iraqi society."[27] The order decreed that anyone previously holding the top four ranks in the party, Udw Qutriyya (Regional Command Member), Udw Far (Branch Member), Udw Shu'bah (Section Member), and Udw Firqah (Group Member), were to be "banned from future employment in the public sector [and] evaluated for criminal conduct or threat to the security of the Coalition."[28] The order went on to target those with any affiliation with the Ba'ath Party if they had held senior positions in top three ranks in government; such people "shall be removed from their employment. This includes those holding the more junior ranks of 'Udw' (member) and 'Udw 'Amil' (Active Member)."[29] The three senior positions were minister, deputy minister, and directors general, roughly comparable to American cabinet ranks of secretary, deputy secretary, and assistant secretary. The senior two positions in Iraq were normally political appointments, but the third rank, while political in stature, was frequently held by senior bureaucrats or technocrats, those who were most needed to get the Iraqi government back on its feet. Despite their party rank, in practice many directors general were only nominal party members but of great importance to their respective ministries. At the time the order was drafted, however, virtually no one working for Garner or Bremer knew the full nature of the Ba'ath Party. In actuality, there were a total of nine ranks in the party with the lowest four of token status. Furthermore, for several decades, there had been only one legal political party in Iraq and as such most senior civilians in government were necessarily Ba'athists.

While Bremer was allowing Raphel to redraft the de-Ba'athification order, he did not mention it to Garner. But Raphel knew Garner should be involved and cornered him near the dining facility in the palace the next morning.[30]

"Have you seen this?" she asked, handing him a copy she had redrafted.

"No, what it is it?" Garner asked. After reading it quickly, he exclaimed, "There's no way in hell we can do this."

Raphel grabbed him by the arm and told him, "This is exactly why you need to stay here. You must remain."

No one was sure how long Garner would stay after Bremer's arrival; nor had Garner set a date to leave. "Robin, I'm going to be here a while, but I don't know how long, because I don't know if I can work with this guy. But I'll go see him and we'll get this changed." With Raphel's draft, Garner headed down the long hallway to Bremer's office. On the way he met the CIA station chief in Baghdad, Charlie Sidell.

"Have you read this?" Garner asked him.

"Yeah, I just read it. That's why I'm coming over here." Together they went in to see Bremer.

Garner deferred to Sidell. "Okay, Charlie, tell him what is going to happen if he does this."

"If you implement this," began Sidell, "you will have between 30,000 and 50,000 Ba'athists go underground by sundown; the number is closer to 50 than to 30."

"Jerry, this is too stiff," Garner piled on. "Give Charlie and me an hour. We'll do all the pros and cons on this, we'll come back to you with them, we'll get on the phone with Rumsfeld, and we'll soften this." Garner was convinced the order had been imposed on Bremer and that with a group effort they could modify it.

But Bremer wanted no assistance. "Absolutely not. These are my instructions and I'm going to execute them."

"It's too firm," Garner objected. "It's too hard, Jerry. We won't be able to run any of the ministries if you do that."[31]

Bremer responded to Garner as he had to Raphel. "I told you I have my instructions, and I'm going to execute them." Clearly Bremer had taken Garner's protest, though intended as assistance, as an affront to his authority; henceforth Garner would have little input for policies that Bremer would implement.

When redrafting the order, Raphel had others review the details; eventually that included UK Ambassador John Sawers, who arrived in Baghdad just after Bremer. He helped Raphel modify one aspect of the order. The final document was more coherent than the original Bremer brought with him, but the essence retained the draconian effect.[32]

When Bremer and Sawers arrived in Baghdad, much of what they observed both in the palace and around the city was chaotic. There had been recent progress they could not fully appreciate, however. Communications within the palace had improved and internet service was available to more people than a week earlier, although deficiencies remained. Hot meals were available three times a day. Some plumbing in the palace was working and the number of shower and toilet trailers had doubled outside. Temporary living quarters, four-person trailers, were being erected behind the palace to make room for office space inside; rooms in the Al-Rashid Hotel would soon be available. Air conditioning was working for communications equipment and would soon be available in the work areas. Security in and around the building was adequate.

Baghdad had been burning, but by Bremer's arrival ORHA had established contact with every ministry in the city and was holding meetings with each one. There was a plan in progress to renovate the buildings that had been looted, or if they had been destroyed to replace them. Emergency payments were in motion, and records had been obtained for much of the government to begin salary payments as funds became available; despite bottlenecks, cash was arriving in theater for those payments. Without unity of command, Garner had developed a working relationship with General Webster and the military command to work together on a range of projects. Beyond Baghdad there were many problems, but three regional ORHA components were up and operational. To appreciate such progress by mid-May, one had to have been there in April.

On the morning of 13 May, the day after Bremer's arrival, Garner had arranged a meeting for Bremer with the principal civilian and military personnel in ORHA. To provide Bremer a free hand, Garner, Adams, and Bates did not attend. Bremer listened as two dozen ORHA members made short presentations about their tasks, which allowed him an opportunity to take the measure of each of them. The briefings expressed both optimism and concern. Although they had made progress during the previous weeks and had established contact with senior Iraqis in their ministries, everyone mentioned the crippling effects of the looting and vandalism on their ministries.[33]

Having achieved a remarkable military victory at little cost in Coalition casualties, it was unclear to Bremer why security was such a challenge. He stated his intention to change the rules of engagement for the Coalition military forces, specifically to allow them to shoot looters, which he alleged had been done during comparable operations in Haiti in the 1990s. Those in the room familiar with the operations in Haiti felt Bremer misunderstood how force had been used there, but no one took issue with him. When he was met by dismayed silence on his intent to shoot looters, he repeated it several times. While there was no question that looting had been devastating throughout Iraq, particularly in Baghdad, there was no relief expressed with the proposition that looters should be shot. Rather, there was disbelief that the Coalition would or could implement such a change overnight. With little knowledge of how the police system worked in Baghdad or elsewhere in Iraq, Bremer stated that they had to get the police back to work, oriented on guarding the government buildings and other important fixed sites in the city.

In his effort to be decisive, Bremer said that the Ba'athists would be removed from power and their replacements would be vetted. The senior advisors had been trying to find and establish new Iraqi leadership in the ministries for which they were responsible. Initially it was unclear what removing the Ba'athists would mean in practice; the implication was that more vetting was in order, but how much more would not be clear for a few days. Bremer told them that he would soon establish a formal policy on the removal of Ba'athists.

Bremer went on to state that the main Coalition objective was to rebuild civil society in Iraq and that would begin with getting the ministries up and working, adding that "democracy cannot work if the government systems don't work." They had to re-vitalize the private sector in Iraq, which was more important in the short term than elections. He urged those present to be careful in using the term "elections" and said that when putting Iraqis into positions of control the appropriate term should be "selections," for which no definition was provided. On internal security and justice, he stated what many had already determined: Iraq needed responsible police, credible courts, and a functional prison system.

Inadequate electricity in Baghdad and the rest of the country was addressed in several of the briefings. Bremer said the Coalition would have to be careful not to impose American standards for adequate electricity in Iraq, but that they would have to get it up to the prewar level as soon as possible. He said that while the senior Coalition personnel present knew what should be best for Iraq, everyone should be on the watch for the appearance of institutional arrogance. He suggested that the Iraqi expatriates, arriving in greater numbers as the IRDC, might cause some problems. He did not develop the issue further, leaving many to wonder about Bremer's alignment with those in Washington who had been trying to get Garner to make better use of the IRDC and expatriates.

Ambassador Sawers sat next to Bremer throughout the meeting and on several occasions reinforced him. Both wore white dress shirts in contrast to the more casual clothes worn by others. Despite the number of presentations and Bremer's efforts to make a decisive statement, it was shorter than meetings that Garner, Bates, and others had run in the Pentagon, Kuwait, and Baghdad. It would soon become apparent that in the large meetings, Bremer wanted others to pass him succinct information and he in turn would provide direct guidance. What was missing in Bremer's meetings was the aggressive dialogue that Garner had favored, a dialogue that often regressed to squabbles but identified conflicts, differences in priorities, and misunderstandings—all of which took time to bring out and more time to resolve. While Bremer's shorter meetings might appear more businesslike and efficient—soon the norm for other working groups—there would be less interaction among those present and less resolution of concerns and disagreements.

With Bremer's arrival there were key changes within the media component as well. Margaret Tutwiler had managed media relations for Garner, but she remained only one week after Bremer's arrival and left on short notice in response to a bombing in Morocco, where she was the U.S. ambassador. When Tutwiler departed, Larry Di Rita assumed her position for a short period. Di Rita and Bremer initially shared a room in the palace until separate accommodations could be arranged, but Di Rita did not join Bremer's inner circle. Within a few days he returned to Washington to work for Secretary Rumsfeld, working with media affairs for the Pentagon.

Di Rita was in turn replaced by Dan Senor, a thirty-two-year-old who had been working media issues in the White House before he joined Tutwiler in Kuwait. Di Rita might have been replaced by Captain Nate Jones, the Navy reservist and Garner's original Public Affairs Officer. Jones had been constrained in the Pentagon and Kuwait to keep the media at arms length. That had changed with Tutwiler's arrival, but Jones found Tutwiler of an older school on media relations, more interested in controlling those in the media rather than exploiting them. Jones wanted to employ the embedded media concept used by the military forces. Tutwiler was unimpressed with the technique and did not want journalists embedded with Garner's group either in Kuwait or in Iraq, although she agreed with Jones that Garner was a good news story and a charismatic figure.[34]

ORHA was easily criticized from a distance, but full of interesting and talented people that could best be appreciated up close. The media could not see them up close if restrained by Tutwiler's methods or those of the UK press handlers, Charles Heatly and Elizabeth Hand, who had managed the press pool that accompanied Garner earlier into Iraq. It was disappointing for Jones to see the senior media position turned over to Senor, twenty years his junior. But if Senor lacked the professional media background Jones brought to Baghdad, he had better political connections in Washington and the confidence of those in the White House. He soon gained Bremer's confidence and helped set up a series of press conferences for him in the Convention Center.[35]

Like Tutwiler, Senor had no interest in embedding journalists, and, worse, he treated them with a disdain that led him to be regarded as a political hack. But with Bremer's arrival, the embargo imposed on ORHA was lifted, perhaps because Bremer had more clout with the White House and was considered more cautious about what he said. The initial press conferences Senor arranged for Bremer were conducted in English with limited facilities for translation into other languages. Most of the journalists attending the conferences in late April and early May were from Western countries, a phenomenon that concerned Meghan Gregonis, the State Department Public Affairs Officer who had joined Nate Jones in Kuwait. Jones had been happy to get her; she was one of the few people he had who spoke Arabic. Barbara Bodine had taken Gregonis as part of her staff, but when Bodine left Iraq Gregonis migrated back to work for Jones, by then subordinate to Senor.[36]

Gregonis knew that the Coalition media focus was weighted on the Western media, which had an impact upon Washington. She proposed to Jones and his assistant, John Kincannon, also from State and an Arabic speaker, that they reweight their attention on the emerging Iraqi media and that of the Middle East region at large. Jones and Kincannon concurred. Later in May Bremer began conducting Arabic media press conference on Saturdays. To keep the Western media from dominating, they required that the questions be asked in Arabic.[37]

Senor did not take an active interest in the Iraqi media and discouraged Kincannon from participating in the Arabic language press conferences. Gregonis felt that "we lost the information battle. A lot of people are watching the Iranian news channels, getting the news from their sources. . . . We had an opportunity to get in and provide information, but we didn't fully leverage the opportunity."[38]

Several days after Bremer arrived in Baghdad, Garner learned of his intention to disband the Iraqi army. Robin Raphel had noted a draft order to disband the Iraqi security services, but it was not immediately clear that the new policy would disband the regular army. There was little question that the Republican Guards and those intelligence agencies intensely loyal to Saddam Hussein, guilty of many atrocities, would have to be disbanded. But the regular army was one of the few national institutions that still had the respect of most Iraqis. Again Garner went to Bremer to protest.[39]

"We've always planned to bring back the Army," Garner told him.

"Well, the plans have changed. We're not going to do that anymore," Bremer responded.

"Jerry, let me tell you something," Garner said. The old soldier was exasperated. "You can get rid of an army in a day, but it takes you years to bring one back."

Bremer indicated that he would defer to Washington. "The instructions are that we're not going to do that. We're going to build a new army." He showed Garner the draft order for what would become CPA Order Number 2, which also disbanded the Ministry of Defense.

Garner was flabbergasted. "You can't have an army without a Ministry of Defense," he exclaimed. Reading more closely, he realized that the draft would also do away with the Ministry of Interior. "You just said yesterday how important it was to rapidly bring the police back. Well, they're all in the Ministry of Interior, and if you abolish the Ministry of Interior, they'll all go home tonight."

In the United States, the Department of the Interior is responsible for agencies such as the Bureau of Land Management, not law enforcement. But in most countries, including those in the Middle East, the Ministry of Interior means the national police and internal security forces. It was apparent to Garner that Bremer was unaware how Iraq's police force was structured under the centralized control of the Ministry of Interior. That included recruitment, training, salaries, and retirement. He tried to explain that standing down the Ministry of Interior would not only cause the police to go home, it would disband the structure that put them in place.

"Then go tell Walt Slocombe he can't do that," Bremer said.

Slocombe left Washington one day after Bremer, but arrived in Baghdad several days later. He had stopped in Europe for a day in Brussels, where he had meetings with senior NATO officials. A State Department official there encouraged Slocombe to try to get other NATO members to participate in Iraq as some were doing in Afghanistan. While there was less enthusiasm in NATO for providing military forces for Iraq, Slocombe was told that there might be some willingness to provide trainers for a new military establishment and police forces; he requested contributions for both. Spanish officials suggested that they might provide a contingent from their national police force, to work with the Iraqi Ministry of Interior rather than provide an infantry formation to work with the Ministry of Defense; the formation they later sent was used as infantry.

The next day, Slocombe was in London to talk to senior British officials, including Ministry of Defense Geoffrey W. Hoon, Lieutenant General Rob Fry, a Royal Marine on the Defense staff, and Baroness Amos of DFID, the UK counterpart to USAID (Claire Short, the previous head of DFID, had resigned to protest the invasion of Iraq). Slocombe outlined his mission and the structure of the proposed New Iraqi Corps. He indicated that there would be no early provisional Iraqi government (which would have been news to Garner), and that there would be a substantive de-Ba'athification program, which might entail some loss of effectiveness and efficiency in the short term, particularly for the security sector.[40] Slocombe assumed that the majority of the Iraqi senior military leaders were Ba'athists and would be removed for that alone.

The British officials felt that the Coalition should address security reform in a comprehensive manner that would go beyond military formations, including police and internal security functions; and that it should also address in a comprehensive manner de-Ba'athification, reconstruction, and an information campaign. Hoon offered to set up a military training base to train the Iraqi army, but Slocombe was concerned about standardization of such training and did not encourage a separate UK training effort.[41]

From London, Slocombe flew to Kuwait and then on to Baghdad. When he arrived on 15 May, Garner had just learned of the intention to disband the Iraqi army. Slocombe had discussed disbanding the army with Feith, Wolfowitz, and Bremer (but not with Ron Adams) in Washington and a few days prior with the British officials in London, but neither he nor Bremer had discussed it with Garner or anyone in Baghdad before their arrival.[42]

Since his designation as senior advisor for the Iraqi armed forces, Slocombe had been a dilemma for Garner. Their prior association in the Pentagon in the 1990s was not positive and there was no bond between them. Slocombe had phoned Garner several times from Washington, but those calls were not substantive and did not indicate his intentions. Slocombe had remained in Washington to go over case studies on regime change in Eastern Europe. The greater cost of Slocombe's delay in joining Garner was that he missed the emerging conditions under which the other senior advisors were working and the internal security chaos in Iraq.[43]

After Garner deployed to Baghdad, Slocombe sent Colonel Greg Gardner to make initial contact with ORHA and find workspace and accommodations. Colonel Gardner left within a few days of his arrival. He left no one as an interim senior advisor for the Ministry of Defense during the critical early days in Baghdad when other senior advisors were busy locating their respective ministries and trying to get them operating.

Prior to his departure from Washington, Slocombe read an op-ed piece in the *Washington Post* by an Iraqi general that argued for entitlements for the Iraqi military forces. Slocombe commented to Colonel Gardner as if he were responding to the Iraqi author: "You guys lost. What do you mean rights—that they should have?"[44]

After his discussion with Bremer about disbanding the regular army and the Ministries of Defense and Interior, Garner went to see Slocombe.

"You can't get rid of the Ministry of Interior," Garner told him, "because all the police are there and they'll go home."

Slocombe appeared uninformed that Iraq had a centralized police system controlled by the Ministry of Interior. He admitted that perhaps the ministry should not be disbanded. When Garner asked about the Iraqi army, Slocombe said that they did not want to bring the army back. They wanted a new army.

"That will take years," Garner exclaimed, but Slocombe just shrugged with indifference. Garner was stunned.[45]

In the absence of Slocombe earlier in April, Garner had tasked his C-5 Plans officer, Colonel Paul Hughes, to monitor the Ministry of Defense. Hughes had been assisted by Mike Ayoub and Lieutenant Colonel Jim Torgler. Garner had asked General Carl Strock to oversee the effort run by Hughes (Strock was also a firefighter for reconstruction, electricity, and oil and a deputy for Baghdad Central). Garner had to stretch his staff to cover the Iraqi army. He knew that Hughes was in contact with planners at Central Command about reconstituting the Iraqi army with contractors. He knew that Hughes, Ayoub, and Torgler had contacts with senior Iraqi officers and were trying to obtain personnel information on the Ministry of Defense. Ayoub was trying to stand up an Iraqi military police battalion for security in Baghdad.[46]

When Slocombe arrived in Baghdad, he had Colonel Gardner and Torgler focus on setting up the team he wanted to form in Iraq. He did not display an active interest in the Iraqi army or Ministry of Defense. According to Ayoub, that had the "unfortunate consequence of freezing any payroll disbursement, freezing my MP training initiative, and locking out our Iraqi interlocutors. Considering the desperate need for Iraqi security forces to augment our own thinly stretched combat troops, this seemed ludicrous."[47]

Ayoub was concerned about the consequences of not reconstituting at least part of the Iraqi army right away. He felt that inattention to the plight of Iraqi soldiers was morally wrong after the promises made to them through the pre-invasion information campaign. That message had indicated that if the Iraqi soldiers did not fight they would be taken care of. Most of them had not fought; in fact, in most cases, they had simply gone home with their weapons. Now some soldiers, particularly officers and NCOs with a career investment in the army, wanted to come back on active duty. Others simply wanted some sort of termination pay from military service. But there were no clear plans for either employment or compensation for the soldiers. Perceptively, Ayoub wrote in his journal, "If the military understand anything, it is that you don't surrender the initiative. If putting the Iraqi military on hold for a few months isn't surrendering the initiative, I don't know what is. Slocombe's team won't even arrive in force for another three months. In the meantime, people with very lethal skills will not be paid or allowed to work."[48]

Ayoub was tracking and contributing to the intelligence on Iraqi soldiers;

he wrote further, "The opposition is paying. Rumors are $50 for any U.S. Soldier killed, $250 for a Bradley and $500 for an M1 Abrams. I feel we are losing any ability we may have had to influence positive change in Iraq. Jim [Torgler] spends his time and considerable talent arranging suitable living and office quarters for the carpet-baggers' eventual arrival."[49]

Prior to and during the invasion in March and April, Lieutenant Colonel John Agoglia at Central Command had monitored a Psychological Operations campaign to prevent the Iraqi regular army from fighting. Leaflets dropped on Iraqi ground forces informed them that if they did not fight, they would not be targeted, and that if they cooperated with Coalition ground forces, they would be taken care of (no specifics were addressed). During the invasion most of the regular army did not fight, about 6,000 surrendered, and the rest slipped away to go home, which reduced casualties on both sides. From different locations Agoglia and Ayoub could not understand the new policy track of the Coalition.[50]

Slocombe was not responsible for the Ministry of Interior as Garner had thought. Bernie Kerik, the former New York City police chief, arrived as the new senior advisor for the Ministry of Interior. He was appointed at the suggestion of former New York mayor Rudy Giuliani with the approval of President Bush. Kerik arrived in Baghdad with no staff or preparation. Bob Gifford, who had been the senior advisor for Interior, became Kerik's deputy. But Kerik exhibited little understanding or interest in the Iraqi police system.

Garner approached Kerik and asked, "Bernie, why are you here?" Kerik told him he had been on the speaking circuit giving speeches, but that he was running out of material. A trip to Iraq should provide him more material. Garner shook his head and walked away.[51]

On the morning of Friday, 16 May, Bremer signed General Order 1 to remove Ba'athists from senior government positions in Iraq. Garner had not been consulted in advance on the pronouncement, nor was he invited to Bremer's office when it was signed. Bremer drove to the Baghdad Convention Center, where he held his press conferences, and spoke for twenty minutes to the assembled journalists about the de-Ba'athification order he had just signed: "The process shall be guided by three principles. . . . It will be fair, transparent, and consistent. . . . We are prepared to accept that the policy will result in some temporary inefficiency in the administration of the government. . . . As soon as possible we will turn the implementation of the de-Ba'athification process over to an Iraqi interim government."[52]

Ambassador Sawers spoke briefly after Bremer to reinforce the de-Ba'athification order as Coalition policy. A journalist from CBS asked how many Iraqis would be affected, noting that there were at least 600,000 Iraqi civilians with government positions. The reporter was told that the order would only affect between 15,000 to 30,000 people, comprising those in the top four ranks of the Ba'ath Party.[53]

Another journalist commented that the Ba'ath Party "extends broadly over the Middle East and that not all Iraqis were in the Ba'ath due to Saddam Hussein." Bremer was unmoved and said that the Iraqi Ba'ath Party had been under Saddam Hussein's control and the party lacked any legitimacy that might exist elsewhere.[54]

The press conference was short; Bremer returned to the palace for a meeting with his senior advisors. When he announced earlier that a de-Ba'athification policy would soon follow, few foresaw the impact. When it became clear that it would remove those of the top four ranks of party members from all government positions, there were immediate protests. Bremer anticipated the protests but he held his position, almost indifferent to the concerns expressed. Frustration was greatest with those senior advisors who had made the most progress with putting Iraqis in senior ministry positions. As the ministry coordinator and a senior advisor, Robin Raphel was particularly distraught. She had been the first to see the order when Bremer arrived and the first to anticipate its impact. One of the reasons she had volunteered to redraft the order (ostensibly so it would be more coherent) was to see if it could be modified. Even after it was signed Raphel felt there was room to negotiate the impact of the order; activation might be delayed to allow time to put a waiver system in place to vet party members, thus allowing them to continue to serve and get critical work done. Bremer, however, wanted to make a decisive statement rather than make compromises. And the order was decisive.[55]

That evening, Bremer made another decisive decision, and again he took Garner by surprise. Garner wanted Bremer to meet the Iraqi leaders of the IIA with the general goal of empowering them in the transition of authority and accelerating the withdrawal of Coalition forces. He arranged for Bremer to meet six of the seven Iraqi leaders in the IIA: Ahmed Chalabi of the INC; Ayad Allawi of the INA; Massoud Barzani of the KDP; Jalal Talabani of the PUK; Naseer Chaderchi of the NDP; and Ibrahim al-Jaafari of the Shiite Dawa Party. Abdul Aziz Hakim of SCIRI did not attend, but he was represented by Dr. Adel Mendi and Hamid al-Bayati.[56]

Of the eight Iraqis who would sit at the table for the conference, two were Sunni Kurds (Barzani and Talabani), five were Shiites (Chalabi, Allawi, al-Jaafari, Mahdi, and al-Bayati), and one was an Arab Sunni (Chaderchi). All but the two Kurds had been exiles or expatriates prior to the invasion, and Barzani and Talabani had been living in northern Iraq beyond the control of Saddam Hussein. Thus while these Iraqis included the key leaders of each of the major opposition parties, only two of them were recent residents of Iraq, a subtle point that Bremer would soon exploit.

The meeting, Bremer's first with Iraqi leaders, began at 5:00 P.M. The Coalition contingent included John Sawers and General Tim Cross of the UK, as well as Garner, Adams, Ryan Crocker, Hume Horan, and Generals Abizaid and McKiernan representing the military forces. It was conducted in English and Arabic with translators.

Entering the conference room, Bremer noted that Garner was in a suit. "Look at that," said Bremer. "You're wearing a tie. I didn't think that you owned one."

"I thought I'd put it on for this night's occasion," Garner said modestly. Bremer was aware he had an edge over Garner in formality, and he did not miss an opportunity to drive it home.[57]

There was a cluster of bodyguards outside. Inside, Coalition leaders sat on one side of the table; Iraqis sat on the other. The room was packed with people sitting along the wall as well. In Bremer's opening address, he emphasized the importance of a partnership between the Iraqi groups represented in the room to ensure movement in the direction of representative government; then he qualified that goal: "We expect the progress along this path to be incremental. . . . But we are prepared to cede increasing responsibility to responsible Iraqi leaders." The reaction from the Iraqis was muted. Colonel Tony Puckett noted, "The mood of the meeting in the opening half hour was polite and somewhat formal, with only a hint of the more urgent exchanges that were to occur later."[58]

Bremer's remark was a signal that there was not going to be an immediate transfer of power, in contrast to what Garner had been planning and had promised those very Iraqis in the room. Garner was both surprised and disappointed, and he was unsure how the Iraqis in the room would respond. As it turned out, most of those present who spoke began by praising Garner for his efforts in Iraq before addressing what they knew of Bremer's intentions.[59]

To the surprise of some Coalition members at the meeting, there was no objection to the de-Ba'athification order issued earlier that day. Several Iraqis at the table praised the order; in fact, they expressed concern that the Ba'athists in Iraq might be regrouping to challenge the regime change that had just been imposed. This reinforced Bremer's position, countering the resistance he had received earlier from his own people. But none of the Iraqis in the room were Ba'athists, and so the order obviously did not apply either to them or those close to them. Most of the senior Ba'athists that would be affected were Sunni Arabs. Perhaps trying to be clever, Chalabi suggested that the Coalition go further with de-Ba'athification, but then undercut his own argument by adding, "We must also realize that many Iraqis have been forced to join the party."[60]

The common concern expressed by the Iraqis was security. General Abizaid, representing Central Command, said he would "organize a meeting early next week with my senior commanders and the members of this council to discuss practical solutions to the security problem."

The first half hour of the meeting had been cordial, but this began to change as Bremer emphasized again "that the path to representative government will be incremental."

Talabani and Bayati suggested in response to accelerate the political process, noting that "the Street is waiting for the freedom promised." Chalabi added that they had been promised a transitional government within a few weeks. But Bremer had not suggested such a transition; Garner had. Bremer made it clear he was in charge and he said that the IIA would be discontinued. He would initiate a new process and that "a representative government will have to include many Iraqis who lived here and suffered under Saddam for decades."[61] The hint Puckett had detected in the initial exchange had materialized as a substantive position. The Iraqis at the table would lose power if more Iraqis were added to a transitional government. It was Bremer who would gain power by adding more. The larger body would be fractious and weak, but the Iraqis that Bremer would add would be beholden to him.

The meeting was followed by a press conference with brief statements by Bremer and Barzani, speaking for the Iraqis present. Bremer recapped the main issues discussed: security, de-Ba'athification, and interim political arrangements. No mention was made to the press of discontinuing the IIA; nor did Bremer mention his plan to assemble a much larger group of Iraqis as an interim government. When Barzani addressed the journalists, he supported Bremer, saying that the Iraqi leaders were generally satisfied with the Coalition invasion of Iraq and with the de-Ba'athification order Bremer had signed that morning. The journalists were given no opportunity to ask questions.

The participants at the meeting then moved to the main dining facility for dinner. Bremer, Sawers, Garner, Abizaid, and McKiernan sat with the senior Iraqis; at the next table, their deputies sat with Ryan Crocker. The meal was cordial but Garner was disturbed. In his view, Bremer had told those in the IIA he had put together, "You're not the government; we're the government. You're not needed and you can go home. And the next morning they all left Baghdad."

During the dinner, an Iraqi who had been raised in the United States and was working for General Abizaid approached Garner and pulled him aside. "You have to stay."

Garner was distraught but replied, "I'm not staying."

The Iraqi insisted. "You have to stay because everybody fears what will happen after you leave. [Bremer] will not go over with the Iraqi people."

Garner looked at him. "You need to tell John Abizaid or somebody else. I'm not the guy to tell."[62]

The next day Bremer took a small party to Mosul in northern Iraq. He did not invite Garner to go with him, nor did Garner ask to go. Developments in northern Iraq contrasted with those in the southern and central regions, both in their political chemistry and through the nature of the invasion. While the main Coalition invasions had been from Kuwait, in the north the Kurdish Peshmerga swelled to over 60,000 and overran part of Arab-populated area in northern Iraq, aided by Special Forces and Coalition airpower. Some assumed that northern Iraq meant only the Kurdish areas, but half of it was Arab, with the large Arab population in Mosul and Kirkuk; most of Iraq's minority populations were also in the north: Turkmen, Yazidis, and Assyrian Christians.

Bruce Moore and Dick Naab had established the ORHA-North office initially in the Kurdish city of Erbil, and only gradually reached out to work in the Arab areas. The 101st Air Assault Division under Major General David Petraeus was established in Mosul and focused on the Arab areas, keeping the Kurds at arm's length. Petraeus had been in Mosul almost a month with 20,000 soldiers and had achieved a great deal. He concentrated his division in Nineveh Province from the Turkish border in the north, along the border with Syria to the west, and extending to Anbar Province further south with his headquarters in Mosul, the provincial capital.[63]

Petraeus was a veteran of operations in Haiti and Bosnia, with more post-conflict experience than many other generals serving in Iraq. He knew that security for the Arab areas was his dominant task, and he needed to get local political leaders back to work and the economy up and working to offset the chaos following the invasion. He knew the Kurdish areas east of Mosul were little affected by the invasion and did not require occupation by his forces for stability. With little guidance from the Coalition military or civilian leaders, Petraeus achieved the security required and moved to other tasks, operating gently when conditions allowed, firmly when he met resistance. When he arrived in Mosul, Petraeus found many armed elements in the city. Most were not enemy forces and he either disarmed them or reformed them under his control.[64]

The Kurdish Peshmerga, the largest armed group, had a good relationship with ORHA; Bruce Moore and Dick Naab considered the Peshmerga heroes for their past resistance to Saddam Hussein and for their more recent role as

Coalition surrogates fighting the Iraqi army during the invasion. Petraeus had another view: the armed Kurdish groups were often a dangerous nuisance. They were clearly anxious to de-Arabize areas that had earlier been predominantly Kurdish. Saddam Hussein had for several decades imposed an Arab population upon northern Iraq with some ethnic cleansing of the Kurds to make room for them. When Petraeus found the Kurds trying to displace the populations of twelve Arab villages near Mosul, he told them he would not stand for it and that they should withdraw the Peshmerga to the Kurdish areas to the east.[65]

Petraeus sought to put a representative group of Iraqi leaders in power. With his subordinate commanders, military lawyers, and other staff officers, he convened a group of 270 delegates representing Mosul's ethnic, religious, and tribal groups. Under his guidance, they elected twenty-five officials to help manage Mosul and Nineveh Province during the period of occupation. It was an ambitious program with no structured guidance from Coalition leaders in Baghdad or Washington.[66]

To get the regional economy going, Petraeus wanted businesses operating and people working. That required an infusion of capital; he used the phrase "Money is ammunition." Petraeus stopped the looting and vandalism as soon as his forces arrived by instituting extensive patrolling, not by shooting looters. When the Iraqi governing council he put into operation asked for export and import approval, Petraeus told them to begin without formal approval (Bruce Moore and Dick Naab told Iraqis the same thing). The first week of May, Petraeus went to the Syrian border and opened it to cross-border trade, which resulted in a flood of exchange, a useful international economic operation conducted on the authority of a major general, which surprised those in CPA.

When Bremer arrived in Mosul on 17 May, Petraeus had established security, conducted elections for local and provincial leaders, and had the economy operating. What Petraeus had accomplished in a month might have been a useful model for other regions, but some members of Bremer's team considered Petraeus a salesman and a loose cannon. Scott Carpenter would later tell visitors going to Mosul to see Petraeus, "Don't look into his eyes when he talks."[67]

Bremer wanted to exploit what Petraeus had in motion, but also harness and control it. He was surprised that the Syrian borders had been opened for trade without his approval and he did not want northern Iraq exporting grain or medicine needed for the rest of the country. The drive into northern Iraq to export rather than sell domestically was driven by price controls of the previous Iraqi regime. Altering domestic prices could have unanticipated consequences. Bremer needed time to assess the overall system to restructure it. Petraeus was too far ahead of him.[68]

If Petraeus had moved on the economic front without consulting Baghdad, Bremer had moved on the political front with the de-Ba'athification order without consulting the military commanders in advance. Many of those Petraeus had recently installed in power were former Ba'athists he had vetted to ensure they were not guilty of atrocities, but he relied on their specific conduct as his guide, not their arbitrary rank in the Ba'ath Party. Furthermore, he had required them to pledge their allegiance to the new structure. Once he acknowledged the de-Ba'athification order, he determined that it made provision for waivers for former Ba'athists. He was quick to exploit this provision with Bremer, who conceded more waiver autonomy to Petraeus than to any other military commander.

One project Petraeus put in motion was getting schools back into operation, with a particular focus on Mosul University, one of the largest universities in the country. Saddam's regime had required more party membership in the Ministries of Education and Higher Education than in other ministries to ensure educational matters were consistent with Ba'ath policies. In Mosul University alone, Petraeus found 180 professors who had held Ba'ath membership in one of the top four ranks. Forced to comply with the de-Ba'athification order, Petraeus fired all 180, then immediately hired back 120 on a provisional basis for six months. His rationale was that it was essential to get students back into classrooms, and classrooms had to have teachers. That applied to elementary and secondary schools, too. The students, particularly the older ones, could be a volatile element who should continue their studies rather than be left outside the classroom and be available for mischief. Petraeus found that some professors had their own following among the students, which could cause problems if those professors were dismissed arbitrarily. By assigning officers under his command to work with the university officials—to vet them, fire them, selectively hire them back for six months, and subsequently establish a process for additional waivers—Petraeus kept the university functioning despite the de-Ba'athification order.

With token approval to continue with the procedures he was implementing for the Mosul/Nineveh educational system, Petraeus had his officers contact Drew Erdmann, the ORHA interim advisor for the Ministry of Higher Education. With Erdmann they developed procedures and assistance programs to keep their universities in operation. What Petraeus had put in motion on his own initiative provided a basis for Erdmann to work around the full impact of the de-Ba'athification order for other universities, an advantage he would have over the Coalition senior advisors working with other Iraqi ministries.[69]

When Bremer made his trip to Mosul, he was accompanied by Lieutenant Colonel John Agoglia, his new liaison from Central Command. Walt Slocombe and Colonel Gardner also joined the party to see what military training facilities might be available in northern Iraq. On the trip, Slocombe and Agoglia discussed the Iraqi army, a continuation of video-teleconferences that allowed those in Washington, Qatar, Kuwait, and Iraq to develop a concept for dealing with the Iraqi military forces. In April, Agoglia and General Abizaid had represented Central Command from Qatar in those discussions, with Slocombe, Feith, and Wolfowitz in the Pentagon, and General Strock, Colonel Hughes, and Lieutenant Colonel Torgler representing ORHA from Kuwait. The key, then, was how to reconstitute the Iraqi army and how to employ it.

On the trip to Mosul, Slocombe told Agoglia, "John, I'm having a hard time with how I justify to the American people recalling an army that didn't have the courage to stand and fight us, an army that deserted and ran like a bunch of cowards."

Appalled, Agoglia responded, "Sir, they did exactly what we wanted them to do."

"What do you mean?" Slocombe asked.

Agoglia explained. "Sir, we've been running a PSYOP campaign against these guys since July of '02. We told them to desert or surrender so that we could make them part of a new Iraqi force to protect a new Iraq . . . for the people of Iraq. That's the message we've been sending to these folks."

Slocombe was not convinced. "Yeah, but . . . but they deserted."

Agoglia again tried to explain. "Sir, they did exactly what we asked them to do. I honestly think it's a good thing that they chose not to fight us. That shows that they did not support the dictator. We've put a lot of energy . . . into this and they believe that we're going to recall them. This is a key piece of the plan."

"Hmm, I've got to think about that," replied Slocombe.[70]

Agoglia was concerned that Slocombe did not understand or support the plan to reconstitute the Iraqi army. Like others, Agoglia had been surprised that the regular Iraqi army had capitulated so easily and that the main resistance had come from the irregular Fedayeen forces. By mid-May, Agoglia knew through intelligence sources that the reason the regular soldiers went home was to protect their families. The Fedayeen would not only fight the Coalition, they would punish any Iraqi soldiers who refused to fight, and that included attacking their families. Agoglia explained that to Slocombe, but the latter refused to see any credible value in the regular army. Agoglia noted that Slocombe did not distinguish between the regular army and the Republican Guard and other special military and intelligence forces. Slocombe referred to all the Iraqi forces as "Saddam's army." Determined to sustain the plan to recall the regular army, Agoglia began to watch Slocombe closely.[71]

Soon after Slocombe and Colonel Gardner returned to Baghdad, they decided to go to Kuwait to discuss their plans for the Iraqi army with McKiernan's officers responsible for planning. Mike Ayoub made the arrangements for transportation and accommodations and cleared their movement with the military command. Since he had been working with Iraqi officers in Baghdad, he put himself on the orders for the conference.

But just as the group was about to leave, Colonel Gardner asked Ayoub, "And why do you need to go, Mike?"

"I'm your State Department representative. I'm here to offer you policy guidance from the civilian side." Ayoub might have also mentioned his work with senior Iraqi officers who wanted to bring their military forces back on active duty.

"This is a military operation. I don't need you there," Colonel Gardner told him. "I need you to stay here." Suddenly Ayoub was off the trip.[72]

Ayoub was frustrated with Slocombe and Colonel Gardner. When they departed for Kuwait he went to Robin Raphel and asked to be reassigned because he was having no substantive impact with the Ministry of Defense. She reassigned him as interim advisor for the Atomic Energy Commission with Colonel Puckett.[73]

On 19 May Slocombe and Colonel Gardner went to Camp Doha to receive a briefing from Colonel Kevin Benson, the senior planner for General McKiernan. Benson laid out the original plan to reconstitute the Iraqi army and how it was to be used for labor and other tasks in Iraq. Since the Iraqi army had not remained intact after the invasion, the CFLCC planners had to adjust their concept on how to bring it back. Benson presented several proposals, some from General Abizaid. The main effort would be to reconstitute the Iraqi army at bases in the north, south, and central regions of the country. They would bring in a division at a time at each location and vet the officers and soldiers, demobilizing many and retaining those that wanted to stay to build brigade-size formations at each base, repeating the process every ninety days, and incrementally reconstituting the army at about one-third or less of its original strength.[74]

General McKiernan's staff had made contact with ten Iraqi generals who wanted to help reform the army. In Baghdad, Paul Hughes, Jim Torgler, and Mike Ayoub had met with senior Iraqi officers to obtain data on army personnel. Although Hughes had sustained email contact with Colonel Gardner in early April, he had missed Gardner when he briefly visited Baghdad in April. With Slocombe's arrival in Baghdad, General Strock dropped his oversight position for the Iraqi army and concentrated on other tasks. When Ayoub decided he could not work effectively with Colonel Gardner and asked to work with another ministry, Lieutenant Colonel Torgler was the only member of ORHA still working with Slocombe's team, with most of his effort on administrative tasks; he did not attend the briefing Colonel Benson gave to Slocombe in Kuwait.

When Benson finished his presentation, Slocombe simply thanked him. Unsure how to proceed further, Benson explained that what he had provided was a decision briefing, meaning that he had just proposed several courses of action and that one should be selected and put in motion, or with additional guidance another course of action could be developed. But Slocombe had little to say. Army Lieutenant Colonel Robert Newman, a Middle East Foreign Area Officer serving as an advisor for political issues for McKiernan, attended the meeting. He asked several pointed questions, which apparently indicated his dissatisfaction with Slocombe's attitude on the Iraqi army. After the briefing, Benson noted that Major General Rusty Blackman, McKiernan's chief of staff, took Newman aside and "chewed his ass" for being rude during the briefing. Agoglia returned to Baghdad with Slocombe and Colonel Gardner. Agoglia notified General McKiernan the next day that Slocombe had taken little interest and provided no feedback on plans to reconstitute the Iraqi army. Colonel Gardner was contacted and told that McKiernan "wasn't happy with it."[75]

Over the next few days, Slocombe and Colonel Gardner had several discussions about the Iraqi army with Ambassador Bremer. Slocombe proposed that Bremer issue the draft order to disband all the Iraqi military and intelligence organizations. Agoglia, present for that discussion, stated strongly that this should be based on the intended recall of the regular army. Slocombe reluctantly agreed, but it was an issue Agoglia had to stress in several meetings. Slocombe expressed concern about the number of Iraqi officers in the army that were Ba'athists, an issue that could not easily be resolved until the files that Hughes, Torgler, and Ayoub were trying to recover could be reviewed. When they were vetted, Agoglia learned that only 50 percent of the generals and less than 20 percent of the colonels were Ba'ath Party members. Slocombe also expressed concern about the state of the Iraqi military facilities that were looted. Agoglia told him some had been looted and some had not; with a smaller army, they would not require all the facilities. "We can work through this," Agoglia told Slocombe.[76]

Another issue was compensation for the soldiers—emergency payments, salaries for those who wanted to remain in the army, and pensions. Slocombe asked rhetorically, "Since when do we pay a vanquished army?" While conscript soldiers could be demobilized and sent home without great hardship, the loss of salaries and pensions would be severe for career officers, NCOs, and their families. Civilian government employees were being given emergency payments in May, but Slocombe was opposed to providing such payments to the military services. Eventually a stipend was paid, but there was doubt in May if any would be paid at all.[77]

Slocombe and Colonel Gardner, accompanied by Agoglia, flew to Kuwait on 22 May for another meeting. They made it clear that soon Bremer would sign an order to disband the Iraqi military services with all its components, but he indicated that the regular army would be recalled. Although drafts were supposedly sent to offices in the Pentagon and to Central Command, Agoglia never saw a copy of the order before it was final. Anyone who read it would have found it awkwardly written, with no mention of the Iraqi army except in the annex on the fourth page of the order, where it listed "Institutions dissolved by the Order (the Dissolved Entities)":

The Ministry of Defense
The Ministry of Information
The Ministry of State for Military Affairs
The Iraqi Intelligence Service
The National Security Bureau
The Directorate of National Security (Amn al-'Am)
The Special Security Organization
The Army, Air Force, Navy, the Air Defense Force
The Republican Guard
The Special Republican Guard
The Directorate of Military Intelligence
Saddam Fedayeen
Ba'ath Party Militia

The order allowed the Coalition to confiscate all assets of the dissolved organizations while at the same time suspending their financial obligations, with the stipulation that the Coalition would establish provisions for the reinstatement of pensions. The order left doubt about what those procedures would be and when they would be in effect. All military rank previously granted by the Iraqi government or armed forces was cancelled, all employees were dismissed, and all conscripts were released from service obligations. Conscription was suspended indefinitely. Citing provisions from the Coalition Order Number 1, Coalition Order Number 2 stated that all those in the rank of colonel and above would be "deemed a Senior Party Member," with the implication that they and their family members would not be entitled to pensions or other obligations of the government. Yet more than half of those officers were not party members.[78]

As Bremer signed the order, he had a video-teleconference with the president and the National Security Council. Frank Miller was present in the NSC room when Bremer announced that he had just disbanded the army. Miller noted stunned silence and shock on the faces of Secretary Powell and National Security Advisor Rice. They had no advance warning of the decision that suddenly reversed what the NSC had earlier agreed upon.

The president simply responded to Bremer, "You are the man on the ground," suggesting no objection.

Miller felt someone in the room should have demanded that they have forty-eight hours to review and staff the issue, but no one suggested that during the meeting. After the meeting Miller went to Stephen Hadley, Rice's deputy, to protest Bremer's uncoordinated action. Hadley said it was too late and expressed no interest in resisting.[79] Powell asked General Peter Pace, the Deputy Chairman of the Joint Staff, if he had been consulted or otherwise knew about the decision to disband the Iraqi army.

"Hell no," Pace exclaimed.[80]

Feith participated in Pentagon discussions with Slocombe and Bremer about disbanding the Iraqi army, yet he stated, "It appears I did not bring the matter to the Deputies Committee." Feith said he told Bremer to get Rumsfeld's approval for the decision, but he cannot confirm that Bremer did so before it was announced.[81]

When Miller told Colonel Greenwood and Major Kojac about Bremer's move to disband the army, Kojac could tell Miller was upset that there had been no effort to staff the decision in Washington. Everyone on the NSC had intended for the past year to retain most of the regular Iraqi army for post-conflict tasks to keep the soldiers from joining the ranks of the unemployed, and to avoid their role in any resistance movement. Miller had worked for Slocombe at the Pentagon during the Clinton administration and considered him both a friend and mentor. Miller thought Slocombe should have warned him in advance about the decision to disband the army. Later Miller said he could not bring himself to discuss the issue with Slocombe.[82]

Meanwhile, Colonel Hughes was in Washington working on contracts with RONCO for DDR in order to gain control of the Iraqi army, and with MPRI to retrain those that would be retained for active duty. Negotiations for both contracts had begun over a month earlier. One day Hughes "turned on the morning news and there's NBC announcing that Bremer has abolished the

Army and I thought, Holy shit! How can he have done that? The Joint Chiefs of Staff didn't find out until after Feith sent them a hand-written note."[83]

Hughes worried about an emergency payment plan ($20 to each soldier) he had tried to put in motion before he left Iraq. By mid-May, the Coalition was making emergency payments to Iraq's civil servants and Garner intended that those payments be extended to the regular army. Before leaving Iraq, Hughes had promised a group of Iraqi officers that the army would get the emergency payment. When Hughes asked Garner about the order to disband the army, Garner told him, "I had no idea it was coming."[84]

Hughes could not understand why officers at Central Command and CFLCC had not tried to stop the order. He did not know that Colonel Ago-glia had an agreement with Slocombe that the regular army would be dis-banded with the Republican Guards and intelligence services, but with the army to be recalled and reconstituted. Agoglia had kept senior officers in the-ater informed of the agreement. Agoglia did not know that Slocombe would not honor it.[85]

General Abizaid, Deputy Commander at Central Command, flew into Baghdad several times during May to try to assist the transitions taking place in Iraq. On one occasion he had difficulty making a long-distance call and was soon aware that there were communications problems in the palace. He contacted Brigadier General Moran at Central Command and directed him to look into it. Moran flew to Camp Victory and sent a message to Colonel Conway instructing him to meet him there to discuss his situation. Conway and his deputy, Tim Phillips, drove to the airport and gave a presentation on ORHA communications to Generals Moran and Detamore. Afterward they had a friendly dinner together. Phillips thought all had gone well. They in-vited Moran and Detamore to the palace the next day to sit in on a C-staff meeting and to have an office call with Jerry Bates, who ran the C-staff.[86]

The next day, Moran, Detamore, and several other officers arrived early and went straight to the C-6 staff office; Colonel Conway was in a C-staff meeting with Bates. Moran wanted to see Phillips, not Conway. Phillips called in Major June and Captain Macias, two officers in the C-6 shop. Moran was not in a pleasant mood and opened with a complaint directed at Phillips.

"Tim, you've gone native on me—you're now part of the problem," Mo-ran stated in front of the junior officers. "You were sent here to do plan-ning . . . you are not doing planning. You are too close to the situation and involved in current operations. There's no strategic planning, this is broke, and we're going to fix it. I want you to identify every communicator and we're going to put together a staff."[87] The others involved in communications were the Raytheon team and the Department of State personnel providing communications to the ambassadors.

When Phillips tried to explain they had a system, Moran responded forcefully, "No. We . . . we're going to reorganize this place."

Moran directed them to draw up a new organization chart for the staff section, moving several officers into different positions, with Captain James Baladad as the operations officer; Baladad commanded D Company, the 86th Signal Battalion, and the military signal detachment supporting ORHA.

Phillips tried to reason with Moran. "Sir, that company commander has a job. He maintains a satellite shop 24/7; he's a company commander. . . . He already has a job."

Phillips expected General Detamore to support him given that Baladad worked for Detamore through the battalion commander of the 86th. But Detamore "remained silent. . . . He didn't say a word. I think he was intimidated."

When Colonel Conway returned from his meeting, he was surprised to find Moran and Detamore in his office trying to restructure his staff. He began to argue with Moran. "We are not going to do it that way."

Moran ordered everyone out of the room below the rank of colonel. Knowing that Conway had a short temper, Phillips went to tell Bates what was taking place. Bates immediately went with Phillips to Conway's office.[88]

Bates pointed at the two generals. "Get one thing perfectly clear. Nobody walks into my command, criticizes my officers, or relieves anybody without talking to me. Is that clear?"

Moran paused and looked hard at Bates. "Crystal," he responded icily.[89]

Bates turned and walked out. Moran and Detamore left and went to another meeting with the senior advisor for the Ministry of Telecommunications and Transportation. No one from the C-6 section attended that meeting. Conway and Phillips had their efforts devoted to sustaining communications for ORHA, not larger issues of communications for Iraq.[90]

Moran and Detamore could have made useful contributions to ORHA several months earlier, and they had provided a small signal detachment in mid-April. But it was far from what ORHA required. Detamore would not help Conway in Kuwait because ORHA could not operate at Camp Doha. Moran had sent Phillips to fix the problems for ORHA, but there were more problems than he could fix. When Moran came to Baghdad at Abizaid's direction, he did not stop by to meet Jerry Bates, for whom Conway worked. When Bates found he had been improperly bypassed, his response was to protect his staff rather than to use Moran and Detamore to help correct ORHA's communications problems. Everyone knew there were communications problems with ORHA, but strong personalities all around prevented a cohesive approach to resolving them.

When Garner flew from Baghdad on 10 May to meet Bremer in Qatar, he spent the night at the Sheraton Hotel in Kuwait en route. That evening he met an Iraqi expatriate, Mowaffak al-Rubaie, who wanted Garner's assistance. Al-Rubaie had met Garner on 17 April at the conference in Tallil, arriving with other expatriates to participate in the conference. A Shia Muslim and physician educated in Great Britain in the 1980s and living in London, he had ties with two Iraqi opposition parties, the Dawa and United Iraqi Alliance (UIA). He wanted Garner to help him go to Baghdad and join the effort to form a new Iraqi government. Garner was impressed with him and later sent Colonel Mike Murphy, his legal advisor, to Kuwait to bring al-Rubaie to Baghdad. A few days later Murphy took al-Rubaie to Najaf to meet Shia leaders to try to obtain their assistance with a new government.[91]

Subsequently, al-Rubaie told Garner he was coordinating with important Shia leaders in Iraq, including the Grand Ayatollah Ali al-Sistani. Aware that key Shia leaders could be useful or obstructionist, Garner told al-Rubaie to sustain his contacts. In mid-May he told Garner that al-Sistani wanted to meet Garner and discuss governance issues in Iraq. But by that time Garner did not have the authority in Iraq that al-Sistani assumed. Garner did not feel he could take on such a high-profile role with Bremer in charge, nor did he think Bremer would allow Garner to do so. If al-Rubaie was correct and al-Sistani did want to meet Garner, it was an opportunity missed. Later, when Bremer tried on multiple occasions to meet with al-Sistani on important governance issues for Iraq, al-Sistani refused to meet him.[92]

On Monday, 19 May, just after Bremer's return from Mosul, Garner had a meeting with Generals Abizaid and McKiernan and key members of their respective staffs to work on the high-priority tasks Garner had defined earlier: salaries, police, courts, prisons, services for Baghdad, fuel, crops, food distribution, town councils, health, and security. Garner and Adams had representatives present for each task: David Nummy, Bob Gifford, General Strock, Gary Vogler, Robin Raphel (with several tasks), Chris Milligan, and Steve Browning. With Abizaid and McKiernan were Generals Webster, Stanton, Bromberg, Hawkins, Christianson, Crear, and Kern, and Colonels Stanton and Stafford. It was an important meeting.[93]

David Nummy and General Stanton began with a briefing on paying salaries. As they were speaking, Clay McManaway entered the room and told General Abizaid, "Ambassador Bremer wants to see you."

Abizaid said he would be glad to see Bremer as soon as they were through, underscoring the importance of the meeting. Dismissive, McManaway said, "He wants to see you now." Abizaid turned and looked at Garner.

Disappointed, Garner told him, "Well, if he wants to see you, go ahead and go." Abizaid excused himself and left. Adams was appalled that McManaway would ask a key member of the meeting to leave in such a rude manner.

A few minutes after they resumed, McManaway returned and went to General McKiernan and said Bremer wanted to see him. Embarrassed, McKiernan looked at Garner as Abizaid had before him.[94]

Garner said, "Dave, he's in charge. You need to go." After McKiernan left, General Webster, the next senior officer in the room, asked Garner if they should continue. Garner said yes, but without Abizaid and McKiernan present, it would be more difficult to resolve conflicts. After the meeting, Garner returned to his office. Abizaid and McKiernan came by and apologized for leaving the meeting.

Garner told them, "Hell, you didn't have any choice. You had to leave."

They told Garner that the issue Bremer wanted to discuss did not justify pulling them from the meeting so abruptly. Garner was greatly annoyed and went to see McManaway.

"Damn him," Garner exclaimed. "He knew I was having this meeting, and he knew this was important. These are things we have to get done."

Again McManaway was dismissive. "Well, he's just that way."

"What do you mean, 'he's just that way'?" Garner demanded.

"Well, you know Jerry. He didn't want to wait till you got through."

"Is this a demonstration—to show me who's the boss?" Garner demanded.

"I don't know, it's just his way of doing things."

Furious, Garner went to Bremer's office, opened the door with no announcement, and said, "Jerry, I'm leaving." Bremer looked at Garner, surprised. "I came to tell you I'm leaving," Garner repeated.

Bremer stood up. "You can't leave," he said.

"The hell I can't," Garner responded.

"Why are you leaving?" Bremer demanded.

"Because you are an asshole," Garner said bluntly, "and I can't work for you. There will never be a day when you and I could work together."

"Jay, you can't do that," Bremer said.

Garner's fury was unabated. "What you just did to me—pulling Abizaid and McKiernan out of a meeting focused on rectifying major problems we have right now—I can't forgive that, and if that's the way you work, I don't want to deal with you."

"Look, you and I have the same objective," Bremer said.

"I don't think so," Garner replied.

"We do. Our objective is to make the United States successful in this endeavor," Bremer said, with no reference to interrupting Garner's meeting.

"It's true, I do have that objective."

"I do, too. In order to do that, the two of us have to work together."

Garner was not appeased. "Jerry, I don't see how I can work with you," again referencing the disruption caused in the meeting. Bremer said he would not do that again, but he offered no apology or explanation.

"Look, in order for me to remain here and to accomplish anything, I have to have access to the staff," Garner said.

"I don't think I can give you that."

"Well then, Jerry, how can I do anything? How can I accomplish anything if I don't have access to the staff?"

"Well, I've got to think about that." Bremer clearly did not want to concede.

Garner tried to reason with him. "It's very important that we get the public servants paid and to get a process in place. I will stay until I'm sure that process is in place to continue unless you and I have another problem like this one."

Approaching a draw in the discussion, Bremer attempted to break off. "Okay, we'll talk some more."

"Fine," Garner said as he left. But he rarely talked to Bremer again.

Ron Adams, Garner's deputy, had a similar experience with Bremer. The day after Bremer's arrival, Adams was one of several people from Garner's team that had been scheduled for an interview with him. The meticulous Adams arrived at Bremer's outer office just prior to his appointment and waited. Colonel Scott Norwood, the U.S. Air Force officer who served as Bremer's military assistant, managed the outer office. When Adams asked him about his appointment, Norwood told Adams simply to wait. Finally Bremer emerged from his office. Adams approached Bremer to introduce himself, annoyed that Colonel Norwood made no effort to do so.[95]

Bremer looked at Adams impatiently. "Who are you?" he asked.

"I'm Ron Adams. I'm Jay Garner's deputy. I am here to brief you."

Bremer looked at him quickly. "I don't want to talk to you."

Adams was embarrassed. "Okay, sir," he said simply. "Thank you very much."

Later that day, Adams had a visit from McManaway. Adams assumed he might have come to apologize or explain. That was not the case.

"Adams . . . what do you do here?" McManaway asked directly.

"I'm Jay Garner's deputy," he said. "I'm a kind of jack-of-all-trades for him."

"When are you leaving?" McManaway asked.

"What do you mean?" Adams asked, surprised at the abrupt opening.

"Are you leaving with General Garner?" McManaway asked.

"Yes, I am leaving when Jay leaves. That's the contract I had."

"Good," McManaway said, breaking off the conversation.

A few days later Adams had a meeting on financial issues with David Nummy, some others from Treasury, and their counterparts from the military command. McManaway entered the room and remained for some time to listen to the discussion.

Later he came to see Adams and asked him, "Would you consider staying on and take the role of chief of staff?"

"Under no circumstances," Adams replied. "I am leaving when Jay Garner leaves." This time Adams had the satisfaction of terminating the conversation.

A week later Ambassador Pat Kennedy arrived from the State Department. His specialty was administration and he soon came looking for Adams.[96] Put off with McManaway's style, Adams found Kennedy altogether different and they hit it off. Kennedy made a point to learn something about Adams before they met and treated him with more deference than Bremer, McManaway, or Norwood had.[97]

Kennedy wanted Adams to lay out the nature of Garner's organization, point out deficiencies, and suggest appropriate corrections. For several hours Adams went through the structure of ORHA, how it worked, how it had matured, the eclectic nature of the interagency team, the mismatched personnel that the U.S. government had provided, and the challenges working with the adjacent military command. Adams went over the difficulties since their arrival in Baghdad—living conditions, communications, transportation, and security. It was a constructive dialogue between two senior officials.[98]

Adams brought up issues Kennedy did not anticipate. Concerned about money to get the economy moving, Adams told him, "We have been asking for auditors from OSD and we thought they were coming for several days." But he explained that the small OSD group stayed for only three hours. The money that they required in Iraq warranted oversight and the Coalition needed a team of full-time auditors, stationed right in the palace, but there were none in Iraq and no one in the Pentagon seemed concerned.

He told Kennedy, "You've got to get them back over here. This is going to bite you if you are not careful." Adams said they had no inspector general and lacked capacity for their own oversight and investigation.

When some people look at an organizational diagram, they study what is on it and how it works. When Adams looked at an organizational diagram, he looked for what was not on it but should be. That had been his impulse in mid-January when Garner faxed him the original organizational diagram Feith's team had put together. He instinctively wrote in the margins the additional components necessary to make it work properly. Adams had been successful in adding some components—legal and PAO sections, and a small contracting component for ORHA—but he had been unable to obtain the auditors or the IG sections he wanted. During their talk, Kennedy listened closely. They agreed to continue the discussion the next day, with both taking some time for reflection.

When they continued the following day, Kennedy tactfully asked him, "Why don't you stay on?"

"No way," Adams responded. "Not the way we have been treated. I'm out of here. I should not have come back to begin with, but now that I have, I don't like what I see."[99]

Adams had joined ORHA with less enthusiasm than Garner. He had no cowboy tendencies like Jerry Bates or Buck Walters. Garner could get those two to join him with the offer to "go soldier again." The businesslike Adams did it out of loyalty to Garner.

There was much Adams had to pass on to Kennedy, but there was much he found futile—the interagency challenges in Washington, the lack of national-level planning, the reluctance to provide money and resources, and the efforts of the military forces to withdraw from Iraq. To Adams, the whole affair had gone wrong. In his eyes, Jay Garner had become the scapegoat. Despite his affinity for Pat Kennedy, that was not enough to get him to remain in Iraq—a project he had never asked for and for which he had no more enthusiasm.

Despite Bremer's interruptions of the 19 May meeting with Garner and McKiernan's key personnel, some advances had been made. Prior coordination between the subgroups working on common tasks ensured the meeting was substantive. At that meeting the first set of slides was presented by David Nummy, the Coalition senior advisor for the Ministry of Finance, and Brigadier General Edward Stanton, McKiernan's senior finance officer.

Together they were able to report that the Coalition had made payments to 40,000 (nonmilitary) pensioners during the previous four days; more payments would continue to be made. On 21 May, Nummy and Stanton would announce a plan to begin paying salaries to (nonmilitary) government employees, commencing in Baghdad on the twenty-fourth and nationwide four days later, with the goal to have the process fully implemented by the end of June. Without a functional credit system in the country, cash was required for all payments. That required transportation and security to move money. Only the Coalition military forces had sufficient transportation and security to make that work, and they relied mainly on the Government Support Teams (GSTs), composed of Civil Affairs personnel. General Stanton provided the procedure for the military commands to implement such payments. The GSTs were scheduled to meet with Iraqi leaders from each province on 25 May to establish arrangements to continue payments.[100]

In May, Iraq was still operating with several Iraqi currencies and the American dollar. Nummy had a plan in motion to establish a single Iraqi currency without Saddam's picture and reduce the reliance on American dollars, but it would take several months for implementation. All currencies would be used in the meantime. Nummy's team had reset the salary pay scales with four levels for government positions. In one meeting Nummy was asked why entry level teachers started at the lowest level. General Strock said that put teachers on a salary par with unskilled workers in government shoe factories. Nummy explained that school teachers accounted for almost half the Iraqi civilian workforce and that with the new pay scales they would be making five times what they had made before the invasion. Garner later conceded he missed an opportunity to upgrade the teaching profession in Iraq by not moving them up one pay level, above unskilled government labor.[101]

Nummy was not indifferent to the impact of pay levels and he knew that teachers were underpaid, even though within his interim system their salaries were higher than before the invasion. He had raised the payments for pensioners, who had only been paid two dollars a month prior to the invasion. His team had grown since his arrival in Baghdad and would continue to expand with people from Treasury and from monetary institutions from other Coalition members.

Following Nummy and Brigadier General Edward Stanton at the meeting were Bob Gifford, senior advisor for the Ministry of Interior, and Brigadier General Howard B. Bromberg, USA, representing McKiernan's command. Gifford and Bromberg presented slides addressing the police, courts, and prisons. There were eighteen police stations in operation in Baghdad. They had secured a police academy and had plans to stand up twenty-five more police stations. Over 7,000 of the 8,000 police in Baghdad had returned to duty, although they had only seventy-three police vehicles on hand. Working with Coalition forces, they were making thirty-five joint patrols a day in the city. Their coordinated approach to policing nationwide was to increase police numbers, obtain more equipment, set up more police academies with interim short-term police courses, establish more effective communications and reporting systems, and improve the public attitude toward the Iraqi police.

What they needed was the funding to implement their plans. So far there was little money available, a problem that went back to Frank Miller, who dismissed requests for funds to rebuild the Iraqi police.[102]

On prisons, Gifford and Bromberg had inspected six, five around Baghdad and one in al-Hilla, and identified detention centers and jails that would require renovation after the looting and vandalism. They were working on penal codes and procedures and wanted to set up interim short-term training programs for prison employees that would include enlightened standards. The key obstacles were the lack of funding, interpreters, and translators; they needed more Coalition military oversight and assistance and a long-term database.

With regard to the courts, Gifford and Bromberg indicated that 40 courthouses in Baghdad and 160 elsewhere in Iraq had been identified, but that 135 had been vandalized, requiring renovation to make them operational. A judicial college building was also being assessed for renovation. The 1969 Iraqi Penal code and the 1952 Civil Code (both under review), more humane than the legal codes employed under Saddam Hussein, were beginning to be implemented. Emergency payments had been given to 2,500 court employees. A de-Ba'athification questionnaire had been developed to vet those in the law enforcement system. In the near term, Gifford and Bromberg wanted to expand court operations throughout Iraq, continue work on the legal codes, coordinate with the Ministry of Justice on court issues, assist with de-Ba'athification countrywide, and seek more judges. What they needed was funding, a military presence to secure the court facilities, and continued assessments of the court system.

Next up were Generals Strock and Hawkins to address infrastructure services and electricity. They wanted to align the military units occupying Baghdad with the municipal boundaries for better overall management of their efforts. By mid-May, they were meeting 40 percent of the electricity demand in Baghdad and were working to get it up to 75 percent of prewar capacity.[103]

For water and sewage, they were working toward the prewar target of 32 percent of the sewage treated, with an eventual goal of 100 percent. Much of the raw sewage was going directly into the Tigris River. Despite concern that such pollution could lead to a cholera outbreak, there were no signs of cholera. On solid waste, beginning with Don Eberly's trash removal scheme put in operation earlier in May, they had removed over 230,000 cubic meters of garbage from the city and anticipated having it all removed by the beginning of June. The Iraqi military vehicles destroyed in the city had been removed and the streets would be cleared of all rubble by 15 June. They reported that the majority of municipal buildings in the city had been looted with many severely damaged. They had plans to repair eleven important buildings by 15 June. Continued Coalition military security was required to protect the buildings that were operating and those that would be renovated.

Gary Vogler, interim senior advisor for the Oil Ministry, General Crear with TF RIO, and General Christianson, the military command logistics officer, addressed the fuel situation in Iraq. Prior to the invasion, the Coalition focus was to get the oil exports moving to produce revenue for Iraq. By mid-May, their attention was on the domestic consumption of fuel. The daily demand in Iraq was 15 million liters of gasoline and 5,000 metric tons of natural gas. But Iraq could refine less than a third of its requirements of gasoline and less than 9 percent of its requirements for natural gas, despite the country's enormous reserves of both. Imports from other Gulf states brought supply up to half the demand for gasoline and 17 percent for natural gas, funded by the Coalition through a KBR contract—a cost unanticipated prior to invasion.[104]

The object was to increase fuel extraction and refining in Iraq to meet the demands of the country, then to expand further to provide national revenue through exports. Fuel imports were available from Turkey, Kuwait, and Jordan but at significant cost.[105] Existing refineries and distribution systems required security. In the short term, security would have to be provided by Coalition military forces. Funding was required to recruit and train an Iraqi security force that would be designated the Oil Police.

Robin Raphel, senior advisor for the Ministry of Trade, and Colonel Marty Stanton, McKiernan's senior staff officer for Civil Affairs, addressed purchasing crops in Iraq and food distribution. On the former, they indicated that the World Food Program would provide $150 million for the harvested crops, taking over for the UN Oil for Food program, soon to be discontinued. Payments would have to be made in cash throughout the agricultural areas, and Raphel and Stanton had a plan to move the cash through the Iraqi banking system for distribution, supported by military security.[106]

Raphel and Stanton requested authority to spend the money the UN had collected through the Oil for Food program to purchase crops harvested in Iraq. They needed storage facilities and security to protect it, with funding and equipment to set up a security training program. Most of the grain harvest came from northern Iraq; the greater consumption was in the south. Distribution required extensive transportation, storage, and security. For immediate requirements, the World Food Program would help set up a "food basket" issue as storage sites were developed. Government contracts were moving along and Raphel and Stanton planned to schedule distribution through the provincial government systems.

For regional and local government structures, Chris Milligan represented

Garner and General Kern represented McKiernan. They presented a plan to install town councils using the Civil Affairs GSTs, augmented with the USAID-contracted Local Governance Teams (LGTs). The latter had been slow to mobilize in Iraq, meaning that the GSTs would have to carry most of the burden through the summer. So far, they had set up seventeen of the twenty-six projected interim town councils for cities with populations in excess of 100,000 each.[107]

The Coalition had deployed GSTs in fifteen of the eighteen provinces in Iraq (they were not needed in the three Kurdish provinces) and had established a reporting system through military channels back to Baghdad. In the process they were establishing a screening and database system that was projected would be working by 15 June. The challenge was to monitor and manage the councils as they were established with the involvement of local military commanders, necessary to identify and vet appropriate Iraqi leaders and help chair the initial meetings.

Steve Browning, the interim senior advisor for the Ministry of Health, and Lieutenant Colonel Stafford, representing the military command, opened with a slide entitled "Meeting Pressing Public Health Issues." At the top of their list of objectives was continued prevention of cholera, dysentery, and epidemic disease in the face of the water, sewage, and solid waste problems throughout the country. They were working on the payment of salaries to ensure the continued employment of those in the health professions and on the protection, maintenance, and development of health facilities throughout Iraq with the medical supplies to sustain it. They had made contact with appropriate international organizations, notably the World Health Organization and the UN Children's Emergency Fund, which could assist their endeavors with assets and, it was hoped, personnel. Those efforts would require funding, security, and time.[108]

Browning and Stafford planned to establish an International Aid Committee by 21 May and to have salary payments underway, a medical waste disposal system established, and vaccinations nationwide in motion by 15 June. Continued medical assessments of the systems were required to monitor diseases. They also needed assistance for the movement, storage, and security of medical supplies, as well as access to radio and TV broadcasts to keep the public informed on health issues.

Tying up the issue of getting the ministries up and running, Robin Raphel, in her role as coordinator for the ministry advisors, and General Kern, as the Civil Affairs commander for the Coalition, emphasized limited progress in four key areas: security, communications, buildings and facilities, and the payment of salaries to civil servants. It was essential to make further progress in those areas. Only eight of twenty-four ministries had sufficient protection of their facilities, and all the senior advisors were trying to refine their security requirements. The dominant requirement was a guard force independent of police and military forces in Iraq to provide protection for their facilities; and a guard force that had to be recruited, trained, and equipped, which required funding. Many of the ministries had substantial transportation requirements and their vehicle fleets needed upgrading and better maintenance systems.[109]

Raphel and Kern made it clear that the ministries could not resume their full functional roles until there was a nationwide communications system. The ORHA communications system would soon provide adequate support for the ministry advisors to communicate among themselves, they reported, but it could offer no assistance to the Iraqis in government employment or to the population at large. What was necessary was distribution of cell phones throughout Iraq by the beginning of June to connect the local, regional, and national government institutions. The slides Raphel and Kern presented included payments of salaries and funding requirements for the ministries.

Security had been a consistent theme throughout the meeting, but it warranted a separate presentation for which Garner did not provide a representative, given that he had no capacity to implement a security program. General Webster made the presentation alone. He stated that the Iraqi military forces had been defeated by the Coalition and that the environment in twelve of the eighteen provinces was generally permissive. Police were being hired and trained throughout the country by military formations; a policy was in force to keep weapons off the street; joint Coalition-Iraqi patrols were being conducted; key sites were being secured throughout the country; and there was planning for additional security forces. He wanted Iraqis to play a larger role in security, which would require money, assistance, and time.[110]

ORHA had been studying and working on all these tasks since April; Garner wanted further progress before his departure. He felt such progress was crucial for Bremer, although Bremer displayed little interest in the momentum Garner was trying to generate. Rather than attend the meetings Garner set up, Bremer arranged his own meetings with many of the same personnel, duplicating much of Garner's efforts rather than complementing them.

The ministry senior advisors had common challenges (security, funding, looting, and vetting Iraqis), and they had challenges unique to their respective ministries. Many had interrelated issues that had to be coordinated. Despite ORHA communications problems, within the palace it was possible to walk down the hall and find a counterpart for another ministry to initiate such coordination. It was more difficult for the Iraqis to do that in Baghdad with ministries spread all over the city, and harder still to monitor ministry activities in the provinces, cities, and towns throughout Iraq.

In Kuwait, Bob Polk had proposed a fusion cell to crosswalk issues within ORHA. Such fusion cells were needed on a larger level for the management of the Iraqi ministries and other functions of government. David Nummy, Van Jorstad, and George Mullinax of the Finance and Central Banking ministries often worked on economic issues with Robin Raphel and Sue Hamrock of the Ministry of Trade. They put together working groups to tackle issues that would put the Iraqi government and economy back into operation, when possible with a free-market architecture; for the American advisors this was a transition more attractive in the summer of 2003 than it would be later.

General Hawkins helped put together a reconstruction working group to integrate the efforts of USAID, the Army Corps of Engineers, and the ministry advisors for the Electricity Commission (with the status of a ministry) and the Ministries of Irrigation, Housing and Construction, Transportation and Communications, and Industry and Materials. Most of those ministries were originally controlled by the Reconstruction pillar under Lew Lucke, who had restrained participation from the Corps of Engineers. Under Robin Raphel as ministry coordinator, there was room for Hawkins to weigh in to assist with coordination, an important progression.

Dan Hitchings from the Corps of Engineers had been designated the ministry advisor for the Ministry of Housing and Construction, but until he arrived (in May), Lieutenant Colonel Joe Morgan, chief of the public works section with the 352nd Civil Affairs Command, was the acting ministry advisor in April. In Kuwait Morgan had worked with engineers in JTF-4, then later in JTF Fajr, USAID, and with the Forward Engineer Support Teams (FEST). In mid-April, Morgan worked on infrastructure in Basra and Nasiriyah. Throughout Iraq, he met Iraqi engineers, impressed at "how smart and capable they were. . . . This was not Africa, nor even Kuwait where the Arabs were not technically competent."[111]

When Morgan moved to Baghdad with General Kern later that month, he set up his Public Works Section a few blocks from the palace. When the Civil Affairs Command began to provide officers to assist Garner's team with ministry advisors, Morgan joined ORHA to work for the Ministry of Housing and Construction. He found the ministry buildings in the capital looted and vandalized. But he found ministry personnel and had them draw up an organizational diagram of the ministry structure, objectives, and personnel strength. Morgan determined that the ministry undertook three areas of construction: bridges, roads, and mosques; residential and public buildings;

and maintenance of civil airports and seaports. The Iraqis told Morgan there were 6,300 personnel in the ministry and it controlled twelve state-owned enterprises (SOEs) in construction with another 8,000 personnel. Half the ministry's work was public housing, noteworthy in a country with a housing shortage and with military commanders requesting momentum to accommodate the homeless population.[112]

With his ministry building looted and out of operation, Morgan found office space in one of the ministry's SOEs in Baghdad that was not extensively looted to use as the ministry headquarters. When the Coalition de-Ba'athification order came out, he had to fire 140 personnel in senior leadership positions. Reluctantly Morgan accepted the order, finding that while firing so many people at one time was unfortunate, it did not greatly degrade the work of his ministry; it also allowed him to remove some deadwood and move others around. The Iraqis that remained in the ministry accepted de-Ba'athification with more grace than anticipated, perhaps because they were professional engineers rather than politicians. He was surprised when they put up a sign that read "No More Ba'athists in the Ministry of Housing and Construction."

Morgan was concerned with the lack of security for the property and construction materials the ministry owned or controlled. Coalition forces had divided Iraq into spheres of responsibility and had occupied many installations belonging to ministries. Morgan accepted such occupation of his ministry installations and worked through it with the respective military commanders; in time he recovered what he needed or found a means to share it. But he felt the coordination between those working for Garner (later with Bremer) and the military commanders involved in reconstruction projects was poor.[113]

The Ministry of Industry and Minerals had several SOEs, including two dozen large cement plants, almost two per province. Production of cement was a mundane endeavor, but illustrative of how the projects and ambitions of one ministry could affect another. Most of the cement plants had been looted and vandalized during and after the invasion. Putting them back into operation required equipment, expertise, and funding. Iraq produced high-quality cement and construction projects there relied more heavily on cement than some Western countries, which used more wood, glass, and metal in general construction, particularly in housing. In Iraq, there was little wood for construction and virtually every building, large or small, public or private, was constructed of concrete and masonry.

Cement produced in Iraq could generate domestic economic activity and construction, and, if produced in sufficient quantity, it could be exported to bring in external revenue. Each cement plant could employ 800–1,000 workers; in aggregate numbers, those employed in cement production in Iraq were comparable to those employed in the oil industry. Like the oil industry, cement production would provide other means of employment through its requirements for storage, transportation, and marketing. Cement would be a stable for the Ministry of Housing and Construction. With large and extended families typically living together in Iraq, for every 1,000 men employed in a cement plant, perhaps 8,000 people would be sustained through their incomes.

Early estimates indicated that many cement plants could be put back into operations for a few million dollars per plant. More critical was the electricity required to support cement production. It took thirty-two to forty constant megawatts to operate a cement plant. For two dozen cement plants, the requirement would be about a thousand constant megawatts.

General Hawkins estimated that the total electricity projection in Iraq after the invasion was just over 3,000 megawatts. His object was to increase it to 4,000 megawatts by mid-summer. For those unaccustomed to using megawatts as a standard of measurement, one engineer explained that a single constant megawatt would provide the electricity for about 1,000 Iraqi homes. If each domicile housed an average of eight people in a country where extended families frequently lived together, a single constant megawatt could provide the domestic needs of about 8,000 people. With a population of 25 million, Iraq required just over 3,000 megawatts alone just to sustain family homes. Electricity to sustain schools, hospitals, and municipal buildings and utilities could easily double the requirement. Sustaining domestic industries and factories in Iraq could double it again.

But if a cement plant required thirty-two to forty constant megawatts to employ 1,000 people and by extension to sustain 8,000 people, it would also displace the domestic home requirements for almost a quarter of a million Iraqis. The costs of producing cement to provide employment, produce revenue, and sustain the building industry would thus be at cross-purposes with providing electricity for Iraqi homes and civil infrastructure. As General Hawkins and TF Fajr worked to increase electricity in Iraq, they would also become involved with contentious issues involving how to distribute the electricity.

In early May, Gene Stakhiv, senior advisor for the Ministry of Irrigation (subsequently renamed the Ministry of Water Resources), was trying to increase electricity production with the hydro-electric power managed by his ministry. That meant a constant movement of water from the large reservoirs into the Tigris and Euphrates river systems. The more water he moved, the more electricity he could generate, but often that would not be the best management of water for irrigation purposes and beyond. Iraqi agriculture relied heavily on its irrigation system. Surging the flow of water to produce electricity could push so much water downstream that the irrigation system would be unable to absorb it, allowing it to flow unused into the Persian Gulf. Fortunately, 2003 was a good year for water flowing into the Tigris and Euphrates from Turkey, Syria, and Iraq, which allowed Stakhiv some latitude. But he worried about the out-years, when there might be less water. When that occurred, an increased reliance on hydro-electrical power might come at the expense of irrigation projects.[114]

The no-nonsense Stakhiv was soon drawn into a major social engineering issue involving the Marsh Arabs, a unique cultural group. This Shiite ethnic group had subsisted for thousands of years in large marsh areas created by the Tigris and Euphrates rivers systems in southern Iraq. But during recent decades, the marshes had been drained and the Marsh Arabs had been forced to move to urban areas where they joined society at the lowest economic level. With little study, many members of the Coalition were determined to reverse the draining of southern marshes to allow the Marsh Arabs to return to their original environment, to recover a lifestyle they were thought to prefer.

Stakhiv studied the water systems in Iraq and found that draining the marshes did not start with Saddam Hussein, nor was it abusive by design. Reclamation of the marshes began in the 1950s with British engineers who "followed the same conventional thinking of that time that we had in the United States, [to] drain the marshes because they're swamps causing malaria, and a threat to public health, and . . . reclaim the land to encourage agriculture. That was perfectly sound thinking at that time, and we did it in the Everglades." Yet the weight of Coalition opinion and of a few Iraqis—some of it informed, some not—was to reflood the marshes. Jeremy Mawdsley, a British army captain working with ORHA-South and interested in the Marsh Arabs, noted that when the marshes were flooded, water buffalos had thrived there. A byproduct from water buffalo milk was yogurt, a staple for the Marsh Arabs. Thus when the marshes were drained, the water buffalo yogurt market dried up with the marshes.[115]

Mawdsley also found there were those who did not want to reflood the marshes, primarily NGOs who argued that the Marsh Arabs were adjusting in the urban areas and were better off there even if they had to start at the bottom of the socioeconomic ladder. In the marshes, their plight was that of the "noble savage," but that was a hard life with few social benefits in terms of education and health services. After the marshes were drained, the land was used to grow wheat and other grains and for grazing, with the water buffalo replaced by cattle. If those were dairy cattle, their milk might be used to produce yogurt that would be as desirable to most people as yogurt produced by water buffalo.[116]

Stakhiv and his ministry had to consider many variables with the use of water in Iraq, and they urged caution when some in the Coalition simply wanted to produce the maximum amount of electricity or reflood the marshes without considering the consequences for other domains, economic and social. With adequate water in 2003, the challenges would not be difficult, but with the dams Turkey and Syria had built on the Tigris and Euphrates, there would be drier years in the future. Stakhiv's object was to make the alternative costs known for those with the political power to make the decisions regarding Iraq's water resources.[117]

When Bernie Kerik arrived in Iraq the second week of May and assumed the role of senior advisor for the Ministry of Interior, Raoul Stanley approached him and explained that the Ministry of Interior had the Department of Technical Services under its control. Stanley explained that Technical Services included water purification, sewage, sanitation, garbage removal, and road maintenance. It had been part of another ministry before being moved to Interior. Stanley proposed splitting it off as a separate ministry. Interested only in the police aspect of the Ministry of Interior with its many law-and-order challenges, Kerik was supportive and by mid-May Bremer approved standing up a new Ministry of Public Works, the first of several new ministries created by the Coalition.[118]

When the de-Ba'athification order came out, Stanley found it did not greatly affect his new ministry. In fact, it was useful in some ways as Stanley wanted to reduce the number of directorates from thirteen to five. De-Ba'athification allowed him to remove or shift personnel around, as Colonel Morgan had done with the Ministry of Housing and Construction. Most of the Iraqis Stanley inherited were engineers, and most were junior enough in rank that the order didn't apply to them; as a result, there was only one waiver that Stanley requested, one of the few approved by Bremer in May.

Stanley began with one assistant, Major Pete Veale, the Air Force engineer who helped move ORHA into the Republican Palace and fix its plumbing and electrical systems. In the process, Veale learned how such infrastructure worked in Iraq. Together, Stanley and Veale vetted 850 Iraqis for their new ministry, but looting and vandalism of its assets included the theft of 250 new utility vans. Lacking equipment, Stanley and Veale had to stand aside as Don Eberly, working with military formations in Baghdad, took charge of garbage removal in Baghdad. Their lack of equipment meant that Coalition engineers or contractors had to undertake road maintenance.

Fixing water and sewage systems was an immediate concern to prevent disease. In early May, Stanley made a trip to northern Iraq to study the Tigris River, where it crossed the border from Turkey. He found the water there remarkably pure. He knew that the pollution caused in Iraq was due to raw sewage dumped into the rivers, with only 7 percent of Iraq serviced by sewage systems. In Mosul, the first Iraqi city the Tigris passed, there was no central sewage system at all. There were septic systems in many areas of Iraq, but their overuse polluted the rivers indirectly.

Without adequate sewage disposal, water purification plants were essential to clean the water. There were 256 such plants in Iraq; many had been looted and vandalized and were out of operation. Not unlike cement plants, it would take parts, technical talent, and money to put sewage systems back into operation. And as with cement production, water treatment absorbed a great deal of electricity, which led Stanley to join the group General Hawkins convened to determine electrical and reconstruction priorities in Iraq.[119]

Tony Puckett had a secondary role after his position as deputy for Robin Raphel and ministry coordination; he was the senior advisor for Iraq's Atomic Energy Commission. As an artilleryman, Puckett had worked in a nuclear weapons program earlier in his career. With Mike Ayoub, he made several trips to the Tuwaithe Nuclear plant outside of Baghdad, where the commission had offices and laboratories. They wanted to determine if the program had been active prior to the invasion. They found nuclear material at the plant, known as yellow cake, but they found no nuclear threat or indication of activity to construct nuclear weapons.

On one visit Puckett found a threat directed at him. Walking into a building with poor lighting, he surprised a looter, who pulled a bayonet on him. Puckett wrestled the man to the ground and took the knife away. He said it happened so fast he forgot he was armed with a pistol.[120]

Puckett was also responsible for integrating Iraqi expatriates who came to Baghdad individually or through the IRDC. That included rating their performance. While some of them were hard working, others were self-serving or had disruptive political agendas. Complaints from the senior advisors went to Puckett, who imposed discipline or sent miscreants home. He wrote evaluation reports on each one. When he left Iraq in late June, he went to the Pentagon to process out of ORHA. As he completed his paperwork, he was told there was a directive for him to report to Doug Feith, though Puckett could not imagine why Feith would want to see him. In the brief office call, Feith asked if Puckett had written negative reports on the Iraqi expatriates. When Puckett said that he had, it set Feith off on a tirade. Puckett realized he was "having his ass chewed." He had never met Feith before. Puckett offered no response and left quietly. He returned to Fort Sill where he had been assigned before going to Iraq, packed up his family, and moved them to Washington before he began attending the National War College. The following year he was selected for command. Feith's dissatisfaction with Puckett did not affect his career.[121]

During the last week of May, Bremer rarely consulted Garner. He was conscious of the negative media coverage he had received and it hurt. Several articles indicated he spent all his time in the Green Zone where it was safe. Garner had been all over Iraq using an unarmored SUV (in contrast to Bremer's armored SUV), accompanied by only a few bodyguards. Throughout April and May he toured dangerous areas in Baghdad to stay informed. Captain Nate Jones wanted better news coverage and lined up reporters to travel with Garner. The journalists liked him, but their positive coverage came too late to alter his image after the negative coverage ORHA had received in April and early May.

On 26 May those from the original ORHA group gave Garner a farewell party by the swimming pool behind the palace. The pool would not be opened for use for another month, but it was a pleasant setting. Over a hundred people attended. When Garner arrived, everyone cheered and maneuvered to have their picture taken with him. Bremer came out briefly with McManaway, Ryan Crocker, and Pat Kennedy. Garner and Bremer tried to be gracious, but it was the last time they spoke in person.[122]

The next day Garner took a small group for an overnight trip to al-Hilla to see Buck Walters at ORHA-South Central. Walters had fixed up the hotel and had a KBR dining facility that was smaller than the one in the palace, but it had ice cream, which was not yet available in Baghdad. Walters told Garner there was a great deal of tension in his region. In the heavily Shiite area there was little evidence of Ba'athists, but that absence had left a void. Mike Gfoeller, Walters's political advisor, saw evidence of Iranian influence flowing into the country, despite the fact that most of the people he talked to did not want an Iranian-style system. What they wanted wasn't clear either. They thought they wanted democracy; they were not sure just what it was. Garner listened, but there was little he could do.[123]

Garner returned to Baghdad on 29 May, and then with the same group he left for Erbil to visit Bruce Moore and Dick Naab at ORHA-North. Nate Jones sent Malcolm McPherson of *Newsweek* along. They drove to Tikrit for a brief stop to see Major General Ray Odierno, commanding the 4th Mechanized Infantry Division. That evening in Erbil, Moore and Naab held a dinner for Garner with many Kurdish leaders. After dinner, Moore took Garner and a few others upstairs for a drink. Moore, a colorful character, was in rare form with many entertaining stories. There was little mention of Bremer, and Garner had a good time.[124]

The following morning, Garner attended a meeting with Moore and Naab, comparable in format to the one he had attended earlier with Buck Walters. Garner told them about the transitions in Baghdad. After the meeting Garner took his group to visit Barzani at his retreat at the nexus of the Turkish, Iranian, and Iraqi border. It was a long drive over difficult roads. Barzani's home was modest, with a magnificent setting overlooking an extraordinary gorge. In contrast to the drab colors throughout the Arab areas in Iraq, the vegetation in the northeast Kurdish region was in full bloom with the temperature remarkably cool for early June. Barzani and his male family members wore the colorful tribal dress. There were no women present in contrast to the social events hosted by Talabani. The food was comparable—a traditional Kurdish banquet. The normally austere Barzani was more talkative than normal and told Garner the Kurds considered him a hero and that they were disappointed he was leaving Iraq.[125]

On the return trip to Baghdad the Arab areas were surreal. Garner's convoy passed several abandoned military vehicles in flames. The local population did not wave as in the Kurdish provinces and there was an air of discontent and danger. Back in the capital, Tim Cross had invited Garner to a dinner at the new British embassy. Cross and Garner had worked well together and they had become friends. Garner was disappointed in his relationship with Bremer, and Cross felt the same about Ambassador Sawers. Garner and Cross were both lame ducks, ready to leave.

Garner left Baghdad on 1 June. With four SUVs, his South African bodyguards, and no military escort, his group included Colonel Kim Olson, Colonel Mike Murphy, and two others from Murphy's legal section. The weather was hot but otherwise pleasant. The convoy stopped at Hilla, where Garner had lunch with Buck Walters and Mike Gfoeller.[126]

Walters was loyal to Garner and sanguine about Bremer's arrival. When they left for Kuwait, Olson rode in the lead vehicle, while Murphy and his legal team rode in the rear vehicle. Garner rode alone in the back seat of one of the middle vehicles with two bodyguards in the front seat. The normally vibrant and charismatic Garner was subdued and reflective. For anyone watching him drive away, it was a moving experience.[127]

They arrived in Kuwait that evening and checked into the Hilton. The next day Colonel Olson and the bodyguards returned to Baghdad. Ron Adams, who flew down from Baghdad, joined Garner for a late plane back to the United States with a layover in Dubai and Paris. When they arrived at Dulles

Airport, Garner and his party went their separate ways. Murphy returned to the White House. Ron Adams returned to Carlisle.

Garner went from the airport to an apartment he maintained in Crystal City. Later he recalled, "I was embarrassed to see my friends. I was embarrassed to go home to my family. I was embarrassed over all the negative press that I had been relieved. . . . It was the worst period of my life." A few days later Garner flew home to Florida. Larry Di Rita called from the Pentagon, but Garner did not take his calls.

A week later Di Rita called and Garner answered.

"The secretary has to see you," Di Rita said.

"He doesn't need to see me. Hell, he fired me."

"He didn't fire you. He didn't do that," Di Rita replied.

And so Garner went to see Rumsfeld, who pinned a medal on him and said, "You need to get your thoughts together because you've got to report to the President."

Stunned that the president would want a report, Garner decided to present his views first to Rumsfeld.

"We have made three mistakes in Iraq, but it's not too late to reverse them," he told Rumsfeld. The de-Ba'athification program was too severe and should be moderated. Disbanding the Iraqi army had been unnecessary: it put trained soldiers out of work, made them angry, and denied the Coalition a useful labor pool and a base to rebuild a new army. And the IIA that Garner had helped to package was essential to put an Iraqi face on a transitional government.

Those were not thoughts Rumsfeld wanted to hear. He told Garner that the train had left the station and there was no turning back.

Garner was deflated. He believed the changes imposed by Bremer represented the wrong track—one that would cause the Coalition to remain in Iraq at a greater cost than anyone in Washington imagined. But his views no longer mattered since Bremer was in charge.

Rumsfeld took Garner to the White House to see President Bush, who asked Garner to tell him some stories about Iraq. It was apparent to Garner that the president did not want an analysis on Iraq; he wanted entertainment.[128]

"I spent about an hour with the president," Garner later recalled. "It was really a nice meeting. I told him some stories about Iraq. He laughed and asked questions—and then I said, 'Mr. President, before I leave I've got to tell you that you've made an outstanding choice. I watched Jerry Bremer for three weeks. I'm impressed with him. He's one of the hardest working guys I've ever seen. He's bright, articulate, and will do you a tremendous job.'"

The president looked at Garner and said, "Hell, I didn't select him. Rummy selected him, just like he did you."

Garner was aghast. The call from Rumsfeld on 24 April was firmly etched in his mind: "I've got to tell you the president has selected Jerry Bremer as your replacement," Rumsfeld had told him. When Garner asked the secretary to delay Bremer's arrival, Rumsfeld had said, "I can't do that. That's not my call."

Sitting in the White House, Garner realized that if the president was being truthful, what Rumsfeld had told him in April "had been a lie."

Rumsfeld was sitting at Garner's side, but he said nothing in response to the president's comment. Nor did he look at Garner as they left. Garner later reflected, "From that day forward I still respected Rumsfeld, but I couldn't trust him. I never have trusted him since then."

Later that summer Rumsfeld invited Garner and his wife to a barbecue at his residence. While it was a social event, Iraq inevitably came up and Rumsfeld expressed interest in what Garner thought. On that occasion and several times afterward Garner sent him letters urging changes that could still be made, but Rumsfeld took no action on Garner's recommendations.

That summer, Malcolm McPherson of *Newsweek* contacted Garner to tell him he had written a very positive article about him but that his publisher had refused to print it. He said it was too late for such coverage of Garner.[129]

Jay Garner departed Iraq as profound transitions were taking place. The most obvious was the emergence of the Coalition Provisional Authority (CPA) from ORHA, which included major changes in personnel, structure, and policy, and left Jerry Bremer clearly in charge. Concurrently, General McKiernan's CFLCC was relieved by its subordinate V Corps, commanded by Lieutenant General Scott Wallace. General Wallace in turn was replaced by the newly promoted Lieutenant General Ricardo Sanchez. Those who replaced much of the V Corp staff, which had managed the invasion of Iraq, were new to the region. Bremer dissolved the seven-member Iraqi Interim Authority (IIA) that Garner had established and by mid-July replaced it with the twenty-five-member Iraqi Governing Council (IGC). These changes were abrupt, disruptive, and time consuming, involving significant personnel turbulence.

The most important transition was conceptual—the shift from the liberation to the occupation of Iraq, with consequences for which the Coalition was poorly prepared. Occupation brought the ire of many Iraqis who anticipated a greater role in reforming their country than the CPA would allow. The IGC formed by Bremer had less power than Garner had intended for the IIA. Rather than put Iraqis in charge of their country as soon as possible, Bremer marginalized Iraqi participation, taking control of the country himself to impose changes far grander than those previously envisioned. The Coalition forces that were to have been reduced to 30,000 by September would remain over 130,000 for several years, attempting to provide law and order in the absence of adequate Iraqi security forces. The Coalition was ill prepared for such stability operations and soon had on its hands an insurgency without a clear ideology or leadership structure.

Neither Bremer nor General Sanchez began with a clear strategy for Iraq, and what strategy they developed was poorly coordinated between them, despite the efforts of their planners. The Iraqi people believed they had been promised liberation, but when the Coalition delayed transfer of power and military forces were heavy-handed in response to violence, the elation that accompanied the removal of Saddam Hussein gave way to humiliation and discontent.

The Coalition's intention, often amateurish and self-righteous, to reform Iraq as a democracy was accompanied by an effort to impose a free-market system on a controlled economy. The American view was that democracy and a free market naturally went hand in hand, as freedom inspires entrepreneurship. There was little reflection that in the West, modern political and economic institutions had evolved over extended periods and were driven by insiders, not imposed by outsiders with a different cultural base.

During the previous year, much thought had been given to postwar Iraq, but without a refined methodology little of that thought could qualify as planning or preparation. What planning there was had been sporadic, uneven, and lacking in cohesion. The interagency process driven by policy makers in Washington did not translate into an integrated interagency operation in Iraq. In-fighting and egocentric personalities at several levels compounded the problem, dynamics that would continue to plague Bremer and his military counterparts as they had plagued Garner and his.

ORHA had gone through significant organization changes prior to Bremer's arrival and the emergence of CPA. Without the anticipated humanitarian crisis, George Ward dissolved his Humanitarian Assistance pillar and returned to the United States; his personnel moved to other positions or left with him. When Garner replaced Mike Mobbs with Robin Raphel, he gave her all the ministries to coordinate. The physical reconstruction tasks were greater than anticipated, and Lew Lucke, managing USAID in Iraq, would remain until mid-summer until he was replaced by Spike Stephenson, who would also have to contend and compete with the Army Corps of Engineers' greater capacity for contracting and reconstruction.

By early May, ORHA had established four regional components on the ground in Iraq that CPA would inherit and soon rename: ORHA-North in northern Iraq under Bruce Moore; ORHA-South Central in central Iraq under Buck Walters; ORHA-South in southern Iraq under Ambassador Ole Olsen; and Baghdad Central under Ted Morse (after Barbara Bodine was sent home). Moore left in early June, turning the northern region over to Dick Naab. Walters left a month later, succeeded by Mike Gfoeller. Olsen lasted through the summer, to be replaced by a UK official. By that time, all of Garner's original key leaders had left: Ward, Mobbs, Lucke, Bodine, Moore, and Walters, along with Ron Adams, Jerry Bates, Tim Cross, and Margaret Tutwiler. Of the most senior civilians to remain who had served under Garner, Robin Raphel and

Ted Morse would both leave before the end of the year. Many of the senior advisors for the Iraqi ministries would remain from ORHA to serve in CPA through the summer as others joined CPA (those noted with one asterisk in Table 5).

By mid-summer, Garner's original military C-staff was broken up and in most cases replaced by contractors from KBR, MPRI, Raytheon, and RAND. The ORHA C-1 Personnel section was renamed Human Resources and the ORHA C-4 Logistics section was split into KBR sections for supply, maintenance, accommodations, laundry, and messing. By June, KBR had over 1,200 employees working in Iraq and supporting CPA at all its locations, half of them in the palace. Colonel DeGraff sent his military personnel home individually in May and June. Colonel Costello literally packed up all his logistics personnel in mid-June, drove to Kuwait in a small SUV convoy with no military escort, and then flew home. Colonel Tom Baltazar's C-3 Operations staff was gradually replaced by contractors from MPRI, all retired military officers and NCOs, dressed in matching polo shirts with the company logo. Baltazar left for a week in June, then returned to work for another month in operations as a regional director for CPA elements setting up in Iraq. Baltazar left CPA in late August.[1]

Colonel John Frketic and the personnel in the C-2 Intelligence section were replaced by others with intelligence backgrounds. Colonel Gary Minor, the C-8 Comptroller, left in May due to a death in the family; his small military staff was soon replaced by civilian comptrollers from several government agencies. From the C-5 Plans staff, Colonel Tom Gross left in July and Colonel Paul Hughes left in August, replaced by a combination of contractors, several from RAND, and a few military officers who came for brief periods. Lieutenant Colonel Bob Polk and Dayton Maxwell volunteered to stay into the fall to assist with the transition.[2]

Most of the C-6 Communication staff stayed longer. Colonel Conway told his staff in early May that they would all be home in thirty days, replaced by Raytheon contractors. Conway himself left quietly in June; his officers and NCOs were surprised that he was the first to go. They were surprised again when Conway's replacement told them that their stay would be extended ninety days through the summer to complement Raytheon, given the importance of communications and the fact that Raytheon could not handle it alone. The C-6 staff was understandably resentful.[3]

Colonel Glen Collins, managing the palace grounds, put the Al-Rashid Hotel into operation in July, with several hundred rooms, two restaurants, a bar, and a disco. By the Fourth of July Collins had the swimming pool behind the palace available for swimming. For the rest of the summer, CPA personnel

Table 5. June 2003: CPA Senior and Interim Advisors for Iraqi Ministries

Ministry	Senior Advisor	Interim or Deputy Advisor
Ministry Coordinator	Robin Raphel: DOS	
Program Review Board	Sherri Kraham: DOD*	
Legal Coordinator	CPT Brad Clark: USAR*	
1. Oil	Phil Carroll: DOD	Deputy: Gary Vogler: DOD Contractor*
2. Defense	Walt Slocombe: DOD Contractor	
3. Interior	Bernard Kerik: DOD Contractor	
4. Information	Bob Reilly: DOD Contractor	
Director of Economic Policy	Peter McPherson: DOD Contractor	
5. Agriculture	Lee Schatz: USDA*	
6. Central Bank	George Mullinax: Treasury Contractor*	
7. Electricity Commission	Pete Gibson: USACE*	Tom Wheelock: USAID Contractor*
8. Finance	David Oliver: DOD Contractor	
9. Housing & Construction	Dan Hitchings: USACE	Deputy: LTC Joe Morgan: USAR*
10. Industry & Minerals	Tim Carney: DOS Contractor*	
11. Irrigation	Eugene Stakhiv: USACE*	
12. Planning	Simon Elvy: UK FCO*	
13. Public Works (new ministry)	Raoul Stanley: AUSAID*	
14. Trade	Robin Raphel: DOS*	
15. Transportation & Communication	Steve Browning: USACE*	

were seen around the pool day and night, a surreal sight in what was otherwise a nonpermissive environment.[4]

As CPA expanded, everyone living in the palace was moved out to make room for more office space. Many moved into the Al-Rashid, others into the trailer complex expanding behind the palace. The Al-Rashid was more popular, with its spacious rooms and various amenities. For some who had arrived in April, the Al-Rashid's bar, pools, and disco seemed decadent and inappropriate. Those who arrived afterward had little reservation about taking advantage of the comforts there, until the hotel was hit with a rocket in late August.

Table 5 (*continued*)

Ministry	Senior Advisor	Interim or Deputy Advisor
Director of Civil Affairs Policy	Robin Raphel, DOS*	
16. Education	Dorothy Mazaka: USAID*	
17. Higher Education/ Scientific Research	Drew Erdmann: DOS*	
18. Foreign Affairs	David Dunford: DOS Contractor	
19. Health	James K. Haveman***	Steve Browning: USACE*
20. Justice, including Prisons	Donald Campbell: USAR*	
21. Labor & Social Affairs	TBD: USAID**	Karen Walsh: USAID Contractor*
22. AWQAF/Religious Affairs	TBD: DOS**	Andy Morrison: DOS*
23. Youth	Don Eberly: SAIC Contractor*	
24. Culture	John Limbert: DOS*	
Governance	Scott Carpenter: DOS	Asst.: Meghan O'Sullivan, DOS* Asst.: Roman Martinez, DOD intern

NOTES. AWQAF = Ministry of Religious Affairs; TBD = to be determined; USDA = U.S. Department of Agriculture; USAID = U.S. Agency for International Development; USACE = U.S. Army Corps of Engineers; DOS = U.S. Department of State; DOJ = U.S. Department of Justice; DOD = Department of Defense; USAR = U.S. Army Reserve; UK FCO = UK Foreign and Commonwealth Office; AUSAID = Australian Agency for International Development.
*Arrived with ORHA/Garner.
**Not identified.
***Identified, but not in Iraq.

The departure of the military personnel from the original C-staff did not diminish the military presence in the palace. The security and communications personnel remained: the National Guard infantry company securing the exterior; the Military Police Company providing escorts downtown; and the army signal detachment supporting Raytheon with the residual C-6 staff. The Civil Affairs Command had over fifty officers attached to the CPA ministry advisor teams. During June, General Sanchez moved part of his CJTF-7 headquarters into the palace, although most of it remained at Camp Victory at the airport. Other soldiers were frequently in the palace for coordination or meetings.

On 15 June ORHA was formally redesignated as CPA. Many key people working directly for Bremer were new; almost all were civilians. Bremer rearranged the functional components with a flat structure (see Figure 8). There were seven directors under his immediate control, with the ministry advisor staffs split among four of them (under Garner they had been split between two, then consolidated under Raphel). Under the new organization, there was a Director of Civil Affairs Policy controlling ten ministries and the Governance Team;[5] a Director of Economic Policy controlling eleven ministries;[6] and the Director of Oil controlling one. A Director of Security Affairs initially had two: the Ministry of Defense and the emerging new army; and the Ministry of Interior with the police. The Ministry of Defense was deactivated for a period, and the Director of Security and his staff functioned as that ministry rather than advising it. The senior advisor staff for the Ministry of Interior was initially under the Director of Security, and then for a period was a stand-alone advisor working directly for Bremer.

Garner's Reconstruction pillar was retained and renamed the Director for Aid, with Lew Lucke replaced by Spike Stephenson, also from USAID. A Director of Press and Public Affairs expanded from ORHA's small media element that had focused on the Western media rather than the Iraqi or regional media. The four regional components were renamed CPA South, CPA South-Central, CPA North, and CPA Baghdad Central under a Director for Regional Operations. The new structure would prove too flat for Bremer to control; it would be reorganized several times to include several levels of middle management, notwithstanding Bremer's disruptive tendency to bypass his immediate subordinates and work directly with someone several levels below.

Ambassadors Clay McManaway, Hume Horan, Pat Kennedy, and later Dick Jones were soon established as the senior members of Bremer's inner circle. In marked contrast to ORHA, many of those in Bremer's inner circle were young, some in their twenties. Several were government interns from departments in Washington; a few were just out of college or graduate school. In contrast, almost all of those close to Garner had been forty or older.

McManaway and Horan, much older than Bremer, could not match their boss's dynamism. Kennedy, in contrast, was full of energy and also had both the personality and sense of procedure and protocol to work effectively with the military officers. In fact, Kennedy was soon the favorite civilian of military officers in the palace, who were ill at ease with the often dismissive Bremer and McManaway and reluctant to deal with those they called the "Kindergarten Kids" of Bremer's inner circle.[7]

Arriving with Bremer were two key officials who would replace Nummy and his team, Peter McPherson and David Oliver. McPherson had broad credentials as an economist with prior government service as an assistant secretary in the Treasury Department and as administrator of USAID. He also had political connections within the Bush administration. He was designated

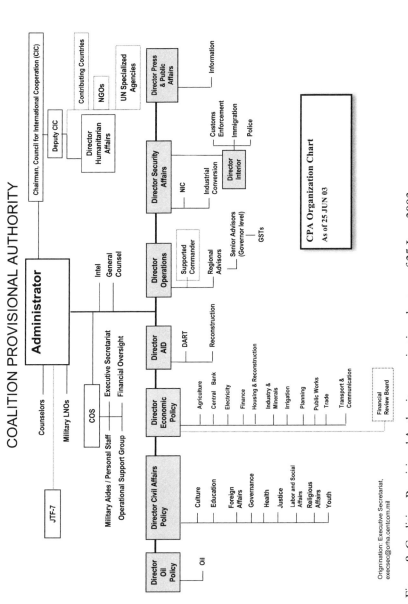

Figure 8. Coalition Provisional Authority organization chart, as of 25 June 2003.

Senior Economic Advisor for the Coalition, responsible for integrating economic policies in Iraq. Oliver was a retired admiral with political connections, designated as the Coalition's Director for Management and Budget. McPherson and Nummy had different financial philosophies regarding regime change. Nummy believed the principal object should be to jumpstart the economy, then to consider changing its structure after stability is achieved. With grander ambitions, McPherson and Oliver wanted to make structural changes right away. In particular, they wanted to disband the State-Owned Enterprises (SOEs) and proposed that 108,000 Iraqi SOE employees be fired or forcibly retired. Other Coalition members and many Iraqis were opposed to such moves, noting high unemployment and emerging violence in Iraq. McPherson and Oliver soon found it difficult to disband the SOEs as they had planned.[8]

Despite their management credentials, McPherson and Oliver were not grounded in nor guided by the nature of Iraqi culture and institutions. Like Bremer, they soon had their minds made up about what to fix in Iraq and how to fix it. They had few questions for those who had been there longer. Nummy and his team quietly left within a month while McPherson and Oliver built an economic cell that included few Iraqis, and none with substantial influence. Bremer and his economic managers assumed their authority to impose their will on Iraq was tantamount to having the capacity to impose changes, which was often at odds with what the Iraqis and their complex institutions could handle.

The important Governance cell was initially managed by Ambassador Ryan Crocker, with Scott Carpenter as his deputy. Crocker had more regional qualifications than anyone else joining Bremer. Like Hume Horan, he was an Arabic speaker with substantial time in the region, and he had served previously as ambassador to Syria, Kuwait, and Jordan. Unlike Horan, who was coming out of retirement, Crocker was one of the most senior diplomats serving in the State Department, with strong connections there and in the National Security Council. Crocker did not join Bremer's inner circle, nor was he in tune with the Bush administration policies for Iraq. In 2002, Wendy Chamberlin noted that he had taken positions against invading Iraq, but he did not sound his objections as loudly as others. The concerns and the quiet protests he had raised over the past year were frequently dismissed.[9] He left Iraq within two months, but he did not return to State, where he might have continued an important role on Iraq. Instead, he took a one-year sabbatical as a visiting professor at the National Defense University, inexplicable when his unique qualifications were so desperately needed for Iraq, either at State or on the NSC.

Scott Carpenter was a decade junior to Crocker without the latter's regional experience when he assumed the senior position for Governance. He was savvy, had political connections in the Bush administration, and worked well with Bremer. He arrived in Baghdad just prior to Bremer and claimed to be the first civilian to wear combat boots on a regular basis, a habit Bremer would assume. Carpenter had five critical tasks: implementing de-Ba'athification; standing up the twenty-five-member IGC; putting in motion a new constitution for Iraq; developing regional and local governments; and establishing a plan for elections in Iraq.

De-Ba'athification was assigned to Meghan O'Sullivan, whom Bremer had moved to Governance. Like Carpenter, O'Sullivan had no regional expertise, but she was willing to make the transition from Garner's team to Bremer's and remain in Iraq with CPA. Robin Raphel felt O'Sullivan's approach to de-Ba'athification was not malleable enough for those seeking to negotiate the process. Bremer reserved the authority to grant waivers for himself, and for the first few months he granted very few. Informally, Raphel told the ministry senior advisors they should use their discretion in removing Ba'athists, but Raphel felt she was being watched closely and had to be discreet. Most questions went to O'Sullivan, who would read them the letter of the CPA order. It was a tedious and unpopular task that O'Sullivan neither requested nor enjoyed. She said that before she arrived in Baghdad, she had never heard of the term "Firqah," the critical fourth rank and the most numerous group of Ba'athists removed from government positions.[10]

During the brief period when she worked for Raphel, who wanted a more lenient application of de-Ba'athification, O'Sullivan deferred in her direction. But once she began working for Carpenter, she interpreted according to the letter of the CPA order: senior Ba'athists "were all [to be] dismissed immediately on the basis of their party affiliation." The CPA order included removal of all those in the top three ranks of government even if they had been more junior Ba'athists.[11]

O'Sullivan also helped Carpenter inaugurate the IGC on 13 July. It had greater ethnic and religious diversity than the seven-member IIA that Garner had put together, with more Sunnis and three women, the latter a particular CPA objective. Garner had chosen those in the IIA for their leadership in opposition parties and political stature with Iraqis. The IGC included the seven members of the IIA, but many of those added were not political leaders. Nor did they have comparable clout or name recognition in Iraq. The expansion of Iraqi leadership in the IGC tended to weaken the impact of the group, despite the diversity.

The Governance Team also tried to assemble a committee of Iraqis to draft a new constitution and set up a legal basis to ratify it. There was a consensus between Bremer and those close to him that a ratified constitution should precede national elections, while Coalition members from other countries (rarely consulted) were skeptical that sequence would work. In early July, Grand Ayatollah Ali al-Sistani issued a *fatwa* (decree) "insisting that the constitution must be written by Iraqis and that the constitutional conference must be elected, not appointed by the Coalition." Bremer, Carpenter, and O'Sullivan always intended that the constitution would be written by Iraqis; the problem imposed by al-Sistani's *fatwa* was finding a basis to elect those who would write it.[12]

Don Campbell, the Army Reserve major general and New Jersey judge serving as senior advisor for the Ministry of Justice, thought otherwise: "There are people here on the Governance Team who are salivating at the thought of writing the Constitution." In particular, he referred to Noah Feldman, a professor of constitutional law at New York University who had been part of the group Scott Carpenter put together in Washington. Feldman, a Rhodes Scholar fluent in Arabic, had written extensively about constitutional issues in the Middle East.[13]

Carpenter felt that Feldman had "allowed himself to be labeled as the person who was writing Iraq's constitution." When al-Sistani forced a delay on the constitution, Feldman joined Campbell to work with the Ministry of Justice, where his legal skills could be put to use. But what Feldman really wanted was to work on the constitution, and so he returned to New York a month later. Feldman later wrote countless articles about Iraq for the *New York Times Magazine*, often describing himself as a senior advisor with CPA; it was Campbell, however, who held that position with the Ministry of Justice, not Feldman.[14]

A dozen people arrived with Carpenter as the original Governance Team. They were also ambitious: when they realized there were more senior positions available within CPA, many left Carpenter for better jobs. For his part, Carpenter was not an empire builder and did not object to the defections. As a result, the Governance Team remained small with junior players. Ryan Crocker was fifty-three with extraordinary regional expertise; Carpenter was ten years younger; O'Sullivan was thirty-two; and Roman Martinez was twenty-four. Martinez had just completed a master's degree at Cambridge University and was serving as an intern under Abe Shulsky in OSD when he volunteered to go to Iraq. He joined the Governance Team and took on the CPA project for the Iraqi constitution, a task that might have gone to someone more senior.[15] Carpenter, O'Sullivan, and Martinez would work within Bremer's inner circle for the next year, despite their lack of regional expertise, a deficiency that was not lost on the senior Iraqis with whom they would work. At one meeting, senior Iraqis approached the CPA interpreter, Haig Melkessetian, and, referring to O'Sullivan, asked, "What is she doing here?"[16]

With attention on de-Ba'athification, standing up the IGC, and putting an Iraqi constitutional process in motion, Carpenter had less time for regional and local governance. When he learned in May that Major General David Petraeus had run a caucus-type election in Mosul, Carpenter was determined not to allow other military formations to do the same. When the Marines tried to hold elections in Najaf, Carpenter went to see the Marine commander, Lieutenant General James Conway.

"You can't have elections in Najaf," Carpenter told him.[17]

Surprised, General Conway asked, "What do you mean—we can't?"

"If you have elections in Najaf," Carpenter explained, "they're going to want to have elections in Karbala, and Hilla. What political parties are registering? What about the influence of Iran in Najaf and Karbala? How [would we] identify who's going to vote? There's no voter registration."

Carpenter felt that the military commanders "hadn't thought through anything." He asked General Conway who was in charge of Najaf at the time. Conway told him it was the U.S. Marine Command.

"Who is going to be in charge of Najaf after a legitimate election in Najaf?" asked Carpenter. "Now everybody understands who's in charge, but once you [hold elections], then no one's going to understand who's in charge."[18]

For Carpenter, the Coalition had to occupy Iraq as a course for democracy was charted. Liberation would come in time, but on CPA terms—not on Iraqi terms.

On 3 June, Walt Slocombe briefed Secretary Rumsfeld in the Pentagon on his concept to disband the Iraqi army and to begin building a new and much smaller army. He would not return to Baghdad for another week to explain that plan to those who had been working with a different concept. When Mike Ayoub and Lieutenant Colonel Jim Torgler told Slocombe and Colonel Gardner what they had developed with senior Iraqi officers, they were told to cease such efforts and were directed to more mundane administrative tasks. When Colonel Kevin Benson laid out the military options for the Iraqi army that his planners had developed, Slocombe was indifferent and noncommittal.

On 13 June, Bremer asked Colonel John Agoglia to attend a meeting with him and Walt Slocombe in his office in the palace. Agoglia was serving as the liaison officer from Central Command to Bremer and CPA; Slocombe had just returned to Baghdad. The subject was the regular Iraqi army.

As the meeting began, Slocombe explained to Agoglia, "Look, we are going to recall the Iraqi army, but not the way it's currently planned."[19]

"Excuse me?" Agoglia was surprised and agitated.

"We're going to recall the Iraqi army," Slocombe continued. "But we're only going to recall three divisions . . . over two years, not over ninety days." He explained that this meant they would recruit new soldiers to fill those three divisions over two years, which could include those who had served previously if there were no problems with them.

Agoglia responded with rising agitation. "Excuse me, sir? Does General Franks know about this?"

"It doesn't matter," Slocombe said.

"What the hell do you mean it doesn't matter?" Agoglia demanded.

"Just what I said, John, it doesn't matter. The Secretary of Defense has already made the decision."

"Well, that's bullshit, sir," Agoglia continued. "Has anybody talked to General Franks about this, or to General Abizaid?"

"John, I told you it doesn't matter."

"I told you, that's bullshit!" exclaimed Agoglia, feeling betrayed.

Bremer had had enough. "John, you need to step outside and cool down."

"Yes, I do sir. I need to call General Abizaid," Agoglia said as he stormed out.

When he called for Abizaid, Colonel H. R. McMaster, Abizaid's executive assistant, answered. Agoglia told him what Slocombe had said and asked him to pass it on to Abizaid as soon as possible. When he was told, Abizaid was surprised and livid.[20]

Slocombe had expressed doubts all along to Agoglia and others about reconstituting the regular Iraqi army. And all along, Agoglia had explained that bringing the regular army back was part of the military and interagency plan. He knew Slocombe had doubts and he had tried to counter them. Agoglia wanted to make it clear that the psychological operations, before and during the invasion, were designed to convince the regular Iraqi army not to fight, with the implication that the Coalition would take care of them. Garner had asked that the army be reconstituted right after that invasion to keep idle soldiers from getting into trouble, and to create a labor force that could be used in reconstruction. General Abizaid wanted to immediately stand up three brigades each month over a number of months to form a constabulary force to assist with internal stability in Iraq. Doug Feith had briefed such concepts to the president and the Principals Committee on 12 March. They had all agreed to retain the Iraqi army.[21]

When Bremer informed the NSC in mid-May that the army was to be disbanded, many of the principals present were surprised and shocked. When Bremer added that senior military officials had been informed, the implication was that they did not object. But military commanders and key staff officers had objected on multiple occasions. To placate them, Slocombe told them that CPA Order Number 2 would disband the regular army, and then they would recall it. Abizaid was thinking in terms of bringing back several divisions within a few months, to be followed by several more; his intent was always to put an Iraqi face on regime change and he knew the regular army was a key component of Iraqi identity. He also knew that the Iraqi army would be required for internal security, something Slocombe had dismissed out of hand. Abizaid would soon be proved right and Slocombe wrong.[22]

Slocombe's concept to build only three divisions over two years would include only 40,000 soldiers. Many of those would be new recruits, not former soldiers. Only a small fraction of the 300,000 soldiers that had been in uniform a few months earlier would join Slocombe's new army. The greatest impact would be upon the regular officers and NCOs who had a career investment in the army. Slocombe believed that all officers over the rank of lieutenant colonel were senior Ba'athists. By June, Agoglia and others had determined that only half the Iraqi generals were Ba'athists and most of the colonels were not party members at all or of nominal party rank. Slocombe was not interested in what Agoglia had learned—his mind was made up.[23]

On 13 June, the day Slocombe informed Agoglia that the regular army would not be reconstituted, Major General Paul Eaton arrived in Baghdad to assume responsibility for the training of the new Iraqi army. Eaton had just completed a tour as the Commandant of the U.S. Army Infantry School at Fort Benning. Slocombe wanted a light infantry army for Iraq with no armor or artillery, in contrast to the heavy forces it had for several decades. Presumably three light divisions could secure Iraq's borders without threatening Iraq's neighbors. No provision was made for internal security.[24]

Eaton had strong credentials for training infantrymen, but he had never served in the Middle East and knew little about Arab armies or institutions. He had not been involved in the invasion of Iraq, nor the discussions to reconstitute the regular army. The only briefings he received before flying to Baghdad were in the Pentagon. Eaton arrived with no staff of his own and the staff he received would be severely undersized for a year. Nor was he provided an army Middle East FAO, who might have helped him gain an understanding of the nature of Arab armies in general and of Iraq's in particular. Eaton would learn with time but mainly on his own.[25]

Originally Garner and the military Coalition planned to bring back most of the 300,000 Iraqi soldiers to identify and disarm them, to provide severance pay to those who wished to leave the army, and to provide work for those who wanted to remain. They could be used for security and reconstruction. In the process they could be kept under observation, employed, and out of mischief. With the concept Slocombe put in motion, the vast majority of the Iraqi army of 2003 would never wear a uniform again, nor would they be disarmed. He was convinced most of the conscripts had been Shia who would not want to serve. But there were many Sunnis that had served in the army, and many of them were unemployed and angry. Some would take up arms against the Coalition.[26]

General Order Number 2 also disbanded the Ministry of Defense, so as Bremer's new Director for Security Affairs, Slocombe and his staff functionally became the Ministry of Defense with the mission to form a new army. The other critical component for Security Affairs was the Ministry of Interior, which included all the police in Iraq as well as responsibility for immigration and customs. Bernie Kerik had arrived in Baghdad earlier as the new senior advisor for Interior. Initially, Interior was not under Slocombe's control, but with a reorganization in June, it made sense to both Slocombe and Colonel Greg Gardner, his assistant, that the Director of Security Affairs should supervise the Ministry of Interior, hopefully with the assistance of paramilitary police from Italy or Spain.[27]

Kerik told Slocombe such paramilitary police forces would be inappropriate for Iraq. Kerik had no experience with such police systems and they did not interest him. Furthermore, he did not want Slocombe involved in his work and refused to work for him. When Slocombe gently tried to explain that the new structure placed the Ministry of Interior under his purview, Kerik told those above him that if he had to work for anyone other than Bremer, he would quit. McManaway later called Slocombe to tell him that Kerik would not come under Slocombe's control.[28]

Colonel Gardner knew there were not enough CPA personnel assigned to the ministry advisor team to work with Interior. He knew that Kerik had served in the Army as an enlisted soldier years earlier, but he had no understanding of how the military components of the Coalition worked. He told Kerik he had a contact in the Pentagon, Colonel Aleksandra Rohde—a military lawyer interested in coming to work in Iraq. Kerik told Colonel Gardner he would be happy to have her join him. She arrived in July and became his deputy. Unfortunately, Rohde did not get on with Kerik or adapt well to his methods, and she was not the only one. When Jay Garner left Iraq, his team of South African bodyguards stayed behind with a contract to protect Kerik. They had worked well for Garner and bonded with him. In contrast, they found working for Kerik difficult and quietly told others that Kerik was arrogant, self-serving, and out of touch with the Iraqis he was supposed to assist. Kerik left within a few months of his arrival, without making a substantive contribution in a role that greatly needed one.[29]

When Slocombe returned to Iraq in June, he was soon contacted by the senior military commander in northern Iraq. The 101st Air Assault Division, under Major General David Petraeus, had responsibility for that region, with large Arab and Kurdish populations. The latter areas were the least affected by the invasion and regime change, but there was instability in the northern Arab areas. Petraeus concentrated most of his division in those areas, particularly Mosul, the largest city in northern Iraq. There were about 100,000 former Iraqi soldiers in that region who had recently served in the regular army. Most were Sunni Arabs. Slocombe thought most of the Iraqi soldiers were Shia, which was not the case in the north.[30]

The critical problem was paying the soldiers. Immediately after the invasion, government institutions stopped operating and no salaries were paid. Garner had been insistent in the Pentagon, in Kuwait, and in Iraq that the Coalition would have to begin paying salaries to get government employees and soldiers working and under control. To jumpstart compensation, he had started emergency payments of $20 in early May, followed by salaries later that month. Despite Garner's efforts, money was not made available for soldiers in May, and it was questionable if it would be.

With Slocombe's absence from Iraq during the second half of May and early June, providing emergency payments and salaries for the regular army had gone unaddressed. As Petraeus began making payments to civilian employees in May, groups of soldiers began to ask when they would be paid. Petraeus sent requests to CPA for funding for the soldiers. He was told there were reservations about paying a defeated army. Petraeus explained that as a practical matter paying them would enhance the stability in his area.[31]

Petraeus passed the word to the soldiers that he was working on getting the payments and urged them to be patient. During the first week of June, unrest continued to build in Mosul. By the second week, soldiers were becoming more aggressive and the mayor asked Petraeus if his police could fire on them if they became violent. Petraeus told him to do what was necessary and reinforced his police with American forces. On 11 and 12 June, a group of soldiers staged a protest in the city. On the first day protesters threw stones and bricks, then shot two policemen. The next day someone threw a grenade and there was more gunfire. The Iraqi police and American soldiers returned fire. In all, two were killed and sixteen, including American soldiers, were wounded during the protests.

Petraeus complained to Baghdad, after which Slocombe sent word that CPA would pay stipends to the soldiers. Within a week Petraeus had payments in motion and calmed the situation. When Slocombe later visited Mosul, Petraeus confronted him and told him that his policies to disband the regular army and his reluctance to make the payments had needlessly led to American and Iraqi casualties. The soldiers of the Iraqi army, which Slocombe and Bremer had defined as nonexistent, did not want to be ignored.[32]

As the transition period in Iraq encountered greater turmoil than anticipated, those on the NSC staff began to express concern and confusion. In the late spring National Security Advisor Condoleezza Rice and her deputy, Stephen Hadley, instructed Frank Miller to reactivate the Executive Steering Group for Iraq. By that time Colonel Greenwood had departed to take command of a Marine Expeditionary Unit and his replacement had not yet arrived. Major Kojac was no longer a novice on the NSC staff and he helped fill the void left by Greenwood with frequent exposure to the senior members of the NSC. Kojac held Rice in high regard for her professionalism and capacity to avoid the petty conflicts he observed elsewhere in the administration, but "in May and in June she was very frustrated with the situation. . . . She just couldn't get past how jacked up it was and she was very frustrated. . . . I remember her getting kind of fussy. I mean she is a very cool personality . . . she's not very easily fazed at all . . . but you could see her face get a little flushed and get a little tight in the voice when she talked about the military and Secretary Rumsfeld."[33]

About the time Garner left Iraq, Kojac was conducting a briefing on Iraq in Rice's office with Andrew Card, the White House chief of staff, Hadley, and Miller. Card asked Kojac about the source of "all the violence and chaos. . . . Why are things completely out of control, and violent? . . . What's going on?"

Perhaps thinking of his first presentation to the NSC staff in early February about force ratios for stabilization in countries like Iraq, Kojac said, "Well, it's just like [General] Shinseki briefed to Congress . . . you need a significant footprint of security forces on the ground to guarantee security and without that you get chaos."

To the surprise of Kojac, "Hadley jumped me and said that's not what Shinseki said, that's not what he was talking about. . . . But I know that Card heard me. . . . It registered with Card because I'm looking at his eyeballs. . . . I know he heard me . . . he got it."[34]

Kojac could tell that Hadley did not agree with him. He did not want to acknowledge that Shinseki might have been correct with the projection of several hundred thousand soldiers necessary to stabilize Iraq, nor did he want to give up on Afghanistan as a useful model for which to measure stabilization forces for Iraq. He was not alone in the administration in this regard, but there were those such as Card who were beginning to express reservations about their prior assumptions on Iraq.[35]

MILITARY PLANNING

In June 2003, Major Wesley Odum, an army infantryman, deployed to Germany and then to Baghdad, becoming one of the key planners for the Coalition in Iraq. He would observe firsthand transitions at several levels and help write a military campaign plan for Iraq, an experience fraught with frustration and sporadic guidance. Odum had spent the two previous years at Fort Leavenworth. The first year he was a student in the Command and General Staff College when the 9/11 attacks occurred.[36] For his second year at Leavenworth, Odum attended the School of Advanced Military Studies (SAMS), which educated selected officers to become planners. With the run-up to the invasion, Odum participated as part of a SAMS study group on Iraq. By graduation in May, Odum had orders for Germany where he was designated to serve as a planner in the V Corps headquarters. On 16 June he arrived at the V Corps base in Heidelberg. He was soon joined by three classmates from his SAMS class, also assigned to V Corps: Majors Dan Soller, Dan Stempniak, and Charlie Constanza. A week later they flew to Baghdad where they would spend another year together.[37]

During the week they were in Germany, Major Lou Rago, a SAMS graduate of 2001, was completing his year as a planner with V Corps in Iraq. He had just returned to Heidelberg for a new assignment. Rago had deployed to Kuwait in November 2002 and remained in theater until 14 June 2003 when he left Iraq with Lieutenant General Wallace, as Wallace turned over command of V Corps to Lieutenant General Sanchez. During the previous year Rago worked for Lieutenant Colonel E. J. Degan, USA, Chief of War Plans for V Corps, with Majors Chuck Eassa and Major Kevin Marcus (all SAMS graduates). Marcus and Rago had been the lead planners for V Corps deployment to Kuwait and the invasion of Iraq through to Baghdad.[38]

In Germany, Rago spent a day with Odum and his peers from Leavenworth. He "briefed us using charts that laid out the organizational structure of CJTF-7 . . . as we made the transition from V Corps to being a CJTF." A U.S. Army corps headquarters is designed to manage ground operations employing U.S. Army formations, whereas CJTF-7 Headquarters would manage forces from several countries, mainly ground formations, but also some air and sea units or support from such units.

Rago returned to Baghdad several weeks later to serve as a battalion operations officer in the 1st Armor Division occupying the city, spending twenty months altogether in theater.[39] In Baghdad, Odum met Degan, Eassa, and Marcus, all due to leave Iraq within the month. Two weeks earlier, V Corps under General Sanchez assumed the role of CJTF-7 from McKiernan's command; McKiernan and his staff redeployed to the United States. Sanchez and Odum had missed the invasion. They would soon observe another kind of war emerge, but their views would differ on its nature.

By the end of July the original four SAMS planners on the V Corps staff—Degan, Eassa, Marcus, and Rago—were replaced by Odum, Soller, Stempniak, and Constanza. Unlike their predecessors, who were of sequential SAMS classes with more diversity in experience, Odum and his peers were all of the same vintage, each coming straight from Leavenworth. There were several officers from Australia and the United Kingdom working in plans during this transition period, but they also rotated from Iraq by the end of August, replaced by others. In November, Brigadier General Daniel Keefe, USA, arrived in Baghdad to take over the C-5 Plans sections for CJTF-7. Sanchez had difficulty filling senior staff positions, and many of those officers arrived late in the year.[40]

When Odum had asked Rago, Degan, Eassa, and Marcus, the outgoing Corps planners, about the transition, they told him that "NATO was going to come in and replace us. V Corps was only going to be the CJTF headquarters for a limited period." They also told Odum a UN military headquarters might replace them. Odum and Soller knew there was "no way the UN was coming," based on what they had observed on the news over the past year at Leavenworth.[41]

Degan, Eassa, Marcus, and Rago had been intensely focused on the tactical planning for the invasion over the previous year, perhaps with little time to monitor news coverage on Iraq. They may have been unaware of the reluctance of other NATO countries to join the American-led Coalition in Iraq. Odum and Soller were correct—there was no NATO headquarters, and certainly no UN military formation, headed for Iraq. The Army V Corps, reflagged as CJTF-7, would be the senior military headquarters in Iraq into the middle of 2004, a critical year in Iraq.

The transition of the senior headquarters in Iraq from CFLCC to V Corps, now reflagged as CJTF-7, was more profound than it appeared—and poorly managed. The U.S. Third Army staff, larger than a corps staff to start with, had been expanded to become the CFLCC staff. If V Corps was to assume the role of CFLCC in Iraq, it should have been expanded. But V Corps was not expanded and as it assumed the role of CJTF-7 and control of military formations in Iraq, many of the V Corp staff officers returned home. As most of the CFLCC staff redeployed to the United States, so did many staff officers from Central Command; what they left in theater were skeleton staffs in Qatar and Kuwait.

The turnover within V Corps was critical. As the veteran General Wallace was replaced by General Sanchez in his first three-star position, almost all the primary staff officers and their assistants in V Corps rotated back to Germany during the summer of 2003. Not only was the V Corps staff going through a turnover of personnel, it was going to assume the senior headquarters role in Iraq.

Odum observed a "great discontinuity in institutional knowledge occurring in a very short period. . . . Our impression was that Central Command and CFLCC had walked away from the problem. They declared victory and went home." Rago told Odum that the Joint Manning Document for CJTF-7 would take time to fill and there would be many vacancies until December, an accurate projection. E. J. Degan told Odum in Germany that he had better hurry up and get to Iraq before it was all over. "Everyone was thinking post–Desert Storm—wash your gear and go home."[42]

There was also a turnover of ground formations. The 1st Armor Division arrived in Baghdad to replace the 3rd Mechanized Infantry Division as the latter returned home. The 1st Marine Division remained until the end of summer, replaced by a multinational division with a Polish headquarters. The 1st UK Division remained in southern Iraq, reduced to less than half its original strength with some internal turnover by battalions. The 101st Air Assault Division, controlling northern Iraq, and the 4th Infantry Division (Mechanized), which arrived the month after the invasion to occupy the region between the 101st and Baghdad, were the only original divisions to remain a full year. The aggregate strength in divisions would remain comparable to those that invaded Iraq. In mid-April General Franks and Secretary Rumsfeld had decided not to send the armored 1st Cavalry Division, previously designated to go to Iraq. As many senior headquarters and divisional formations rotated in and out of Iraq, so did many supporting formations (see Figure 9).[43]

Some military engineer battalions would remain in Iraq, but not the 416th Engineer Command or the eight construction battalions that had come with it. They redeployed that summer, just as it was becoming clear that the Iraqi infrastructure was decrepit. When the Marines departed, they took ten Marine and Navy seabee engineer battalions with them. The multinational division that replaced the Marines brought only one engineer battalion to replace ten. Of the engineer formations that remained in Iraq, most were combat engineer battalions with less utility for reconstruction projects than construction battalions. Most of the engineer units were attached to the maneuver divisions; few were left under centralized control for major projects. With the shortage of infantry battalions, some combat engineer units were employed

CPA & CJTF-7

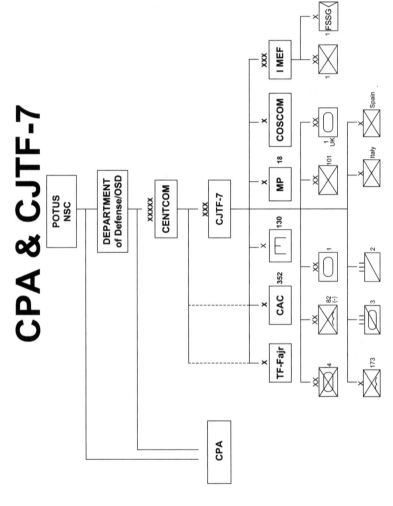

Figure 9. Coalition Provisional Authority (CPA) and Combined-Joint Task Force 7 (CJTF-7).

as infantry, making important contributions but not for reconstruction. Nor would they be managed by a single engineer headquarters comparable to the 416th ENCOM.

In contrast, the Army Reserve Civil Affairs formations, almost 2,000 reservists, were ordered to remain in Iraq for a year as many regulars and most reservists, including those in the 416th ENCOM, returned home. There were only about 6,000 Civil Affairs soldiers in the army inventory, but a third of them were still in a training status or otherwise were nondeployable. Other Civil Affairs units were serving in Afghanistan, the Balkans, or in Africa. A year later, when those 2,000 Civil Affairs soldiers left Iraq, there would be little left in the Civil Affairs inventory to replace them.

In April, General Franks told General McKiernan and his subordinate commanders to take as much risk getting out as they had getting in.[44]

When Garner heard that, he went to McKiernan and said, "Dave, that's the dumbest thing I ever heard. . . . You were never going to lose the war no matter what you did, but you can sure as hell lose the peace."[45]

Sanchez felt the redeployment guidance from General Franks was clear but strategically flawed. By the end of May it was clear that the actions Bremer was taking would lead to an occupation for an unknown period. General Abizaid agreed with Sanchez, but he could not stop the departure of ground forces until he replaced General Franks at Central Command in July. Although late, Abizaid was decisive and refused to allow any more forces to depart unless they were replaced. Army generals in the United States had been told forces would be reduced to 30,000 in a few months. They were unprepared to sustain forces in Iraq and resisted. One senior general flew to Baghdad and demanded that Sanchez back off on the forces for Iraq. Sanchez refused, despite the general's threat that the Army would look unfavorably on his actions.[46]

By early June, Sanchez and Abizaid realized that with the Iraqi army disbanded and Slocombe slowly building a much smaller one, U.S. forces would have to provide security for Iraq, which was going to be more demanding than anyone had anticipated. As Sanchez and Abizaid saw violence and instability increase throughout Iraq, they went to Bremer and asked to take over the police training and to raise an Iraqi Civil Defense Corps (ICDC) to provide internal security for Iraq. Bremer refused and told them he would manage the Iraqi military forces and police. By late July Bremer relented on the ICDC, though with precious time lost, but he would not relinquish control of police training that was to be managed by Bernie Kerik. Kerik, however, was more interested in running police raids in Baghdad than rebuilding police forces for the whole country. Sanchez complained to Kerik that his raids were not coordinated with American military forces in Baghdad and that the police training program was lagging. When Kerik left in September, Sanchez went to Bremer again to explain that little had been done with the police and asked to take over. Bremer again resisted; it would be several more months before the military command was allowed to manage a training program for the Iraqi police. The failure of CPA and the military command to cooperate on rebuilding the Iraqi army and police with violence escalating throughout Iraq placed greater demands on American forces in Iraq, as those in Washington tried to bring them home.[47]

Major Odum was initially consumed with managing the summer rotations taking place, but he was soon assigned to write the campaign plan for CJTF-7 in Iraq. There was no V Corps plan available, although he inherited the Eclipse II plan developed by Colonel Benson. Digging through the work of those who had just departed, he found their final product, a thirty-slide show with the Phase IV plan in three sub-phases. It was not much, but it was a place to start. Odum reduced it to four tasks: security, governance, economic assistance and essential services, and communications.[48]

Odum knew that planning a campaign was a collaborative process involving guidance from the headquarters above and participation from those formations adjacent, in support, and subordinate. But in July, CJTF-7 had received no detailed guidance from CFLCC on its departure or from Central Command. Odum wanted "to get some buy-in and feedback from the divisions. Part of that whole dynamic was that the plans officers for the most part changed that summer" and the new group "was largely composed of SAMS graduates from the class" from which Odum had recently graduated.[49]

In his planning conference, Odum had the advantage of everyone knowing each other from their previous year at Leavenworth together, but the disadvantage that all of them were new with little institutional knowledge of what had taken place in Iraq in the past few months. With the assistance of the division planners, Odum developed a mission analysis he provided General Sanchez at the end of July. He proposed a campaign mission statement oriented on stability operations based on "a low intensity conflict" environment in Iraq.

Sanchez rejected Odum's proposal and "wanted to keep it offensively focused," with an orientation on the destruction of residual elements of the Saddam Hussein regime. Odum suggested to Sanchez that the Coalition was facing an adversary with a strong criminal element that had not yet "coalesced into a coherent insurgency." Sanchez wanted to stay on the offensive on the sort of "search and destroy campaign" used in Vietnam. For Odum the violent resistance in Iraq was not so much residual Ba'athists but rather "anti-Saddam elements, such as Muqtadr al-Sadr's Mahdi Army and some Sunni groups that had no obvious ties to the former regime. It was also apparent that those groups were clearly against the Coalition."[50]

In November, when Brigadier General Keefe took over as C-5 for CJTF-7, he asked Odum to define the center of gravity for the Coalition in Iraq. Odum had been in Iraq for six months and told him it should be "the support of the Iraqi population for their government." Keefe rejected that concept. Like Sanchez, he wanted a military object that could be attacked. Odum realized that the momentum within the military command was "hunting people in an urban environment." That required more precise intelligence than the Coalition had available. In Odum's view, the population was soon alienated by Coalition night raids, use of firepower, and the use of checkpoints. He watched as the general insecurity increased. Earlier in August, "Colonel Agoglia and some other officers from CENTCOM came to look at [Odum's] campaign plan but they did not really offer any advice" beyond "positive reinforcement of the way we were developing it."[51]

Meanwhile, Major Dan Stempniak began to assist with planning for the new Iraqi army, the responsibility of Major General Eaton, working for Walt Slocombe, not General Sanchez. Eaton's task was to create only a few battalions before the end of the year. The military commanders and their staffs knew that they needed far more Iraqi forces to assist with stability. At the pace Slocombe and Eaton were progressing, Stempniak, Odum, and others could see that "we were never going to create an Iraqi Army of sufficient size in a sufficient period." The planners proposed that the Coalition divisions recruit, train, and employ interim Iraqi forces to assist with internal security. That led to competition between CJTF-7 and CPA over resources and control of Iraqi security forces, and friction between Eaton and Sanchez.[52]

In an effort to align military operations with the other components of the Coalition, Odum began coordination with CPA planners. In August Colonel Paul Hughes left Iraq, leaving Lieutenant Colonel Bob Polk and Dayton Maxwell as the last planners from ORHA working with CPA. Polk and Odum soon had a good working relationship, and in October Odum moved from the airport at Camp Victory to live and work in the palace with Polk and Maxwell, trying to align military operations with CPA efforts.

Just as Odum was slow to gain the confidence of General Sanchez, it took several months before Polk and Maxwell could gain Bremer's confidence. When Bremer arrived in Iraq, he did not bring planners with him, nor did he develop an early relationship with those planners working within ORHA. Polk and Maxwell did not gain his attention for several months after Bremer realized he needed something like a campaign plan. When Polk and Maxwell showed him what they were working on in July, Bremer took an interest as they produced a strategic plan for CPA entitled "A Vision to Empower Iraqis," which identified security as the top priority.[53]

Bremer and CPA had little capacity to provide security for Iraq. Without viable Iraqi police or military forces, only CJTF-7 could provide internal security. Odum, Polk, and Maxwell were aware that some policies developed by CJTF-7 and CPA were at cross-purposes. Odum felt CPA was determined "to make a transition from a socialist economy to a free market economy." In the short term that would put people out of work and disrupt Iraqi institutions, both increasing instability and violence. The challenge with CPA planning was dealing with grand concepts for Iraq with limited means to impose them. The challenge for CJTF-7 planning was getting the military commanders to provide stability and security rather than pursuing offensive operations that would alienate the Iraqi people. Odum later wrote that "we were too enemy-centric and not population-centric, too much whack-a-mole and not enough clear, hold, build, and transition."[54]

In November, Central Command sent a planning team to work with CPA to develop a strategy and integrate it with military planning. To Odum, it appeared as if after a summer break of "three or four months they were ready to pick up an oar and continue rowing again. They brought over a planning team really to help CPA." At that time CJTF-7 had not yet published a campaign plan.[55] In January 2004, over halfway through his tour in Iraq, General Sanchez finally signed the plan Odum had written in July. By that time, the divisions had established their own campaign plans, with their planners working from Odum's draft but with little input from General Sanchez.[56]

ORHA AND CPA

The evolution of ORHA into CPA was erratic with major policy shifts, and a change in leadership and staff. Bremer and many he brought with him were not interested in the institutional knowledge acquired by those in ORHA from January through May. Garner and his team had tried to empower non-Ba'athist Iraqi leaders to form a new government. Bremer set out to impose a grand vision on Iraq, driven by Western democracy and capitalism, with little consideration for Iraqi values or institutions. Bremer and his team were determined to define what was best for Iraqis; that included imposing a free-market system and discarding the Iraqi-controlled economy when much of the physical, political, and cultural components of Iraq were in turmoil and unemployment was rampant.

The Coalition was surprised to find the physical infrastructure of Iraq in such poor condition, weakened by decades of sanctions and neglect and poorly addressed or acknowledged in pre-invasion intelligence estimates. The original reconstruction concept was to fix what was broken from the war, returning services to prewar standards with the assumption that oil exports would provide revenue to cover the costs. War damage was minimal, but regime change unleashed looting and vandalism that crippled Iraq's fragile infrastructure and its ability to export oil, with the Coalition unprepared to put Iraq back together. With Bremer controlling CPA and General Sanchez controlling CJTF-7, each reporting to different superiors, the Coalition lacked unity of command in Iraq. Both organizations drifted in different directions as the situation deteriorated. Secretary Powell complained about the lack of unity of command to Condoleezza Rice and the others on the Principals Committee but without result.[57]

The greatest obstacle to progress was lack of security. In June 2003 there were 250 attacks on Coalition forces; in July there were 500.[58] Attacks on the population of Iraq also increased, perhaps with greater casualties than those suffered by Coalition forces. Despite the best efforts of individuals such as Dick Mayer from the Justice Department, there had been no resources before the war to put a package in place for law enforcement in Iraq or to rebuild the Iraqi police forces. By disbanding the regular army with plans to bring back only a small force over a period of several years, there was no other Iraqi component to provide internal security.

Only Coalition military forces could provide internal security, but those forces were poorly focused for that task. In April, military commanders subordinate to Central Command (and Army generals in the Pentagon) were told that the goal was to reduce American forces to 30,000 by September, with some other component not yet defined, perhaps NATO or UN, to take over. Once Baghdad was taken, there was a rush driven by Secretary Rumsfeld and General Franks to send American forces home. The military forces that remained in Iraq were predominantly mechanized and armored heavy forces trained and equipped to fight a conventional war. They were not prepared for an insurgency or to conduct stability operations.

Rather than focus on winning the hearts and minds of the Iraqi people, General Sanchez tried to take the offensive against those attacking his forces, with methods that often alienated the Iraqi population. The Coalition in Iraq had two components that were never properly integrated. CPA laid out grand economic and governance designs it could not implement, and CJTF-7 sought an offensive campaign that could not provide security necessary for those designs. Neither CPA nor CJTF-7 made effective use of the Iraqi people and institutions in their efforts to reform the country. Those in Washington who should have provided corrective guidance and additional resources were slow, even resistant, to grasp the seriousness of the situation or to reverse plans to pull out of Iraq.

8
REFLECTIONS

How do you learn?
—Ted Morse[1]

Regime change in Iraq constitutes a major endeavor in a new century. American forces successfully removed the regime of Saddam Hussein with "rapid decisive operations," yet the United States was not prepared to effectively replace that regime. As stated in the preface, the focus of this study is the formation and actions of ORHA with Jay Garner as the central figure. The purpose of this chapter is to provide a summation and assessment of its subject. Such an evaluation should include a review of the prewar planning for regime replacement and the transition from ORHA to CPA with the arrival in Iraq of Ambassador Bremer.

The process of regime change in Iraq was adversely affected by the management, or lack thereof, of the National Security Council and other U.S. government departments and agencies. Given that many events might have occurred differently, some counterfactual considerations may be in order, which in turn may help qualify lessons from the experience in Iraq. As discussed throughout this study, there were notable deficiencies in the planning, preparations, and execution of regime change in Iraq, or—as Jay Garner might suggest—missing pieces on the mosaic. The absence of those pieces ensured that early success would be elusive and that the costs would be far greater than anticipated.

On 17 January 2003, Secretary of Defense Donald Rumsfeld and Undersecretary for Policy Doug Feith asked Jay Garner to put together an organization to execute the planning for the post-conflict phase in Iraq. Garner was given a line diagram as a guide two months before Iraq would be invaded. He was told the American objective was the liberation of Iraq with political control to be handed off to Iraqi leaders as soon as possible. At the end of the meeting, Garner reflected on the relevant World War II experience and commented, "Marshall had two years—you are giving me two months."[2]

Almost every great endeavor has some historical precedent, and the United States had many precedents for post-conflict going back to World War II. And for that conflict General Marshall and other army officers of his generation had several precedents they could rely on. They knew the U.S. Third Army had secured part of the Rhineland at the end of World War I, and they had a long Army experience in the Philippines and Panama prior to the 1940s. For the U.S. Marine Corps there were the extended mid-war experiences in Haiti, the Dominican Republic, and Nicaragua, where American military forces would return to fight oppression and insurgencies or assist with stability operations.

During or after World War II, American forces participated in the liberation or occupation of North Africa, Italy, France, Germany, Austria, the Philippines, Okinawa, Japan, and Korea. Those experiences were well documented in official histories and memoirs, but only Germany and Japan received any attention prior to the invasion of Iraq. John Dower, the noted historian of Japan, took that case study out of general consideration, in part by noting that the occupation of Japan had important characteristics that would not be present in Iraq following an invasion. The absence of those criteria for Iraq should have given planners pause rather than lead them to simply dismiss Japan as a useful case study.

In September 2010, Dower published *Cultures of War: Pearl Harbor / Hiroshima / 9-11 / Iraq*, a comparative study of the occupation of Japan after World War II and the functional occupation of Iraq following the invasion in 2003. Drawing from his earlier work on Japan and on recent developments in Iraq, Dower confirmed critical differences that allowed occupation in Japan to be progressive and nonviolent, while the experience in Iraq was remarkably violent with success more challenging. Dower condemned those in political power for misuse of or indifference to history in the preparation for Iraq. He made little reference to other post-conflict case studies that might have offered greater perspective for occupation or liberation.[3]

For policy makers who did not look for other examples, that left Germany as the main reference for Iraq, ironic given that Germany was to endure an extensive occupation with a punitive design, while Iraq was to be liberated quickly with intended benevolence. When American political leaders sought a model to deal with the Ba'athist party of Iraq, no attention was directed to how that phenomenon was handled in the countries that had been liberated: how the Fascists of Italy or the Nazis of Austria were vetted and reformed. Instead, the model chosen was the draconian purge of Nazis in Germany, leading to disastrous results in Iraq.

Peter Rodman, a policy advisor for Rumsfeld, promoted the French resistance during World War II and the nationalism harnessed by General Charles

de Gaulle as a model for the liberation of Iraq, with analogy to Iraqi opposi-
tions groups and, perhaps, Ahmed Chalabi of the INC as a national leader.
General John Abizaid objected to such a model for Iraq, noting that while the
French were nationalistic, Iraqis were more tribal: "This will not be like the
liberation of France. In that case you had two things that were important—a
free French Army and a Free French Government [in exile]. In the case of Iraq
there is no free Iraqi Army and no free Iraqi government." He might have
added that where General de Gaulle was a credible unifier, Ahmed Chalabi
would polarize Iraqis.[4]

Little mention was made during prewar planning of the military and interagency operations conducted during the Cold War (Greece, Korea, the
Dominican Republic, Grenada, Lebanon, Panama, and Honduras/Nicaragua)
other than cursory references to Vietnam and the interagency experience with
the Civil Operations and Revolutionary Development Support (CORDS)
program. Nor was there mention of the many peacekeeping operations of that
period. More contemporary were the experiences of the 1990s—Bosnia, Somalia, Haiti, and Kosovo—but those were mainly during the Clinton administration and involved nation-building programs that the Bush administration
disdained. Few members of the Bush administration had shared those experiences, and they did not want to undertake nation building on their watch.

There was one consistent lesson from World Wars I and II that continued
through the contemporary experiences of the 1990s: if large ground formations are available at the beginning of a liberation or occupation, unexpected
challenges can be contained with a dominating military presence, allowing
time to adapt to conditions as they develop. General Peay and General Zinni
at Central Command in the 1990s and General Shinseki and Major Kojac in
Washington in 2003 confirmed the need for large formations following an
invasion, but political leaders on the NSC and in the Pentagon did not want
to hear it. Thus for regime change in Iraq there was a great deal of institutional American experience, but little of it was studied. The history that was
reviewed by policy makers was often distorted or used improperly.

An illustrative, if minor, example of misconstrued U.S. history was that of
the army planner who proposed Cobra II as the name for the invasion of Iraq,
intended as a reference to the Cobra operation in Normandy led by General
George Patton and the U.S. Third Army in 1944. But the original Cobra operation was actually planned and conducted by the U.S. First Army commanded
by General Omar Bradley. A more useful historical reference for an invasion of
Iraq might have been the U.S. Third Army occupation of the Rhineland at the
end of World War I or the Third Army occupation of the American sector in
Germany following World War II. Such comparisons should have suggested

that the Third Army, configured as CFLCC to invade Iraq in 2003, would be needed after the invasion to stabilize the country, rather than pass that role on to the smaller and less capable V Corps reflagged as CJTF-7.

The military planning for Iraq had started on a sound footing following Desert Storm in the 1990s, under the stewardship of the commanders at Central Command: Generals Hoar, Peay, and Zinni and their dedicated planners. Using the successful Desert Storm as a model for planning, those officers argued tenaciously for large ground formations for and after an invasion of Iraq. They did so in the face of those in the Pentagon and elsewhere who wanted to reduce those formations by offsetting them with enhanced technology. While such technology could help defeat the Iraqi army, it could not displace ground forces for stability operations that must follow an invasion. When Rumsfeld coerced Central Command to severely reduce the size of the invasion forces and told the planners not to worry about the post-conflict phase, their energy went into planning for the invasion, not what would follow. Later, when Rumsfeld decided the Pentagon should manage the post-conflict phase, military planners took on that assignment late in 2002. At Central Command the effort was led by Major Tom Fisher; for Coalition ground forces it was driven by Colonel Kevin Benson's Eclipse II plan. But neither effort was integrated with the formation of JTF-4 under General Steve Hawkins or ORHA under Jay Garner.

Interagency discussions began at the National Security Council early in 2002 with weekly meetings by the Principals Committee. Later in the year, several agencies had small groups working on Iraq part-time. Frank Miller set up the Executive Steering Group in the NSC with a subordinate working group under Elliot Abrams and Robin Cleveland to prepare for humanitarian assistance and reconstruction in Iraq. At USAID a similar group did the same under Ambassador Wendy Chamberlin. A team at Treasury studied the Iraqi economy and currency issues. The Pentagon put together a small group to study oil in Iraq. In the Department of State Tom Warrick managed the Future of Iraq project, which involved Iraqi expatriates. No one exercised overall control of these groups, nor did they effectively share information with each other or with the planners at Central Command. By the time Jay Garner stood up ORHA "to operationalize the planning that had been done," there had been significant study of Iraq by these groups, but there was no national plan to pass on to ORHA.

Once Garner agreed to take on the operation, he had to recruit personnel from across the U.S. government, organize them into working components, integrate and develop planning for Iraq, and prepare his organization for deployment. Within a week Garner had recruited over a dozen people; by mid-

February he had over 100. By the time he deployed to Kuwait in mid-March, he had almost 200. Most of them came from the Departments of Defense and State and from USAID. A few came from other government agencies and departments: Treasury, Agriculture, Commerce, and the CIA. In the process Garner experienced many challenges.

There was resistance to provide the military personnel Garner requested, and those that joined came from different staff sections in the Pentagon and other military bases throughout the Washington area. They did not know each other and it took precious time for them to build cohesion. The tension between senior civilian leaders in the Pentagon and the Department of State led many Foreign Service Officers with Middle East experience to avoid join- ing ORHA. Of those that volunteered, many were civil servants from State with little or no Middle East experience. Of the half-dozen ambassadors State offered Garner with Middle East experience, many were retired and lacked current connections. The Pentagon also rejected some of those ambassadors in March, leaving Garner with gaps that would not be filled until later, with critical time lost. Rumsfeld, for example, told Garner he could not take Tom Warrick, who managed the Future of Iraq project. The documents from that project lacked form and qualification and had not been integrated in the State Political-Military plan for Iraq, despite the best efforts of Mike Ayoub. As such, the Future of Iraq project had little utility for ORHA without Warrick.

In January, Doug Feith led Garner to believe that OSD-Policy had under- taken substantial planning that he would share with ORHA. If there had been such planning, however, none of it was made available to Garner. As people joined Garner, they instituted daily meetings and various coordination tasks in order to jumpstart their own planning. The largest and most high-profile meeting was the February rock drill, conducted at the National Defense Uni- versity. The rock drill suggested more questions than resolutions. Garner and others in the administration anticipated the first task following the invasion would be humanitarian assistance. For that task Garner structured a Hu- manitarian Assistance pillar within ORHA. He also had a pillar working on Reconstruction and another on Civil Administration for Iraq. Most of the reconstruction effort would repair what was damaged during the invasion. That work was to be outsourced to contractors and managed by USAID. Ma- jor General Carl Strock had to work his way into ORHA to make the case that the U.S. Army Corps of Engineers could help, but most USAID person- nel did not want help from the Corps of Engineers unless it was essential to achieve their tasks. Strock and his engineers had to wait for an opportunity to make a contribution.

The main focus of the Civil Administration pillar was the ministries in the

Iraqi government, about which little was known. The Pentagon insisted on providing the leader of the Civil Administration pillar, eventually designating Mike Mobbs. Though talented, Mobbs was not cut out for such a large management role and knew little about the Middle East or the ministries in Iraq. Regarding civil administration, Garner was concerned about large governance issues—elections, a constitution, and political policies that should guide a new regime in Iraq. He asked Rumsfeld to form a group of experts from academia and government for that role. Two assistant secretaries of state, Liz Cheney and Scott Carpenter, were chosen to package that group, but it was slow to form and provided no assistance to Garner; the group did not even arrive in Iraq until Bremer took over.

Garner assumed the NSC would provide support and personnel unavailable through the Pentagon. He had weekly meetings with National Security Advisor Condoleezza Rice and her deputy Stephen Hadley. Rice and Hadley could not or would not task the U.S. governmental departments and agencies to provide the personnel Garner needed when those personnel were not forthcoming. Nor did they provide Garner the funding he sought to allow him to pay salaries for Iraqi civil servants who would have to go back to work after an invasion to get the country running again.

When Garner presented a plan to Rice for police trainers to reform and put the Iraqi police back into operation, Rice was ambivalent. Garner did not know that Frank Miller had forcefully argued that providing such police trainers from the American law enforcement system would be too difficult and therefore should not be done. When Garner presented his plan for the police with an estimated cost to Rumsfeld, the secretary said the United States would not pay for it. He told Garner that funding for Iraqi police would have to be paid for by the Iraqis. Garner, however, needed the money up front to get police trainers lined up. He could not wait until after the invasion for funding when it would be imperative to have trainers on hand. Garner knew the Iraqi police would have to be reformed and retrained. The NSC's and Rumsfeld's refusals to provide police support would cost the Coalition dearly within the year. An inadequate plan for internal security for Iraq after the invasion would be the most expensive deficiency in the planning.

What assessment is appropriate for Garner and for ORHA as it was developed and employed? Working against time limitations, Garner formed ORHA from scratch, filling positions with the most capable people he could obtain. When he could not obtain the appropriate people, he designated interim personnel until the arrival of those deemed qualified. Without the developed plans promised by the Pentagon, he began his own planning in Washington, which would continue through deployment to Kuwait. With chaos and danger following the invasion and austere living conditions, Garner and those in ORHA established and improved a headquarters in Baghdad and the outlying regions. His senior and interim advisors established contact with their ministries, and put together a skeleton ministry component of the government executive branch to put it back into operation. When Bremer arrived, he did not have to create CPA from scratch; he had a viable base in ORHA from which to expand. Even many of those that arrived with Bremer, such as Scott Carpenter's Governance Team, had been put in motion earlier at Garner's initiative.

Throughout the process Garner was a beacon of energy and inspiration. He provided decisive leadership consistent with his guidance to provide a basis for liberation of Iraq. Despite the obstacles he faced, Garner consistently displayed determination and enthusiasm. Only after Bremer changed the scope to occupation and reversed much of what ORHA had in motion did Garner exhibit disappointment. For those who observed both Garner and Bremer as managers, it is difficult to imagine that Bremer could have forged the organization that Garner began in the Pentagon. For many of those in ORHA, Garner was the indispensable man.

What criticism is in order for Garner? Given his shortages in key personnel and resources, arguably he should have pushed harder for more assistance. Given the limited knowledge those in ORHA had about Iraq, perhaps he should have developed a better relationship with Iraqi expatriates in the IRDC and integrated them earlier within ORHA. When it was clear in Kuwait that Mike Mobbs was not the aggressive leader he needed and Barbara Bodine was difficult to work with, perhaps he should have replaced them before he went into Iraq. In Kuwait and Iraq he might have demanded more military support: military police, transportation, Civil Affairs, and communications units. Augmentation with such units would have ensured greater capacity for ORHA.

There are plausible counterviews. Garner did push hard for personnel and resources. Arguably, if he had pushed harder he might have caused more problems than he solved. As for the Iraqi expatriates and the IRDC, Garner found some had self-serving agendas, more interested in imposing their individual vision on Iraq than helping ORHA. Determining who would be useful and who would not required more energy than Garner or others in ORHA could give. As for Mike Mobbs and Barbara Bodine, Mobbs was the senior representative from OSD-Policy and Bodine was the senior representative from the Department of State serving with Garner. Firing either early on might have caused Garner more turmoil than waiting and trying to get them to adjust. In an effort to assist them, Garner assigned both a full colonel as a deputy.

On working with the military commanders, many assumed that Garner's prior service would make that smoother than it did. It is unclear what pushing harder for support from General Franks or General McKiernan might have achieved, particularly when they were heavily involved in the invasion. When Garner asked for military support in Baghdad, he was given modest support with a small communications detachment, an MP company, and some Civil Affairs officers. Obtaining more was difficult in late April when most of the support units were attached to maneuver divisions. Perhaps Wendy Chamberlin summed it up best: "I always suspected that a General would emerge from the woodwork. I didn't know he would be retired and would lack the support of the uniformed services."[5] Indeed, Garner was poorly served by senior officers in uniform.

Were there alternatives to Jay Garner, and how might they have done in his place? Within ORHA four were plausible: his two deputies, Ron Adams and Tim Cross, his chief of staff, Jerry Bates, and his senior military officer, General Carl Strock. Adams clearly had the management skills to run ORHA, but he became ill prior to going into Iraq. He also lacked the clout with OSD and with those in CPA that followed Garner; much the same could be said for Bates. Cross was certainly one of the most insightful leaders in ORHA, but he was a non-American in an American-dominated organization and an American-dominated invasion. The popular Strock was the one person in ORHA who could approach Garner's charisma, but he would have been junior to run ORHA as a major general.

Beyond ORHA, who might have matched the skills and traits Garner brought to ORHA? On the NSC there was no obvious candidate, nor in OSD. It is hard to imagine Stephen Hadley, Frank Miller, Paul Wolfowitz, Doug Feith, or any of their immediate subordinates matching Garner's management skills, charisma, or leadership. At State and USAID, the senior candidates might have included Richard Armitage, Marc Grossman, Ryan Crocker, Andrew Natsios, Wendy Chamberlin, or one of their immediate subordinates. Again, none were clearly in a league with Garner. Other retired generals? Generals Peay and Zinni, prior commanders at Central Command, were qualified, but they had demanded more troops for Iraq, incompatible with the views of those in the NSC and the Pentagon. And what about Bremer? What if he had been selected in January instead of Garner? Without a connection in the Defense Department, it is difficult to imagine him standing ORHA up from scratch. In sum, there is no indication in this study that another person could have matched the achievements of Garner, much less surpassed them.

How should others in ORHA be judged? Garner is on record in interviews for this study and elsewhere that he assumed Washington would give him a

C-team of marginal personnel, but what he got was an A-Team. Garner had reason to be proud that the civilians that went with him were all volunteers. Those in uniform participated with comparable zeal. All were prepared to go in harms way and endure hardship, which they did. The inconveniences were more difficult for those from civilian agencies unaccustomed to austere and dangerous environments, but they adapted. In that respect the members of ORHA were remarkable. But they were not an A-Team in terms of what Garner needed, and in that sense Garner is incorrect.

Many members of ORHA were underqualified for the positions they eventually filled. Many of those from State were civil servants rather than experienced Middle East Foreign Service Officers; many of the ambassadors that joined were recalled from retirement. Many from USAID were contractors; the same could be said for some of those sent by other agencies. There was a reason many advisors to the Iraqi ministries were assigned the title interim advisors; those so designated were junior and often without the appropriate skills for the assignments they were given. Some were well qualified: Robin Raphel, Donald Campbell, Dayton Maxwell, Mike Gfoeller, Chris Milligan, Lee Schatz, Don Eberly, David Nummy, George Mullinax, and Van Jorstad. The Corps of Engineers sent technically qualified personnel with leadership skills: Major General Carl Strock, Steve Browning, Mark Held, Gene Stakhiv, those on the FEST, and others who came later. However, even most of these individuals had never worked in Iraq before and only a very few spoke Arabic.

As Garner left, his most senior leaders left with him: Ron Adams, Tim Cross, Jerry Bates, George Ward, Bruce Moore, Buck Walters, and earlier Mike Mobbs and Barbara Bodine. Many stayed on through the summer. Some stayed longer, such as Steve Browning, Robin Raphel, Dorothy Mazaka, Sherri Kraham, Meghan O'Sullivan, Dayton Maxwell, Bob Polk, Mike Gfoeller, and Dick Naab. Many of those who made substantial contributions to ORHA would provide a critical base for Bremer in CPA.

No one in ORHA was prepared for the de-Ba'athification program Bremer implemented, or the disbanding of the Iraqi army and the Iraqi Interim Authority. That cannot be blamed on Garner, given his aggressive protests. It is fair to ponder what might have occurred had Bremer not taken those actions. Without the de-Ba'athification order, there would have been less turmoil with the Iraqi ministries during May and June. As more information became available about individual Iraqis whom the Coalition put in power, some would have to be removed based on previous transgressions; those untainted could have remained in leadership positions.

Retaining the Iraqi army might have been more complicated, particularly if

Bremer had insisted that it be vetted and reformed by Slocombe and General Eaton through the RONCO and MPRI contracts that Colonel Hughes had in motion. There is reason to be skeptical that RONCO could have designed an appropriate plan for the Iraqi army when the company's expertise was clearly minefields. MPRI had the contract to retrain the Iraqi army, a task it had undertaken in other countries. Yet when MPRI later worked with General Eaton to train a new Iraqi army on a limited scale, there were complications and problems. It is doubtful that MPRI could have handled the much larger task that Garner and Coalition military commanders had in mind during 2003.

If the Iraqi army had been recalled as Garner and others anticipated, it is probable that the U.S. Army and Marines would have had to take on much of the management, which would have stretched their capacity for stabilization. It is probable that any effort to reactivate the Iraqi army would have reduced the number of those that took up arms against the Coalition in 2003 and later. As Garner told Bremer and Slocombe, "You can get rid of an army in a day, but it takes you years to bring one back." Garner was right—it did take years.

To have made the IIA effective—assuming Bremer did not disband it—would also have been challenging. Once Garner had seven members for the IIA, he had difficulty getting them to achieve functional cohesion. Few of them had a strong base in Baghdad, as all were opposition leaders with their base elsewhere. There was only one Sunni Arab in the group, a problem since the Sunni population was the most loyal to Saddam Hussein and it was important to win it over and bring it under control. It is possible, even probable, that the IIA would have floundered under Bremer if he had tried to work with them. An advantage to retaining them would have been the appearance of putting an Iraqi face on the face of the liberation.

How should the prewar planning be assessed? There were efforts to plan for the post-invasion phase of Iraq throughout the U.S. government, yet that planning had little utility. An assessment should begin with the National Security Council, its staff, and a review of the planning conducted by the Department of State, USAID, and several levels with the Department of Defense.

The National Security Council has responsibility for interagency policy for international endeavors. Shortly after the attacks on New York and the Pentagon in September 2001, the Principals Committee of the NSC began discussions about changing the regime in Iraq. Just as military planning often begins with discussions at several levels rather than with top-down directives, so the principals had their deputies meet to develop objectives for Iraq. The Deputies Committee began meeting for lunch once a week early in 2002, but it was not until the summer that Condoleezza Rice directed Frank Miller to form the Executive Steering Group and begin planning for Iraq.

As National Security Advisor, Rice had two fundamental responsibilities. One was to advise the president on national security issues, as the title clearly suggests, a task that requires an understanding of international institutions and dynamics as well as the political policies of the American government, which are frequently evolving. For that role, some academic knowledge of the international arena is in order. Rice had previously worked on the NSC staff and had academic credentials, but her expertise was with arms control and the Soviet Union; she did not have first-hand experience with the cultural, economic, and political issues endemic to the Middle East, or to Iraq in particular.

The other role of the National Security Advisor is to manage the interagency process, integrating the efforts of large governmental agencies for effective operations overseas. That requires a different set of qualifications, developed through executive management, skills that are not inherently academic and typically acquired through leadership of large multi-dimensional organizations. Most National Security Advisors are not selected with such skills in mind, and in turn few are strong executive managers. Rice was no exception during a period when the country desperately needed such a manager.

In fairness, no leader at the senior level can be expected to possess every appropriate capacity in a changing environment. But a leader should be able to identify subordinates who can fill the gaps and offer key support. In that regard, Rice was poorly served by Steve Hadley, and to some extent by Frank Miller. Like Rice, both had their credentials in the field of arms control, not in the Middle East. Hadley had worked at senior levels in government most of his career, but he was a lawyer with little management experience.

Miller was a better manager, but he was poorly served by the NSC system. A senior military staff, such as Central Command, consists of almost a thousand people and may expand to twice that during periods of conflict, as it did during the invasion of Iraq. In contrast, the size of the NSC staff is fewer than two hundred, and it did not expand appreciably for the invasion. While a military staff has officers with comparable training, education, and experience, the staff on the NSC is eclectic, representing many backgrounds, without a common professional base. Few on the NSC had intermediate training or education comparable to military staff colleges and war colleges, nor does the NSC have common procedures and systems for planning and preparation.

For several months in early 2003, Garner had weekly meetings with Rice and some association with Hadley and Miller. Colonel Baltazar accompanied Garner to each meeting. They presented Rice and her associates with what ORHA needed from the other Departments and Agencies. Rice was receptive and sympathetic, but she did little to assist Garner. Both Garner and Colonel

Baltazar believed that Rice and Hadley were weak in their respective roles, failing to manage the NSC staff in an effective manner to harness the U.S. government to support ORHA. Bremer had similar problems obtaining support for CPA.[6]

Central Command had a core of people on its staff with proven planning qualifications, assigned to work on Iraq full-time in 2002, and when the load became heavy, officers such as Colonels Fitzgerald, Halverson, and Agoglia could request, and successfully obtain, additional qualified officers to augment their staffs at Tampa and Qatar on a full-time basis. Frank Miller had only a few people working directly for him. Those that he brought in to form his Executive Steering Group to study Iraq were not fully under his control and met with him only two or three times a week. He certainly did not have a structured planning process comparable to those in a senior military command. Miller established only one working group under his direct supervision, to provide humanitarian assistance and limited reconstruction in Iraq.

Robin Cleveland and Elliot Abrams, who led that working group, did not possess developed experience with the Middle East in general or Iraq in particular. Abrams had some experience with humanitarian assistance, and Cleveland had been involved in funding international programs, but when events unfolded there was no substantial requirement for humanitarian assistance in Iraq, and the reconstruction tasks in Iraq were far greater than anticipated. Once the cost of reconstruction soared and she was no longer in a leading role, Cleveland restricted the flow of money to ensure it was properly accounted for, rather than push it forward aggressively when there was such critical demand. The result was chokepoints for money that should have been readily available.

Working groups were set up by the other government departments. USAID put together a team to expand upon the reconstruction tasks of Cleveland's working group. It brought more talent and experience to reconstruction, but it was not prepared for the grand scope of what would be required for Iraq. Treasury had a small team study the Iraqi finance and banking system, but it did not foresee the magnitude of the task before it, nor the extensive economic changes that would eventually be imposed upon Iraq when Bremer took over. The State Department put the Future of Iraq project into motion under Tom Warrick, but there were few from State involved in the project and there was no coherent plan in the written papers produced. When Ron Adams studied the working groups early in 2003, he drew a line diagram that had them all reporting to Frank Miller's ESG. But Miller said that only Abrams and Cleveland's Humanitarian Assistance group worked for him. The problem with the

NSC was that no single person controlled all the working groups trying to prepare for Iraq and no one brought them into a national plan.

When it became clear that someone in government had to take charge of Iraq for the post-conflict period, Rumsfeld argued that the Department of Defense could do it best. He was correct, but in their dealings with the rest of the government, Rumsfeld, Wolfowitz, and Feith were heavy-handed and arrogant. Secretary Powell agreed that Defense should manage postwar Iraq and conceded that State was improperly equipped to do so. Not everyone agreed with Powell; some felt that the post-conflict phase should not be under military control. Those that felt the State Department should have been in charge, rather than Defense, may not have understood the depth of management and resources required for the task.

The American regular military establishment had over a million uniformed personnel in 2003, with over 150,000 commissioned regular officers, while the total number of State Department employees was only 50,000. Even that number is deceiving, however: about 35,000 of those working for State are foreign nationals working in embassies and consulates overseas; they cannot be deployed to other countries. In 2003, of the Americans working for State there were about 7,000 diplomats or Foreign Service Officers (FSOs)—not many more than the officer strength of the U.S. Coast Guard. There is nothing in the State Department comparable to an NCO corps, much less battalions of trucks, engineers, military police, or Civil Affairs units that can go to a nonpermissive region under austere conditions to put a broken state back into operation.

Those on a diplomatic career track at the Department of State are not in the business of executive management, nor are they recruited for such skills. While ambassadors have rank for pay and protocol purposes comparable to general officers, senior military officers are far more familiar with the task of managing large numbers of people, equipment, supplies, and massive budgets. General officers have supervised extensive installations with schools, hospitals, dependent housing areas, commissaries, exchanges, police and fire departments, jails and prisons, rail yards, and even port facilities. That type of broad-based management is uncommon for senior diplomats. The infighting and bad blood within the American government during the planning and operations for Iraq was indeed unfortunate, but arguably not because the overall responsibility for managing the post-conflict phase was under the Department of Defense. It would have been far more difficult—probably impossible—for the NSC to do it directly with its small staff or for the Department of State to do it with the lack of infrastructure necessary to manage the operations of another country.

What about USAID with its mandate for international development? Some of the same problems apply. In 2003 the total strength of USAID was about 2,000, including its Foreign Service Officers. Most of them were already overseas on USAID projects. The FSO from USAID is less of a diplomat than an FSO from State, with management capacity based on their projects overseas. But those are normally small projects run by small teams. Many USAID personnel have not worked in upper management of large postconflict endeavors like those in Iraq and Afghanistan, although they are certainly involved. When USAID is involved, they must use contracts to obtain trucks, equipment, storage facilities, and communications support. Such contracting assumes a permissive environment for contractors to move freely. In an austere environment with little security, and limited contractor support, USAID will be unable to lead the overall effort.

If the Department of Defense was the appropriate agency to manage the post-conflict phase for Iraq in 2003, what assessment of its performance is in order? First, planning began far too late. When Rumsfeld threatened to fire anyone distracted from war planning by post-conflict concerns, military planners were happy to focus on what they knew best. Later, when Rumsfeld acknowledged that Defense would have to take on the post-conflict role, planning and preparation lacked cohesion and central guidance. There were four uncoordinated planning efforts within Defense: Central Command planning began in December 2002 under Major Tom Fisher; the Joint Staff stood up JTF-4 under Steve Hawkins the same month; in January OSD-Policy had Jay Garner stand up what would become ORHA; and that month the Coalition ground component command produced the Eclipse II for Phase IV, which gained little from Major Fisher's efforts, and had no developed role for JTF-4 or ORHA.

The Army War College Crane-Terrill study was also an unintended victim of the emergence of ORHA for the postwar role. When a draft copy of the study was given to the Department of the Army staff and to General McKiernan, who was visiting the Pentagon at the end of January, there was a sudden lack of interest if an interagency group under Garner was going to take on that role. When the study did not reach Garner or many others in ORHA who might have benefited, the value of the study found no utility. It was Con Crane's view that if ORHA had not been created, the Army Staff would have pushed Central Command and McKiernan's CFLCC to pay more attention to it.[7]

Both JTF-4 and ORHA were started from scratch rather than from a standing headquarters, excusable perhaps for another governmental agency or department without organizational depth, but not for the Department of

Defense with its many well-structured headquarters and standing task forces, some specifically designed for sustainable deployment. Compounding the problem, both organizations were poorly supported by a department deep in resources. When JTF-4 and ORHA were sequentially passed to Central Command under General Tommy Franks, little effort was made by that command to provide resources or attention. Rear Admiral Robb, the J-5 for Plans and Policy at Central Command, repeatedly told Garner to expect little assistance from military formations, and specifically said there would be no security forces provided. JTF-4 was placed under Central Command's subordinate CFLCC, in time for some integration, but it was an unhappy affair. Central Command did not pass ORHA to CFLCC control until the invasion was in progress, a time when General McKiernan did not "have the intellectual energy to talk about Phase IV."[8]

JTF-4 was deactivated prior to the invasion, but fewer than half a dozen of its officers joined ORHA. In Baghdad, military support for ORHA was minimal. Worse, General Franks began a redeployment of military forces from Iraq, telling his commanders, "Take as much risk getting out as you took getting in."[9] In the eyes of one observer, that led "to a rush at the port in Kuwait to get out of theater."[10] That rush was not stopped until General Abizaid took command in July. By the end of the summer the aggregate combat forces in Iraq were comparable to the invasion forces, but much of the support formations had redeployed. That included the military construction capability with the 416th Engineer Command and the I MEF Engineer Group, which left Iraq with fourteen engineer construction battalions. Meanwhile, reconstruction requirements greatly exceeded previous estimates, with contractors such as Bechtel assigned projects and unable to get established or move in Iraq due to inadequate security.

When the U.S. Third Army Headquarters, the core of the ground force command, left Iraq and handed off control to V Corps, the command and support capability was reduced beyond what numbers suggested. To make the situation worse, when V Corps assumed the role of CJTF-7, much of the original V Corps staff was allowed to depart on a peacetime rotation schedule, including all the planners, with the loss of institutional knowledge acquired over the previous year and during the invasion of Iraq.

That all these changes were allowed to take place with so little foresight and attention is unconscionable for a professional military system. Who should be held responsible? Starting at the top, the senior leadership in the Pentagon must be held accountable, both civilian and military—specifically Secretary Rumsfeld and Chairman of the Joint Staff General Richard Myers along with their respective subordinates. The senior leadership of the Department of the

Army, while not in charge, should have taken a strong interest, but by June 2003 the Secretary of the Army had resigned over a scandal, and General Shinseki, the Army Chief of Staff, was retiring. That does not remove responsibility from other senior Army officers who should have been intensely concerned with the operations in a theater employing four of the Army's ten divisions.

At Central Command, General Tommy Franks must be held responsible as the overall commander for operations in Iraq. General Abizaid expressed concern about the rush to redeploy during the summer; when he replaced Franks in mid-July he took measures to stop it, but he could not recall many of the formations that had left. General McKiernan bears some responsibility. It was not his decision that his headquarters leave Iraq, but he did not resist that decision. It does appear, however, that he did not take an active interest in the personnel turnover that took place within V Corps during the summer. That responsibility must be shared. Even if it was under control of Central Command, the senior U.S. Army headquarters in Germany still maintained administrative control over V Corps personnel in Iraq and managed individual officer rotations.

There has been little outcry over the transitions with military formations and personnel in Iraq during the summer of 2003, beyond what General Sanchez has written.[11] His challenges were more extensive than they appeared when he took command. The overall management of the senior military officers for the forces in Iraq during this period warrants a more critical assessment than this study allows.

COUNTERFACTUALS

What might have taken place differently within the same context during the planning and execution for the post-conflict phase in Iraq? Starting with the Department of Defense, acknowledgment that the Pentagon would have to provide the initial post-conflict management could have come sooner in 2002 and could have been better integrated in the overall planning for the invasion.

Even coming together only in December 2002 as it did, there could have been greater unity of purpose and effort with OSD-Policy and the Joint Staff working together in the Pentagon. Those in OSD could have provided the policy guidance and assisted with interagency contributions. The Joint Staff could have provided the military guidance and coordination to package the right capabilities to go into theater. Properly done, there would not have been a separate ORHA and JTF-4 for comparable tasks; there would have been a single organization with civilian and military personnel. Rather than stand the overall formation up from scratch, an existing headquarters, complete with a cohesive staff, communications, and other appropriate equipment for some self-sustainment, could have been identified and used as a base for ORHA. Colonel Tony Puckett later suggested that the headquarters staff of III Corps Artillery at Fort Sill, Oklahoma, could have performed such a task. It had staff sections comparable to the ORHA C-staff, but it was more robust and had a substantial communications capability. The III Corps Artillery headquarters did not deploy for OIF and was otherwise available in the United States for the role Colonel Puckett proposed.[12]

With such a single formation forming in January 2003 with someone such as Jay Garner in charge, those in the Pentagon should have coordinated with Central Command to ensure it fit with the invasion plans. That would have entailed alignment with the ground component plans. In January, Colonel Kevin Benson was writing Eclipse II for General McKiernan's command. Rather than wait until April to place ORHA and Garner under control of General McKiernan and his command, it could have been done in January, which would have made it appropriate for Benson to plan Eclipse II with ORHA as the central element rather than write a post-conflict plan that left ORHA out. Placing ORHA under McKiernan in January would have allowed a thoughtful allocation of forces to ORHA as they became available and as ORHA could use them. (See Figure 10 for the April 2003 situation with ORHA under control of General McKiernan and CLFCC alongside other units available for post-conflict not otherwise associated with ORHA or under ORHA control.)

A more useful alignment of forces would have been to merge ORHA and JTF-4 to form a single headquarters, ideally with a core staff from something like III Corps Artillery as its base. Adding a signal battalion would have ensured ORHA had organic communications to work in Baghdad and to manage its regional subordinate components. Adding a full MP battalion would have ensured ORHA had more security and more armed escort for movement. To enhance the governance and the Civil Administration pillar, the 352nd Civil Affairs Command, with one CA brigade and one CA battalion, could have been attached to ORHA (the other CA brigades and battalions would have remained attached to the maneuver formations). To enhance Reconstruction until contractors like Bechtel were operational, the 416th ENCOM with its eight subordinate construction engineer battalions could have been attached and aligned under the ORHA Reconstruction pillar (see Figure 11).

CFLCC Phase IV Assets

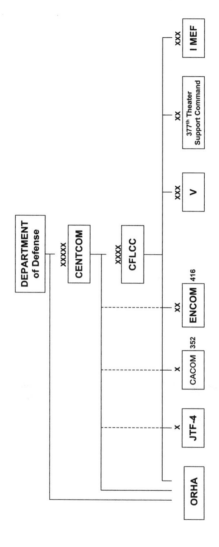

•ORHA was not under CFLCC control until April 2003;
•other units were under CFLCC control as they came into theater

Figure 10. Combined Forces Land Component Command (CFLCC) Phase IV Assets.

Possible Eclipse II forces for ORHA

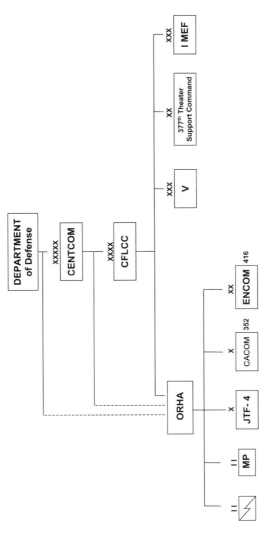

Figure 11. Possible Eclipse II forces for ORHA.

With JTF-4, the 352nd CAC, the 416th ENCOM, and signal and MP units attached to ORHA, they could have been integrated with the ORHA functional and regional pillars (see Figure 12). With such a structure, Garner and ORHA would have had security, communications, a reconstruction capability as contractors arrived, and an enhanced capacity for governance to manage the Iraqi ministries. The attached military units could have had subordinate units aligned with the ORHA regional components as required to empower those as well. Such an arrangement designed in January 2003 as part of the Eclipse II plan could have set Garner and ORHA up for a much more successful operation in Iraq, allowing greater depth to adapt to challenges on the ground. In turn, such an organization could have been extended to CPA under Bremer.

And the rest of the U.S. government—how might it have made a greater contribution? In the State Department, the Future of Iraq project could have been managed better with the wealth of information collected. It could have been integrated into a rigorous political-military plan for Iraq that could have been taken to the Department of Defense and on to Central Command. When Mike Ayoub took the existing political-military plan from the State Department files in 2002, there was only a shell format. But the format had utility if used for a detailed planning effort. Ayoub took the plan to his superiors in an effort to bring it up to date, but he was rebuffed. At some level above Ayoub, there could have been direction to merge Ayoub's and Tom Warrick's efforts to produce the State portion of a political-military plan for Iraq. With USAID as a subordinate agency to the Department of State, the planning effort for Iraq by Wendy Chamberlin and her team could also have been integrated with Ayoub's political-military plan. The problem at State and USAID was that there was not a rigorous system for planning to make it natural to fuse such efforts together.

If someone such as Deputy Secretary Richard Armitage or even Secretary Powell (both with military backgrounds and planning experience) had taken greater interest in the efforts of Warrick, Ayoub, and Chamberlin, it should have been possible to better focus the efforts of State and USAID on providing greater unity of effort to work with the NSC and the Department of Defense. Perhaps personalities at State and Defense may have made such a connection problematic, but if State had managed its efforts better, it is also possible that those at Defense might have seen more utility in working together. On a larger level it would have been useful if State had brought in more Coalition partners and the United Nations, as it had during the lead-up to Desert Storm. When Garner went to the United Nations in February

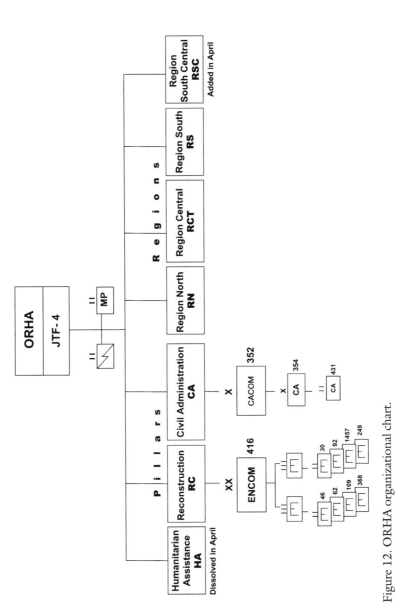

Figure 12. ORHA organizational chart.

2003, no one from State went with him and the U.S. ambassador to the UN was lukewarm in his support.

Management by the National Security Council could have been greater at several levels. There was utility in the Executive Steering Group set up by Frank Miller, but his authority was limited to coordination, and when Garner started to recruit for ORHA, Miller stopped the ESG meetings on Iraq and did not reconvene them until after the invasion. Miller might have been given more power, a larger staff, with ESG designated as the point of contact for Garner and ORHA. Instead, Garner attempted to coordinate for assistance with Condoleezza Rice, who lacked Miller's management skills and Pentagon connections.

During 2003 and into 2004 it was clear that there were serious deficiencies with interagency management. In July 2004, Congress authorized the creation of the Office of the Coordinator for Reconstruction and Stabilization, known as S/CRS, within the Department of State. The intention was to establish an operational component that could integrate the interagency efforts of the American government for overseas endeavors. If there had been such an office in 2002, it could have been used to integrate the efforts of Mike Ayoub, Tom Warrick, and Wendy Chamberlin, representing separate efforts for Iraq within the Department of State and USAID. Integrating the efforts of other government departments and agencies remain as problematic as it was for Frank Miller and the Executive Steering Group, as there is no indication S/CRS will be able to task or coerce the rest of government to provide the personnel or resources necessary for operations overseas. Although S/CRS has a larger staff than Miller had in 2003, it does not have the same proximity to the National Security Advisor and the NSC that Miller enjoyed.

Looking back on the period when the U.S. government attempted to plan and prepare for regime change in Iraq, Colonel Tom Greenwood, who served with Frank Miller on the NSC staff, reflected, "We ran out of strategic patience and paid dearly for our impetuosity. At the highest level, the United States failed to build a robust and cohesive coalition required to sustain a global undertaking that would last years and not weeks. The United States also failed to provide General Jay Garner sufficient time to organize, train, and equip his corps of civil servants so essential to running Iraq's government ministries after Baghdad fell."[13]

Observing the president and the Principals Committee on the NSC, Greenwood felt the decision to invade by a particular date was allowed to offset the requirements for proper preparation. "A strong desire to start the war in the spring of 2003 meant that U.S. forces did not have adequate Arabic interpreters, stay-behind forces, or international police trainers. In short, a 'cake walk' mentality was complemented with artificially derived deadlines which permeated virtually all aspects of prewar planning."

In Greenwood's view, the central flaw in planning for Iraq was to first set the date for the invasion—not later than mid-March 2003—then to try to adapt the planning and preparations for the invasion and what would follow in place to fit that date. "This leaves us with the lesson that unless attacked first, nations should fight preemptive wars when they are politically and militarily optimized to do so. My sense is historians will continue to discover in the years ahead that this was not the case with Operation Iraqi Freedom."[14]

Arguably, the president should have demanded that everything was ready, both for the invasion and what was to follow, before he authorized the invasion to be launched. Just hours before the invasion took place, the president did ask the military commanders if they were ready to go into Iraq to remove the regime of Saddam Hussein. They told him they were indeed ready, and they proved it with dramatic results.

The president did not ask his military commanders or Jay Garner if they were ready for what would follow the invasion. The number of ground forces was inadequate to stabilize the country, the post-conflict planning was incomplete, and there were no preparations to reform Iraqi police forces. Garner and ORHA had not been properly supported for their role in personnel, resources, interagency planning, or time. Nor were the military commanders or Garner prepared for the dramatic changes that Bremer would impose upon the American intentions for Iraq—shifting from liberation to an occupation that would require more resources and time, when the intent by the NSC and the Department of Defense had been to keep them to a minimum. Bremer's changes had token approval from the president, but were otherwise uncoordinated with the rest of the U.S. government or the Coalition. The results were painful, prolonging the overall effort in Iraq with significant costs in time, lives, treasure, and American prestige.

Iraq had a fragile and complicated domestic and economic structure that was poorly understood by American policy makers and planners. Those who saw Saddam Hussein correctly as a tyrant did not discern that his ruthless regime provided much of the glue that held Iraq together. Once that regime was removed from power, the Iraqi opposition parties and the population at large were unprepared for the liberation American policy makers intended.

In Garner's metaphor, there were many missing tiles on the mosaic for Iraq prior to the invasion and for what followed. The most critical deficiencies were those noted at the highest level of the American government. And

there were deficiencies as well with every department and agency that participated or should have participated in the planning and preparation for regime
replacement. Those deficiencies can be used to help explain the prolonged
recovery for Iraq. The American experience in Iraq provides a new chapter in
the history of nation building. It is a chapter as worthy of study and reflection
as the American experiences following World War II.

NOTES

PREFACE

1. Gordon W. Rudd, *Humanitarian Intervention: Assisting the Iraqi Kurds in Operation Provide Comfort, 1991* (Washington, D.C.: U.S. Army Center of Military History, 2004).

2. Interviews with Jay Garner, 30 March, 22 April, 14 September 2005, 15 October 2007.

INTRODUCTION: A COLD START

1. In 2003, General James Jones, USMC, was Supreme Allied Commander Europe and U.S. European Command, which supported American operations in Iraq. Lieutenant General John Abizaid, USA, was the U.S. Central Command deputy commander; in July 2003 he would replace General Tommy Franks as commander of Central Command and be promoted to full general.

2. Interviews with Jay Garner, USA (Ret), 30 March and 22 April 2004, 14–15 September 2005, 30 October 2006, and 15 October 2007. Garner believed that General Jones, who had served under him as a colonel on Operation Provide Comfort and was the NATO commander in 2003, had suggested him to Rumsfeld for work in Iraq.

3. Ibid.

4. Ibid.

PROLOGUE: MARSHALL HAD TWO YEARS

1. Earl F. Ziemke, *The U.S. Army in the Occupation of Germany, 1944–1946* (Washington, D.C.: U.S. Army Center of Military History, 1975), 6.

2. *United States Army in the World War, 1917–1919,* Volume 11, *American Occupation of Germany* (Washington, D.C.: U.S. Army Center of Military History, 1948).

3. Ibid., 3, 9, 135. On the right, the French had advanced to Mainz; on the left the British had closed on Cologne; and the Belgian army was further north before Düsseldorf.

4. Ibid., 2, 86.

5. Ibid., 159. The French staff system is often referred to as the Napoleonic staff system, but the French army staff system in World War I, copied by the U.S. Army and the basis for contemporary American military staffs, was far more sophisticated and integrated than what Napoleon developed a century earlier; "Napoleonic" does not fit the twentieth-century model.

6. Ibid., 146; the original Hunt Report is at the U.S. Army Military History Institute, Carlisle, Pa.

7. Ibid., 60–170; Ziemke, *U.S. Army in the Occupation of Germany,* 3.

8. *FM 27–5 Military Government* was succeeded by *FM 41–10 Civil Affairs Operations*; Ziemke, *U.S. Army in the Occupation of Germany,* vi, 4.

9. Harry L. Coles and Albert K. Weinberg, *Civil Affairs: Soldiers Become Governors* (Washington, D.C.: U.S. Army Center of Military History, 1986), 3–11.

10. Ibid., 12–13, 19, 80; Ziemke, *U.S. Army in the Occupation of Germany,* 9–10; Arnold G. Fischer, *Military Government in the Ryukyu Islands, 1945–1950* (Washington, D.C.: U.S. Army Center of Military History, 1988), 12–13.

11. Coles and Weinberg, *Civil Affairs,* 22–27.

12. Ibid., 21–24, 27.

13. Ibid., 25–29; George C. Marshall, *George C. Marshall: Interviews and Reminiscences for Forrest C. Pogue,* ed. Larry I. Bland (Lexington, Va.: George C. Marshall Research Foundation, 1991), 452–454, 612.

14. Coles and Weinberg, *Civil Affairs,* 56.

15. Ibid., 171–172.

16. Ibid., 173, 177–179.

17. Ibid., 190–199, 209; the Civil Affairs experience in Sicily was portrayed in the novel *A Bell for Adano* by John Hersey, which General Bradley read the night before the Normandy invasion; it later won the Pulitzer Prize. John Hersey, *A Bell for Adano* (New York: Random House, 1944); David Hogan, *First Army Headquarters in Europe, 1943–1945* (Washington, D.C.: U.S. Army Center of Military History, 2000), 68.

18. Coles and Weinberg, *Civil Affairs,* 371–372.

19. Robert Murphy, *Diplomat among Warriors* (New York: Doubleday, 1964), 224.

20. Ibid., 194.

21. Ibid., 187, 283–285, 290–294.

22. Ibid., 230–232, 392–393, 471–474.

23. Formations in German-occupied Italy, the Balkans, and Greece were disbanded by the Germans or joined the Germans. Albert N. Garland and Howard M. Smyth, *Sicily and the Surrender of Italy* (Washington, D.C.: U.S. Army Center of Military History, 1965), 532–549.

24. Martin Blumenson, *Salerno to Cassino* (Washington, D.C.: U.S. Army Center of Military History, 1969), 184–185, 236, 253, 285, 418; Ernest F. Fisher Jr., *Cassino to the Alps* (Washington, D.C.: U.S. Army Center of Military History, 1977), 29, 253, 402, 415.

25. Stanley Sandler, *Glad to See Them Come and Sorry to See Them Go: A History of U.S. Army Tactical Civil Affairs/Military Government, 1775–1991* (Fort Bragg, N.C.: Special Operations Command, 1988), 187, 191, 202.

26. Coles and Weinberg, *Civil Affairs,* 553–556, 671–673, 697–699; Marcel Vigneras, *Rearming the French* (Washington, D.C.: U.S. Army Center of Military History, 1957), 74–90.

27. Coles and Weinberg, *Civil Affairs,* 84–85, 861.

28. Forrest C. Pogue, *George C. Marshall: Organizer of Victory, 1943–1945* (New York: Viking Press, 1973), 463–467.

29. Sandler, *Glad to See Them Come,* 229; Ziemke, *U.S. Army in the Occupation of Germany,* 381–383; Lucian K. Truscott, *Command Missions: A Personal Story* (New York: E. P. Dutton, 1956), 503.

30. Ziemke, *U.S. Army in the Occupation of Germany,* 320; James J. Carafano, *Waltzing into the Cold War: The Struggle for Occupied Austria* (College Station: Texas A&M University Press, 2002), 15, 36, 52.

31. Ziemke, *U.S. Army in the Occupation of Germany,* 341; Truscott, *Command Missions,* 507–531.

32. Sandler, *Glad to See Them Come,* 230–232. Clay remained as the deputy for military government when Eisenhower was replaced by General Joseph T. McNarney, then assumed the senior position in March 1947.

33. Ibid., 231–234; Murphy, *Diplomat among Warriors,* 281–282.

34. Ziemke, *U.S. Army in the Occupation of Germany,* 348–351; Sandler, *Glad to See Them Come,* 237n43.

35. Sandler, *Glad to See Them Come,* 240.

36. Ziemke, *U.S. Army in the Occupation of Germany,* 83–84; Hajo Holborn, *American Military Government: Its Organization and Policies* (Washington, D.C.: Infantry Journal Press, 1947), 36–37.

37. Ziemke, *U.S. Army in the Occupation of Germany,* 84–90, 380–387.

38. Ibid., 240–242, 430–431.

39. Ibid., 445–446.

40. Michael Beschloss, *The Conquerors: Roosevelt, Truman, and the Destruction of Hitler's Germany, 1941–1945* (New York: Simon & Schuster, 2002), 283.

41. Carafano, *Waltzing into the Cold War,* 53; Sandler, *Glad to See Them Come,* 262–268; Holborn, *American Military Government,* 75, 132–135, 139.

42. Sandler, *Glad to See Them Come,* 262–268; Holborn, *American Military Government,* 82–83.

43. Sandler, *Glad to See Them Come,* 262–268.

44. Carafano, *Waltzing into the Cold War,* 97–115.

45. Ibid., 129–133, 162–164, 173–178, 193–198.

46. M. Hanlan Cannon, *Leyte: The Return to the Philippines* (Washington, D.C.: U.S. Army Center of Military History, 1954), 198–201; Holborn, *American Military Government,* 87.

47. Cannon, *Leyte;* Robert Ross Smith, *Triumph in the Philippines* (Washington, D.C.: U.S. Army Center of Military History, 1963), 40–41; Sandler, *Glad to See Them Come,* 211–212; Charles Willoughby, ed., *Reports of General MacArthur,* vol.1, *The Campaigns of General MacArthur in the Pacific* (Washington, D.C.: U.S. Army Center of Military History, 1994), 4–22, 295–326.

48. Karl C. Dod, *The Corps of Engineers: The War against Japan* (Washington, D.C.: U.S. Army Center of Military History, 1966), 650–654.

49. Ibid., 653.

50. Roy E. Appleman, James MacGregor Burns, Russell A. Gugeler, and John Stevens, *Okinawa: The Last Battle* (Washington, D.C.: U.S. Army Center of Military History, 1948), 35, 417–419.

51. Ibid.; Fisch, *Military Government in the Ryukyu Islands*, 15–21.

52. Fisch, *Military Government in the Ryukyu Islands*, 24–29.

53. Ibid., 38–45, 49–70.

54. Ibid.

55. Ibid., 74–80; Dod, *Corps of Engineers*, 657–660; Holborn, *American Military Government*, 92–97.

56. John W. Dower, *Embracing Defeat: Japan in the Wake of World War II* (New York: New Press, 1999), 222–224, 525; *Reports of General MacArthur*, vol. 1, *The Campaigns of General MacArthur in the Pacific*, 431–450.

57. Dower, *Embracing Defeat*; Charles A. Willoughby, ed., *Reports of General MacArthur*, vol. 1, suppl., *The Occupation: The Military Phase*, 12–27; Sandler, *Glad to See Them Come*, 268.

58. Willoughby, *Reports of General MacArthur*, vol. 1, suppl., *The Occupation: The Military Phase*, 24–25.

59. Ibid., 220–222, 225, 231–232.

60. Willoughby, *Reports of General MacArthur*, vol. 1, *The Campaigns of General MacArthur in the Pacific*, 403–405, vol. 1, suppl., *The Occupation: The Military Phase*, 53–54, 117–147; Dower, *Embracing Defeat*, 113–114.

61. Willoughby, *Reports of General MacArthur*, vol. 1, suppl., *The Occupation: The Military Phase*, 65–66, 194–196.

62. Ibid., 195–230; Dower, *Embracing Defeat*, 224.

63. Willoughby, *Reports of General MacArthur*, vol. 1, suppl., *The Occupation: The Military Phase*, 219–222; Sandler, *Glad to See Them Come*, 277.

64. Sandler, *Glad to See Them Come*, 213, 216–217, 296.

65. Dower, *Embracing Defeat*, 277–301.

66. Ibid.

67. Sandler, *Glad to See Them Come*, 278.

68. *Reports of General MacArthur*, vol. 1, suppl., *The Occupation: The Military Phase*, 6–7, 14–16; also see Allan R. Millett, *The War for Korea, 1945–1950: A House Burning* (Lawrence: University Press of Kansas, 2005), 52–60; Holborn, *American Military Government*, 99–100.

69. Sandler, *Glad to See Them Come*, 308–310; Ronald H. Spector, *In the Ruins of Empire: The Japanese Surrender and the Battle for Postwar Asia* (New York: Random House, 2008), 149–151.

70. Spector, *In the Ruins of Empire*, 152–153.

71. Sandler, *Glad to See Them Come*, 228–236.

72. Ibid., 336–338.

73. Ibid., 351–366; Thomas W. Scoville, *Reorganizing for Pacification* (Washington, D.C.: Government Printing Office, 1982).

74. Sandler, *Glad to See Them Come*, 351–366.

75. Ziemke, *U.S. Army in the Occupation of Germany*, 446–447.

76. Douglas Feith, *War and Decision: Inside the Pentagon at the Dawn of the War on Terrorism* (New York: Harper, 2008), 277–279, 402–403. Feith states in his book that his office in the Pentagon in 2002–2003, the Office of the Secretary of Defense—Policy,

"consistently promoted liberation rather than occupation" for Iraq. He further states that President Bush was committed to "liberation, not occupation."

CHAPTER 1. MILITARY PLANNING

1. Russell Weigley, quoted in Richard M. Swain, *Lucky War: Third Army in Desert Storm* (Fort Leavenworth, Kans.: U.S. Army Command and General Staff College Press, 1994), xxvii. Here Weigley is called the "dean of American military historians" by Roger Spiller, a prominent military historian in his own right.

2. Swain, *Lucky War,* 338.

3. *Joint Vision 2010* (Washington, D.C.: Government Printing Office, 1996).

4. Admiral William Owens noted his role in *Joint Vision 2010* in his book *Lifting the Fog of War* (New York: Farrar, Straus & Giroux, 2000), 208–209.

5. William Owens, *High Seas: The Naval Passage to an Uncharted World* (Annapolis: Naval Institute Press, 1995), 25.

6. For World War II U.S. Army and Navy planners, see Mark S. Watson, *Chief of Staff: Prewar Plans and Preparations* (Washington, D.C.: U.S. Army Center of Military History, 1950); and Edward S. Miller, *War Plan Orange: The U.S. Strategy to Defeat Japan, 1897–1945* (Annapolis: Naval Institute Press, 1991).

7. Of the best-known books published about Iraq after 2004, only Michael Gordon and Bernard Trainor, in *Cobra II* (New York: Pantheon Books, 2006), address any of these planners, and then only briefly. Tom Ricks, in *Fiasco: The American Military Adventure in Iraq* (New York: Penguin Press, 2006), mentions only two—Agoglia and Benson—while none are mentioned in Bob Woodward's *Plan of Attack* (New York: Simon & Schuster, 2004) or *State of Denial* (New York: Simon & Schuster, 2006), nor do other books such as George Packer, *Assassins' Gate: America in Iraq* (New York: Simon & Schuster, 2005), or Rajiv Chandrasekaran, *Imperial Life in the Emerald City* (New York: Alfred A. Knopf, 2006).

8. Memorandum from Colonel Richard Stouder, USA (Ret), to author, 4 July 2007.

9. Ibid.

10. Interview with Colonel Roland Tiso, USA (Ret), 30 May 2008.

11. Stouder memo; Tiso interview.

12. Stouder memo; interview with General Binford ("Bennie") Peay, USA (Ret), 8 December 2006.

13. Stouder memo; Peay interview.

14. Stouder memo.

15. Peay interview.

16. Stouder memo; Peay interview.

17. Interview with Colonel Steven D. Kidder, USA (Ret), and Colonel Michael D. Fitzgerald, USA (Ret), 24 September 2006; Kidder interview, 13 October 2006; Tiso and Fitzgerald interviews, 31 May 2008.

18. Tiso, Fitzgerald, Kidder interviews.

19. Kidder interview, 13 October 2006; Peay interview.

20. Kidder, Fitzgerald, Peay interviews.

21. End of Tour report of General Binford Peay III, Commander in Chief, United

States Central Command, August 1994–August 1997, dated 3 November 1997, declassified December 2006, 12, 16, 25.

22. Peay interview; Peay, End of Tour report, 39, 41–42.

23. Peay, End of Tour report, 42, 45; Peay interview.

24. At that time Colonel Stouder was G-3 Operations officer working for Lieutenant General Tommy Franks at the Third Army; Stouder retired in the summer of 2001. Stouder memo; Tiso, Kidder interviews.

25. Kidder, Fitzgerald, Tiso interviews; Kidder email, 25 May 2007; interview with General Anthony Zinni, USMC (Ret), 28 April 2008.

26. Kidder, Fitzgerald interviews.

27. Zinni interview; email message from Zinni to author, 8 May 2008.

28. Kidder, Fitzgerald interviews.

29. Kidder, Zinni interviews.

30. Kidder interviews.

31. Zinni interview; Desert Crossing Seminar (U): After Action Report (U) 28–29 June 1999, declassified 2 July 2004 by Brigadier General G. J. Trautman Jr. USMC, Deputy J5, Central Command; Action Officer: Mr. Michael D. Fitzgerald, CCJGP Civilian Contractor.

32. Colonel Mike Madden, USA, was Chief of War Plans for one year between Kidder and Fitzgerald; Kidder, Fitzgerald interviews.

33. Kidder, Fitzgerald interviews.

34. Kidder, Fitzgerald interviews.

35. Fitzgerald, Zinni interviews; Desert Crossing Seminar (U): After Action Report (U), 28–29 June 1999.

36. Kidder, Fitzgerald interviews.

37. *Joint Vision 2020* (Washington, D.C.: Government Printing Office, 2000).

38. Kidder, Fitzgerald interviews.

39. Tommy Franks, with Malcolm McConnell, *American Soldier: General Tommy Franks* (New York: Regan Books, 2004), 315, 348–349. Kidder, Fitzgerald interviews; Christopher Kirchhoff summary paper of an interview by the Special Inspector General for Iraqi Reconstruction with Brigadier General Mark E. Scheid, 20 September, 2006.

40. Franks, *American Soldier*, 331, 342–344.

41. Scheid interview summary; Fitzgerald interviews.

42. Franks, *American Soldier*, 362.

43. Interviews with Colonel John Agoglia, USA, 28 June 2003, 22 September, 2006, 15 October 2007; the SAMS program began at Fort Leavenworth in the early 1980s and provided key planners during Operation Desert Storm. In the early 1990s, the U.S. Marine Corps established a comparable program with the School of Advanced Warfighting (SAW) and the U.S. Air Force with the School of Advanced Air and Space Studies (SAASS). In 2002, the U.S. Navy established the Naval Operational Planners Course (NOPC). Officers attended SAMS, SAW, SAASS, and NOPC after completion of staff college. Upon graduation they were senior majors or lieutenant colonels; many would serve in key planning positions for operations in Iraq. Interview with Eric B. Yonkee, 3 June 2008; Franks, *American Soldier*, 362, 411, 420.

44. Agoglia, Fitzgerald interviews.

45. Interview with Colonel Kevin B. Benson, USA, 10 June 2006.

46. Campaign Planner Primer, Department of Military Strategy, Planning, and Operations, Army War College, 2006, 5.

47. Janet A. McDonnell, *After Desert Storm: The U.S. Army and the Reconstruction of Kuwait* (Washington, D.C.: Government Printing Office, 1999).

48. Agoglia, Benson interviews; email from Colonel Michael D. Fitzgerald, USA (Ret), 31 August 2006; Franks, American Soldier, 350–353.

49. Agoglia interviews.

50. Benson interview; email from Benson, 31 August 2006; Stouder memo; Franks, *American Soldier,* 545.

51. Agoglia, Zinni interviews.

52. Douglas J. Feith, *War and Decision: Inside the Pentagon at the Dawn of the War on Terrorism* (New York: Harper, 2008), 292–293.

53. Interviews with Colonel Tom Baltazar, USA (Ret), 22 and 29 June 2006; email from Colonel Martin Stanton, USA, 16 October 2006; the four CA Commands are 350th CA aligned with Southern Command (SOUTHCOM), the 351st CA aligned with Pacific Command (PACOM), the 352nd aligned with Central Command (CENTCOM), and the 353rd CA aligned with European Command (EUCOM); Army field manual FM 41–10 Civil Affairs Operations, 14 February 2000, 100.

54. Interview with Colonel Aldo R. Calvi, USAR, 13 July 2003; interview with Colonel James D. Owens, USAR, 14 July 2003.

55. Benson interview; email correspondence with Martin Stanton throughout 2006. Stanton wrote two books, *Road to Baghdad: Behind Enemy Lines* (New York: Valentine Books, 2003), and *Somalia on $5 a Day* (San Francisco: Presidio Press, 2003).

56. Benson, Calvi, Owens, Agoglia interviews.

57. Calvi, Owens interviews.

58. Calvi, Owens interviews.

59. Agoglia interviews; interview with Lieutenant Colonel Paul A. Shelton, 14 December 2005, Quantico, Virginia. At Central Command, Shelton replaced Marine Lieutenant Colonel John Buford, also a SAW graduate sent there as an augmentee earlier in 2002.

60. Shelton interview.

61. See McDonnell, *After Desert Storm.*

62. Shelton, Agoglia, Fitzgerald interviews.

63. Interviews with Gary Vogler, 18 June 2003, 31 December 2007; Shelton interview. John Agoglia did not remember the events the same way. He felt that General Renuart was an "agnostic" on the issue and did not push back to the degree Shelton remembered. Agoglia interview; Franks, *American Soldier,* 436–440; see also Colonel Nicholas E. Reynolds, *U.S. Marines in Iraq, 2003: Basrah, Baghdad, and Beyond* (Washington, D.C.: History Division, U.S. Marine Corps, 2007), 21–23.

64. Agoglia interviews; interview with Major Thomas S. Fisher, Central Command Headquarters, Tampa, 27 August 2003.

65. Paper by Colonel Kevin Benson, USA, undated; Benson, Fisher interviews.

66. Interview with General George W. Casey, USA, 19 February 2010; interview with General Casey by Stuart Bowen, Special Inspector General for Iraqi Reconstruction (SIGIR), 30 July 2008.

67. Casey interviews.

68. Feith, *War and Decision,* 292–293.

69. Casey interviews; interviews with Brigadier General Steven R. Hawkins, USA, 23 June 2003, 2 January 2004.

70. Hawkins interviews.

71. Casey, Hawkins interviews.

72. Casey, Hawkins interviews.

73. Baltazar interviews.

74. Agoglia interviews.

75. Agoglia, Baltazar interviews.

76. Hawkins, Agoglia interviews.

77. Agoglia interviews.

78. Hawkins interviews.

79. Ibid.

80. Ibid.

81. Agoglia interviews.

82. Agoglia, Benson interviews.

83. Benson interview.

84. Agoglia, Garner interviews.

85. Richard Haass, *War of Necessity, War of Choice: A Memoir of Two Iraq Wars* (New York: Simon & Schuster, 2009), 212–220. Haass had several discussions with Rice during this period and also made repeated arguments against a war, but he found that Rice was not interested and had her mind made up: the United States was going to invade Iraq.

86. Quantico hosts such presentation events as the Erskine Lectures. By design such presentations are not for attribution, although they are recorded. In 2008, General Zinni agreed to allow the Marine Corps University, which hosted the Erskine lectures, to release the tape to the author to use for this book.

87. Zinni interview; Tenet stated that "policy makers have a right to their own opinions, but not their own facts." George Tenet, *At the Center of the Storm: My Years at the CIA* (New York: HarpersCollins, 2007), 315–317.

88. Zinni presentation, 11 September 2002.

89. Testimony before the Senate Armed Services Committee, 23 September 2002; General Jay Garner commanded the ground forces, under General Shalikasvilli, that entered Iraq.

90. Testimony before the Senate Armed Services Committee, 23 September 2002.

91. Zinni interview.

CHAPTER 2. INTERAGENCY PLANNING

1. National Security Presidential Directive-1: Organization of the National Security Council System, 13 February 2001.

2. Ibid.

3. Interviews with Frank Miller, 20 November 2007, 30 July 2008; Douglas J. Feith, *War and Decision: Inside the Pentagon at the Dawn of the War on Terrorism* (New York: Harper, 2008), 237–238.

4. Tommy Franks, with Malcolm McConnell, *American Soldier: General Tommy Franks* (New York: Regan Books, 2004), 330, 363, 375, 545.

5. Ibid.

6. Miller interviews; Feith, *War and Decision,* 237n276.

7. Miller interviews.

8. Feith, *War and Decision,* 276–277.

9. Miller interviews.

10. Interviews with Lieutenant Colonel Jeffrey S. Kojac, USMC, 12 and 19 October 2007, 9 November 2007; Major Kojac began working for Frank Miller and Colonel Greenwood in January 2003.

11. Interview with Colonel Joe Collins, USA (Ret), 29 August 2006. In 2002 Collins was Deputy Assistant Secretary of Defense for Stability Operations within Feith's Policy office and represented OSD at meetings in Robin Cleveland's office beginning in August 2002; he also served on Dworken's Humanitarian Relief Working Group. A retired army colonel with a Ph.D., Collins had been the military assistant to Paul Wolfowitz when he was the Undersecretary of Defense for Policy in the early 1990s. Interview with Wendy J. Chamberlin, 14 July 2008; Robin Raphel interview with Chamberlin, 18 April 2007.

12. Miller interviews.

13. Chamberlin interviews.

14. Interviews with Thomas S. Warrick, 10, 15, and 17 November 2004.

15. Ibid.

16. Ibid.

17. Ibid.

18. Ibid.

19. Warrick, Future of Iraq project slides.

20. Future of Iraq project (FOI): Transitional Justice Report, CD produced by the Bureau of Legislative Affairs, State Department, May 2003.

21. Warrick interviews.

22. FOI: Transitional Justice Report, 26.

23. Ibid., 29.

24. Ibid., 27–31.

25. Warrick interviews.

26. Future of Iraq briefing, Department of State, 30 January 2003, slide 10.

27. FOI briefing, slide 16; FOI report: Economy & Infrastructure, 60–88; Warrick interviews.

28. FOI report: Economy & Infrastructure, 60–88; Warrick interviews.

29. FOI project report: Economy & Infrastructure, 178–179.

30. Warrick interviews.

31. David Philips, *Losing Iraq: Inside the Postwar Reconstruction Fiasco* (Boulder, Colo.: Westview Press, 2005), 45–46.

32. Ibid., 38, 46–47, 76.

33. Warrick interviews.

34. Ibid.; Philips, *Losing Iraq,* 49.

35. Warrick interviews.

36. Ibid.

37. Ibid.

38. Ibid.

39. Ibid.

40. Ibid.; Feith, *War and Decision,* 378–381.

41. Philips, *Losing Iraq,* 89–90.

42. Ibid., 90–91; interviews with Jay Garner, 30 March 2004, 22 April 2004, 14–15 September 2005, 30 October 2006, 15 October 2007.

43. Philips, *Losing Iraq,* 90–92.

44. Ibid., 100–101.

45. Ibid., 94–95.

46. Warrick interviews; interview with John S. Kincannon, 9 June 2003.

47. State Department biography, Michael N. Ayoub, 2006; email from Ayoub to author, 31 August 2006.

48. Mike Ayoub, "ORHA Inshallah: A Baghdad Diary of ORHA," unpublished manuscript, 6–8; interviews with Colonel Tom Baltazar, USA (Ret), 22 and 29 June 2006.

49. Ayoub diary, 6–8; interview with Mike Ayoub, 7 June 2003.

50. Collins interview.

51. Ayoub diary, 8–10.

52. SIGIR interview with Andrew Natsios, 17 March 2008; Chamberlin interviews.

53. Interview with Thomas Christopher Milligan, 13 July 2003.

54. Ibid.

55. Interviews with Douglas J. Feith, 27 December 2004, 27 January 2005; interview with Abram N. Shulsky, 7 December 2006; Feith, *War and Decision,* 293–294.

56. Interview with Michael Mobbs, 12 December 2005.

57. Interviews with Gary Vogler, 18 June 2003, 31 December 2007; interview with Clarke D. Turner, 24 June 2003.

58. Vogler interviews.

59. Ibid.; Jack Herman, "A Whole New Ballgame Overseas," *St. Louis Post-Dispatch,* 20 February 1989, 1D.

60. Mobbs interview.

61. Interview with Paul Shelton, 14 December 2005.

62. Ibid.

63. Interview with Brigadier Robert Crear, USA, 25 June 2003.

64. Collins interview; interview with Colonel Paul Hughes, USA (Ret), 26 June 2006.

65. While POLADs were normally Department of State personnel assigned to senior commands in the Department of Defense, V Corps was not senior enough to warrant someone from State. Determined to have a POLAD for its role in Iraq, V Corps simply hired an academic for the role; Dale had a Ph.D. from Harvard in political science, but little knowledge of the Middle East.

66. Hughes interview. The CA officers were Colonel George Pogge of the 352nd CA Command and Lieutenant Colonel Chris O'Gara of the 354th CA Brigade.

67. Institute for National Strategic Studies, Workshop Report: "Iraq: Looking Beyond Saddam's Rule," 20–21 November 2002, 1; no mention was made of the maintenance status of Iraq's infrastructure after over a decade of economic sanctions.

68. Ibid., 2–3, 7–16.

69. Ibid., 3.

70. Ibid., 3, 17–26.

71. Ibid., 5, 26–34.

72. Ibid.

73. Ibid.; Hughes interview.

74. Interviews with Conrad C. Crane, 15 June 2006, 22 September 2006; interview with Colonel Robert L. McClure, USA (Ret), 21 September 2006.

75. Conrad C. Crane and W. Andrew Terrill, *Reconstructing Iraq: Insights, Challenges, and Missions for Military Forces in a Post-Conflict Scenario* (Carlisle, Pa.: Strategic Studies Institute, February 2003); Crane interviews; interview with W. Andrew Terrill, 15 June 2006.

76. Crane and Terrill, *Reconstructing Iraq,* 3–18; Campaign Planner Primer, Department of Military Strategy, Planning, and Operations, Army War College, 2006, 5; in 2002 the four operational phases were Phase I Deter/Engage; Phase II Seize Initiative; Phase III Decisive Operations; and Phase IV Transition.

77. Crane and Terrill, *Reconstructing Iraq,* 12; Crane, Terrill interviews.

78. Crane and Terrill, *Reconstructing Iraq,* 14–15.

79. Ibid.

80. Ibid., 14.

81. Crane interviews; John Dower, "Lessons from Japan about War's Aftermath," *New York Times,* 27 October 2002.

82. Dower, "Lessons from Japan about War's Aftermath," *New York Times,* 27 October 2002.

83. Ibid.; John Dower, *Embracing Defeat* (New York: W.W. Norton & Co., 1999).

84. Crane and Terrill, *Reconstructing Iraq,* 3–5.

85. Ibid., 5–8.

86. Ibid., 8–11.

87. Ibid., 18–36.

88. Interviews and discussions with Conrad Crane.

89. The issues and proposals in these studies were comparable; there were also similar efforts by other think tanks in 2002, including "Iraq: A New Approach," Carnegie Endowment, August 2002, and Laurence Meyer, "After an Attack on Iraq: The Economic Consequences," Center of Strategic and International Studies (CSIS), March 2003.

90. Miller interviews. Miller saw only a few slides in September and was never provided the text of the FOI Project. The final FOI papers included 956 pages of English text, 92 slides, and 187 pages in Arabic, presumably translations; the INSS "Workshop Report" was 41 pages. Crane and Terrill, *Reconstructing Iraq.*

91. Miller interviews; Feith, *War and Decision,* 347–348.

92. Miller, Casey interviews.

CHAPTER 3. IN THE PENTAGON

1. Interviews with Lieutenant General Jay Garner, USA (Ret), 30 March and 22 April 2004, 14–15 September 2005, 30 October 2006, 15 October 2007;

interviews with Lieutenant General Ronald E. Adams, USA (Ret), 16 June, 22 September, and 13 October 2006, 26 September 2007.

2. Garner, Adams interviews.

3. Garner interviews.

4. Adams interviews.

5. Adams interviews; Douglas Feith, *War and Decision: Inside the Pentagon at the Dawn of the War on Terrorism* (New York: Harper, 2008), 348–349. Feith writes that he told Garner that he would be replaced in Iraq. But nowhere in his book does he mention General Adams.

6. Adams interviews.

7. Feith, *War and Decision,* 34–35.

8. Garner, Adams, interviews; interviews with Colonel Tom Baltazar, USA (Ret), 22 and 29 June 2006. Hanauer joined OSD in 1995 as an intern and served under Bill Luti, Feith's Deputy Assistant Secretary for the Near East and South Asia. Hanauer fell out with Luti and became an assistant for Feith.

9. Interview with Paul Hughes, 29 June 2006.

10. Garner, Baltazar, interviews with Frank C. Miller, 20 November 2007, 30 July 2008; interviews with Colonel Robert D. Costello Jr., USA, 15 and 18 June 2003; Feith, *War and Decision,* 347–348.

11. Adams interviews.

12. Adams, Garner, Miller interviews.

13. Garner interviews.

14. Ibid.

15. Ibid.

16. Ibid.

17. Ibid.; interview with Wendy J. Chamberlin, 14 July 2008.

18. Garner, Chamberlin interviews.

19. Chamberlin regretted she had not spoken out in the meeting in Garner's defense; Chamberlin interview. Robin Raphel interview with Chamberlin, 18 April 2007; Garner interviews.

20. Interview with Thomas Christopher Milligan, 13 August 2003; Garner, Adams interviews.

21. Milligan, Garner interviews.

22. Garner interviews.

23. Ibid.; interview with Lieutenant General Jared L. Bates, USA (Ret), 2 August 2006.

24. Interviews with Stephen B. Browning, 25 April 2006, 21 and 27 July 2007; Garner interviews; interview with General George W. Casey, USA, 19 February 2010. General Casey told the author that he was reluctant to provide military personnel for a 24/7 operation for ORHA. He did not recall refusing Garner communications support, but he did not deny doing so.

25. Garner interviews.

26. Ibid.

27. Interview with Lieutenant Colonel Robert B. Polk and Dayton L. Maxwell, 14 August 2003.

28. Interview with Ambassador George F. Ward, 29 June 2006; Garner interviews.

29. Garner, Baltazar interviews.

30. 31 January 2003 task list, Tom Baltazar papers.

31. Author's observations.

32. Crane-Terrill briefing for Lieutenant General Ron Adams, "Military Missions and Challenges in Post-Saddam Iraq," 28 January 2003; email message to the author from Conrad Crane, 23 July 2009.

33. Memo by Marc Powe, 8 August 2006.

34. Ibid.

35. Interview with Gary L. Vogler, 18 June 2003.

36. Interview with Clarke D. Turner, 24 June 2003.

37. Vogler, Turner interviews; interview with Michael Mobbs, 12 December 2004.

38. Mobbs interview.

39. Garner interviews.

40. Polk and Maxwell interview.

41. Garner interviews; Tommy Franks, with Malcolm McConnell, *American Soldier: General Tommy Franks* (New York: Regan Books, 2004), 422–423.

42. Garner interviews.

43. Ibid.; email from Colonel Michael E. Williams, USMC (Ret), 10 July 2007.

44. Garner interviews.

45. Ibid.

46. Ibid.

47. Ibid.; Bates interviews; FOI Project, 24 May 2002, 1–2.

48. Interview with Andrew P. N. Erdmann, 21 July 2003; interview with Meghan O'Sullivan, 29 December 2003; Richard Haass, *War of Necessity, War of Choice: A Memoir of Two Iraq Wars* (New York: Simon & Schuster, 2009), 174, 200, 252–253.

49. Interview with Michael Gfoeller, 10 August 2003.

50. Garner interviews; interview with Sherri Kraham, 13 August 2003.

51. Kraham interview; author's observations.

52. Interview with Henry Lee Schatz, 26 June 2003.

53. Interview with Dorothy M. Mazaka, 16 June 2004.

54. Adams interviews.

55. Interview with Captain Nathan E. Jones, USNR, 9 June 2003.

56. Adams interviews.

57. Interview with Lieutenant General Carl A. Strock, USA, 30 October 2006. Wendy Chamberlin felt the USAID road project in Afghanistan was a success; Chamberlin interview.

58. Strock, Garner interviews.

59. Browning, Garner interviews.

60. Browning interviews.

61. Ibid.

62. Interviews with Lieutenant Colonel Jeffrey S. Kojac, 19 October, 9 November 2007.

63. Ibid.; see also Michael Gordon and Bernard Trainor, *Cobra II: The Inside Story of the Invasion and Occupation of Iraq* (New York: Pantheon Books, 2006), 102–103.

64. Kojac interviews; emails from Lieutenant Colonel Kojac, 28 May 2009.

65. Garner, Bates, Casey interviews; Casey did not recall or deny refusing communications support to Garner.

66. Garner interviews.

67. Colonel Tom Baltazar, February calendar for General Garner; Garner interviews.

68. Baltazar interviews.

69. Garner interviews.

70. Powe memo; Baltazar, February calendar.

71. Baltazar, notes on meeting with Secretary Rumsfeld, 19 November 2003.

72. Baltazar, notes from 19 November for projected meeting with Rice on 20 November 2003; Baltazar interviews.

73. Interagency Rehearsal and Planning Conference: Summary and Analysis, Washington, D.C., undated, 1; author's observations.

74. Interview with Colonel Anthony J. Puckett, USA, 22 January 2008.

75. Message to the author from Conrad Crane, 23 July 2009.

76. Ibid.

77. Ibid.; Garner interviews.

78. Garner interviews.

79. Interagency Rehearsal and Planning Conference: Summary and Analysis, 4; author's observations.

80. Author's notes.

81. Garner interviews.

82. Interagency Rehearsal and Planning Conference: Summary and Analysis, 10.

83. Hawkins, Puckett interviews.

84. Garner interviews; Garner phone conversation with author, 16 August 2006; Hawkins, Puckett interviews.

85. Interagency Rehearsal and Planning Conference report; author's observations.

86. Raphel interview with Chamberlin; USAID Bureau for Asia and the Near East, "Vision for Post-Conflict Iraq," February 2003.

87. Chamberlin, Garner interviews.

88. USAID, "Vision for Post-Conflict Iraq," 3–10.

89. Milligan interview, 13 July 2003.

90. Milligan, Chamberlin interviews; Raphel interview with Chamberlin.

91. David Philips, *Losing Iraq: Inside the Postwar Reconstruction Fiasco* (Boulder, Colo.: Westview, 2005), 127.

92. O'Sullivan interview, 29 December 2003.

93. Ibid. O'Sullivan's publications on sanctions include *Honey and Vinegar: Incentives, Sanctions, and Foreign Policy* (Washington, D.C.: Brookings Institution Press, 2000) (co-edited with Richard N. Haass), "Sanctioning 'Rogue' States: A Strategy in Decline?" *Harvard International Review* (Summer 2000), and *Shrewd Sanctions: Statecraft and State Sponsors of Terrorism* (Washington, D.C.: Brookings Institution Press, 2003).

94. O'Sullivan interview.

95. Adams email, 14 August 2006.

96. Garner, Baltazar interviews.

97. Garner, O'Sullivan interviews.

98. Baltazar, Garner, O'Sullivan, Warrick interviews.

99. Barbara Bodine, telephone interview with Dr. Terry Beckenbaugh, Combat Studies Institute, Fort Leavenworth, Kansas, 15 February 2006; Baltazar interview.

100. Ibid.; Garner, Adams, Baltazar interviews; Mike Ayoub, "ORHA Inshallah: A Baghdad Diary of ORHA," unpublished manuscript, 2003, 16.

101. Author's observation.

102. Ibid.

103. Interview with Simon Elvy, 22 June 2003.

104. Ayoub diary, 15–16.

105. Garner interviews.

106. Ibid.

107. The UN agencies represented were UNICEF, the United Nations Development Program, UNHCR, the United Nations Office for the Coordination of Humanitarian Affairs, OIP, and the World Food Program (WFP); Ward, Garner interviews.

108. Garner interviews.

109. Garner's personal papers, copies in author's possession; Garner, Baltazar, interviews; interview with Colonel Joseph J. Collins, USA (Ret), 29 August 2006.

110. Garner, Browning interviews; Powe memo.

111. Garner, Baltazar interviews.

112. Miller, Kojac interviews.

113. Kojac emails, 26 and 27 May 2009.

114. Garner interviews.

115. Interview with Major General Tim Cross, UK Army (Ret), 28 January 2008.

116. Author's notes.

117. Garner interviews; interviews with J. Scott Carpenter, 18 and 29 June 2003. In *War and Decision,* 378, Feith asserts that Ambassador Ryan Crocker was Garner's top political advisor, but he had little association with Garner during 2003 and Garner did not consider Crocker his political advisor.

118. Feith, *War and Decision,* 401–407.

119. Ibid.

120. Miller interviews; Feith, *War and Decision,* 408–410.

121. Miller interviews.

122. Ibid.

123. Puckett interview.

124. Garner interviews.

125. Interview with Colonel Michael J. Meese, USA, 27 July 2003; Colonel Meese was teaching at West Point when he was directed to participate in the eleven-man group. Later in June, he deployed to Iraq to serve as a Political Advisor for Major General David Petraeus commanding the 101st Air Assault Division.

126. Jones interview.

127. Ibid.; author's observations at the press briefing.

128. Author's observations.

129. Ibid.

130. Ibid.; Jones, Garner interviews.

131. Garner interviews.

132. Ibid.; Jones interviews.

133. U.S. Senate Hearings, Committee on Foreign Relations, "The Future of Iraq," 11 February 2003 (Washington, D.C.: Government Printing Office, 2003), 59.

134. Email to author from a participant at Fort Meade, 30 July 2007.

135. Elvy interview.

136. Interview with Major Keith L. June, USA, 14 June 2003.

137. Interviews with Robin L. Raphel, 15 November 2005, 12 September 2007.

138. Interviews with Sue Hamrock, 12 and 15 June 2003.

139. Ayoub diary, 17.

140. Garner interviews.

141. Ayoub diary, 17–18.

CHAPTER 4. IN KUWAIT

1. Memo from Marc Powe, 8 August 2006.

2. Interview with Michael W. Page, 16 July 2003; interviews with Colonel Robert D. Costello, USA, 15 and 18 June 2003; interview with Lieutenant Colonel Steven M. Elliot, USAF, 12 July 2003.

3. ORHA C-1 personnel roster, 17 March 2003. Garner, Bates, Adams, Walters, and Moore held temporary Senior Executive Service rank. The Iraqi IRDC was not part of ORHA at that time, and Scott Carpenter's Governance group, still forming in Washington, had little or no contact with ORHA.

4. Author's observations and notes. SIPRNET stands for Secret Internet Protocol Router Network, a system of interconnected computer networks used by the Departments of Defense and State.

5. Author's notes.

6. Clare Short, *An Honourable Deception? New Labour, Iraq, and the Misuse of Power* (London: Free Press, 2004), 184–186.

7. Interview with Captain Nathan E. Jones, USNR, 9 June 2003; interviews with Jay Garner, 30 March and 22 April 2004, 14–15 September 2005, 30 October 2006, and 15 October 2007.

8. Lieutenant Colonel Evan Heulfer, one of Colonel Benson's planners, proposed the name COBRA II for the CFLCC/Third Army plan for Iraq, in reference to General Patton's Third Army breakout in World War II; interview with Colonel Kevin C. Benson, USA, 10 June 2006. But it was General Bradley's First Army that planned and conducted COBRA in 1944, not Patton or the Third Army.

9. JFLCC OPLAN COBRA II (U), 13 January 2003.

10. Benson interview.

11. CFLCC presentation, "Oplan Eclipse II," slides 5–6; Eclipse was the occupation plan for of Germany.

12. Ibid., slides 14–15. "A-Day" stood for Air Attack Day.

13. Ibid., slide 7.

14. Ibid., slide 21; six more brigades were to come from the 1st Cavalry and 1st Armor Divisions.

15. Ibid., slides 22–23.

16. Ibid., slide 19; email from Colonel Kevin Benson, USA, 25 August 2006.

17. Slides in author's papers; copies of Garner's private papers.

18. Author's papers; Feith, *War and Decision,* 401–411.

19. Interview with Major Lawrence F. Miller, USMC, 16 July 2003.

20. Ibid.

21. The C-1 was Colonel Dennis DeGraff, USAF; C-2 Colonel John Frketic, USA; C-4 Colonel Costello, USA; C-6 Colonel Randy Conway, USA; C-7 Captain Kiser, USN; and C-8 Colonel Gary Minor, USAF.

22. Mike Ayoub, "ORHA Inshallah: A Baghdad Diary of ORHA," unpublished manuscript, 20.

23. Interview with Andrew Goledzinowski, 1 January 2004.

24. Interviews with Lieutenant General Ronald E. Adams, 16 June, 22 September, and 13 October 2006, 26 September 2008.

25. Ibid.; author's observations and notes.

26. Jones interview.

27. Ibid.; interview with Colonel Guy Shields, USA, 4 August 2003.

28. Jones interview; interview with Meghan Gregonis, 9 June 2003.

29. Interview with John S. Kincannon, 9 June 2003.

30. Interview with Major Keith L. June, USA, 14 July 2003.

31. Ibid.

32. Interview with Lieutenant Commander Jonathon F.A. Rollins, USNR, 29 June 2003.

33. Ibid.; Jones interview.

34. Interviews with Mike Ayoub, 7 June 2003, and 30 October 2006.

35. Interview with Simon D. Elvy, 22 June 2003.

36. Interview with Colonel Paul B. Hughes, USA (Ret), 29 June 2006; interviews with Colonel John F. Agoglia, USA, 28 June 2003, 22 September 2006, 15 October 2007.

37. Agoglia, Benson interviews.

38. Garner interview; interviews with Colonel Thomas P. Baltazar, USA, 10 June 2003, 22 and 29 June 2006.

39. Baltazar interviews.

40. Janet A. McDonnell, *After Desert Storm: The U.S. Army and the Reconstruction of Kuwait* (Washington, D.C.: U.S. Center of Military History, 1999), 55, 65, 73–74, 82–83, 119.

41. Gregory Fontenot et al., *On Point: The United States Army in Operation Iraqi Freedom* (Fort Leavenworth, Kans.: Combat Studies Institute Press, 2004), 446–447.

42. Garner interviews; email from General Carl Strock, USA (Ret), 19 August 2008.

43. Author's notes.

44. Interviews with Steven E. Browning, 21 June 2003, 25 April 2006, and 21 July 2007; interviews with Lieutenant General Carl A. Strock, USA, 30 October 2006, 20 September 2007.

45. Strock, Browning interviews. The author accompanied Strock to visit the oilfields; author's notes.

46. Interview with Lieutenant Colonel Robert B. Polk, USA, 14 August 2003.

47. Garner interviews.

48. Costello interviews, 15 and 18 June 2003.

49. Interviews with Timothy A. Phillips, 12 and 13 July 2003.

50. Ibid.

51. Ibid.

52. Ibid.; June interview.

53. Benson interview.

54. Author's observations; Garner interviews.

55. Kim Olson, *Iraq and Back: Inside the War to Win the Peace* (Annapolis: Naval Institute Press, 2006), 39–40.

56. Ayoub interview.

57. Interview with Susan E. Hamrock, 12 and 15 June 2003 interview; Ayoub diary, 21–22; author's observations.

58. Interview with Andrew N.P. Erdmann, 21 July 2003; Ayoub interview.

59. Erdmann, Elvy, Ayoub interviews.

60. Ayoub diary, 31.

61. Elvy, Erdmann interviews; Ayoub diary, 31–34.

62. Telephone conversation and email exchange with Dick Mayer, 30 July 2007.

63. Author attended both briefings; author's notes.

64. Ibid.

65. Interviews with Ted D. Morse, 18 and 20 July 2003.

66. Interview Michael W. Page, 16 July 2003.

67. Page, Costello interviews; T. Christian Miller, *Blood Money: Wasted Billions, Lost Lives, and Corporate Greed in Iraq* (Boston: Little, Brown, 2006).

68. Garner memorandum: Procurement Management Review Process, 9 April 2003.

69. Ayoub diary, 21.

70. Ibid., 30.

71. Benson interview.

72. Ibid.; Bates interviews.

73. Memorandum, Jay Garner to Ryan Henry, ORHA Humanitarian Update, 10 April 2003, Garner papers.

74. Ibid.

75. Hughes interview.

76. Garner interviews.

77. Garner, Hughes interviews.

78. Hughes interview.

79. Ibid.

80. Jones, Kincannon, Shields interviews.

81. Garner interviews; Burkle flew to Baghdad on 20 April with Colonel Glenn Collins and Steve Browning.

82. Author's notes; author observed the meeting on 6 April.

83. Interview with Thomas Wheelock, 23 June 2003. Wheelock stated that Bechtel competed against several other large corporations for the contract awarded by USAID: KBR, Parsons, and the Washington Group.

84. Interview with David Dunford, 13 June 2003.

85. Ibid.; Wendy Chamberlin confirmed that Ryan Crocker expressed reservations about invading Iraq; Chamberlin interviews.

86. Ambassador David J. Dunford papers, 1–3.

87. Feith, *War and Decision*, 386–389.

88. Dunford papers, 9.

89. Ibid., 13–15; Dunford interview.

90. Interviews with David M. Nummy, 23 and 27 June 2003.

91. Ibid.

92. Nummy, Garner, Baltazar interviews; Garner and Baltazar also believed Cleveland was obstructive.

93. Nummy interviews.

94. Statement by White House press secretary, 2 December 2002. Khalilzad held two other positions on that date: Special Presidential Envoy for Afghanistan and NSC Senior Director for Southwest Asia, Near East, and North Africa Affairs. He would retain the Afghanistan position and relinquish the NSC position.

95. The author accompanied Garner on the trip to Tallil; author's notes.

96. Author's observations and conversations with those present that evening.

97. Author's observations.

98. Garner interviews.

99. Author's notes; author was present for the first Easter service and Garner's talk at the tennis court.

CHAPTER 5. IN IRAQ: GARNER'S FIRST THREE WEEKS

1. Colonel Michael E. Williams, USMC (Ret), in April 2003, email to author, 14 July 2007.

2. Interview with Simon Elvy, 22 June 2003.

3. The author accompanied Garner from Kuwait to Iraq.

4. Interviews with Lieutenant General Jay Garner, 30 March 2004, 22 April 2004, 14–15 September 2005, 30 October 2006, and 15 October 2007.

5. Interview with Brigadier General Stephen R. Hawkins, 23 June 2003.

6. Email from Colonel Michael E. Williams, 12 July 2007.

7. Garner interviews; notes by Colonel Anthony Puckett, USA, mid-May 2003.

8. Feith makes a developed argument that he did not overly promote Chalabi as a leader for Iraq: Douglas Feith, *War and Decision: Inside the Pentagon at the Dawn of the War on Terrorism* (New York: Harper, 2008), 242, 279, 281, 380, 383, 420–421, 487–490. This was not, however, Garner's impression from his discussions with Feith and Wolfowitz; Garner interviews.

9. Garner interviews.

10. Matthew Bogdanos with William Patrick, *Thieves of Baghdad* (New York: Bloomsbury Press, 2005), 20–23, 57, 130, 140; interview with Zainab Bahrani, CPA Senior Advisor for Iraqi Ministry of Culture, 21 June 2004.

11. Interview with Major Keith L. June, USA, 14 June 2003.

12. Ibid.

13. Ibid.; PowerPoint presentation, D Company, 86th Signal Battalion, 1 August 2003.

14. Interview with Colonel Glenn C. Collins, 17 July 2003.

15. Interviews with Stephen E. Browning, 25 April 2006, 21 and 27 July 2007.

16. Interviews with Colonel Thomas P. Baltazar, USA, 10 June 2003, 22 and 29 August 2006.

17. Mike Ayoub, "ORHA Inshallah: A Baghdad Diary of ORHA," unpublished manuscript, 36–39; email from Colonel Anthony Puckett, USA, 3 June 2007.

18. Ayoub diary; Puckett email.

19. Interview with Ambassador David Dunford, 13 June 2003; interview with Ambassador Timothy Carney, 12 June 2003; interviews with Ambassador Robin Raphel, 15 November 2005, 12 September 2007; Don Eberly, *Liberate and Leave: Fatal Flaws in the Early Strategy for Postwar Iraq* (Minneapolis: Zenith Press, 2009), 72–75.

20. Interview with Michael W. Page, 16 July 2003.

21. Collins interview; Ayoub diary.

22. Interview with Major Lawrence E. Miller, USMC, 16 July 2003.

23. Ibid.

24. Garner interviews.

25. Ibid.

26. Ibid.

27. Browning, Garner interviews; Burkle later returned to Iraq to work with USAID personnel; interview with Dr. Frederick M. Burkle, 15 July 2008.

28. Email from Williams, 12 July 2007; letter from Williams, 14 August 2007.

29. Interview with Stephen Browning conducted by John Lonnquest, U.S. Army Corps of Engineer Office of History, 28–29 July 2003.

30. Browning interviews.

31. Author's notes; author went with Goledzinowski and Schollum to the ANZAC ceremony.

32. Email from Puckett, 3 June 2007; Garner interviews.

33. Ambassador David J. Dunford papers.

34. Collins interview; author's observations, author's notes.

35. Don Eberly, "My Two Years Working on Iraq," unpublished manuscript, 105; Eberly, *Liberate and Leave,* 138–139; Dunford papers, 21.

36. Dunford interview; Dunford papers, 21; author's notes.

37. Dunford papers, 20.

38. Ibid., 19.

39. Puckett email, 3 June 2007.

40. Dunford papers.

41. Author's observations; author's notes.

42. Browning interview with Lonnquest. Author attended the meeting with Browning; author's notes.

43. Interview with Henry Lee Schatz, 26 June 2003.

44. Ibid.

45. Raphel interviews.

46. Interview with Colonel Greg Gardner, USA (Ret), 12 June 2006.

47. Interview with Colonel Paul D. Hughes, USA (Ret), 29 June 2006.

48. Gardner, Garner interviews.

49. Garner, Gardner, Hughes interviews.

50. Dunford interview; Dunford papers, 1.

51. Dunford interview; Dunford papers, 20.

52. The Australian Wheat Board was later found guilty of providing kickbacks to the Iraqi government as part of the Oil for Food program: "AWB Halts Iraq Wheat Trade," Australian Broadcasting Company, 22 December 2006.

53. Author was present at the meeting; author's notes.

54. Interview with John Eugene Bulla, 21 July 2007; interviews with Timothy A. Phillips, 12–13 July 2003.

55. June interview.

56. Interview with Captain Jaime Macias, USMC, 20 July 2003.

57. Bulla interview.

58. Phillips interviews.

59. Ibid.

60. Ayoub diary, 44–45.

61. Ibid., 42–46.

62. Interview with General David McKiernan, USA, by Stuart Bowen, Special Inspector General for Iraqi Reconstruction (SIGIR), 5 November 2007.

63. Dunford papers, 28 April 2003.

64. Eberly, *Liberate and Leave,* 138–45; Eberly, "My Two Years," unpublished manuscript, 35, 105–110.

65. Eberly papers, 109–110.

66. Garner interviews.

67. Author was present at the first meeting; interview with Colonel Anthony J. Puckett, USA, 22 January 2008.

68. Puckett and Dunford papers; Baltazar, Puckett interviews; Ayoub diary, 49–50.

69. Garner interviews; Bradley Graham, *By His Own Rules: The Ambitions, Successes, and Ultimate Failures of Donald Rumsfeld* (New York: Public Affairs, 2009), 397; interview with Colonel Kevin Benson, USA, 10 June 2006.

70. Garner, Benson interviews; interviews with Ambassador L. Paul Bremer, 18 October 2007, 7 January 2009.

71. Memorandum, Colonel Michael E. Williams, USMC, 2 May 2003.

72. Ibid.

73. Email from Stephen E. Browning, 13 July 2007; email message from Captain Dennis E. Ammundson, USN, 14 July 2007.

74. Email from Williams, 12 July 2007.

75. Letter from Williams, 14 August 2007.

76. Interviews with David M. Nummy, 23 and 27 June 2003; Garner interviews.

77. Nummy, Garner interviews.

78. Nummy, Garner interviews; interview with Lieutenant General Jared Bates, USA (Ret), 2 August 2006.

79. Nummy interview.

80. Ibid.

81. Author was present at the meeting; author's notes.

82. Nummy interview.

83. Emails from David Nummy, 22 and 23 August 2007.

84. Nummy interview.

85. Nummy emails.

86. Interviews with Susan E. Hamrock, 12 and 15 June 2003; Raphel interviews.

87. Raphel, Hamrock interviews.

88. Interview with Dorothy M. Mazaka, 16 June 2004.

89. Ibid.; interview with Pamela A. Riley, 9 June 2004.

90. Mazaka, Riley interviews.

91. Ayoub diary, 43.

92. Interview with Andrew P. N. Erdmann, 21 July 2003.

93. Interview with Eugene Stakhiv, 20 July 2003.

94. Ibid.

95. Ibid.

96. Author's observations.

97. Garner interviews; interview with Major General Donald F. Campbell, USAR, 14 July 2007; Ayoub diary, 37–38.

98. Campbell interview.

99. Greg Fontenot, *On Point: The U. S. Army in Operation Iraqi Freedom* (Fort Leavenworth, Kans.: Combat Studies Institute, 2004), 476, 485–487; emails from Colonel Terry Spain, USA (Ret), 1 December 2006, 29 January 2007, 13 March 2007, and 16 August 2009.

100. Garner interviews.

101. Interview with Raoul Percy Stanley, 12 August 2003.

102. Ibid.

103. Ibid.

104. McKiernan interview, SIGIR.

105. Hawkins, Strock, interviews; interview with Brigadier General Robert Crear, USA, 25 June 2003.

106. Strock, Garner interviews; interviews with Ted Morse, 18 and 20 July 2003.

107. Eberly, "My Two Years," unpublished manuscript, 115; Ayoub diary, 51.

108. Interview with Colonel Joseph Anderson, 29 July 2003.

109. The author accompanied Garner on the trips to Hilla and Basra; author's notes.

110. Interview with Ambassador Ole Olsen, 1 July 2003.

111. Olsen, Macias interviews.

112. Olsen interview; interview with Brigadier Andrew Gregory, UK Army, 1 July 2003.

113. Garner interviews. Author was present at the meeting; author's notes.

114. Garner, Benson interviews.

115. Garner, Benson interviews.

116. Interviews with Lieutenant General Ronald E. Adams, USA (Ret), 16 June, 22 September, 13 October 2006, 26 September 2008; interviews with Colonel Dennis J. DeGraff, USAF, 27 June 2003, 25 June 2004.

117. Adams interviews; in Feith, *War and Decision,* there is no mention of Ronald Adams.

118. Adams interviews.

119. Browning interviews.

120. Browning interviews; multiple discussions between author and Williams.

121. Browning interviews; author's discussions with Williams and others.

122. Browning, Garner interviews; letter from Said Haki, 7 May 2003, in author's possession.

123. Author was present for the meeting; author's notes.

124. Garner, Strock interviews.

125. Garner, Strock interviews.

126. Garner interviews.

127. Dunford interview; Ayoub diary, 58.

128. Transcribed directive from Iraqi security services, originally dated 23 January 2003.

129. Ayoub diary, 51–52; interviews with Mike Ayoub, 7 June 2003, 30 October 2006; also see Aram Roston, *The Man Who Pushed America to War: The Extraordinary Life, Adventures, and Obsessions of Ahmad Chalabi* (New York: Nation Books, 2008), 262–264.

130. Ayoub diary, 52–53.

131. Ayoub, Hughes, Benson interviews; interviews with Colonel John F. Agoglia, USA, 28 June 2003, 22 September 2006, 15 October 2007.

132. Author attended the meeting. Author's notes; Garner interviews.

CHAPTER 6. BREMER ARRIVES

1. Interviews with Lieutenant General Jay Garner, 30 March 2004, 22 April 2004, 14–15 September 2005, 30 October 2006, and 15 October 2007.

2. Ibid.

3. Ibid.; L. Paul Bremer, *My Year in Iraq: The Struggle to Build a Future of Hope* (New York: Simon & Schuster, 2006), 3–4.

4. Garner interviews; interviews with Lieutenant General Ronald E. Adams, USA (Ret), 16 June, 22 September, 15 October 2006, and 26 September 2008.

5. Interviews with Ambassador L. Paul "Jerry" Bremer, 18 October 2007, 7 January 2008.

6. Ibid.

7. Ibid.

8. Garner interviews; Bremer, *My Year in Iraq,* 6–9; interview with Colin Powell and Richard Armitage by Stuart Bowen, Special Inspector General for Iraqi Reconstruction (SIGIR), 4 February 2008.

9. Garner interviews; Bremer, *My Year in Iraq,* 10–11.

10. Adams, Bremer interviews.

11. Douglas J. Feith, *War and Decision: Inside the Pentagon at the Dawn of the War on Terrorism* (New York: Harper, 2008), 404–411, 427–435.

12. Ibid., 427–435; Garner interviews.

13. Bremer, Garner, Adams interviews; Roger Cohen, "The MacArthur Lunch," *New York Times,* 27 August 2007, 17.

14. Bremer interviews.

15. Bremer, *My Year in Iraq,* 11–12.

16. Cohen, "The MacArthur Lunch."

17. Ibid.; Garner interviews; Powell and Armitage interview, SIGIR.

18. Interviews with Douglas Feith, 17 December 2004 and 27 January 2005; Feith, *War and Decision,* 427–435; Bremer interviews.

19. Interview with Walter B. Slocombe, 18 July 2003.

20. Bremer, *My Year in Iraq,* 54; interview with Colonel Paul D. Hughes, USA

(Ret), 29 June 2006; Center for Public Policy: "Windfalls of War," http://projects
.publicintegrity.org/wow/bio/aspx?act=prp&ddlC=50.

21. Silverberg remained in Iraq as an assistant to Bremer into the fall of 2003;
her subsequent resume lists her as senior advisor in Iraq. See http://georgewbush
-whitehouse.archives.gov/government/silverberg-bio.html; also http://en.wikipedia
.org/wiki/Kristen_Silverberg.

22. Garner interviews; interviews with Ambassador Robin L. Raphel, 15 November 2005, 12 December 2007.

23. Raphel interview; interview with Colonel Anthony J. Puckett, USA, 22 January 2008.

24. Raphel interviews.

25. Richard Haass, *War of Necessity, War of Choice: A Memoir of Two Iraq Wars*
(New York: Simon & Schuster, 2009), 174, 200, 252–253.

26. Raphel interviews; interview with Meghan O'Sullivan, 29 December 2003.

27. Coalition Provisional Authority Order Number 1, "De-Ba'athification of Iraqi
Society," 16 May 2003.

28. Ibid.

29. Ibid.

30. Garner, Raphel interviews.

31. Garner interviews.

32. Raphel interviews.

33. Author was present for the meeting; author's notes.

34. Interview with Captain Nathan E. Jones, USNR, 9 June 2003.

35. Ibid.

36. Ibid.; interview with Meghan Gregonis, 9 June 2003.

37. Jones interview.

38. Gregonis interview.

39. Garner interviews.

40. Geoffrey W. Hoon interview with BBC, 18 January 2007.

41. Ibid.

42. Slocombe interview; Mike Ayoub, "ORHA Inshallah: A Baghdad Diary of
ORHA," unpublished manuscript, 60; Feith, *War and Decision*, 427–435; Adams,
Garner interviews.

43. Garner interviews.

44. Interview with Colonel Gregory C. Gardner, USA (Ret), 12 June 2006.

45. Garner interviews.

46. Garner, Hughes interviews; interview with Mike Ayoub, 7 June 2003.

47. Ayoub diary, 61; Ayoub interview.

48. Ayoub diary, 61; Ayoub interview.

49. Ayoub diary, 61; Ayoub interview.

50. Interviews with Colonel John F. Agoglia, USA, 28 June 2003, 22 September
2006, 15 October 2007.

51. Garner interviews.

52. Bremer, *My Year in Iraq*, 44–45; author was present at the press conference.

53. Author's notes.

54. Ibid.

55. Raphel interviews. Author was present at the meeting; author's notes.

56. Bremer, *My Year in Iraq*, 45–49.

57. Garner interviews.

58. Bremer, *My Year in Iraq*, 45–49; Colonel Anthony J. Puckett, USA, Memorandum: Meeting with Iraqi Interim Authority, 16 May 2003, personal papers, copy in author's possession.

59. Garner interviews; Puckett memo.

60. Puckett memo; Bremer, *My Year in Iraq*, 46–49.

61. Bremer, *My Year in Iraq*, 49.

62. Garner interviews.

63. Interview with Colonel Joseph Anderson, 29 July 2003.

64. Interviews with Major General David H. Petraeus, 28 July 2003, 30 June 2004 (as Lieutenant General).

65. Petraeus, Anderson interviews.

66. Petraeus, Anderson interviews.

67. Interviews with J. Scott Carpenter, 18 and 29 June 2004.

68. Interview with Colonel Michael J. Meese, USA, 27 July 2003; Carpenter interviews.

69. Petraeus, Meese interviews; interview with Andrew N.P. Erdmann, 21 July 2003.

70. Agoglia interviews.

71. Ibid.

72. Ayoub diary, 61; Ayoub interview.

73. Ayoub diary, 61–62; Ayoub interview; Puckett interview.

74. Interview with Colonel Kevin B. Benson, USA, 10 June 2006; interview with General John Abizaid, USA (Ret), by Stuart Bowen, Special Inspector General for Iraqi Reconstruction (SIGIR), 4 February 2008.

75. Email from Colonel Kevin Benson, USA (Ret), September 2007; Agoglia interviews.

76. Agoglia interviews.

77. Agoglia, Ayoub interviews.

78. Coalition Provisional Authority Order Number 2, "Dissolution of the Entities," 23 May 2003; Agoglia, Hughes interviews.

79. Interviews with Frank Miller, 24 November 2007, 30 July 2008.

80. Powell interview, SIGIR; other sources indicate that no one on the Joint Staff, including the chairman, General Richard Myers, knew about Bremer's intention to disband the Iraqi army before the decree was issued. See Bradley Graham, *By His Own Rules: The Ambitions, Successes, and Ultimate Failures of Donald Rumsfeld* (New York: Public Affairs, 2009), 402–403.

81. Feith, *War and Decision*, 432–433.

82. Interviews with Lieutenant General Jeffrey S. Kojac, USMC, 12 and 19 October 2007; Miller interviews; email message from Lieutenant Colonel Jeff Kojac, 2 June 2009.

83. Hughes interview.

84. Ibid.

85. Agoglia interviews.

86. Interviews with Timothy A. Phillips, 12 and 13 July 2003.

87. Ibid.; interview with Major Keith L. June, USA, 14 June 2003, interview with Captain Jamie Macias, USMC, 20 July 2003.

88. Phillips, June, Macias interviews.

89. Phillips interviews.

90. Ibid.

91. Garner interviews; author accompanied Colonel Murphy and al-Rubaie on the trip to Najaf. Al-Rubaie later became a member of the Iraqi Governing Council under CPA; in 2004 he was appointed Iraqi national security advisor by the CPA and held that position in several Iraqi administrations.

92. Garner interviews.

93. Garner, Adams, Raphel interviews; interview with Gary L. Vogler, 18 June 2003.

94. Garner interviews.

95. Adams interviews.

96. Interviews with Ambassador Patrick F. Kennedy, 18 June, 25 June 2004.

97. Adams interviews.

98. Adams, Kennedy interviews.

99. Adams interviews.

100. ORHA briefing slides, 19 May 2003.

101. Interviews with David R. Nummy, 23 and 27 June 2003; Garner interviews; author's notes from meetings.

102. ORHA briefing slides; Miller interviews.

103. ORHA briefing slides.

104. Ibid.

105. Ibid.

106. Ibid.

107. Ibid.

108. Ibid.

109. Ibid.

110. Ibid.

111. Interview with Lieutenant Colonel Joseph L. Morgan, III, USAR, 12 August 2003.

112. Ibid.

113. Ibid.

114. Interview with Eugene Z. Stakhiv, 20 July 2003.

115. Ibid.; interview with Jeremy C. Mawdsley, 4 July 2003.

116. Mawdsley interview.

117. Stakhiv interview.

118. Interview with Raoul Percy Stanley, 12 August 2003.

119. Ibid.

120. Ayoub interview; Ayoub diary; author's conversations with Colonel Tony Puckett, USA; papers of Colonel Tony Puckett, in author's possession.

121. Author's conversations with Puckett.

122. Author was present at the party; author's notes.

123. Author's notes; author traveled with the group to al-Hilla.

124. Jones interview.

125. Author traveled with Garner on this trip.

126. Author's notes; author rode with Garner from Baghdad to Hilla, then returned to Baghdad as Garner drove on to Kuwait.

127. Author's notes.

128. Garner interviews.

129. Garner interviews.

CHAPTER 7. TRANSITION

1. Interviews with Colonel Dennis J. DeGraff, USAF, 25 June 2003, 26 June 2004; interviews with Colonel Robert D. Costello, USA, 15 and 18 June 2003; interviews with Colonel Tom Baltazar, USA, 10 June 2003, 22 and 29 June 2006.

2. Interview with Lieutenant Commander Jonathon F.A. Rollins, USN, 29 June 2003; interview with Colonel Paul D. Hughes, USA (Ret), 29 June 2006; interview with Lieutenant Colonel Robert B. Polk, USA, and Dayton Maxwell, 14 August 2003.

3. Interviews with Tim Phillips, 12 and 13 July 2003; interview with Major Keith L. June, USA, 14 June 2003; interview with Captain Jamie Macias, USMC, 20 July 2003.

4. Interview with Colonel Glen C. Collins, USA, 17 July 2003.

5. Ministries under the Director of Civil Affairs Policy included Culture, Education, Higher Education, Foreign Affairs, Health, Justice, Labor and Social Affairs, Religious Affairs, and Youth.

6. Ministries under the Director of Economic Policy included Agriculture, Central Bank, Finance, Electricity, Housing and Reconstruction, Industry and Materials, Irrigation, Planning, Public Works, Trade, and Transportation and Communications.

7. Interview with Major Susan K. Arnold, USA, 29 July 2003. The term "kindergarten kids" was used by Major Arnold and others working with CPA personnel.

8. James Dobbins, Seth Jones, Benjamin Runkle, and Siddharth Mohandas, *Occupying Iraq: A History of the Coalition Provisional Authority* (Washington, D.C.: RAND, 2009), 224–227.

9. Interview with Wendy J. Chamberlin, 14 July 2008; Robin Raphel interview with Chamberlin, 18 April 2007.

10. Interviews with Ambassador Robin Raphel, 15 November 2005, 12 September 2007; interview with Meghan L. O'Sullivan, 29 December 2003.

11. Raphel and O'Sullivan interviews.

12. L. Paul Bremer, *My Year in Iraq: The Struggle to Build a Future of Hope* (New York: Simon & Schuster, 2006), 94; interviews with Ambassador L. Paul Bremer, 18 October 2007, 7 January 2009; interviews with J. Scott Carpenter, 18 and 29 June 2004; interview with Meghan O'Sullivan, 29 December 2003.

13. Interviews with Major General Donald F. Campbell, USAR, 14 July, 13 August 2003.

14. Carpenter interviews.

15. Carpenter, O'Sullivan interviews; interview with Roman Martinez, 13 December 2003.

16. Interview with Haig Melkessetian, 13 December 2005.

17. Carpenter interview.

18. Ibid.

19. Interviews with Colonel John F. Agoglia, USA, 28 June 2003, 22 September 2006, 15 October 2007; interviews with Frank C. Miller, 20 November 2007, 30 June 2008; interview with General John Abizaid, USA (Ret), by Stuart Bowen, Special Inspector General for Iraqi Reconstruction (SIGIR), 4 February 2008.

20. Agoglia interviews.

21. Agoglia, Miller, Abizaid interviews.

22. Agoglia, Miller, Abizaid interviews.

23. Agoglia interviews.

24. Interviews with Major General Paul D. Eaton, USA, 1 January, 27 December 2004.

25. Ibid.

26. Interviews with Jay Garner, 30 March and 22 April 2004, 14–15 September 2005, 30 October 2006, and 15 October 2007.

27. Interview with Walter B. Slocombe, 18 July 2003; interview with Colonel Gregory Gardner, USA (Ret), 12 June 2006; interview with Slocombe by the BBC, 15 September 2007.

28. Slocombe, Gardner interviews.

29. Gardner interview; author's discussions with the bodyguards.

30. Interview with Colonel Michael J. Meese, USA, 27 July 2003.

31. Ibid.; Colonel Meese served as a political advisor in Mosul for General Petraeus in 2003; interviews with Major General David H. Petraeus, 28 July 2003, 30 June 2004 (as Lieutenant General).

32. Meese, Petraeus interviews.

33. Miller interviews, 20 November 2007, 30 July 2008; interviews with Major Jeffrey S. Kojac, 19 October, 7 November 2007.

34. Kojac interviews.

35. Ibid.

36. Interview with Lieutenant Colonel Wesley R. Odum, USA, and Lieutenant Colonel Daniel E. Soller, USA, 10 January 2007; telephone interview with Lieutenant Colonel Wesley R. Odum (in Germany) conducted by Dr. Don Wright of the Combat Studies Institute (CSI), Fort Leavenworth, Kans., 17 March 2006.

37. Major Constanza flew to Iraq earlier than the others; Odum interviews.

38. Interview with Lieutenant Colonel Louis Rago, USA, 9 January 2007.

39. Odum and Soller interview.

40. Odum, CSI interview.

41. Odum and Soller interview.

42. Odum interviews; Odum email to author, 28 February 2010.

43. Donald P. Wright and Timothy R. Reese, *On Point II: Transition to the New Campaign, The U.S. Army in Operation Iraqi Freedom* (Fort Leavenworth, Kans.: Combat Studies Institute, 2008), 141–142.

44. Ibid., 142.

45. Garner interviews.

46. Ricardo S. Sanchez, with Donald T. Philips, *Wiser in Battle: A Soldier's Story* (New York: HarperCollins, 2008), 368–369, 227–229; interview with Lieutenant

General Ricardo Sanchez, USA (Ret), by Stuart Bowen, Special Inspector General for Iraqi Reconstruction (SIGIR), 26 October 2007.

47. Sanchez, *Wiser in Battle,* 213–215, 323–333, 249–251; Wright and Reese, *On Point II,* 165; Agoglia, Abizaid interviews; Sanchez interview, SIGIR.

48. Odum, CSI interview.

49. Ibid.

50. Ibid.; Odum and Soller interview.

51. Odum, CSI interview; Agoglia interviews.

52. Odum, CSI interview; Odum email to author.

53. Maxwell and Polk interview; *Bremer, My Year in Iraq,* 114–117.

54. Maxwell and Polk interviews; Odum, CSI interview; Odum email to author.

55. Odum, CSI interview.

56. Odum and Soller interview.

57. Interview with Colin Powell and Richard Armitage, by Stuart Bowen, Special Inspector General for Iraqi Reconstruction (SIGIR), 4 February 2008.

58. Wright and Reese, *On Point II,* 32.

CHAPTER 8. REFLECTIONS

1. Interviews with Ted Morse, 18 and 20 July 2003.

2. Interviews with Lieutenant General Jay Garner, 30 March 2004, 22 April 2004, 14–15 September 2005, 30 October 2006, and 15 October 2007.

3. John W. Dower, *Cultures of War: Pearl Harbor / Hiroshima / 9-11 / Iraq* (New York: W.W. Norton & Company, 2010).

4. Bradley Graham, *By His Own Rules: The Ambitions, Successes, and Ultimate Failures of Donald Rumsfeld* (New York: Public Affairs, 2009), 351–352.

5. Interview with Wendy J. Chamberlin, 14 July 2008; Robin Raphel interview with Chamberlin, 18 April 2007.

6. Garner interviews; interviews with Colonel Tom Baltazar, USA (Ret), 22 and 29 June 2006; interviews with Ambassador L. Paul "Jerry" Bremer, 18 October 2007, 7 January 2008.

7. Memo from Conrad Crane, 2 May 2010, author's files.

8. Interview with Colonel Kevin B. Benson, USA, 10 June 2006.

9. Donald P. Wright and Timothy R. Reese, *On Point II: Transition to the New Campaign, The U.S. Army in Operation Iraqi Freedom* (Fort Leavenworth, Kans.: Combat Studies Institute, 2008), 142.

10. Email to author from Colonel Gregory Fontenot, USA (Ret), author of *On Point: The U.S. Army in Operation Iraqi Freedom* (Fort Leavenworth, Kans.: Combat Studies Institute, 2004).

11. Ricardo S. Sanchez, with Donald T. Philips, *Wiser in Battle: A Soldier's Story* (New York: HarperCollins, 2008), 193–195.

12. Interview with Colonel Anthony J. Puckett, USA, 22 January 2008.

13. Email from Colonel Tom Greenwood, USMC (Ret), to author, 28 June 2009.

14. Ibid.

BIBLIOGRAPHY

In writing this book, I have relied predominantly on primary sources. These include 282 interviews I conducted with those associated with regime change in Iraq; 210 of those interviews were conducted in Iraq in 2003 and 2004. Most of the remaining interviews were conducted in or near Washington, D.C.; half a dozen were conducted in other countries. I have also consulted interviews conducted by others as listed in the bibliography.

In addition, the bibliography includes the papers, unpublished diaries, and manuscripts of those who worked in ORHA and CPA. During the time I was in Iraq, I collected documents on Iraq produced by ORHA, CPA, military commands in Iraq, and U.S. Central Command in Tampa, Florida. Unpublished sources include military and civilian after-action reports, command briefing slides, chronologies, journals, memoranda, and evaluations generated before, during, and after the period in which ORHA was deployed to Iraq. In addition, I have had extended email correspondence with many participants in ORHA, CPA, and the U.S. government in Washington, as well as others based in Iraq.

INTERVIEWS

The interviews listed below were conducted by the author and include the names of those interviewed, the date and location of the interview, and, if applicable, their military rank, service, and organization. These interviews were transcribed by Ann Roundtree, under contract with the Special Inspector General for Iraqi Reconstruction (SIGIR), and come to a total 10,022 pages. The transcripts and audio versions of these interviews will be provided to the National Archives.

Adamcyk, Joseph W., Colonel, USA (Ret), 31 December 2003, 1 July 2004, Baghdad

Adams, Ronald E., Lieutenant General, USA (Ret), 16 June 2006, 22 September 2006, 13 October 2006, 26 September 2007, Carlisle, Pa.

Agoglia, John F., Colonel, USA, 28 June 2003, Baghdad, 22 September 2006, 15 October 2007, Carlisle, Pa.

Agristo, John, 1 January 2004, Baghdad

Albergottie, Angela D., Lieutenant Commander, USN, 27 June 2003, Baghdad

Allgood, Buddy M., 15 June 2004, Baghdad

Anderson, Joseph, Colonel, USA, 29 July 2003, Mosul

Arnold, Susan, Major, USA, 29 July 2003, Erbil

Ayoub, Mike, 7 June 2003, Baghdad, 30 October 2006, Washington, D.C.

Bahrani, Zainab, 21 June 2004, Baghdad

Baltazar, Thomas P., Colonel, USA, 10 June 2003 Baghdad, 22 and 29 June 2006, Washington, D.C.

Bartlett, Joseph Terry, Lieutenant Colonel, USA (Ret), 25 June 2004, Baghdad

Bates, Jared, Lieutenant General, USA (Ret), 2 August 2006, Crystal City, Va.

Bayley, Gareth (UK), 26 June 2004, Baghdad

Bearpark, Peter Andrew, 18 December 2003, 21 June 2004, Baghdad

Benson, Kevin B., Colonel, USA, 10 June 2006, Fort Leavenworth, Kans.

Betros, Fareed M., Lieutenant Colonel, USA, 25 June 2004, Baghdad

Bien, Lettie, Colonel, USAR, 23 June 2004, Baghdad

Blackledge, David N., Brigadier General, USAR, 2 January 2004, Baghdad

Block, William, 27 December 2003, 10 June 2004, Baghdad

Bowen, Stuart W., SIGIR, 6 April 2006, Crystal City, Va.

Boyd, Martha L., Major, USAR, 9 June 2004, Baghdad

Bremer, L. Paul ("Jerry"), 18 October 2007, 7 January 2008, Washington, D.C.

Brooks, Robert M., CWO3, USMC, 10 July 2003, as-Samawah, Iraq

Brown, Larry F., Colonel, USMC, 9 August 2003, Hilla, Iraq

Brown, Lyn S., Major, CA, USAR, 22 June 2004, Baghdad

Brown, Manson, Captain, USCG, 28 June 2004, Baghdad

Browning, Steven E., 21 June 2003, Baghdad, 25 April 2006, 21 July 2007, northern Virginia

Bucci, Steven P., Colonel, USA (Ret), 2 May 2006, Pentagon

Bulla, John Eugene, Raytheon, 21 July 2003, Baghdad

Byergo, Laura G., 2 July 2004, Baghdad

Calvi, Aldo R., Colonel, USAR, 13 July 2003, Baghdad

Campbell, Donald F., Major General, USAR, 13 and 14 July 2003, Baghdad

Carney, Timothy, Ambassador, 12 June 2003, Baghdad

Carney, Timothy J., 11 June 2004, Baghdad (not the same as individual above)

Carpenter, J. Scott, 18 June 2004, 29 June 2004, Baghdad

Casey, General George W., 19 February 2010, Pentagon, Va.

Casteel, Steven W., 3 July 2004, Baghdad

Castle, Edwin Scott, 24 June 2004, Baghdad

Chapman, Kay M., 21 June 2004, Baghdad

Coffman, James H., Colonel, USA, 21 September 2006, Crystal City, Va.

Collins, Glenn C., Colonel, USA, 17 June 2003, Baghdad

Collins, Joseph J., Colonel, USA, 29 August 2006, Washington, D.C.

Cooper, Kenneth S., 1 August 2003, Mosul

Corum, James S., 8 June 2006, Fort Leavenworth, Kans.

Cossin, Rene, Major, USAR, 30 July 2003, Mosul

Costello, Robert D., Colonel, USA, 15 June 2003, Baghdad, 18 June 2003 Kuwait

Couvillon, David W., Lieutenant Colonel, USMCR, 7 August 2003, al-Kut, Iraq

Coxin, Natasha, Major, UKA (Territorial), 8 June 2004, Baghdad

Crane, Conrad, C., Lieutenant Colonel, USA (Ret), 15 June 2006, 22 September 2006, Carlisle, Pa.

Crangle, Tommy F., 13 June 2004, Baghdad

Crear, Robert, Brigadier General, USA, 25 June 2003, Baghdad

Cross, Timothy, Major General, UK Army (Ret), 28 January 2008, Aldershot, UK

Davidson, Charles H., Brigadier General, CA, USAR, 30 June 2004, Baghdad

Davis, Walter J., Lieutenant Colonel, CA, USAR, 18 June 2004, Baghdad

Day, Kirkpatrick J., 20 June 2004, Baghdad

De Luca, Perar A., Colonel, USA, 20 September 2006, Quantico, Va.

Dean, Leslie ("Cap"), 22 June 2004, Baghdad

DeGraff, Dennis J., Colonel (S), USAF, 27 June 2003, 25 June 2004, Baghdad

Denham, J.R. Giles, 22 June 2004, Baghdad

Diddams, Richard E., 29 April 2006, Quantico, Va.

Dittoe, Michael J., 29 June 2004, Baghdad

Duklis, Peter S., Colonel, USAR, 1 July 2003, Basra, 20 June 2004, Baghdad

Dunford, David J., Ambassador, 13 June 2003, Baghdad

Dunford, Joseph F., Colonel, USMC, 9 August 2003, al-Hilla, Iraq

Durant, Edward C., Major, USMCR, 7 August 2003, al-Kut, Iraq

Eaton, Paul D., Major General, USA, 1 January 2004, 2 January 2004, Baghdad, 27 December 2004, Fort Monroe, Va.

Egli, George T., Captain, USMC, 31 July 2003, Erbil

Eiriz, Ray (with CENTCOM J-5 in 2003), 7 December 2006, Pentagon

El-Haery, Nadia, 20 December 2003, Baghdad

Ellery, James W.M., Brigadier General, UKA (Ret), 9 June 2004, Baghdad

Elliott, Stephen M., Lieutenant Colonel, USAF, LOGCAP, 12 July 2003, Baghdad

Elvy, Simon D., UK Foreign Ministry, Planning Ministry, 22 June 2003, Baghdad

Erdmann, Andrew P. N., 21 July 2003, Baghdad

Fein, Bruce E., 1st Lieutenant, USAR, 19 June 2004, Baghdad

Feith, Doug, 17 December 2004, 27 January 2005, Pentagon

Fellinger, Matthew W., Major, USAR, 10 July 2003, as-Samawah, Iraq

Ferrell, Robert S., Colonel, USA, 11 June 2004, Baghdad

Fisher, Thomas, Major, USA, 27 August 2003, Tampa

Fitzgerald, Michael D., Colonel, USA (Ret), 24 September 2006, Carlisle, Pa.

Fleischer, Michael P., 20 June 2004, Baghdad

Foote, Christopher L., 6 August 2003, Baghdad

Forster-Knight, Edward, Lieutenant Colonel (UK), 4 July 2003, Basra

Gardner, Gregory C., Colonel, USA (Ret), 12 June 2006, Reston, Va.

Garner, Jay, Lieutenant General, USA (Ret), 30 March 2004, 22 April 2004, 14–15 September 2005, 30 October 2006, 15 October 2007

Gfoeller, Michael, 10 August 2003, al-Hilla, Iraq

Gibb, Thomas W., 24 June 2004, Baghdad

Glover, Audrey F. (UK), 24 June 2004, Baghdad

Glover, Edward C. (UK), 30 June 2004, 2 July 2004, Baghdad

Godson, Margaret N., 25 June 2004, Baghdad

Goledzinowski, Andrew (Aus), 1 January 2004, Baghdad

Gompert, David C., 13 June 2004, Baghdad

Grant, Oliver M., Captain, 3 July 2004, Basra
Gregonis, Meghan, 9 June 2003, Baghdad
Gregory, Andrew, Brigadier General (UK), 1 July 2003, Basra
Groves, Jeremy H., Lieutenant, USN, 8 August 2003, al-Kut, Iraq
Hageman, Douglas D., 2 July 2004, Baghdad
Hamrock, Sue, 12 and 15 June 2003, Baghdad
Hatch, Richard O., Colonel, USA, 28 June 2004, Baghdad
Hawkins, Niel, 21 June 2004, Baghdad
Hawkins, Steven R., Brigadier General, USA, 23 June 2003, 2 January 2004, Baghdad
Hermann, Joseph M., Major, USAR, 8 August 2003, al-Kut, Iraq
Hodgkinson, Sandra, 26 June 2003, Baghdad
Holzman, John C., Ambassador, 25 June 2004, Baghdad
Hughes, Paul B., Colonel, USA (Ret), 29 June 2006, Washington, D.C.
Hunter-Chester, David E., Colonel, USA, 25 May 2006, Baghdad
Jeffrey, James Franklin, Ambassador, 27 June 2004, Baghdad
Jepsen, Ole S. (Denmark, civilian), 1 July 2003, Basra
Johnson, Jennifer J., 23 June 2004, Baghdad
Johnson, Ronald L., Major General, USA, 27 June 2004, Baghdad
Jones, Nathan E., Captain, USNR, 9 June 2003, Baghdad
Jonson, Charles, 27 June 2004, Baghdad
June, Keith L., Major, USA, 14 July 2003, Baghdad
Kader, Tania A., 25 July 2003, Sulaymāniyyah, Iraq
Kanewske, Patrick J., Colonel, USMC, 3 June 2008, Tampa
Keijzer, Rodolf, Major (Netherlands), 10 July 2003, as-Samawah, Iraq
Kellogg, Keith, Lieutenant General, USA (Ret), 2 January 2004, Baghdad
Kelly, Michael J., Colonel (Aus), 12 June 2004, Baghdad
Kennedy, Patrick F., 18 June 2004, 25 June 2004, Baghdad
Kepchar, Allen J., 13 June 2003, Baghdad
Khalil, Peter B. (Aus), 2 January 2004, Baghdad
Khedery, Ali, 24 June 2004, Baghdad
Kicklighter, Claude M., Lieutenant General, USA (Ret), 29 June 2004, Baghdad
Kidder, Stephen D., Colonel, USA (Ret), 24 September 2006 (with Colonel Michael Fitzgerald), 13 October 2006, Carlisle, Pa.
Kincannon, John S., 9–10 June 2003, Baghdad
King, Peter D. (Aus), 21 June 2004, Baghdad
Kiser, Richard J., Captain, USN, 15 July 2003, Baghdad
Kojac, Jeffrey S., Lieutenant Colonel, USMC, 12 and 19 October, 9 November 2007, Quantico, Va.
Kornatz, Stephen D., Captain, USN, 28 June 2004, Baghdad
Kraham, Sherri G., 13 August 2003, Baghdad
Krawczel, Timothy, Lieutenant Colonel, USAR, 11 June 2004, Baghdad
Kuklok, Kevin B., Major General, USMCR (Ret), 8 June 2004, Baghdad, 26 September 2005, Quantico, Va.
Lovelady, Catherine T., Lieutenant Colonel, USAF, 3 July 2004, Baghdad
Luft, Rolf D., 11 June 2004, Baghdad
Macias, Jaime, Captain, USMC, 20 July 2003, Baghdad

Marsh, Schappi, Lieutenant Colonel, USAR (Ret), 30 July 2003, Mosul
Martin, Mark W., Major, USAR, 31 December 2003, Baghdad
Martinez, Roman, 31 December 2003, Baghdad
Martins, Mark S., Lieutenant Colonel, USA, 29 June 2004, Baghdad
Matta, Aline Y. (Aus), 8 July 2003, Basra
Mawdsley, Jeremy C.W., Captain (UK), 4 July 2003, Basra
Maxwell, Dayton L., with Robert B. Polk, Lieutenant Colonel, USA, 14 July 2003, Baghdad
Mazaka, Dorothy, 16 June 2004, Erbil
McClure, Robert L., Colonel, USA (Ret), 21 September 2006, Crystal City, Va.
Meese, Michael J., Colonel, USA, 27 July 2003, Mosul
Melkessetian, Haig, 13 December 2005, Quantico, Va.
Mendofik, John J., 2nd Lieutenant, USAR, 9 August 2003, al-Kut, Iraq
Meyer, Ronald G., 9 July 2003, Basra
Miley, Stephanie A., 2 July 2004, Baghdad
Miller, Frank C., 20 November 2007, 30 July 2008, Alexandria, Va.
Miller, Lawrence F., Major, USMC, 16 July 2003, Baghdad
Milligan, Thomas Christopher, 13 July 2003, Baghdad
Mills, Ainsworth B. ("Andy"), Colonel, USA, 4 July 2004, Baghdad
Mobbs, Michael, 12 December 2005, Pentagon
Mollen, James C., 27 June 2004, Baghdad
Morgan, Joseph L., Lieutenant Colonel, USAR, 12 August 2003, Baghdad
Morse, Ted, Baghdad Central, 18 and 20 July 2003, Baghdad
Mott, Gordon B., 28 June 2004, Baghdad
Mott, Robert L. Jr., Lieutenant Colonel, USA, 22 June 2003, Baghdad
Mulaney, Michael J., 31 July 2003, Mosul
Mulhern, Matthew D., Colonel, USMC, 23 June 2004, Baghdad
Naab, Richard L., Colonel, USA (Ret), 1 August 2003, Mosul
Naji, Ammar A., 15 July 2003, Baghdad
Nash, David H., Rear Admiral, USN (Ret), 1 July 2004, Baghdad
Nations, Kenneth T., Commander, USN, C-8, 27 June 2003, Baghdad
Norman, Jeffrey E., Staff Sergeant, USMCR, 23 June 2004, Baghdad
Nummy, David R., 23 and 27 June 2003, Baghdad
O'Donohue, Lieutenant Colonel, USMC, 10 July 2003, as-Samawah, Iraq
Odum, Wesley R., Lieutenant Colonel, USA, and Major Dan Stoller, USA, 10 January 2007, Heidelberg, Germany
Oleen, James R., 3 July 2004, Baghdad
Olsen, Ole W., Ambassador (Danish), 1 July 2003, Baghdad
Oster, Jeffrey W., Lieutenant General, USMC (Ret), 26 June 2004, Baghdad
O'Sullivan, Meghan, 29 December 2003, Baghdad
Ott, Richard L., Lieutenant Colonel, EN, USAR, 1 August 2003, Mosul
Owens, James D., Colonel, USAR, 14 July 2003, Baghdad
Page, Michael W., KBR, 16 July 2003, Baghdad
Parker, Matthew C., 1 July 2004, Baghdad
Paul, Joshua M., with Matthew Sherman, 4 July 2004, Baghdad
Peak, James H., 31 July 2003, Baghdad
Peay, Binford ("Bennie"), General, USA (Ret), 8 December 2006, Lexington, Va.

Peterson, Harry W. ("Bucky"), Colonel, USMC, 26 June 2003, Baghdad
Petraeus, David H., Major General, USA, 28 July 2003, Mosul; Lieutenant General, USA, 30 June 2004, Baghdad
Phillips, Timothy A., 12–13 July 2003, Baghdad
Polk, Robert B., Lieutenant Colonel, USA, with Dayton L. Maxwell, 14 July 2003, Baghdad
Puckett, Anthony J., Colonel, USA, 22 January 2008, Garmisch, Germany
Purrington, Roliff H., 14 June 2004, Baghdad
Rago, Louis, Lieutenant Colonel, USA, 9 January 2007, Milan, Italy
Raphel, Robin, 15 November 2005, 12 September 2007, Washington, D.C.
Rassam, Amal, 17 July 2003, Baghdad
Reed, Gilbert R., 30 June 2004, Baghdad
Riley, Pamela A., 9 June 2004, Baghdad
Robison, Gordon R., 22 December 2003, Baghdad
Rollins, Jonathon F.A., Lieutenant Commander, USN, 29 June 2003, Baghdad
Schatz, Henry Lee, 26 June 2003, Baghdad
Shelton, Paul, Lieutenant Colonel, USMC, 14 December 2005, Quantico, Va.
Sherman, Matthew, with Joshua M. Paul, 4 July 2004, Baghdad
Shields, Guy T., Colonel, USA, 4 August 2003, Baghdad
Shorey, Alan B., Major, USA, 19 June 2004, Baghdad
Shortridge, Robert J., Group Captain, RAAF (Aus), 20 December 2003, Baghdad
Shulsky, Abram N., 7 December 2006, Pentagon
Sievers, Marc J., 12 June 2004, Baghdad
Simoni, Julie Ann, Captain, USA, 24 June 2004, Mosul
Sincinski, Stephen J., Lieutenant Colonel, USA, 8 January 2007, Pisa, Italy
Sky, Emma M. (UK), 1 August 2003, Erbil
Slim, Wassim, Captain, 8 July 2003, Basra
Slocombe, Walter B., 18 July 2003, Baghdad
Smith, Sondra M., 1st Lieutenant, USAR, 8 August 2003, al-Kut, Iraq
Spear, Christopher T., 15 July 2003, Baghdad
Spear, Robert M., Colonel, USA, 28 June 2004, Baghdad
Squatrinto, Joseph P., Colonel, USAF, 4 July 2004, Baghdad
Stakhiv, Eugene Z., 20 July 2003, Baghdad
Stanley, Raoul Percy, 12 August 2003, Baghdad
Stevenson, James ("Spike"), 24 June 2004, Baghdad
Stinson, J. Michael, 12 June 2004, Baghdad
Strock, Carl A., Lieutenant General, USA, 30 October 2006, Washington, D.C., 20 September 2007, Quantico, Va.
Summers, Guy, 4 July 2003, Basra
Tappan, Robert A., 15 June 2004, Baghdad
Tarantino, David, CDR, USN, with John S. Walker, Kenneth W. Backes, Lieutenant Colonel, USAF, 25 June 2004, Baghdad
Terrill, Andrew, 15 June 2006, Carlisle, Pa.
Thames, Gerald W., 26 June 2004, 1 July 2004, Baghdad
Theriot, Edwin A., 11 June 2004, Baghdad
Thoele, Daniel T., Major, USMC, 29 July 2003, Mosul
Thomas, Matthew, Lieutenant Colonel, USAF, 29 June 2003, Baghdad

Tiso, Roland J. Colonel, USA (Ret) with Michael Fitzgerald, USA (Ret), 30 May 2008, Tampa
Trollinger, Matthew G., Major, USMC, 15 June 2004, Baghdad
Tucker, Pamela Y., Sergeant, USAR, 31 July 2003, Mosul
Turner, Clarke D., 24 June 2003, Baghdad
Valentine, Harold D., Lieutenant Commander, USN, C-4, 19 June 2003, Baghdad
Valenzano, Terry C., Bechtel, 14 August 2003, Baghdad
Vogler, Gary L., 18 June 2003, Baghdad
Walker, John S., with Kenneth W. Backes, Lieutenant Colonel, USAF, and David Tarantino, Commander, USN, 25 June 2004, Baghdad
Ward, George F., 29 June 2006, Washington, D.C.
Warlick, James B., 13 June 2004, Baghdad
Warrick, Thomas S., 10 November 2004, 15 November 2004, 17 November 2004, Washington, D.C.
Wheelock, Thomas R., 23 June 2003, Baghdad
Whitaker, Richard M., Lieutenant Colonel, USA, 2 August 2003, Mosul
Whitehouse, Anthony W., 1 July 2004, Baghdad
Wismer, Frank E., Colonel, Chaplin, USAR, 31 December 2003, Baghdad
Wolfe, George B., 13 June 2004, Baghdad
Yonkee, Eric B., Lieutenant Colonel, USMC (Ret), 3 June 2008, Tampa
Zinni, Anthony C., General, USMC (Ret), 28 April 2008, Quantico, Va.

INTERVIEWS BY THE SPECIAL INSPECTOR GENERAL FOR
IRAQI RECONSTRUCTION (SIGIR)

Chamberlin, Wendy, special UN consultant on development, former USAID Assistant Administrator Near Eastern Affairs, 3 May 2006, 18 April 2007
Dworken, Jonathan, former NSC director, Participant in Reconstruction and Humanitarian Working Group, 11 October 2006, 29 March 2007
Jones, Michael D., Brigadier General, USA, Director, JCS J-5 Middle Eastern Affairs, 13 April 2007, Pentagon
Maxwell, Dayton, 28 March 2008
Milligan, T. Christopher, 27 March 2007
Natsios, Andrew, 17 March 2008
Scheid, Mark, BG, USA, 15 September 2006

BBC INTERVIEWS

Transcripts of the following interviews were provided to the author by the British Broadcasting Corporation (BBC). Most of the interviews were conducted in 2003–2004, but otherwise are undated with no indication of the interview location.

Allawi, Ali
Anderson, Andrew
Bearpark, Andrew
Bodine, Ambassador Barbara

Bowen, Stuart, Special Inspector General for Iraqi Reconstruction (SIGIR)
Bremer, Ambassador L. Paul
Chalabi, Ahmed
Chandrasekaran, Rajiv, *Washington Post*
Cross, Timothy, Major General, UK Army (Ret)
Dodge, Toby
Garner, Jay, Lieutenant General, USA (Ret)
Greenstock, Jeremy, Ambassador
Hoon, Geoffrey, Minister of Defence, UK
Hughes, Colonel Paul, USA (Ret)
Jackson, Sir Michael, General, UK Army
Short, Claire
Slocombe, Walter
Stewart, Rory
Tripp, Charles
Wilkerson, Larry, chief of staff to Secretary of State Colin Powell

DOCUMENTS

CFLCC presentation, Oplan Eclipse II
Coalition Provisional Authority Order Number 1. "De-Ba'athification of Iraqi Soci-
    ety." 16 May 2003. http:/www.cpa-iraq.org/regulations/20030823_CAPORD_1
    _De-Ba_athification_of_Iraqi_Society_.pdf
Coalition Provisional Authority Order Number 2. "Dissolution of the Entities." 23
    May 2003. http:/www.iraqcoaliton.org/regulations/20030823_CAPORD_2_Dis
    solution_of_Entities_with_Annex_A.pdf
JFLCC OPLAN COBRA II (U), 13 January 2003
Desert Crossing Seminar (U): After Action Report (U) 28–29 June 1999.
U.S. Senate Hearings, Committee on Foreign Relations, "The Future of Iraq," 11 Feb-
    ruary 2003. Washington, D.C.: Government Printing Office, 2003.

PERSONAL PAPERS

I have copies of these manuscripts in my possession.

Adams, Ronald, Lieutenant General, USA (Ret)
Baltazar, Tom, Colonel, USA (Ret)
Dunford, David, Ambassador. Original papers are in Dunford's possession.
Garner, Jay, Lieutenant General, USA (Ret). Original papers are in Garner's pos-
    session.
Mullinax, George
Puckett, Anthony, Colonel, USA (Ret)

UNPUBLISHED MANUSCRIPTS

I have copies of these manuscripts in my possession.

Ayoub, Mike. "ORHA Inshallah: A Baghdad Diary of ORHA." Personal diary. 2003.
Eberly, Don. "My Two Years Working on Iraq." N.d. This unpublished manuscript

used for Eberly's book, *Liberate and Leave: Fatal Flaws in the Early Strategy for Postwar Iraq*. Minneapolis: Zenith Press, 2009.

Memo sent to author by Colonel Richard Stouder, USA (Ret), 4 July 2007.

BOOKS AND PUBLISHED MONOGRAPHS

Allawi, Ali A. *The Occupation of Iraq: Winning the War, Losing the Peace*. New Haven, Conn.: Yale University Press, 2007.

Appleman, Roy E., James MacGregor Burns, Russell A. Gugeler, and John Stevens. *Okinawa: The Last Battle*. Washington, D.C.: U.S. Army Center of Military History, 1948.

Bensahel, Nora, et al. *After Saddam: Prewar Planning and the Occupation of Iraq*. Santa Monica, Calif.: RAND Corp., 2008.

Beschloss, Michael. *The Conquerors: Roosevelt, Truman, and the Destruction of Hitler's Germany, 1941–1945*. New York: Simon & Schuster, 2002.

Blumenson, Martin. *Salerno to Cassino*. Washington, D.C.: U.S. Army Center of Military History, 1969.

Bremer, L. Paul, III. *My Year in Iraq: The Struggle to Build a Future of Hope*. New York: Simon & Schuster, 2006.

Campaign Planner Primer. Department of Military Strategy, Planning, and Operations. Carlisle Barracks, Carlisle, Pa.: Army War College, 2006.

Cannon, M. Hanlan. *Leyte: The Return to the Philippines*. Washington, D.C.: U.S. Army Center of Military History, 1954.

Carafano, James J. *Waltzing into the Cold War: The Struggle for Occupied Austria*. College Station: Texas A&M Press, 2002.

Chandrasekaran, Rajiv. *Imperial Life in the Emerald City: Inside Iraq's Green Zone*. New York: Knopf, 2007.

Clark, Wesley K. *Winning Modern Wars: Iraq, Terrorism, and the American Empire*. New York: Public Affairs, 2003.

Coles, Harry L., and Albert K. Weinberg. *Civil Affairs: Soldiers Become Governors*. Washington, D.C.: Government Printing Office, 1964.

Collins, Joseph L. *Choosing War: The Decision to Invade Iraq and Its Aftermath*. Washington, D.C.: National Defense University Press, 2008.

Crane, Conrad C., and Andrew W. Terrill. *Reconstruction Iraq: Insights, Challenges, and Missions for Military Forces in a Post-Conflict Scenario*. Carlisle, Pa.: Strategic Studies Institute, February 2003.

Diamond, Larry. *Squandered Victory: The American Occupation and the Bungled Effort to Bring Democracy to Iraq*. New York: Times Books, 2005.

Dobbins, James, et al. *America's Role in Nation-Building: From Germany to Iraq*. RAND Corporation, 2003.

———. *Occupying Iraq: A History of the Coalition Provisional Authority*. Santa Monica, Calif.: RAND Corporation, 2009.

Dod, Karl C. *The Corps of Engineers: The War against Japan*. Washington, D.C.: U.S. Army Center of Military History, 1966.

Dower, John W. *Cultures of War: Pearl Harbor / Hiroshima / 9-11 / Iraq*. New York: W. W. Norton & Company, 2010.

——. *Embracing Defeat: Japan in the Wake of World War II*. New York: W.W. Norton & Company, 1999.

Eberly, Don. *Liberate and Leave: Fatal Flaws in the Early Strategy for Postwar Iraq*. Minneapolis: Zenith Press, 2009.

Fallows, James. *Blind into Baghdad: America's War in Iraq*. New York: Vintage Books, 2003.

Feith, Douglas J. *War and Decision: Inside the Pentagon at the Dawn of the War on Terrorism*. New York: Harper, 2008.

Fisch, Arnold G. *Military Government in the Ryukyu Islands, 1945–1950*. Washington, D.C.: Government Printing Office, 1988.

Fisher, Ernest F. *Cassino to the Alps*. Washington, D.C.: U.S. Army Center of Military History, 1977.

Fontenot, Gregory, et al. *On Point: The U.S. Army in Operation Iraqi Freedom*. Fort Leavenworth, Kans.: Combat Studies Institute Press, 2004.

Franks, Tommy, with Malcolm McConnell. *American Soldier: General Tommy Franks*. New York: Regan Books, 2004.

Galbraith, Peter W. *The End of Iraq: How American Incompetence Created a War without End*. New York: Simon & Schuster, 2006.

Garland, Albert N., and Howard M. Smyth. *Sicily and the Surrender of Italy*. Washington, D.C.: U.S. Army Center of Military History, 1965.

Gordon, Michael R., and Bernard E. Trainor. *Cobra II: The Inside Story of the Invasion and Occupation of Iraq*. New York: Pantheon Books, 2006.

Graham, Bradley. *By His Own Rules: The Ambitions, Successes, and Ultimate Failures of Donald Rumsfeld*. New York: Public Affairs, 2009.

Haass, Richard N. *War of Necessity—War of Choice: A Memoir of Two Iraq Wars*. New York: Simon & Schuster, 2009.

Hashim, Ahmed S. *Insurgency and Counter-insurgency in Iraq*. Ithaca, N.Y.: Cornell University Press, 2006.

Herring, Eric, and Glen Rangwala. *Iraq in Fragments: The Occupation and Its Legacy*. Ithaca, N.Y.: Cornell University Press, 2006.

Herspring, Dale R. *The Pentagon and the Presidency: Civil-Military Relations from FDR to George W. Bush*. Lawrence: University Press of Kansas, 2005.

——. *Rumsfeld's Wars: The Arrogance of Power*. Lawrence: University Press of Kansas, 2008.

Hogan, David. *First Army Headquarters in Europe, 1943–45*. Washington, D.C.: U.S. Army Center of Military History.

Holborn, Hajo. *American Military Government: Its Organization and Policies*. Washington, D.C.: Infantry Journal Press, 1947.

Joint Vision 2010. Washington, D.C.: Government Printing Office, 1996.

Joint Vision 2020. Washington, D.C.: Government Printing Office, 2000.

Kelly, Terrence, et al. *Stabilization and Reconstruction Staffing: Developing U.S. Civilian Personnel Capabilities*. Santa Monica, Calif.: RAND Corp., 2008.

Komer, Robert W. *Bureaucracy at War: U.S. Performance in the Vietnam Conflict*. Boulder, Colo.: Westview Press, 1986.

Mann, James. *Rise of the Vulcans: The History of Bush's War Cabinet*. New York: Penguin Books, 2004.

Marshall, George C. *George C. Marshall: Interviews and Reminiscences for Forrest C. Pogue.* Ed. Larry I. Bland. Lexington, Va.: George C. Marshall Foundation, 1991.

McDonnell, Janet A. *After Desert Storm: The U.S. Army and the Reconstruction of Kuwait.* Washington, D.C.: Government Printing Office, 1999.

Miller, Christian. *Blood Money: Wasted Billions, Lost Lives, and Corporate Greed in Iraq.* Boston: Little, Brown, 2006.

Miller, Edward S. *War Plan Orange: The U.S. Strategy to Defeat Japan, 1897–1945.* Annapolis: Naval Institute Press, 1991.

Millett, Allan R. *The War for Korea, 1945–1950: A House Burning.* Lawrence: University Press of Kansas, 2005.

Murphy, Robert. *Diplomat among Warriors.* New York: Doubleday, 1964.

Olson, Kim. *Iraq and Back: The Inside War to Win the Peace.* Annapolis: Naval Institute Press, 2006.

Owens, William. *High Seas: The Naval Passage to an Uncharted World.* Annapolis: Naval Institute Press, 1995.

———. *Lifting the Fog of War.* New York: Farrar, Straus, & Giroux, 2000.

Packer, George. *The Assassin's Gate: America in Iraq.* New York: Farrar, Straus and Giroux, 2005.

Phillips, David L. *Losing Iraq: Inside the Postwar Reconstruction Fiasco.* Boulder, Colo.: Westview Press, 2005.

Pogue, Forrest C. *George C. Marshall: Organizer of Victory, 1943–1945.* New York: Viking Press, 1973.

Pollack, Kenneth M. *The Threatening Storm: The United States and Iraq—The Crisis, the Strategy, and the Prospects after Saddam.* New York: Random House, 2002.

Rathmell, Andrew, et al. *Developing Iraq's Security Sector: The Coalition Provisional Authority's Experience.* Santa Monica, Calif.: RAND, 2005.

Reynolds, Nicholas E. *U.S. Marines in Iraq, 2003: Basrah, Baghdad, and Beyond.* Washington, D.C.: History Division, U.S. Marine Corps, 2007.

Ricks, Thomas E. *Fiasco: The American Military Adventure in Iraq.* New York: Penguin Press, 2006.

Roston, Aram. *The Man Who Pushed America to War: The Extraordinary Life, Adventures, and Obsessions of Ahmed Chalabi.* New York: Nation Books, 2008.

Rudd, Gordon W. *Humanitarian Intervention: Assisting the Iraqi Kurds in Operation Provide Comfort, 1991.* Washington, D.C.: Government Printing Office, 2004.

Sanchez, Ricardo S., with Donald T. Philips. *Wiser in Battle: A Soldier's Story.* New York: HarperCollins, 2008.

Sandler, Stanley. *Glad to See Them Come and Sorry to See Them Go: A History of U.S. Army Tactical Civil Affairs/Military Government, 1775–1991.* Fort Bragg, N.C.: U.S. Army Special Operations Command, 1998.

Scoville, Thomas W. *Reorganizing for Pacification Support.* Washington, D.C.: Government Printing Office, 1999.

Short, Claire. *An Honourable Deception? New Labour, Iraq, and the Misuse of Power.* London: Free Press, 2006.

Smith, Robert Ross. *Triumph in the Philippines.* Washington, D.C.: U.S. Army Center of Military History, 1963.

Special Inspector General for Iraqi Reconstruction (SIGIR). *Hard Lessons: The Iraqi Reconstruction Experience*. Washington, D.C.: Government Printing Office, 2009.

——. *Iraq Reconstruction: Lessons in Contracting and Procurement*. Crystal City, Va.: SIGIR, 2006.

——. *Iraq Reconstruction: Lessons in Human Capital Management*. Crystal City, Va.: SIGIR, 2005.

——. *Iraq Reconstruction: Lessons in Program and Program Management*. Crystal City, Va.: SIGIR, 2007.

Spector, Ronald H. *In the Ruins of Empire: The Japanese Surrender and the Battle for Postwar Asia*. New York: Random House, 2008.

Swain, Richard M. *Lucky War: Third Army in Desert Storm*. Fort Leavenworth, Kans.: U.S. Army Command and General Staff Press, 1994.

Tenet, George, with Bill Harlow. *At the Center of the Storm: My Years at the CIA*. New York: HarperCollins, 2007.

Toland, John. *The Rising Sun: The Decline and Fall of the Japanese Empire, 1936–1945*. New York: Bantam Books, 1970.

Truscott, Lucian K. *Command Missions: A Personal Story*. New York: E. P. Dutton, 1956.

Vigneras, Marcel. *Rearming the French*. Washington, D.C.: U.S. Army Center of Military History, 1957.

Warrick, Thomas, ed. *Future of Iraq Project*. Washington, D.C.: Bureau of Legislative Affairs, Department of State, May 2003.

Watson, Mark S. *Chief of Staff: Prewar Plans and Preparations*. Washington, D.C.: U.S. Army Center of Military History, 1950.

Willoughby, Charles A., ed. *Reports of MacArthur: The Campaigns of MacArthur in the Pacific, Volume 1*. Washington, D.C.: U.S. Army Center of Military History, 1966.

——. *Reports of MacArthur: The Occupation – The Military Phase, Volume 1 Supplement*. Washington, D.C.: U.S. Army Center of Military History, 1966.

Woodward, Bob. *Bush at War*. New York: Simon & Schuster, 2002.

——. *Plan of Attack*. New York: Simon & Schuster, 2004.

——. *State of Denial: Bush at War, Part III*. New York: Simon & Schuster, 2006.

Wright, Donald P., and Timothy R. Reese et al. *On Point II: Transition to the New Campaign: The United States Army in Operation Iraqi Freedom May 2003–January 2005*. Fort Leavenworth, Kans.: Combat Studies Institute Press, 2008.

Ziemke, Earl F. *The U.S. Army in the Occupation of Germany, 1944–1946*. Washington, D.C.: U.S. Army Center of Military History, 1989.

INDEX

Abdula, Aamer Sheaa, 300
Abizaid, John, 2, 33, 53, 57, 110–11, 118,
    144, 172, 196–97, 210, 265, 302–3,
    304, 307, 308, 323, 324–25, 328, 329,
    333, 334, 335–36, 366–67, 375, 383,
    395, 396
Abrams, Elliot, 67, 80, 92, 98, 105, 121,
    127, 150, 321, 384, 392
Adams, Ron, 94–98, 100–101, 103, 104,
    105–8, 113–14, 120–22, 125, 127,
    130–32, 138, 144, 149, 150, 161, 164,
    165–66, 169–70, 182, 187–90, 202,
    210, 213, 222, 247, 294–95, 305, 306–
    7, 314, 319, 323, 335, 336, 337–39,
    352–53, 356, 388, 389, 392
Afghanistan operations, 41–42, 46, 48, 55,
    58–59, 64, 65, 66, 67, 69, 78, 82, 86,
    91, 114, 115, 116, 117–18, 142, 159,
    172, 201, 306, 318
Agoglia, John, 33, 43–44, 46–48, 50–51,
    52, 55, 56, 57, 121, 165, 170, 191–92,
    197, 305, 321, 328–31, 333, 365–67,
    377, 392
Albergottie, Angela, 168
al-Dhari, Sulayman, 278
al-Janabi, Ali Shanan, 249, 257, 271
Al Jibouri, Ma'an, 264
Allawi, Ayed, 69, 237, 322
al-Qaeda, 41, 58, 59, 64
al-Rubaie, Mowaffak, 335
al-Shibib, Ahlam, 71
al-Sistani, Ali, 335, 364
Ammundson, Dennis, 243, 248, 257, 271
Amos, Baroness, 318
Anderson, Joe, 291
Annex V (Interagency Coordination), 40, 52,
    78, 156. *See also* OPLAN 1003
Armitage, Richard, 64, 69, 75, 93, 99, 103,
    133, 139, 150, 388, 400
Australian Wheat Board, 260
Austria, occupation of in WWII, 5, 13, 16–
    17, 20, 24, 27, 28, 33, 90, 382

Ayoub, Mike, 77–79, 85, 92, 112, 131, 132,
    145, 148, 150, 169, 185–86, 191, 194,
    197, 214, 241, 250, 264–65, 269, 279–
    81, 284, 299–300, 320–21, 329–30,
    350, 365, 385, 400, 402
Aziz, Riyadh, 240

Ba'athists, 74, 87, 89, 105, 124, 132, 142,
    147, 249, 261, 270–71, 307, 308, 310,
    312–13, 315, 319, 321, 323, 327, 330,
    346, 351, 363, 367, 382
Badoglio, Pietro, 11, 13
Bahrain, 39, 44
Baltazar, Tom, 54–55, 97, 105, 111, 114,
    120, 130–32, 134–35, 162, 165, 172,
    176, 179, 183–84, 188, 197, 208, 220,
    244, 245, 261, 269, 270, 296, 357,
    391–92
Barkey, Brett, 113–14
Bartlett, Dan, 167
Barzani, Massod, 206, 219, 235, 237–38,
    239, 247, 252, 290, 322, 324, 352
Bates, Jared "Jerry," 101–4, 106, 111, 114,
    118–19, 133, 142, 144–45, 162, 164,
    165, 168, 169–70, 182, 184, 188, 191,
    192, 196, 201, 207, 208, 212, 244–45,
    247, 251, 252, 261, 267, 270, 274,
    292, 295, 300, 305, 314, 315, 333–34,
    339, 356, 388, 389
Bayati, Hamid al-, 322, 324
Bechtel, 83, 128, 199, 260, 280, 395, 397
Beltz, Jan, 112
Benson, Kevin, 33, 44–45, 47, 52, 56–57,
    121, 156–58, 159–60, 161, 170, 181,
    192, 210, 294, 329–30, 365, 376, 384,
    397
Biden, Joseph, 143
bin Laden, Osama, 41
Blacklist, Operation, 20
Blackman, Robert R. "Rusty," 45, 192, 330
Blackwell, Paul, 119
Bloomfield, Lincoln, 66

447